Between the Denaby and Cadeby Main Collieries Limited. Appellants and The Yorkshire Miner's Association, and Others. Respondents

Anonymous

Between the Denaby and Cadeby Main Collieries Limited. Appellants and The Yorkshire Miner's Association, and Others. Respondents

Miner's Federation of Great Britain - In the House of Lords between The Denaby and Cadeby Main Collieries, Limited and The Yorkshire Miners' Association and Others - 1906
HAR06249
11/30/1914
Court Record
Harvard Law School Library
Manchester: T. Ashton, Junr., Printer, Toxteth Street, Higher Openshaw, c.1906

The Making of Modern Law collection of legal archives constitutes a genuine revolution in historical legal research because it opens up a wealth of rare and previously inaccessible sources in legal, constitutional, administrative, political, cultural, intellectual, and social history. This unique collection consists of three extensive archives that provide insight into more than 300 years of American and British history. These collections include:

Legal Treatises, 1800-1926: over 20,000 legal treatises provide a comprehensive collection in legal history, business and economics, politics and government.

Trials, 1600-1926: nearly 10,000 titles reveal the drama of famous, infamous, and obscure courtroom cases in America and the British Empire across three centuries.

Primary Sources, 1620-1926: includes reports, statutes and regulations in American history, including early state codes, municipal ordinances, constitutional conventions and compilations, and law dictionaries.

These archives provide a unique research tool for tracking the development of our modern legal system and how it has affected our culture, government, business – nearly every aspect of our everyday life. For the first time, these high-quality digital scans of original works are available via print-on-demand, making them readily accessible to libraries, students, independent scholars, and readers of all ages.

The BiblioLife Network

This project was made possible in part by the BiblioLife Network (BLN), a project aimed at addressing some of the huge challenges facing book preservationists around the world. The BLN includes libraries, library networks, archives, subject matter experts, online communities and library service providers. We believe every book ever published should be available as a high-quality print reproduction; printed on-demand anywhere in the world. This insures the ongoing accessibility of the content and helps generate sustainable revenue for the libraries and organizations that work to preserve these important materials.

The following book is in the "public domain" and represents an authentic reproduction of the text as printed by the original publisher. While we have attempted to accurately maintain the integrity of the original work, there are sometimes problems with the original work or the micro-film from which the books were digitized. This can result in minor errors in reproduction. Possible imperfections include missing and blurred pages, poor pictures, markings and other reproduction issues beyond our control. Because this work is culturally important, we have made it available as part of our commitment to protecting, preserving, and promoting the world's literature.

GUIDE TO FOLD-OUTS MAPS and OVERSIZED IMAGES

The book you are reading was digitized from microfilm captured over the past thirty to forty years. Years after the creation of the original microfilm, the book was converted to digital files and made available in an online database.

In an online database, page images do not need to conform to the size restrictions found in a printed book. When converting these images back into a printed bound book, the page sizes are standardized in ways that maintain the detail of the original. For large images, such as fold-out maps, the original page image is split into two or more pages

Guidelines used to determine how to split the page image follows:

• Some images are split vertically; large images require vertical and horizontal splits.
• For horizontal splits, the content is split left to right.
• For vertical splits, the content is split from top to bottom.
• For both vertical and horizontal splits, the image is processed from top left to bottom right.

MINERS' FEDERATION

OF

GREAT BRITAIN.

In the House of Lords.

MONDAY, 12th MARCH 1906

LORDS PRESENT

THE LORD CHANCELLOR
LORD MACNAGHTEN
LORD DAVEY
LORD JAMES OF HEREFORD
LORD ROBERTSON
LORD ATKINSON

BETWEEN THE

Denaby and Cadeby Main Collieries

LIMITED   *Appellants*

AND

The Yorkshire Miners' Association,

AND OTHERS   *Respondents*

[Transcript from the Shorthand Notes of Messrs MARTEN MEREDITH, HENDERSON & WHITE 8 New Court, Carey Street, W.C., and Mr WILLIAM ROGERS 8 New Court, Carey Street W.C.

MANCHESTER
J. ASHTON Junr., Printer, Toxteth Street, Higher Openshaw

In the House of Lords

Monday 12th March 1906

LORDS PRESENT

The LORD CHANCELLOR
Lord MACNAGHTEN
Lord DAVEY
Lord JAMES OF HEREFORD
Lord ROBERTSON
Lord ATKINSON

BETWEEN

THE DENABY AND CADEBY MAIN
COLLIERIES, LIMITED

Appellants

AND

THE YORKSHIRE MINERS' ASSOCIATION
AND OTHERS

Respondents

--

Transcript from the Shorthand Notes of Messrs MARTEN, MEREDITH HENDERSON & WHITE, 8 New Court Carey Street W C and Mr WILLIAM ROGERS, 8, New Court Carey Street W C

Counsel for the Appellants Mr ELDON BANKES K C, Mr MONTAGUE LUSH, K C and Mr H T WADDY (instructed by Messrs JOHNSON WEATHERALL and SPURR Agents for Messrs BROOMHEAD WIGHTMAN & MOORE Sheffield)

Counsel for the Respondents THE YORKSHIRE MINERS ASSOCIATION and CRAGG, SMITH (since deceased) and KAYE (Trustees) Mr RUFUS ISAACS K C M P Mr DANCKWERTS K C and Mr CLEMENT EDWARDS, M P (instructed by Messrs CORBIN, GREENER & COOK, Agents for Messrs RALEY & SONS, Barnsley)

Counsel for the Respondents JOHN WADSWORTH and FRED HALL Mr ATHERLEY JONES K C M P Mr S T EVANS K C M P and Mr J A COMPSTON (instructed by Messrs CORBIN, GREENER & COOK Agents for Messrs RALEY & SONS Barnsley)

FIRST DAY

Monday, 12th March, 1906.

— —

Lord JAMES of HEREFORD. Looking through the Petition in this case I see that the strike apparently originated out of a vote of the Conciliation Board. I should not like to take part in the hearing if that vote in any way directly or indirectly comes in question. I should feel myself precluded from doing so. Will you tell me if you or your opponent have any view on the subject?

Mr. ELDON BANKES. My Lord, it comes in question merely in this way, that it is part of our case that the fact that your Lordships Award was given, and the result was an immediate reduction of wages, was raised as an argument to induce the men to break their contracts. It is only in that way that it comes in question. Of course it is not whether the Award was right or wrong. That is not in question at all.

Lord JAMES of HEREFORD. I do not quite see how it affects the legal question. All I can say is that if I find that it does in any way I will cease to take any part in the hearing. If you have no objection I will leave it in that way for the present.

Mr. ELDON BANKES. I am much obliged to your Lordship. If your Lordship pleases. My Lords, in this case I appear with my learned friends Mr. Lush and Mr. Waddy, for the Appellants who are the Denaby and Cadeby Main Collieries Limited, a Company who own and work two collieries situate in South York-shire. They brought this action claiming damages against the Defendants in respect of alleged wrongful acts committed by the Defendants at the time of and in connection with the strike which commenced at those collieries in the month of June 1902. The action was tried before Mr. Justice Lawrance with a Special Jury. The trial occupied a very considerable time, and at the end of the trial, at the end of the evidence, I formulated with the assistance of my learned friends certain questions to which I shall have to call your Lordships attention directly, and which in our view covered all the grounds upon which the opinion of the Jury was necessary, and Mr. Justice Lawrance accepted those questions and he put them to the Jury, and the Jury answered them all favourably to the Appellants. Upon that Judgment was entered for the Appellants. The present Respondents appealed to the Court of Appeal, and their grounds of appeal were shortly first of all that there was no evidence to support the findings of the Jury, and, secondly, an alleged ground of misdirection and non-direction by the learned

Judge   The Court of Appeal was divided in opinion   All three of the Lords Justices ---

Lord DAVEY   It was a motion for a new trial I suppose?

Mr ELDON BANKES   Yes, my Lord, a motion for a new trial or in the alternative to enter Judgment upon the ground that there was no evidence to support the findings   There was a division of opinion in the Court of Appeal the three Lords Justices were in favour of the present Respondents upon the ground that there was no evidence to support the findings on one branch of our action, but the Master of the Rolls was of opinion that there was evidence to support the finding of the Jury on another branch of our case and that the Judgment which had been entered for us ought to be allowed to stand   I need only tell your Lordship before opening my argument that it was agreed between the learned Counsel on both sides that the question of damages should stand over and be assessed subsequently and that the question to be determined in the first instance should be the question of liability only

Now my Lord, under these circumstances it is that the case comes before this House and your Lordships will see from the size of this book what a mass of material there is for consideration but I will endeavour to occupy as short a space of your Lordships time as I can and I will endeavour to present the material facts to your Lordships in a moment in chronological order   but there are one or two matters which I must mention first of all in order to explain to your Lordships the position

I told your Lordships that this Plaintiff Company owned and worked certain collieries in South Yorkshire   There were two of those collieries one was called the Denaby Main Colliery and the other the Cadeby Main Colliery   They were situate about a mile apart and in a district in South Yorkshire about 12 miles from Barnsley the town at which the head office of the Yorkshire Miners Association is situate   The Denaby Colliery was much the older colliery   That has been in existence for a great many years   The Cadeby Colliery was opened and commenced working in I think the year 1896   The number of men employed at these collieries at the time of the strike was between 4000 and 5000 of which number 700 were colliers   that is to say   men actively engaged in cutting coal   the remainder were men employed in the various incidental operations in connection with the collieries   and of those 4000 or 5000 men about half were Unionists   members of the Yorkshire Miners Association

Lord ROBERTSON   About half?   I understood you to say 700

Mr ELDON BANKES   No my Lord half the total number I think as far as we can judge there was employed at the collieries at the time of the strike somewhere about 2,000 members of the Yorkshire Miners' Association. The total output of those two pits was about 1,200,000 tons a year, and when I tell your Lordship that the strike lasted from the 29th June 1902—certainly into the month of March 1903—during the whole of which time there was an entire stoppage of work at these pits, your Lordships will realise what a great loss was suffered by the Colliery Company, apart altogether from the enormous damage that was done underground by the closing of the roads and ways owing to the fact that it was impossible under existing conditions to get any men even to work to keep the roads and airways of the pits open.

The gentleman who was employed as the manager of these mines was a Mr. Chambers and his name, your Lordship will see, is frequently mentioned during the course of the strike, and therefore I should just like to tell your Lordships a word about him as it appears upon the evidence, so that your Lordships may consider the various facts of this case with a true appreciation of that gentleman's character. My Lord, he had been employed at these collieries for a great number of years. He was not at all one of those men who opposed the Trades Unions or opposed the Trades Unionists, and I think I could show your Lordships by reference to three passages in this book that he was not only a man who was anxious that his men should belong to the Union but that it was acknowledged by the witnesses who were called on behalf of the Defendants that he was a man who showed every willingness and readiness to meet the men—at any rate in discussion—although, of course, it was not always possible for him to accede to their demands. If your Lordship will turn to page 307 of the Appendix your Lordship will find a letter of the 28th January 1901, which Mr. Chambers wrote to Mr. Parker Rhodes of Rotherham who was the secretary of what was known as the Joint Committee—that was a committee of masters and men which was formed in order to, if possible, arrange the differences that arose between masters and men in this district, and if, as I say, your Lordship will turn to page 307 under letter B your Lordship will find the passage in this letter to which I desire to refer in this connection from Mr. Chambers. Writing to Mr. Rhodes about the settling of these disputes he says "You will readily understand that it is very much adverse to the Company's interest to have these actions, and I would rather they were all in the Union than not." And at page 607, under letter F, your Lordships will find what Mr. Chambers himself says with reference to deputations of men which were in the habit of calling upon him about questions relating to wages and so forth. Mr. Lush asked Mr. Chambers "As long as you are satisfied about that. We have heard so much about it that perhaps I might put this. The deputations have been necessarily pretty frequent always at large collieries like this?" "It is very necessary and it is beneficial too, we could not carry on without it." And then there is Mr. Wadsworth who was one of the Defendant, whom I asked the question as to Mr.

Chambers reputation and position At page 803, under letter F Question 2400 I say to him "And until this strike occurred you have never known any disinclination on Mr Chambers part to receive a deputation?– No Mr Chambers has always met a deputation when I have requested him Of course it is not possible for your Lordships to see Mr Chambers and to hear him as the Jury did therefore I only wished at this early stage to indicate the kind of man Mr Chambers was and the attitude which he adopted with reference to the men employed in the collieries and to Unionists employed in the collieries

Now my Lords the practice in this district with reference to wages is this– that each colliery has its own fixed price list The price list is fixed as between the masters and men having reference to the local conditions and any increase upon the rate of wages is arrived at by a percentage upon the fixed price list for the colliery The price list for the Denaby Main had been revised from time to time I need not give your Lordships any reference to the earlier price list but the price list which was in force at the time of this strike was a price list dated the 18th June 1890 I shall have to call attention to that in a moment The price list for the Cadeby Mine was dated the 27th November 1894

Now there are in this district my Lords two bodies who assist masters and men with reference to questions which arise between them and the one body is a body called the Joint Committee and that is a body which consists of members of the South Yorkshire Coalowners Association on the one part and the Yorkshire Miners Association on the other part Their secretary is Mr Parker Rhodes a solicitor of Rotherham I think the gentleman to whom Mr Chambers wrote the letter to which I have called attention and the Joint Committee are referred to upon matters which arise local disputes between masters and men either as to prices or as to work or hours and any questions of that kind which they cannot settle between themselves are referred to the Joint Committee Then, my Lords in addition to that body there is a wider body which is called the Conciliation Board That body has jurisdiction over a wider area and it is to that body that the question is referred of any increase or decrease in the rate of wages That body consists also of representatives of masters and men, with an independent chairman the chairman at the time of this strike being my Lord James of Hereford That body was established (the Conciliation Board) in the year 1893

Now ever since the establishment of the Conciliation Board circumstances had been such that whenever the question of a revision of the rate of wages came up for discussion the circumstances of the coal trade justified there being an increase on the percentage and the state of things was that in 1894

Lord JAMES of HEREFORD   An increase on the standard rate, I think you ought to say

Mr ELDON BANKES   If your Lordship pleases, on the standard rate   In the year 1894, the percentage over standard was 30 per cent; in the year 1902, it was 60 per cent   It had been raised from time to time—not all at once, but from time to time as occasion required and as applications were made to the Board, and the position was that in 1902 the rate of wages was 60 per cent over standard, the standard, of course, in the case of these collieries being the price lists to which I have drawn your Lordship's attention

Now, my Lord, application had been made, in the summer of 1902, for a reduction in the rate of wages, and the matter had come before Lord James, and he had made his Award, it was dated the 14th June, 1902

Lord JAMES of HEREFORD   It is very immaterial, but it is not an "Award", it is simply that the Board meets, and they always vote, the men one way, and the masters the other, as far as my experience goes, and then the casting vote on the motion is given by the chairman

Mr ELDON BANKES   If your Lordship pleases

Lord JAMES of HEREFORD   It is substantially the same as an Award

Mr ELDON BANKES   I am obliged for your Lordship's correction   It has been called in this case "the Award," but your Lordship has explained really what it is, it is really a casting vote which, in substance, is the deciding vote, and it was given in favour of a reduction of 10 per cent on this occasion

Lord ROBERTSON   I did not catch the date, Mr Bankes

Mr ELDON BANKES   My Lord, the date was the 14th June, 1902   The casting vote was given in favour of a reduction of the standard by 10 per cent, and that was to come into operation in the week following the 29th June, and, in the case of these collieries, I think, the first pay day——

Lord DAVEY   Does that apply to both collieries?

Mr ELDON BANKES   Oh, yes, both collieries   The date at which the reduction is to come into force applies to the whole district under the Conciliation Board

Lord DAVEY   The whole District?

Mr ELDON BANKES The whole district, and it includes, my Lord, not only Yorkshire, but Derbyshire and Lancashire, and a very wide district I think the first pay day at these collieries which would have been affected by the reduction was the pay day of July 3rd

Lord JAMES of HEREFORD This is all 1892, I think

Mr ELDON BANKES 1902, my Lord, not '1892" Now there is another fact to which at this stage I must call your Lordship's attention, and that is this that all the men employed at these collieries were employed under written agreements The written agreements took the form of the men signing the contract book There is no dispute about this, that they were all employed under written agreements and it was one of the terms of the written agreement that 14 days' notice should be given on either side

Lord DAVEY Were they fortnightly pays or weekly pays?

Mr ELDON BANKES Weekly pays, my Lord There is another fact to which I wish to call your Lordship's attention at this stage, and that is this, that this Colliery Company had undoubtedly done a great deal for their men, and they had provided for them some 1,400 or 1,500 houses, which were occupied by some between 2,000 and 3,000 of their men Those houses were all occupied under written agreements, and your Lordships will hear in the course of this case the steps the Colliery Company had to take for the welfare of the men in the way of recreation rooms and reading rooms and places to work in their leisure and so forth

Lord DAVEY We have not to express an opinion upon the merits of the strike, surely!

Mr ELDON BANKES Oh, no, my Lord, I am not asking your Lordships to express an opinion upon the merits of the strike at all The strike began, my Lord, on the 29th June, 1902 That was a Sunday, and it began on the night shift of that day, and it lasted into the month of March, 1903 There are two leading dates I should like to give your Lordships in connection with the strike at this stage, and they are these, that on the 24th July a resolution was passed by the Defendant Union to grant the men strike pay as from the 17th July

Lord JAMES of HEREFORD 17th of July—what year did you say?

Mr ELDON BANKES 24th July, 1902—a resolution to grant strike pay as from the 17th July and the other leading date is the 16th January of 1903, which was the date of the decision of the

Court of Appeal granting an Injunction restraining the Union from any further grants of strike pay. The amount that was paid in strike pay between those dates your Lordship will find at page 764 if you wish to verify my statement—the amount paid in strike pay between those two dates was, I think, 22,600 odd pounds.

Lord JAMES of HEREFORD. Of course, Mr Bankes, you will come back to tell us whether the strike was with notice or without notice?

Mr ELDON BANKES. I can tell your Lordships now.

Lord JAMES of HEREFORD. Just as you like.

Mr ELDON BANKES. The men came out without giving any notice. I was now coming to tell your Lordship shortly what our points were. The action, as I have told your Lordship, was by the Colliery Company against the Union and certain of its officials—I will deal more fully in a moment with who the officials were—and broadly speaking, our case was divided into two parts. First of all, we alleged that the Union by its officials had procured the men to break their contracts, and the second branch of our case was—put quite broadly—that whether that were so or not the Union had interfered in the strike, and by its officials had unlawfully maintained and continued the strike by unlawful means.

Now, I propose, my Lord, to address myself, first of all, to that first branch of our case, and I can tell your Lordships quite shortly what happened. There had been no suggestion or rumour of any strike or anything in the nature of a strike in June, 1902, and Mr Chambers the manager, was away on his holiday. On the Saturday night, the 28th June, a bellman was employed by the branches of the Union (as I say for the moment—I will say the officials of the Union) to go round and summon a meeting of the men of both collieries.

Lord JAMES of HEREFORD. Would you mind telling me what is the fact—were they officials of the branch, or of the main body?

Mr ELDON BANKES. Of the branch, my Lord. I use that word, because I do not for the moment wish to use any word that would convey a wrong impression. The bellman was employed by the officials of the branches to summon a meeting for the Sunday morning, and a meeting was held on that Sunday morning in a field in Denaby village, at which the number of persons present was variously estimated at from 200 to 400. It was addressed by the officials of the branches who advocated an immediate strike going to the length of stopping all work at the colliery immediately; and following on that meeting pickets were placed, and men were prevented going to work at the night shift on that Sunday.

Lord JAMES of HEREFORD Can you tell me, Mr Bankes, were these people that you have spoken of as officials workmen in the collieries?

Mr ELDON BANKES Yes

Lord JAMES of HEREFORD Occupying that position?

Mr ELDON BANKES Yes, my Lord I am only putting it quite broadly I hope to fill up the information I will try to bring to your Lordship's mind what the point is?

Lord JAMES of HEREFORD Yes

Mr ELDON BANKES They made these speeches, and they caused pickets to be posted, and men to be prevented from going to work at that night shift

Lord DAVEY What do you mean by "prevented"?

Mr ELDON BANKES Well, told that they were not to go I will call your Lordship's attention to the evidence

Lord DAVEY That is not prevention

Mr ELDON BANKES I will call your Lordship's attention to the evidence in a moment I hope I am not using a phrase that is not fair under the circumstances—at any rate, they used such means that the fact was that only four colliers went to work out of the 700, and four continued to go to work till the following Tuesday, when one of them was so grievously assaulted that he ceased to go to work, and so did the others, and from the Tuesday no collier worked at all until the following March, and our case was that the branch officials procured the men to break their contracts on that Sunday night and Monday and not to go to work, and as evidence in support of our proposition that the branch officials had procured the men so to break their contracts, we relied upon the fact that at this meeting the branch officials had (as we said) inflamed the men's minds and endeavoured to get them to come out, by using as an argument an inducement that unless there was a general strike throughout the Federation the 10 per cent reduction would come into operation

Now, as against that, it had been pleaded by the Defendants that there were certain grievances in existence at the collieries, and of course the object of referring to those grievances at all was to endeavour to show that our case was wrong, that the men had not been procured at all by anybody, but that they had come out spontaneously because of these alleged grievances and a number of grievances were enumerated in the Particulars, but at the trial two only were referred to, one was a grievance, or an alleged grievance, in connection with what was called the 'bag dirt' question, the other was a grievance, or alleged grievance, in relation to what was called the timbering question

Now, my Lord, in opening this case, and throughout this case, we have always said that from our point of view it was not material really for us to discuss or consider whether these grievances were real grievances or whether they were not real grievances, and in opening this case I said that so far as we were concerned we were quite prepared to leave it an open question, because it did not seem to us to be a necessary part of our case at all to establish that these were not what people might call real grievances. But on the other side my learned friends I suppose thought that it was necessary to their case to establish that these were real grievances, and therefore the matter was gone into particularly with regard to the " bag dirt "

Lord JAMES of HEREFORD. Did they go to the extent of saying that they were such grievances in their reality that they would justify the breach of contract?

Mr ELDON BANKES. No, my Lord. I think the way in which it was put—and the only logical way in which it could be put—was not that it justified the breach of contract, but that we were wrong in suggesting to the Jury that there was any procurement at all by anybody, that it was the spontaneous act of the men, that they went out on account of their grievances, and according to the wild language that was used they were burning grievances. As I say, we did not invite discussion about this, but my learned friends went into the facts, and the facts are now in evidence, and I propose to call your Lordships' attention quite shortly to the facts with regard to this bag dirt question, because as they are out—and though it was not necessary for them to bring them out—they are, I submit, conclusive to show that there was no grievance existing at these collieries in relation to the " bag dirt " question (not sufficient, at any rate, to put it at the lowest) which affected such a number of men that any strike of the whole body would have been possible unless severe pressure had been brought upon the men, and the rules of the Union which were in force for the safeguarding of the interests of the men themselves had been deliberately avoided

Now my Lord, the history of this " bag dirt " question is this, and I think I can put it before your Lordships quite shortly. The seam that is worked in this colliery is, I think, called the " Barnsley seam," it is altogether about 9 feet in thickness, and it consists of five different layers (I think I may use the word layer), the three lower layers of coal, and then there comes an intervening layer of " bind," which is called the " bag dirt," and above that there are two layers of coal again, and the system of getting this coal has been first of all to get the three lower layers of coal, and then it is necessary to get down the "bag dirt." The bag dirt being (some portion of it, at any rate) of a sufficiently hard description, is used by the men to build up the walls which keep the roof in place. They get down the "bag dirt" in connection with bringing down the two layers above, and if your Lordship will now turn to the price list, which your Lordship will find at page 129 of the Appendix, there are three items to which I must call attention, because it is in connection with those that this dispute arises—it is the first, the third, and the sixteenth. Now the first is "coal getting, wooding, packing and top cutting large coal 1s. 4½d. per ton." No. 3—"For stalls under 35 yards in length the coal getting and wooding large coal 1s. 2d." "16. Cutting tops in gates (including dropping bag dirt) 11d."

Now, my Lords, your Lordships will see this price list has been in force at this colliery at the time of the strike (this particular one) for 12 years, and the 1s. 4½d. (the first item) in a stall which is over 35 yards in length, includes the whole of the work done by the collier—including getting down the bag dirt and everything. In stalls which are less than 35 yards in length the man has not got the same opportunity of making a large wage, because he cannot get down the coal with the same facility as he can in a stall which is more than 35 yards in length, and therefore Item 16 is introduced, which gives an extra 11d. for cutting tops in gates, including dropping of bag dirt in stalls, which are less than the 35 yards.

Lord JAMES of HEREFORD. Where does that occur "less than the 35 yards"?

Mr. ELDON BANKES. "Less than the 35 yards."

Lord JAMES of HEREFORD. Where do you get it?

Mr. ELDON BANKES. Well, my Lord, that is the practice. That is the meaning of the price list.

Lord JAMES of HEREFORD. That is agreed, is it?

Mr. ELDON BANKES. That was a subject of discussion. I will show your Lordship what happened. That is what the price list was intended to be, and that is how it has been acted upon. It is upon those points that the dispute arose, and I can tell your Lordship now what happened. It began in the year 1897, and if your Lordship will turn to page 142 of the Appendix your Lordship will see at that time the men asserted that under the price list they were entitled to the 11d. in addition to the 1s. 4½d. They sought to say that that was the meaning of the price list, and thereupon not being paid the 11d. in addition, they brought an action in the county court on the 16th December, 1897, claiming the 11d., in addition to the 1s. 4½d., and that matter was fully discussed and argued, and the county court judge decided against them—that it was plain that the price list was drawn up upon the footing and understanding that I have mentioned to your Lordship, that the 11d only applied to gates under 35 yards.

Then, my Lord, the matter rested until 1900, and then in 1900 the men asked that the matter should be brought up before the Joint Committee, and it was brought up before the Joint Board, and at the discussion which took place before the Joint Board the men said if they were not going to have the 11d they would sooner not get down the "bag dirt," and Mr. Chambers said Well if you do not want to get down the "bag dirt," I am quite prepared to get it down, and that he would deduct the cost of doing it, and thereupon some of the men in some of the stalls ceased getting the "bag dirt" down and Mr. Chambers did it and he deducted a halfpenny, or claimed, at any rate, to deduct a halfpenny—which was the halfpenny of the 1s 4½d —upon the ground, as he asserted, that that halfpenny had been originally inserted in the 1s 4½d as being the price of getting the "bag dirt"

Then, my Lord, at page 301 your Lordship will find a letter of December 19th, 1900—the letter at the bottom of that page 301—a letter written by Mr. Dixon (who was one of the branch officials) to Mr. Pickard (who was the General Secretary of the Defendant Union) in reference to this matter. He writes from the "Denaby Main Branch" "At the last Council meeting the bag dirt question at our colliery came before them for their consideration. They referred the case to the Joint Board for them to deal with it. The Board met on the 30th, and the question was referred to Messrs. Longbotham, Thirkell, Hall, and Annables for them to deal with it the day following this meeting" (now Longbotham and Thirkell were the representatives of the masters, Hall and Annables were the representatives of the men) 'No 1 stallmen" (that is No 1 stall) "were paid halfpenny per ton less than the usual price, the halfpenny being scratched off the pay-sheet, this amounted to 10s 9d. A deputation saw the manager and told him that they should not allow this kind of thing to be done, and if not refunded steps would be taken for its recovery. He admitted it was not right for him to take the course he had, but, says he, I'll pay it back, and I'll charge these stallmen the cost we have been put to in getting this bag dirt down and removing it"

Lord JAMES of HEREFORD Is the "manager" Chambers?

Mr. ELDON BANKES Yes, my Lord "On the 8th inst, 19s 6d was deducted from their wages, this sum being equal to 2d per ton for two weeks. We don't intend him to do this kind of thing, and we ask the Council's advice on the question and hope immediate action will be taken for its recovery"

15

Then, my Lord, Mr Pickard sends that letter on to Mr Chambers—which was the ordinary course taken in this district—Mr Pickard writes to Mr Chambers and says "I am desired by your branch and our Council meeting to ask you not to make any further deductions off the wages of the workmen with regard to the bag dirt question, and also to ask you to refund the money already deducted from the men until such time as the arbitrators meet and if possible settle the whole question," and Mr Chambers answers the next day "I am in receipt of your letter of the 31st ultimo. I cannot think that you are serious in requesting us to pay wages to workmen for work they have not done and which they refuse to do. I do not propose now to argue the rate of payment for top cutting, including dropping and removal of bag dirt, as arbitrators have now the question to hand. It is a fact the men for 15 years have done the work under the same contract as now in operation. Without any notice whatever, one set of men neglected and refused to do the work. Under these circumstances I think I should be justified in reducing the tonnage rate by the amount I can prove the men have been receiving for this portion of their contract. In order to alleviate the impression of dissatisfaction as much as possible, and it being imperative to rip the gate in order to enable the colliers to send out the coal got, ordinary datallers, whose rate of wages is less than that of the collier, were employed to do sufficient ripping to enable the work to be carried on, and only the actual money paid to them was charged against the colliers, who received the full contract price, less this deduction. If I were to accede to the suggestion named in your letter it would be just the same in principle as admitting the liability to pay the full usual wages to all the men employed if they went on strike for an advance on the rate of payment."

Now, my Lord, your Lordship will see that letter is dated the 1st January, 1901, and in February of 1901 the arbitrators met, and the question that they had had referred to them was What was the price in the price list for getting down the "bag dirt"? and their Award is at page 155 of the Appendix. I do not think, my Lord, I need read the whole of the Award. It shows what the dispute was. Well, perhaps I ought to read it, because the matter crops up later. It is addressed "To the chairman and members of the Joint Committee of the South Yorkshire Coalowners' Association and the Yorkshire Miners' Association. Gentlemen, Denaby Main. On the 30th November last you appointed us to act as a sub-committee to investigate questions in dispute at this colliery, with respect to the payment for bag dirt. At this Joint Committee meeting it was stated on behalf of the men (1) That they wanted more money for it (2) Or that the Company take it into their own hands. We have had several meetings, both amongst ourselves and also with Mr Chambers and the men, and have made an underground inspection. On behalf of his Company, Mr Chambers said he was willing to accept the proposal made at the Joint Committee meeting that the Company do the work themselves He stated the amount now paid for it was ½d a ton Messrs Hall and Annables would not admit this ½d a ton unless a document wherein it was clearly stated (such document being the original price list drawn up and signed on behalf of the men by some person authorised to act on their behalf) was produced On February 9th (this day) this document was produced, and submitted to Mr William Chappell, who we were informed had written and signed it and in the presence of the four arbitrators" (Mr Chappell was the gentleman who had originally made the price list) "Mr Chambers on behalf of the Denaby Company, and three workmen, Nolan, Crofts and Rounds, Mr Chappell declared that the document was in his writing all of it, and he was authorised to act on behalf of the men It is here made clear that cutting tops, coal in gates, and waste, and dropping and removing bag dirt, is included in the 1s 4½d a ton, and that ½d a ton is clearly stated as appertaining to this work We now beg to report that it has been established to our satisfaction that the price fixed for doing this work is ½d a ton"—so that the first———

Lord JAMES of HEREFORD And I suppose in the 1s 4½d ?

Mr ELDON BANKES Oh, yes, and in the 1s 4½d Now, my Lord, the men were not satisfied with that Of course, the position, your Lordship will see, was that the County Court Judge had decided that the 11d was not additional to the 1s 4½d The men then did not do the work, and Mr Chambers had it done, and deducted, not exceeding ½d , as your Lordship will see it was—not really ½d , but "not exceeding ½d " Then the men understood that the ½d was not to come off it, but now it is decided that the ½d was the proportion of the 1s 4½d which was allowed for this work

Lord JAMES of HEREFORD I am sure it is my fault I cannot see the great difference between the 11d that the County Court Judge has not allowed and the ½d

Mr ELDON BANKES My Lord, their first position was under the price list we are entitled to 1s 4½d plus 11d , the County Court Judge said "No, the 1s 4½d is an inclusive price Then they did not do the work, and Mr Chambers did it, and claimed to deduct the ½d , because, as he said, the ½d was the originally agreed price in the 1s 4½d for doing this work , therefore, if you do not do the work, and I do it———

The LORD CHANCELLOR One is per ton, the other is per yard

Lord JAMES of HEREFORD Oh I beg your pardon , that is it, that is so I do not doubt that the Lord Chancellor's explanation is correct

Mr ELDON BANKES My Lord, may I just look—will your Lordship forgive me for one moment (Referring) My Lord, the 1s 4½d is per ton and the ½d is per ton

Lord JAMES of HEREFORD Yes

The LORD CHANCELLOR One is "per yard"

Mr ELDON BANKES No

Lord DAVEY The 11d is per yard

Mr ELDON BANKES Yes, the 11d is per yard—I beg your Lordship's pardon I was not following

The LORD CHANCELLOR That explains the difference

Mr ELDON BANKES Now, my Lord, the men are not satisfied with the position of things and they applied for leave to take a ballot I will come to the rules in a moment It is at page 220 I may just say that under the rules—and I am sure your Lordship will see that it is a very proper rule—a strike under the rules of this Association is not to be permitted, unless, first of all, a ballot is taken A ballot shall be taken in a way which shall allow the expression of the free opinion of the men, and the two branches applied to the Defendant Association for leave to ballot, and then application, it appears, is dated the 18th, 19th February, 1901—or rather, their application, appears in the resolution of the ordinary Council meeting of the 18th, 19th February, 1901, page 220 This is the resolution "That Mr Parrott write Mr Parker Rhodes, asking him to summon a Joint Committee as early as possible on the question of a revised price list for Denaby and Cadeby Main Collieries, on the bag dirt question, and the manager not carrying out the agreement made at the last joint meeting in Sheffield, and, in the meantime, both collieries be allowed to take a ballot vote and forward the result to Mr Pickard" Now, they did take a ballot, and the result of the ballot, my Lord, appears at page 312 of the Appendix, and, of course, the question before the men was then, whether or not there should be a revised price list, and, as your Lordship will see, the number of men in favour of having a revised price list was very considerable, as one would imagine, of course, that was a matter upon which it would be easy to understand that the men would be anxious if they could, to get their terms

Now, it is quite plain what the men thought the effect of Hall and Annables' Award was, because, if your Lordship will turn to page 221, there is a letter from Hirst (who was an official of the Cadeby Branch) to Pickard on the 7th June 1901, in these terms, "That this meeting condemn the action of F Hall and W Annables for signing a document unknown to the workmen, which,

B

in our opinion, gives away the bags and bag dirt question entirely, and that they be asked for an explanation at the council meeting "

Now, my Lord, your Lordships will remember that in March of 1901 the men had balloted in favour of having a revised price list, and now the question came up as to whether or not they should strike for a revised price list, and on page 222 your Lordship will find the minute of the ordinary Executive Committee Meeting of the Defendant Association—of the Union—under date the 21st August 1901, page 222 at the top "That seeing the Denaby Main and Cadeby Main members have not taken a ballot of their men to terminate their contract of service they be now advised to take a ballot on this question and the result sent into the office immediately after taken, so that the next Council meeting can deal with the matter "

Lord JAMES of HEREFORD This would still be on the bag dirt ?

Mr ELDON BANKES Oh yes, my Lord, they were now asking for a revised price list

Lord JAMES of HEREFORD Yes, quite so I quite understand that

Mr ELDON BANKES And they were saying that the conditions had altered because, at any rate in certain stalls in the mine, the bag dirt was thicker and harder than it had been at the time when the original price list was fixed

Now, my Lord, they took that ballot in September, and your Lordship will find the result of the ballot is given, at any rate with regard to the Cadeby Main Branch, at page 321, but I can tell your Lordship what the figures were, in the case of the Cadeby Main there were 423 in favour of giving the 14 days' notice and 423 against

Lord JAMES of HEREFORD Give the number again, please.

Mr ELDON BANKES 423 in favour of giving 14 days' notice and 423 against

Lord DAVEY · A tie ?

Mr ELDON BANKES A tie, my Lord—yes, and the Denaby Main were 713 in favour of giving 14 days' notice and 484 against, I will give your Lordship the rule in a moment, but we are all agreed that those numbers fell far short of the majority required by the rules for permitting a strike, and if your Lordship will now turn to page 321, you will see there is a letter at the bottom of page 321 from the Secretary of the Denaby Main to Mr Pickard, and that shows the position the men then took up He says "I am instructed by a joint meeting of the Denaby and Cadeby workmen That seeing that we have failed in our ballot to secure the necessary majority to give in our notice we send the following resolution in to be dealt with by the the Council on Wednesday, September 11th Resolution That we be allowed to enter an action in the County Court for the recovery of the money that has been deducted from the workmen at Denaby Main, and that we try to establish in a Court of Law our right to be paid 11d per yard for cutting tops in gates, including dropping bag dirt as stated in our price list Hoping you will bring this on before the Council on Wednesday and oblige'

Lord JAMES of HEREFORD There had been a previous action in the County Court to try this very question

Mr ELDON BANKES To try part of it Your Lordship will see it was to try the question as to whether the 11d was an addition to the 1s 4½d , but now they tried a different action, which was whether they could get back the ½d , it was the same action only in another form They brought an action in the County Court, and that action was decided on the 13th February of 1902 against the men

The LORD CHANCELLOR Substantially the same subject matter ?

Mr ELDON BANKES Yes, my Lord, substantially The decision is at page 181 Now, perhaps, I ought to mention this, that the evidence was only given there, I think, for the men— I think Mr Chambers was not heard, and in the course of his Judgment the County Court Judge did say, I think, that he thought the bag dirt was harder (page 188, my Lord, B and C) This is the part of the Judgment, if I may begin at B "This concluded the case for the defence His Honour said that the contract was based upon the price list made between Mr Chambers on behalf of the employers, and Mr Pickard on behalf of the men, on the 18th June, 1890, and then price was 1s 4½d per ton At the time the contract was made it was within the knowledge of the men and of the employers that the situation was practically the same in point of material as it was now Gradually since that time, he believed, that what was known as the strata of bag dirt had been getting broader and tougher, until at last the upper part had become so tough that the men practically declined to get it This was pre-eminently a case that ought to have been referred to a practical man to say what was fair between the parties He was not there to say what was fair between the parties He was not there to say what was fair between the parties, but to administer what was just in law He had to say what he thought was a contract between the men and the Company, and he thought top cutting included the removal of bag dut It was very hard that the labour should be increased without increase of payment, but it was a question for an arbitration, and it was for the consideration of the parties whether the time had not arrived when another price list should be put upon the work He was inclined to think that the work was harder, and that the material would not come down nearly so readily as it came down 12 years ago, but the undertaking had been that it should be removed and taking that view of the meaning of the contract he was bound to give Judgment for the Defendant Company with costs"

Now that statement by the County Court Judge was relied upon naturally by the men, and relied upon by my learned friend in argument, but it was also complained of very much by the masters upon the ground that it was an *ex parte* statement, made, as your Lordship will see the learned Judge says—he believes—he really had not got both sides before him, but I think the evidence at this trial—which was not contradicted, as I shall show your Lordship in a moment—puts, at any rate, this point of the case outside and beyond controversy Now that Judgment was given on the 13th February, 1902, and in March the position taken up by Mr Chambers at this time and throughout was this—he said If you men do the work I shall not pay you more than 1s 4½d, but if you do not do the work I will do it or have it done for you, and I will deduct the price not exceeding a halfpenny He said I say that I am entitled to deduct a halfpenny, but I shall deduct the cost not exceeding a halfpenny, and we proved in this case that in every instance in which Mr Chambers had had the work done, instead of the men who would not do it, it had cost him a farthing, and that the amount which he deducted from the men amounted to the farthing and no more, so that he was generous If they would not do the work he was entitled, as a matter of right, to say If you do not do the work I shall take a halfpenny, but he was generous, I submit, in saying I will do it and only deduct the actual cost, because I can show your Lordship when we come to figures in a moment that the amount was only a farthing.

My Lord, at page 329 would your Lordship kindly turn to a letter of the 4th March, 1902, in which Mr Wadsworth, who was one of the Defendants and an official of the Union, reports the result of a deputation, which he had attended with the men, to Mr Chambers on certain matters, including the "bag dut," and he says "I attended along with deputation at Cadeby and Denaby to-day on the following, viz (1) Market men (2) Timber question (3) Complaints about props at different distances (4) Bag dut *re* new price list (5) Thomas Forcett's case (6) Home coal (7) David Butler's compensation We got Mr Chambers to allow Forcett to restart work again (No 5 case) In Nos 1, 2, 3, 4, 6, and 7 cases we got nothing whatever done. In No. 4 Mr. Chambers offers us his old terms, viz. He would take the work if we would give him the ½d per ton "

Well, the next step, my Lord, was that the men applied for leave to take a partial ballot—that means to say they wanted to ballot a certain proportion only of the men—and on the 2nd June the Council refused that application (your Lordship will find that on page 224 under letter B) " That seeing that the application from Denaby Main only asks for a partial stoppage of the pit this Executive Committee Meeting cannot grant it inasmuch as it is contrary to all precedent "

Now I have brought down the history of the "bag dirt" question into the month in which the strike occurred, and the fact which I so strongly rely upon as evidence for the Jury is that this grievance, whatever it was, was not one of the kind that would influence the whole body of men, is the fact that every conceivable means had been tried and the only occasion on which they balloted the men on the direct question of whether they should come out on it, the men had refused

The LORD CHANCELLOR Just explain the " Ordinary Executive Committee Meeting " Is that the Union ?

Mr ELDON BANKES Yes, my Lord, of the Union Your Lordship will see there is a Council and an Executive Committee Now if your Lordship would not mind turning to page 19 of our case, your Lordship will find there summarised in a short form—and I have verified the statements—the points we established It is paragraph 38 on page 19 of our case Your Lordship will remember our case comes first We there summarise the evidence, my Lord, that was given in addition as we did go into it, and I want to call your Lordship's attention pointedly to this, that of course our main complaint here was against the officials of the branches (their conduct), and we gave a great deal of evidence as to what they had done, and also a good deal of evidence on this question of " bag dirt," and so forth, which dealt with the question of whether the " bag dirt " had increased or whether it had not increased

Now the Defendants called no evidence at all except through what I will call their principal officials from Barnsley , they did not call a single man from the pit, and they did not call a single branch official, and therefore our evidence upon all these points stands uncontradicted, and this is a summary of the evidence with the references—if your Lordships desire I can refer to them, but I have verified it myself, and I think it is an accurate statement of the evidence, and I should like to read the paragraph, because I think it puts it in a summary form This is what we say " In the course of the hearing of this present case before the Honourable Mr Justice Lawrance and the Jury, the Appellants called evidence which was not contradicted by evidence called by the Respondents which established

(A) That there had not been any alteration in the character of the bag dirt for the last 20 years, and that it had not got thicker or harder " (Then we refer to the witness, Mr Soar, who was the underground manager) "(B) That though the bag dirt exists in degree at both pits, complaints were made by the men working at the Denaby Pit only (Chambers, Questions 410, 411 and 428), such complaints being confined to 6 out of 85 stalls, and that 24 men (colliers) only were affected (Soar, Questions 640, 642, 765 and 766) (C) That those men who did not get down the bag dirt were getting the highest rate of wages, viz , 9s 4d per day against the general average of wages throughout the collieries of 9s 1½d per day (Chambers, Question 71), or 1s a day over the average of the rest of the districts in the same pit (Chambers, Question 533), and that in all cases where complaint had been made Mr Chambers had offered to transfer the men complaining to other stalls in the pit, an offer which had been invariably refused (Chambers, Question 412) (D) That the total amount of the deductions for bag dirt from the men's wages, from December, 1900, to June, 1902, a period of just over 18 months, amounted to £61 15s 10d , and affected 17 stalls only at the Denaby Pit, comprising 68 colliers altogether (Chambers, Question 548) (E) That the total amount of the deductions for bag dirt for the six months from 1st January, 1902, to June, 1902, amounted only to £17 5s (Soar, Question 648) (F) That the £8 15s deducted on the 25th June, 1902, represented the accumulations of deductions, extending over a previous period of from 10 to 12 weeks (Soar, Question 650), and, in the case of Stall 55, extended from the 13th November, 1901 (Barnard, Questions 1370 and 1371) , and, in the case of Stall No 1, extended from the 1st day of February, 1901, in fact, in each case from the date of the last previous deductions (Barnard, Questions 1365 to 1366) (G) That as to Stall 55, in respect of which the largest deductions were made during the 18 months from December, 1900, to June, 1902, viz , £17 0s 4d , the men during this period worked altogether 18,839 tons of coal, of which 16,113 was large coal, in respect of which the men received their full 1s 4½d per ton, and that the deductions worked out at the rate of only one farthing a ton

Now, that summarises the position The fact was that there was an insignificant number of colliers affected by the question at all , that these men—although as they said, the "bag dirt" was thicker and harder in their stalls—were enabled to get coal at such a rate that their average rate of wages amounted to 9s 4d a day as against (I think the average was) 8s 7d , but it says 9s 1d here, and that the total amount of deductions which was made upon their wages (your Lordship will remember they having been paid during the full period the whole 1s 4½d) amounted to a farthing a ton

Now, if your Lordship will kindly turn to the statement of deductions (which is the next thing in order of date to which I wish to call your Lordship's attention), which is at page 83 of the

Appendix, your Lordship will see this—it begins at page 81—these were given in the form of Particulars by the Defendants, and these were given as Particulars of, as they said, illegal deductions which had been made from the colliers' wages, and your Lordship will see it runs from December, 1900, down to June of 1902, and it gives the number of the stall, and it gives the name of the men working in the stall, and it gives the amount of the deduction, and if your Lordship will kindly turn to page 85 you will find there the deductions were made on the 25th June, which was the day immediately preceding the calling of the meeting which resulted in the strike

Now, if I may just read that, your Lordship will see what it states, and it is the fact "Week ending 25th June, 1902, deductions were made from four stalls, 62,' it gives the name, and the deduction was 5s, "40" stall (it gives the name, including the collier and other men) deduction, £2 12s, "55" (it gives the name and the deduction) £2 12s Stall No 1 (it gives the name and the deduction) £3 6s, and I have told your Lordship in the evidence which I have just read summarised what those deductions represent If your Lordship will turn your eye to page 84, under letter F you will see a deduction was made for stall 55 under date the 13th November, 1901 Now, the last deduction made from Stall 55 was made in November, 1901, and this £2 12s is the accumulations of work which had been done between November, 1901, and June of 1902— accumulations of work done under Mr Chambers' orders by datallers because the men would not do it themselves, they had been drawing the full 1s 4½d during the whole period, and the accumulations, instead of deducting it a few pence at the time it was allowed to accumulate, and it amounted to £2 12s, and the only possible thing that I think the men could really reasonably say about that was that it would have been much better for us if you had deducted it week by week instead of allowing it to accumulate to that amount, but it is the fact that it represented that period The men could have asked that it should be deducted at more frequent intervals, and I have no doubt the men who were actually affected by this felt that it was rather a large amount when the day came that it was deducted from their wages They were earning at the rate of 9s 2d a day, and I think this works out at an average deduction for the week of about 1s or something like that per man No 1 stall Your Lordship will see there had not been a deduction in respect of No 1 stall for for some time I need not go into the details—it is sufficient that your Lordship has got the position

Now, that brings me to the date of the 25th June That brings me very near to the date when the first step was taken towards the strike Now, this deduction was made on the 28th the books are made up to the Wednesday, I think, and they are paid on the Saturday, they would therefore be paid on that Saturday the 28th The men were all paid and these were the only deductions made, and therefore these were the only men who could be affected Out of the whole 4,000 or 5,000 men there were no men who could be affected on that Saturday except these men, and it was on that Saturday night that the bellman was sent round

Lord JAMES of HEREFORD What day of the month would that be—the 28th?

Mr ELDON BANKES The 28th, my Lord He was sent round between 6 and 7 in the evening How far exactly he went or how far he got one does not know, but I must explain this to your Lordship I have told your Lordship that the Denaby village consists, I believe, entirely of the houses of the Colliery Company, and the men who cannot be accommodated there live away at a distance, at Conisbrough and other villages and towns around and presumably therefore the bellman could only have conveyed the notice to those people who happened to live in Denaby However, he was sent round and the meeting was called, and now I think I had better call your Lordship's attention to what happened at the meeting, because that will, at any rate, very nearly complete what evidence I have got to produce upon one particular branch of the case at the moment All I want to say is to summarise the case which we put before the Jury, and which I submit there was ample evidence to justify the Jury in finding, that up to this 28th June, there was no cause of dissatisfaction existing at these collieries sufficient to account for the men breaking their contracts and coming out *en masse*, and that no reasonable man upon this evidence could come to the conclusion that the men had come out spontaneously As your Lordship will see by the evidence, a large number of them never knew even when they went to work on the Sunday or the Monday that the question of a strike had been suggested or discussed, and our case was that the necessary steps were taken by the branch officials to bring together a number of sympathisers who were determined to have a strike, and who realised that no strike would be possible if they followed the machinery laid down for their guidance, and they were determined to bring the men out straight, and to take the necessary steps to stop the work at these collieries absolutely, and to ensure that no man should go to work

Now, my Lord, the speeches of the men at these meetings were taken by a shorthand writer, not employed at all by us, but apparently a man who took them with a view to publishing them in the local press

Mr ATHERLEY JONES In the newspaper

Mr ELDON BANKES And those notes were agreed upon between the parties as being a fair representation of what was said and they were used in the trial as fairly representing what the men had said in some cases where the shorthand writer's notes were not available we had to have recourse to the local press, but in those cases also it was by agreement that the extract of newspaper account that we had fairly represented what took place

Now if your Lordship will turn to page 388, I will read the account of this meeting—I will read it all, but I ought before doing that to tell your Lordships who the officials of these two branches were. There was a branch of the Union for each colliery, and they each had their own officers, and these were the officers. First of all, I will take Denaby. Of the Denaby Branch the president was Croft, he presided at nearly all the meetings, the secretary was Smith, the treasurer was Baughan (his name does not appear very frequently), the delegate was Nolan—his name occurs very prominently.

Mr ATHERLEY JONES He is one of the Defendants

Mr ELDON BANKES He is one of the Defendants—yes. I will deal with them in a moment. I am explaining who the delegates are. Then in addition to those named officers they have a Committee

Lord DAVEY I do not see anything about "the Defendants"

Mr ELDON BANKES Nolan and Humphries were Defendants, they did not appear, my Lord, but they were originally made Defendants

Lord DAVEY "Nolan" I see

Mr ELDON BANKES The Committee of Denaby were Birch, Follows, Raybould, and Mannion, now of the Cadeby Branch the president was Phil Humphries the secretary, G H Hurst, the treasurer, Casey, the delegate, H Humphries

Mr ATHERLEY JONES "Harry"

Mr ELDON BANKES "Harry Humphries"—yes, and the Committee, Moon, Collier, Mounsey, Donellan, and Fleming. Your Lordships will find them at pages 6 and 7 of the Appendix I think if your Lordships want the reference. My friend tells me they are set out there

The LORD CHANCELLOR Now we have got them

Mr ELDON BANKES Yes, my Lord. Now, my Lord, I propose to read those speeches. Your Lordship will remember the meeting called and held in the field at Denaby, I think held in the morning about 11 o'clock

Now, the speech of Mr Croft is at page 388 ' Fred Croft, presiding. Addressing the meeting he said they could not rest on the

Sunday without knocking about and seeing what they could do with regard to the question at Denaby and Cadeby Main. The Committee at Cadeby had said whatever they did at Denaby they would do, and had pledged themselves to do whatever was done by the Denaby officials." Now, may I stop there to say that that is plain to show that there had been a meeting of the Committees of Denaby and Cadeby, and that the two Committees had pledged themselves to stand by each other in whatever was done; therefore, there must have been a previous meeting of the Committee, the result of which was this meeting. Then he says they "had pledged themselves to do whatever was done by the Denaby officials, whether they had the opinion or not as to whether anything should be done soon with regard to the 'bag dirt' question', that is to say, they pledged themselves to stand by the Denaby people whether they thought there was anything in the "bag dirt" question or whether they did not. "When it came to nearly £10 on a Saturday being stopped from their fellow workmen it was time something was to be done when 18s went out of a man's wage, it was hard lines. It was hard lines when a penny was deducted, but when it comes to £3 12s being stopped from four men it was a bit thick. It was for them to say what they were going to do." If your Lordship wants to refer to the deductions the reference is page 85. He is wrong in saying there was £3 12s deducted from any man, but that is an immaterial circumstance. Then he says "If any speaker treads on your toes this morning, don't cry out, but bear it. The district was prepared at the previous meeting—September." Now that, my Lord, I think must have had reference to the ballot, because your Lordship will find they complain about this. Apparently, in September, the men had had a meeting at which, by show of hands, it appeared that the meeting was ready to "go out,' but when it came to balloting it was plain that the men were not ready to go out, and what he is saying here is "The district was prepared at the previous meeting in September." He means by that, that at some previous meeting in September, by show of hands, they had said they were willing to go out. "He had told them, as a gentleman had said, they had winter before them, and he had said, if they had, they had summer still. It was beautiful weather, and they could stand it" That means that when they met in the previous September he must have said to the men. If you strike now, you have got the winter ahead; if you do not strike now, you have got the summer. "They stood it in '93 for about 10 weeks without anything, and the feeling had been throughout the Federation that they would suffer again before they would suffer a 10 per cent reduction" Now, may I stop there, my Lord? It is plain that what this man is advocating is a strike because the 10 per cent reduction was imminent. Your Lordship will remember it would have been deducted from the next week's pay

Lord JAMES of HEREFORD: Is Croft a workman in the Denaby Main Colliery?

Mr ELDON BANKES Yes, my Lord   "They stood it in '93 for about 10 weeks without anything, and the feeling had been throughout the Federation' ——

Lord JAMES of HEREFORD Pardon me   Is your point that all this, that this man Croft said, was said as a member of the Branch Union ?

Mr ELDON BANKES Yes

Lord JAMES of HEREFORD You do not allow for him being speaking for himself as a workman ?

Mr ELDON BANKES No   Our case is that he is speaking here as representing the Union—as a local official of the Union

Lord JAMES of HEREFORD It was a meeting of the men

Mr ELDON BANKES It was a meeting of the Union men

Lord DAVEY A meeting of the Cadeby Branch only ?

Mr ELDON BANKES Yes   Our case with regard to this is that the Union are responsible for the acts of the local officials

Lord JAMES of HEREFORD I was only wishing to tell you what was in my mind   If the man was there in a double capacity, he may be there as a workman, or he may be there as an official—if as an official I presume he was speaking for the Union as an official, not as a workman

Mr ELDON BANKES Yes, that is our case

The LORD CHANCELLOR In order to get it clear, do you say that he was speaking as an official of the Branch, or as an official of the Union ?

Mr ELDON BANKES My Lord, as an official of the Branch, but because he was an official of the Branch he is a local officer of the Union   That is our case

The LORD CHANCELLOR I understand

Mr ELDON BANKES I will call attention to the rules I am coming to that in a moment

Lord DAVEY It is not enough to bind an association or body by an individual official

Mr ELDON BANKES May I come to that part of my argument in a moment ?

The LORD CHANCELLOR That is one of the facts you go upon ?

Mr ELDON BANKES Yes, my Lord This is upon the question whether or not the strike was procured by anybody The next step is, who procured it, and who is responsible for what they did ? That is the order of the points

Lord DAVEY You will deal with them in order ?

Mr ELDON BANKES I am only now reading what he said

Lord DAVEY Certainly

Mr ELDON BANKES " It was beautiful weather, and they could stand it They stood it in '93 for about 10 weeks without anything, and the feeling had been throughout the Federation that they would suffer again before they would suffer a 10 per cent reduction The wage question was a one-sided affair When Judge Ellison was then Arbitrator, he had given another 10 per cent advance for them, but the owners had broken away from it " That must have reference to some decision when Judge Ellison occupied the position of independent Chairman of the Conciliation Board He says, " They never ought to have had it, and they ought to break away Trade was as good as ever it had been for the last four years, yet they could not interfere for a year and nine months, and they were allowed to take the coal up as high as £1 per ton When Lord James gave in his decision against them, they ought to say, We will not stand it The owners had said so when Judge Ellison gave his advance It was not the cry in that district only, but in every district They would stop throughout the Federation, and they would do right if they never started until they got 60 per cent " Now, 60 per cent, of course, was bringing it back to what it was before the 10 per cent reduction, and the Federation your Lordship will see (I ought to explain) means the whole area affected, and not merely this district He is here advocating that there should be a strike " throughout the Federation, and they would do right if they never started until they got 60 per cent Men with 60 per cent could earn a fair wage He and Nolan had been told that they would let the men work for 4s or 5s per day " (Now) " If they would support them they would support the men in getting a fair wage on Saturday " Now that clearly is a statement as an official of the Union He is calling upon the men to support him " It was time that the ' bag dirt ' was settled There was not another colliery where they got coal so cheap as they did at Denaby Main "

Lord DAVEY " He and Nolan had been told "—so-and-so " If they " (that is the Committee) " would support them " I should understand that to mean " he and Nolan "—practically

Mr ELDON BANKES He and Nolan were the two principal speakers

Lord DAVEY Oh, I daresay—yes

Mr ELDON BANKES "If they would support them they would support the men in getting a fair wage on Saturday It was time that the 'bag dirt' question was settled There was not another colliery where they got coal so cheap as they did at Denaby Main In 1885 they stood to be turned out of their houses, and they were then supported a lot better out of Yorkshire than they were in their own county"

Lord JAMES of HEREFORD What do the words ' on Saturday" mean—" a fair wage on Saturday '

Mr ELDON BANKES I think it means the next Saturday— or, at any rate pay day I suppose he means pay day I should think so

Lord DAVEY Would there be the operation of the 10 per cent reduction until a fortnight after that?

Mr ELDON BANKES No, July 3rd, my Lord

Lord DAVEY Which would be " the next Saturday '

Mr ELDON BANKES *The* next Saturday "?

Lord JAMES of HEREFORD No, this is Sunday the 29th

Mr ELDON BANKES, July 3rd, if I am right, would be the Saturday I do not know why I have got "July 3rd" here My Lord, I am quite right July 3rd would be the making up day for the wages—the first making up day—although the Saturday would be the pay day

Lord DAVEY If Sunday was the 29th, the 1st would be the Tuesday, and the 3rd would be the Thursday

Mr ELDON BANKES Wednesday, my Lord

Lord DAVEY Surely if Sunday is the 29th of June, there are only 30 days in June, Tuesday would be the 1st, Thursday the 3rd, and Saturday would be the 5th

Mr ELDON BANKES Yes At any rate, I may have got the dates wrong, but the decision under Lord James' casting vote was that it should come into operation the first week after June 29th I gave your Lordship the 3rd, but perhaps it ought to have been the 4th, at any rate, it would be the first making up day

Lord DAVEY I daresay it would be an oversight July 12th was the first pay day affected

Mr ELDON BANKES It would be a mistake At any rate, I meant to say the 3rd

Lord DAVEY Then which would be the Saturday?

Mr ELDON BANKES I do not mind which day it is, my Lord

The LORD CHANCELLOR The meaning here is plain

Mr ELDON BANKES Yes, I think so Now he says " If the miners would only stand behind them who were going to fight for them they need not be in the position they were in then When one man was affected it ought to affect every man They ought not to pay their 6d per week to say they were Union men, but they ought to stick to their principle On one occasion, when they interviewed Mr Chambers, he turned round in his chair and said to him, ' Croft, come and take my chair ' He said he did not want the chair, but only wanted him to answer his question There were some there who had stood the question in 1885, and they were willing to do so again "

Lord JAMES of HEREFORD This latter portion refers to bag dirt, I think, does it not?

Mr ELDON BANKES Yes

Lord JAMES of HEREFORD If you go back to " C "

Mr ELDON BANKES Yes, my Lord, I think it does Our case was There is no doubt they talked about bag dirt, but they did not think that the bag dirt alone would bring the men out, and probably the men who were collected there would have come out whether they talked about bag dirt or anything else , but no doubt these speeches would come to the ears of other men, and the fact that they used this argument about the 10 per cent was in our submission a clear indication that they were using arguments which they thought would influence the men and for the purpose of inducing the men to come out straightaway and break their contracts Then Mr Humphries " Harry Humphries said so far as the ' bag dirt ' question was concerned it had always been contended that they had nothing to do with it save in the getting of it down or in the removing of it, as it was not on the price list according to the contract under which they worked The bag dirt some years ago was not so thick then as it was now, neither was it so hard to get down He remembered the time when they were only too glad for the bag dirt to stop up so that they could get the coal from under it They had

had to set props under it to hold it up, and when they took the props away, the stuff fell. It was the same now as then in some districts, but in the drift district the bag dirt had stiffened and took four times the amount of labour to get it down as it used to do. Formerly it was so handy to get in for the 'packs' and came down so easy that they never took the question into consideration. They continued to do it until it became so hard to get down that they said they ought to be paid for it, or ought to let it alone. The men in that particular district were that day getting the bag dirt down where it was so hard that they were leaving the strong 'bind' up so far in the cutting until they got 20 yards or so. The Company were sending men down to get the 'bag dirt' down, and stopping the money off the men's wages; £8 and £9 had been stopped off men. It was time that the men should not have this to contend with, and if it was their cause they should want the men to fight the cause for them. They were met there to ask the men who were not affected to help these men. The reason was because of a principle, and he thought every Union man, when one man had a grievance, should make every man's grievance his own. There were two large districts, and where there were a lot of men to deal with there was a lot of trouble to get all the men in one mind. They had tried them by ballots and had failed." This is important from our point of view. "They had tried the districts to get men to throw down their tools; and they had said that it was not right for one part of the pit to be working and the other playing. They were being trodden on, and they would have to turn like the worm. He hoped that when the resolution was put before them that morning that they would not be like the previous meeting of 800 or 900 men put their hands up, and when it came to the time they refused to put the X in the right place. He hoped they would go by the show of hands in the morning. It was a thing which he did not like to advocate; but when it came to a Company stopping the money off men, and they considered they had no right to do, it made them say things which they did not like to say. He hoped they would do what was right and just." Now it is plain that "Harry Humphries" (who was a delegate of the Union—I will deal with his position in a moment) is there referring to the point that he knew quite well that they had no right to ask the men to strike until they had taken a ballot; but he is telling them "They had tried them by ballots and had failed," and that on the last occasion, in September, by show of hands they were in favour of a strike, but when it came to a ballot they failed, and though he does not like to advocate it, he says. Well I hope you will go by the show of hands to-day.

Then "Fred Croft" makes a short speech, which I do not think is material—I will read it. He "said datallers were getting 1s per box, where miners were only getting 4d, and they were getting a good percentage out of the miners' earnings. He was present with Pickard when the price-list was drawn up. Pickard asked for a ½d per ton for shift work, but he could not get it." Then Nolan (who is a delegate from Denaby) 'said they had the question before their district, before the County Court Judge, and before the Joint Board, and they were pleased to have Arbitrators on the Joint Board to say that the ½d covered the lot" (I think that must be sarcasm) "He might inform them that two Arbitrators agreed to come down to one Joint Board meeting of these collieries and report on what they did, and said of the document which they had never seen They had asked for the document to be produced, but they could not get one sight of that supposed document, whether it said a ½d per ton should be paid for 'bag dirt' whether it ran 6 feet thick The deductions had been made seeing that the two men were coming down to try the men and see what they were made of with regard to the question' Now I want to pause there to say this A resolution had been passed by the Union that Hall and Annables should come down and explain to those Denaby men what had happened and Nolan, apparently, is rather sarcastic about them and then he says "The deductions had been made seeing that the two men were coming down to try the men and see what they were made of with regard to the question" What exactly he means by that is not very obvious, but it seems as though he was suggesting Is it likely that the men would be satisfied or persuaded by Hall and Annables ? However, it is not very material "The grievance had existed for two years The County Court Judge on a point of law had given his decision between 'bag' and 'bag dirt' which had got to be 6 feet thick" Now there really is not any foundation for that statement "The time had arrived when the price list should be revised At that time there were only 14 or 15 places, and at the present time there were 26 places"

He means affected by the "bag dirt" Your Lordship will see by their own Particulars the numbers which are affected, and that it is not accurate to say there are anything like 267 'Seeing that the Judge in his final remarks wound up by saying that the case ought not to have been brought before him, but that a practical man should have the case in hand, they thought that it was an incentive to them that the time had arrived when they ought to let the Council put the case before the Joint Board and let them decide what they should have for the extra bag dirt At the present time there was some of it nearly 40 inches thick and it had got so hard that men had to work hard for a whole shift to remove it Then the men had ripped down 2 feet the contractors had removed a further quantity and drawn the money which had been stopped out of the miners' wages It was everybody's question So far as he was concerned he had not touched a bit of 'bag dirt' He was not qualified to work in a bank He was surprised to see men stand the tyranny in that district If he was leading them wrong let them put someone else in his place" Now, it is quite plain, I submit, that that is a statement made by a man by virtue of his position as an official He says Here I am, I am advocating this and I am leading you, if you do not like it, put someone in my place, which means, elect somebody in my position instead of me, and it is quite plain that he is there speaking in his official position and saying If you do not like what I say put somebody in my place "Any hard work that he had to do he was going to be paid for it, and he wanted other men to say the same thing. If they would all do that they would get more satisfaction In going back on the ballot they had done wrong" Now, that is not quite accurate He does not mean "going back on the ballot" What he means is this When in balloting you did not come up to your resolution as given by show of hands, you did wrong "In going back on the ballot they had done wrong The district had decided, previous to them taking a ballot, to have a revision of the price list The men had said 'No' If they could only form into one body at both pits they would be a lot better off He would not be pointed out as one man who was always causing bother, because they stood up they were hounded all over South Yorkshire The tyranny was more than human nature could stand They came to the deputation and asked for their grievances to be remedied They had men working for less than 4s a day, and they ought to attend the meetings and ventilate their grievances He knew a place where there were 200 victims, and where a levy of £20 a week was made to make them up to 30s a week while they were at play They had men as good at Denaby and Cadeby, as well as they had at South Kirby, Hemsworth, or anywhere else"— those were two pits that had quite recently been out on strike "If, instead of complaining, they would place their cause before them, they would be better off than they were Since the Judge had made his decision, they had collected £30 to put the men right who were suffering from the deductions Now, a resolution was passed as follows "That this meeting is of the opinion that the time has now arrived when some steps should be taken with reference to the reduction of men's wages for 'bag dirt,' and fines for different things at Denaby and Cadeby Collieries, and that having tried to come to some amicable understanding, and failed, the only thing that is left for us to do is to stop the wheels at both collieries" That resolution was passed at this meeting Stopping "the wheels" means stopping the work It was not that the men should strike only, but that they should stop the work "Stop the wheels"—stop the work And that is what they did, as your Lordship will see

Now "Harry Hirst said the question had been labouring in his own mind, and he thought it had been explained very well There was an understanding that they ought to have a few words with reference to the wages question With regard to the 10 per cent reduction, when they were about to enter on it he would refer to it in a few remarks Some few weeks ago they had held a joint general meeting of the Denaby and Cadeby Main workmen, including surface men The question before them was with reference to the recommendation from their officials connected with the Association to accept the 10 per cent His opinion was at that time that they should not hear of the reduction In Northum-

berland and Durham their wages had gone down very seriously.
The wages had gone down 33⅓ per cent. In Yorkshire they had
said their wages had not gone down at all, and that they could not
go into the market and compete with the owners of Northumberland and Durham because those mines were submitting to their
wages a matter of 1s or 1s 6d less per ton than the Yorkshire
owners were paying. The owners said they had had to drop the
price 1s per ton, but they had not said what enormous profits they
got in 1900. When the wages went to 60 per cent, and they could
not go higher, he thought they ought to recognise this and send
someone to Northumberland and Durham to teach them that they
were friends and not enemies. The selling price ought to be in the
hands of the working classes. If they could get them into the
Federation there would be no doubt about it, they could get re-
munerated on a sliding scale and could even rule as far as wages
were concerned. Some might not agree with the Eight Hours Bill,
some might not agree with him, but every man had a right to his
opinion. He thought the time had arrived when they ought to
drop the Eight Hours Bill, as it was the only thing which was
keeping Northumberland and Durham out of the Federation. There
were only 340,000 miners in the Federation and 410,000 outside, so
that the Federation was practically in the minority, instead of
spending money to send men to the House of Commons, he thought
they should drop that and send men to Northumberland and
Durham to get the men to join the Federation, that would be the
best thing. He hoped they would follow out the resolution which
had been so unanimously carried." Now what happened, my Lord,
upon——

The LORD CHANCELLOR: May I ask you a question of
fact?

Mr ELDON BANKES: Yes, my Lord.

The LORD CHANCELLOR: Was this meeting attended
wholly by members of the Union (Unionists) or by others?

Mr ELDON BANKES: My Lord, we do not know. All we
know is——

The LORD CHANCELLOR: That is enough.

Mr ELDON BANKES: All we know is that there was quite
a small attendance. One witness said, I think, two hundred (200)
men and boys. I think one witness put it rather higher.

Lord JAMES of HEREFORD: It was said that it varied
from 200 to 400—the estimate.

Mr ELDON BANKES Yes, I think so, my Lord Now I think I can best indicate what happened by calling attention to the evidence of one or two men, but there is no dispute about what happened That resolution to "stop the wheels" must have been passed on the Sunday morning In the ordinary course of events the next shift to go to work after this meeting would be the evening shift on the Sunday night They would not be working in the day on the Sunday, but they did go to work as a night shift on the Sunday, and by that Sunday evening the organisation was complete to stop the men going to work, because your Lordship will follow that as regards a large number of the men it would not have come to their knowledge that a proposal even to strike had been made, so that the roads leading to the colliery (you had to go along one road to get to another colliery) were picketted, and the men were turned back, and the steps taken were so effectual that as a matter of fact the work was stopped

Now I want to call your Lordship's attention, quite shortly, to the state of things I will call attention to the evidence first of two men on this point There is a man named Howden His evidence is on page 667 He is a man who was not stopped He was one of the very few who refused to stop At Question 1159 he is asked "Were you a miner in the employ of the Denaby Company," and he says "Well I worked for the Denaby Company, but I was not a coal getter Q Were you present at the meeting of June 29th, when the strike was arranged?—No, I was not present Q Did you know that there was a meeting?—Well, I heard the bellman come round between six and seven on the Saturday night that there was going to be a meeting on the Sunday morning Q That was on the Saturday night, was it?—Yes, as far as what I remember Q Between six and seven?—Yes, as far as what I remember Q Did you hear what the bellman was calling?—That there was going to be a meeting in the Croft by the Station Hotel on the Sunday morning Q On the Sunday evening were you going back to your work?—On the Sunday evening I was going to my work just before six o'clock, Q Did anything unusual happen to you when you were going back to your work?—When I got to the bottom of the street into the main road there were part of the committeemen and others stood there, and they asked me if I was aware of what had passed at the meeting I said Well, I had heard rumours, but I was not aware of the transactions altogether, so they said it had been passed that the wheels were to stand until there was some grievance or something—there was nobody to go to work anyway Well, I said, I pay into the Union, and I am going to work according to their rules I said This is an illegal affair, and for that reason I am going to my work" And then he did go to his work for a short time Then at Question 1168 he is asked "Was that about all that passed then?—That was about all that passed at the time Q Now can you give me the names of the committeemen who were there, or any of them?—Well, there was Brog, Collier,

Mounsey, and Casey," so that it is quite plain what was going on, although it did not affect this man

Now if your Lordship will turn to page 709——

The LORD CHANCELLOR "Brog," who was Brog?

Mr ELDON BANKES "Brog" was Moon It was the nickname for Moon

Lord JAMES of HEREFORD The Cadeby delegate?

Mr ELDON BANKES Yes, his nickname

The LORD CHANCELLOR Yes, that will do

Mr ELDON BANKES He went to work These men went to work It is a pretty good indication of what was going on, and of what they said Now I will take another man—Gill, page 709 "Q Are you a dataller employed at the Denaby Main?—Yes Q Were you at the meeting on Sunday, 29th June?—No Q Did you hear of the meeting at all before you started to work that night?—No Q Did you start to work intending to go on at the night shift on Sunday?—I went to work on Sunday night to go to work Q You started to work?—I started off to work Q Who did you meet by the way?—Benjamin Raybould and John Nolan Q Where were they?—They were on the middle of the highway Q Was that the highway leading to the colliery?—Yes Q Did Nolan speak to you?—Yes Q What did he say?—Wanted to know where I was going Q What did you say?—I told him I was going to work Q What did he say next?—He said they had had a meeting that morning and had settled it to stop the wheels Q Did he say anything more?—No He said they were there at 6 o'clock at night to stop the 6 o'clock shift, and had come down to stop the 10 o'clock shift Q What did you say then?—I said if that be it it is no use going any further Q What did you do then?—I turned round and emptied my bottle and set off home again Q Did you go to work after that?—No Q Why not?—Because they stopped us going. They were there night and morning'

Now that is only to give an indication, and a sufficient indication, my Lord, I think, to show what was going on, and the result of it was that nobody at all went to work with the exception of the four colliers to whose case I will call attention in a moment

————

(Adjourned for a short time)

(After a short adjournment.)

Mr ELDON BANKES: My Lord, I had just given your Lordship an indication of the state of things on the Sunday night, and as a matter of fact practically all the men stopped work, and stopped work without having given a notice. So that with very few exceptions the whole of these 4,000 or 5,000 men broke their contracts with the Colliery Company.

Now I should like just to call your Lordship's attention, quite shortly, to what happened with regard to the colliers on the Monday and the Tuesday; but before I do that I should just like to emphasise the position so that your Lordships may realise what had happened and what was likely to happen. Your Lordships will remember that of these 4,000 or 5,000 men there were about 2,000 Unionists, so that assuming these men and this strike were under the control of the local officials, there would not be much difficulty in keeping the Unionists out if they could get strike pay for them. And so far as the non-Unionists were concerned, of course it depended upon their attitude, but only so much intimidation and coercion was necessary as was found to be sufficient to keep them out. And there is this fact, which is probably peculiar to this strike, that the masters, the Colliery Company did not attempt for many months to bring in any outside labour, and, as your Lordships know, the violence that is unfortunately associated with some of these strikes generally occur in connection with the bringing in of this outside labour. There was no attempt to do that in this case, and therefore you would only expect such an amount of molestation and intimidation as was necessary to keep out the men who were in the regular employ of the Colliery Company. And from the evidence which we adduced at the trial I think your Lordships will be of opinion that the Jury were amply justified in finding, as they did find, that molestation and intimidation was used, and used to such an extent as to keep out such men as were desirous of coming back.

Now, I should like just to call your Lordship's attention, quite shortly, to what happened on the Monday and Tuesday with reference to the men coming back. I think I gave your Lordship the page, 695, and that is the evidence of a man named Berry. I had better begin at page 693, or indeed page 692—I had better read his evidence, it is not very long, and on page 692, Question 1425, he is asked "On your way to the colliery the next morning—that would be on 30th June—did you see any of the committeemen? –I did. Q. Who?—Harry Hirst and Arthur Dickinson, the two present check-weighmen of the colliery at Cadeby. Q. Did you see what they were doing? –When I saw them they were just crossing the road to go into a shop, which was called Morton's shop, at the end of Kilner's Bridge. Q. Did you see them speaking to the men? No. Q. On the 1st July did you go to work again?—Yes. Q. Did you see the committeemen there?—I saw several standing on the

other side of the road, but I did not notice anyone in particular. Q.
Did you see what they were doing. Were they doing anything?—
Not particularly when I passed." Then I will pass to 1436, when
we come to the 2nd of July. "Q. Now on the 2nd July?—That was
the third shift. Q. Did you go to work then?—Yes, I went to work
then. Q. On your way back from the colliery did you see many
people about?—I might say as I was going to work on the 2nd July,
which was the third shift, when I was going down at the back of
Firbeck Street in the morning to work, a lot of men called out to me
'blackleg'—that was as I was going to work—and booed and hooted
at me. Q. Were you followed by them?—No further than the
bottom of the street. Q. They did follow you?—Yes, at the backside
of the building." Then I asked. "Did anything else happen that
day?" and he said. "I went to my work and worked the shift, and
when I was coming home, as I got to Kilner's Bridge, there was a
large crowd assembled on either side of the road—that was,
commencing from Kilner's Bridge; that is where the main turnpike
road commences. There was a large crowd gathered on either side
of the road, and as I was walking I had to walk between the crowd
in the middle of the road. There was no alternative for me. I could
not get on to the causeway for the largeness of the crowd. Well, I
should say there would be between 700 and 800 people; that is men
women, and boys." Your Lordship will remember at that time
there were quite a few men going to work, and therefore it was
only necessary to stop these few men to make the stopping of the
wheels complete. Then he says. "An old lady came behind me
to offer to shove me to the ground." Mr. Isaacs said. "I object
to the old lady." Then I said. "Go on." And the witness said
"I managed to gather myself, without falling altogether to the
ground. The crowd still followed closed in upon me, and hooted
and booed, and called out 'Blackleg.' When I got outside
Whittaker's pawnshop, and the 'Denaby Main' hotel, there were
several stones thrown at the back of me, which whizzed past my
head, one catching me at the back of my head. Of course, I did not
take very much notice of that, seeing that it did not hurt me. I
went a little further, and just as I got to the entry of the 'Denaby
Main' hotel, at the door I was caught at the back of the head with
half a brick." Then he describes how it hurt him, and then he
says, after D. "As I was going on the way home, as soon as ever I
got out of the hotel, I was escorted by three of the officers, and the
crowd still continued to follow, hooting and booing, right away to
my home, and remained outside—a great quantity of them—for a
long time, and threatened that they would blow the house up."
Then I said there was nothing to laugh at. Then. "How long
were you laid up by this assault?—Well, I was laid up several
weeks. Q. When this took place on the 2nd July did you see any
of the Committeemen amongst the crowd?—I saw, on the 2nd July,
when I was going to work in the morning, amongst the pickets,
Phil Humphries and William Collier. (Mr. Rufus Isaacs). This is
a different thing. (Mr. Cautley). This is on the morning?—On the

morning of the 2nd July I saw amongst the pickets Phil Humphries and William Collier that I recognised."

The LORD CHANCELLOR: Was that the same occasion as the last?

Mr ELDON BANKES: No, my Lord, that was when he was coming back; it was when he was coming back from work that he was assaulted. "Q After this assault you did not go to work?—No, I dared not go to work. I dared not go outside the house very often unless I was very careful where I went. Q How many colliers had gone to work on the 30th June?—There was myself, and a father and son named Davey, and a man named Joseph Cooper—four on the Monday, and on the Tuesday there was myself and Cooper, and on the Wednesday there was only myself." So that that shows exactly what had happened on those days, and he was the only one left on the Wednesday, and then he was assaulted in the way he describes, he says he was afraid to go on; and from that time until the following March there was not a single collier working in the pit.

Lord JAMES of HEREFORD: It does not say whether Berry was a Unionist or not, I do not know that it makes any difference.

Mr ELDON BANKES: I do not think that that was proved, my Lord, but I may say at once in this case that there was no sort of feeling as between Unionist and non-Unionist, as you will find in some cases, and so far as this colliery was concerned, there was no feeling against the Unionists; and our case here is as against the Union that we are not complaining of them as a Union, but we are complaining of this strike, because they did not follow their rules, and our case is that if they had followed their rules there never would have been this disastrous strike, and the consequent enormous damage to the Colliery Company.

Lord JAMES of HEREFORD: I do not quite understand your saying you do not complain of them as a Union, but you are seeking to make them liable as a Union.

Mr ELDON BANKES: Oh, certainly.

Lord JAMES of HEREFORD: That is rather complaining of them as a Union if you seek to make them liable.

Mr ELDON BANKES: In that sense; but I mean we have no complaint against our men for belonging to the Union, and we have no complaint against the rules or regulations or composition of the Union provided they follow their rules and do not behave in the way they behaved in this case.

Now, my Lord, I have now got to a point at which I think it is convenient to call your Lordships' attention to the questions that were asked of the Jury, because I think when your Lordships are in possession of the Jury, because I think when your Lordships are in possession of the questions I shall be better able to direct your minds to the points I want when I am discussing the rules of the Association, which is the next point I propose to deal with My Lord, those questions are at page 1009 The first question is this " Did the Defendants Nolan and Humphries or either of and which of them unlawfully and maliciously procure the men to break their contracts of employment by going out on strike on June 29th without giving notice ?—Yes " Now there was a special question asked with regard to those two men because of their special position as delegates, which I will explain in a moment Then Question 2 " If you answer the first question in the affirmative then were Nolan and Humphries or either and which of them in so doing purporting to act as agents of the Association and for its benefit —Yes " Then " 3 Did the members of the Committee of the Denaby and Cadeby branches or any of them unlawfully and maliciously procure the men to break their contracts of employment by going out on strike on June 29th without giving notice ?—Yes " 4 If you answer the third question in the affirmative then, were the members of the Committees in so doing purporting to act as agents of the Association and for its benefit ?—Yes " Now your Lordship will see that the third and fourth questions are the same, only applied to the members of the Committees as a whole instead of being confined to the two men Then 5——

Lord JAMES of HEREFORD Have you given us all the evidence there is of what we will call " Inducement "?

Mr ELDON BANKES Of the procurement?

Lord JAMES of HEREFORD The consequence of the resolution of the 29th June

Mr ELDON BANKES Not all, my Lord

Lord JAMES of HEREFORD Substantially

Mr ELDON BANKES The Jury would be influenced by what took place afterwards

Lord JAMES of HEREFORD Substantially

Mr ELDON BANKES The main part—what I rely upon—yes not on all these points Then " 5, Did the Defendant Association by its Executive Council or by its officials ratify the acts of Nolan and Humphreys or of the members of the Committees in so procuring the men to break their contracts ?—Yes ' Now, of course, that is directed to the assumption that the men were not agents, or the Committee were not agents—that they had no prior mandate, as it were, but that their conduct was subsequently ratified. That is what the question is directed at, and that the Jury found in the affirmative. Of course, your Lordship has none of the evidence directed to that point yet. The questions following on after that are directed to the second branch of our case, upon which the Master of the Rolls thought that the verdict was right. "6. Did the Defendant Association by its officials or by the members of the Committees of Denaby and Cadeby Branches maintain or assist in maintaining the strike by unlawful means, that is to say (A) By molesting or intimidating men who were working for the Plaintiffs with a view of inducing them to cease from so working?— Yes. (B) By inducing or attempting to induce men who were willing to enter into contracts of service with the Plaintiffs or to work for them to refrain from so doing?—Yes. (C) By the grant of strike pay against the rules of the Association?—Yes. 7." (and this is directed to certain individual Defendants) "Did the Defendants Wadsworth, Parrott, Firth, and Hall, or any and which of them, maintain or assist in maintaining the strike by unlawful means, that is to say, by any and which of the above means?—Not personally, but as servants of the Association."

Lord JAMES of HEREFORD. Is that what you wanted, Mr. Bankes, or not—I am looking at the answer. Did you prefer that answer or not?

Mr. ELDON BANKES. I do not think the qualification affects the answer. I daresay perhaps the Jury thought it might, but I do not think it does. "8. Did the Defendants, or any, and which of them, conspire with each other, or with workmen in the employ of the Plaintiffs, to do any and which of the matters mentioned in Question 6?" Now, of course, that might under certain circumstances give a cause of action other and beyond that indicated in Question 6, but, my Lord, I am not sure that that question arises here.

The LORD CHANCELLOR. Is it answered?

Mr. ELDON BANKES. Oh, yes, my Lord.

The LORD CHANCELLOR. But is that an answer? It does not say "any" or "which", it does not describe "which."

Mr. ELDON BANKES. I think that was accepted as a general affirmative answer. There has been no complaint of the answer, at any rate, up till now. Then, my Lord, those were the nine questions that were answered.

Lord DAVEY. Mr. Bankes, inducing men not to enter into contracts is not actionable, is it?

Mr ELDON BANKES   You mean without the finding of conspiracy ?

Lord DAVEY   With or without, but we will leave out the finding of conspiracy for the moment   Inducing a man not to contract with another is not actionable, is it ?

Mr ELDON BANKES   My Lord, that is a matter which has been a good deal discussed   I do not know that I want that individual one, but I will not say any more about it for the moment   That point is a matter for discussion, but I do not think except on that point there will be any doubt as to the law applicable to these answers

Lord DAVEY   Giving strike pay, again, is not actionable

Mr ELDON BANKES   That, again, is a matter of discussion

Lord DAVEY   What has that to do with you ?   If I out of my private means relieve men on strike, am I liable to an action ?

Mr ELDON BANKES   Put in that way, I should think very likely not

Lord JAMES of HEREFORD   It is a case of maintenance

Mr ELDON BANKES   I agree that a good deal of discussion may range over findings B and C , but it is not necessary for my purpose that I should support those if I support A   It must not be thought I am for a moment relinquishing my position   There is a great deal to be said, but at this point I do not propose to address your Lordships on the law until I have made the facts plain, if I can

Lord DAVEY   Very well

Mr ELDON BANKES   I think I have read all the questions

The LORD CHANCELLOR   Nine

Mr ELDON BANKES   Yes, those were the nine questions

Mr ATHERLEY JONES   You have not read nine

Mr ELDON BANKES   I beg pardon   "9   Did the Defendants or any and which of them unlawfully and maliciously conspire together and with workmen formerly in the employ of the Plaintiffs to molest and injure the Plaintiffs in the carrying on of their business, and were the Plaintiffs so molested and injured ?— Yes "   I thought I had read that   Now there is only one further fact I ought to mention before I come to the rules, and it is this   I called your Lordships' attention to the meeting on the 29th June, the Sunday, and to the speeches, but I have not called your Lordships' attention yet to the fact that that resolution which was passed was entered in the books of the branches as a resolution of the branches, and if your Lordship would turn to page 226 you will find the minute I must call attention to this, your Lordship will see there are two resolutions there, one is from the transcript of the Shorthand Writers' Notes (that is in the middle of the page) which I have read, but the official minute as entered in the Cadeby and Denaby branches was rather different, and that is at the bottom of the page Now, it is in this way "Minutes of Cadeby Branch Meeting held June 29th, 1902, between the Denaby and Cadeby men in the Croft adjoining the Station Hotel, at 10 o'clock" Now, it is recorded as a meeting of the men, and the resolution is "That this meeting is of the opinion that the action taken by the Colliery Company deducting money out of men's wages is wrong, and that we stop the wheels at Denaby and Cadeby until such time as Mr Chambers refunds the money stopped and remedies our long existing grievances" Now, that is undoubtedly the resolution of the branch It treats the meeting as a meeting of the joint branches and resolves "that we" (that is the branches) "stop the wheels"—which they proceeded to do, and did So that when I come to address your Lordships on the question as to who it was who induced the men, and on the question as to ratification, if it is necessary, I rely upon this, amongst many other things, as indicating that it was treated as being the action of the branches (I have used that expression for the moment) throughout

Lord JAMES of HEREFORD You used the word 'branch,' no doubt, but the language is "The Denaby and Cadeby Men" which in fact, as you say, might probably be different

Mr ELDON BANKES Of course, it ought only to have been a meeting of the Union men, because no one else was entitled to vote according to their rules at all

Lord JAMES of HEREFORD Have you got the terms of the summons to the meeting?

Mr ELDON BANKES Only the bellman went round

Lord JAMES of HEREFORD So I recollect, but have you the terms of the bellman's summons?

Mr ELDON BANKES No, all we know is what I read to your Lordship from the evidence of Howden "Did you hear what the bellman was calling?—That there was going to be a meeting in the Croft by the Station Hotel on the Sunday morning" That is all we know about it

The LORD CHANCELLOR What page was that?

Mr ELDON BANKES: Page 667

Now, my Lord, I think I had better go to the rules, because I think it is convenient at this time that your Lordships should be in possession of the constitution of this Union, and your Lordship will find them set out at page 93   I am afraid I must go through them all, but it is very important to see exactly what the rules are   Of course, people talk as though as a question of law you could say whether or not a branch official was an agent of a Union, but it must depend upon the rules of the particular Union, and must depend not only upon that, but upon the particular acts done on each occasion   Now the rules are at page 93 "Rules of the Yorkshire Miners' Association, registered under the Trades Union Acts, 1871 and 1876   (1) This Society shall be known as the 'Yorkshire Miners' Association,' and shall consist of as many members employed in and about the various collieries as may think proper to join   It shall be divided into as many branches as may be deemed expedient" (now my case here is that the Union consists of the branches)   "It shall be divided into as many branches as may be deemed expedient, and shall remain in existence under the above title , nor shall its funds, books, emblems or other property be appropriated to any other use than as provided for in these rules so long as fifty members in one or more branches remain together in the district, and are willing to carry out its objects   The place of meeting and office of this Association shall be at the offices, Huddersfield Road, Barnsley, in the County of York, where the business of the Association shall be carried on   The place of meeting and office may be from time to time changed,' and so forth   Now, "(2) These rules shall be for the government of the Association, and the protection of the members, and no new rule shall be made, nor any of the rules herein contained or hereafter to be made, shall be amended, altered or rescinded unless with the consent of a majority of the members present,' and so on   Now, "(3) This Trade Union is established for the following objects, viz ' (this is equivalent to the Memorandum of Association of a Company) " (A) To raise funds by contributions, fines, donations and levies for mutual help   (B) To try for improved enactments for more efficient management of mines, whereby the health and lives of miners may be protected   (c) To secure the prices and wages bargained for by the members   To prevent all illegal stoppages at the pay office, and to protect members when unjustly dealt with by the masters or managers ' (your Lordships will remember by the resolution which I last read that what was stated to be the cause of the strike was the illegal stoppages from the wages)   "(D) To try for compensations for accidents (whether fatal or otherwise), if such accidents have been caused by negligence on the part of employers or managers   (E) To secure the true weight of the material sent to bank by the miners, which will give justice to both employers and workpeople   (F) To shorten the hours of labour in the pit to eight hours per day, and to improve the moral and social position of the mining classes

(G) To provide a weekly allowance for the support of members and their families who may be locked out or on strike, and to resist any unjust regulations in connection with their employment (H) An allowance to all full members, half members, and members' wives at death, who are financial on the books (I) To extend the principles of self-help in other mining districts, and to aid all other Associations which have for their object the protection of labour and kindred objects (J) The whole of the moneys received by this Association shall be applied to carrying out the foregoing objects according to rules, and any officer misapplying the funds shall repay the same, and be excluded" Now, those are the objects "4 That the supreme government"—now, I lay stress on the word "supreme"— "of this Association shall be vested in a Council, which shall consist of a president, general secretary, financial secretary, and agent, treasurer, and one experienced member, duly elected (as delegate)"— this is where the delegate comes in—"by and from each of the financial branches composing the Association, and each delegate appointed to attend Council meeting shall present to the president a credential from his branch empowering him to act" I think it would be convenient if I were to give your Lordships at this stage who the various officers were at the time of this strike, as I am on this rule The president ——

Lord DAVEY Are they printed anywhere?

Mr ELDON BANKS They are the Defendants in the action, really, my Lord The president was Mr Cowey, the general secretary was Mr Pickard, the agent was Mr Parrott, the financial secretary was Mr Frith, and the treasurer was Mr Hall The Denaby delegate was Nolan, one of the speakers at the meeting, and the Cadeby delegate was Harry Humphries Now your Lordships will appreciate why we drew the distinction in the questions between Nolan and Harry Humphries, and the other members of the Committee, because these men—I mean, for what it is worth, and I do not say at the moment what the value of it is, but these two men were members of the Council at the time

Lord JAMES of HEREFORD There are no Committeemen of the general body but only of the branch body?

Mr ELDON BANKES No, there are not, there is an Executive Committee

Lord JAMES of HEREFORD Out of these.

Mr ELDON BANKES There is an Executive Committee under the rules

Lord JAMES of HEREFORD. Out of the Council

Mr ELDON BANKES Not necessarily out of the Council, but so far as the central office is concerned there is the Council which is defined in this rule and there is an Executive Committee with limited powers which we shall come to in a moment Then the next rule is No 5 My learned friends say I did not finish reading 4 "And each delegate appointed to attend Council meeting shall present to the president a credential from his branch, empowering him to act as their representative, before being allowed to take part in the business of such Council meeting" I thought I read it Then "5 The ordinary Council" (now they do not mean there a different Council from the other Council, but they mean an ordinary Council meeting as opposed to a special Council meeting) "shall meet to transact the business of the Association, at the offices, Barnsley, once every six weeks or as often as may be required, and shall deal with all questions relative to the interests and welfare of the Association in such a manner as is directed in these rules" I want to call attention to the fact that the ordinary meetings are every six weeks, but there is power to call a meeting whenever one is required, because when we come a little later on to deal with the facts I have relied, and do rely, on the fact that no meetings of this Council were called, and, as I say, they left the control of the strike to the local officials

Now comes the voting power "6 No branch shall be allowed to send more than one delegate to the Council meetings, and each recognised branch having 50 members or under have one vote, but any branch having more than 50 members, such branch shall be allowed one vote extra for every other clear 50 members or fractional part of 50 members, and every delegate shall exercise his vote or votes on all questions that may come before the Council, no delegate being alllowed to remain neutral" I do not think, unless my learned friends wish it read, the rest of this rule is material, it has only reference to the appointment of the delegates, and the importance of this rule to bear in mind is this, that the officials of the Union have no vote Mr Pickard, Mr Cowey, Mr Parrott, Mr Frith, and Mr Hall have no vote at all, and the only persons who have any votes are the delegates

Lord DAVEY Is that so?

Mr ELDON BANKES Yes, my Lord, we are agreed as to that, the officials were asked whether that was the meaning of the rule, and that is so The only provision for a vote is that the delegates are to have a vote, and therefore the scheme of this constitution is that the paid officials are not to have any votes at all, but the votes shall be given by the members, as it were, acting through their delegates sent specially to the Council Then "7 That the expenses of all delegates to Council meetings," and so forth, shall be paid, they get their expenses of going to the meetings, but nothing else Then No 8 is as to the time of meetings, and so forth, there is nothing in that, I think, my Lord   Now 9 is important   'The Council shall not have power to lay levies on the members or make grants to any cause, member or purpose whatever until the same has been submitted to the branches for their approval or otherwise " Now that indicates on those matters that it is not even the delegates whose votes are to be accepted, but those matters are to be sent down to be voted on at the branches by the individual men   There is no point in 10   " 11 Any branch appropriating the funds of the Association to any purpose whatever not specified in these rules, shall be dealt with by the Council, or as the law directs '   Now that is important from my point of view, because these rules, I submit, throughout are plain to show that the funds are the funds of the Association, because Lord Justice Mathew made the point that the branch is a Union, and if anybody has cause of complaint against the officials of a branch you must sue the branch, but these rules are plain, as I submit, to show that the branches are local habitations, if I may use the word of the Union, but the funds are the funds of the Union, and the officers are local officers of the Union   " Any branch appropriating the funds of the Association to any purpose whatever not specified in these rules shall be dealt with by the Council, or as the law directs "   Then   ' 12 A registered vote shall be taken throughout the entire Association, whenever any number of branches, numbering one-fourth of the Council, demand such vote on the following questions, viz   The adoption or prolongation of a strike, alteration of rule or rules, voting away large sums of money either in our own district or to other districts, or dismissal of general secretary or other district officials, such registered vote to be taken by ballot in the local branch room, and recorded in their books, a copy of which shall be forwarded to the offices to be counted up either by the Council, executive, or whom they may direct to do so   No branch allowed to remain neutral unless the Council decide otherwise, and the majority of such registered votes to be decisive and binding upon the whole of the branches and members composing the Association "   Now there is a provision that in certain cases the registered vote of the Association shall be taken in what they call the local branch room   Then   " 13 The President of the Association shall be nominated from the branches "   I do not think that the appointment or duties of these gentlemen are material, unless my learned friends think so   I will just pass through the rules hurriedly   There is a rule as to the appointment of the " President and his duties," the " Duties of Corresponding Secretary," the " Duties of Financial Secretary," and the " Duties of Agent "

Now 17 is important for my point of view   " The wages of the secretaries and agent shall be fixed by the Council, and shall be paid by the treasurer of the Association every week, they shall be under the control of the Council, and must obey their directions during the time he or they are in their service," so that it is plain that these gentlemen, what I may call the permanent staff, are mere servants (I do not use that word in any offensive sense) of the Council, because it is provided that they must obey their directions, they have no independent powers, they may advise but they have no vote, and they are bound to do as they are told, and who it was who was to control this strike when I come to it except the branch officials, my submission is that it is impossible to find from these rules

Lord JAMES of HEREFORD Mr Bankes, with great respect, is it your case that if a branch of the Association, small or great, acts independently, and in relation to some local injury that it feels it is suffering from and takes a certain course, that action would find the whole of the Association in all its branches?

Mr ELDON BANKES Yes, my case is that under these rules (I do not speak of any other rules) the branch officials are the local officials of the Association

Lord JAMES of HEREFORD That is your case Do you rely upon these rules for that purpose?

Mr ELDON BANKES Certainly

Lord JAMES of HEREFORD You could not get on without them?

Mr ELDON BANKES No, I do not think so, I say you cannot submit as a general proposition of law with regard to any voluntary association of individuals is registered association of individuals that any particular person or their agent or not without looking into their constitution, and I think I have seen other rules in which the state of things might be quite different from these rules I am now merely dealing with these The next I have got marked is material (of course I will refer to any my learned friend wishes me to) is 22 "The general treasurer shall be nominated by a branch and elected by a majority of members throughout the Association His duties shall be to receive and pay all moneys belonging to the Association, and shall under no circumstances pay, lend or appropriate the funds of the Association to any purpose whatever, except the same be in accordance with the rules," &c I need not read the rest of these rules about the treasurer except that at page 100, my Lord, 26B, with regard to the treasurer, there is this provision which I think is material " He shall receive three months' notice from the president, by direction of the Council previous to any alteration taking place as to the terms of his situation, or previous to his being discharged; the Council shall not have the power to discharge the treasurer until sanctioned by the branches" Then as to "trustees," it is not material to read that rule Now we come to the Executive Committee, 28, and that is material "There shall be an Executive Committee always in existence, which shall be composed of not less than 13 members elected from and nominated by the branches. And the general

secretary and other district officials included, and to have a vote at
all Committee meetings" (so they have a vote at the Committee
meetings), "and the said Committee shall be elected or re-elected at
and confirmed by the Council, half of whom respectively shall retire
half-yearly, which shall be in the months of June and January, and
the ordinary Executive shall meet once in every six weeks" "29
The duties of the Executive Committee shall be to consider and
decide upon all cases of emergency arising between council meetings,
such as preparing programme for Council meetings, branch
grievances, accepting and ordering the payment of victims, and all
minor questions, but the Executive shall not decide upon questions
relating to strikes, lock-outs, or of voting money to other districts, or
any amount in the district exceeding five pounds,' so that for any of
the purposes that are material to this case we may eliminate the
Executive Committee they had no power to deal with the strike, or
with any lock-out, or with any question of strike pay

Lord JAMES of HEREFORD But had the Council?

Mr ELDON BANKES Yes, the Council had the right, we
will see later on about the strike pay

Lord JAMES of HEREFORD Do you put it that the branch
had power to deal with the strike question, or the Council?

Mr ELDON BANKES The branch had, and the Council
had too

Lord JAMES of HEREFORD You have to say both

Mr ELDON BANKES Both clearly had, I think Then, my
Lord, the next is 31—we now come to the branches "The president
of every local branch shall be elected or re-elected by a majority of
members of the branch, and shall serve for six months, he must
zealously watch the interests of the branch, superintend all business
relative thereto, preside at all meetings, and see that all cases are
dealt with according to the rules, he shall have power to instruct
the secretary to call special meetings when requested to do so by two
or more members of the Committee, and he shall have 2s 6d for
every 100 and under, and then for every other clear 50 members 6d
extra" So that he is a paid official of the Association, he is paid
out of moneys of the Association although it is collected at the
branch

Lord DAVEY Yes, but is that quite enough?

Mr ELDON BANKES My Lord, I am only going by steps

Lord DAVEY The office boy is a paid official

Mr ELDON BANKES Official? I do not know

The LORD CHANCELLOR A paid servant

Mr ELDON BANKES ' (32) The secretary of every branch shall be elected or re-elected every six months His duty shall be to keep a correct account of all moneys received and expended He shall strictly attend to all money received by the branch in the manner set forth in these rules and minutes of Council He shall attend all Committee and general meetings, take minutes of the same, and have charge of the books, documents, papers and correspondence relative to the business of the Association and his branch He shall also attend strictly to all moneys being returned to the Council and appropriated as directed by rules, keep the books clean and respectable, and have them ready for inspection at any time the Council or branch may desire to see them He shall fill up or make out correct returns of income" I do not think the rest of the rule is material Then branch treasurer and his duties "The treasurer of each local branch shall be elected or re-elected every six months, and shall receive and pay all moneys connected with the branch He shall see that proper receipts for all payments are returned to the Committee and kept in possession of the branch, he shall not on any account pay, lend or appropriate any of the funds to any member, cause or purpose whatever beyond the rules, resolutions or minutes of the Council, he shall attend all meetings, answer all questions relative to money matters," and so forth And then " 34 All local secretaries shall be paid for their services quarterly and in the following manner " Then there is a scale of payment " 35 Local treasurers shall be paid for their services quarterly, and in the following manner " So that the treasurer and the secretary are both paid officials, and paid as the president is, out of the moneys of the Association " 36 All local Committees shall be allowed, for their attendance at the Committee meeting, 6d each No member of the Committee shall be allowed to absent himself from the meeting, or leave the meeting, before the business is finished, and the meeting closed." So, again, the Committeeman is paid, but in a different sense, he does not get a salary, but he is paid for each attendance

Lord JAMES of HEREFORD Mr Bankes, what are the words which justify what you have just said, that these persons are paid out of the moneys of the Association, as distinguished from the branch money?

Mr ELDON BANKES Because there is no branch money, my Lord I will read the rules through, and I shall satisfy you

Lord JAMES of HEREFORD What is the meaning of Rule 33 " That the treasurer shall receive and pay all moneys connected with the branch " ?

Mr ELDON BANKES That means that there are certain expenses connected with the branch, for instance, there is the treasurer's salary, and the secretary's expenses, and the expenses of the bellman

Lord JAMES of HEREFORD " Shall receive "

Mr ELDON BANKES They are the contributions of the members

Lord JAMES of HEREFORD Then there is that money of the branch

Mr ELDON BANKES It is collected locally, the money of the Association is collected locally, but it is, as your Lordship will see, all the money of the Association   The member contributes to the Association, and his money is collected by the branch

Lord JAMES of HEREFORD That is very important, if you could just give the exact reason why you say it is the money of the Association

Mr ELDON BANKES I shall come to it in a moment, but I have passed one of the rules——

Lord JAMES of HEREFORD You know best, Mr. Bankes, if you are coming to it, pray go on

Mr ELDON BANKES I think your Lordship will be satisfied, but I passed one rule which dealt with it   It is Rule 11, and may I just turn back to that " Any branch appropriating the funds of the Association to any purpose whatever not specified in these rules shall be dealt with by the council, or as the law direct " Now, there is no money comes into the hands of any branch except the contributions of members, and, therefore, this rule must be directed to appropriating the contributions of members, because there are no other funds of the Association which come to its hands, and that is made plainer by later rules, I think

Lord JAMES of HEREFORD Are there no fines ?

Mr ELDON BANKES Yes, there are fines of members, as well as contributions of members

Lord JAMES of HEREFORD Are they distinguishable as between the branch and the Association ?

Mr ELDON BANKES. No, there is no distinction in these rules.

No 37 is a very important rule, I think the most important of all the rules almost from my point of view "All local branches shall be conducted by a Committee of not less than five or more than nine financial members, president, secretary and treasurer included, whose duty shall be to attend all meetings, whether regular or special, and shall at all times transact the business of the branch as directed by the rules and minutes of the General Council' Now, it is plain that the General Council have a controlling influence over these men. They may say "You shall do this, or "You shall not do it," or "You shall do it in a particular way", but subject to any such direction, or subject to any of the standing rules, the business of the branch, whatever it is, to be conducted by the Committee including the officers who, as I have said, are the paid officers

Lord JAMES of HEREFORD. But the direction that can be given by the General Council can only be by rule and minute

Mr ELDON BANKES. That is all

Lord JAMES of HEREFORD. It would not include saying to the branch "Go and advocate a strike'

Mr ELDON BANKES. No, but "minute" means merely the record of some decision of the Council. When this strike began it was perfectly competent for this General Council to have called a meeting and passed a resolution that no branch official should take any part in it, perfectly competent, and my submission is that not calling any meeting and not passing any resolution, but interfering with it in the way they did by advice and assistance, they left the branch to manage its own affairs, as directed in this rule, as being the local officials of the Union

Now, 38 I do not think is material. It is only for the election of the Committee, 41 is very important "In the event of any alteration at any of the collieries"——

Mr COMPSTON. You ought to read 40, I think

Mr ELDON BANKES. I will read any you wish "40 The Committee of local branches shall meet once in every fortnight (unless warned by the secretary, after consultation with the president, that there is no business to transact), to investigate all grievances and complaints of members, and deal with them as per rule, they shall attend to all moneys being received and paid in accordance with these rules and minutes of Council and Executive Committee, they must know the amount of income and expenditure at all Committee meetings, and shall lay all transactions and business of the branch and the Association before the general meeting of the branch, which shall be held once in every fortnight, or oftener if required' Well, I have read it as I was asked to read it "41 In the event of any alteration at any of the collieries in the mode of working that tends in any way to take away the interest of the members, the branch (through the Committee) shall at once investigate the matter, and shall lay all facts before the Council or Executive Committee" I think it must be the "Council or Executive Committee or General Secretary immediately"

Lord JAMES of HEREFORD Yes

Mr ELDON BANKES "42 That in all cases of emergency arising at any of the branches where prompt action is required, such branch shall forthwith lay all information before the general secretary, who shall report the same to the Council or Executive Committee as early as possible"

I think that exhausts the rules directing what the branches are to do, at any rate for the moment Then there come the class of rules which deal with the property, and if your Lordship will look at 46 "All branches shall be supplied by the financial secretary with contribution books, cash book, branch stamp, and stationery necessary to carry on the business of the branch, out of the funds of the Association, which shall be the property of the Association and under their control" Then with 48 we begin the class of rule which deals with the auditing, and this is important, from my point of view It provides that "Two or more auditors shall be nominated by the branches and elected by the General Council, half of whom must be elected every year, and stand for two years They shall audit all books and other documents and accounts used by the Association, whether local or general" (now, that is a good illustration, I submit, of what these rules are) "once in every quarter' The rest of the rule I do not think is material Then "52 That each and every branch be provided with a ballot box for the purpose of taking a registered vote"———

Lord JAMES of HEREFORD Is it quite clear that "local' means branches?

Mr ELDON BANKES Yes, my Lord, I think quite plain I do not think my learned friend can point to any rule which indicates the contrary application of the word Then "53 There shall be for this Association one general fund, which shall be applied for the relief of those members and families who may have been thrown out of employment by strikes, lock-outs, or victimised, and for management, and also to financial members at the time of death, whether accidental or natural, or to such other legal and necessary purposes as may arise from time to time amongst our members, such as grants to other trades, hiring rooms, interment of members, half members and members' wives at death This fund shall be under the guidance and control of the Association's Council, and shall be supported and disbursed as provided in these rules " Then " 54 The entrance fees of all new branches that are wishful of joining the Association shall be fixed and determined in accordance with the funds of the Association The entrance fee shall be 2s 6d for full members and 1s 3d for half members The workmen employed at any pit or colliery, who are not connected with this Association and are wishful to enter, may form themselves into a branch and pay the entrance fee as above All information respecting conditions of membership, and the benefits to be allowed, shall be given on application to the registered office " Your Lordship will bear in mind that these two pits each had a branch, the Denaby Branch and the Cadeby branch Then " Removal of Officers " is not material No 57 is material " The regular contributions to this Association's general fund shall be 6d per week " (that is the contribution to the general fund, and I think this bears on the point Lord James asked me), " but should this fund at any time be so reduced as to be inadequate to meet the claims of its members, the general secretary shall lay the facts before all the branches, at a general meeting convened for that purpose, and if decided by a majority of members composing the Association, the Council shall be empowered to lay an extra levy upon all (in proportion to the amount of contributions they pay) until such time as the fund may have gained its preponderance, and the Council be able to discharge the liabilities and permit the contributions to be reduced to their ordinary standard That all moneys collected in the name or entered in the books of the Association, and entrusted to the care of the local treasurers of the Association, be forwarded by post office order to the financial secretary, made payable to the district treasurer for uses of the Association, and that all local treasurers take the receipt received from the financial secretary " Now one of these officers is called in terms the local treasurer of the Association, there is no sort of doubt about that, and he is in exactly and precisely the same position as the president, secretary, and other members of the Committee He is the local officer of the association, and there he is so called Then " Members in arrears "— I need not trouble about that

Now we come to the two rules which were before this House in Howden's case, and they are with regard to strike pay, 64 and 65 May I read, as Lord James asked me to deal with this point, Rule 60 ?

Mr ATHERLEY JONES That is just what I was going to ask you to do

Mr ELDON BANKES " 60 No branch shall be allowed to make use of the funds of this Association for processions, flags, banners, or any other personal or public use not specified in these rules, unless the same be submitted to the Council, and approved by a majority of the branches," but it is plain to show that the funds in their hands are the funds of the Association. Then "64. If any branch member or members have grievances affecting their wages, mode or manner of working, or the hours of labour, if the employers refuse to remedy those grievances, and after all proper and peaceful means have been tried to effect a settlement by deputations from members, with the advice and assistance of Council, and such member or members be permitted to cease work by the sanction of the Association in accordance with the rules, such members shall receive 9s per week for full members, 4s 6d per week for all half-members and 1s per head per week for all children under 13 years of age, until such time as they can resume work either at the place they left or some other colliery, or the Council with the sanction of the majority of members decide otherwise." "65. Any branch or portion of any branch which may be locked-out, or otherwise thrown out of employment, in consequence of any action that may legally have been taken by the Association to keep up the price, or remedy any grievances, either at that or any other colliery connected with the Association, the members of such branch shall be supported after the same rate as the members on strike until such time as they can get work, or the Association decide otherwise."

Now, it is quite plain that under those rules the authority to decide whether strike pay is to be granted is the Council; the rules do not give them any right to say whether a strike shall take place, or whether a strike shall not take place, but it is quite plain to show that they are the only people who are to say whether strike pay shall be granted or not. It is quite consistent with these rules that a branch as I call them, the local officials of a branch may procure a strike, and maintain a strike, in the hope of getting strike pay, and, if they did not get it, naturally the strike would collapse, but whether they get it or not depends on the Council.

Lord JAMES of HEREFORD, Was any strike pay found by the Council here?

Mr ELDON BANKES Yes, my Lord, they passed a resolution—I gave your Lordship the date, on the 24th July—that strike pay should be paid as from the 17th July, and they paid it from the 17th July until the Injunction in Howden's case, for over six months; but, of course, I have not told your Lordships the circumstances under which they justified it yet.

Then the next, and I think the last, rule I need refer to is 72, which is a very important rule, and of course, affects the branches, and this is a rule directed to the strikes which the branches must work themselves "No branch or portion of a branch shall be allowed to strike or leave off work with a view of causing the works to stand, unless sanctioned by two-thirds of the members composing the branch, when such strike shall be determined by registered ballot such vote to be obtained by the branch officials calling a special meeting of said branch for that purpose, and each member shall have delivered to him one black and one white ball" (I do not think I need go through the details of the vote, but if your Lordship will turn over you will see) "but in no case shall such vote be legal unless three-fourths of the members composing such branch record their votes, and two-thirds of such votes be in favour of such strike" Now, there is a very wholesome and salutary rule, one would think, which, if properly carried out, would do two things, it would first of all give the workman the opportunity of expressing his own free will, and, secondly, it does provide that there shall be no strike until there is a great preponderance of opinion of men acting voluntarily in favour of the strike, but the importance of it, from my point of view, is this, that this is a direction that the taking of the ballot which is the first step in the initiation of a strike shall be the proper business of the branch officials, because a good deal has been said in this case about *ultra vires*, and so forth, but I only wish to emphasise that on this point These are all the rules

Mr S T EVANS You might read the end of 72

Mr ELDON BANKES "In all cases where a registered vote is taken, such votes shall be counted up by four experienced members of the branch, and forwarded to the offices, to be dealt with by the Executive or Council meeting" I do not follow that, but I have read it

Those are the rules, and, of course, if I am right in saying that these rules do constitute the branch officials local officials of the Union, I submit there was abundant evidence to support the answers of the Jury when they answered the questions which were put to them as to whether or not the members of the Committee and Nolan and Humphries were purporting to act and did act as the agents of the Association Of course, the Court of Appeal have decided that, as a matter of law, there was no such evidence, because upon these rules I think Lord Justice Mathew went so far as to say that the branches were constituted independent Unions, and that therefore they are responsible for what they do, and do not involve the Association in any liability for anything they do, but my first submission is that, take the rules by themselves, they do create an Association with officials The central officials, if I may so call them, the salaried officers of the Association, have a very limited authority, they are directed to do what the Council tells them to do, and they have no independent initiative and no independent authority whatever There is no officer of this Association in existence that does such a thing as take charge of a proper strike except the branch officials, the local officials, with such assistance as they may get under the authority of the Council from the salaried central authorities.

That is my first proposition, but the second proposition upon the rules is this, that whether I am right, or whether I am wrong, as a matter of construction, it is plain, I submit, upon these rules that the Council have the authority to say what the branch officials shall do, or shall not do, and if you find the Council refraining from telling these branch officials that they must no longer interfere and maintain this strike, but on the contrary you find them, as you will find them when we come to the evidence, directly interfering and assisting the men by advice and by sending down men to speak, and so forth—when you find them directly advising the branch officials whom they knew were in charge of the strike, even if the branch officials did not follow that advice, it is the clearest evidence, as I submit, for a Jury that the Council did in this particular case allow the branch officials to have the conduct of this strike Whether they had the right to have it under the rules is one thing, at any rate, they had the right to prevent them exercising it, and they did not attempt to prevent them but on the contrary, as I submit, they clearly acted in such a way as to justify any Jury in finding, as this Jury did, that these people were, under the circumstances which I shall now proceed to detail to your Lordships, acting as the authorised agents of the Union

Now I think, my Lord, I can pass back to the point at which I broke off——

Lord DAVEY Where is the rule you refer to about them acting under the direction of the Council ?

Mr, ELDON BANKES That is 42, I think

Lord DAVEY No, I think 37 is the one you refer to

Mr ELDON BANKES Yes

Lord DAVEY " And shall at all times transact the business of the branch as directed by the rules and minutes of the General Council " Does that mean more than this, that in transacting the business of the branch they must pay regard to the rules and minutes of the General Council ?

Mr ELDON BANKES Yes, it includes that, of course

Lord DAVEY Does it mean more than that ?

Mr ELDON BANKES I submit it clearly gives the Council a right to pass a resolution and minute it, so that now as from this moment——

Lord DAVEY I daresay , but supposing they have not passed the resolution ?

Mr ELDON BANKES If they have not passed a resolution then first of all I will assume against myself for the moment that the true construction of the rules is not that they are the local officials, assuming that for the moment, then, at any rate, the Council are aware that the branch officials at Denaby within twelve miles of Barnsley are in charge of this strike, and under those circumstances, knowing that and sending down their treasurer every week with the strike money, it was their strike from the time they paid the strike money

Lord DAVEY I understood your argument I should like to ask you this Supposing a strike has been properly initiated, that there has been a proper ballot and the proper number of people have voted and so forth, the General Council have no control then to say "Notwithstanding all this has been done, you shall not strike,' have they ?

Mr ELDON BANKES I think the only hold that the Council have is that they may say to their officers "Now, you shall take no part in this "

Lord DAVEY That may be

Mr ELDON BANKES And they might say under the rule about strike pay——

Lord DAVEY Could they refuse strike pay saying, which you say is not the case here, and I quite appreciate that because we have had all this before "We will not pay strike pay," assuming that a strike of the branch alone has been determined upon by the proper number of members, voting in the proper way, and by the proper majority, and so forth ?

Mr ELDON BANKES I think if all the rules were carried out they have no power to refuse strike pay

Lord DAVEY I do not think they could, that was my impression

Mr ELDON BANKES I think that is so Now, might I go back, my Lord, to where I broke off, and I had better go now in order of date through this rather long history to show your Lordship what happened, and of course, what I am going to draw your Lordships attention to now is material on the second branch of our case about maintaining the strike by unlawful means, It is material also upon the question, if it is necessary to go into it as to whether or not the Council ratified what had been done previously, and it is material also on the question, if it is necessary to go into it, as to whether or not they did constitute the branch officials their agents for the purpose of carrying on the strike Now, that is what the evidence is directed to, and, of course, as to the existence of intimidation and coercion, the existence of these unlawful means

I said just now that the first branch of our case involved three questions, and, first of all, was the strike procured by anybody? That is the first question—or was it spontaneous, if I may so say? I mean, to put it in precise form, was the breaking of the contracts by the men procured by anybody? That is the first question Upon that I submit there is abundant evidence for the Jury to find upon the materials which are before your Lordships, that the men were procured to break their contracts, because they all broke their contracts on the Sunday night and the Monday morning Now, why did they do it? I am not here to suggest that there may not have been grievances existing in some people's minds, I think he would be a bold man who would say that at any place or under any circumstances you could not find grievances, but I do submit this, that upon the facts before the Jury it was plain there was no grievance existing of such a character as would have induced the men to go out spontaneously. And you do find this, as we call it, hole and corner meeting called by the officials of the branches, and addressed by officials in the way in which the men were addressed followed by effective picketing. From those materials any Jury is entitled to find that there was a procuring of breach of contract on the part of the men, and particularly in the absence of any suggestion to the contrary, and every one of the members of the Court of Appeal accepts that they accept the finding of the Jury that the breaking of contracts was procured. Now, the next point was, who was it procured by? If it was procured at all, it is quite plain that it was procured by the men who took active part in the calling of the meeting, and the addressing of the meeting, and the organisation and rendering effective of the picketing. There is no suggestion that anybody else did it, or could have done it

Lord JAMES of HEREFORD What was the object in not having a ballot, Mr Bankes?

Mr ELDON BANKES We have always said, and I submit it is the only answer, that they knew quite well, if they took a ballot, the men would not come out. There was not a strong enough feeling about this question of the bag dirt, whether it was that there were not a sufficient number of men involved, or whether it was that the men realised that there was no real grievance in it, we do not know, but the fact is that they said themselves at the meeting "We have tried the ballot and failed" There were not a sufficient number of men in favour of striking on this particular point Then the third question is If it was procured by these men, were they the agents of the Union?

Lord DAVEY For that purpose?

Mr ELDON BANKES Yes, for that purpose.

Lord JAMES of HEREFORD Acting against the rules?

Mr ELDON BANKES Yes, they went against the rules

The LORD CHANCELLOR Agents in procuring, you mean?

Mr ELDON BANKES Agents in procuring Now, I have dealt with the rules so far as they relate to and deal with that third branch of this part of our case Of course, the evidence is material upon that, because your Lordships will see what was done and what was said, and so forth, and if it is convenient——

The LORD CHANCELLOR Before you go to the evidence your point induces me to put this to you, so that you may explain it to-morrow, or some other time I observe you do not ask any questions of the Jury as to whether these persons were in fact authorised by the Association

Mr ELDON BANKES No

The LORD CHANCELLOR I do not want to argue it, I only want to put that to you

Mr ELDON BANKES I will answer that in a moment, we do not suggest that the branch officials were authorised by the Association to bring the men out in the way in which they did bring them out

The LORD CHANCELLOR That is what I thought

Mr ELDON BANKES We do not suggest that, we suggest that the central officials, if I may use that expression, knew that the men were going to be brought out

Lord JAMES of HEREFORD You rely on the ratifying

Mr ELDON BANKES No, I rely, my Lord, upon the fact, first of all, of the agency, as I submit, created by the rules themselves I submit that these men were the local officials of the Union to conduct the business of the branch, and if they conduct the business of the branch contrary to the rules, they offend against the rules, but that does not affect the position of an outsider

Lord DAVEY But were they the agents for this purpose, Mr Bankes?

Mr ELDON BANKES Yes, my Lord, our case is clearly——

Lord DAVEY That they were agents in some sense I suppose most people would admit, but were they the agents for this purpose? They were not general agents

Mr. ELDON BANKES No, in one sense they were not general agents They were agents to do anything connected with the business of the branch, as they call it, which is a wide word, and it clearly includes strikes, because there is a rule directed to taking a ballot preparatory to a strike which is defined to be part of the business of these local officials, and, as I say, and have said before, Who is to control and direct a properly initiated strike of a branch unless it is the branch officials under these rules? Who is there to do it?

The LORD CHANCELLOR Might I, in order to get rid of this—and you need not answer it now—point out the other observation I want to make upon the first branch of those questions to the Jury You did not ask the Jury whether it was within the scope of the authority of these men to act on behalf of the Association, and, again, you do put it and only put it as a case of them purporting—that is to say, affecting or professing to act as agents, and that being ratified afterwards I do not know if I make myself clear, but the first five questions seem to me to have no relation except to original defect of authority, purporting to act, ratified afterwards, when the thing came to the knowledge of the Association That is your case as regards the first five questions I may be wrong, but will you think of that by to-morrow morning?

Mr ELDON BANKES, Yes, my Lord

Lord DAVEY And at the same time will you consider whether you can have a ratification of an act not purporting to have been done on behalf of the central association?

Mr ELDON BANKES My Lord, there has been a good deal of discussion about how far ——

Lord DAVEY I do not want an answer now

Mr ELDON BANKES We propose to deal with that

The LORD CHANCELLOR You will deal with these questions?

Mr ELDON BANKES Yes May I say at once with regard to the scope of authority that I submit that would not be a question for the Jury, that is a matter of law as to whether the agent is acting within the scope of his authority

The LORD CHANCELLOR, It may be so, Mr Bankes,

Mr ELDON BANKES I submit the question for the Jury is—first of all I think it is necessary to ask whether he purports to act, and secondly, whether it is for the master's benefit

Lord JAMES of HEREFORD For the benefit of the principal, you mean?

Mr ELDON BANKES Yes I will come to Monday the 30th, and your Lordship will find the state of things that was going on upon the Monday pretty well described by two witnesses I will just refer to, a man of the name of Legg, and a man of the name of Watkinson Legg's evidence on this point your Lordship will find at page 716, Question 1599 "Q Do you remember going to work on the Monday, June 30th?—Yes Q As you went to work did you see any of the Committee men?—Yes I saw them at the corner of Kilner's Bridge on the way to the work Q Who did you see?—Brog, Collier and several others of the Committee as I was going to work on the Monday morning Q Whereabouts were they as you went to work?—They were on the right hand side of were I had to turn to go over the bridge Q What time in the morning was this?—Between half-past five and six Q Where you told anything on your way to work as to the pits?—Yes, they asked me whether I had heard about a meeting as was held on the Sunday I said I had They said they had come to the conclusion that they were going to stop the wheels till such times as there were some terms come to with the management Q Did you go on and go to work?—No, I went back home after that Q Why did not you go to work?—Because when they said that I was frightened to go (Mr Justice Lawrance) What are you—a collier?—I was a filler before the strike" Then another man—Watkinson—at page 721 "Q Are you a driver at the Denaby Pit?—No, I am employed at the Cadeby Pit I was employed at Denaby before the strike I had signed on on the 29th June Q On Monday, 30th June, did you go to your work at the Denaby Pit?—I was proceeding on my way Q You started to go to work?—Yes Q Do you remember getting to the railway crossing?—Yes Q That is very near the pit?—Yes Q Tell us what you saw and what happened?—As I was proceeding to work on the 30th June, on the morning shift, about half-past five, I got nearly to the crossing and I saw a group of men in the middle of the road One of them came to me and says 'Where are you going?' I said 'I am going to work, I suppose' Q Do you know who it was?—Yes, John Nolan, and he says 'Well, do you know as we have decided to stop the wheels until we get more money?' I says 'No, I dont, I suppose I shall have to go back home then now?' He says 'Yes, you will have to go back home' He says 'The other men and boys have gone back, and you will have to go back,' and with that I turned round emptied my bottle, and went back home again" I think that is an indication sufficient to satisfy your Lordship as to what was going on

Now, at 11 o'clock on that morning, they had one of these meetings, and I may tell your Lordships that they had what they called a joint meeting every week throughout the strike; I think they had one certainly every Monday throughout the strike, which was addressed by these branch officials sometimes, and sometimes by the central officials who were sent down from Barnsley. The minute of the joint meeting is at page 227. We do not seem to have got a report of the speeches, but this is the resolution "1 That the resolution of the previous day be confirmed"—that is, that we stop the wheels "2 That a deputation be appointed to wait on Mr Chambers, with a view to arriving at some amicable understanding 3 That the deputation consist of '—then the names are given "4 That the joint secretaries write asking Mr Chambers to meet a deputation from both branches '

Now, on that same day, information is sent from the branches to the central office at Barnsley of the fact of the strike, and your Lordship will find the telegrams on page 334, B. At 10 10 in the morning, Smith, the secretary of Denaby, wires to Pickard "Denaby Pit playing over stoppages Bag dirt question" And Hirst at 9 7 wires from the Cadeby Branch the next document "Denaby and Cadeby Pits set down this morning Bag dirt Now, that is in accordance with their resolution, as entered in their book, that they determined to stop the wheels because of the illegal deductions from the pay Upon receipt of these two telegrams, the Executive Committee, who happened to be meeting at Barnsley that day, considered them, and they passed a resolution which is at page 227, at the bottom of the page This is a very important resolution "That Mr Cowey be instructed to wire the secretaries of Denaby and Cadeby main branches, stating that in the opinion of this Executive they ought to have a meeting and agree to resume work at once as they are out contrary to the rules and resolutions of this Association ", and the telegram which he sent is at page 334

Lord DAVEY It is a copy of the resolution.

Mr ELDON BANKES It is, my Lord, verbatim Now may I pause there to say this First of all, it is a plain indication that the Executive realised upon the scanty materials that they had got in these telegrams that the men were out, as they called it afterwards, illegally, contrary to the rules and regulations; they were out without notice Therefore, it is brought home to the Executive Committee that these men are wrongly out Now what do they do? They treat this matter as one which is clearly within the competency of the local officials to deal with; they realise that the branches have got charge of this, because they wire instructions to the branches of what they are to do in connection with it Therefore, I submit that it is a plain indication that they realised what I submit was the real position under the rules, that it was for the branch officials to deal with this matter, and they proceed to give them advice, and very good advice too, if it had been followed "That Mr Cowey be instructed to wire the secretaries of Denaby and Cadeby main branches, stating that in the opinion of this Executive they ought to have a meeting and agree to resume work at once"

Now will your Lordships please bear this in mind, although I have some facts to call attention to meanwhile, that the Council did not meet until the 14th Their ordinary day for meeting was the 14th of July

Lord JAMES of HEREFORD They met on the 30th of June first

Mr ELDON BANKES Not the Council

Lord JAMES of HEREFORD That was the Executive Committee

Mr ELDON BANKES Yes These wires happened to come on a day when there was an ordinary Executive Committee meeting, and the next ordinary Council meeting was on the 14th July, and no attempt was made to call a special meeting, nor was anything attempted to be done by the Council or Executive Committee at all to control this strike or to do anything indeed until the 14th, when it came before them in ordinary course I will tell your Lordships when I come to it in order of date what they did

Then Tuesday was the 1st July, and there is nothing material that I call your Lordships' attention to On the 1st July, as you have heard from Berry's evidence, I think two colliers went to work On Wednesday the 3rd July, Berry was assaulted, and from that date no colliers went to work to get coal at all until the following March There was a joint meeting on Wednesday July 2nd, and the minute of what happened is at page 228 We have not got the speeches, but the resolution was "That seeing that Mr Chambers will neither return the money deducted from the stallmen's wages, nor will he undertake to discontinue the practice, this meeting confirms the previous resolution of June 29th to let the pits lay idle" What did happen was that directly the strike had been notified to Mr Chambers, who was in Ireland, he came back, and he arrived back on this Wednesday A deputation of men met him, but he would not go back from his former attitude that he would either do the work and charge them an amount not exceeding a halfpenny, or let them do it and they would be paid the 1s 4½d, and then afterwards this resolution is passed Then nothing material happens until the 7th July, which was the Monday in the week following On that Monday there was, as usual, a meeting, and to that meeting the two men Hall and Annables came down They were, as your Lordship will remember, the two Arbitrators who had been parties to the Award, and whose action the men had said had given the bag dirt question away, and apparently the Executive at Barnsley had thought it was wise to send these men down, and they do pass a resolution that they should go down to explain the matter, but that resolution had been passed before the strike commenced. Still, in pursuance of the resolution, I suppose the men came down. Now the report of this meeting is at page 393. Croft is again in the chair.

Lord DAVEY. Did the meeting only consist of these four men?

Mr ELDON BANKES. No, my Lord, there was a considerable attendance, but the reporter records the presence of these as principal men, I suppose; they were all officials, and my learned friend suggests they may be called the platform men. The chairman "said he thought they had behaved themselves since the previous Monday night in a proper manner, and he was glad to see it. No one was more pleased than himself to see how quiet they have been at Denaby and Cadeby. They had not been so very quiet since the first time they met Mr Chambers on their grievances. There was something in the papers that morning which scarcely had a word of truth in it. Mr Chambers had not told the Press what had taken place at an after meeting held the next day, and what Ben Pickard had told him. He had put the bright side in to suit himself " (it is here if it is necessary to refer to it) " he (Croft) was disgusted with what he saw in the papers. They must have a price list to work by, and it was only left to them and other men to fight it out. He (Mr Chambers) had had one side of it, and had not told the public that the men had taken half a yard down before the 'muck' was taken away by the men set on for the job. One side was good until the other was told. He hoped they would take his advice, and not interfere or interrupt any of the speakers. Some men said 'How are we going on for money?' They had been out for seven months in 1885. They would never give in, but stand like braves. He and Nolan had told the manager time after time on deputations that unless the grievances were remedied the wheels would stand, and their reply was 'Let them stand.' It was the wrong way, but when a man came to have 17s 9d stopped out of a three days' wage they could not let it slip by. In one case a man had had to borrow money to finish paying his trammer. (Shame on them.) Some men with large families might ask 'How are we going to get on?' The Committee had sent circulars to each branch in the district asking them to call meetings to consider their case at every branch in the district. They would have strike pay, no one could stop them. Grass would grow over the top of the wheels before they would work if they got strike pay." Now there is a plain indication of what Croft intended the men should do, if they could only get strike pay; it was that they would never come in, and that grass should grow over the tops of the wheels, and that was said in the presence of Hall, who was one of the central officials, the treasurer of the Union, and therefore he was at that time made fully aware of what the attitude of the men was,

E

and what they intended to do if only they could get strike pay. Then he goes on to say, "Some of the neighbouring collieries had cried shame on the Denaby men that they had no pluck in them. He had many a time gone into a 'best room' in Mexbro' and had been told that they would work for any price at Denaby. The last time they met the manager over the lads they said that unless the 'fineings' was stopped something would happen. The manager had replied, 'I shall be there.' If the dispute should last for one month or go for two years, he hoped they would be in the same mind as they were now, as they could not be worse off when they were 'playing' than when they were working. The report said 1s 4½d per ton, but he should not take off the price of the pillars. It would become 11d per ton, a good price for a yard of coal if they did not look out. When he and Nolan went to Sheffield they had reported every fact and truth. Mr Pickard told him (Mr Chambers) that he was not a gentleman, and that nothing was left for the men but to fight it out, and the sooner the better. He and the rest of his colleagues were prepared to go into the western portion. They had been treated as beasts of the field and not men." Now that is plainly an exhortation to the men to stand out, and a statement in the presence of Hall as to what they intended to do if they got strike pay. Then Mr Hall makes a long speech, but his speech is directed to explaining his conduct as treasurer, and I do not think that this is material at all on any——

Mr ATHERLEY JONES. You had better read it, perhaps.

Mr ELDON BANKES. I am afraid I cannot read it. Then Mr Annables was called, but the men would not hear Mr Annables, you will see on page 400 at the end of Mr Annables' remarks "The speaker was prevented from proceeding in consequence of the uproar and sat down." Then Croft begins again, and he says "The thing you have to work at was that which he pointed out at Sheffield. Never mind Mr Chambers or anyone else, they are not paying according to the price list. The average wages they were getting had been given by Mr Chambers. Some men were getting 4s 6d and 5s per day. What would be the result if 50 per cent was to come off? He only wished that every man starting with a 10 per cent reduction they would all throw down throughout the Federation districts."

Then Nolan again speaks. He said "Mr Hall had made a fine statement, and had gone a long way round to tell them what he had told them about the document had not brought them a bit nearer than what they had told them at their meetings from time to time. They had asked for a copy of the document to be sent on. Judge Masterman had said, on a point of law, he would have to decide in favour of the Colliery Company, but in his summing-up he had said that he believed the time had come when the stuff had got harder and thicker, and that there should be a different price fixed, and that the case should have been settled by different people They were all trying to do their best on that day, and he was one who was put in the witness-box They did not want any more gulling, as it was said in the morning papers that they were trying to mislead the men It was no benefit to himself any more than any other man He felt that he would act as straight as he could and do his duty, but since they found it different he would move on and make room for someone else" (Now here again it is quite plain he is speaking as an official, and saying to the men "If you are not satisfied with me as such, you can get somebody in my place") "Who authorised the two men to draw up the document of ½d per ton to cover the question? It was time so far as the document was concerned Annables had told him that he had signed a document, because he saw Mr Hall's signature attached to it Until then officials acted in a different manner to that they would never be able to do any good in their own local branches Mr Chambers was prepared to take the ½d off and pay for the whole of the work"

Then Harry Hirst says "He was pleased they had got Hall and Annables down to explain the document It was not an agreement which had been drawn up, it was only an arrangement It was not an agreement and did not stand for what Mr Chambers said it stood for He would like Hall and Annables to answer that question one way or another Providing the district would not allow them strike pay, it would be for them to make the best possible arrangement they could, appeals would be given to the district branches stating the case Mr Chambers would see that the men took down two feet, and men had been sent to take down the remaining ten inches He hoped they would stand out Mr Hall told them that their only hope lay in changing their venue and giving in their notices for a revision of the price list"

(Adjourned to to-morrow at half-past ten o'clock)

SECOND DAY.

Tuesday, 13th March, 1906.

Mr ELDON BANKES If your Lordships please My Lord, if it suits your Lordship's view, I prefer to continue with the narrative before breaking off to answer the particular point which your Lordship put to me last night

The LORD CHANCELLOR Pray do not break off

Mr ELDON BANKES I had got to the point of Monday, the 7th July, which was the meeting, your Lordships may remember, at which Messrs Hall and Annables were present, and my point upon that is that it was then directly brought to the knowledge of one of the principal of the officials of the Union—Hall, the treasurer—the view of the men and the view of the branch officials, as disclosed in the speeches on that day, namely, that if they got strike pay the grass would grow before they would go to work again, and I am not sure whether I had called your Lordships' attention to the resolution that was passed at that meeting, but, if not, I desire to call your Lordship's attention to it It is on page 228 It is in these terms "Joint meeting held on the 7th July, 1902, in the 'Reresby Arms, Croft, at 6 p m, attended by Messrs Hall and Annables (1) After hearing the report of Hall and Annables the following resolution was carried (2) That the joint secretaries write in to the Council which is to be held on Monday, July 14th, asking for strike pay to be granted to the men at Denaby and Cadeby for the time they play" Then there is a similar minute in the Denaby minute book I may pass on now to the 11th

Lord JAMES of HEREFORD Mr Bankes, in what capacity did Hall and Annables attend?

Mr ELDON BANKES Hall and Annables attended that meeting, my Lord, in pursuance of a resolution of the Council passed prior to the strike, that they should go down and explain to the men their action as arbitrators That was how they came to go there, but, of course, Hall was in fact the treasurer, and my point upon that meeting is that he left that meeting with the knowledge that he must have acquired as to the attitude of the men and the attitude of the branch officials as disclosed in the speeches at that meeting

Then, my Lord, the next date I want to refer to is Friday, the 11th July There is a letter which was written on the 11th July (page 342) a letter written by Smith, the secretary of the Denaby branch, to Mr Pickard It is in these terms "Dear Sir, I am instructed to ask you to bring before Council Meeting the case of the Denaby Main Miners. You will have heard that the pit has been stopped owing to the excessive tyranny that has been imposed upon the men and also through the stoppages that have been made off the men's wages for the so-called bag-dirt." May I stop there, my Lord, to refer to the expression? "You will have heard that the pit has been stopped." I am not sure that I sufficiently emphasised our view with regard to the terms of the resolution. The original resolution was that "the wheels be stopped," and of course the reference to the wheels there is to the winding wheels of the pit. It means that no one shall be employed at the pit either to come up or to work down, not only to work the coal, but nobody shall be allowed to take part in the necessary work of either raising or lowering the men in the pit, either for the purpose of feeding the horses, or for the purpose of keeping the ways open and so forth. It is the most comprehensive term that could be used, that the wheels be stopped,—and here he speaks again and says "You will have heard that the pit has been stopped." Then he goes on to say "It was unanimously agreed at a meeting of 3,000 men and boys to put the pit down." Now I ought to call attention to that, I think, because it emphasises, in my view, the attitude that the branch men were taking towards the officials. There is no doubt that this was an exaggeration, and I assume an exaggeration purposely made for the purpose of getting Mr Pickard to take a more favourable view of their position than he might otherwise take. "It was unanimously agreed at a meeting of 3,000 men and boys to put the pit down. This was done. At general joint meetings which have been held this proposition has been unanimously confirmed with the addition that we have a revised price list something that will be definite not (as Mr Chambers calls the present one) a myth to work on as we are at present. I am instructed to ask you to put before the Council our case with a view to obtain strike pay for the men and boys affected. I wish to bring to your notice, and before Council, that Mr Chambers repudiates the revised price list signed by you in 1890, and falls back upon Mr Chappell's Agreement that was made in 1885, a thing which we cannot entertain. Please bring this before Council and oblige." Well, that was a misconception. That was not so at all, and on page 343 (that is the same page, my Lord) Hirst, the secretary for the Cadeby Branch, writes a similar letter only in different form. He says I am instructed by a Joint Meeting of Denaby and Cadeby main workmen to write asking you to bring this letter before the Council Meeting on July 14th. Our men along with Denaby men set the pits down on Monday June 30th." Now your Lordships will see, there is a distinct statement as to whose action it was "Our men" (that is our branch—our Union men) "along with Denaby men set the pits down on Monday, June 30th", and of course your Lordships will bear in mind that all these expressions are material upon the question as to who procured, and upon the question as to whether these men were purporting to act on behalf of the Union. "Our men along with Denaby men set the pits down on Monday, June 30th, without giving any notice through the action of the Colliery Company by deducting £8 15s 6d from the men's wages in one particular district in the Denaby Main Pit, which amounted in some cases to 17s 9d per man (for as the management alleges) refusing to do work that the price list told them to do But we say that it is not in the contract We have tried all that lays in our power to get the grievance remedied but have failed, Mr Chambers saying that if it was only 2½d we wanted he would not give it us to settle the case So our branches think that the time has come when some stand should be taken to get a revised price list, a list that the men can understand, and seeing that we are now out in the field it ought to be thoroughly gone into before we commence again, and we are now making application for strike pay Hoping that the Council will grant us pay and oblige yours truly" "P S Anything further you may want our delegates will be able to explain" That of course has reference to the fact that in ordinary course Nolan and Humphries would attend the Council on the 14th, at which this application came up

Now, my Lord, we come to the 14th, and it is the most material date from our point of view, because this was the date at which the whole matter came up before the Council It was their first meeting since the strike had commenced It was an ordinary meeting, and, of course, there came now an opportunity for them to disaffirm what had happened, if they wished to disaffirm it Now was the opportunity for them to say, if they wished to say it, that the branch officials could take no part in the conduct of this strike, but what I think your Lordships will find did happen was this—that although they disapproved of the particular course that was taken in going out without notice, they approved of the strike as a strike, and they intervened for the purpose of putting the thing in order if they could, and they entrusted the branch officials with the duty of putting it in order, and, of course, our case is that if they intervene and entrust the branch officials with the conduct of the strike, those branch officials are then agents from that moment, even if they have not been before, and it is no answer to say that the branch officials did not do exactly what we wished them to do

Now, my Lord, the resolution is at page 228 It is the resolution at the bottom of the page "Ordinary Council Meeting, held at the Miners' Offices, Barnsley, on Monday, July 14th, 1902, Mr J Wadsworth (Vice-President) in the chair I think at that time, my Lord, Mr Pickard was ill, and he was unable to be present, no doubt he continued to be ill, and ultimately he died, I think, during the progress of the case I beg your Lordship's pardon, it was Mr Cowey—I think Mr Cowey was President—I am not sure It was Mr Cowey who was the President, and who was ill, and not able to be there However, this is the resolution—page 228 "That Messrs Wadsworth and Walsh accompany Messrs Nolan and Humphries to a meeting to be held to-morrow morning at 11 o'clock, and tell the men they must resume work, and then take a ballot of Denaby and

Cadeby Main Collieries the first day they work as to whether or not they will give in their notices to terminate their contract of service to get their grievances settled That Mr Pickard be instructed to write Mr Chambers asking him to meet a deputation along with Messrs Wadsworth and Walsh to-morrow afternoon to try and arrange for the men to resume work"

Now I must stop to emphasise the language of that resolution, and to point out to your Lordship exactly what it means If your Lordship will look at the last line on page 228, what they tell the men to do is "to resume work and then take a ballot" Now the point of this is this It was recognised by the Council, as I submit, that the men had broken their contracts and were no longer in the employ of the Colliery Company, and that being out of their employ they could not take a ballot and give notices, but they would have to go back to work and again become the servants of the Colliery Company, and having done that, they were to ballot, and then of course they could give their notices if the ballot was taken Now the point of that is this, my Lord Our case was and is that if the men had only been allowed to come back to work there would have been an end of the strike, because our case was and is, that there was no universal grievance affecting these men, which, if they had been allowed to exercise their own free will, would have influenced them to remain on strike, and if only the men had been allowed to come back we were confident that the strike would have come to an end, and our view is emphasised by what happened Our case was and is that the branch officials recognised this, and they were determined that the men should not go back to work, but that some scheme or another should be devised which would enable them to say they were acting upon the suggestion of the Council and enable them to bring themselves, as they thought, within the orders of the Council, without allowing the men to go back to work, and I will proceed to show your Lordship how that took place

Now, the only other observation I want to make about this resolution is this that the Council direct that a ballot is to be taken Now, of course, under the rules that ballot had to be taken under the direction and control of the branch officials The rule is plain about that, because there is a special rule directing that it is the duty of the branch officials, and here we have the Council not repudiating the strike in the sense of saying It is all wrong, and we will have nothing to do with it, not repudiating the branch officials in the sense of saying You have no right to interfere in this, and we will not allow you, as officers of the Association, to do it, but simply to propose a course which, in the view of the Council, would make this a strike which under their rules they were entitled to support

Now that, my Lord, is the resolution, and in consequence of that resolution, or following upon that resolution, Mr Pickard gets into communication with Mr Chambers, because your Lordship will see that under the second branch of the resolution "That Mr

Pickard be instructed to wire Mr Chambers asking him to meet a deputation" Now, of course, I ought to say before passing from this resolution of the Council that that is a resolution of a meeting at which presumably the whole facts were before the Council, because Hall had been down and he knew what was going on, and the two delegates, Nolan and Humphries, were present, and in the letter from the Secretary of the Cadeby Branch, it had been pointed out to Mr Pickard that if they wanted any information about the strike they could get it from the delegates who were to attend in the ordinary course

Then at page 344 your Lordship will find the wires which passed At the top of page 344 Mr Pickard wires to Chambers "I am desired by our Council Meeting to ask you to meet a deputation of your men along with Messrs Wadsworth and Walsh to-morrow afternoon to try and arrange for the men to resume work" Answer from Chambers "No need to wait for meeting, the pits are open when the men wish to resume work," and Mr Chambers emphasised that in his evidence—that the one desire of the Colliery Company was that the men should come back They did not believe that they would stay out if they got a free opportunity of exercising their own judgment, and their one wish and desire was that they should come back

Then, my Lord, at that time the position of things began to improve slightly in this sense—that more men were coming back gradually, and by the 14th of July ten men had come back and had resumed work at Denaby, and from 60 to 70 had come back and had resumed work at Cadeby The importance of that to the Colliery Company was very great indeed, because the damage that was being done to the pits at that time was enormous owing to the closing of the ways, and if the Colliery Company could only have got a sufficient number of men to continue working at the ways, an enormous amount of damage that was afterwards suffered would have been avoided Your Lordships will understand that these men were not getting coal, there was no attempt made to get coal, but they were employed in keeping the ways open

Lord JAMES of HEREFORD Did they go back of their own accord, or in any way in consequence of what they knew was the view of the Central Council?

Mr ELDON BANKES No, there is no evidence of that, and so far as we know they came back of their own accord, and there is no doubt, I think, from the evidence that there were a great many men who would have come back and were anxious to come back, your Lordships will bear this in mind also, that of the total number of men employed, half of them were non-union men who got no strike pay at all The only inference is that with regard to these men who had got no grievance and were getting no strike pay, some influence or another of a sufficiently strong kind had been brought to bear to keep those men out

Lord JAMES of HEREFORD Why do you say they had no grievance? They were in the same position as the Union men as regards their supposed grievance

Mr ELDON BANKES Yes What I meant was, there is no universal grievance affecting anything like that number of men I do not want to minimise it the least There was this question about the bag dirt which did affect, at the outside, some 40 to 60 men out of 4,000 or 5,000

The LORD CHANCELLOR Were the non-union men affected by the 10 per cent reduction?

Mr ELDON BANKES Oh, yes, they were

Lord JAMES of HEREFORD I have looked very carefully into that They did not seem to make much of that as causing the strike at all, it is the bag dirt at present

Mr ELDON BANKES Now, your Lordship will see there is no doubt that the 10 per cent was never officially put forward in any way as the ground of the strike, nor could it be, but our case was that whether it was a potent argument or not, it was undoubtedly used by the men who were desirous of getting the men to come out on strike It was held out to them as an inducement that if they came out there would be a general strike throughout the Federation in respect of the 10 per cent Now the next day is Tuesday, the 15th, and on that day a meeting of the men is held at which Messrs Wadsworth and Walsh attend in pursuance of the resolution of the Council, which I have read "That Messrs Wadsworth and Walsh accompany Messrs Nolan and Humphries to a meeting to be held to-morrow" So now we get one of the paid officials of the Council sent down specially, accompanied by a man named Walsh, who was chosen because he was an exceptionally good speaker, and they were sent down to attend a meeting of the men, and that meeting your Lordship will find recorded at page 402

The LORD CHANCELLOR Wadsworth and Walsh were sent down?

Mr ELDON BANKES They were sent down

The LORD CHANCELLOR Accompanied by Nolan and Humphries?

Mr ELDON BANKES Nolan and Humphries were the delegates, and who would be there in the ordinary course It was Wadsworth and Walsh who were sent down, and they were to attend the meeting at which Nolan and Humphries would, presumably, be present in ordinary course, and the account of this meeting is at page 402, and my summary of this meeting is that it shows that, so far from disapproving of the strike as a strike, the men were told that Pickard and the officials of the Union sympathised with it, and if it had not been for the Taff Vale decision, they would have had their strike pay, as a matter of course, straight off, but I had better read the speeches

Lord DAVEY   Is this a meeting of Cadeby or Denaby?

Mr ELDON BANKES   A joint meeting   I must read these speeches, I am afraid, my Lord, they are all material   This is the record   "Present   Fred Croft (Chairman), Messrs Wadsworth, Walsh, Hirst, H and P Humphries, and Nolan"   And the Chairman says that   "they had been anticipating a meeting since the previous Wednesday night to know the decision of the Council, and the feeling of their officials and delegates   There was scarcely a delegate at Council" (now the delegates, your Lordship will remember, are the only people who are entitled to vote) "who did not sympathise with the Denaby and Cadeby men   Walsh and Wadsworth would give them good advice   They had dealt with the question for the past two years, and it had been a burden to them   No one could say that they had not tried to settle the grievances on amicable terms   Their manager would never reason with them   Now that it had come to what it had, if they would agree that morning, they would be in a position to fight and stand"   (That means to say   If you will accept the suggestion that is going to be made to you, we shall then be in a position to fight and stand)   ' He was proud to learn that Mr Ben Pickard would only be too pleased if he could allow them strike pay   He could not help them with strike pay, but he would be glad to do all he could for outside support"   Now, what that means, my Lord, is this —that we cannot give you strike pay as things are at present, because you have come out without notice, but we will appeal to the various branches to support you voluntarily, and if evidence of sympathy and so forth is required, I submit, for what it is worth, that that is strong evidence that, at any rate they did not disapprove of the fact that they had struck   "He could not help them with strike pay, but he would be glad to do all he could for outside support   (A Voice   Why doesn't he come down?')   Croft   'He's too ill   He (Croft) wanted them to come to a calm decision at the finish   They had not done wrong and could not stand it any longer   It would be as good a thing as had ever been decided at Denaby and Cadeby   The summonses did not frighten him, but only made himself and his colleagues all the more eager to fight '   (That had reference to the fact that the Colliery Company had summoned a number of these men for damages for going out without notice)   "There would be a deputation to meet Mr Chambers at two o'clock   To have 17s 9d stopped out of wages was enough to rile any man   It was time to stop work when they got to working for nothing   He was fully confident that it would end in a right way '   Well, of course, one does not want to criticise language used on occasions like these, but to speak about working for nothing when the men of this Union were getting 9s 4d a day—a shilling a day more than the other men who were not affected—it is exaggerated, in plain language, but there it is

Now Walsh speaks He "said that along with his colleague Wadsworth he had come there that morning" (now what?) "to assist them out of their difficulty, and in the first place he must congratulate them on the spirit they had displayed during the past fortnight in resenting the conduct of their manager during the past two years in regard to their grievances" (Now can anything be stronger? Language of deliberate approval) "I am sorry to think that you placed yourselves in such a position that you were not able to strike that terrible blow at Mr Chambers that you originally intended you could (A Voice 'We knew that before we started') If you had struck this blow three years ago, from the feeling that was displayed in Council yesterday, the Council would have given you strike pay" Now he goes on to explain that He says The only reason we decided we could not was because of the Taff Vale decision, but here again is the language of deliberate approval If this strike had taken place under the circumstances in which it did take place, three years ago, you would have had your strike pay yesterday "They had rules in their Society, but the position was changed by virtue of the decision being given in the House of Lords nearly 18 months ago against the Railway Servants' Union, known as the Taff Vale decision The leaders in that case caused the men to stop work illegally, and agreed to pay them their Union money from the funds of the Association The Taff Vale Company at once sued Mr Bell, M P, the leader of their Union, for £28,000 for loss of profits and other expenses The case was tried before the Queen's Bench, and a decision given for £7,800 against the Amalgamated Society Mr Bell went to a higher Court and it was confirmed, and every day afterwards, as long as they remained out of work, the Society was practically in the hands of the Railway Company Mr Bell applied for the legal expenses of himself and Mr Holmes, the arbitrator objected, and even Mr Bell's Union could not pay the legal expenses of Mr Bell and Mr Holmes out of the funds of the Union, and they were now appealing for a voluntary levy to the railway servants to enable them to defray the legal expenses which they were put to by the Taff Vale Company That decision had gone against the tailors in London, cotton operatives in Lancashire Three cases already decided Are we going to make the fourth as Yorkshire miners? If they had decided to grant them their pay against the law of the land and under the Employers' and Workmen's Act, £1,250 per week would go out of their funds Mr Buckingham Pope' (he was the chairman of the Company, my Lord) could take Mr Pickard into Court and sue the Society through Mr Pickard and claim at least £1,000 a week for 14 days Was there any man amongst them who would like to see Mr Pope in that position ? They would not like to see Mr Pope in that position It then money had been granted yesterday, Mr Pope could sue Mr B Pickard for so many thousand pounds damages and compensation (A Voice What have you brought us out for then ?) (Walsh) You have the fullest sympathy of the officials and the whole of the members of this Society They saw by the unanimous vote of yesterday of the delegates they would like to vote for money to help them to fight the battle, but dared not Their fear was that they would have Mr Pope getting money out of the same funds How could we remedy this ? Your grievances are burning grievances, and your management have not been as discreet as the majorities of managements are in Yorkshire If there was one thing more than another which would convince Mr Chambers to alter his policy towards them it was the decision of Judge Masterman given in the County Court They were there to decide how they could make an impression upon him, that you try and do is to take a ballot of yourselves within the rules, give in your notices, and come out and let us all be in behind you in the county and fight this to a finish It won't last more than 15 days Humble yourselves I have been in a position at end of six weeks, when my committee were defeated, when the district was flooded with police—Kirkley and Hemsworth When they dogged his footsteps, and he was tyrannised most abominably in the pit bottom, yet at the end of six weeks they would not pay, and they went back to work to put themselves in proper order There was no shame in it He was glad to see the spirit displayed amongst the men, because it gave the lie to those men who had said there were so many 'rats' at Denaby We know there are many rats You have got them out of their holes, see if they will be manly enough to take a ballot in accordance with the rules of their society From 14 days from that moment Mr Pickard would be heart and soul behind you He wants to meet the employers on the Denaby Main grievances, so that he may bring Mr Chambers to a rational frame of mind and to treat them as men and not as 'hewers of wood and drawers of water' He hoped they would take the advice of his colleague They had no support, the men had done their best in the county, but they would have to bring in about £750 a week to give them 5s each It would be better for them to have 9s a week and let them go about and get money and bring in what they could They could settle down then when they would always get strike pay If a two years' battle was fought at Denaby, it would bring that gentleman to his senses who was treating them so cruelly He hoped there would be no cavilling amongst them when future speakers got up as they had done their best They were not humiliated, they wanted to get into one boat and row together into the harbour of success In the public houses they were grumbling at them, but he thought when they were earning money they ought to put 1s a week into the funds instead of putting on the public and fight for a living wage , 6d a week more would not break any man and would provide means to fight the battle 18s a week or 2s each child—that would keep them ought of starvation Hunger would force men to open their eyes There was before them a terrible time They had stepped off the precipice of prosperity, they called it prosperity"—and so forth I do not think I need read the rest of it, my Lord I do not think there is anything that is material, but my criticism of that speech is this—that it is an appeal to the men to put themselves right, and it is a distinct statement that if they put themselves right, they will get all the support the Union can give them, and it is anticipated even that the fight may last two years Further, there is this reference to "rats" and congratulation that the "rats" had been got out of their holes ("Rats" meaning blacklegs) It is perfectly obvious that the man who was using this language knew that there were men who had been coerced into refraining from work against their will, because a "rat" or a "blackleg" is a man who wants to go to work and is not in line with, at any rate, a number of men who desire to stop work, and he is recognising the fact that there were these "rats," and congratulating the men that they have used the proper means, as he puts it, "to get them out of their holes," and with regard to the past the language is the language of approval of the fact that they had struck, and the language of regret that the Taff Vale has prevented the Union, *pro tem*, providing them with the means of keeping out

Now Mr Wadsworth speaks, and he says "He was sorry they were not on a better mission He was sorry that the men at those two large and important collieries, and in that great industrial centre, were not that morning within the rules and regulations of their own Society, and outside altogether the clutches of the law If that had been the position, himself and Mr Walsh would have been able to have said a few more things than what they would be able to say under the circumstances He trusted that every man at that particular meeting, and those away from it, would try, and especially at that particular time, to keep a cool head They had got to a crisis, and it was now felt absolutely necessary that they should discuss without any opposition or feeling, but to come to the best decision in the interests of the whole of men, women and children They all knew that they had had this particular dispute about 'bag dirt,' and other disputes on hand for a considerable time He had been down at Denaby on one or two deputations, but he had never been able to get Mr Chambers to do what, in his opinion, he ought to have done as a colliery manager over an important firm like the Denaby and Cadeby Collieries If he had met the men in a reasonable spirit, if he had met them as he considered he should have done, with justice and fair play, and shown a disposition to sympathise with them in difficulties, these collieries, in his opinion, would never have come to stand" With regard to that language, may I say this Of course, there must come a time in the affairs of any concern when the manager, whoever is in control, must take a stand upon a definite, particular point—for instance, with regard to this payment for the "bag dirt," rightly or wrongly, the view Mr Chambers had taken was that the men were getting a fair pay, to which they had already agreed, and that if he did the work he was doing it at a cost to them of less than the halfpenny which was allowed in the agreement, and he met them whenever they asked him to meet them, but his answer was always the same, and they had tried all methods that they could think of to get some decision that Mr Chambers was in the wrong and that they were in the right, and had failed, and language like this, I submit, is hardly justifiable. It is not a case of where a man refused to discuss the matter, but a time had come when he said I am very sorry, but there is only one view I can take, and it is no good discussing it any more

Then he says at the bottom "For the time being the manager had the advantage. They were outside the law, and there was not the slightest doubt but what Mr Chambers was trying all that he possibly could to play that card to the uppermost. It was not always a matter of getting everything at the time being, but it was a question of whether it was right, just and equitable, and whether it would succeed in the future. If Mr Chambers had met them and put aside the supposed document which Chappell signed, which he ought to have done, and dealt with the price list in a proper and fair manner, they would have met him in a fair, honest and amicable spirit. Instead, Mr Chambers had rushed everything to the gate. He had made his mind up before the deputation had gone to him, and had said certain things, and they could not drive him from them. It was not a manly position for a man to take up in such a position as he held. Whether they liked it or not, they would have to swallow the pill. They would have to put themselves within the rules of the Association. If they took the advice which had been given to them by Mr Walsh and which they had come down from the Council to advise them, they would then put themselves in a legal position and would be able all the better to deal with Mr Chambers and his firm than what they were at the present time. It was a hard thing for men to accept a position of this description. Previous to 1871 they were in a little worse position than they were even to-day. Right away down from 1876 (the Trades Union Acts were passed in 1871 and they were amended in 1876) they had always been in a fortunate position compared with what they were this morning. It was on account of the apathy of the men that this had come about. It had taken 30 years to find that this was not the law of the land. All the Courts and House of Lords had, till 18 months ago, declared that it was the law that Unions were not a corporate society. The decision in the Taff Vale case was the most important thing which had taken place in the history of coal miners, so far as workers' interests were concerned, which had taken place during the last 50 years. They would have to pledge every man who went to the House of Commons that he would give his vote, voice and energy to amend this law and to bring them back into the position which they were in previous to that decision The men would not care to put themselves in a position so as to incriminate the Union Political exigencies had had something to do with the bringing about of the decision which had recently been arrived at Instead of the men being at the poll and voting for the men who would uphold Trades Unions, there were only 50 per cent attended The higher classes knew more than to stay away and they were left to do as they liked They had to recommend to them what was not a very nice thing, but when a man took a position he ought to be in a position to assist his Union and carry out the rules of his Union In the meantime they should ballot the whole of the men whether they are disposed to give in a 14 days' notice to terminate their contracts They would then be within the rules of the law and their Association They would have officials, the whole of their delegates and collieries in the county to help and assist them in fighting this battle " Now, may I pause there I do not know how that came about—whether Mr Wadsworth had had communication with the branch officials or not, but he there is apparently using language consistent with what the men did, and not consistent with what he was sent down to advocate, because he says " In the meantime they should ballot the whole of the men whether they are disposed to give in a fourteen days' notice to terminate their contracts " He does not refer to the fact that they had first got to go back to work, then ballot, and give their notices, he simply does not refer to it, my Lord—whether it was intentional or not I do not know, but we shall see in a moment what happened " They had authorised Mr Pickard to wire Mr Chambers asking him to meet a deputation that evening along with Mr Walsh and himself and local men They had wired Mr Pickard, asking him if he had heard from Mr Chambers, and the following was the answer from Mr Chambers 'No need to wait for meeting, pits are open when men wish to resume work, Chambers' There was no need for a deputation If they took their advice " (now this is the point) " they would agree to return to work at as early a date as possible, and in the meantime they would take a ballot of the men Take a ballot to-day and then give your notices in " Now that seems more pointedly to suggest that they were to take the ballot and give their notices before they went to work

The LORD CHANCELLOR Might I ask Suppose they had gone in and resumed work and then had given their notices,—they could not have given them until they resumed work

Mr ELDON BANKES No

The LORD CHANCELLOR Do you contend that there was anything wrong in their balloting and deciding before they resumed work what they would do afterwards ?

Mr ELDON BANKES I think they might take the ballot at any time, provided, of course, my Lord, that the ballot was taken in the proper way   Our case is not only did they not let them go back to work, but that they did not ballot them in the proper way

The LORD CHANCELLOR   That is another thing, I see what you mean

Mr ELDON BANKES   Oh no   I think they might ballot at any time   It was independent of their being workmen   They would ballot as Unionists and not as workmen

The LORD CHANCELLOR   Yes

Mr ELDON BANKES   "With regard to the summonses, they were in possession of a nice little bill—£6—which was 10s a day for 12 working days   Colliery owners made statements which were not true   They would have to prove they had lost 10s per man   Would that each man had earned 10s a day   What Chambers had done was proof that they were getting profits   If they were getting 10s a day they were worth it   They were worth it more than the director who got a thousand a year   All they wanted was a fair day's wage for a fair day's work, and fair conditions of employment   If he was a gentleman he would withdraw the summonses and make peace and contentment at the collieries for weeks, months and years"   (Now comes the resolution)   "That this meeting of the Denaby and Cadeby workmen agree to resume work at the earliest convenience and that the men be ballotted as to whether they are prepared to serve 14 days' notice to terminate their contract of service"   Of course, that leaves it indefinite as to whether they were to go to work first

The LORD CHANCELLOR   That is why I asked the question   I do not want to interrupt you, but do you think it signified if they went back to work, whether they ballotted first and went back afterwards, or not?

Mr ELDON BANKES   From our point of view ——

The LORD CHANCELLOR   I only want to see whether you think it matters

Mr ELDON BANKES   Our point of view is that if the men had gone back to work we should have been in a better position if they had balloted after they had gone back to work, but I cannot contend as a matter of right that they were bound to go back to work before they balloted

The LORD CHANCELLOR   Thank you

Mr ELDON BANKES   Now Mr Walsh says "the men had their salvation in their own hands and it would hurt him to the core

if they did not take the ballot unanimously and come out and fight
They would disgrace the county   Now there is no language that
could be more emphatic to show that the advice of these people, who
came down from the Council, was that they should strike and
continue the strike   Hirst says they had brought the men out
Now here is strong evidence, my Lord, upon all the points - —

Lord DAVEY   Where are you reading ?

Mr ELDON BANKES   I am reading at page 409   I have
finished Wadsworth—after the resolution

Lord DAVEY   I thought you were reading Croft

Mr ELDON BANKES   There is a short passage of Walsh
It is higher up on page 409—letter A   Then Hirst says "They
had brought the men out to prove to the district that they had
grievances, and that they intended if they could get strike pay to
get those grievances remedied before they took the men back to
work"   Now this is the language of the branch official in the
presence of the two persons sent down from the Council, one of
whom was Mr Wadsworth, the Vice-President—a definite statement
that the men had been brought out by the branch officials, and
that they were not going to let them go back until a certain event

Then he says (this is a delegate) "Every delegate went so far
as to say in his opinion they ought to have strike pay   If they only
had strike pay they would get what they were entitled to   It was
decided to take the ballot of datallers and fillers on Wednesday
night, and colliers on Thursday morning '

Mr ATHERLEY JONES   Hirst was not a delegate

Mr ELDON BANKES   I did not say that Hirst was a
delegate

Mr. ATHERLEY JONES   Yes, you did

Mr ELDON BANKES   I beg your pardon, I meant to say in
referring to that passage on page 409 he is purporting to give the
men a statement as to what the delegate's views were at the Council
Meeting.

Lord DAVEY   Hirst was the Secretary

Mr ELDON BANKES   Hirst was the Secretary of Cadeby
Then, my Lord, the recorded minute is at page 229   I do not think
I need refer to that   That is only in the same terms, I think
Now, my Lord, this is important   It is a minute entered in the
books of both branches of the joint meeting held on July 15th,

1902, in the Station Hotel, Croft, attended by Messrs Walsh and Wadsworth "1st That we take a ballot to decide whether our men are in favour of returning to work with a view to giving 14 days' notice" Now that is a perfectly fair way of taking the ballot if they had carried that out It indicated to the men what they were asked to vote about—whether they were in favour of returning to work for the purpose of giving 14 days' notice and then going out "2 That the ballot be taken at once" Now, that is a flagrant violation of what they ought to have done No, I beg your pardon, I will reserve that for a moment I will withdraw that remark if I may "3 That the whole of the Committee assist with the ballot boxes and giving ballot papers out," so that is only indicating what would naturally happen under the rule, but there is a definite statement that this ballot was to be taken by the Committee Mr Wadsworth, at page 344 (at the bottom), wired to Mr Pickard as the result of that meeting The wire is not very definite, but it is at the bottom of the page "Men agree to resume work and terminate notices" What he meant by "terminate notices" I do no know, but apparently his idea was that the men were going to resume work, probably the particular point was not present to his mind, although he seems to have used ——

Lord DAVEY It is an inexactitude of terminology I think he means terminate by notice

Mr ELDON BANKES Probably, my Lord

Lord DAVEY I do not think he means anything contrary to the fact He means that they would give notice to terminate their contracts

Mr ELDON BANKES I think so, my Lord Of course he ought to have been more guarded in his language at the meeting if the point had been present to his mind about the men going back

Now my Lord, the ballot was to be held the next day, the 16th, and I want to call your particular attention to the form of the ballot paper which was issued to the men, and that is on page 195 Now that is the form of the ballot "Are you in favour of giving 14 days' notice, until such times as your grievances are remedied?" Now will your Lordship contrast that form of the ballot paper with the form of the ballot paper that had been used on the previous occasion in the September of the previous year, which is at page 322, when they had taken the ballot under which the men decided they would go out "Are you in favour of giving 14 days' notice to terminate your contract of service, until such times as your grievances are rectified" Now, the position is this, obviously those words were left out because the persons who are responsible for the drawing up of this realised that the men were not at that time 'workmen" That is the first thing, and realising that they left out those important words, and they left a form of ballot paper which really conveyed nothing direct to the man's mind "Are you in favour of giving 14 days' notice until such times as your grievances are remedied" does not bring it to the man's mind pointedly The question he is asked is "Will you go out on strike? If you go back to work, will you then give the 14 days' notice for the purpose of going out on strike?" However, there is the form of the ballot paper, but what happened was——

Lord DAVEY Do you suggest that one of these workmen would not know what was meant by giving 14 days' notice?

Mr ELDON BANKES The point is that they were asked to ballot at a time when they really were not "workmen"

Lord DAVEY That is quite true Whether they would give the 14 days' notice or not under those conditions is another question, but do you suggest that they did not know what was meant by giving notice?

Mr ELDON BANKES I think under the circumstances in which the ballot was taken I do not think they did know But there is the form of it I do not want to exaggerate any point It is an element in the case, I think, especially when your Lordship comes to see now as to how this ballot was taken

Lord JAMES of HEREFORD What has become of the Council recommendation that they should go back to work?

Mr ELDON BANKES My Lord, it was not followed, and it was not followed, as we say, deliberately, because if the men had once got back to work they would not have got them out again What they did is only consistent with that view, I think

The LORD CHANCELLOR If that is the case, and you may be right about it, it looks to me as if you were right The men very likely would have been willing to stay on, so far as I see at present, but if you gave them a ballot that would be the most effectual way of enabling them to say what they wished to do

Mr ELDON BANKES Yes, if it was a fair ballot If it was a fair ballot we should not criticise it at all

The LORD CHANCELLOR We shall hear more about it

Mr ELDON BANKES Now we come to the ballot I do not make any point about this The rule, as your Lordship knows, says there is to be a ballot box and balls Well, as a matter of fact, instead of balls the practice had been to use papers We make no point at all about that, but, of course, if a man uses a paper in order to put him in the same position as the man who uses the ball

he must be given the opportunity of putting his cross upon the
paper at some place where he is not under the direct supervision of
a Union official, because if the man is brought up to a table and is
there told to put his cross on the paper he is not, in any proper
sense of the word, balloting, because he is exercising his right of
voting under the direct supervision of a man who, we say, was
exercising at that time an improper influence over him, and he was
exposing himself to the effect of all the intimidation and
molestation which would follow if he did not put his cross in the
place the man wished it to be put. And I understand that your
Lordship will find that no steps at all were taken to see that every
man got a paper, or that one man did not get twenty papers. It is
quite consistent with the way they took the ballot that twenty
papers might have got into the hands of a sympathiser, and he put
twenty crosses on them, and that in that way they arrived at the
numbers that they ultimately got.

Now, my Lord, the story about the ballot, I think, you will find
in a man named Chapman's evidence at page 655.

Lord JAMES of HEREFORD: Will you kindly explain to
me—how is this irregularity of the ballot necessary to your
argument?

Mr ELDON BANKES: For this reason, my Lord—because
our case is that this is one of the acts done by the branch officials—
and illegally done—for the purpose of maintaining and continuing
the strike. There is a conspiracy to molest and injure us, my Lord,
and it comes in as part of the evidence under that.

Lord DAVEY: I do not at the present moment see how you
connect that with the Association.

Mr ELDON BANKES: Oh, yes, because our case is this—
at any rate, this act of balloting was an act which was directly
entrusted to these men to carry out, and we bring ourselves directly
within the principle of such cases as Barwick and those cases which
I will refer to in a moment. It is one of the class of acts which
were entrusted to these people to do—this ballot. We directly
bring this ballot home to the Executive, and if it is necessary to
bring it home, because they deliberately entrusted the taking of this
ballot to these men.

The LORD CHANCELLOR: That you will do afterwards.

Mr ELDON BANKES: Yes, my Lord. Now take page 655.
He speaks (at the top of the page) about the meeting. Will your
Lordship come to the bottom of the page (I read the two minutes)
Question 1022. "How many men were employed in giving the
papers out?—The majority of the Committee. Q. Was any check

kept on the number of papers given to any man ?—None whatever "
Then my friend Mr Isaacs objects, and there is a good deal of
discussion about the objection, but your Lordship will find we get
on again to the point at page 658 Question 1024 "Was this
ballot taken by means of papers ?—Yes Q Were any ballot boxes
used ?—Yes Q How many ?—Two Q Were the papers signed,
or did the men make marks on them before they put them in the
ballot boxes ?—Yes Q Where were these ballot boxes ?—Against
the gate coming out of the Croft Q Where did the men sign
these papers ?—In the Croft Q Was there a table for the purpose ?—
Yes Q Who was sitting at the table ?—Brog " Then there is an
objection Mr Isaacs says "I object I really cannot understand
where we are getting to This again is suggestion and innuendo
(Mr Justice Lawrance) You have got enough, Mr Bankes, to
show how it was done The question of the numbers seems to me
cut both ways really and truly (Mr Eldon Bankes) Did you go
to the pit on the morning of Thursday, 17th July ?—Yes " Now
we come to another point

Lord DAVEY The man "Brog' is Moon

Mr ELDON BANKES Yes, he is one of the Committeemen,
and the result of that ballot, my Lord, was —your Lordship will find
it at page 230—that upon that paper which I submit was at any
rate not sufficiently clearly expressed to bring home to the men
what the precise point was—especially after the speeches which had
been addressed to them, and the way in which the ballot was taken—
your Lordship will find the numbers at page 230 —"For giving in
notices, 1967 Against 59, spoilt papers 3, neutral 4 ' My Lord, I
ought to read—my friend Mr Waddy kindly reminds me—on page
720, the evidence of a man named Legg about this ballot I do not
want to take up more time of your Lordships than I can help in
calling attention to the details of the evidence It is at the bottom
of page 720, Question 1637 This is in cross-examination by Mr
Danckwerts "When the ballot was taken anybody was at liberty
to take the paper where he liked to mark it ?—The ballot was taken
as anybody could see Q You do not answer my question When
a man got a paper he could go where he liked in order to mark it ?—
Of course he could go where he liked, but the table was there and
the biggest majority were filled up at this table Q Nobody was
compelled to fill it up at the table ?—They were what you may say
compelled to fill it up at the table Q How do you mean by
compelled ?—Because they could not pass the table The papers
were given out to them, and the pencils were there for them to be
marked," and of course one knows the state of things existing at
these pits at the time, and what the effect of that resolution on the
Sunday had been, and I think a Jury might fairly assume that these
men were not exercising—or, at any rate, were not allowed the
opportunity of exercising their own free will

Now the next thing that happened was this. After this ballot had been taken—and indeed before the ballot had been taken—men began to present themselves at the colliery to work, numbers of whom were willing to work, and when they got to the colliery they were required to sign the contract book. It was proved to be the invariable practice of the colliery when a man absented himself for more than a shift or two shifts, to require him to sign the contract book when he came again, and so in ordinary course the men were asked to sign the contract book when they came to present themselves for work, and a number of them did sign, but apparently, I assume—at least I suggest, that it came to the branch officials' knowledge that men were signing on too readily, and then this point was taken, it was said the men were asked to sign a fresh contract— a new contract—it was not the old contract, and this "hare" was roused in this way. Some time before the strike the Home Secretary had promulgated some new timbering rules, and according to the practice of the colliery those timbering rules had been printed and had been attached to the books which were given to the men, they could not be printed in the books but they were attached to the books— a fly-leaf, and when any man signed on he was given the book of rules with the fly-leaf attached. During the stoppage of the colliery the opportunity had been taken to reprint the books and to put these rules in the books in ordinary order, instead of on a fly-leaf, and thereupon somebody as we suggested who was looking about for an opportunity to prevent the men coming back, as he saw they were likely to do, started this suggestion that these were new contracts— that the men were asked to sign new contracts—and indeed we had evidence that the men were told that if they signed these new contracts they bound themselves for 12 months, and, of course, the object of a statement like that was to prevent the men signing on and going back to work

Lord JAMES of HEREFORD. How could they give in their notices unless they did go back to work, in the terms of the resolution?

Mr ELDON BANKES. They could not, and it was a sham, what happened was a mere sham. What happened was that when this "hare" was started about signing a fresh contract the men came up on the morning of the 17th in quantities, and they knew then that they would have to sign the contract book. They were told by the officials that they were not to sign the contract book, and, therefore, they just walked up to the colliery and they threw notices into buckets which had been placed outside the colliery office, and then went back again, and then having done that they asserted—or assumed, poor fellows—that they had done as they were told, and that, therefore, they were putting themselves in the right. Well, of course, the position then was one in which somebody had to exercise ingenuity to suggest a way in which it could be said that the men had put themselves in the right and entitled themselves to strike pay, and the view then suggested by Mr Pickard (and in our view it was merely the counsel of desperation) was that the men had never broken their contracts, that the old contracts were still subsisting, that the management in asking them to sign fresh contracts were refusing to employ them, and that the men were in their right in giving in their notices without signing the fresh contracts, because the existing contracts were already in operation, and that, therefore, they were entitled to give their notices without signing on again, and that the management were wrong in refusing to employ them without signing

Lord DAVEY They said   A breach of the contract does not necessarily terminate it

Mr ELDON BANKES No, my Lord, that is quite true May I finish my sentence and then answer that?

Lord DAVEY Yes

Mr ELDON BANKES Mr Pickard assumed the position that after what had happened this was not a strike at all, but that it was a lock out by the masters, and that, therefore, being a lock out by the masters strike pay was payable, and strike pay was paid

Now, may I answer what Lord Davey said?

Lord DAVEY I only suggest what their views were

Mr ELDON BANKES My Lord, that is quite so

Lord DAVEY It is not a suggestion of my own

Mr ELDON BANKES I quite accept that, but may I remind your Lordship of what the resolution of the Council was on the 14th—that the men resume work and give notices

Lord DAVEY Yes

Mr ELDON BANKES Clearly indicating that at that time the view of everybody was that the contracts were at an end   I can call attention in a moment, and I will, to Mr Parrott's evidence at page 855, if it is necessary to call attention to it   At page 855 he was asked about that (Question 2884) " We know that it has now been decided that the contracts were at an end at that time   Was that your belief?—Yes   Q Was that your belief at that time?— That the contracts were at an end ", and there is no sort of doubt about it, as I submit, that upon this evidence the procedure which was recommended on the 14th by the Council was a procedure upon the assumption that the contracts were at an end

Now, if your Lordship will please turn to page 345 you will see what Mr Smith, the Secretary of the Denaby, writes to Mr Pickard about this

Lord JAMES of HEREFORD I forget for the moment what day they went out, the meeting was on the 29th

Mr ELDON BANKES They went out on the night of Sunday, the 29th

Lord JAMES of HEREFORD They had been out at this time nearly a fortnight

Mr ELDON BANKES They had been out a fortnight—rather more than a fortnight On the 16th July your Lordship will see this is the day the ballot was taken, and before the men were recommended to go back to work some of them had been already going " I have to inform you that when our men present themselves asking for their lamps to be got ready for Thursday morning they are told they cannot start work until they have signed a contract book with a heading on it which we have not heard of before According to the information received they will not be allowed to resume work for the purpose of serving their notices Shall we be in order in refusing to sign a fresh contract ' Then he gives the number " We are intending serving the notices out on each shift and have urged the men and boys to present themselves for work on their respective shifts and if their lamps are refused to return home after giving in their notices "

The LORD CHANCELLOR Was there any answer to that ?

Mr ELDON BANKES My Lord, yes Well, there are telegrams which pass, but I do not think there was a letter to Mr Smith—not at that time, my Lord I will now come to the events of the 17th, and I had better call attention to the evidence of some of the men upon this point , but before I do that will your Lordship kindly turn to page 195, where the notice is printed that the Colliery Company issued Directly it came to their attention that this point had been raised about there being an alteration of contract, they had printed and stuck up the notice at the bottom of that page (it was issued at once on the 17th) " As it is reported there is an impression that the form of contract now required to be signed by persons engaging for work differs from that in force at the cessation of the work, Take Notice that no variation has been made in the conditions of employment for the Denaby and Cadeby Main Collieries, Limited W H Chambers, managing director," and books that the men were asked to sign were produced at the trial, and the men were asked to sign on immediately in consecutive order after the last man had signed I do not think I need elaborate that

Lord DAVEY I suppose the Secretary of State's timbering rule was binding, quite apart from the contract, was not it?

Mr ELDON BANKES It was, my Lord A point was attempted to be made by Mr Isaacs at the trial that there might be a difference in this sense, that so long as they were merely the Secretary of State's rules they were binding, and had the ordinary force of law, but if they were put into the Contract Book they had an additional contractual force That was a perfectly true observation to make, but the rules had been in the books

Mr DANCKWERTS We said they were *ultra vires*

Mr ELDON BANKES I hear my learned friend, Mr Danckwerts, say they are *ultra vires*, but it did not make them more or less *ultra vires* putting them into the books, and a good deal of discussion took place about this, but I cannot think that your Lordships will be troubled about those timbering rules Our evidence was—and it was not contradicted—that the effect of these timbering rules upon the Colliery Company was to put them to a very considerable expense, because they had to provide a good deal more timber, but as far as the men were concerned, they put them in rather a better position than they had been in before, because the timber was placed rather nearer to the working places than before That is the uncontradicted evidence There is no other evidence to the contrary, so far as I recollect I do not want to get into discussion about this it is not material from my point of view, either way

Lord DAVEY I think it is unfortunate that Mr Chambers' notice did not explain a little more about the timbering, because I suppose many of these men had signed contracts which did not contain timbering rules, before the timbering rules were issued

Mr ELDON BANKES That was not shown, my Lord The timbering rules had been issued some years before

Lord DAVEY Oh, had they?

Mr ELDON BANKES But how many years I do not know There may have been men working there before they were issued, but at any rate they had been in force for some years

Lord JAMES of HEREFORD If the timbering rules had not been in would the men have signed the new contract?

Mr ELDON BANKES Oh, no, my Lord Our view is that it was a mere device I can show your Lordship by the evidence the men were told If you sign these you are bound for 12 months

Lord JAMES of HEREFORD Suppose the contract book had been produced without the insertion of the timbering clause in, would the men have signed it, or not, as a new contract?

Mr ELDON BANKES Our case is that they were not allowed to sign anything, that it was the deliberate policy that they should not come back

Lord DAVEY I do not see what harm the signing would do the men as regards giving the notice I do not see what difference it would make They might at once give the notice notwithstanding

Mr ELDON BANKES Oh, yes, certainly

Lord DAVEY If they signed, they must give a fortnight's notice in any event

Mr ELDON BANKES Yes, certainly

Lord DAVEY I do not see what difference it would make

Mr ELDON BANKES Our case is that it was an absurd, objection

Lord DAVEY When people are in delicate relations like this you know a small misunderstanding does so much mischief

Mr ELDON BANKES My Lord, I am not saying it is not so for a moment, but I think I can show from this evidence that it was not the intention of the branch officials that the men should go back, and this was merely made a pretext for keeping them out It is a matter your Lordships may have to decide

Lord DAVEY What is the use of balloting to give in notices, if they were not intended to go back?

Mr ELDON BANKES My Lord, I do not suppose the men were told what was in the minds of the branch officials

Lord DAVEY Take the branch officials themselves The branch officials were a party to the ballot, and they wished for a majority

Mr ELDON BANKES Yes, because the Council at Barnsley said they had to ballot, and of course there was no chance of getting strike pay unless they could satisfy the Council at Barnsley that they were doing what they told them to do, therefore, they have at any rate to pretend to do what they are told to do, and it is an essential element in that, that they should take the ballot Well, they took the ballot

Lord JAMES of HEREFORD In the form in which they took it?

Mr ELDON BANKES No, the Council never anticipated that they were going to take a ballot in a form in which the men would not have the free opportunity to exercise an independent judgment

Lord JAMES of HEREFORD That is another matter It is the sending in of the notices That is the point in my mind

Mr ELDON BANKES Whether or not the Council would have approved the ballot paper if it had been submitted to them, my Lord, I do not know But no doubt the Council intended that the men should go back to work and then ballot, and then there would be the decision as to whether they should give the notices in order to go out on strike

Lord DAVEY Yes, but I do not understand Mr Wadsworth and Mr Walsh to have recommended that

Mr ELDON BANKES Mr Walsh did not deal with it definitely, and Mr Wadsworth unfortunately used very indefinite language upon the particular point, but it is not very material for my purpose to say that Wadsworth or Walsh definitely approved of this scheme Our point is that they went down there to counsel and advise and left in the hands of local officials

Now, may I come to the evidence? If your Lordship will look at page 684, there is a piece of evidence given by Bury which is material as to whether or not the local officials did not realise that the contracts had been broken, and that the men would have to sign on again 1350 I had better read from

Lord DAVEY I suppose you would say the Colliery Company would have the right to elect how to treat the contract?

Mr ELDON BANKES Yes, and they did

Lord DAVEY They might have elected to treat it as not at an end, or as a matter of ballot

Mr ELDON BANKES Certainly

Lord DAVEY It was a matter for the Company to elect as to the way in which they would regard it

Mr ELDON BANKES Certainly, my Lord, I agree, and they treated it as broken

Lord DAVEY I only wanted to understand

Mr ELDON BANKES Quite The Colliery Company had definitely elected to treat the contract as broken

Lord DAVEY No, not "as broken," but as at an end

Mr ELDON BANKES As at an end, if your Lordship pleases Of course, if the men could have shown that there was any real impression about that, that the contract was not at an end, they might have had something on the point to say, but they begin on the 14th July with the resolution which shows that they recognised that it was at an end I have given you Mr Parrott's evidence Now I am going to give the evidence which a man named Bury gave about "Croft" But before I begin that I will, if I may, read on page 683 He gives an account of how these notices were signed, and so forth Question 1341 "Now a question about the 17th July, when the notices were put into the buckets or baskets Were you there on that day at the colliery?—Yes Q Which pit were you at?—At Denaby Q Did you see what occurred when the men came?—Yes, I saw a good deal of it Q Were you there in the morning?—Yes, about half-past five" (This man is a manager of the colliery—one of the colliery officials) "Q Tell us shortly—I would rather you gave it in your own words—what happened?—As I was going to work, going down towards the pit, I saw the road was filled with a great number of men going to and coming from the pit, and at a short distance from the pit, before we got to the railway crossing, I saw a table on which were a lot of papers and ink and pens, and some of the committeemen standing at and near the table, and in the street facing the men as they came towards the works, and I saw some of these papers being distributed to the men, and I also saw the writing – what I do not know Then I passed them and I went into the yard There I met Mr Soar, the under manager, and one or two others, and I watched the proceedings more or less as the men came in, and I took up a position at about halfway between the yard gates and the lamp cabin, where the men called for their lamps, and I saw them putting papers into the buckets that were near the yard gates and going across to the lamp cabin asking for lamps, I suppose and coming back again and going out Q Now I want you to tell me this if you can Can you give me the names of any man that you saw at the table or in the yard I do not mean the mere working men but others?—Yes, I saw George Smith Q He was the Secretary?—The Secretary of the Denaby branch He, I think, was standing behind the table Birch was in the street facing the men as they came I saw Nolan and I saw all the Committee at 6 o'clock because they came to speak to me Now, may I stop there, to show that the Committee not only took charge of the ballot, but they took charge of the giving in of these notices which was the next step Then "Q In the morning?—In the morning That was after the men were supposed to be down the pit—after the working hour had begun I saw Croft Q You say you saw them as they came to speak to you?—

Yes Q What about?—They came to ask me to accept the notices that were in the buckets I cannot remember who the man was I fancy it was Croft asked me if I would take the notices I said 'No' He said 'Why not?' I asked him if the men who were supposed to have written these notices had not left the work some 14 days beforehand He said 'That is right enough' I said 'Then they are not men of ours' We looked at one another, and I do not know what he said, and they went away" I mean it is not very strong evidence, but it is evidence to show that at any rate Croft realised what everybody else realised—that these men were no longer the Company's men at the time they were giving these notices

Lord JAMES of HEREFORD I suppose the notice treated the contract of service as in existence

Mr ELDON BANKES It must have

Lord JAMES of HEREFORD You have not got the form here, have you?

Mr ELDON BANKES Yes, my Lord, we have, it is at page 196 "I hereby give 14 days' notice to terminate my service with the above Company' I ought to mention this fact, too, which I had forgotten—that it was proved that not only the ballot papers, but these notice papers were all paid for out of the Union funds That is material.

Then, my Lord, the next evidence I should like to read is the evidence of a man named Soar, at page 620 He is being asked about the talk at the colliery, and he is asked (at the top of the page) "Can a man have his lamp if he has missed more than two shifts there?—Not without he has been ill, or something of that Q Unless he has been ill he cannot have his lamp if he has missed two shifts?—No, without he brings a doctor's certificate Q If he does not do that, what has he to do?—He has to see me Q He has to come to you, and what has he to do then?—If he stops out above a week I sign him on again Q He has to be signed on again?—Yes Q Is that the invariable practice—that he has to sign on again if he has been away above a week?—Yes"

Lord DAVEY "Above a week?"

Mr ELDON BANKES Yes I said "two shifts," my Lord I made a mistake, I was confusing it with the doctor's certificate, if they were away a week they had to sign on again "(Q 690) After these men went to the lamp house did they come to you in the office?—No, they did not come to me I stood there and asked them to sign Q You asked some of them to sign on?—Yes Q Did they sign on?—No, they did not. There were two or three. Q

They refused?—Well, I asked them to sign and they said they had a better job on now, they had got on the right track, they said, now." So that it is a clear indication that by some means or another they had got it into their heads, or had had it put into their heads, that they were not going back to work—that they were all right—that "they had got on the right track."

Lord JAMES of HEREFORD) What do you say that meant?

Mr ELDON BANKES That they had been advised that all they had got to do was to give in this notice and then they would get strike pay

Then at page 644, would your Lordship turn to the evidence of a man named Brealey At page 646 he gives an account of the men coming to the pit At one time we made the point that some of these men came, not in their working clothes, but there was nothing in it, or very little in it if anything, and I do not now rely upon that Would your Lordship turn to Question 950 (646 page) Mr Lush said "Did you go outside the office and say anything among the men?—I went outside and asked them to come and sign the book for work again They said if they did so they had to sign new rules and new contracts (Mr Justice Lawrance) They said? (Mr Montague Lush) The men said?—Yes, and also if they started to work again they would have to work twelve months before they could come out again ' Now, of course, that is repeating something that somebody told them 'Q What did you say to that?—I told them it was a great mistake, there was no alteration whatever, and I asked them to come and look at the books, and also the rules to see for themselves if there was any alteration Q Did they do that?—Not until the bulk of them had gone away, and then there were several came in, and it was after that when I signed these Q After the bulk had gone away several came in?—Yes Q Did they look at the book?—Yes Q And then what did they do?—Some of them signed the book Q What did the others do?—The bulk of them went away, and I might say, some of them said " Then there was an objection to what they said, so we did not get that

Then will your Lordship turn to page 658? At Question 1032 I asked him "Did you go to the pit on the morning of Thursday, 17th July?—Yes Q Did you go in your working clothes?—Yes Q Did you intend to go to work?—Yes Q And desired to go to work?—Yes Q As you went to work did you see any of the Committeemen in the road?—Yes Q Whom did you see?—Moon, Collier, Humphries, Dickinson and Hurst (Mr Eldon Bankes) Hurst is the secretary of the Cadeby branch? (Mr Justice Lawrance) Is Moon the same man as Biog?—Yes, my Lord (Mr Eldon Bankes) Had they a table?—Yes Q Tell us what took place—The Committee stood together, and they shouted at the people that were going by, 'Here; come here and fetch this paper—sign this notice paper Q Did the men go and get a paper?—Yes.

Q From the table?—Yes Q Was that one of those notices that was used in this case—the 14 days' notice?—Yes Q Was anything said about signing on?—'You must not sign on' We were told not to sign anything Q Were you willing to sign on?—Yes Q Did you sign on?—No Q Why not?—I was afraid of signing on"

Lord JAMES of HEREFORD Mr Bankes, if they did not sign on, I do not sign on I do not see what was the use of the notices

Mr ELDON BANKES My Lord, the use of the notices was this—that it had the desired effect, because it enabled Mr Pickard, ultimately, to take this entirely erroneous view, that the men were within their rights in having given in these notices, that they were in the right and the Company was in the wrong in refusing to allow them to come back without signing a fresh contract—that it was a lock-out, and, therefore, strike pay was payable

Lord JAMES of HEREFORD When absent 14 days from work, I do not quite see that Mr Pickard's view could have come to that in effect

Mr ELDON BANKES Well, my Lord, ought not to have come to that

Lord DAVEY· The view Mr Pickard put forward was that the contract although broken was not at an end

Mr ELDON BANKES Yes, that is so The Master of the Rolls deals with that

Lord DAVEY If that view was correct the notices would be in order

Mr ELDON BANKES Yes It was not a justifiable view to take, but our case was that Mr Pickard was in this position he was only too anxious to grant these men strike pay, that if he saw what we said was "half a chance" of saying the strike was a legal strike he would grant them the strike pay, but he took this view perfectly erroneously, but deliberately

Lord JAMES of HEREFORD I should have thought that the contract was broken—if one man engaged to work for another and says I will continue to work for you until I give you such and such notice to determine the contract, and then he goes out without notice, I should have thought that then there was a breach of contract

Mr ELDON BANKES There is no doubt it was a breach, but the point was whether the contract was at an end The master might elect to say —The contract is broken, but still subsisting, and the point here was whether the contract was at an end, and there is no doubt that both parties viewed it as at an end

Lord DAVEY I suppose the fact of the Company requiring the men to sign a fresh contract would be an expression of their opinion and election?

Mr ELDON BANKES Certainly, if they had not done it before Then at page 723 is the evidence of a man named Leadbitter, who went to work He says that he was at work at the Cadeby Pit—that he was a member of the Union, and that he did not hear anything about the meeting on the 29th "Did you go to work as usual on the Monday?—Yes Q Did the way from your house to the pit lay by the high road or did you go some other way?—By the canal side,' (This was a man who got to the pit by a by-way) "Did you meet anybody on your way to the works?—Not that morning Q Then when you got there you found the pit was stopped?—Yes Q What is your work?—A dataller Q Did you continue working at the pit until the 15th August?—I continued to work at the pit up to two days before they stopped it Q That would be the 17th Now during that time did any member of the Committee speak to you about your working?—Yes Q Who was that?—Brog Q What did Brog say to you?—He said I wanted hurling into the cut for going to work," and "Brog" is one of the Committeemen, and it is an indication of the line these men were taking towards those who wanted to go to work and those who were going to work

Then at page 763 in the evidence of a man named Scott—I say to him "I want to ask you about the 17th July—the day when the men signed the notices Were you going to the pit on that day?—Yes Q On your way to the pit did you see any of the Committeemen?—Yes Q Who were they?—Smith, James Burch, and a man named Stokes Q Where were they when you saw them?—On a little plot of land that lies off the highway, just by Mr Soar's house Q Had they got a table?—They had a table there, and Smith and these men were round it, and they called me and said 'Scott come here, we want you to sign one of these notices to go and give your notice, us will get our union pay if we sign these notices' I said 'What are you giving notice for, you are not employed here, you have left their employ'" (this was, of course, after the ballot) "Q What did you say when he said he wanted you to give notice?—I said 'How can you give notice when you are not employed there?' I said, 'You must work there before you can give notice,' and they made an answer to me as the reason they were not going to sign on was that the Company had brought a new rule out which was to the effect that any one signing on signed on for twelve months I asked them if they had seen that rule, and they said 'Yes' I said 'Well, I cannot believe you I shall go and see for myself, and shall believe myself. It is ridiculous if I have got to sign on for twelve months. I can understand giving 14 days' notice, but as far as regards signing for twelve months, I cannot agree with it.' Q. What happened then?—I left them and proceeded through the crossing, and I met a man called Nolan. Q. Is that the Committeeman?—Yes. He asked me if I had got my notice. I said, 'No, I do not need one.' He said, 'you b———y old cripple, you want to take a notice,' and I said, 'I shan't take one.' I said, 'I do not see what there is to give notice for, I have not got anything to include your grievances at all, as far as it concerns me they have been all right to me and I am going to see what is the difference between signing on now and signing on before.' He told me I should have to sign on for twelve months, so I proceeded through the gates to the pits." Now, there is clear evidence. Here are the Committee sitting there telling the men to come and sign the notices, telling them that they have actually seen the new rule which compels them to remain at work for twelve months if they sign. This old man is not satisfied with them. He goes on, and then he is overtaken by Nolan, who tells him again that if he signs he will have to sign for twelve months.

Lord JAMES of HEREFORD. He seems to have been a very shrewd old man.

Mr ELDON BANKES. Yes, my Lord, he was. Then will your Lordships turn to page 662—the evidence of a man named Smeaton, and he is a man who was anxious to go to work—he went to sign on the day before—the 16th. (Q. 1083.) Then page 662, at Q. 1082 "You told me you went up to the colliery on the 16th July?—Yes. Q. Why did you go on the 16th?—I went to sign on. Q. Why did you go to sign on that particular day. Had anybody asked you?—I had heard of there being a meeting at Conisboro' to give the notices and start work. Q. That you were to go to work?—Yes. Q. Had you seen the deputy, Shelton?—Yes. Q. Had he asked you to go to work?—He told me to go down and see the manager. Q. So you went on the 16th and signed on?—Yes. Q. Did you go to work?—Not that afternoon. Q. Did you the next day?—Yes. Q. How long did you work?—14 days. Q. Then did you stop work?—Yes. Q. Why did you stop then?—I was afraid."

Now, my Lord, I think that I have sufficiently indicated what was going on, and it is—impossible, I submit, to resist the conclusion—it is for your Lordships to come to the conclusion but at any rate it was for the Jury to form their opinion as to really what this indicated, and now I will just pass on to show what was passing between Mr Pickard and the local officials in reference to this matter, and I will begin at page 346—I had better read at the bottom of page 345, F Mr Pickard got into communication with Mr Chambers on this 17th July (page 345, letter "d")—Pickard to Chambers "I am desired by your men to ask you to meet a deputation to-day. 2 30,

Colliery offices wire reply   Pickard—" Then over the page, Chambers to Pickard—' I adhere to my telegram, pits are open and all men who have applied and signed on have been employed   Every effort will be made to prepare the stalls for turning ' Now that was perfectly genuine   Any man who signed on was taken back and we were only too anxious to get the men back   Then Pickard wires to Smith—the same day   He passed on Mr Chambers' telegram   " Discussion impossible with men on strike without notice Chambers "   And then he wires to Smith   " I adhere to my telegram pits are open and all men who applied and signed on have been employed   Every effort will be made to prepare the stalls for the turning   Chambers " Therefore he repeats to him what Mr Chambers had wired, then he goes on   " Present yourselves for work at every shift   Consulting solicitors   Either send or bring first thing in morning the two copies of rules, those you are working under and the new one you are expected to sign   Don't fail to go to work, and don't sign any new rule '

Lord JAMES of HEREFORD   What date is that ?

Mr ELDON BANKES   That is the 17th, my Lord   Of course all the circumstances had not come to Mr Pickard's knowledge then, but he is told that they are new rules, and, therefore, at that moment his attitude was quite consistent   He is told that they are new rules, and on the assumption that they are new rules presumably he says " Do not sign anything ", but he asks for copies of the rules and he gets them   As your Lordships have got this in your minds I would just call attention to these wires on the 18th (at the bottom of the page) , then I shall have to finish about the 17th by calling attention to a meeting   On the 18th (on that same page) Pickard wires to Chambers   " Why should men sign on again, is not the contract they previously signed still existing " That is the question   Answer " Regular custom at these collieries when men have left to sign again before restarting "

Now I must ask your Lordships to go back, please, to finish the 17th, because on that day there was an important meeting

Mr ATHERLEY JONES   Would you mind reading the telegram of the 18th ?

Mr ELDON BANKES   Certainly, I will read the one at the top of the page

Mr ATHERLEY JONES   It completes it

Mr ELDON BANKES   Yes   " The men have not left your employ, and therefore why should they sign on again?"   That is what Mr Pickard says   Then, my Lord, at page 409 the meeting is , and it is again presided over by Croft , and he says that " he had been to see Mr Pickard   Wires were going in to Mr Pickard from different quarters every five minutes   They had had a fair interview with him, and all the grievances at Denaby were gone into, and he might tell them that he (Mr Pickard) was heart and soul with them " Well it is difficult after that, if it is true—and nobody denied it—for the Association to say that they were in any sense setting their faces against the state of things that was going on   " They had had a lot of talk what went on with Nolan, Rounds, and himself at Sheffield, and he could tell them that, if there was ever a man to have got at him, he was the man   He was prepared to do everything—that it had come to a fight   Mr Pickard said ' They had done perfectly right not to sign, and telling the men not to sign on under any circumstances, and to go every morning to the pit to every shift, and they would see what they could do   While he was there he (Mr Pickard) wired to Mr Chambers to ask him to meet a deputation, but they had not received a reply as yet   Men would be there at the pits to serve notices, and they were to go until every shift—until they heard something different   He hoped every man would have to go to Doncaster at the week end to show Mr Chambers   Thirty or forty places stood out through Yorkshire on the wage question ' Now there was a strike at this time, and it was contended by us that the men had gone out about this 10 per cent , but it was suggested on the other side that they had gone out on another question   I do not know that it is very material, but he refers to this on this point, and he says " Mr Pickard had the opinion that it would have to be a Federation job again as it was in 1893   (A Voice ' That's what we want ')   It would soon be all over then   If they did not get their grievances remedied, they would stop out at Denaby '   Then Mr Humphries said " Mr. Chambers said they wanted to work out their notices on the old contract, and did not want to sign a new one   If Mr Chambers would not allow them to work their notices out on the old contract, Mr Pickard would call a general meeting for the next Saturday to see what could be done   Mr Pickard wanted them to get into a legal position and then they would do all they could " Now my point about that is this, that it is immaterial for my purpose whether Mr Pickard really thought the contracts were at an end or not If he took this line at this stage   I will help you all I can , I will try and put the thing in order , I will assist, and if it is got into order we will support you through thick and thin , how can the Union after that dissociate themselves from what was happening, or refuse to recognise the liability for what happened ?

Then " John Nolan said he did not think when they started that they would be a bit further that morning   They had been trying to play their cards in the best possible manner, and in playing their hand had lost their hand in not coming out legally They had appealed to their higher authority, and they had said it was no use, they would have to go back and work the notices in the best possible way to get everything in order   Men had presented themselves at work that morning, and the manager had told them they would have to sign new rules. There was an alteration in the new rules, and seeing this was the case, and there was an unpleasantness over the 10 per cent, he should like to take this when they had their joint meeting. If the whole district had gone in the same way as they had, the 10 per cent would never have taken place yet. They felt the time had come when they should protest to the 10 per cent. They ought to pay it, and all the lads had the pluck to say they would never go back until their grievances were remedied with regard to the wages question." (Now that, no doubt, had reference to the other pits that were out because the lads had struck.) "If they had been working they would have been in a similar position to what they were at other places. Some boys worked at 2s 3d per shift, when they boasted of 60 per cent on '88 wages. Instead of 2d, 4d was taken off and in some cases 11d. They had been summoned for £6 for 12 days, and 3s 6d, the cost of the summons. Even at Denaby 'market men' were worth a little more to the Company than they themselves were asking for. Hurst and himself had been engaged to seek advice and engage a solicitor to see what they could do. He (the solicitor) had informed him that if they wished to 'go down the line' they could not. The law provided that under that Act they had to pay the fine or have their homes distressed. They had had a resolution to the effect that they would go down the line rather than pay, but, seeing that this was so, it meant pay. They had a few more points with the solicitor, and when they had met on Saturday they would be able to show that the tale was not as black against them as at the present time. He had told them that he could not get them off, and they did not expect that he could. It seemed hard when the manager could come down on them for 10s a shift, when some of the men had been working for less than 5s. Seeing they had taken the stand they had, they ought to go for what they intended getting from the first—a price list for the fillers and lads."

Now, your Lordship will see what that means shortly. These men put forward a new price list, and they resolved by various resolutions that they would stand until they got the new price list, and we proved that the new price list made an advance in wages— of 26 or 28 per cent in wages—all round. That is what they were really after. Then Hurst "said the position they had been in for three weeks was altered that morning. They had tried to put themselves in a legal position, and it had been decided amongst them that a deputation should be appointed to wait on Mr Chambers. Mr Chambers had wired 'No need for a meeting, pits are open when men wish to resume work.' It was generally known after that that they were bound to go back after passing the resolution independent of signing any new contract whatever. Yesterday afternoon 44 people went on and signed at Cadeby, and only two at Denaby. It proved beyond doubt that there was better loyalty at Denaby than at Cadeby Main." Now is not that conclusive of what was in these men's minds, and they were talking about a man who was ready to sign on—he was a blackleg—44 had signed on at Cadeby and only two at Denaby, and he is praising the Denaby men because they are more loyal than the Cadeby men "He hoped that after the meeting there was no man would sign the contract after the advice they had had from Mr Pickard" They give the result of the ballot and then Croft, the Chairman (at page 412) says this "The Chairman said that Mr Parrott had said they could go to work without signing the new rules"

Mr ATHERLEY JONES You did not read what is said at the bottom of the page

Mr ELDON BANKES Do you wish me to read that?

Mr ATHERLEY JONES Yes

Mr ELDON BANKES My Lord, I will read it I did not think it was material, but I will read it "As one of the Committee he advised them to take the advice which had been sent down from the General Secretary, and present themselves to work until such times as Mr Chambers thought fit to let them work Their turn would come We then dealt with the various new rules" Then "The Chairman said that Mr Parrott had said they could go to work without signing the new rules He (the Speaker) had said 'We shan't sign them' They paid men to look after their interests and he was always there when he was wanted" (speaking of himself as an official) "Mr Pickard had told him that morning, 'Tell your men to be calm' He had said that they had been playing a month, and many of them wanted bread, and it was so in many cases They had better be wanting bread than going to work for nothing They wanted to start with a new price list before they consented to go to work They had been told they would be out of work for 12 months They could fight for four years if they got strike pay" I do not think I need, my Lord, comment upon that language—your Lordship will follow the drift of it, and the impression it might very properly have upon a Jury

Now, if your Lordship will turn to page 230 your Lordship will find the resolution that was passed on that day That "After the report of Messrs Croft and Humphries of the interview with Mr Pickard with reference to the Colliery Company refusing to allow us to return to work until they had signed a fresh contract (had been given, it was then)," I do not know what that means It was "Moved and seconded, That a deputation be appointed to wait on Mr Chambers asking him to allow the men to work their notices out on the old contract That the old deputation be appointed for that purpose That each man go to the lamp house and ask for his lamp each working day during the running of his notice That we still adhere to the old resolution of June 29th, 1902" That is to "stop the wheels" I think that exhausts all that took place on this very important day

Now, my Lord, some important correspondence follows between Mr Pickard and the officials of the branches, which is to be found at pages 346 and following pages. There is a letter, my Lord, of July 21st on page 347, and this is an important letter, because it is the letter which Mr Pickard writes after an interval between the 17th—after he had seen Croft and after he had seen Nolan and Humphreys, and after he had had the rules, he writes on the 21st July to Mr Smith, the Secretary of Denaby "I have had Mr Nolan and Mr Humphries here to-day, and talked the situation over at your collieries along with Mr W E Raley, who endorses what Mr I Raley said, and they only confirm my opinion with regard to the present position. First of all, we cannot recommend you to sign on again, but earnestly recommend you to continue presenting yourselves for work" Now, of course, it was idle to do that. It was quite plain that the Colliery Company would not take the men back unless they signed on, and therefore presenting themselves for work was merely an idle form.

The LORD CHANCELLOR. The Colliery Company may have been perfectly wise, as well as within their right, but what harm would it have done to them if they had taken the men on?

Mr ELDON BANKES. Of course, if they had taken them on without a fresh contract it would have been open to the men to dispute the terms under which they were engaged. The Company having said, and let it be known that they considered the old contracts at an end, if they had let the men come back then, without signing on again, it would have been left in such a position that any man might have gone away at a day's notice, there was no provision for 14 days' notice except the contract which, according to the Colliery Company's own view, was at an end, therefore, if the men had just walked back when they liked, they could have gone out again at a day's notice, and what the Colliery Company wanted to do was to get the men back under the original contract, and they felt confident that if they did it, they would stay—or the bulk of them would stay. I wish to point this out, that it was in the Colliery Company's own interest to get the men back. They had no idea of bringing in outsiders, therefore, unless these men came back, the pits would go to rack and ruin.

The LORD CHANCELLOR. Was there any explanation given of why they did not take them back? One wants to get at the motives of the whole thing.

Mr ELDON BANKES. So far as the Colliery Company is concerned, of course, they always considered it very important that the men should sign the contract, not only because it provides for the length of notice, but because it provides for the men complying with the various by-laws.

Lord DAVEY Would there have been any doubt, if they had allowed the men to come back, that they came back upon the old terms ?

Mr ELDON BANKES Our view is this If we had given way on this point these men would have found some other device to keep them out It is very well to suggest after the event that we had better have taken this course or that course It seems to me that possibly if we wanted to get them back we might have taken that course, but in the start of it the thing was—they being controlled by the men who undoubtedly had the control of it—if we had given way on that point there would have been some other device found (this was obviously a device) to prevent the men coming back

Lord JAMES of HEREFORD May not the Company have said If we let you come back after an absence of 14 days' without signing the contract it might be taken against us that any workman might go away for 14 days and then come back ?

Mr ELDON BANKES Certainly

Lord JAMES of HEREFORD It would establish a precedent against them ?

Mr ELDON BANKES Yes

The LORD CHANCELLOR Thank you You have answered the question

Mr ELDON BANKES The letter of July 21st I was reading " First of all we cannot recommend you to sign on again, but earnestly recommend you to continue presenting yourselves for work I am also of opinion that whilst you are not entitled to pay and which the Council considered also, at the same time I think from the time you presented yourselves for work and they refused to allow you to do so according to Mr Chambers' first telegram, from that date you will come within our rule We are also of opinion that your contract is not broken, and if Mr Chambers persists in refusing to allow you to restart work without signing on he comes under the same law he brought you under, namely, he summoned you for leaving work without notice, and we shall be able to sue him for wages for the whole of the time he refuses to allow you to resume work However, under the circumstances, you as Secretary must present a requisition to come within rule from the date when you offered to resume work and were refused As you are aware your application for pay will have to be laid before the district before any payment can be made So far as I am concerned I think that if a voluntary levy could be obtained that might be done for the time that has gone by, and I can only hope if one is laid you will have a fair response   I want also to impress upon you this letter is not for publication "

Now just conceive the position that letter created   Here the Council had it absolutely in their power to stop this thing at the moment if they had taken the line and said, No, we do not approve of this strike, whether you are wrong or right as to your grievances you are out against the rules, no strike pay for men out against the rules the thing would have collapsed, but here the question as to how strike pay may be obtainable comes from the General Secretary himself   Nobody had ever thought of it before   It is an ingenious way of suggesting how these men may get what I think the Master of the Rolls calls "the life blood" for this strike, namely, the strike pay, and your Lordship will please read the next letter, which is from Smith of the Denaby   He says   " I am instructed to ask you if it would be possible to get a week's strike pay for our men   We have played six days on Wednesday, July 23rd, 1902, and seeing that our men have not had a pay day for one month they are getting uneasy, and will doubtless break away and sign the contract book, or would it be possible to make a grant equal to a week's strike pay until our case was settled by district, as we consider that seeing we are inside rule there should certainly be some signs of some money being forthcoming   Trusting that this application may meet with a favourable reply "

Now, see what the secretary of the branch says   ' If money is not forthcoming they will break away ", and what will they do when they break away?   They will sign the contract book   They have no objection to signing the contract book, but we have told them they are not to   and if strike pay is forthcoming they will not do it, but if strike pay is not forthcoming they will do it

Then, my Lord, there is a meeting on the 23rd   This question about strike pay had got about, and that is at page 471   Now, my Lord, this is not a very long meeting, and the bulk of it is not material, and if your Lordship will allow me I will read the passages that are material   This is a report from a newspaper report   I do not want to leave out anything that is material, but the passage I want to read is between "E" and "F '   He (Mr Croft) says "He was pleased they had not given the police any trouble, and they did not intend to do   Some women had told him that if they could only get two loaves a day they would fight   Those were the sort of Union women he liked   He hoped every man would stand as he had said 'like the brave with their face to the foe '   When they got strike pay they would be as contented as lambs   Then children would not be 'clamming for bread" and so forth   Then Smith "urged the men to carry out the advice of the officials at Barnsley and continue presenting themselves for work until the period of notice had expired and on no account to sign a contract   The speaker read a letter from Mr Benjamin Pickard, M P, which dealt with the question of strike pay and also the legality of the notices tendered "

I assume that is the letter "not for publication." The minute of that meeting is at page 231. This is an application for strike pay. "That the joint secretaries write in to the special Council Meeting to be held on Thursday, July 24th, asking them to grant strike pay for the financial members of both branches from July 17th seeing the manager refused to allow our men to go to work. (2) That we still adhere to the resolution of June 29th, 1902" (that is to "stop the wheels," again). (3) That we ask Mr. Rowlands, solicitor, Wakefield, to continue to defend us at Doncaster Court re summonses for damages by Colliery Company. (4) That the Committees draft a revised price list up and submit it to the men." That price list I shall have to deal with in a moment.

Then on that same page—231—your Lordship will find a resolution of the Council Meeting that was held on the 24th, when they dealt with the application for strike pay. "Special Council Meeting held at the Miners' Offices, Barnsley, on Thursday, July 24th, 1902, Mr. J. Wadsworth (Vice-President) in the chair. (8) That the financial members at Denaby and Cadeby Main Collieries be paid strike pay from the first day when they presented themselves for work and Mr. Chambers would not allow them to resume work unless they signed a new contract. (9) That this Council Meeting recommend every branch to do what they can in a voluntary manner to help the Denaby and Cadeby Main men during the time they were out illegally." Now *there* are the two branches of the resolution, the one is to grant them strike pay as from the 17th and the other is to ask the branches, not "ask" but to recommend the branches, to provide pay for the men during the time they have been out illegally.

The LORD CHANCELLOR. I have been trying to think what there is illegal in that. Supposing people commit an illegal act, and they have gone out, why should they not ask others to subscribe and give them relief for the consequences of their illegality?

Mr. ELDON BANKES. My Lord, there is no cause of action *per se* in it at all, but we use that as some evidence of ratification, that they adopted the act that these men did. Of course it is open to question, assuming there was no prior mandate under the rules.

The LORD CHANCELLOR. I understand the contention. That is an answer. You say it is evidence of ratification of an illegality.

Mr. ELDON BANKES. Yes, that is so.

The LORD CHANCELLOR. That you ask others to subscribe to relieve the suffering, if there be suffering. You say that is evidence of ratification of illegality,

Mr ELDON BANKES Some evidence—yes my Lord   Taken with——-

The LORD CHANCELLOR I understand   I see your point

Mr ELDON BANKES I can pass on   The first payment of strike pay was made on the 25th July and it dated from the 17th July, and from that time until the granting of the Injunction by the Court of Appeal in Howden's Case, strike pay was paid every week, and the strike pay was brought by Hall the Treasurer down and disbursed to the local treasurers

Lord DAVEY What is the date of the Injunction?

Mr ELDON BANKES The 16th January, 1903   I think that is the date   Then, my Lord, at page 232 (the next page) there are resolutions of the 30th July   My Lord, I am sorry I gave you a wrong date   The last payment of strike pay was on the 23rd January, 1903   I am afraid I gave Lord Davey the wrong date   On the 30th July, having got their strike pay, we now find that the resolutions take a different form, and on the 30th July there is a resolution of the joint meeting held 30th July, 1902 ' That we stand till we get a fresh price list", and there is a meeting held at which that resolution was passed   The meeting is at page 474, but I do not think, my Lord, that there is anything to which I need call your Lordship's attention pointedly in that meeting   At page 474, under letter E, Croft says this "One thing that pleased him on Saturday was that Mr Ballance and the other official who came down to pay strike money said the Denaby and Cadeby men were the best conducted in Yorkshire, and he would be only too pleased to tell every branch never to call Denaby and Cadeby men any more   Proceeding, Mr Croft said so long as the bags with the Union pay kept coming, he was sure they would go on fighting   They were more determined than ever   The password was "Be calm"   Now that is important, because this man, Croft, undoubtedly had advocated from the first that the men should be calm   They had put on such pressure as was necessary, and with the exception of the man Bury, there had been no actual assault, but they had put on sufficient pressure and prevented the men going to work, but your Lordship will find later on, when the men began to go back, that Phil Humphries, presiding at a meeting, says that the time has gone by for the watchword "Be calm"   and then we find a very different state of things   I may pass on now, my Lord, to the 7th August   Your Lordship will find a minute on page 233 of the 7th August

Lord DAVEY A minute of what?

Mr ELDON BANKES Of the Cadeby branch, my Lord—of both branches   "That the price list submitted by the Committee to the men be accepted as satisfactory and that it be forwarded on to

Mr Pickard asking him to submit it to Mr Chambers That we ask our officers to assist us in getting Manvers Main Price List for our boys That we still adhere to the Resolution of June 29th, 1902, till we get a new price list" Now that was that they would "stop the wheels," I think, and would get a new price list, and the price list (as shown by the evidence of Mr Chambers) was not any idea of mere alteration of the bag dirt question but a general rise in wages— I think he said of 26 per cent

Lord DAVEY Standard wages?

Mr ELDON BANKES Yes my Lord

Lord JAMES of HEREFORD No

Mr ELDON BANKES Of the price list for the colliery?

Lord JAMES of HEREFORD Yes, yes, but——

Mr ELDON BANKES I suppose it would be the standard for the colliery

Lord JAMES of HEREFORD A standard percentage

Mr ELDON BANKES I think now, my Lord, I may pass to the 13th August I was going to give your Lordship one fact On the 13th of August it is proved by a man named Barnard one of the officers of the Company—on page 687 if it is necessary to verify it— that 87 men had come back to work—that there were at that time 87 men working in the two pits, and it is apparent that the branch officials were realising that unless more active steps were taken the men would come back in increasing numbers, and there was a meeting held on this 13th August (which is at page 477) My suggestion to your Lordship is—and it is plain, I submit, by the evidence—that this speech of the Chairman's here (Phil Humphries) was a deliberate instigation to the men to adopt a stronger line with regard to the men who were at work, and that they must stop those who were at work, and they did it in the way I shall describe in a moment, but his "opening remarks were brief He said the time had come when they ought to throw away the password 'Be calm' and get another It was 'Be calm' in 1885 and they lost", and I will now proceed to show your Lordships——

Lord DAVEY Croft took a different view, apparently

Mr ELDON BANKES Yes, Croft was there, apparently, but he was not in the chair "Croft took a different view He said in regard to 1885, what he witnessed and experienced taught him that the moment they began noting their case was over and they were beaten" So that there is no doubt as to what everybody understood

and what Phil Humphries meant However, they took Phil
Humphries advice, and not Croft's advice And it was not the men
only, it was the Committeemen took part in all this It your
Lordship will turn to page 669, you will find what Howden said I
ought to tell your Lordship that by the 18th the course of conduct
which was adopted by the men (as we say, with the sanction and
approval and at the instigation of the branch officials) resulted in the
numbers of men dropping, I think, to five or six, and when they
dropped to five or six the police advised the Colliery officials that it
was dangerous to allow any men to go on, and they shut down the
colliery I will call attention to it I will give your Lordship the
evidence of a few of the men This is Howden, page 669 He
speaks about an assault which took place on the 18th August (1178)
"We have got to that date Between the day when you first heard
of the strike and the day when you were first assaulted in August, I
want you to give me some account of what had taken place You
had been working every day, had you?—Sometimes I was working
at night and sometimes in the day time,—every day I worked six
days a week Q First of all, about how many men were working
besides yourself?—As near as I can say, with the officials and the
men that was working at the time when they met us in full force on
the Wednesday, there would be about 70 or 80 of us working
altogether, as near as I can say, at Cadeby Q Did the number of
men working get larger or smaller as time went on?—Well, after
they began to meet us in full force, when they lined the roadway
where we had to pass, and we had just a narrow passage to walk
down in the middle, they fell off They dared not come to their
work Q That is to say, the men at work fell off?—Yes, those who
were at work Q About how long before the 18th August, which
was the day when you were assaulted, had the crowd been lining the
roadway?—There had been several in the roadway every day from
the strike starting, but they came in full force on the Wednesday
before the 18th Q That will give us the date—about the 13th
August Do you recollect there being a mass meeting of the men
about this time?—As I was given to understand I was at my work
Q If you do not know yourself, say so Do you know of your own
knowledge whether there was or was not a mass meeting of the
men about that time?—There had been a mass meeting that day on
the Wednesday, and they came from that mass meeting to meet us
as we left the colliery" Then at 1186 Mr Lush says "I will pass
from it Before the 13th August, the Wednesday when the
men came in full force you said some had been in the road What
exactly had occurred as you were going to your work before that
Wednesday?—If I was working on the night shift when I was
coming home of a morning there were several of the Committeemen on the Glasshouse Bridge, Kilner Bridge, whichever it may be
represented, and other men that had worked at the colliery with
them Q There were several Committeemen and other men who
had worked at the Colliery with them at some bridge What was the
name of the bridge?—Kilner's Bridge Q Is that the bridge on

the road leading to the Colliery?—Yes Q To the Cadeby Pit
When these Committeemen and other men were there what
occurred? Did anything unusual happen?—They were booing us a
little bit as we passed backwards and forward to our work, behind
our back, as soon as we got that we could not see They tried to hide
it a little bit that way, so that we could not see the individual who
did it—but as soon as we got anywhere near them they were at it—
we had just got by them (Mr Justice Lawrance) What did they
do?—They were booing us and calling us black sheep (Mr
Montague Lush) About what time in the morning would that
be?—Betwixt five and six Q That had happened up till the
Wednesday, had it?—Yes, of a regular thing Q On the Wednesday you saw they come in full force?—Yes Q Was that on your
way to work or on your way home?—That was on my way home?
Q When they were there in full force, just tell the Jury what
happened What did you say or what did they do?—We had to
walk down between them They lined the road from the bridge
down to the bottom of the street where I live, and they were hissing
and booing us and calling us black sheep, and carrying sheeps'
heads blackened on broom handles, and throwing old tin cans about
and drumming them Q That was on the Wednesday?—This
occurred from the Wednesday to the Monday that I was assaulted
Q That occurred from the Wednesday till the following Monday?—
Barring the Saturday They were not throwing at us on the
Saturday They were away collecting on the Saturday the majority
of them Q What effect had this upon the number of men working
at the mine" Then there was an objection, and then, my Lord,
on pages 672 and 673 he describes the assault upon himself which
took place on the 18th The details of that are not material, but if
your Lordships will go to page 673, I will begin at 1210 'Can you
tell me the names of any prominent men who were there in the
crowd on those few days between the Wednesday and the Monday?—
There was the biggest part of the Committeemen there Q Did
you hear any one of them, or anybody, endeavour in any way to
stop this booing and so on?—No, I never saw them try in any way
to stop it, but they were in carriages" Now that goes to show, as
I submit, that they were there controlling this There would be no
other reason for them being in carriages except for the purpose of
giving them a commanding position and controlling

Now that is Howden Legg I have read, I think Then, my
Lord, there is a man named Witty at page 681 He is asked at
Question 1313 "Now on the 13th August did you see anything
that was out of the common?—I saw a great crowd of people on
the bridge leading to the colliery Q Has the bridge got a name?—
Kilner's Bridge Q That is the one spoken of by Howden?—Yes
Q What was the crowd doing?—Hooting and shouting Q What
were they hooting and shouting at?—At the men who were leaving
work at 2 o'clock from the pit Q Had you noticed that occurring
on any days previous to the 13th August?—Yes, on several days

Q To the same extent or not?—No, it varied—sometimes more and sometimes less Q On the 13th, what was the character of the demonstration then?—Very wild Very wild shouting I was 200 yards away, and it was very plain Q Were there a large number of people congregated there?—Yes, a great number Q Did you see the same thing happening on any days between the 13th and 19th?—Yes, especially on the 18th August I think it was a Wednesday On the 18th there was a tremendous crowd" Then Barnard—I do not think I need read all the evidence, my Lord, if I give your Lordships a selection There is a man named Hill at page 728——

The LORD CHANCELLOR Make your selection, but give us the references to the other passages that you do not quote

Mr ELDON BANKES There is Turner speaks of it at page 752 I think your Lordship will find our case on this point summarised in our case—I think I am right in saying—at page 40 and 41 of our case, and I think your Lordship will find all the references in our case It is paragraphs 73 and 74 of our case at pages 40 and 41, but if I may I will give it in my own way

The LORD CHANCELLOR If you please

Mr ELDON BANKES Your Lordship will find all the references there, I think There is a man named Hill at page 727 He is one of the men who worked throughout He is describing what happened on the 13th (Question 1711) "What happened to you on that day on your way home?—When I got to Kilner's Bridge I met a large crowd of people As soon as we got going into the crowd they started to throw stones and sticks and shoved their feet out trying to throw us down (Mr Justice Lawrance) I am afraid I cannot follow that I think you said when you got to Kilner's Bridge you met a crowd What did they do?—They started shouting at us ' blackleg,' and then they started to throw stones at us, and shoved their feet out trying to throw us down Q You say us—who was with you?—No others but me, I was by myself (Mr Montague Lush) Were they carrying anything or doing anything?—They were carrying flags, and they wrote on the flags 'No road for blacklegs' Q Were they carrying anything else?—They were carrying sheeps' heads (Mr Rufus Isaacs) Where?—As soon as we got in the crowd these lads would come up with their flags and go in front of us with these sheeps' heads, blackleaded on sticks (Mr Montague Lush) Did you see any of the Committeemen there?—Yes, I did Q Can you give us any of the names? I saw Nolan, Harry Hirst, Phil Humphries, Arthur Dickenson, and others I know by sight but not by name Q Did you work any more after that day—August 14th?—No, I was in the doctor's hands for a day or two Q What made you go into the doctor's hands?—

I was struck in the back with half a brick   Q   On this day, the 14th August?—Yes "

Then Westlake (at page 732, Question 1778) says he worked there until the 13th August   He says   "I went to work "   "Q   Was that immediately after you signed on and commenced work?—Yes   Q   And right away on till the time you gave up?—Right on till I gave up   Q   In what way were you interfered with?—Well, we had to pass through a crush—women, men, children and every one else were so far beasts as to spit at us as we passed by, while the language is scarcely necessary to come out with   (Mr Justice Lawrance)   We need not have that   (Mr Cautley)   Bad language was used?—Very bad   Q   What else happened?   Tell me subsequently what happened?—I do not know that I can recollect at all, but I can recollect one important point   The last time we were going home there were sticks and stones flying, and I had my head cut open here by a piece of wood   Q   Can you tell us when that was?—That would be about the 11th or 12th August   I do not keep all those dates in my mind   If I had expected this we might have had the dates properly ready   Q   Did you then cease to go to work?—I did   I thought it was time "   Then Wall, at page 740——

Lord JAMES of HEREFORD   Are these all mentioned in your case that you gave us the reference to?

Mr ELDON BANKES   I think they are   Probably I need not go through them   They are all of the same character, and I may say that they indicate that between this 13th and 18th August there was a deliberate organised intimidation and molestation at which the Committeemen, or a large number of them, were present, and, of course, the force and significance of that is made much stronger when one realises that no single one of those Committeemen was called to deny the reasonable inference which would be drawn from the fact that he was present there   My Lord, there is one policeman   He describes the assault upon Howden   I do not know that I need read that if I give a reference to it   At page 754 I should like to read Q 2073 (this is important)   " From what you saw on that day " (that is the 18th August) " was it safe for any man to go on working or not?—It was not safe to continue working   Q   Did you happen to have a man stationed by Howden's house?—Yes   Q   When Howden was assaulted, did you see any Committeemen among the crowd there?—Yes, I saw Moon and Collier   Q   Moon is the man called 'Brog'?—Yes, 'Staley' and Collier and I believe there were several more about   Q   Now taking that day was any single one of the Committeemen doing anything to stop the violence?—No   They seemed more to encourage it   Q   Taking the period generally through between the commencement of the strike and the closing of the pits, you often saw, you say, Committeemen about?—Oh, yes.   Q   Did you report to the Denaby Company in consequence of what you have seen as to whether it was safe to keep the pits open ?—Yes, I did   Q We know that in accordance with your advice the pits were closed on the following day ?—Yes " Then Mr Isaacs says " I protest against your saying in consequence of his advice " Then a little lower down   " Mr Montague Lush " (2081) " In accordance with your advice is what I said ?—The pits were closed next day "

My Lord, the only other fact I want to mention is that it was proved that the numbers of men had dropped from the 80 or 90 which there were on the 13th August to 9 or 10, and your Lordship will find that stated by a witness on page 673   That was Howden stated it—Question 1208, page 673 " How many about ?—I do not think there were above 9 or 10 '

The LORD CHANCELLOR You gave us the first date the 13th August ——

Mr ELDON BANKES Down to the 18th On the 18th Howden was assaulted That was the day that the numbers of men had dwindled down to nine or ten, that was the day the police advised the officials that it really was not safe to keep the pit open There was a notice, my Lord, issued by the Colliery Company, which is at page 197 I just ought to mention that, because a point was made about it at the trial, and it was explained At page 197 the Colliery Company issued a notice They said " Since the commencement of the strike on June 30th the Company have employed a certain number of hands underground in order to render the workings safe while standing for a long time These operations were as much in the interests of the men as of the Company, nevertheless, the strikers have molested, intimidated and assaulted these few men This work having now been completed, the men will be withdrawn and the pits closed " Well, Mr Chambers was asked about that, and what he said was this He said that the Company did not like to acknowledge that they had to give in to this intimidation It was not a correct statement to say that the work was completed It was far from completed, and really in the case of several of the pits it was necessary to keep them going if they could, but they did not like to publicly acknowledge that they had had to give in to this intimidation

Now, my Lord, I will ask your Lordship's attention to a meeting which took place on the 21st August, which is very important as connecting the committeemen with what had happened It is at page 482 Croft speaks, but there is nothing in his speech that I want to call your attention to I do not think there is anything I ought to read at all there, but Nolan's is a very important speech from our point of view Nolan also spoke at page 483 He " first alluded to the work done by the women in connection with stopping the men from going to work He said it had become a question between the police authorities and the Colliery management " ——

The LORD CHANCELLOR What does that mean—' a question between the police authorities and the Colliery management"?

Mr ELDON BANKES He means It is a great shame to bring the police in That is what he means In a later speech he refers to the work of the women again, and it is quite plain that what must have happened was that there was an organisation of the women, which was, I assume, carried through at the instigation of these Committeemen—at any rate, with their approval—to stop the men They thought that they would be able to stop the men without actually assaulting them, if they organised these demonstrations of women "Before the management would pay the wages the men were entitled to according to the price list, they had thought fit to pay thousands of pounds for police protection for a few black sheep The time had come when it was thought these men ought to be stopped The Taff Vale decision had been hanging over their heads and they had not been able to say what they would like to say Their position had been circulated throughout the length and breadth of Yorkshire and every man and lad who worked at a pit knew it exactly The Chief Constable, Captain Russell, at Wakefield had informed the colliery management, if they were going to insist upon those few men working in the way they were doing he would not be responsible for any rioting that might take place and he did not want to see a second Featherstone"

Now it is quite plain there that Nolan is recognising the advice which had been given by Phil Humphries—the men had got to be stopped and stopped they were Now I may pass on to page 485 The next thing I want to call attention to is a stoppage on the 3rd September, and at this meeting the full details are given the fresh price list is set out I do not think I need go into it, it is not material to go into it, but Nolan's speech is material (487) " Nolan said since the last meeting he was pleased that the ladies had done their duty " (Of course, the pits were shut and there was nobody coming to them at all) "He could not say that of all men, for there were a few probably there that morning who had not done their duty, and instead of helping the Committee had been trying to stop the funds from coming in " There was very considerable dissatisfaction undoubtedly amongst a number of the men as to the strike at all

The LORD CHANCELLOR May I ask you this The last meeting is the 21st August, this meeting was the 3rd September. Had there been any men employed in the interval?

Mr ELDON BANKES· No, my Lord, no, not that we know of

The LORD CHANCELLOR Therefore this referred, not to stopping the men from going to work, but some other thing—"that the ladies had done their duty"?

Mr ELDON BANKES I am not sure I think what he means is this I assume the organisation of women had been kept on foot, and that, inasmuch as no men had in fact gone to work, he was congratulating them upon their——

The LORD CHANCELLOR Stopping them

Mr ELDON BANKES They had not in fact stopped them, but they were there ready to stop them, but his view was that so long as they were there ready to go on doing what they had hitherto done, things were satisfactory And Mr Chambers' evidence, my Lord, I may refer to on this question of the price list, because this is the first time that it has been formulated At page 513, Question 173, I ask him "Then you saw this revised price list which the men had published in September?—1 am not sure about it, but I think it is very likely I did then Q At any rate, you have seen it I want to know generally with regard to that price list, how did it compare as a whole with the price list in existence at the time of the strike ? —There was a very considerable advance in the standard rates they were asking for Q An advance all round?—Not on all items, but the general effect of it was to advance the rates of wages that they had been having about 28 per cent —at least that Q At least 28 per cent over and above the standard rate?—Yes "

Lord JAMES of HEREFORD Were they asking for special rates of wages for these two collieries only as against the Federation?

Mr ELDON BANKES Yes, they were asking for special rates of wages for those two collieries only Each colliery has its special price list This was a special price list

Lord JAMES of HEREFORD You said a question arose on the standard The "standard" is general I do not know that it is very material, they wanted a rise of wages

Mr ELDON BANKES They wanted a rise of wages I suppose the standard rate would be the price list rate, I should imagine so I think I may pass now to the 17th September and a meeting at page 412 Mr Croft "said he was pleased to see the way which they had stuck to their word Rumours had been going about that there was a settlement at Denaby and Cadeby If that was so on a right basis, the Committee and himself would be glad They had fought 12 weeks "

I do not think there is anything else that is material on that page, but on the next page at the top, he says "They suffered in '85, and then they were turned out of their homes, pitched in tents, nothing coming forward, no Union pay, they fought for some months on nothing They had now Union pay in front of them They had winter coming, and they had winter then and no pay It was better to suffer a little now than to suffer when they got back again the way in which they had before they came out The price list had been before the Council, and had been discussed by their leaders It was not in their hands alone, but in their leaders' hands "

Then I do not think there is anything else in his speech that is material If your Lordship will turn over, at page 414 you will see " Nolan said, that in fairness to the Committee he should like to say that before people went through the district saying the pits were open for Thursday, they should come to their Committee as they were in direct communication with Barnsley The Committee were as anxious to get back to work as any men, but they were not anxious to have ' peace at any price '" There is evidence again Here are the Committee in charge of this direct communication with Barnsley, and saying that they were not going back to have " peace at any price " First, my Lord, a little higher up, between " B " and " C," on page 414 says " He hoped every man would still be as loyal as on the 30th June, when he assisted in passing the resolution to stop the wheels " The resolution that they passed on that day (at page 235) is simply this " That we adhere to the resolution of June 29th, 1902 " That again is " to stop the wheels " until, now, they get their fresh price list Then September 23rd— My Lord, I think the next one I must pass to for the moment is October 29th

The LORD CHANCELLOR If it helps your argument, it is nearly time for luncheon, and if you would like to have the interval now we will rise

Mr ELDON BANKES I am obliged to your Lordship For the moment I have lost my reference

(Adjourned for a short time)

Mr ELDON BANKES My Lord, the next date I want to refer to is October 29th, and your Lordships will notice that I have passed over a very considerable interval, and the reason of that is this, that the pits had been closed down, and so during these weeks there was really no invitation to men to go to work—direct invitation I mean—and the strike pay was being paid, and therefore one would expect that nothing particular would have occurred But you find that the same kind of speeches are made with reference to what will happen to men if they do go back to work, and if your Lordships will kindly turn to page 420 you will find a reference there to a meeting which took place on the 29th October These meetings had been taking place every week, and the substance of them I think was, wherever we find a report of them, that the men were exhorted to stand together and stand out, and they passed a resolution about stopping wheels and so forth, and now we come to October 29th, page 419, and Croft says " they were not going to be defeated They

had come out together and they were going to go in together."
Then at page 420 there is a passage I want to read beginning
between D and E The earlier part of the speech was taken up by
an explanation by Croft, apparently somebody had published in a
newspaper that Croft was making money out of the strike, and that
he had started a shop, and he deals with that, it is not material but
between C and D he says "During the past six years, up to 18
months ago, he had never saved a penny, but up to then he had put
a few shillings in the Post Office Savings Bank, and in the Barnsley
Co-operative Society, and since he came out on strike with the rest
of the men he had had to draw from the Barnsley Co-operative Any
man could go, and they would tell him what he had drawn from there
since the strike commenced That kind of thing was not very nice,
but could they wonder at it when they had 'rats' amongst them
They were crawling about, but they ran into their holes when the
dog came, because they were frightened" That was the kind of
language that was used with reference to any men who wanted to
break away, and at page 421 he refers to that again between B and
C He says "There are some rats in here, and we know them,
and we will send a ferret into the hole and get them out" And
again between D and E ' He said yes there are some women and
children knowing something, 9s was not enough, but if they could
hold out to the end of the year they would get 14s instead of 9s,
and if it was so the rats could go into their holes and stop there"
Then at page 422 Berry, the miner, the man who had been
assaulted, tries to speak, and they will not let him speak, and then
Nolan speaks "With regard to that man in the corner (Cries
'Throw him out') That man was the Chairman of the Cadeby
branch 12 months ago He was one picked to draw up the price
list to submit to the manager, and he was quite willing when they
were yielding to put it to Mr Chambers This man worked black
sheep whilst he was out This man left Denaby and Cadeby and
went to work at Manvers, and he is going back, and he is on our
funds Has he any right to be on? He ought to go outside" Then
I do not know that there is anything else my Lord that I need refer
to, it is only an indication and whenever they a had meeting the
same kind of language was used about men working black sheep,
and all holding together, and so forth

Now, I may pass on to November 6th where there is a letter
from Mr Chambers to Mr Parrott, at page 367 I may as well
read the letter before, at page 367, from Mr Parrott from the
Miners' Offices, Barnsley, showing that they were keeping in touch
with what was going on "I am requested by the members of our
Council Meeting and also by your late workmen to ask if you will
arrange to meet a deputation along with the district officials in
order, if possible, to arrange a proper settlement of the dispute at
your two collieries An early answer will oblige", and Mr
Chambers writes on the next day "Dear Sir, in reply to your
request that I should meet a deputation of our late workmen I am

unable to comprehend that any good result would be attained by it
I have previously endeavoured to make perfectly clear it is quite
impossible for the Company to give any advance on the standard
rate of wages or to interfere with the price lists which have existed
for many years, and on which the men entered the Company's
employment, and the Company desire there should be no misapprehension on this point If the men are disposed to resume work
they are at liberty to do so If afterwards any matters arise which
cause dissatisfaction I will try to remove them, failing that the men
can appeal to the Joint Committee appointed by the South Yorkshire
Coal Miners' Association and the Yorkshire Miners' Association
for the purpose of settling disputes which cannot be settled between
the managers and men at the various collieries" My Lord, I
submit that it is a perfectly fair and proper attitude to take up, and
is an indication of the attitude which was taken up throughout

Now we come, my Lord, to an important incident which marks
another phase in this strike, and that is this I told your Lordship
that the Company had built for their men a large number of houses
and the men were occupying those houses under agreements by which
the rent was deducted from their wages Of course the result of
the men being out on strike was that they continued in occupation
of these houses without paying any rent, and they had been allowed to
remain in possession from the 29th June up to this date in November—
it being the wish of the Colliery Company to keep these men on as
their workmen if they could, and under the continual impression
that this, as they considered it absurd strike could not continue for
an indefinite length of time But in November the Company came
to the conclusion that it was impossible to let that state of things
continue any longer and Mr Pope thereupon drafted and issued a
circular to the men setting out what the condition of things was, and
enclosing with it a paper which the men should sign stating whether
they were willing to come back and work or not and stating that if
men were not willing to come back to work they would be obliged
to turn them out of their houses Now all these documents are very
material and the incident is material for this purpose, it was at once
realised by the branch officials that a step had been taken which
would very likely induce the men to go back to work, and they were
very concerned about this They immediately appealed to the
Council at Barnsley, and the Council at Barnsley realising the
position sent down men, as they had sent them down before, as I
suggest when you read the speeches, to strengthen the position, and
strengthen the backs of those who were inclined to give in

Now, my Lord, I will refer to the documents Mr Pope's
pamphlet is at page 200 I am afraid it is rather a long document,
but I must read it.

Lord DAVEY Who was Mr Pope?

Mr ELDON BANKES Mr Pope was the Chairman of the Company, my Lord I do not think I need read it at all, I may summarise it I think, my Lord He first of all begins by stating that having been more than a quarter of a century chairman of the collieries at which you have worked, I think it my duty to address you personally on the subject of the present strike For many years past Mr Chambers has, in good times and bad times, persistently brought to the attention of the Board every suggestion he could think of for increasing the comfort of the inhabitants of Denaby Main," and then he sets out the very many things that had been done for the comfort and improvement of the men, and he talks about the houses they live in, and at page 201, letter A, he says " The Board have done what they consider to be right—they do not expect gratitude but they look for fair play, and certainly did not expect that you would try to injure the Company without ' rhyme or reason ' A large proportion of your number were perfectly satisfied, and would have continued to work peaceably enough had they not been made a catspaw of by certain men amongst you who have grown rich upon your misery, men who, after being on strike for over 18 weeks, find themselves all of a sudden men of capital, who can afford to buy pigs," and so forth Then he deals with the question about wages, and between E and F he says " I find on examination of the books that the miners' wages at Denaby and Cadeby during the six months previous to the strike amount to an average of 9s 2d per day, and if this statement is questioned the books are open for the inspection of any properly qualified accountant In addition to this you have had a further very great advantage over nearly all other collieries, because work has been provided for you every working day in the year, very often at a heavy cost to the Company in paying your wages when stacking coal which they could not sell I find that the standard of wages was arranged 17 years ago, and since then advances and reductions have been made on it in accordance with the advances and reductions in the district, and not a word has been said Seventeen years ago these collieries only employed 1,113 men and boys underground, but at the time of the stoppage they employed 3,110 " Well, I think Mr Pope under estimated the figure, and then he gives reasons

Mr H T. WADDY That is right—' underground

Mr ELDON BANKES Oh, underground Then he says " I will now remind you of what led to this strike " I do not think, my Lord, I need read that, though I should like to read it, but I do not want to occupy your Lordships' time It is not directly material But on page 203 he points out that the Company could not afford to give them an increase of wage, and between E and F he says " In fact, if the Company were as anxious to give as you are to receive an increase in wages they would not be able to keep the pits working for a month, because they would be absolutely unable to dispose of their coal except at a heavy loss, therefore you must clearly understand that the Company have no more power to advance your wages and continue to work the pits than your wives have to make a stone of bread out of a pound of flour. I must now refer to another subject. You have been living in the Company's houses for 18 weeks without paying any rent, and you are not only doing this, but you are trying by remaining in the houses to prevent other men from going to work, so as to force the Company to pay you impossible wages. Some of you have done even more than this, and have acted more like savages than Englishmen by assaulting, stoning and otherwise annoying and injuring men who had no dispute with the Company, and who were only anxious to be allowed to work peaceably. The Company have exercised very great patience with you, as they hoped that before this common sense would prevail, but the Company have now determined, as you do not wish to work for them, that you must give up your houses, so that those men who are anxious to work peaceably shall be allowed to do so. I do not for one moment mean to apply these strictures to all, knowing, as I do, that a large number of you are as good as any set of working men in the kingdom, but I believe, through fear, a great number have failed to assert their rights as free-born Englishmen, and now for the first time you really find yourselves in a position of slavery, but your slave masters are the tyrants amongst your own number. I wish it to be distinctly understood that there will be no necessity for any of you to leave your houses. Any one, after he has signed on and resumed work, if he becomes dissatisfied with that work, or knows of some place where he can obtain higher wages, has nothing more to do than to give 14 days' notice at any time, and he is free to go away and receive those wages. Those men who are content with the wages paid at these collieries can remain, and the Company are determined that they shall not be molested by the others. I will just give you a homely illustration of a parallel case. Supposing you had a housekeeper, and one day when you went home expecting your dinner to be ready you found her sitting idle and nothing done, and when you wished to know what was the matter she told you that she would do no more work until you raised her wages, and further that she would remain in the house to prevent anyone else doing it. What would you do? Of course you would turn her out, and unless you will go to work the Company will act exactly as you would yourselves act under similar circumstances. Who can question the fairness or justice of such action? In conclusion, let me draw your attention to the following facts. During the last few years you have received advances in wages to the extent of 60 per cent on the standard. Why? Because coal rose in price, and this enabled the coalowners to pay the advance. The 60 per cent advance has now been reduced to 50 per cent. Why? Because coal fell in price, so that it could not be sold for sufficient money to pay the men for getting it. No one has ever yet been able to extract 'blood from a stone.' You have been trying to do so for over 18 weeks, and the attempt has cost you more than £100,000 in wages, and you are not a bit nearer than when you started. Perhaps some of you will say this is only a 'gaffer's story,' but I think you will do me the justice to admit that I have never deceived you in the past, and I pledge you my word of honour I am not deceiving you now."

Then, my Lord, with that was the circular which is next on page 205. It begins "If you are desirous of terminating the strike, you may sign the enclosed form. If you are unwilling to resume work, do not sign it. In any case place the form in the envelope in which you receive it, and seal it up. You may then either post it or cause it to be delivered at the Company's offices by hand, or keep it till one of the Company's officers calls for it. The Company will give you every assurance that no individual's name who signs the form will be divulged, and the utmost secrecy will be observed." The form is No 51. "I, the undersigned, of so-and-so, agree to return to work when required, on the same terms as existed on the 12th July, 1902." I do not think anybody could say of that that it is not a perfectly fair circular to send out, and one which anybody reading it would see would be likely to influence men who were in occupation of these houses, and who had no real dispute with the Company, but were anxious to come back to work. That was how it was interpreted, because at page 368, on November 7th, Smith, the secretary of Denaby, writes to Mr Pickard "Enclosed find copy of notices which have been served out to-day to occupiers of houses under Colliery Company, which my Committee have authorised to forward for your perusal, and also to ask your advice on. I also have to ask if it is possible for an official to come to assist in addressing a meeting which is called for Monday at 12 o'clock at the Mason's Arms, Mexbro', as you will understand that the proceedings the Company are taking is causing great uneasiness among the men and they wish for a district official to come in our midst to see if there is any possibility of coming to some arrangement whereby the proposed proceedings may be deferred. You will see by Mr B Pope's manifesto that he is trying to undermine the stability of our men to cause a break, the ultimate result of which would, no doubt, cause disorder and further prosecutions. Our Committee's wish is to avoid any rupture if possible, but what can we do in the face of the ultimatum which we had given us? You will readily understand that these notices are a kind of threat which are intended to intimidate the men, besides which there have been imported into the village about 40 extra police. We contend that there is no necessity for these, except they are for the purpose of inciting the men to commit acts which otherwise they would not do, as the place has been extremely quiet since the pits were closed. If you think it possible for an official to come you will confer a great favour on our branches." Now, of course, the Colliery Company having issued this notice and intending to act upon it, took the wise and reasonable precaution of drafting in extra police, and here the man realises what the effect is likely to be, and he appeals that a district official may be sent down "to assist us in addressing a meeting of the men."

Now the next thing that happens is this—that in order to as far as possible ensure that the men should not do what Mr Pope desired them to do—sign these notices stating whether they were willing to come back or not—a resolution is passed that these circulars are all to be brought into the branches. It is at page 237, my Lord, minute on November 10th. "That the ballot papers issued by the company to the men be brought into the respective branch rooms." Now this is a very effective means of shutting the men off from the possibility of exercising their free will, because if an order goes forth that the papers are to be brought into the branch offices then it is known at once whether a man is a blackleg or not; if he brings it in, well and good, there it is, it is in the control of the branch and it cannot be used; if he does not bring it in, it leads to the inference that he is a blackleg and he would be treated accordingly. Then they go on to say, "That we stand firm to the resolution of June 29th, 1902." Now there again it is plain from this, and all this evidence that the branch officials were determined to keep this matter in their own hands and to keep the men out.

Then there is a meeting on this same day and at page 425 Croft addresses the meeting, and at the middle of page 426 between C and D he says this. "Nine weeks ago Mr Cowey had tried to get a deputation—they would not meet them. If Mr Chambers had said then, 'I will meet a deputation,' the thing would have been amicably settled. It was stupidness on his part, not on the men's side. They were prepared to get ready for work on a proper basis. Some people said, 'We shall take another ballot,' but the Society would not allow them to take a second ballot." Now, this is something we had not heard of before, but apparently people were saying, "Let us take another ballot, a proper ballot, to see whether we ought not to go back to work"—and Croft is here saying they were ready for work. "Some people said 'we shall take another ballot,' but the Society would not allow them to take a second ballot. Mr Chambers was going to take another ballot, and when he had taken it he might get a little more sense. There might be a 'rat or two' who would sign on, but they would have to go into their holes out of the road." That is a pretty plain indication of what was intended to be done to the men who signed Mr Pope's circular. Then at page 427 at the bottom of his speech between C and D, he says, "Use your own judgment, and whatever you do be careful of your words, and the old story 'be calm.' They had had no intimidation yet, but there might be some, but he hoped not." Of course, for some weeks there had been no necessity for intimidation since they had taken the effective step which resulted in the closing down of the pit. Then Nolan speaks, my Lord. At the bottom of page 427 he begins, but just between A and B, at page 421, he says, "Mr Pope's ballot only came to prove what people had been writing, that the Colliery Company were trying to find the weak place of some of the men who were not heart and soul in the dispute. Some said the dispute was not a properly constituted dispute. He said it was. They had admitted that they had done wrong What was the reason, because when they tried to take a ballot 12 months ago they could not get two-thirds majority in favour of coming out on strike to settle the dispute? The reason was that the ministers in the various churches criticised him and other members of the Committee in trying to bring men, women, and children out to a point of starvation If it had not been for the priests and ministers in church and wirepullers going round to weak men in the pit, the ballot would have been as good on that day as it was when they decided to stop the wheels " Now, there is the explanation according to Nolan of why they failed in the September of the previous year, and there is a statement of why they took the course they did—a deliberate statement He says "We could not get the men to come out in the previous year by ballot, so we brought them out without a ballot,' and the reason why they did not vote by a sufficient majority in the previous year was that they were weak men who were influenced by the priests and ministers

Lord JAMES of HEREFORD Why do you say there was not a ballot? There was a vote, at any rate, taken—that vote of 1,400 and odd

Mr ELDON BANKES In September?

Lord JAMES of HEREFORD No, when they did come out on June 29th

Mr ELDON BANKES No, there was no ballot

Lord JAMES of HEREFORD There was a vote

Mr ELDON BANKES No, there was no vote or ballot at all On June 29th they had a meeting on the Sunday morning, and they had a show of hands

Lord JAMES of HEREFORD Ah, that was a vote

Mr ELDON BANKES Yes, by show of hands, but no ballot

Lord JAMES of HEREFORD I correct myself, it was a vote that was taken What were the numbers they sent up to the Central Office, 1,400 odd?

Mr ELDON BANKES No, there were no numbers recorded of that meeting

Lord JAMES of HEREFORD But at a subsequent meeting they recorded the numbers

Mr ELDON BANKES Yes, your Lordship is thinking of the ballot that was taken as to whether or not they should give in their notices

Lord JAMES of HEREFORD   Fresh notices, yes, that was the substantial matter

Mr ELDON BANKES   Then, my Lord, there is a passage at the end of Hirst's speech on page 432   He says at D   "He hoped the men would use their own judgment after taken in consideration the case, and that they had played for nearly the 20th week   Was it sense that a sensible body of men should hold a meeting on a Sunday morning and pass a resolution to stop the pits down and stand three weeks without any pay, and then believe the statement that Mr Pope was making that they had no grievances?   They had big grievances, and burning grievances, and until such time as Mr Chambers and Mr Pope would agree to meet them amicably, they were prepared to say they had great grievances   If any man thought fit to put his signature to go to work, let him do so, but it would be 'God help him'"   Now, of course, the object of that language and the object of the resolution, that the ballot papers should be taken into the branch, was to make it plain that no man was to sign those notices, and although I am told a few did sign them, we have not got the evidence about that

Then, my Lord, I think I can pass on to the 17th, and on that 17th a fire broke out in the colliery   That fire, of course, was a matter of most serious moment, and unless it was checked it might result in the entire destruction of these collieries   Every endeavour was made to get men to come to do the necessary work, to isolate the fire or to put it out, and the attempt succeeded to a certain extent, men came and worked   Again an occasion arose therefore which, according to the view of the branch officials, called for their interference, and they took active and deliberate steps to get the men out who had responded to the call for help in connection with the fire   I will call your Lordship's attention to what happened, but first of all I must call attention to the meeting which was attended by Mr Parrott and Mr Walsh, who were sent down in pursuance of a resolution of the Executive Committee, and that resolution is on page 238   Your Lordship will remember the application for an official to come down, that application came before the Executive Committee on the 17th November, page 238, and the resolution is   "That Messrs Parrott and J Walsh attend the meeting at Mexborough on Monday, November 24th, 1902"   Walsh was the same man who had gone down before, and Mr Parrott was the agent of the Defendant Association

Now at page 371 your Lordship will find a further letter which I think I ought to have read first, it is dated November 13th, and I am afraid I am a little out of date, but Hirst, the secretary of the Denaby and Cadeby branches, or writing for the Denaby and Cadeby branches, writes to Mr Pickard   "Dear Sir   We have arranged for a mass meeting to be held in the Mexbro' Market Hall on Monday night, November 24th, on the Denaby and Cadeby case, and I am instructed to write and ask if two officials will be able to come down to that meeting I may say that we should very much like you to come , failing you, either Mr Cowey, Mr Walsh, or Mr Wadsworth Hoping to have an early reply and oblige " The answer is on the next page, a wire at the bottom of page 372, dated November 22nd " Parrott and Walsh will attend your meeting, Monday morning, 11 o'clock "

Those two gentlemen, Parrott and Walsh, came down, and the report of the meeting is at page 434 Walsh was not called, but Mr Parrott was called, and we had an opportunity of cross-examining him about the language used there and about his attitude Although, as your Lordship will see, he used the strongest possible language, and the strongest possible language was used about Mr Pope's circular, he had to admit that he had not even taken the trouble to ask for a copy of it or to read it or to ask what was in it, and it is quite plain that these two men came down to encourage the men in the attitude which they had been told to take up to resist any advances on Mr. Pope's part at all cost The meeting is on the 24th November, and Mr Parrott makes a long speech, but I do not think there is anything material to read until you get to the bottom of page 435 He talks about the Boers and between E and F he says " Lord Kitchener could do so , then owners were taking a very unmanly stand, and one which would not hold good to the intelligent public of the country They were doing even worse things They were giving them notice to quit the Company's houses They knew that wintery weather had already set in, and they would have very severe weather to contend with between now and spring He considered that that was a very unmanly step to take The women and children, who had done nothing amiss to Mr Buckingham Pope, but because they had refused to work on certain conditions the management were revenging themselves on innocent people connected with their families It was a shameful thing to do They had partly done it, and he understood from what he read that they were getting ejectment summonses to ' chuck ' them out if they would not go without being thrown out They would submit a resolution to them, and he hoped that they would fairly consider that resolution To turn them out of their houses if he required them would be a different thing, but then it would be nothing like what was expected in a Christian age, but to turn people out of their houses and let them remain empty was a most devilish thing in his opinion The Coal Owners' Association were supporting their owners in that stoppage " Now, really this is language which is likely to inflame people's minds, but those gentlemen had no right to say that they had no right to say that there was an intention to turn people out of the houses and keep them empty There was an honest intention of substituting these workmen by other workmen who should come and occupy the houses Then he said " They had not only to fight Mr Buckingham Pope and management, but the whole of the Coal Owners' Association as well Whether they had agreed to Mr Pope turning them out of then houses he did not know He would not go so far as to say that the coalowners had done it The notices had come in the name of Mr Pope, and he was the person whom they could lay the blame upon for taking that dirty action at a time of the year like the present" Then, my Lord, on page 437, between B and D, he says ' He was not there to stroke men down their backs if they ought to be told their duty, and he wanted to say that while he blamed, and severely so, and condemned the action of their masters and managers, he thought that the workmen themselves sometimes got a little wrong He was an official of nearly 30 years standing, it was 30 years since he became a checkweighman, and he had been connected with that class of work 26 years They should always obey the advice of their officials, and never take it into their own heads that they knew how to settle disputes better themselves than those who had been in the work 20 or 30 years or more Men had been taken before the Doncaster magistrates"—and so forth, I do not think there is anything else I need read

Then on page 438 D—it is still Mr Parrott—he says "They wanted to be working and earning good wages to be able to save a trifle for the rainy and stormy days (A Miner 'There's nothing to put the percentage on ') I have come down to see if there is a decision on the part of the men to arrange something to get the pit wheels working again He did not see any prospect unless they came to some understanding about meeting the officials of the colliery or someone else they might appoint to do the work for them He felt that he had done his duty, but he thought some authority ought to step in to prevent Mr Pope from driving them from the houses in which they now resided It was a most cruel thing of anything They had read of cruel things during the war in South Africa, and they had said it would not occur here, but things were being done which thoughtful men would never think would happen Being thrown about in the country, their wives and families weakly and wan, they were subject to catch colds, and colds brought on other diseases, and he was afraid that during winter, if there was not something done by way of getting them properly housed and made comfortable, they would have cause to mourn on account of the loss of some dear little one or wife if that kind of cruelty was persisted in He hoped Mr Pope would withhold his hand from ejecting them, and he hoped, if he did not, he would receive the condemnation of the whole universe He hoped they would take his words thoughtfully, and, when the resolution was submitted to them, they would think it over He was trying to make himself plain He believed there was a way out of the difficulty, but to do that they would have to show that they were willing either to resume work on the understanding that things were to be remedied, or they would have to do something on their part to show that they had a disposition to be reasonable and show proper treatment to the workmen who made them their fortunes."

Then Walsh speaks "He was proud to see the ruddy faces about the platform at the end of 20 weeks of the struggle."

The LORD CHANCELLOR The pith of it is that he wanted to continue the strike

Mr ELDON BANKES Yes, of course my Lord if I may put it in that way, that is all I want to say about it If I might turn to page 442 now, because this is in a different point——

The LORD CHANCELLOR I mean of course unless they could come to terms

Mr ELDON BANKES Yes Walsh uses stronger language on the general questions, but he uses language here which is very important from one point of view in our case

Lord JAMES of HEREFORD Who was Mr Parrott?

Mr ELDON BANKES Mr Parrott was the agent, he was one of the paid officials

Lord JAMES of HEREFORD Of the central body

Mr ELDON BANKES Yes Then at page 442, letter C "If the men did not feel satisfied they wanted to get to work let the manager meet them, and he had no doubt they would resume work in a few days from now" (He knew quite well they would) "It was their duty now to stand by the strike Committee The Committee were men highly respected at head quarters, and it was the least they could do to support them He hoped that if Mr Chambers would let them meet him they would have an opportunity of discussing the matter in every way in order that the district might resume its calm state once more, and that then every one of them would have cause to thank the men who had had the courage to lead them on in the struggle, and they would be glad they had not taken the advice of the men writing in the public press to vilify their Committee Such men were their enemies"

Then Nolan says "They had been out 20 weeks and had tried to carry the strike on in the best way they could, and seeing that some seemed to be dissatisfied with what was going on they thought it best to have an official down to support or renounce the strike" Now I rely upon that language very strongly to show the exact relative position between these men, the branch officials were left and allowed to conduct it, but if they felt a difficulty or felt the men were breaking away they sent for somebody to come and assist them from the central office I do not think I need read more of that meeting

Then, my Lord, we find that on the 1st December at page
239, the Council passed this resolution "Denaby Main (1) That
this Council Meeting hereby again confirms Resolution 8 of Special
Council Meeting, held July 24th, 1902, viz, in reference to paying
the Denaby and Cadeby Main men their lock-out pay" Your Lordship will see they call it the lock-out pay I am getting now, I am
glad to say, towards the end of the history, but there is a meeting
on the 4th December which is important I was going to read from
page 449, but it begins at page 446

Lord JAMES of HEREFORD Has not some trouble been
taken in framing this Appendix to make the documents as confused
as possible?

Mr ELDON BANKES No, my Lord, if your Lordship
realises that they are in groups, there are the speeches together, the
correspondence together, and the Minutes together

Lord JAMES of HEREFORD It does not make it less
confused

Mr ELDON BANKES The speeches are all together, and
this speech begins at page 446, my Lord

The LORD CHANCELLOR Is it not very much the same
thing?

Mr ELDON BANKES The same thing, except that at page
449, between D and E Nolan speaks and says this—at C I had better
begin "They had a lot of men saying officials ought to come down
When they had gone away, it was the old tale over and over again
They had suggested that someone should be sent down Mr Parrott
had come down and given a nice little speech, and Harry Howden
had been able to find a thread and get up his nice little case in
London If Mr Parrott had not come down, and he did not respect
him for the attitude he had taken in regard to the men, if Mr
Parrott had only had the rule, he would have advised them to go
back to work on the same lines on which they came out If wrong
was done, then officials ought to have come down on the first outset
and told them they were wrong" Now that is exactly our position,
and the men realised it as clearly as, I submit, the Jury did The
branch officials were saying "What is the good of the men
quarrelling with our action and saying 'the officials ought to have
come down, it is not our fault, it is the officials' fault' If they
thought we were wrong from the outset why did they not come
down at the outset and tell us so?"

On December 17th there is another meeting, and then Nolan
again speaks, the speech begins at page 454 and if your Lordship
will turn to page 458, the passage I wish to read is there Your

Lordship will remember that the fire was at this time in progress and Nolan makes this speech at page 458 "With regard to men working, they had deputies at Denaby and managers at Denaby going round and telling the men that they had the full consent of the Association for men to go to work, and that a young man who went to work could go back on the funds He would deny that No authority had been given He would see the blazes out of the top of the shaft before any men should go to work"

The LORD CHANCELLOR Read the next sentence

Mr ELDON BANKES "If the management had written them asking them to allow a few men to go, they would have done so Barnard was going about the pit saying he had seen him and others It was a lie The men who were working were black sheep They had given them no authority He would say nothing more about it, but would leave it in the hands of the women" I am obliged for your Lordship's suggestion, I ought to read the passage as a whole What he says is, "If you will come and ask us for a few men we will let you have a few men, but if you do not ask for a few men the men who go are black sheep and we will let the Colliery be utterly consumed before we will allow men to go back, and we will leave them in the hands of the women," which means that no men shall be allowed to go back and the intimidation shall be resumed and made as effective as it was when men had desired to go back before

Now my Lord, I think I ought to call attention just to the evidence of Turner, the police constable, as to what happened at the time of the fire, on page 755, it is Question 2082 'About the fire that happened afterwards in November?—December, was it not Q The end of November?—Yes Q Do you recollect the fire occurring?—Yes, I do Q And you know that the Company employed men with a view to putting it out?—Yes Q Did you see what occurred when men went to the colliery when there was a fire?—Yes Q Tell us shortly what occurred Did they go and return peaceably or not?—For the first day or two there would be just a few on the road The first day when the fire broke out there was a few men watching it on the road, then the crowd seemed to increase day by day, and they were shouted and hooted at, called 'blacklegs,' and that kind of thing, and one man, Stonehouse, when he was returning from Denaby Pit, was rushed at (Mr Rufus Isaacs) I am not quite sure whether this comes within the particulars" Then we say we have a particular, and at Question 2090 "Were the men able to go and do their work, or were they interfered with?—They were interfered with on their return from work Q Did you hear what they were called by the crowd?—Yes They were called 'blacklegs' and 'baa' (Mr Montague Lush) In the particulars, page 32 of your Lordship's copy, it is stated that one man was assaulted (To the Witness) Were women there among the crowd?—Yes About how many were there in the crowd on those two or three days?—I should think there would be 1,000 to 1,500 Q Did you hear what they said to those men besides calling them blacklegs—what sort of things?—I forget now what was said to the men (Mr Justice Lawrance) Were these men who had been taken on, or men who were still in the pit? (Mr Montague Lush) No, the men who were taken on with a view to putting out the fire, as I understand (Mr Justice Lawrance) There were some fresh men taken on when there was a fire?—There were some of the old hands taken on" And that is all, it is an indication of what took place

Now I think I may pass on fairly rapidly, my Lord, because at this time Howden had issued his writ and the Judgment was proceeding, in the Court below the case was tried and Judgment was given on the 16th January Of course the Union recognised that when the injunction was granted the strike was practically at an end They passed on the 2nd February a resolution which I think is very significant, it is at page 241 "That the question as to whether the Denaby Main men should resume work be and is hereby relegated to the branches and a registered vote be taken thereon and that the vote be sent in by first post on Monday morning, February 9th, 1903" Now I do not understand that to mean these two particular branches, I think it means the branches generally, and it is an indication——

The LORD CHANCELLOR Is that so?

Mr ELDON BANKES I think it is the branches generally, I think it is one of those votes which is referred to in the rules, as your Lordship will remember, there are certain things to be decided by the branches, that is to say, it is a matter which the Council even have not the right to deal with, but which has to be dealt with by the branches generally And it is only an indication of the position of this Council, they were not themselves supreme in any sense as to whether or not this strike should go on or whether it should cease, and the suggestion which has been made by the Judgment, particularly of Lord Justice Mathew, that each branch was a separate Union in itself, is, I think, completely met by such a resolution as this We are agreed about that, your Lordship has the rule, and it is Rule 12

I do not think there is anything else I need call attention to The men began to come back very shortly after the Injunction was granted in Howden's case Apparently, during the continuance of the strike the Union men got not only the strike pay but they got, what they called, "nipsey money," which was the result of the collections that were made up and down the country Your Lordship will remember I called attention to one passage in the evidence, that there was no intimidation or molestation on the Saturday, because the men were away collecting, and apparently this "nipsey money" lasted for some little time beyond the date of the Injunction in

I

Howden's case, and the strike flickered on for a little time after the Injunction, but ultimately the men came back, and they came back on precisely the same terms as they went out on, and they have worked since perfectly contentedly upon precisely the same terms

That is the whole history of this lamentable strike

Lord DAVEY What date do you give to the cessation of the strike?

Mr ELDON BANKES My Lord, it is difficult to say

Lord DAVEY Approximately

Mr ELDON BANKES I think it went on into March, but it is difficult to say the exact date Men were coming back, but certainly no strike pay was paid after the date I have given to your Lordship The men did not all come back until the middle of March, certainly

Lord DAVEY Did even Croft and Nolan come back?

Mr ELDON BANKS I am not sure whether all the men were allowed to come back, and I do not know whether these two men did Certainly they were not all allowed to come back, some exceptions were made, but they practically all came back

I think the next best thing I can do, if your Lordships will allow me, is to read the Judgments of the Court of Appeal, because your Lordship is now in possession of the history, and I would like to read the Judgments before I summarise the matter and put my propositions to your Lordship The Judgments begin at page 1025, and the Master of the Rolls says "This is an Appeal by the Defendants against a Judgment entered against them by Mr Justice Lawrance, in a case tried before him and a Special Jury The Plaintiffs are the owners of the Denaby and Cadeby Main Collieries The Defendants are a Trades Union, its trustees and principal officials, and the officials and the Cadeby and Denaby branches thereof The Action was brought to recover damages for a conspiracy by the Defendants other than the trustees, to injure the Plaintiffs by bringing about a strike amongst their workmen involving breaches of their contracts of service with the Plaintiffs, and, as a distinct cause of Action, for conspiring to maintain the strike by unlawful means, embracing intimidation, molestation and the illegal payment of strike money The trial occupied many days, and, the Jury having answered in favour of the Plaintiffs a number of questions carefully framed to cover all the points involved, the learned Judge gave Judgment for the Plaintiffs for damages to be assessed as agreed between the parties The Defendants other than the two branch officials, who did not appear, now apply for Judgment, or a new trial, on the ground that there was no evidence to go to the

Jury, that the verdict was against the weight of evidence, and that the learned Judge misdirected the Jury. The collieries in which the strike took place form two out of a large number of branches which together make up the Association, and the first group of questions put by the learned Judge relates to the procuring or bringing about the strike as distinct from the maintaining it after it had been begun, to which latter point another series of questions was addressed. Very different considerations applied to these two groups. First, as to the initiation of the strike. It was not disputed by the Defendants that this was illegal. The men were under contracts requiring 14 days' notice to determine them, and they left their work without notice. The strike was also resolved upon in flagrant disregard of the rules of the branches which provide for the method and conditions by which such resolutions are to be taken. It was hardly, if at all, disputed before us that the strike so procured was the work of the officials of the branches, and the evidence that such was the case was in fact overwhelming. It may be necessary to refer to this in somewhat greater detail later on in reference to another aspect of the case. The responsibility of the branch officials was only material, however, from the Plaintiffs' point of view as establishing or tending to establish the responsibility of the Union itself whose liability alone was of any pecuniary importance. It was accordingly strenuously pressed upon us by the Plaintiffs' Counsel that the officials of the branch were really by the constitution of their Association the agents of the Union itself, to whom the duty of organising and superintending strikes was delegated, and that, therefore, the Union was responsible for their Acts. In my opinion the rules do not admit of this contention." Now there with great submission we entirely join issue with the Master of the Rolls, our submission is that that is not a correct view of the rules.

Lord JAMES of HEREFORD. Would you just kindly read the passage again—only the last three lines?

Mr ELDON BANKES. "It was accordingly strenuously pressed upon us by the Plaintiffs' Council that the officials of the branch were really by the Constitution of the Association the agents of the Union itself, to whom the duty of organising and superintending strikes was delegated, and that, therefore, the Union was responsible for their acts. In my opinion the rules do not admit of this contention. Their effect seems to be to leave to the branches the right to determine for themselves whether they will strike or not, though the Union, if it sanctions the strike, is empowered to grant strike pay to the strikers. If the rules do not make the Union responsible for the acts of the branch officials, I agree with my colleagues that they did not become liable by ratification. I think there was no evidence of 'purporting' on the part of the branch officials to act for the Union." (Now there we join issue again with the Master of the Rolls if it is necessary in a matter of law to prove 'purporting' in the sense in which he uses the word) "and I am not prepared to say, since the decision of Durant *v* Roberts in the House of Lords, that 'purporting' is not a necessary condition of possible ratification even in the case of a tort, nor am I satisfied that ratification was legally *intra vires* of the Association, and therefore possible See Poulton *v* The London and South-Western Railway, Law Reports 2, Queen's Bench, page 534 The case upon the rules is more fully dealt with by my learned brothers with whom on this part of the case I agree It follows, therefore, that on that part of the case which rests on the responsibility for the initiation of the strike the Plaintiffs fail as against the Association and its officers Here, I regret to say, I part company from my brethren and have the misfortune to differ from them as to the second part of the case I am of opinion as to the issues raising the question of the responsibility of the Union for the maintenance as distinguished from the initiation of the strike that there was evidence fit for the consideration of the Jury of concerted action between them and the officials of the branch to maintain the strike by illegal means It is not my province to decide anything more, unless it is made out, that there was misdirection which may have affected the verdict Of this, on this part of the case, I can find no trace On this second branch of the case it becomes necessary to examine the evidence in somewhat greater detail The fact that the strike had begun at both collieries was communicated by wire to Mr Pickard, the General Secretary, by the respective secretaries of the two branches on the 30th June, and by a minute of the Executive Council of the Union of that date it appears that the President, Mr Cowey, was instructed to wire the secretaries of the Denaby and Cadeby Main Branches stating 'That in the opinion of this Executive they ought to have a meeting and agree to resume work at once as they are out contrary to the rules and regulations of the Association' So far, no exception could be taken to the attitude of the Association, and this resolution would *prima facie* indicate a desire on their part that the strike should be ended by the men resuming work If this was their original view, the evidence seems to me conclusive that it was changed shortly afterwards It was clear to all parties that the strike could not go on unless the Association could see its way to grant strike pay, and to put an end to the strike the Association had nothing to do but to withhold it There were also legal difficulties in their way which, unless surmounted, debarred them, as they quite understood, from granting strike pay in respect of a strike illegally begun as this was On the 11th of July, 1902, application for strike pay was made by the two branches to Mr Pickard, with a request that their demand should be laid before the Council at the meeting to be held on the 14th At the meeting of that date a resolution was passed 'That Messrs Wadsworth and Walsh accompany Messrs Nolan and Humphries to a meeting to be held to-morrow morning at 11 o'clock, and tell the men they must resume work, and then take a ballot of Denaby and Cadeby Main Collieries, the first day they work, as to whether or not they will give in their notices to terminate their contract of service to get their grievances settled' The terms of this resolution passed as it was in answer to an application for strike pay, are sufficient to show that the Association were desirous of making the strike effectual by granting strike pay, and were pointing out to the branches the steps to be taken in order to enable them to do so But if these were not evident from the fact and terms of the resolution itself, it is quite clear from the statements of speakers at a meeting of the branches held on the 15th of July, which was addressed by Wadsworth and Walsh, who attended as a deputation from headquarters The Chairman, Croft, of the Denaby branch, said 'There was scarcely a delegate at Council who did not sympathise with the Denaby and Cadeby men' 'He was proud to learn that Mr Ben Pickard would only be too pleased if he could allow them strike pay' Walsh said 'They saw by the unanimous vote of yesterday of the delegates they would like to vote for money to help them to fight the battle, but dare not Their fear was they would have Mr Pope (the Plaintiffs' managing director) getting money out of the same fund What you must try and do is to take a ballot of yourselves within the rules, give in your notice and come out, and let us all be behind you in the county and fight to the finish' Wadsworth spoke to the same effect 'They should ballot the whole of the men, whether they are disposed to give in a 14 days' notice to determine their contracts—they would then be within the rules of their Association They would have officials, the whole of their delegates and collieries in the county to help and assist them in fighting this battle The resolution was then passed 'To resume work at the earliest convenience, and that the men be ballotted as to whether they are prepared to give 14 days' notice to terminate their contract of service' And Walsh added, 'that the men had their salvation in their own hands, and it would hurt him to the core if they did not take the ballot unanimously and come out and fight, they would disgrace the county' H Hirst the secretary of the Cadeby Branch, followed and said 'They had brought the men out to prove to the district that they had grievances, and that they intended, if they could get strike pay, to get their grievances remedied before they took the men back to work Every delegate went so far as to say that in his opinion they ought to have strike pay If they only had strike pay they would get what they were entitled to These speeches, coupled with the resolution, seem to me to furnish very cogent evidence—it is not necessary to say more—that matters had thus far developed that the Association now intended that the men should resume work, not with a view of ending the strike but with a view of legalising their position so as to enable them to strike effectually with the resources of the Union behind them It will be seen from what follows that the position never was legalised, but that nevertheless the resources of the Union were thrown into the scale, and life blood supplied to the strike in the shape of strike pay furnished week by week from the funds of the Association I think there is cogent evidence that from and after the stage which I have now reached the Association itself directly intervened in guiding the course of the strikers in such fashion as to give such a colourable semblance of legality to their proceedings as should make it possible for them the Association, to assist the movement by the granting of strike pay. It may be that their hand was forced by the active spirits of the branches, but certain it is that they immediately found themselves confronted with a situation which was not quite what they had contemplated, and probably forced Mr Pickard to take the movement into his own hands. Instead of resuming work as suggested by the resolutions I have set out, the strikers attended with notices in their hands which they presented before signing on, and in point of fact refused to sign on, on the ground, as they alleged, that new terms had been introduced into the contract contained in the book which, in the ordinary course they would have had to sign on returning to work after an interval. Thus the condition precedent originally insisted upon by the Association that they should resume work before giving notice was not performed. It had not occurred apparently to Mr Pickard or any one else up to that time that having been on strike for a fortnight they were, nevertheless, in a position to give valid notices without resuming work. Mr Pickard was at once informed what had happened. Then followed a correspondence by letter and wire between him and the branches and the manager of the Collieries which is strongly relied upon by the Plaintiffs as evidence of malice. That is to say, of persistence in an illegal course with full notice of facts which must have been brought home to the minds of the Executive a sense of the illegality had they not allowed their judgment to be disturbed by their desire to attain the end in view, namely, to maintain the strike. The position assumed originally viz., that the men on strike were out of employment and must get back into it before they could legally give notice was not at first abandoned when the new emergency of the men not having signed on arose, but objection was taken that a new condition was sought to be imposed. When this suggestion was proved to be unfounded, Mr Pickard does not withdraw his direction given to the men on the 17th July, 1902 'Do not sign any new rule' and, writing in the name of the Council on the 21st July, 1902, he says 'We cannot recommend you to sign on again. Why should such advice be given unless for some reason it was thought undesirable then that the men should be allowed to go back into employment at all? It was suggested by the Plaintiffs that the risk which the letter of the next day from the Secretary of the Denaby Branch shows to have been a real one was present to the minds of the Council, who gave the advice conveyed in Mr Pickard's letter. Asking for a week's strike pay, the Secretary of the Denaby Branch says on the 22nd July, 1902 'Seeing that our men have not had a pay day for a month they are getting uneasy and will doubtless break away and sign the contract book.' If this was regarded as a danger to be averted if possible it suggests a clue to the shifting of positions on Mr Pickard's part in finding justification for the timely intervention of the Association. Driven from the positions which he had hitherto relied upon as justifying his attitude, Mr Pickard finally falls back upon a third which is that upon which, apparently, he sought to justify the right of the Association 'to grant strike pay within the rules' The third position thus taken was that the men on strike had never left the employ, that the manager, therefore, had no right to insist upon their signing on even upon the old terms, and, therefore, that the case was not one of strike by the men, but of lock-out by the employers This contention was advanced and adopted by the Council as their ultimate justification, although it was proved that it was the invariable rule of the colliery that every workman who had been absent more than two or three days must sign on on returning to work, and Mr Parrott, a leading member of the Council, who played a prominent part in this controversy, had to admit that he knew that such was the case" (I did not call your Lordship's attention to that evidence, but the Master of the Rolls is quite right) "The course ultimately recommended after full consideration with the two branches appears in Mr Pickard's letter 'not for publication' of the 21st July, 1902, and as appears by a minute of a special Council Meeting of the 24th July, 1902, the following resolutions were passed on that day "That the financial members at Denaby and Cadeby Main Collieries be paid strike pay from the first day when they presented themselves for work, and Mr Chambers would not allow them to resume work unless they signed a new contract' 'That this Council Meeting recommend every branch to do what they can in a voluntary manner to help the Denaby and Cadeby men during the time they were out illegally' It would seem from a statement in one of the letters that the Council, before passing these resolutions, had consulted a solicitor, but the Defendants gave no evidence of what facts were laid before him, or what evidence was given I desire to speak with all respect for the memory of the late Mr Pickard, but he was placed in a difficult position He was acting with and for other persons who were very desirous of finding means of supporting the strikers—witness the passages from the speeches which I have referred to—and it was no doubt difficult to maintain a judicial attitude under the circumstances But after all, his conduct does not stand outside criticism The standard of illegality was inflexible, and could not be made to accommodate itself, as the occasion required to two opposite courses of conduct And it is for the Jury, and not for the Court to Judge whether the opinion adopted by the Executive as to the legality of granting strike pay was influenced by considerations other than legal Pausing for a moment at this stage, it is quite clear that the course thus adopted by the Association was illegal It has been so held by the House of Lords As pointed out in Lord Macnaghten's speech, it was not merely *ultra vires* but (if that makes any difference) positively prohibited He says 'Clause 3 Sub-section (J), declares that the whole of the moneys received by the Association shall be applied in carrying out the objects specified in the preceding sub-section in accordance with the rules In an earlier clause, Clause 1, there is an express direction that the funds of the Association shall not be appropriated to any other use' and at his instance the word 'illegal' was added to 'ultra vires' in the declaration The means actually used, therefore, to maintain this strike were certainly illegal, and if any other element is required to fill up what is covered by 'maliciously' in the wrong charged, it seems to me impossible to say there was no evidence of malice to go to the Jury, evidence founding the inference that a colourable pretext rather than an assured opinion was sought and acted upon the Defendants, and that in their eagerness to accomplish the object they had in view, they had allowed their judgment to be warped and patent facts to be ignored in coming to their resolution But even if I am wrong in this view, there are other considerations which in my judgment could not have been withdrawn from the Jury The payment of strike pay week by week necessarily kept the Association in continuous touch with the strike which was going on within some 12 miles of Barnsley, and there is evidence of constant communication between the branches and the central authority, and in critical emergencies, i e, when the zeal of the strikers was felt to be flagging, the aid of the central body was sought, and leading members of the Council were sent down to encourage and advise, and speeches were delivered by them and in their presence, which I think could not be withheld from the Jury, speeches which contained no word of rebuke for illegalities already committed, and which must have been known to the speakers, but which did contain allusions to 'rats' and 'blacklegs' which might well be construed as incitements to intimidation There was clear evidence that not only was this strike illegal in its inception, as already pointed out, to the knowledge of the Defendants, but that it was carried on by illegal means Intimidation by large bodies gathered to intercept and beset those workmen who had gone to work and were returning or who wanted to go to work, violent language and threats, and in some instances actual physical violence I do not propose to follow out these facts in detail As pointed out by the Plaintiffs when demonstrations of this kind were needed they were forthcoming, when their purpose had been served and would-be workmen had been deterred from returning intervals of calm ensued, and were not disturbed until some fresh emergency arose It cannot, I think, be disputed that the officials of the two branches were prominent in encouraging the illegalities I have referred to, and as I have already pointed out there is evidence of a common purpose shared by the officials of the central authority and of the branches to assist in maintaining the strike Was it possible, then, for the former, while furnishing from week to week the most powerful support in the shape of strike pay, to wash their hands of responsibility for the methods adopted by their confederates in carrying out the common purpose?"

The LORD CHANCELLOR Will you not now but before you finish, consider whether if you give strike pay that involves of necessity for all the methods adopted in keeping up the strike

Mr ELDON BANKES I should not contend that *per se*

The LORD CHANCELLOR I gathered that to be what the Master of the Rolls says

Mr ELDON BANKES I think not He says "Was it possible then for the former, while furnishing from week to week the most powerful support in the shape of strike pay, to wash their hands of all responsibility for the methods adopted by their confederates in carrying out the common purpose?" but, of course, that must be read in connection with the statement read before, when he pointed out that there was evidence of common purpose shared by the officials of the Central Authority and the branches to assist in maintaining the strike I think he means the two passages to be read together

The LORD CHANCELLOR It may be so

Mr ELDON BANKES "The inferences to be drawn from the proved facts appear to me to be essentially for the Jury and not for the Court, and that to withdraw them from their cognisance would be to usurp their functions There are three distinct elements of illegality in the maintenance of this strike, two of them affecting the means actually used, the third affecting the immediate object aimed at They are (1) Aiding the strike by misapplying to its maintenance funds which the law expressly forbade to be so applied"

Lord DAVEY The law there means the contract between the parties

Mr ELDON BANKES Yes, I think it must, my Lord

Lord DAVEY Nothing more than that?

Mr ELDON BANKES I think it must Of course it has been put against us that it is something more than that, because when they, a registered Society and "*ultra vires*" and so forth, they seek to put us exactly in the same position of an incorporated company However, I think that must be meant Then "(2) Intimidation in different forms (3) Inducing the men to break existing contracts, an illegal act in itself and not mitigated by the fact that the means used to bring it about were themselves illegal I have dealt with the first and second heads I will add a few words as to the third Passing over the cases of those men who did not join the strikers in the first instance, but who were forced to come out afterwards of whom there were several, but who may have come out before the date at which it may be inferred that the co-operation of the Association in the common movement began, I will confine myself to the case of those who had signed on after the meeting of July 15th, when the majority refused to do so   There can be no doubt that these men were induced to break their contracts and come out at a time when there was evidence that the co-operation between the Association and the branches in a common purpose had begun   How is it possible to say that the Association who were finding funds for the carrying out of such a purpose, that is of inducing or compelling those who had returned to their employment to break their contracts and come out—how is it possible to say that they are entitled to have Judgment entered for them as a matter of law?   The fact that a certain number of men had resumed work was a most critical element in the strike, and might in all probability have defeated it had they been permitted to remain in, and yet it was just at such a moment that assistance came from the Association   Who is to draw the inference from these facts—the Jury or the Court?   I am of opinion that Mr Justice Lawrance was abundantly justified in leaving the case to the Jury and that it is quite impossible for us to enter judgment for the Defendants   It still remains, however, to be considered whether there was any misdirection which obliges us to interfere to the extent of ordering a new trial   Misdirection, or want of direction, if any, upon the questions relating to the initiation of the strike is not material, since we are all of opinion that, as against the Association, this cause of action is not made out   With regard to the questions relating to that part of the case as to which I hold that there was evidence to go to the Jury I think they were quite separate from those addressed to the other part, and that there is nothing to complain of in the Judge's direction, or in the questions put   In my opinion, therefore the Plaintiffs are entitled to retain their verdict in respect of the causes of action dealt with in question 6, and those that follow it, and against all the surviving Defendants   As, however, my brothers are of a contrary opinion, this appeal must be allowed with costs, and Judgment entered for the Defendants

Now, my Lord, Lord Justice Mathew's is the next Judgment, and he says   "This action was brought to recover damages from the Defendants for a conspiracy to procure a strike of the workmen at the Denaby and Cadeby Collieries   It was contended for the Plaintiffs in the first place, that an easy solution of the matters in dispute would be arrived at if the Defendants were regarded as an Association for carrying on a business   (Now with great submission to the learned Lord Justice it was not our case at all—however)   "The Defendants, it was said, carried on their so-called business in defence of workmen by means of strikes, and this operation in all cases was entrusted to the branches   When the workmen struck they acted on behalf of all their fellow members in the Association, who became responsible as if express authority had been given   But the ordinary firm, carrying on its business for profit is in no way analogous to a trade union   The true nature of the trade union, and the rights and obligations of its members   must be ascertained not from any superficial comparison with ordinary partnerships, but by an examination of the rules under which the Trade Union is constituted (Now that has always been our case) ' But it was argued for the Plaintiffs that even if this was so the rules show that the branches were agents of the Association This position seems to me as untenable as the former one The consideration of the Association under the rules seems to be this The units are the branches, of which there were about 150 Each of these was independent of the others, and was in itself a small Trade Union." Now with great submission the rules cannot bear on the construction, and it is because the learned Lord Justice assumes that to be the meaning of the rules that the rest of his Judgment is founded upon that assumption Then it goes on, " It had its officers and its rules" (well it is not correct to say that it had its rules except as part of the rules of the Association) "and the members of each branch were entitled to strike when their grievances seemed to them to justify that course The funds collected by each branch, after deducting the necessary expenses for carrying on its affairs, were remitted to the charge of the Council, a body consisting of delegates from each of the branches The Council were assisted by a secretary and other paid officials, whose ordinary duty was to assist in the settlement of any differences that arose between members of each branch " (Well, with great submission, that is not to be found in the rules I think) " when a strike was threatened or took place the officials of the Council were charged with the duty of endeavouring to bring employers and workmen together and settle their differences amicably " (not the officials certainly), " The principal duty of the Council was not to promote, but to endeavour to prevent strikes," (I think that may be) " The Council had power, out of the funds in their hands, to grant strike pay where it was considered that the workmen were justified in refusing to work until their complaint had been considered by the employers, and a reasonable arrangement had been come to The rules gave the Council no control whatever over the refusal of the workmen to continue in the service of the employers They had no power to prevent or to terminate a strike ' (With great submission, the learned Lord Justice is not correct there, they had two powers to prevent— they could have directed the branch officials to take no part and they could have refused to grant strike pay) " In that respect each branch was independent of the Council And, on the other hand, the branch could not procure for itself strike pay That was a matter with which the Council alone could deal This seems to me the result of the rules, so far as they are material The evidence showed a course of business in no respect inconsistent with their terms" (The learned Lord Justice would not look at the matter from the business point of view with regard to their constitution, but he introduces the question now) " But it was contended for the Plaintiffs that the agency of the branches if not disclosed in the rules was established by the evidence of what took place after the strike had begun, and it becomes necessary to state how and why the strike originated There had been for some time a dispute between the workmen and their employers with reference to the bag dirt in both collieries The coal which had to be won was covered in many parts of the mines by a deposit which was shallow and friable in some places, but in others thick and stubborn The men insisted that the price list for getting coal did not cover the labour for removing the bag dirt The employers asserted the contrary The question had been dealt with by the County Court twice, and by a joint committee of representatives of the employers and workmen on a third occasion, and the decision upon each case was against the latter Thereupon the men demanded an alteration in the price list in their favour The only result had been that the manager was willing, upon terms not assented to by the men, to have the bag dirt removed and to deduct the cost from the men's wages But the men complained that under any such arrangement the burden of the removal fell unequally, and when as much as 17s was deducted from the weekly wages for the cost of removing the bag dirt there were bitter complaints, and much anger with the manager This seems to have been the immediate cause of the strike On the 29th June, 1903, a bellman was sent round " (it ought to be the 28th) " to the two collieries to summon a meeting Some 300 or 400 miners attended, and the following resolution was passed ' That this meeting is of opinion that the time has now arrived when some steps should be taken with reference to the reduction of men's wages for bag dirt and fines '" (It is not " reduction "—it is " deduction " in the resolution)

Lord DAVEY It should be obviously

Mr ELDON BANKES " For different things at Denaby and Cadeby Collieries, and that having tried to come to some amicable understanding and failed, the only thing that is left for us to do is to stop the wheels at both collieries The secretaries of both branches at once informed Mr Pickard, and his reply was that the men were in the wrong for not having followed the rules, and ought to return to their work And he forthwith placed himself in communication with Mr Chambers, the manager of the mines, in the hope of settling the dispute But there were two difficulties in the way The Plaintiffs treated the strike as a repudiation of their contract by the men, and on this ground dismissed them, and refused to permit them to resume work under their former contracts " Well, it is not correct to say that they dismissed them, but it is obvious what the Lord Justice means " On the other hand, there was reason to believe that the men who had struck were resolved, if permitted to return, to give at once a formal notice terminating their contracts The men were told that they might go back if they signed fresh contracts, but no explanation satisfactory to them was given for this requirement and nothing was done " (with submission in face of the evidence that is not a position that can be maintained) " It is possible that the Plaintiffs considered that the workmen were not likely to receive strike pay because of their infraction of the rules, and that without such help they would be compelled to submit. Meanwhile it was not disputed that every exertion was being made on the part of the Council to induce the men and their employers to settle the dispute amicably. The Council obtained legal advice as to the position of the men. It was clear that they were liable in damage for throwing up their work without giving the notice required by their contracts. But the Council appears to have been advised that the men might set themselves right as regard their employers and the Association if they treated their contracts as still subsisting." (Now there is no evidence that any such advice was given as the Lord Chief Justice refers to. It is stated that a solicitor had been employed, but what advice he gave or what facts were laid before him the Master of the Rolls states was not in evidence, and I think he is right) "and tendered their services from the period for which notices ought to have been given. They were advised to take this course. Accordingly, formal application was made from day to day by the men to be permitted to return to work. The applications were refused unless the men signed fresh contracts, which the men had made up their minds they would not do" (well, they had only made up their minds not to do it because of the statements which had been made to them and of intimidation which, as I submit, had been exercised upon them). "After this ineffectual attempt to get back the men applied for strike pay. Their demand as between them and their fellow-members of the Association would seem not to be unreasonable having regard to the advice which had been given. They claimed to have brought their contracts to an end, as if the rules had been followed before the strike. The question for the Council was a difficult one, as it was not clear from the rules that a subsequent sanction of the strike by the Council would be sufficient, and the Council came to the conclusion on July 24th that the men were entitled to strike pay. The strike continued until the month of August, when the pits were closed by the Plaintiffs. I have stated what seems to me to be the result of the evidence relied upon for the Defendants, and if it was believed the charge of conspiracy to procure a strike would seem to have been answered. But the Plaintiffs' counsel insisted that it was altogether untrustworthy" (Your Lordship will see the Lord Justice was there treating it as a matter of evidence. He says ' In my view of the evidence a charge of conspiracy would have been answered." And then he says "The Plaintiffs' counsel insisted that this evidence was untrustworthy") "The true explanation of what happened was said to be this—it was one step in a campaign by the Association against the reduction of wages directed by the Award of Lord James of Hereford"

Lord JAMES of HEREFORD. It ought to be "Federation," ought it not?

Mr ELDON BANKES. Yes my Lord, Federation; but here again, if this is a correct statement of our position, which

I submit it was not, the Lord Justice is stating clearly that it was a question for the Jury "The alleged grievances of the men in the Plaintiffs' collieries were, it was said, a mere pretext The strike was not theirs, but was an act of the Association In support of this startling contention reliance was placed upon the fact that there were strikes about the same time in some 20 collieries out of the 150 which formed the Association, but the strikes in question were clearly shown to have nothing to do with any grievance of the men It appeared that the boys in those collieries were entitled under their contracts to a small advance in wages, and it was said by the employers that the deduction of 10 per cent under the Award deprived them of the small benefit There was much indignation in consequence, and the strikes of the boys were the result. In this state of things it was clear that there was no ground for the allegation that the strike in question was referable to Lord James Award The men acted loyally by the decision of Lord James The next point that was made in proof of the alleged conspiracy was the fact that the men sent by the Council on three occasions ostensibly to assist in bringing about a settlement were, in fact, instructed to encourage the men to continue the strike But I see no reasonable ground for this ' conclusion " (With great submission to the Lord Justice, if there was evidence, and it is impossible to contend that there was not evidence, it is not for the Lord Justice to decide) "The men directed by the Council to attend the meetings of the men at the collieries could not avoid hearing strong denunciations of the contemptuous treatment the men considered they had received from the Plaintiffs and their manager The unreasonable complaint was made by Counsel for the Plaintiffs that the representatives of the Council did not take sides with the employers and censure the men for striking Their doing so would not have helped to bring about a peaceful solution " (What we said was "It you disclaim the strike and are now saying you are not to be responsible for it, all we say is this ' If you really had disclaimed it you would have taken a very different course from the one you did take '") "The further contention of the Plaintiffs was that the Association, if they did not procure them, at any rate encouraged the strike It was said that they must have known that many of the men were unwilling to leave their work, but that they were coerced by their fellows It was said there was molestation and intimidation, of which the officials of the Council must have been aware It was admitted that up to July 14th there was only one case of personal violence A man named Berry was struck with a stone flung by someone in the crowd Up to that period there was no evidence of more than ordinary incidents of a strike which are easily exaggerated into evidence of more than was permissible " (Now there was clear evidence of molestation and actionable intimidation, although it did not amount to violence, which was not contradicted, there was no attempt made to contradict it) "The limits of lawful picketing are uncertain It was not shown that any considerable number of the men were unwilling to join in the strike in the early part of July. By the 14th July there were only some 60 men at work at the Cadeby and 12 at the Denaby Colliery. These were not employed in raising coal, but in keeping the airways and the waterways clear. At a later period when it was clear that the pits were about to be closed there was some disturbance." (With great submission, the disturbance was not when it was clear that the pits were about to be closed; the disturbance was when it was plain that the men were coming in in such increasing numbers that the pits were likely to be opened.) "But whatever complaints may be made of the unruly conduct of the workmen, there is no evidence that the Association authorised what the men were doing. The Council could exercise no control over the men, who were as obstinate as their employers. But the chief ground upon which the complicity of the Association in the original strike, and its consequence was sought to be established was what was described as the illegal allowance of strike pay. That the action of the Council as between them and the members of the Association was *ultra vires* has been settled by the decision of the House of Lords. It was illegal also, but only in the sense that a breach of trust, or a breach of contract, is forbidden by law. It could not be disputed that the right of the men to obtain assistance from the Council was a difficult question. There was reasonable ground for the contention that the Council had power, after the strike had taken place, to assist the men under Rule 64. Grave doubt upon the point was not wholly removed by the argument in the Court of Appeal in Howden's case. It was contended for the Plaintiffs that the grant of strike pay sanctioned the conduct of the men, and made the Association responsible from the 29th June. But there seems to be an answer on two grounds. As a matter of law the Association could not sanction an Act which was *ultra vires*. They could not ratify what they had no power to do." (Now, with great submission, that could have no reference to the granting of strike pay, because the granting of the strike pay was a direct act of the Association itself, and that does not require any ratification.) "In the second place what was done by the Council was not an admission that the original strike was undertaken on behalf of the Association, or a sanction of acts by those who were admitted to be agents." (Now that, in so far as it is a question of fact, is a question for the Jury.) "The resolution of the Council was that strike pay might be granted, although the branches had not acted on behalf of the Association. It was not contended that the Council had been guilty of bad faith, or of any intention to cause injury to the Plaintiffs. It was insisted for the Plaintiffs that it was immaterial whether the payment of strike pay was made in good faith. The argument of the Plaintiffs' counsel seemed to me to envolve the contention that the grant of strike pay, whether in accordance with the rules or not, was evidence of conspiracy to injure the employers. If there had been a conspiracy with any such object Mr. Pickard must have taken the principal part. But the learned counsel for the Plaintiffs paid a tribute to the integrity and ability of Mr. Pickard, and did not suggest that he had said or done anything during the long struggle with Plaintiffs which was in any way discreditable to his memory It seems to me that the grounds upon which the members of the Association were charged with a conspiracy to procure a strike wholly failed But an alternative view was put forward by the Plaintiffs' counsel It was said that if the case of a conspiracy on the 29th June failed the subsequent incidents when put together supplied evidence of another and a later conspiracy, starting from the 24th July, when strike pay was granted But at that date the contracts had been determined, and the position of the Plaintiffs was this They were entitled to damages from each workman for his breach of contract, they could replace the men discharged, and recover possession of the houses they occupied But they could not compel the men to continue to work for them In this state of things, it seems to me idle to talk of a conspiracy to deprive the Plaintiffs of the services of the workmen whom they had themselves discharged If it be sufficient evidence of a conspiracy to injure the employers that strike pay had been granted, it is difficult to see how Trade Unions could continue to exist This alternative view of the liability of the Association seems to me to fail Much comment was made upon the obstinacy of the men But it is well to bear in mind that the dispute about bag dirt had gone on for many years"—with submission to the learned Lord Justice, I do not think we commented on the obstinacy of the men—"and had, at times, become so angry that it was only by the constant efforts of the Council that a strike was prevented Why the efforts which were made after the strike were ineffective to bring about a settlement may, perhaps, be accounted for by the fact that the Plaintiffs were fighting the men in the interest of and on behalf of a Union of employers, the South Yorkshire Coalowners' Association It appeared from Mr Chambers' evidence the Plaintiffs were advised from the first by this Association of employers, and obtained from them a contribution towards the loss which followed upon the strike" (If that is material I do not think the Lord Justice has correctly reproduced the evidence) "No settlement could have been come to without the sanction of the Association Mr Chambers admitted that he had given as his reason for not meeting a deputation of the men that he was bound down by the Coalowners' Association In weighing the evidence and arguments for the Plaintiffs, it should not have been forgotten that it was of great importance to the Coalowners' Association with reference to these and future strikes, that the funds subscribed by the men for their defence in trade disputes should be lost or greatly diminished The questions put to the Jury were prepared by the Counsel for the Plaintiffs with great adroitness, and were adopted by the learned Judge I think Counsel for the Defendants, who insisted that there was no case for the Jury were right, and were not called upon to suggest any modification I do not think any useful purpose would be served by a minute examination of the questions or the answers of the Jury There was, in my judgment, no evidence upon which the Jury could reasonably have decided against the Defendants." I submit that you can take different passages from the learned Lord Justice's own Judgment in which he really treats some of these matters as questions of evidence and decides them in a particular way

Then Lord Justice Cozens-Hardy says "In this case the Plaintiffs, who are a Colliery Company, seek to recover damages occasioned by reason of a strike The Defendants are (1) The Yorkshire Miners' Association (hereinafter called the Union), (2) the Trustees of the Union, who are not charged with any personal misconduct, (3) Wadsworth, Parrott, and Hall, who are three of the officials and members of the Executive Committee of the Union, and (4) Nolan and Humphries, who are delegates of the Denaby and Cadeby Branches of the Union Nolan and Humphries have not appeared The Defendants are sought to be made liable on the ground of conspiracy Judgment has been entered against all the Defendants for damages to be assessed The Defendants have appealed and contend that Judgment should be entered for them, or, alternatively, that there should be a new trial Before dealing with the facts, it will be convenient to consider the nature of the constitution of the Union and the precise position of the branches The Union comprises about 63,000 members, divided into about 150 branches Its object include"—— It is not necessary to read that, and I might pass to between D and E on the next page "Now, under those circumstances, it is clear that it is competent to the Union to order or adopt a strike"

Lord DAVEY Is it clear that it is competent to the Union to order or adopt a strike?

Mr ELDON BANKES It is quite clear that it is competent to them to adopt a strike Whether it is in express terms competent to them to order a strike, I think, is open to criticism on the rules

Lord DAVEY It all turns on the construction of Rule 64 apparently, however, do not delay Mr Bankes

Mr ELDON BANKES "Such action would ordinarily be taken only where the interests of the members as a whole are considered to be affected But it is quite clear that it is contemplated that a branch, as distinct from the Union, may strike In that case great care is taken that the branch members shall have no claim for strike pay out of the Union funds, unless certain forms are complied with, and the sanction of the Council has been obtained A local strike" (now this is what I should rely upon) "will naturally be engineered by the local branch officials, but in my opinion the branch officials are not agents of the Union with authority to bind the Union by their acts in the matter of a local strike" (Now that of course is a matter, amongst others, for your Lordships' decision)

T

" Such agency must be founded on something outside the rules, and its existence must be proved by those who rely upon it " (I assume the Lord Justice means there it must be founded on something outside the rules, because you do not find it inside the rules He does not mean to say that if it is in the rules that will not be sufficient, and where we join issue with him is in the implication that it is not in the rules) "The evidence in this case is very voluminous, but I do not propose to discuss it in detail It will suffice to state the conclusions at which I have arrived (1) The strike of the Denaby and Cadeby colliers on the 29th June was procured and brought about by the Denaby and Cadeby branch officials, who induced the men to break their contracts of service by leaving work without giving 14 days' notice This is the finding of the Jury in answer to the first and third questions' (and he adopts that as right) "(2) The branch officials were not agents of the Union in bringing about the strike In so far as the answer of the Jury to the second and fourth questions assert the contrary, the rules do not justify the finding, and there is no evidence outside the rules of any such agency, in fact "

Now, of course, the learned Lord Justices' view is right if the rules did not justify the finding, because we did not suggest that there is any evidence of prior mandate for the procuring of the breaches of contract unless it is found in the rules

Lord DAVEY What you traverse in what he says is that the local officials are not the agents of the Association

Mr ELDON BANKES Yes "(3) The Union by its Council or Executive Committee or officials did not ratify the acts of the branch officials in procuring or bringing about the strike On the contrary they endeavoured to induce the men to resume work The minutes of the Council and Executive Committee of the Union and the letters written by Mr Pickard, the late secretary, are clear on this point, and I see no reason for the suggestion that they were artfully framed for the purpose of representing the exact contrary of the truth I am of opinion there is no evidence to support the finding of the Jury in answer to the fifth question " If I may pause there, my Lord, there is this criticism that I would like to make upon that passage

The LORD CHANCELLOR I think it is past the time for rising if you are to reason upon it, Mr Bankes Will you continue on Thursday morning?

(Adjourned to Thursday next at a quarter-past ten)

THIRD DAY.

Thursday, 15th March, 1906.

Mr ELDON BANKES If your Lordships please When the House adjourned, my Lord, I was in course of reading Lord Justice Cozens-Hardy's Judgment on page 1044 With your Lordship's permission I propose to finish that I think I had got as far as the letter C If your Lordship will allow me I will begin at what his Lordship numbers 3 just below the letter B He says " (3) The Union, by its Council or Executive Committee or officials, did not ratify the acts of the Branch officials in procuring or bringing about the strike On the contrary they endeavoured to induce men to resume work The minutes of the Council and Executive Committee of the Union, and the letters written by Mr Pickard, the late Secretary, are clear on this point, and I see no reason for the suggestion that they were artfully framed for the purpose of representing the exact contrary of the truth I am of opinion there is no evidence to support the finding of the Jury in answer to the fifth question I do not pause to consider whether ratification of the original tort was legally possible, the branch officials not having purported' to act as agents of the Union (4) The strike thus commenced was continued and maintained by the branch officials and the branch members by unlawful means, viz, by molestation and intimidation But there is no evidence that this molestation or intimidation was directed or sanctioned by any of the officials of the Union Great stress was laid on language used by some of the speakers at meetings of the men on strike It is impossible to deny that several of the local leaders indulged in inflammatory rhetoric which probably increased the intimidation and exasperated the quarrel On the other hand, the speeches of the officials sent down by the Union were temperate and free from objection " My Lord, I think when his Lordship made use of that expression he must have forgotten Walsh's speeches I will not refer to them for the moment, but I specially refer to Walsh's speech on page 403 which I have read to your Lordships because I think that could not have been in the mind of the Lord Justice at the time he made that reference to the speeches of the local men who were sent down Your Lordships will remember the facts with regard to that Three men were sent down, Mr Parrott was sent with Walsh and Mr Wadsworth was sent with Walsh—three altogether but Walsh went twice

"I decline to attach importance to the unwise use at a very late stage of the strike of a particular adjective 'devilish,' even though uttered in the presence of an excited crowd of colliers No illegal act followed this utterance (5) The strike was continued and maintained by the branch officials and the branch members by pickets, and by inducing the colliers who went out on the 29th of June not to enter into fresh contracts of service, and also other men not to enter into contracts of service In so far as this was free from molestation or intimidation it was not an unlawful means, and the finding of the Jury in answer to Question 61B cannot be supported as a ground of action   (6) The strike was continued and maintained by the grant of strike pay by the Union in breach of the rules of the Union   The strike collapsed directly the strike pay was stopped by the injunction granted in Howden's action   In my opinion this is the only act of importance as against the Union Unless this act suffices, I think there was no evidence upon which the Jury could find the Union liable   It is important to observe that the resolution to grant strike pay was not passed until the 24th July, and it was only paid as from the 17th July   The contracts of service had, in my view, been terminated before that date, and the strike was therefore not then open to the original illegality It was a lawful strike unless and in so far as it was continued and maintained by intimidation or molestation or other unlawful means " Well, with submission to the Lord Justice on that point, nothing had happened to alter the character of the strike   It was no more lawful on the 17th July than it had been on its initiation   Nothing had been done to make it a strike in accordance with the rules   I do not know that it is very material, but I submit that it is an incorrect view of the Lord Justice, that it was a lawful strike at that time

Then "D" "It remains to consider whether this grant of strike pay was, under the circumstances, a tortious act rendering the Union funds liable to pay damages to the Colliery Company from the time when it was resolved that strike pay should be given   But probably it is not very easy to see how a gift of money to strikers by a man or body of men can involve any such liability, even though the strikers may, without the sanction of the subscribers, be guilty of molestation and intimidation in the conduct of the strike   Nor will the mere knowledge of the subscribers that such unlawful means have been used or are likely to be used by the strikers alter the legal position Thus far I have assumed that the money belongs to the subscribers to be disposed of at their own free will   Can it make any difference that the subscribers being trustees have improperly taken the money out of the trust fund? This would be a breach of trust as between themselves and their beneficiaries, but I fail to appreciate the argument that it can give any further right to the employers to whom the source from which the money is derived is a matter of indifference   I am not prepared to hold that, in the case last supposed, the persons who subscribed the money could be considered to be maintaining the strike by unlawful means   The members of a Trades Union are not, I think, in any worse position by reason of their having taken advantage of the Trade Union Acts   It follows that, in my opinion, the action must fail against the Union   The case against Wadsworth, Parrott and Hall cannot be maintained if the case against the Union fails on the ground above stated They acted only in their character as agents of the Union They were not guilty of any independent tortious act The case against Nolan and Humphries is abundantly clear, but as they have not appeared and are, I presume, without means, this is not a matter of importance'

I am glad to say I have now put your Lordships in possession, I think, of the material facts of the case, but before I formulate the propositions upon which I desire to address your Lordships, I should like to refer to some passages in this Judgment of Lord Justice Cozens-Hardy because, but for the fact that he takes the view that the branch officials are not agents of the Union under the rules, this Judgment in many of its main features is very much in favour of the contentions which I am submitting to this House

Now I would just refer to the passages to which I allude in that connection, and first of all, upon page 1043, between letters "D" and "E,' the Lord Justice comes to this conclusion when he begins the new paragraph, he says "Now under those circumstances it is clear that it is competent to the Union to order or adopt a strike,' and that is the contention which I am putting forward and upon which I strongly rely Then a few lines lower down, under "F," he says "A local strike will naturally be engineered by the local branch officials' There again that is one of the essential propositions of our case and it is adopted and accepted by the Lord Justice

Lord JAMES of HEREFORD Your proposition is, is it not, that they engineered it as agents for the central body?

Mr ELDON BANKES Yes, my Lord

Lord JAMES of HEREFORD The Lord Justice does not take that view

Mr ELDON BANKES No, there are two separate points. Of course, I have got to establish first of all that is part of the business of the branch that the local officials shall engineer the strike I have got to establish as a second proposition that in doing so they are agents of the Association The Lord Justice accepts the first proposition, but he refuses to accept the second

Lord JAMES of HEREFORD Yes.

Mr ELDON BANKES Then, my Lord, at 1044 the first of his conclusions, I think, must necessarily relieve me from going through a great deal of the evidence again, because the first conclusion he comes to — and your Lordships will notice that he differs from the Master of the Rolls in this — the Master of the Rolls says I have not got to come to a definite conclusion, I have only to say whether there is evidence for the Jury on these points, but Lord Justice Cozens-Hardy goes further He says "It will suffice to state the conclusions at which I have arrived", and his first conclusion is that "The strike of the Denaby and Cadeby Colliers on the 29th June was procured and brought by the Denaby and Cadeby branch officials, who induced the men to break their contracts of service by leaving work"

Now, may I pause there to make my point about that, because, of course, it was an essential part of our case to prove to the satisfaction of the Jury that the breaking of the contracts was procured by the branch officials The Jury found that it was so, and the verdict cannot be set aside by my learned friends, unless they can satisfy this House that it was a verdict which no reasonable man could come to upon the evidence, and my submission is that the Lord Justice, having stated that that was the conclusion at which he himself had arrived, I really need not trouble myself to go at length through the evidence in order to satisfy your Lordship that there was evidence upon which the Jury could properly come to such a conclusion

Then later down, my Lord, in the passage which I have just read this morning under head 4, between D and E, another of his conclusions is that "The strike thus commenced was continued and maintained by the branch officials and the branch members by unlawful means, viz, by molestation and intimidation" That, again, is one of the facts which the Jury have found in our favour, and upon which it is said—or may be said—that there is no evidence Again I pray this in aid, in support of my contention that the verdict was right—at any rate, it was one which this Court would not interfere with upon the evidence

Then later down, under "5," he only repeats again in a different form that same conclusion "The strike was continued and maintained by the branch officials and the branch members by pickets, and by inducing the colliers who went out on the 29th of June not to enter into fresh contracts of service"

Now, my Lord, I think I may pass from this, but before I address your Lordships upon the questions of law which seem to me to arise, my learned friend, Mr Danckwerts, wishes me to call your Lordship's attention to the admission as to the use of the speeches which is contained on page 386 of the Book

Lord JAMES of HEREFORD Mr Bankes, have you concluded your observations on the Judgment?

Mr ELDON BANKES Yes, my Lord, for the time

Lord JAMES of HEREFORD I should like assistance in respect to this question of what constitutes the maintaining of the strike in relation principally to what fell from the Master of the Rolls

Mr ELDON BANKES Of course I am coming to that point in a moment, my Lord , I propose to deal with it separately

Lord JAMES of HEREFORD If you please

Mr ELDON BANKES My learned friend, Mr Danckwerts, thinks that I put my proposition to the House too high when I said that the extracts from the speeches and the Shorthand Notes of the speeches were admitted The exact form of the admission, my Lord, is on page 386—I have just referred to it—between E and F I may begin " It is admitted that the respective reporters would, if called at the trial depose that to the best of their respective beliefs they took down correctly but not fully what was said by the speakers These admissions are intended only to dispense with calling the reporters as witnesses at the trial, but not as admissions that any of the speeches are admissible in evidence or are to be admitted as evidence at the trial, and it is also admitted that the reports may not be full or accurate reports of everything the respective speakers said Neither side is to call the reporters or any of them ' And then, my Lord, at the trial I think my friend, Mr Danckwerts, was not there but a discussion took place between myself and Mr Isaacs and I said " Of course, if my friend has any objection to make with regard to any particular speech or to its being used as evidence then, of course, it will be right to object, but I put that in formally (Mr Isaacs) Quite, that is why I drew your attention to it I do not want to call the reporter so it may be taken to be correct " My Lord, I do not think I put the case too high, because I submit that taking this admission and the form in which it was made, and taking what was said by my learned friend, Mr Isaacs, and taking the fact that Mr Wadsworth was called, and it was not suggested by him that what he was reported as having said was inaccurate , it was not suggested by Mr Hall that what he said was inaccurately reported and nobody else was called . therefore, taking this admission and Mr Isaacs's admission, and the fact that the accuracy of the speeches was not in any way challenged at the trial by evidence, I submit that my observation to your Lordship was justified Of course, my only desire was to put before your Lordships a statement that was absolutely accurate in every respect

Now, my Lord, having put the facts before your Lordships, I would now come back to the questions, and address myself to your Lordships upon the questions and upon the law as applicable to these questions, and as I have said before, may I now repeat, there are four separate points upon some of which I submit, that both as to the facts and the law, we are, if I may use the expression, in " smooth water ' With regard to some of the points the water is not quite so smooth, but still I submit that all our propositions are justified and maintainable

Now the first point is that we have a cause of action because the officials of the Union procured the men to break their contracts, and upon that I submit that there are no difficulties either of fact or law The only question for your Lordships is as to the construction of the rule

My second proposition is that the Defendant Association, by its officials, maintained, or assisted in maintaining, the strike by unlawful means

Lord JAMES of HEREFORD Would it interfere with your statement to say, when you say "officials," do you mean central or branch officials?

Mr ELDON BANKES Well, my Lord, in some cases branch, and in some cases central, but I am contending that the branch officials are officials My proposition is that it is done by officials

Lord JAMES of HEREFORD If you please

Mr ELDON BANKES I will proceed to give your Lordships evidence about that in a moment, that the Defendant Association, by its officials, maintained, or assisted in maintaining, the strike by unlawful means Now, the first class of unlawful means complained of is molestation and intimidation, and down to this point I submit that I am in what I call the calm water Of course, the only effect of failing in my first contention and establishing my second would be that the date of the cause of action, instead of being the 29th of June, would be the 14th July or the 17th July The date of the cause of action is different, but the result is substantially the same

Now, of course, there are other illegal acts complained of One is the granting of the strike pay

The LORD CHANCELLOR Still on "2"?

Mr ELDON BANKES Yes, still on "2," my Lord It is the second of the unlawful means, the granting of the strike pay, and there I admit there are serious questions of law to be decided as to whether or not the granting of the strike pay under the circumstances in which it was granted can be said to be an unlawful act That is the question of law with regard to that Then the third alleged unlawful means, the inducing or attempting to induce men who were willing to enter into contracts, we do not rely on, and never have relied on as an unlawful act per se apart from conspiracy, therefore your Lordships will please understand that our case of maintaining or assisting to maintain the strike by unlawful means is confined to the intimidation and molestation and to the granting of strike pay

Then, my Lord, the third ground is that the Defendants unlawfully and maliciously conspired to molest and injure the Plaintiffs, and, of course, under that, my Lord, all the three grounds ("a," "b," and "c," of Question 6) are evidence That means to say that we rely, as evidence of the conspiracy to molest and injure, not only on the fact that there was molestation and intimidation of our workmen in fact, but there was the granting of the strike pay against the rules of the Union, and there was the inducing, or attempting to induce, men not to enter into contracts with us, and it is plain that that constitutes a cause of action if it is the result of a conspiracy to molest and injure, and the fourth head is that, assuming that our case is not sustainable, that the branch officials were the agents of the Association by virtue of the rules, there was a ratification of the acts of the branch officials *ab initio* And that, my Lord, raises what the members of the Court of Appeal have considered to be a serious question of law as to the meaning of the word "purporting" when used in connection with "ratification" I will deal with that when I come to the fourth head

Now, my Lord, with regard to the first head, of course, everything depends upon the construction of the rules I have read them through to your Lordships once, and I will not attempt to do so again I wish now, looking back, that we had emphasised our case more fully upon the rules before the Court of Appeal I shall have to refer to one or two of the rules, but before I do so I should like to refer to the Trades Unions Act under which these rules are made, because I think that that throws very considerable light upon the position of these branch officials The Trades Unions Act of 1871 is 34 and 35 Victoria, c 31 That is the Act which your Lordship may remember permitted of the registration of Trades Unions, it provided that Trades Unions should have rules, and Section 14 is in these terms "With respect to rules of a Trade Union registered under this Act, the following provisions shall have effect (1) The rules of every such Trade Union shall contract provisions in respect of the several matters mentioned in the first schedule to this Act ' Now, the rules are bound to contain reference to the matters referred to in the first schedule, and the first schedule is a schedule containing six clauses It is stated to be the "first schedule of matters to be provided for by the rules of Trades Unions registered under this Act (1) The name of the Trade Union and place of meeting for the business of the Trade Union (2) The whole of the objects for which the Trade Union is to be established, the purposes for which the funds thereof shall be applicable, and the conditions under which any member may become entitled to any benefit assured thereby, and the fines and forfeitures to be imposed on any member of such Trade Union (3) The manner of making, altering, amending, and rescinding rules (4) A provision for the appointment and removal of a general committee of management, of a trustee or trustees, treasurer, and other officers " Now, the rules are to provide for the appointment of the officers Now, my first point is, therefore, that every person whose appointment is referred to in the rules is, *prima facie*, at any rate, an officer of the society There is no doubt that a Trades Union may appoint agents *ad hoc* They may appoint persons to carry out any particular part of the business

of the Trades Union, but those persons stand in a different category
from what I may call their recognised officers. Now, what do we
find in those rules with reference to the branch officers? They are
treated in exactly the same way (it is at page 93 the rules begin) as
the other officers of the society whose duties are confined to the
central office. If I may just run through them, your Lordship may
begin at Rule 13. There is the president and his duties; 14, there
is the corresponding secretary; 15, the financial secretary; 16, the
agent; 22, the general treasurer; 27, the trustees; then 31, the
election of branch president and his duties—branch secretaries—
branch treasurer. They are officers of the society just as much as
any other of the persons who have been previously named, and if
your Lordship will just carry your eye down to Rules 34 and 35,
you will see them in those rules called "the local secretary" and the
"local treasurer," and in 36 they are called "the local committee."
Now, all those persons, including the local committees, are paid—
paid servants—some of them in receipt of a regular salary, some of
them in receipt of a salary which is measured by the number of
attendances, but equally every one of them paid officers of the
Association.

Now, my Lord, I think the next step I should like to take
would be to read to your Lordship—because I think it would be the
proper place at which to introduce this—the Judgment of Mr Justice
Farwell in the Taff Vale case, where he deals with this particular
point amongst others. I shall have to come back to the rules again in a
moment. It is the Taff Vale Railway Company against the
Amalgamated Society of Railway Servants, and it is reported in
1901 Appeal Cases, page 426. Now the action there, as your Lordships may remember, was against the society, and two gentlemen,
one Mr Bell, the general secretary, and one Mr Holmes, the
organising secretary for the West of England, and the question
which Mr Justice Farwell had to decide was as to whether or not
the Society could be sued as such, and whether they were responsible
for the acts of those two persons. His Judgment is at page 427,
and I think all of it is material in support of my argument. He
says this: "The Defendant Society have taken out a summons to
strike out their name as Defendants on the ground that they are
neither a corporation nor an individual, and cannot be sued in a
quasi-corporate or any other capacity. Failing this, they contend
that no injunction ought to be granted against them. I reserved
judgment last week on these two points because the first is of very
great importance, and Counsel were unable to assist me by citing
any reported case in which the question had been argued and
decided." Then he says: "Now, it is undoubtedly true that a
Trade Union is neither a corporation nor an individual, nor a
partnership between a number of individuals; but this does not by
any means conclude the case. A Trade Union, as defined by S 16
of the Trade Union Act, 1876, 'means any combination, whether
temporary or permanent, for regulating the relations between workmen

and masters, or between workmen and workmen, or between masters and masters, or for imposing restrictive conditions on the conduct of any trade or business whether such combination would or would not, if the principal Act had not been passed, have been deemed to have been an unlawful combination by reason of some one or more of its purposes being in restraint of trade' It is an association of men which almost invariably owes its legal validity to the Trade Union Acts, 1871 and 1876 In the present case the foundation of the argument that I have heard on behalf of the Society is that it is an illegal association—an argument that would have more weight if the action related to the enforcement of any contract and were not an action in tort The questions that I have to consider are what, according to the true construction of the Trade Union Acts, has the Legislature enabled the Trade Unions to do, and what, if any, liability does a Trade Union incur for wrongs done to others in the exercise of its authorised powers? The Acts commence by legalising the usual Trade Union contracts, and proceed to establish a registry of Trade Unions" Then, my Lord, I do not think I need read further there unless my friend wishes it He says at page 429 "Now, although a corporation and an individual or individuals may be the only entity known to the common law who can sue or be sued, it is competent to the Legislature to give to an association of individuals which is neither a corporation nor a partnership, nor an individual, a capacity for owning a property and acting by agents, and such capacity in the absence of express enactment to the contrary involves the necessary correlative of liability to the extent of such property for the acts and defaults of such agents It is beside the mark to say of such an association that it is unknown to the common law The Legislature has legalised it" Then he says it "is not a case of suing in contract' Then he goes on (page 430) "Now the Legislature in giving a Trade Union the capacity to own property and the capacity to act by agents has, without incorporating it, given it two of the essential qualities of a corporation—essential, I mean, in respect of liability for tort, for a corporation can only act by its agents, and can only be made to pay by means of its property The principle on which corporations have been held liable in respect of wrongs committed by its servants or agents in the course of their service and for the benefit of their employer—*qui sentit commodum sentire debet et onus*—(see Mersey Docks Trustees v Gibbs) is as applicable to the case of a Trade Union as to that of any other corporation." Then he says, at page 431 "If, therefore, I am right in concluding that the Society are liable in tort, the action must be against them in their registered name The acts complained of are the acts of the Association They are acts done by their agents in the course of the management and direction of a strike, the undertaking such management and direction is one of the main objects of the Defendant Society, and is perfectly lawful, but the Society in undertaking such management and direction undertook also the responsibility for the manner in which the strike is carried out The fact that no action could be brought at law or in equity to compel the society to interfere or refrain from interfering in the strike is immaterial, it is not a question of the rights of members of the society, but of the wrong done to persons outside the Society For such wrongs arising as they do from the wrongful conduct of the agents of the society in the course of managing a strike which is a lawful object of the society, the defendant society is, in my opinion, liable I have come to this conclusion on principle, and on the construction of the Acts, and there is nothing to the contrary in any of the cases cited by the Defendants' Counsel They were all cases relating to the limitation of the right of enforcing contracts to which I have already referred It is true that in Lyons v Wilkins the name of the Trade Union was struck out as a defendant by Byrne, J , but I have been supplied with a copy of the shorthand notes of this case, and I find that the point was not argued, the Plaintiff's Counsel not thinking it worth while to contest it , and, on the other hand, although the Court of Appeal in Trollope v London Building Trades Federation affirmed an injunction restraining libel by a Trade Union, I find that the Trade Union entered no appearance, and that the injunction went against them before Kekewich, J , in default of appearance, and his order was affirmed, nothing being said about the society The cases having the nearest analogy to the present are those like Ruck v Williams and Whitehouse v Fellowes, where unincorporated improvement commissioners and the trustees of a turnpike road respectively, sued under their respective Acts in the name of the clerk, were held liable in tort I accordingly dismiss the society's summons with costs I have now to consider the question whether an injunction should be granted against the society in addition to that granted last week against Messrs Bell and Holmes, and I am of opinion that it should The objects of the Society comprise promoting the settlement of disputes between masters and men by arbitration or, failing that, by other lawful means, and of course a strike is perfectly lawful , the general management of the society is vested in an executive committee, with powers to represent the members in disputes about hours and wages " Your Lordship will notice the distinction between the rules of that Society and this There the supreme control was in the Executive Committee

Lord JAMES of HEREFORD Just two lines back he says the strike is lawful?

Mr ELDON BANKES Yes "The objects of the society comprise promoting the settlement of disputes between masters and men by arbitration, or, failing that, by other lawful means, and, of course a strike is perfectly lawful "

Lord JAMES of HEREFORD That is what I wanted

Mr ELDON BANKES Then he goes on at page 433 "The Defendant Bell was the general secretary, and the Defendant Holmes was the local organising secretary of the society, they, as agents for the society, and on their instruction and for their benefit put themselves in charge of the strike"

Now, of course, I wish to call attention to this There was this distinction between our case and this case, that in the Taff Vale case Holmes and Bell were expressly authorised by the Executive Committee to go down and take charge That is a distinction, but in my submission there is no difference, because my submission is that under these particular rules which we are now discussing, the branch officials were the local officials on the spot, whose natural duty it was to take charge of the strike unless orders were given to the contrary

Lord JAMES of HEREFORD Holmes and Bell were Central officers, were not they?

Mr ELDON BANKES Bell was, but Holmes was the local organising secretary "The Defendant Bell was the general secretary, and the Defendant Holmes was the local organising secretary of the Society"

Lord JAMES of HEREFORD But I think he was a gentleman who went from locality to locality to organise, was not he?

Mr ELDON BANKES No, my Lord Holmes was stationed in South Wales

Lord JAMES of HEREFORD I know

Mr ELDON BANKES As local organising secretary, he did not move from place to place

Lord DAVEY He was the organising secretary of the Society for that locality?

Mr ELDON BANKES Yes

Lord JAMES of HEREFORD He was there peripatetically, he wandered about?

Mr ELDON BANKES My friend Mr Danckwerts wishes me to remind the House that there was a resolution of the Society in that case sending Mr Bell down I am not disputing that at all

The LORD CHANCELLOR. You have told us that

Mr ELDON BANKES Yes, it is part of my argument, and I desire to lay great stress upon this, because so much is said about the responsibility of branch officials and the Union's liability for the acts of branch officials My submission is that every case must be dealt with on the rules You could make rules, I do not doubt, under which they would not be local officials The Taff Vale case was a case in which a man was expressly sent down by resolution to take charge of the strike Our present case is that under these particular rules these branch officials were stationed there for the purpose of doing this, as I can satisfy your Lordships I hope in a moment "The Defendant Bell was the general secretary and the Defendant Holmes was the local organising secretary of the society, they as agents for the society and on their instructions and for their benefit, put themselves in charge of the strike, and on the evidence that was read last week illegally watched and beset men to prevent them from working for the Company, and illegally ordered men to break their contracts I have already held that the society are liable for the acts of their agents to the same extent that they would be if they were a corporation, and it is abundantly clear that a corporation under the circumstances of this case would be liable See, for example, Ranger v Great Western Railway Company, where Lord Cranworth points out that, although a corporation cannot in strictness be guilty of fraud, there can be no doubt that if its agents act fraudulently, so that if they had been acting for private employers the persons for whom they were acting would have been affected by their fraud, the same principles must prevail where the principal under whom the agents acts is a corporation It is not a question of acting *ultra vires*, as in Chaples v Brunswick Permanent Building Society, but of improper acts in the carrying out of the lawful purposes of the Society In such cases the principal, whether an individual or a corporation, or a body like turnpike trustees, is answerable for every such wrong of the servant or agent as is committed in the course of the service and for the master's benefit, though no express command or privity of the master be proved Granted that the principal has not authorised the particular act, but he has put the agent in his place to do that class of acts, and he is answerable for the manner in which the agent has conducted himself in doing the business—with which the principal has entrusted him, see Barwick v English Joint Stock Bank in the Exchequer Chamber Therefore, if it is any longer necessary to grant an injunction, I grant an injunction against the Defendant society in the same form as that granted last week against the other Defendants."

Now that Judgment was affirmed in this House in terms by some of your Lordships, and the then Lord Chancellor who gave the leading Judgment—the first speech—says in terms of Mr Justice Farwell's Judgment "In this case I am content to adopt the Judgment of Mr Justice Farwell, with which I entirely concur"

Now the proposition which I submit to your Lordships from this Judgment is that a Trade Union is in exactly the same position as any corporation or any individual with regard to the acts of any persons who are proved to be its agents, and my first submission is that upon these rules the branch officials are the local officers of the Association, and if they are local officers of the Association they are the agents of the Association

Lord DAVEY For certain purposes

Mr ELDON BANKES If your Lordship pleases, I am not disputing that for a moment, but if you find that any individual is an agent of another, and in the course of his agency and for his master's benefit he commits a tort the master is responsible

Now the first point that I have got to establish is that the branch officials were in fact agents I rely upon the rules The second point is "You have got to establish that the tort complained of was committed in the course of the agency and for the master's benefit, and what is meant by 'in the course of the agency and for the master's benefit' is to negative the proposition that the agent was doing it on his own behalf If you once find that a man is in the position of an agent and he commits a tort the question for the Jury is Was he doing that for himself, or was he doing it as agent and for his master's benefit? The master is responsible, and the responsibility arises out of the fact of the existence of the condition of principal and agent and the master can only escape liability if he shows that the agent was committing the tort complained of, not on his master's behalf but on his own behalf

Now I will refer your Lordships to the decisions in a moment The question which we submitted to the Jury, I submit, is quite correct and quite sufficient Your Lordship asked me a moment ago—or a day ago I think—whether or not the Jury ought not to have been asked whether the acts complained of were within the scope of the agent's authority

Now if my proposition is right that to establish the agency the question for the Jury is Was the man acting as agent for the master's benefit or was he acting for himself?—that is only another form of expression for saying Was he acting within the scope of his employment? I think I can establish that by reference to authorities And, my Lord, the question the Jury was asked, your Lordship sees at page 1015 The word " purporting " was put into the question, because we were afterwards going to ask them about ratification, but that does not affect it " If you answer the first question in the affirmative " were they " or either and which of them in so doing purporting to act as agents of the Association and for its benefit "? That I submit is a perfectly sufficient question

The LORD CHANCELLOR May I tell you in one sentence the thing that is in my mind?

Mr ELDON BANKES If your Lordship pleases

The LORD CHANCELLOR An agent may purport to act for his principal in doing a thing which was clearly outside the scope of his authority and not lawful What I meant was that there did not seem, at the moment to me, to be involved in this question or in the answer to it, any finding that the agent was in fact acting within the scope of his authority That is the thing I wanted you to tell me

Mr ELDON BANKES I had better deal with that at greater length when I refer to the cases but my proposition is that I have established, as I submit, upon the rules that the branch officials were local officials

Now, of course, it might be a strong argument although it would not be at all conclusive, if it could be shown upon the rules that under no conceivable circumstances could the management or control of the strike be within the scope of their employment, but so far as the rules indicate anything on the point, I submit they are plain to show that the management of a strike is contemplated as being part of the duties which they may have to perform, because, my Lord, all that the rules say about it is this Rule 37 says——

Lord JAMES of HEREFORD What page, please?

Mr ELDON BANKES Page 104, my Lord, Rule 37 All that it says about what they are to do is that they are to conduct the business of the branch—quite true—subject to the rules and minutes of the General Council, but apart from any such rules and minutes, what they are there to do is to conduct the business of the branch Now, do the rules themselves give us any assistance as to what the business consists of? Well, so far as they give us any assistance, the assistance is strongly in the line of showing that the strike would be part of the business—the conduct of it, because the ballot, which is the preliminary step to the strike under Rule 72, is to be taken It says in terms (Rule 72, letter E) "Such vote to be obtained by the branch officials," so that, so far as the Rules give us any assistance, the business of the branch is that done by the local officers, and that business clearly includes the taking of the preliminary ballot Here again I emphasise the fact—the officials of the Union were called—no one suggested that the management and control of the strike was any part of the duty of the branch officials ; they disclaimed the fact that they were acting as the agents of the Society That is another point But to say that it was not part of the business of the branch officials to manage the strike was never suggested in evidence by any of these people And again, I appeal to Lord Justice Cozens-Hardy in a passage in his Judgment that I read before, and I again emphasise this (page 1043, letter F) "A local strike will naturally be engineered ' (he says) "by the local branch officials", and Mr Justice Farwell takes the same view, because in his Judgment that

I read to your Lordship he says the undertaking and management and direction is one of the main objects of the Defendant Society, and is perfectly lawful, therefore I submit that I have established, at any rate so far as the rules go, the proposition that the rules do indicate that this particular business of managing and controlling the strike is part of the duties contemplated by the rules which are to be performed by the branch officials, but it is not necessary for my purpose, I submit, that I should establish that

Now, the next case I should like to refer to, my Lord, is the case of Giblan v National Amalgamated Labourers' Union of Great Britain and Ireland That is reported in 1903, 2 King's Bench page 600 Now, that case is only useful as an illustration It does not carry the law any further than the decision of Mr Justice Farwell, but it is an illustration of a case in which a Union were held responsible for the acts of two of its officials, and again in this case the Lords Justices affirmed the proposition that there was no distinction between the case of a Union and any other corporation or individual so far as the law of principal and agent is concerned, and they again asserted that the principle of Barwick v The English Joint Stock Bank applied to the case of the Union My Lord, that was an action which was brought by a man named Giblan against the National Amalgamated Labourers' Union of Great Britain and Ireland, a man named Williams, the General Secretary, and Toomey the Local Secretary at Newport, claiming damages for loss of wages I can tell your Lordship shortly what the facts were Giblan had been an officer of the Union and he had misappropriated certain funds, he had been ordered to pay the funds back by instalments, he did not do it and the Union took the view that he was defying them, and thereupon Williams and Toomey went round from time to time to the different persons in whose employ Giblan was and threatened that if they continued him any longer in their employ they would call out the Union men, and that was alleged to be a wrongful and actionable act, and in the statement of claim at page 606 it was alleged that Williams and Toomey in doing the acts complained of "acted in unison and each for and with the other and as the agents and by direction of the said Union" Then by their defence the Defendants denied that they had authorised or directed "Williams and Toomey or either of them, to do the acts therein referred to or any of them, and that if those Defendants did any of the said acts, which was not admitted, such acts were beyond their powers and beyond the powers of the officials of the Union, as a registered Trade Union, to do or to authorise and direct to be done, and that they, the Union, were not liable for the said acts" and in argument——

The LORD CHANCELLOR Was it tried?

Mr ELDON BANKES Oh, yes, my Lord, it was tried, and then there was complaint of the summing up It was tried before

k

Mr Justice Walton at Cardiff, and at page 614 this is the argument of the Counsel for the defence, so it raises the point directly. They say 'The action is for conspiracy between the Union, Williams and Toomey to injure the Plaintiff, but no such cause of action is made out by the Pleadings. Neither Williams nor Toomey had any authority from the Union, nor was it within the scope of their authority,' so that there is no doubt the point was directly raised.

Now, the Court consisted of Lord Justice Vaughan Williams, Lord Justice Romer, and Lord Justice Stirling. I will not read the whole of the Judgment, but only such passages as I think are material. At page 617 Lord Justice Vaughan Williams says this "There remains the question of the liability of the Union and Toomey. I think they are both liable. The Union, Williams and Toomey were all parties to acts constituting an actionable wrong — namely, interference with Giblan in the exercise of his undoubted common law right to dispose of his labour according to his will. It is said that the rules did not authorise the acts of Williams and Toomey, but be that how it may, the acts were not *ultra vires* of the Union, but only of its officers, and the Union in general meeting undoubtedly adopted the acts of Williams and Toomey, and took the benefit of them.' Now, there the distinction between that case and this is, that after the acts complained of had been committed the Executive Committee met—or, I think, the Society met in general meeting—and they approved of what had been done. There was that distinction, but it does not raise, in my opinion, any distinction of principle at all.

Then there is a passage which I should like to read which bears upon another branch of my argument, at page 619.

Lord DAVEY. Who is the learned Judge you are reading?

Mr ELDON BANKES. Lord Justice Romer, I was going to read. He says "But I should be sorry to leave this case without observing that, in my opinion, it was not essential in order for the Plaintiff to succeed, that he should establish a combination of two or more persons to do the acts complained of. In my judgment, if a person who, by virtue of his position or influence, has power to carry out his design, sets himself to the task of preventing, and succeeds in preventing, a man from obtaining or holding employment in his calling, to his injury, by reason of threats to or special influence upon the man's employers, or would-be employers, and the design was to carry out some spite against the man, or had for its object the compelling him to pay a debt, or any similar object not justifying the acts against the man, then that person is liable to the man for the damage consequently suffered" Then he goes on "The remaining question is as to the liability of the Defendant Union. That depends upon whether, if the acts complained of had been done by the Executive Committee, the Union would have been liable. I have come to the conclusion that the Union would have been liable on the principle stated in Barwick v English Joint Stock Bank—that the acts were done in the service and for the benefit of the Union." Lord Justice Stirling expressly refers to Barwick, and approves it. I do not think I need read more of that Judgment.

Then, my Lord, I ought to call your Lordship's attention to another decision illustrative of this. My learned friend, Mr. Atherley Jones, was against me in it.

Lord JAMES of HEREFORD. Mr Justice Farwell's Judgment was approved of in terms in this House, was it not?

Mr ELDON BANKES. Yes, my Lord. I read the Judgment of the Lord Chancellor. My Lord, I was in a case in the Court of Appeal against my learned friend Mr Atherley Jones, which is called Airey v Weighill. That is a case which is only reported in the *Times* newspaper, but I thought I ought to call your Lordship's attention to it. In my opinion it really does not affect the question before your Lordships at all. It was a very special case depending entirely upon the special rules of that Society, and the very peculiar circumstances of the finding of the Jury, but undoubtedly the result was that the Court of Appeal held that in that particular case the Union was not liable for the acts of the branch officials.

The LORD CHANCELLOR. You have not given us the date of the *Times*.

Mr ELDON BANKES. My Lord, the date is February 11th, 1905. It was a most peculiar case. I mention it to your Lordships, but in my view it will not assist your Lordships at all. I do not know whether my learned friend agrees as to that?

Mr ATHERLEY JONES. No, I do not.

Mr ELDON BANKES. My Lord, It was a most particular case, because the facts were these. Pressure was sought to be put upon a man to join the Union, and he did not want to join the Union, and thereupon there was a meeting of the branch, and—I think my recollection is right—there was a unanimous vote of the branch that they should not do anything, but, in spite of that unanimous vote, the next day some men, employed in the same works as this objectionable man, took action and struck and came out, and amongst the men who struck and came out was one of the branch officials, and the Jury were asked as to whether or not the branch approved of this strike, and their answer was, Yes, because they did not act upon the unanimous decision of the branch meeting, or words to that effect. A question arose as to what Judgment should be entered upon that finding. It was a hopeless case really to contend, although I had to contend in support of it, that the branch under those circumstances were liable. The rules were very special, and I only mention it to show that I do not pass it by, and I do not think it is necessary to go into the facts of it

Now, I want just to call attention quite shortly to Barwick and the similar cases in which the responsibility of the principal for the act of the agent is laid down, and which cases are by those which I have cited to your Lordship said to be applicable to the case of the Trades Union and its agents. My Lords, there is Limpus v The London General Omnibus Company, and there is Barwick. I should like to refer to Limpus' case. My Lord, Limpus v The London General Omnibus Company is reported in the Hurlstone and Coltman, page 526, and in 32 Law Journal Exchequer, page 35. I think the report in the Law Journal is the fuller, but still I will read it from Hurlstone and Coltman.

Lord JAMES of HEREFORD: It was a "nursing" case, was it not?

Mr ELDON BANKES: Yes, my Lord. The facts were these. It was the case of two omnibuses racing.

Lord JAMES of HEREFORD: Yes.

Mr ELDON BANKES: And the driver of the London General Omnibus Company had been passed by his rival, and when his rival was catching him up again he drew across the road, and the result was that the opponents' omnibus was upset and the plaintiff was seriously injured. Now in that case there were special directions to the drivers to this effect. During the journey he must drive his horse at a steady pace; he must not on any account race with or obstruct another omnibus, or hinder by anything the driver or conductor in his business whether such omnibus be one belonging to the company or not. Therefore, it was the case of a man acting contrary to direct instructions, and there was a division of opinion in the Court, which was a very strong court in the Exchequer Chamber. Mr Justice Wrightman dissented from the view of the rest of the Court, consisting of Mr Justice Williams, Mr Justice Crompton, Mr Justice Wills, Mr Justice Byles, and Mr Justice Blackburn. Mr Justice Crompton, in giving his Judgment, says this—(and I am quoting this from the *Law Journal* report, my Lord, which is rather fuller than the other) "My doubt is whether this was an act within the scope of the driver's employment, in other words, whether he was acting in the course of the driving or management of the omnibus." Now I extract that because I think it assists me with reference to the point which was in your Lordship's mind. It is only another way of stating what is the meaning of "within the scope of his employment." Is the man acting in the course of the driving or management of the omnibus? The Judge having told the Jury what was the test by which they were to determine whether the act was done in the course of the service or not, used language in which he tells them perfectly rightly that if the act is done in the course of the service the defendants are responsible and there is a case which well illustrates that, which is the case of Ward v The London General Omnibus Company in 12 Law Journal, Common Pleas (I should like to refer to that) at page 265 That was a case my Lord, in which there had been a collision between an omnibus and a tramcar and some man had jumped on to the step of the omnibus—no doubt with the object of taking the number of the omnibus driver, and then the omnibus driver slashed him in the face with his whip, and an action was brought against the London General Omnibus Company for that, and the question there was clearly put Did he do this for his master's benefit or did he do it for his own ? Was his object to avoid getting into trouble himself, or was his object to avoid an action against the Company ? and it is put in such plain words here by Mr Justice Blackburn " The question comes before us in a form most unfavourable for the Defendants, because verdict must stand if it be possible to find evidence of negligence in the employment to go to the Jury, and the question is if there be sufficient for the Jury A master is responsible for his servants' act in his business though the servant be excited by drink or passion, but if the servant act for private spite (and I agree with my brother Martin it does not matter whether the action be in contract or tort), if the act be done so as to divest him of his character as servant, the master is not responsible In the present case there was a quarrel and the servant was irritated, but the Jury might find he was acting in the course of his duty, or entirely for his own purposes, and in the former case find one way, viz , for the Plaintiff, in the latter case the other way ' Now, I think, my Lord, that case is a good illustration of what is meant by the " course of employment," and I can follow it by later cases where the masters have been held not to be responsible for the act of the agent, and in those cases it is because it is plain, or by the finding of the Jury made plain, that in the particular case the agent was acting for his own private purposes or for his own private benefit, and all that is meant by " scope of the employment " is that, having established the relation of master and servant or principal and agent you have got to have it found by the tribunal which is in charge of the decision of the question of fact Aye or No, was the man acting for himself or was he acting for his masters ?

Now my Lord, Barwick I want to refer to because——

The LORD CHANCELLOR Do you mean that it is enough to say that he was acting for himself or acting for his master without saying also that he was acting within the scope of the authority given to him ?

Mr ELDON BANKES Yes if you establish the agency that is enough You have got to find that it was for the master and for the master's benefit, you have got to find both

The LORD CHANCELLOR Yes

Lord JAMES of HEREFORD You have got to establish the particular agency sometimes as distinguished from a general agency—if agency is made out   There have been a great many cases tried at *Nisi Prius*, as where the case arose of a coachman driving his master for a certain portion of the evening and then going on his own account to see some friends and meeting with an accident   He was, of course, an agent in one sense because he was the coachman, but he was not an agent in another

Mr ELDON BANKES A case arose the other day of a motor car man   he was told to go to meet his master at such and such a time in the West End of London, and afterwards he went for a drive on his own account up to Hampstead to see a lady friend, and in the course of doing it he ran over somebody, and the Jury in that case found he was not acting for his master ; indeed, I think they said he was acting for his master, but that was the question   This case is reported in Law Reports, 2 Exchequer, at page 259

Lord JAMES of HEREFORD What case is this ?

Mr ELDON BANKES Barwick v The English Joint Stock Bank   The precise language of Mr Justice Wills in that case has been over and over again approved both in the Privy Council and in this House, and therefore I should just like to read the exact language

Lord JAMES of HEREFORD Will you give me the date of that please ?

Mr ELDON BANKES The date my Lord, is 1867

Lord DAVEY It has been very often quoted

Mr ELDON BANKES Yes, he says this   " But with respect to the question whether a principal is answerable for the act of his agent in the course of his master's business and for his master's benefit no sensible distinction can be drawn between the case of fraud and the case of any other wrong   The general rule is, that the master is answerable for every such wrong of the servant or agent as is committed in the course of the service and for the master's benefit, though no express command or privity of the master be proved   That principle is acted upon every day in running down cases ' (then he goes through them)   " In all these cases, it may be said, as it was said here, that the master has not authorised the act   It is true he has not authorised the particular act, but he has put the agent in his place to do that class of acts and he must be answerable for the manner in which the agent has conducted himself in doing the business which it was the act of his master to place him in " Mr

Justice Wills put it in two ways, meaning the same thing, but your Lordship will find, if it is necessary to go through them, that both ways in which Mr Justice Wills put it have been approved in this House and in the Privy Council He says first he "is answerable for every such wrong of the servant or agent as is committed in the course of the service and for the master's benefit," and then he says the reason is "he has not authorised the particular act, but he has put the agent in his place to do that class of acts, and he must be answerable for the manner in which the agent has conducted himself"

Now, my Lord, that has been approved in The British Mutual Banking Company v Charnwood Forest, 18 Queen's Bench Division I want to refer to this and Swire v Francis, in 3 Appeal Cases, and Houldsworth v City of Glasgow Bank, in 5 Appeal Cases

The LORD CHANCELLOR That surely has been settled If anything has been settled, it is the law of agency

Mr ELDON BANKES If your Lordship pleases, except that Lord Selborne says this "It is a principle, not of the law of torts or of fraud or of deceit, but of the law of agency, equally applicable whether the agency is for a corporation (in a matter within the scope of the corporate powers) or for an individual," and so forth

Lord DAVEY Is that on appeal from Barwick?

Mr ELDON BANKES No, my Lord, this was much later This was the case of Houldsworth v The City of Glasgow Bank in the year 1880, but Lord Selborne refers to Barwick and cites it with approval He cites the language of Mr Justice Wills with approval

Now, my Lord, may I just in conclusion of this branch of my case call attention to a very recent case which is an illustration of an instance in which the master was not held liable—that Ruben v Great Fingal Consolidated Company?

My Lord, this case is an Appeal to this House, Ruben v the Great Fingal Consolidated Company It is reported in 1904, 2 King's Bench, at page 712 Now, that was a case where an action was brought because of certain frauds of a secretary of a Company in issuing forged certificates, and the question was whether the Company were liable There are difficult questions as to estoppel arising upon the issue of the certificates, and so forth That is not material for the present purpose The question was raised as to whether or not, inasmuch as the secretary was issuing these forged certificates for his own purposes, merely—for his own private advantage, and for the purposes of getting money, which he used for his own purposes, the Company were liable, and upon that the Master of the Rolls says at page 724 ' The general rule governing the responsibility of a master for the acts of his servant was stated by the late Justice Wills, in delivering the Judgment of the Exchequer Chamber in Barwick v English Joint Stock Bank" Then he reads what I have read "Founding themselves on the principle so stated the Court of Appeal in British Mutual Banking Company v Charnwood Forest Railway Company held that an action of deceit would not lie against a principal for a fraudulent misstatement made by his servant for his own private purposes in reply to a class of questions which it was within his ordinary duty to answer", so that in the Charnwood Forest case it was within his duty to answer, but in that particular case he had given the answer not for his master's benefit, but entirely for his own "The fact that it was made, not in the supposed interest of the master, but for his own private purposes, *ipso facto*, took it out of the scope of the actual authority and also, according to Bowen, L J, and of the class of acts which the agent was put there to do In Thorne v Heard, Kay, L J, refers to this case, to which he was not himself a party, in these terms 'It was deliberately decided in British Mutual Banking Company v Charnwood Forest Railway Company that the words 'for the master's benefit' are essential, and that where an agent in the course of his employment committed a fraud not for his principal's benefit but for the benefit of himself, and the principal did not benefit by such fraud, he could not be made liable for it It was also cited with approval by Lord Brampton in the House of Lords in the recent case of George Whitechurch, Limited v Cavanagh,' and so forth My Lords, I need not read further

Mr DANCKWERTS That case is under appeal

Mr ELDON BANKES It is under appeal, it is shortly coming on, but I do not think that view of the law will be questioned I have only cited it to your Lordship as illustrating, and to complete my argument

Lord DAVEY It is difficult to understand it, because he is there to answer questions —placed there by his master to answer questions So far as the rights of the person who receives the answer go, it is rather difficult to understand why it should make any difference whether the man is defrauding his principal or master, or not.

Mr ELDON BANKES Yes Of course, if you can bring it in another class and "hold out,' if you cannot quite say you hold the man out as your agent, it may under those circumstances not be potent.

Lord DAVEY I put the man there and he answers questions which are properly and rightly asked of me in the course of my business, but suppose he answers fraudulently —wrongfully—in order to cover a fraud of his own, or something of that kind, still so far as my liability to the other man goes it is a little difficult to understand how that is a defence——

Mr ELDON BANKES I think your Lordship will find the defence is clearly accepted I am only putting it to illustrate——

Lord DAVEY It is only what is passing through my mind

Mr ELDON BANKES I was only citing it as an illustration in order to make my point plain to your Lordships as to what is necessary——

Lord DAVEY It does not affect your argument?

Mr ELDON BANKES No, my Lord I have finished now what I have got to say on this branch of the case, and my propositions, put shortly, are these That the rules do constitute the branch officials local officers, that the rules show (if it is necessary for me to say so) in the language of Mr Justice Wills, that they have been put there to do this class of act, but whether that is so or not, the finding of the Jury that in this particular case they were acting as agents and for the benefit of the Association, and, therefore, not as mere workmen for their own benefit is sufficient for my purpose unless that verdict of the Jury can be set aside on the ground that it is against the weight of evidence

Lord DAVEY Which finding of the Jury is that?

Mr ELDON BANKES My Lord, the finding in answer to the second and fourth questions—1015 Their answer is that they purported to act as agents for the Association and for its benefit

The LORD CHANCELLOR That is what struck me, Mr Bankes, at the beginning, and it is still on my mind, and I want you to try and relieve my mind of the difficulty You do not here have a finding that, in fact, these men were acting as agents for the Association, I do not say that it is necessary, but if there is anything further I would like to know what you mean about it

Mr ELDON BANKES Of course, your Lordship must remember the way in which the case was fought, and the facts in relation to which these questions were framed Of course, your Lordship will see we had the point about ratification, and on the question of ratification it is necessary that you should have a finding that the people were purporting to do it On this question as to whether or not they were acting as agents the question which the Jury have got to decide is Were they acting for themselves or were they acting for the Association? That is broadly the question

The LORD CHANCELLOR It does not necessarily follow if they were not acting for themselves that they were acting for the master They might have been acting for a third person I do not say they were in this case

Mr ELDON BANKES That is why I say the question was framed with reference to the proposition in the case before the Jury, and the way in which the case had been fought The real case for the Defendants at the trial was that the Union was not responsible for the acts of these men That is their case on the rules They said We have nothing to do with it Then our answer to that is Well, the rule will decide that point, but in order to succeed we have got to get a finding that the men were not acting for themselves merely, therefore we say We will ask the Jury Were they acting as agents and for the benefit of ?

Now, my Lord, with submission, it is a question for that purpose, and it does answer what is wanted, because if a man is purporting to act as agent for a man it is plain that he is not acting for himself, and all I have got to negative—if it was a question for the Jury as to whether the men were at the time agents—that is to say, whether they had been appointed agents, I agree that the finding does not go far enough because there is not involved in this finding of fact that they had been appointed agents It is consistent with this that the man purporting to act as agent had never been an agent

The LORD CHANCELLOR Does it not come to this, Mr Bankes, that as regards the finding of the Jury on this head of the case you do not require the finding because the rules practically admit it ?

Mr ELDON BANKES Yes

The LORD CHANCELLOR I completely understand your case about that, but is it not the case that these first questions were designed to raise the point of ratification ?

Mr ELDON BANKES Oh no, certainly not, because your Lordship will see we have got the words "for the benefit" These questions were expressly drafted to raise this question, and the Master of the Rolls says so Your Lordship will see

The LORD CHANCELLOR Thank you that is enough

Mr ELDON BANKES We put the words in "for the benefit" and the words "for the benefit" only are directed to this point, and if I may conclude what I have got to say about this If I have got to establish the appointment as agent as a fact, I agree the Jury have not found it I say the rule has appointed them, and then the question of fact I have got to get rid of in order to establish my right to Judgment is that having been appointed they were not acting for themselves, and I submit that I have got that finding, and if it is necessary to go into it your Lordship will know there is this in these rules

Lord JAMES of HEREFORD You have just said that they were not acting for themselves

Mr ELDON BANKES Findings 2 and 4 "in so doing purporting to act as agents of the Association and for its benefit"

Lord JAMES of HEREFORD, You said a short time ago that if they purported to act as agents they could not act for themselves Is that quite sound?

Mr ELDON BANKES Well, it is in this sense, my Lord, I think—it does not matter to me if they were acting for themselves as well I think All I have got to establish is that at the time they were doing the acts complained of they were, in fact, agents, and for this purpose I have assumed that I am in the same position as if I had produced written agreements from the men

Lord JAMES of HEREFORD If they purported to act as agents to the knowledge of the suggested principal, that would carry you a step further?

Mr ELDON BANKES My Lord, I do not think it is necessary at all to establish the knowledge of the suggested principal at the time of the acts complained of, because the essence of the thing is that the agent is put in the position to do this class of act, and does it in the absence of the principal—when the principal is not there

Lord JAMES of HEREFORD Then that brings you back to the rules, you know If you are put into that position, that brings you back to the argument on the rules

Mr ELDON BANKES My Lord, may I make my position quite plain? What I say is this I have to establish that these men were appointed agents

Lord JAMES of HEREFORD By rules?

Mr ELDON BANKES By rules Then they, having been appointed agents by rules, I have got to establish that in doing the acts which we complain of they were not acting for themselves merely, but were acting as agents for, and for the benefit of, the Association Now, I have got the finding of fact in my favour unless the finding can be set aside and it can only be set aside on the ground of being against the weight of evidence

Lord JAMES of HEREFORD I do not see why you bring in the word "purported" Why do not you say "accusation"?

Mr ELDON BANKES Because it is to avoid too many questions

Lord JAMES of HEREFORD You want it independently of ratification?

Mr ELDON BANKES If you look at Question 5, your Lordship will see that we ask the question whether they ratified

Lord JAMES of HEREFORD Yes, I know

Mr ELDON BANKES That question by itself would not be enough In order to establish a valid ratification we have got to establish that the persons whose acts it is said were ratified purported to act for the principal

Lord JAMES of HEREFORD I quite see that, but if you could have got a finding that they did in fact act as agents you would not want your ratification

Mr ELDON BANKES No my Lord I do want it for this reason, because the Jury might say they did act as agent but the Court might say they were not in fact agents, and therefore I wanted ratification in order to meet the case

Lord JAMES of HEREFORD Why did not you take both strings to your bow?

Mr ELDON BANKES We did, my Lord

Lord JAMES of HEREFORD I do not find it My noble friend has pointed out that there is no finding that they were agents in fact, but you rely upon your rules for that

Mr ELDON BANKES I could not submit to the Jury the question whether they were agents under the rules because that is a question on the construction of the rules for the Court Nobody suggested that the Jury should be asked what the rules meant

Lord JAMES of HEREFORD I think it is a question for the Jury When they did these acts did they, as a fact, act under these rules? It is not the *construction* of the rules at all You have to apply the rules to the facts

Mr ELDON BANKES I have got that found

Lord JAMES of HEREFORD No, you have only got "purporting"

Mr ELDON BANKES Yes, my Lord, it is the same thing, and, as I submit, all this is the same thing, because the point is Were they acting for themselves, or were they acting for the Association? And if you choose to say they were purporting to act for the same Association, then it must mean that they were not acting for themselves, and that is the only point in question, indeed, it is not open to my learned friends now, even if they wanted to raise it, because there is a decision of this House that where questions are formulated, although you are not bound by the form of them, if they are not sufficient, and you want anything more and do not ask for it, you cannot say by the Court Let the Jury find, and then say they are not sufficient

The LORD CHANCELLOR I think we understand your view

Mr ELDON BANKES Now, my Lord, I have finished this point except one further observation, and that is this Of course there is undoubtedly a distinction between the position of Nolan and Humphries and the rest of the branch officials, because, whatever my learned friend may say about the branch officials, Nolan and Humphries were members of the Council There is no sort of doubt about that They are members of the Supreme Council They are two of the 150 men who compose the Supreme Council, and therefore if I am wrong in saying that the branch officials were local officers, it seems to me that it is impossible for my learned friends to contend that Nolan and Humphries were not officers of the Association Who else was an officer if they were not?

Lord JAMES of HEREFORD They were delegates

Mr ELDON BANKES Yes, but the word "delegate" means a member of the Council

Lord DAVEY A Member of Parliament is not answerable for the acts of the Government

Mr ELDON BANKES No, and of course Parliament is not responsible for acts of a Member of Parliament We are now, my Lord, dealing with the case of what is a corporation for this purpose, and we are dealing with the question of who are its officers

Lord DAVEY That is rather a stretch

Mr ELDON BANKES I submit that it really is not necessary for me, at any rate at this stage, to go through the evidence to show that there was evidence fit for the Jury, that these men did purport to act as agents for the Association and for their benefit I could go through the evidence, and I submit it clearly shows that it is so, but Lord Justice Cozens-Hardy has said that in his view that was so, because he says at page 1044 "The strike of the Denaby and Cadeby colliers on the 29th June was procured and brought about by the Denaby and Cadeby branch officials" I have mentioned that point before, but I refer to it again, as the particular point is immediately present to your Lordship's mind My submission on that is that it is impossible to say that the verdict of the Jury is one which no reasonable man could find when the Lord Justice expressly found, after a careful consideration of the evidence, that that is the conclusion he himself comes to

Now, my Lord, the second point is this, of course if we are right on this first point nothing further need be said, because if we establish this it carries us the whole way, we are entitled to a verdict and Judgment upon the ground that the Union by its officials procured our men to break their contracts, but assuming that that is not established, then I pass to the second point

Lord DAVEY Would that be enough for you, Mr Bankes? They broke their contracts, it is true, but after a certain date they ceased to be officials?

Mr ELDON BANKES Yes, my Lord, but the whole damage was done because the strike had been brought about by getting the men to break their contracts and come out It is only after that a question of the measure of damages The Judgment would pass for us, of course

Lord DAVEY Did all the damages subsequently flow from that?

Mr ELDON BANKES My Lord, that would be a question possibly to be gone into in assessing the damage Of course our case would be You are responsible because you procured the men to break their contracts, and in face of this evidence we shall ask to assess these damages and say Not only did you bring them out, but you subsequently did everything you could, and said everything you could, to maintain the strike

The LORD CHANCELLOR In damages That comes in on the question of damages

Mr ELDON BANKES I think that comes in on the question of damages

Lord DAVEY. Probably that is so

Lord JAMES of HEREFORD One moment   The Master of the Rolls rather brings in maintenance here as a cause of action

Mr ELDON BANKES Yes

Lord DAVEY That is the cause of action the Master of the Rolls finds

Lord JAMES of HEREFORD That is a restricted case of damages only

Mr ELDON BANKES That is an independent cause of action Now I will explain, if I may, what the cause of action would be It is this, that the Union by its officials maintained the strike by unlawful means Now nobody will dispute that that is a cause of action if we can establish it, that the Union by its officials maintained the strike by unlawful means Now the unlawful means (if I may take the easiest branch of our case to begin with) are molestation and intimidation

Lord DAVEY You gave us a summary of your views?

Mr. ELDON BANKES Yes

Lord JAMES of HEREFORD But, Mr Bankes, if it does not disturb your argument, I have my doubts as to what is the meaning of the words as applied to a cause of action—"maintaining a strike"

Mr ELDON BANKES It means this, my Lord—take this Supposing the strike to be in existence, and a lawful strike——

Lord JAMES of HEREFORD Yes, but the strike is over, of course going out without giving notice of the termination of the contract is an illegal act, but in this case the time had run out, because the employers were asking them to work on fresh contracts and treated the old ones as at an end That being so I do not see that there is any illegality The workmen refused to enter into a new contract That is perfectly legal

Mr ELDON BANKES May I explain my position? I will put a hypothetical case Suppose, for instance, that at any given works there is a perfectly lawful strike, we will assume that it has been going on for a fortnight, it is a strike that the men were entitled to engage in, and it had been going on for a fortnight, and supposing somebody were to come to me and say Now look here, there is a chance of the men going back, and I say Well, I will take very good care they do not go back, I will come down to-morrow with 20 men and I will molest every man who attempts to go back Now if that is so I maintain that strike by unlawful means, by going down there with a *posse comitatus* and molest the men who are desirous to go back Now that is what we mean by "maintaining the strike by unlawful means" It means on this assumption that a strike was commenced —whether it was legal or illegal is immaterial for this purpose

Lord JAMES of HEREFORD Quite right

Mr ELDON BANKES But pending the strike the Union, by its officials, molested and intimidated our workmen

Lord JAMES of HEREFORD Will you excuse me Mr Bankes Maintaining a strike may be perfectly legal

Mr ELDON BANKES Keep it going

Lord JAMES of HEREFORD Keep it going perfectly legally by subscriptions (it did occur not long ago) from persons who desired the strike, they kept the men—supported them

Lord DAVEY Like a man who would prevent scholars coming to a school

Lord JAMES of HEREFORD Yes, I was going to suggest that I do not think this has got much to do with Trades Unions and strikes I was going to give you that very instance It really is individual action which is not unlawful in itself

Mr ELDON BANKES That is it my Lord

Lord JAMES of HEREFORD If it prevents individuals taking a course which prevents the business of the complainant being carried on, I think you will find that you must show that it prevents the business of complainant being carried on It is not a question of strike at all

Mr ELDON BANKES No, my Lord, and I wish very often these things were kept to their real legal principles apart from the questions of strike and so forth This is a legal question pure and simple, whether or not the cause of action can be established by reason of certain individuals having unlawfully molested and intimidated our workmen

Lord JAMES of HEREFORD That is so

Mr ELDON BANKES And in consequence of that we use the words "maintain the strike," or, if you like, "prolong the strike"

Lord JAMES of HEREFORD I have nothing to do with prolonging the strike, I think it is preventing people coming

Mr ELDON BANKES If your Lordship pleases I will confine it to that

Lord JAMES of HEREFORD You will find all these cases most fully collected in the Mogul case—the wild duck and the decoy and the school--that is all as to carrying on the business

Mr ELDON BANKES I quite agree that "maintaining the strike" is not a legal expression or a term of art, but it is a compendious phrase that was used The essence of the cause of action is the unlawful act of intimidating and molesting the workmen And our case is that it was done by the agents of the Union Now, of course, for this purpose I will assume that the argument I have addressed to your Lordships upon the rules is not right, because I need not address any argument to your Lordships if the rule is right and the branch officials were the agents *ab initio*, therefore I have got to establish that there was evidence upon which the Jury could properly come to the conclusion either that the Union appointed these men their agents *ad hoc* to conduct the strike or that the permanent officials at Barnsley so interfered in the strike as, in the language of the Master of the Rolls, to make common cause with the branch officials and direct them Well, of course, again I could indicate to your Lordships the kind of evidence that I rely upon on either of these two grounds There is a passage in the rules to which I wish to call attention, because I have not emphasised this particular point before This is in Rule 12, page 96 It is by inference that I bring this point home Rule 12 says " A registered vote shall be taken throughout the entire Association whenever any number of branches numbering one-fourth of the Council demand such vote on the following questions, viz The adoption or prolongation of a strike ' Now stop there It is quite true that this is a case in which the rule is directed to deal with the cases where a registered vote is to be taken, but upon that point, which is a point which may often come up for decision and be a matter which the Association will have to decide upon —what ? The adoption of any particular strike That is a thing that the rule indicates as a matter which will have to come up for decision, and in certain cases they say if a certain number of branches require it they will have to go before the district, but if that requisition is not made who has got to decide that ? Well of course, the Council have got to decide it They have got to decide whether they will adopt any strike Now, if that is within the purposes—the lawful purposes of an Association—whether they will adopt a strike, could any stronger evidence be given than we have given in this case that they adopted this strike ? There may be many strikes which the Association would have a difficulty in stopping but there was no difficulty about stopping this strike if they wanted to stop it There were two ways they might have adopted if they wanted to stop it They could have passed a resolution forbidding the branch officials to take any part in it I venture to think that any Jury, after reading

L

these speeches and knowing the history of this strike, would have come to the conclusion that if the branch officials had been debarred from taking any part in this strike it would have fizzled out within a week or a fortnight. But whether this view is right or not they could properly have withheld strike pay from these men, and in that way they could have stopped the strike at once.

Lord JAMES of HEREFORD: Suppose the question to arise as to whether it was a legal strike in the sense of breaking the contract or not, is there any ground for suggesting that the paying of strike pay was any offence at all?

Mr ELDON BANKES: No, my Lord, the point is this. Your Lordship will see I have got to go by steps. The question is whether they adopted this strike. I will ask your Lordship to assume for a moment that they adopted it. Very well. Now, having adopted it, to whom did they give the control of it?

Lord JAMES of HEREFORD: Do you mean by "adopting" any more than granting strike pay?

Mr ELDON BANKES: Yes.

Lord JAMES of HEREFORD: What?

Mr ELDON BANKES: Of course, among other things, the granting of the strike pay is also bringing in the forces of the Union to assist in it—bringing to bear all the aid that can be obtained from the officials of the Union. "Adopting" a thing means this. You may adopt it and say, I will not do anything more, but you may adopt it and say, I will adopt it and assist it.

Lord JAMES of HEREFORD: That is your point. Do you include in that what you call the illegal act of stopping the people going to work?

Mr ELDON BANKES: Yes, my Lord. My point is this. First of all, it is clearly within the purview of the rules that they could adopt the strike. My second point is this. Assume they adopt the strike, the next thing is this—to whom do they give the control of it? Now, who did manage this strike? Well, there is no doubt the branch officials managed it. Who were they managing it for? Now, Lord Justice Mathew says they were having a sort of game of their own, they were a "Union" in themselves, and they were doing it for themselves, but apart from any such view of the rules, which I submit cannot properly be taken, who were they managing it for? Now, assume the Association had adopted it,— I submit that the obvious inference of fact is that the Union branch officials were allowed to manage it, and if they were allowed to manage it they were appointed agents *ad hoc*. I could refer your

Lordship to a good many passages in the evidence in support of that, but I should like just to call attention to this,—that every resolution that was passed was entered in the society's books—every payment that was made was made out of the society's money—in the first instance no doubt by the local treasurer, but afterwards passed by the auditor; the expense of the bellman to summon the meeting of June 29th was paid by the branch, and passed by the auditor, the wages of the Committeemen who met and passed these various resolutions were paid by the local treasurer and passed by the auditor, the expenses of that ballot as to whether the men should give in their notices were paid by the local treasurer,—passed by the auditor, the cost of the notices themselves was paid out of the local funds and passed by the auditor. Then, my Lord, again——

Lord JAMES of HEREFORD. There is no local treasurer or branch treasurer. Whose funds were they actually?

Mr ELDON BANKES. They were the funds of the Union. They were collected from the members of the Union who are members of the branch.

Lord DAVEY. I thought the branch paid their own expenses, did not they?

Mr ELDON BANKES. Yes, my Lord. Your Lordships have not had attention called (perhaps it is convenient that I should call attention to it at this moment) yet to the details of the expenses. Your Lordships will see how the books are kept.

Lord DAVEY. If that is so, according to the rules the local treasurer first pays his own expenses—I mean the expenses of his branch.

Mr ELDON BANKES. Yes.

Lord DAVEY. Then he hands over the balance to the general Association.

Mr ELDON BANKES. Yes, but the books are audited and therefore any expenses not properly incurred would be disallowed presumably, and although they were the expenses of the branch they were expenses of the Union. The copies of the books or accounts are at page 244.

Lord DAVEY. When it is said the branch initiates and carries it on, on its own account, they may deduct that; they are at perfect liberty to do it. Whether they could pay strike pay or not is another question, but they are quite at liberty to carry out the strike.

Mr ELDON BANKES. Yes.

Lord DAVEY And they can charge the expenses of their so doing in their accounts

Mr ELDON BANKES Yes, of course That is such a strong argument in my favour from my point of view, I say that that is part of the business of the branch and they could not charge it properly to the accounts, unless it were branch business and it is the branch business that the rules say they are to manage

Lord DAVEY That is what I assume

Mr ELDON BANKES My Lord, the accounts are at page 224 and onwards May I take you to page 249, because that is the material point—the first item of the initiation of the strike If I may, I will just run through the details on that page

Lord JAMES of HEREFORD "Cash to district", is that the District Association?

Mr ELDON BANKES Yes it is paid to Barnsley Your Lordship will see on the other side the amounts First of all they have on the left hand side the contributions from members—paid apparently (sometimes) every fortnight

Lord DAVEY Are these the accounts of the Association or of the branch?

Mr ELDON BANKES This is the Denaby branch, my Lord There are the contributions of members, totalling up from July 5th to September 27th to £400 17s 3d Then on the other side you see "Paid to Branch" (what exactly that means I do not know) "Cash to District" (that means sent to Barnsley) "Deputations —Organising—Collecting—P O Stationery—Joint Deputation— Bellman, 8s —Committee, Special—Organising—Balloting men" (Now, my Lord, the dates are not right, that is not "July 5th"— that was July 17th, perhaps entered on July 19th) "Balloting men—Cash to District—P O and Stationery—Joint Committee and Special—Deputation—Cash to District £90—P O Order and Stationery — Bellman — Organising — Committees and Special— Stationery, &c —Cash to Districts—P O and Stationery—Collecting —Serving out Notices, £3 10s " (those were the notices as to whether they should go back to work or not) "Bellman—Committee's Cash to District—Collecting—P O and Stationery—Joint Committee," and so forth and so forth That is an illustration They are all the same I do not want to occupy more time than I usefully ought I do not want to go through the evidence because I rely so much upon what Lord Justice Cozens-Hardy said about this, because his view again (1044 under the head "4") is this he says "The strike thus commenced was continued and maintained by the branch officials and the branch members by unlawful means—viz, by molestation and intimidation," I respectfully submit that if anybody goes through the evidence (your Lordships have it all before you now) any Jury in the world would be justified in coming to the conclusion that the men were molested and intimidated, and that that molestation and intimidation was organised and controlled and directed by the branch officials. You remember what Nolan says, that the women had done their duty, and so forth, and so forth. Your Lordship will remember it all.

Lord JAMES of HEREFORD: Were the molesters paid— the men who molested, were they paid at all?

Mr ELDON BANKES: Of course, the president the treasurer and the secretary get their wages under the rules, they get a certain amount according to the number of members in the branch. The Committeemen apparently only got paid for the Committees they attended, but whether they had a Committee meeting in order to go out and take charge of these men or not we cannot tell.

Now, my Lord, my submission upon this is shortly that there was abundant evidence upon which the Jury could come to the conclusion that the branch officials were appointed *ad hoc* as agents of the Association to conduct the strike, and that whilst acting as such agents they did take part in the molestation and intimidation which were complained of. Of course, in that view it is not necessary to make out that the Union officials at Barnsley were directly concerned in this from that point of view, but we have included certain of these officials in our action, and the Jury have found a verdict against them, saying that they acted as agents, and I submit there is abundant evidence to support that, and I put that part of the case shortly on this ground—that, assuming for the moment that the Association appointed the branch official agents *ad hoc* to manage, it is plain that the local officials were in constant touch with Barnsley, and that whenever a crisis occurred an appeal was made to Barnsley for the assistance that was required, and it was forthcoming. Your Lordship will remember that early on the 14th July, when the question arose as to how they should convert this unlawful strike into a lawful strike Barnsley was appealed to in order that officials should be sent down who should induce the men to go through what ultimately turned out to be this farce of giving in their notices before they went back to work, therefore you directly connect the Barnsley officials with what is going on, and the second occasion when Mr Pope's circular was thought likely to bring the men back to work again Parrott and Walsh were sent down to strengthen the backs of the faint-hearted, and above and beyond all, the fact that Mr Pickard engineered this scheme of paying the strike pay, it shows a direct control from Barnsley, and the scheme by which the strike pay was ultimately paid was the result of Mr

Pickard's interference and suggestion, and on all these grounds I submit——

Lord JAMES of HEREFORD Where did the strike pay absolutely come from—Barnsley direct?

Mr ELDON BANKES The treasurer, Mr Hall, brought it down every week

Lord JAMES of HEREFORD Can you give me a reference to that?

Mr ELDON BANKES That he brought it every week?

Lord JAMES of HEREFORD I only want to know that Hall brought it Perhaps your junior could tell us where to find it

Mr ELDON BANKES It is so, but I am afraid I cannot put my hand on the reference at the moment It is in Mr Hall's evidence—891, my Lord, I am told, on 912

The LORD CHANCELLOR You can supply it afterwards

Lord JAMES of HEREFORD I only want the date of it

Mr ELDON BANKES The first payment was on the 16th July

Mr DANCKWERTS No

Mr ELDON BANKES Yes, it dated from the 16th July

Mr DANCKWERTS No, it was the 24th

Mr ELDON BANKES The first payment was made on the 24th, but it dated from the 16th

Mr DANCKWERTS It was to date from the 17th, you said the 16th.

Lord JAMES of HEREFORD It runs from the 17th

Mr ELDON BANKES It ran from the 17th, which your Lordship will remember was the day on which the Company refused to allow the men to go back unless they signed on again, and that was stated by Mr Pickard to be a refusal to employ, and therefore a lock-out

Now I do not want to go at length into the decisions of the Court of Appeal or of this House in Howden's case, but I might call attention to this that in the Judgment of the Lord Justices in Howden's case, both Lord Justice Vaughan Williams and Lord Justice Mathew, after going through all these facts about throwing the notice into the buckets and going to work, they both said in terms that in their opinion the thing was a sham. Howden's case in the Court of Appeal is reported in 1903 King's Bench, at page 308, but Lord Justice Vaughan Williams says (on page 333) that "The resolution passed by the men and the correspondence clearly show that the men never meant to resume work as before the strike, but only intended to go back for the purpose of putting the strike which had already commenced in order under Rule 64. It would have been a sham return, and a sham resumption of work." And then Lord Justice Mathew says the proposal to resume employment was a sham under such circumstances, that the men never got back to their employment. The only importance of that, from my point of view is this that on the particular question as to whether there was evidence that the Association made what the Master of the Rolls calls "common purpose" with the branch is that if all this scheme was a sham it was a sham engineered from Barnsley, and it is impossible to say under those circumstances. I submit that the Jury were not justified in finding that not only the Association appointed these local officials agents ad hoc, but that the officials at Barnsley themselves were making common cause and directing the strike from Barnsley, and under those circumstances they themselves would be responsible.

Now, my Lord, that finishes what I have got to say on the second point. The third point I think I mentioned to your Lordship was as to whether there was evidence of a conspiracy to molest and injure. Now again, of course, this is not wanted if we succeed on the other two points. The Jury found that there was such a conspiracy. Your Lordship has pointed out that they did not answer as against which of the Defendants, I think, but no objection was taken at the time, or in the notices of appeal to that, and I think my friends would agree with me that it was understood by everybody that this was intended to be a comprehensive affirmative answer for the Plaintiffs. The question your Lordship will see is 9 "Did the Defendants or any and which of them unlawfully and maliciously conspire together, and with workmen formerly in the employ of the Plaintiffs, to molest and injure the Plaintiffs"

The LORD CHANCELLOR Mr Bankes, upon this it may be that you are right, and that we ought to draw the conclusion that it was intended as a general affirmative answer, it may be, but in point of fact it does not say which of the Defendants conspired and it does not say which of the matters mentioned in Question 6 they conspired to do. You see Question 6 involves three things, one of which is with regard to strike pay. It may be that we ought to put a larger construction upon it

Mr ELDON BANKES My Lord, I was reading 9, 9 has no reference to 6

The LORD CHANCELLOR I was reading 8

Mr ELDON BANKES Oh, 8, I beg your Lordship's pardon

The LORD CHANCELLOR You see that

Mr ELDON BANKES Oh, yes

The LORD CHANCELLOR The same observation does apply to 9, too, but not quite so much

Mr ELDON BANKES There is a double observation with regard to 8, because they do not find which of the Defendants or which of the objects, but in 9 it is simply that they do not answer which of the Defendants, and I submit that those three were clearly accepted by everybody as being a comprehensive affirmative answer

Mr DANCKWERTS No

Mr ELDON BANKES My friend says no All I can say is if they were not, then the time to say it was when the verdict was given

Mr DANCKWERTS We took no responsibility

Mr ELDON BANKES I think it is intended as an affirmative answer, and if there had been any doubt about it my learned friend ought to have said Will you ask the Jury whether they mean that or whether they mean something else It was not for us to say it They answered all as I submit Upon that I will not occupy your Lordships' time, the evidence is all before the House Here again, I submit, that there was abundant evidence if the Jury had thought fit to accept our view, that there was an intention to molest and injure and for this reason the men who are responsible for this strike, it is quite plain from their speeches, adopted a most aggressive attitude towards the manager They for some reason or another had got a grievance against him, whether it was justified or not it is not material for my present purpose to consider I submit it was not, but in the first speech made when Walsh goes down on the 14th July, he says What a pity it is you cannot strike this terrible blow at Mr Chambers that you originally intended It is open to the Jury that where there is a strike which there are no circumstances to justify, having regard to the condition of the men, or the alleged complaint- if you find there is a general strike instituted where there is no general ground of complaint, followed by violent language against the manager on every occasion on which the opportunity offers—violent language and violent attacks upon him—when you find a fire breaking out at a pit the refusal to allow men to go to work, and there is language such as this, that unless you apply to us for leave we will let the blazes out at the top of the pit, and so forth—all these matters are matters for the Jury, and it was quite open to them to say that the people who were engineering this strike were not actuated by any real desire to benefit the men so much as to have a direct, deliberate attack upon the manager and upon those who employ him

My Lord, the fact is that after this disastrous strike lasting all these months the men went back on exactly the same terms as they had been before   They had gained nothing   There was nothing for them to gain, and under those circumstances it is open to the Jury to find, where otherwise they could not properly find   If you prove serious grievances or oppression of the men or unfair conditions you may reasonably say   Well that is a case of men who are on strike to benefit their position, but where you find, as here, men taken out without any rhyme or reason, and as I say, this exaggerated language used, men coerced and intimidated to remain away from work and yet remain in the houses of the Company paying no rent, when you find all this and put all these things together you cannot complain if the Jury find against people who are responsible for this kind of thing that they were not actuated by the legitimate motive of improving the men's condition, that they brought this about in order as they say to strike the terrible blow at Mr Chambers, the manager, who, for some reason or other, some portion of the men at any rate chose to dislike

My Lord, the passage in that particular speech about striking the "terrible blow" is in one of the earlier speeches, it is at page 403, my Lord, "E"   That, my Lord, is the speech I was going to refer to because I asked your Lordship to note it in reference to what Lord Justice Cozens-Hardy said   That no men sent from Barnsley made an inflammatory speech   That is at page 403   This is Walsh He says "that along with his colleague Wadsworth he had come there that morning in order to assist them out of their difficulty and in the first place he must congratulate them on the spirit they had displayed during the past fortnight in resenting the conduct of their manager during the past two years in regard to their grievances   I am sorry to think that you placed yourselves in such a position that you were not able to strike that terrible blow at Mr Chambers that you originally intended you could If you had struck this blow three years ago, from the feeling that was displayed in Council yesterday, the Council would have given you strike pay "   Now that is not the kind of language where men are suffering from a legitimate grievance   It is the language of people who are incensed and inflamed against a particular individual

Now, my Lord, I have almost finished   I come now to deal with this question of ratification   It is quite a secondary part of our case, because if we are right on these other propositions we do not want it   The difficulty about that part of the case is not, as I

submit, a difficulty in fact and is not found to be a difficulty in fact
by the Lords Justices   The difficulty, which they there state as a
difficulty of law, arises from this question of ' purporting "   Now
the whole difficulty arose because of a recent decision in this House
in Keighley Maxted v Durant   My Lord, that was a case of
contract, and it was decided in this House that in a case of contract
where a case of ratification of an act of an agent was sought to be
established it was necessary to prove that the agent purported in
this sense—that he indicated to the other contracting party at the
time of the contract that he was contracting on behalf of the person
who afterwards sought to ratify   That is established with regard to
contract, and, of course, one can see a reason why that should be,
because in a case of contract one contracting party may say   well, it
is a question of contract   It is a question of consensus of mind, you
cannot ratify a contract made by somebody with me as your contract,
unless at the time I made it I was given notice that you were the
person on whose behalf it was made , but such a doctrine, I submit,
with reference to a tort is altogether out of place, and for this
reason   Of course the man who commits the tort must purport to
act as agent in this sense—that he must be intending to do it for the
principal and not for himself, but to say that at the time he commits
the tort he is bound to tell the other man he is doing it, I submit
there is no foundation for at all and no reason for it, if in the
omnibus case the Omnibus Company were not liable unless the
omnibus driver at the time he slashed the man across his face said
this is one from the Omnibus Company   My Lord, I submit that
you are bound to show that he was intending to act as a servant of
the Omnibus Company, you are bound to show at the time that you
do it on behalf of the Omnibus Company, I say that would go beyond
anything that appears in any of the cases quoted, and for which
there is not any foundation   It was upon that ground that the
Master of the Rolls said at the bottom of 1026   " If the rules do not
make the Union responsible for the acts of the branch officials, I
agree with my colleagues that they did not become liable by
ratification   I think there was no evidence of ' purporting ' on the
part of the branch officials to act for the Union, and I am not
prepared to say, since the decision of Durant v Roberts in the House
of Lords that purporting is not a necessary condition of possible
ratification even in the case of a tort nor am I satisfied that ratification
was legally *intra vires* "   That is what the learned Lord Justice is
referring to—not as a question of fact that there was no evidence of
ratification, but that there was no evidence of purporting in the
sense of having announced at the time that they were acting as
agents   My Lord, my case with regard to that is this—that there
is no foundation for that view of the law, and that, so far as the facts
go, these men throughout purported in every sense to act as agents
of the Union   They never purported to do anything else whenever
the matter was referred to

Lord DAVEY   Who are you referring to ?

Mr ELDON BANKES Now, the branch officials They never purported to do anything else Of course, in this connection, the speeches are the main thing Well, now, upon that the Jury had got this before them—that nobody ever spoke at any one of these meetings unless he was a branch official, and the resolutions which followed from these speeches were all recorded in the Minute Book, and on several occasions such language as this was employed by the men Well you grumble, if you do not like what we are doing, appoint someone in our place Your Lordship remembers that occurs on several occasions—language such as this We have brought you out, and if we get strike pay we will not let you go back again The speeches are all before your Lordships and I need not go into them in detail My submission is this Here again if it is necessary to rely upon this part of the case there is abundant evidence to justify the verdict of the Jury

My Lord, I think, I have addressed all the observations which I can to your Lordships upon this very long case and I have endeavoured to summarise it as well as I can May I say in conclusion this, my friend Mr Lush is with me and if your Lordships will allow it, instead of following me now he will reply on behalf of the Plaintiffs—if that view is one which your Lordships will allow

The LORD CHANCELLOR Do you mean only two Counsel?

Mr ELDON BANKES, Only two Counsel my Lord

The LORD CHANCELLOR Then you are within your rights

Mr ELDON BANKES There is one point more I ought to have mentioned—would your Lordship forgive me—that is this Your Lordship will remember that the Master of the Rolls said that as far as this part of the case is concerned he was not satisfied that the matter did not come within Poulton's case, but I wanted to refer to Ashbury Railway Carriage and Iron Company v. Riche, which is reported in Law Reports 7 House of Lords cases, page 653 It is one of the many cases in which it has been held that a Company cannot ratify acts which are *ultra vires,* but at page 668 Lord Cairns points out the distinction between the Memorandum and the Articles of a Company—that the objects of a Company are contained in its Memorandum, and that a Company doing something which is not within its objects that act is *ultra vires* the Company, that these may be acts which are contrary to the directions in the Articles, but those acts may be *ultra vires* the directors, and not *ultra vires* the Company, and that the Company may properly ratify an act which is *ultra vires* the directors when it cannot ratify an act which is *ultra vires* the Company

Now, my Lord, I do not think the question arises in this case of course, but I just wanted to mention it, because it has been said against us that in this particular case this particular strike pay was *ultra vires*, and was held to be *ultra vires*, and that therefore it could not be ratified. As far as I remember the argument, the whole case for ratification does not depend upon anything to do with the strike pay. Our case with regard to ratification has reference to the procuring of men to break their contracts, and that cannot be said to be *ultra vires*, and if it was *ultra vires* at all, it was only *ultra vires* in the sense that it is *ultra vires* the directors, and therefore it is an act which is capable of ratification.

Lord DAVEY. That raises a very curious question. Your Memorandum and your Articles of Association—if I may adopt that language—are all moulded into one document, into the rules, and you have to ascertain from the nature of the rules whether it is "Memorandum," or whether it is "Articles."

Mr ELDON BANKES. Yes, my Lord, and if your Lordship looks at the rules you will find there is a rule which deals with the objects, and that would, I think, be the 'Memorandum,' and the others I should submit would be the "Articles." I think there is great difficulty in saying that any of it is *ultra vires*.

Lord DAVEY. It is a difficulty which I have felt before.

Mr ELDON BANKES. And I quite feel it too, my Lord.

Lord DAVEY. We have had these rules before us in another case.

Mr ELDON BANKES. Quite true, my Lord, in Howden's case.

Lord DAVEY. It is a very curious question.

Mr ELDON BANKES. I only mentioned it so as to show that I had not passed over it. That is what we rely upon but my friend will elaborate it more, if it is made a point of on the other side, when he comes to reply. There is only one other point I will just mention, and it is this. If it is necessary for us to rely as a part of the cause of action upon this payment of the strike pay our case is this—that it has never been decided what constitutes an unlawful act within the meaning of the rule which says that a conspiracy is a conspiracy to do a lawful act by unlawful means. It has never been decided, but "unlawful" in that sense means, and it is plain, as I submit, that it cannot mean indictable or criminal, because you might plainly have, as I submit a cause of action for conspiring to slander a man, which is not a criminal offence, and in this particular case the paying of strike pay has been held by this House to be not only *ultra vires* but illegal.

Lord DAVEY   Not authorised by the rules

Mr ELDON BANKES   And illegal

Lord DAVEY   When was it introduced into the Order of this House ?

Mr ELDON BANKES   I will give your Lordship the reference   It is in 1905 Appeal Cases at page 256

Lord DAVEY   In that sense, of course, it is if the officers of the Association deal with money in a way which they are not authorised to do, that is in a sense illegal

Mr ELDON BANKES   My Lord, I am not saying for a moment in what sense the word was used, but the Decision is in 1905 Appeal Cases, pages 256

Lord JAMES of HEREFORD   What is the case ?

Mr ELDON BANKES   The Yorkshire Miners' Association v Howden   There Lord Macnaghten says this at page 266   "One word as to the form of the order under Appeal   I think it is most objectionable, and I trust it will not form a precedent   I think, and I may add that the Lord Chancellor agrees with me in thinking, that the order should be varied by prohibiting directly and in terms the diversion of the funds of the Union to the particular purpose which the Court holds to be unauthorised   I would suggest (and I may mention that the Lord Chancellor agrees) that the order might go in the following terms   'Declare that the payment of strike pay to the financial members of the Yorkshire Miners' Association in pursuance of the resolution of the Council of the said Association passed on the 24th July and confirmed on the 11th of August, 1902, was in contravention of the rules of the Association, and that the said resolution purporting to authorise such payment was *ultra vires* and illegal "

Lord MACNAGHTEN   That was a branch of the requirements of the Act of Parliament as well as of the rules.

Mr ELDON BANKES   Yes my Lord, that is what I was going to say   Of course, our submission is that the case of a Trades Union is not the same as the case which your Lordship put to me of a trustee, because, of course, a trustee is under a contractual obligation—or I suppose it is a contractual obligation—not to misappropriate the trust funds ; but here this Association is a registered Association, and its rules have, at any rate, something in the nature of the force of an Act of Parliament, and, therefore, if this payment is made it is made illegally in a different and a wider sense than the misappropriation by a trustee of trust money, and if it is necessary for us to contend, we are prepared to contend that the payment of this strike pay was unlawful in the sense in which the word is used where it is said that the conspiracy consists in doing a lawful thing by unlawful means

Lord JAMES of HEREFORD Why do you say "unlawful"? By reason of what Act was it unlawful?

Mr ELDON BANKES Because it was a payment against the rules

Lord JAMES of HEREFORD You come to that, and that is the same in Howden's case—"against the rules"

Mr ELDON BANKES Yes

Lord MACNAGHTEN And against rules prescribed by Act of Parliament

Mr ELDON BANKES Against rules prescribed by Act of Parliament and by the Trades Unions Act Of course, your Lordship will follow that Howden's case was a decision upon this particular payment

Lord JAMES of HEREFORD I know Mr Bankes, are you quite sure of your ground that the employer of labour against whom the strike goes has a better cause of action because the person who is paying and the men break their own rules between themselves?

Mr ELDON BANKES That is the point as to which I said I was not in quite such calm water That, of course, is a difficult question of law, but our proposition is that in this particular case, having regard to the fact that the payment was against the rules which were framed in accordance with and subject to the Act of Parliament, it was an illegal and an unlawful act, and as such it clearly comes within the definition which has always been accepted

Lord DAVEY They might have changed that rule relating to strike pay, in a proper manner, of course, and with proper safeguards provided by the rules themselves They might have altered that rule and made strike pay payable on other events

Mr ELDON BANKES Yes, but, my Lord, that would be an alteration of the rule under statutory authority and creating a fresh statutory authority

Lord DAVEY It would be the authority of the rules themselves The rules themselves give the power to do it.

Mr ELDON BANKES Yes but the Trades Union Act provides, my Lord, for the alteration of the rules

Lord DAVEY Does it?

Mr ELDON BANKES Yes

Lord DAVEY I thought it was in the rules themselves

Mr ELDON BANKES It is in the Act, my Lord It is one of the things I know in the Act

Lord DAVEY They may make rules about strike pay

Mr ELDON BANKES Yes

Lord DAVEY Oh, yes

Mr ELDON BANKES They may make rules for the purpose, and they may alter the rules

Lord DAVEY It is in the rules themselves

Mr ELDON BANKES It is in the schedule, my Lord The Act of Parliament says that their rules shall provide for the matters referred to in the schedule, and one of the matters referred to in the schedule is the manner of making, altering, or rescinding rules

Lord DAVEY If you look at the words you will find it in the rules themselves

Mr ELDON BANKES Yes, my Lord, I think that would be so That is the argument I have to present to your Lordships

Mr DANCKWERTS My Lords, I appear with my friends Mr Rufus Isaacs and Mr Clement Edwards for the Respondent Association My friends Mr Atherley Jones, Mr Evans and Mr Compton appear for the individual Defendants other than the trustees My Lords the trustees are not represented My Lord, it was arranged that Mr Isaacs should open the case for the Respondents, but owing to an accident I unfortunately have at some short notice to begin it myself My Lord, what I have to submit for the consideration of the House is that the Judgments of the majority of the Court of Appeal and of the three Judges so far as they are unanimous are correct, and what I desire to do is to put before the House at once certain propositions which we submit are correct propositions The first is that any act which is *extra vires* of the Association cannot be treated as an act of the Association whether done or authorised by the Council or any one else Second, my Lord, that any act which is *intra vires* of the Association, but *extra vires* of the Council cannot be treated as the act of the Association if done or authorised by the Council Then, my Lord, 3—which is perhaps stating the second proposition in a slightly different form To bind the Association the act done or authorised by the Council must be *intra vires* of both the Association, and the Council, 4th an act *extra vires* of the Association cannot be adopted or ratified by an Association or Council , 5th an act *extra vires* of the Council cannot be adopted or ratified by the Council even though *intra vires* of the Association

My Lord, the next proposition is that the rules, though required to be made by the Statute, are still made binding by way of contract, or are nevertheless made binding by way of contract

Lord JAMES of HEREFORD Give me the first one again, Mr Danckwerts

Mr DANCKWERTS My Lord, that the rules though requiring to be made by the Statute and registered in the case of a Registered Trade Union, are still matters which rest in contract and are binding as matters of contract, and that everyone dealing with a Registered Trade Union must be deemed to have notice of the rules

My Lord, with regard to the rules I have to submit this that under them the delegates to the Council represent nobody but the branch that has elected the delegate, and that the branch officials are not officials of the Union, but officials of the branches for branch purposes , and I submit further that any official of the Union who is such for a particular purpose cannot be treated as representing the Union for all purposes

My Lord, with respect to the doctrine of Barwick v The English Joint Stock Bank, the latest case in which that has been reviewed and applied is in the Court of Appeal in Thorne v Heard, 1894, 1 Chancery 599 Your Lordship will remember that in Barwick v The English Joint Stock Bank Mr Justice Wills, who delivered the Judgment there, began the proposition which has been so often referred to by my learned friend, by saving that when a person has been put into such a position as that people are entitled to assume he is there for doing a certain class of acts, then if he does them in the course of his service and for the benefit of his employer, the employer is bound, whether or not he is given a prior command That is the whole of that proposition And, my Lord, at page 611, the Lord Justice Kaye conveniently sums up the law in a very short passage "In Barwick v English Joint Stock Bank Mr Justice Wills stated the general rule to be 'that the master is answerable for every such wrong of the servant or agent as is committed in the course of the service and for the master's benefit, though no express command or privity of the master be proved" My Lord, as I understand that the whole of that proposition simply comes to this, that if a person is put in a position in which he is to be assumed to have the authority to do a certain class of acts and in the course of his service he does for the benefit of his master an act coming within that class then the master is bound although there be no prior authorisation on the part of the master in regard to the particular matter

The LORD CHANCELLOR. Was not Barwick a "holding out" case?

Mr DANCKWERTS. No, my Lord, it was not a "holding out" case. Then Lord Justice Kaye goes on "This passage was cited with approval by Lord Selborne in Houldsworth v City of Glasgow Bank and it was deliberately decided in British Mutual Banking Company v Charnwood Forest Railway Company that the words 'for the master's benefit' in that statement of the doctrine are essential, and that where an agent in the course of his employment committed a fraud, not for his principal's benefit but for the benefit of himself, and the principal did not benefit by such fraud, he could not" (in fact) "be made liable for it." Your Lordship will see, I think, I am right in saying that the whole of the thing there depends upon the man having been put into the place where, in the course of his assumed service it can be assumed that he was doing the act in the course of his service.

In the case of Keighley Maxted v Durant your Lordship will find that in several of the Judgments the question—particularly if I remember rightly Lord Robertson's opinion—the question whether the doctrine applied to torts as well as to contract is discussed. I will not refer to it further, but there are two express decisions of the Exchequer Chamber upon the point. Buron v Denman is one, 2 (Old) Exchequer 167. In that case the captain of an English man-of-war had attacked a foreign vessel on the ground that it was a slaver, and he did so with his man-of-war as representing the Crown. It turned out that it was not a slaver, I think—at all events, for some reason the act was not in accordance with the law bearing upon the subject.

Lord DAVEY. It was not, but it might have been. It might have been not in accordance with his instructions, but exceeding his instructions.

Mr. DANCKWERTS. I think there was some question of the Slavery Convention there, and the Crown adopted the Act, and thereby said it made it an act of State, which, being committed against a foreigner, was, of course, not examinable in any of our Courts. That was the question decided in that case—that it was open to the Crown in those circumstances to adopt and ratify the act on the ground that the man had done it in his capacity of a servant of the Crown,

M

Lord DAVEY. That he had done it as a duty.

Mr DANCKWERTS. Your Lordship will see if the Crown had not adopted the act (I think it was argued on demurrer—it being in the Exchequer Chamber), it being on the presumption, an unlawful act, he would have been liable for it towards the foreigner.

The LORD CHANCELLOR. No, no, Mr Danckwerts, surely he would not.

Mr DANCKWERTS. Yes.

The LORD CHANCELLOR. Whenever the Crown thinks proper to adopt an act of war, or anything of that kind, there is an end of it. You must look to the Crown as an act of State, surely.

Mr DANCKWERTS. I agree. I said if the Crown had not adopted it—that is what the Court said—if the Crown had not adopted it he would be liable; but because the Crown had adopted it and ratified it therefore it became an Act of State.

Lord DAVEY. Is there any question of adoption as between private individuals?

Mr DANCKWERTS. The Court of Exchequer said the same doctrine applied to subjects.

Lord DAVEY. If I remember the case the Secretary of State wrote a despatch in which it appeared that although it was not strictly within the instructions, or might not be within the instructions, of Captain Denman, it was an act which the State adopted and approved, and there was an end of it.

Mr DANCKWERTS. Yes, my Lord, but there the point was in fact that Captain Denman had no authority at the time he did the act.

The LORD CHANCELLOR. Very well.

Mr DANCKWERTS. Now my Lord, the other case is Phillips v. Eyre, Law Reports, 6 Queen's Bench.

Lord DAVEY. What is the proposition you are quoting this to support?

Mr DANCKWERTS. My Lord, that the doctrine of ratification ended when the man purported to do it on behalf of a principal. That applies both to tort and to contract. My learned friend, Mr Bankes, in his concluding observations, disputed that proposition

Lord DAVEY That was Mr Bankes contention all along.

Mr DANCKWERTS His contention was that it did not apply to torts

Lord DAVEY His contention was that it did

Mr DANCKWERTS No, the other way, my Lord——

Lord ATKINSON His contention was preface to an act

Mr DANCKWERTS I am content in this case to say it does apply, my Lord Mr Justice Wills, in delivering the Judgment of the Exchequer Chamber in that case, lays down the doctrine exactly in the same way as it is laid down in this House with regard to contracts I may take it here from page 246 of 1901 Appeal Cases, where Lord Macnaghten adopts the language of Chief Justice Tindal in Wilson v Tumman, which was a case of contract—" That an act done for another by a person, not assuming to act for himself, but for such other person, though without any precedent and authority whatever, becomes the act of the principal if subsequently ratified by him, is the known and well established rule of law" There Chief Justice Tindal lays it down on the broad lines as applicable to both, whatever the nature of the act is

Now, my Lord, in the case of The Yorkshire Miners' Association v Howden it was an admitted fact that in reality Howden's action was being prosecuted by the present Appellants for their own purposes, and it is so admitted in this case, too, my Lord, and throughout this case from the hearing before Mr Justice Lawrance upwards the parties have assumed that the decision in Howden's case was applicable in this Your Lordship will remember in this House Lord Davey and Lord James of Hereford differed from the rest of their Lordships on the question of whether the action lay at all owing to the provisions of the Trades Unions Act, but all the members of the House agreed that the facts were as they were laid down in the Judgment of the Court below That will be seen very plainly from Lord Macnaghten's Judgment at page 263, where he adopted the views of the Court below, and your Lordship will remember the Respondents were stopped in that case upon the fact and the only question which they were called upon to argue was the question of law

Now, my Lord, in that case there are some useful points which I submit are equally true on the evidence in this case, and I desire to draw your attention to this, in 1903, 1 King's Bench, page 330

Lord DAVEY It was in this House last year was it not?

Mr DANCKWERTS It was in this House in 1905—yes I will give your Lordship the reference there—1205, Appeal Cases page 256

Lord DAVEY In the Court below, 1903, 1 King's Bench

Mr DANCKWERTS 1903, 1 King's Bench The case begins at page 308 I was about to read from the Lord Justice Vaughan Williams' Judgment At page 330 he says "Dealing first with Rule 64, it was admitted by the Defendants' counsel that, on its initiation, the strike was not of such a character as to entitle the members of the Union who were striking to ask for the benefit of the rule or to justify the Association in giving it to them The men undoubtedly ceased work without the sanction of the Association and without giving the fourteen days' notice which by the rules incorporated in their contract of service they were bound to give There having been a failure to give that notice, the effect of which, if given might have been to provide an interval for reflection during which possibly the dispute between the employers and the men might have been settled, and a failure to obtain the sanction of the Association, it is admitted that the condition—Rule 64—was not complied with In my judgment the giving of strike pay under the circumstances would be not merely a matter affecting individual members of the Association, or concerning its internal administration only, but something which would alter the most essential conditions and purposes of the Association One can well understand a workman who had the interests of his class at heart, and who desired to support his fellow workmen in everything that might reasonably be supposed to tend to their advantage and the improvement of their position, gladly joining an association which, at the same time that it efficiently protected its members in their relations with their employers, was so constituted that members of it would not have to throw up their employment by the orders or at the dictation of some members of the association, or unless and all reasonable efforts had been made to preserve peace, and the existence of all the conditions which would justify a strike had been affirmed by the sanction of the Association being given to a strike by the particular branch which was proposing to strike Under the circumstances, in my judgment, the action is one of a character that is maintainable by an individual member of the Union" Then he goes further (page 331) "There is no doubt that the men did cease work originally without the sanction of the Association, and, inasmuch as they have never resumed work, and have ever since remained out on strike, I do not see how it can be made out that they ever ceased work a second time with the sanction of the Association within the meaning of Rule 64. In my opinion it is clear that they ceased work and went out on strike entirely of their own choice, and have remained out of work ever since But it is said that if the case does not come within Rule 64 then Rule 65 applies I cannot assent to that contention It was hardly disputed that, if the words of Rule 65 were construed literally, they would not cover the case. There has been no lock-out by the employers nor have the men been thrown out of employment in consequence of any action legally taken by the Association. The fact is that the men went out of employment and on strike of their own accord, and have never been in employment since."

(Adjourned for a short time.)

Mr DANCKWERTS. My Lords, Lord Justice Stirling agreed with Lord Justice Vaughan Williams in those facts which I have read to your Lordships, but there is a passage in Lord Justice Stirling's Judgment on page 340 to which I feel bound to call your attention. It was said, and, of course, said rightly, having regard to the views of the majority of the Judges who have dealt with the matter, that the payment of strike pay under Rule 64 in this case was contrary to the rules. Your Lordships will remember that Mr Pickard and some of the others came to the conclusion that they were bound to pay strike pay under Rule 64. Now, it has been suggested that that is a peculiar indication of malice on their part. I think that is a very unfounded suggestion, if I may respectfully say so, and for this reason. Lord Justice Stirling certainly would have concurred in that view if he had been permitted to act merely on his own judgment. He said so in his Judgment. You will find that on page 340 of 1903, 1 King's Bench. I ought to begin at the bottom of page 339. "The further questions therefore arise whether the rules of the Union, as they at present stand, have been violated, and, secondly, whether circumstances have occurred which give a right of action to the Plaintiff, as a member of the Association. In dealing with the first question regard must be had to the provisions of Rules 64 and 65. With regard to the construction of Rule 64, I am bound to say that I have felt considerable doubt whether the proposed payment of strike pay might not be justified under it. It provides that, in order that members may be entitled to receive strike pay, they must have been permitted to cease work by the sanction of the Association in accordance with the rules. What took place was this. There has been a continuous cessation of work by the men from the time when the strike originally took place down to the present time. Previously to a date somewhere about July 17th, that cessation was without the permission or sanction of the Association, but subsequently to that period the cessation of work was sanctioned by the Association. It is contended on behalf of the plaintiff that, in order to bring Rule 64 into operation, the sanction or permission of the Association must be given before the men in the first instance cease from working. If that is the true construction of the rule, then that condition has not been satisfied in the present case. It may be said that the construction of the rule contended for by the Plaintiff is more in accordance with what is primarily the meaning of the words used, but I must say that I have felt some doubt whether, without unduly stretching the meaning of the language, the men might not be said to have been permitted to cease work by the sanction of the

Association from the time at which in the present case that sanction was given But, as my brothers take the other view with regard to the construction of the rule, I cannot say that I feel sufficiently clear that the view which I have suggested is correct to differ from them, and I come the more readily to the same conclusion as they have come to, because in my view the rule is capable of being altered so as to authorise the payment of strike pay in such circumstances as exist in the present case without doing any great violence to the existing constitution of the Union " Why I read that, my Lords, and why I bring it to the attention of the House is that if a Judge so learned as the Lord Justice Stirling saw his way to come to the same conclusion, possibly as Mr Pickard and the others came to in this case, I think, and I submit respectfully it is most excusable on the part of Mr Pickard and his associates to have taken the view of the rule that the men were in fact entitled to strike pay As I think Lord Davey and others of your Lordships have pointed out, and as I shall again point out, under the rules once the conditions for the payment of strike pay arise, the Association has no option but to pay strike pay Therefore, really and truly these men acted on the view that this rule had come into operation, and that therefore they had no option but to pay strike pay I submit that having regard to what Lord Justice Stirling said, you cannot say that they are unreasonable in coming to that conclusion

Now I will read what Lord Justice Mathew said

The LORD CHANCELLOR Are you quoting Lord Justice Mathew for the same purpose?

Mr DANCKWERTS No, my Lord, Justice Mathew took the other view What I am quoting Lord Justice Mathew for is his statement of the facts

The LORD CHANCELLOR I do not wish to stop you at all but, of course, that was decided on evidence I imagine, on affidavit

Mr DANCKWERTS No

The LORD CHANCELLOR At all events, it was evidence different from the present

Mr DANCKWERTS No, it was substantially the same evidence

The LORD CHANCELLOR Was it the material that we have here?

Mr DANCKWERTS No If I may put it shortly, it was really a dress rehearsal of the present action between the same parties

The LORD CHANCELLOR We have the full materials Is

it not better to deal with the materials we have actually here, because it rather embarrasses one to read conclusions on different evidence, although it may have been largely the same

Mr DANCKWERTS Why I read it is because it sums up our point of view, and because in the present action it was really treated as one of the axioms of the case which must be accepted in the present action that is to say, all the parties at the trial accepted what was decided on the facts in that case as applying in the present case, and, indeed, it is largely because that view was taken that this case was fought out as it has been May I just put it shortly Our view is that the men on the 29th June, 1902, took the bit into their teeth and, so to speak, in despite of, almost, certainly without, the sanction of the Association, came out The Association instantly pointed out that the men in what they had done were in the wrong, and rightly or wrongly they sought by the conciliation of Mr Chambers, the manager, who was abroad in Ireland at the time, to arrange some means by which the men might get back to work No doubt, I do not think it can be denied, there was some idea that at some future time they might still give their notices in order to finally settle this question—give fourteen days' notice and come out unless they could agree the matter with Mr Chambers meanwhile That was somewhat modified later on, and, finding that the men were obstinate the plan was devised, the plan of getting the men to go back to work and giving their fourteen days' notices, that being done under the advice which they had received from some legal gentleman in the north, and upon the view which they took—that the Association had not elected to treat the breach of contract as putting an end to the contract of service Thence the use of the word "resume," and hence the use in several telegrams from Mr Pickard of expressions which showed that it was unnecessary to sign on on a new contract 'Now that, at the trial it was recognised was a wrong view, and in point of fact, as from the 29th June, 1902, both parties agreed that the men were no longer in the employment of the Colliery Company the Appellants with the result that thenceforward the men were in the position of free men, free from any contractual obligation though, of course, liable to damages for breach of contract—damages which were in fact sued for from the men and adjudications being obtained The view which the Association took was that the men were after the 17th July entitled to strike pay, and they paid strike pay as they thought they were bound to do I think your Lordships will find that there is no evidence at all, as the two Lords Justices and the Master of the Rolls in the Court below all held, no evidence whatever to connect the Association with the breach of contract which occurred on the 29th June and the following days There is no evidence of it

Now, my Lords, having got to that point, may I first draw your attention to the Trades Union Act of 1871 It is 34 and 35 Victoria, chapter 31 As your Lordships know now under the Trades Union

Act of 1876 the definition in the Act of 1871 has been repealed and Trades Unions are under that Act of two sorts—the unregistered and the registered. In this case the Association is a registered Trades Union and by Section 6 the process of registration is initiated. "Any seven or more members of a Trade Union may by subscribing their names to the rules of the Union and otherwise complying with the provisions of this Act with respect to registry, register such Trade Union under this Act, provided that if any one of the purposes of such Trade Union be unlawful such registration shall be void." Then Section 8 is a property section, and it is important for this reason—that it recognises branches as being capable of having property separate from the Union itself. That Section 8 has been amended by Section 3 of the Act of 1876, and if your Lordships would permit me, I will read it in the amended form. "All real and personal estate whatsoever belonging to any Trade Union registered under this Act shall be vested in the trustees for the time being of the Trade Union appointed as provided by this Act, for the use and benefit of such Trade Union and the members thereof, and the real or personal estate of any branch of a Trade Union shall be vested in the trustees of such branch, or of the trustees of the Trade Union, if the rules of the Trade Union so provide." So that it recognises that the branch is capable of having property distinct from the Union and applicable only to the particular branch. Section 13 provides the regulations as to the registration. Section 14 says "With respect to the rules of a Trade Union registered under this Act the following provisions shall have effect. (1) The rules of every such Trade Union shall contain provisions in respect of the several matters mentioned in the first schedule to this Act. (2) A copy of the rules should be delivered by the Trade Union to every person on demand on payment of a sum not exceeding one shilling." Therefore there were means taken to enable the public to have a copy of the rules. You will notice with regard to registration, Section 6, that any seven or more persons may do it by subscribing their names to the rules. The rules, therefore, are supposed to be pre-existent and, of course, anterior to registration, they can only have force and effect as a contract. I submit, with the greatest respect, that there is nothing in the Trades Union Act of 1871 or 1876, that I have been able to find at least which gives any greater force than contractual force to the rules of a Trade Union. All that it requires is that rules shall exist anterior to registration and that those rules shall make provision for certain matters, but apart from that it gives no higher sanction to the rules than they had before registration. There is no section which does so. Then comes the schedule of provisions which are to be in all the rules. I submit, therefore, that under this Trades Unions Act the rules have simply the force of a contract between the parties. No doubt the Act requires that that contract shall contain certain stipulations, but I submit that the requirement that the rules shall contain those stipulations does not alter their contractual character, nor do the stipulations which require publicity to be given to the rules. There is a case which I have not the reference to for a moment of Turquand v the British Bank, a Decision of the Exchequer Chamber reported in Ellis and Blackburn (I cannot remember the volume at the moment) where the Court held that where you have any company (I think it was anterior to the Companies Act), which by Act of Parliament is required to have its rules registered in a particular place, everybody who deals with that Company is obliged to take notice of those rules, and is bound by what they contain. The case which I have mentioned I will give your Lordships the reference to to-morrow if I may be permitted to do so.

Now I propose to deal with the rules, my Lords. I submit this proposition as emerging from a consideration of the rules, amongst others, namely, that so long as a branch does not violate what I may call the rules of the Association there is nothing whatever in the rules preventing that branch from having special rules of its own, special property of its own, and having special aims of its own, always provided that they do not thereby violate or contradict the rules of the Association itself. I submit in that respect that, if you look at this Trades Union the nearest analogy you can have is something like the United States of America. You have independent States federated together in the United States for certain purposes and all other purposes left to the States. That is really substantially the position of these branches as they are called. They are little Trades Unions in themselves, as Lord Justice Mathew said in the Court below. The Association is the *nexus* between the branches, and no doubt every member of the branch is also a member through the branch of the Association. Will your Lordships turn to page 93. The first rule provides "The Society shall be known as the Yorkshire Miners' Association, and shall consist of as many members employed in and about the various collieries as may think proper to join. It shall be divided into as many branches as may be deemed expedient, and shall remain in existence under the above title, nor shall its funds, books, emblems, or other property be appropriated to any other use than provided for in these rules, so long as fifty members in one or more branches remain together in the district, and are willing to carry out its objects." Pausing there for a moment, the language justifies the observation which I have made, namely, that the branches which include in themselves the members of the Association may themselves, particularly when you come to the subsequent rules, be regarded as also capable of doing things other than those prescribed by these rules, provided that they do not violate these rules. The only property which is dealt with there is the property of the parent Association itself. I do not think it is necessary to read the objects beyond this—that it is perfectly clear that none of those objects are unlawful, and if they were unlawful the registration would be void *ipso facto*. Section 6 of the Trades Unions Act provides "If any one of the purposes of such Trades Union be unlawful such registration shall be void, and there is provision made in another part for vacating the registration

I submit therefore that a *prima facie*, treating it as a registered Trades Union, which is the foundation for the Plaintiffs' right of action in this case, because they could not sue it unless it was a registered Trade Union, you come to these objects as being lawful and necessarily to be carried out by lawful means

The LORD CHANCELLOR That is common ground We have been through the rules No doubt some comments of yours will be required with regard to particular rules, but we have been through them

Mr DANCKWERTS I have read my learned friend, Mr Bankes's, comments, and I propose to add some of my own, but beyond that I will not detain your Lordships Now, " The supreme government of this Association shall be vested in a council which shall consist of a President,' and so on, and an experienced member duly elected as delegate (you will notice the word ' delegate " there) " by and from each of the financial branches composing the Association ' You will see that the branches are themselves treated as composing the Association, and the members of the Council are delegates from the branches Each delegate shall present to the President a credential from his branch Then 5 is as to meetings On 6 I have agreed with Mr Bankes, that the executive members, if I may so call them, of the Council have no vote at Council meetings 9, you will see, is the first fetter on the powers of the Council They are not "to lay levies on the members or make grants to any cause, member, or purpose whatever, until the same has been submitted to the branches for their approval or otherwise " That of course, must mean all the branches Then there is the rule prohibiting the branch from appropriating the funds of the Association to any purpose whatever not specified in the rules

Now, I submit that 12 is a most important rule, because it shows that it is absolutely beyond the powers of the Council to adopt or carry on a strike, because nowhere do you see power given to the Council to initiate any strike, nor do you see any power anywhere given to the Association to adopt or prolong a strike The only power with regard to the adoption or prolongation of a strike is to be found in this Rule 12, and you will note that there is to be " a registered vote taken throughout the entire Association whenever any number of branches numbering one-fourth of the Council demand such vote " Now here, *a concesso*, there has been no such vote

The LORD CHANCELLOR Do you say that the Council has no duties except ministerial with regard to a strike ?

Mr DANCKWERTS No because I think they have to determine, for example, certain matters on subsequent rules about conciliation, and so on, and also whether circumstances exist which

entitle the members of the Association to strike pay   But I say that
they have no power whatever to initiate the strike   I do say that
They have no power to adopt the strike and no power to prolong the
strike   The only power is by a registered vote of the whole of the
branches of the Association, as you will see   " Such registered vote
is to be taken by ballot in the local branch room, and recorded in
their books, a copy of which shall be forwarded to the offices to be
counted up either by the Council, Executive, or whom they may
direct to do so   No branch allowed to remain neutral unless the
Council decide otherwise, and the majority of such registered votes
to be decisive and binding upon the whole of the branches and
members composing the Association '   Therefore I submit that this
Association itself has no power except by a registered vote to adopt
or prolong a strike and *a fortiori* the Council have no such power,
nor the Executive Committee   Then there are the President, the
two Secretaries and the Agent referred to there   It is not suggested
that any of them have any powers which could possibly be material
here   Then the secretaries and treasurer are to be under the control
of the Council and must obey their directions during the time they
are in their service

Now Rule 21 is the rule, which refers to the secretary of the
local branch, and your Lordships will note why he has any existence
at all   It is simply for the purpose of having a medium of
correspondence between the secretaries of the local branches and the
general secretary   " Each Branch Committee shall furnish the
Council with the name and address of their Secretary on the first
meeting after his election to the General Secretary, so that all
balance sheets, reports and minutes can be sent to the Local
Secretaries, and not to the meeting rooms of the branches '
Therefore, the Secretary of the branches, so far as the Association
is concerned, is simply a sort of post office, and nothing much more
Then the General Treasurer has to be nominated by a branch and
so on   Then I think the next material rule on which I ought to
comment is Rule 28 on page 101   " there shall be an Executive
Committee always in existence which shall be composed of not less
than 13 members elected from and nominated by the branches (and
the general secretary and other district officials included, and to
have a vote at all Committee meetings ")   There you will see you
have a Committee of 13, which consists partly of the elected
delegates, and partly of the permanent officials who are the Executive
Committee alone, to have a vote   It is the only occasion on which
they have any power at all   They are to meet every six weeks
" The duties of the Executive Committee shall be to consider and
decide upon all cases of emergency arising between Council meetings,
such as preparing programme for Council meetings, branch grievances,
accepting and ordering the payment of victims, and all minor
questions ; but the Executive shall not decide upon questions relating
to strikes, lock-outs, or of voting money to other districts, or any
amount in the district exceeding five pounds '   Now there you see

again all power is taken away from the Executive Committee of dealing with strikes. They are to decide no questions relating to strikes, lock-outs, or of voting money within the district exceeding five pounds, and I submit that they have no power to bind the Association with regard to a strike. Then there are some further duties of the branch secretaries. They are to be elected, and are elected, every six months. Their duty is to keep correct accounts of all monies received. 'Shall strictly attend to all money received by the branch in the manner set forth in these rules and Minutes of Council. He shall attend all Committee and general meetings, also take Minutes and so on," and take charge of the books. There, that is simply clerk's business. He has no particular functions beyond that. Thirty-three is important. "The treasurer of each local branch shall be elected or re-elected every six months and shall receive and pay all moneys connected with the branch; he shall see that proper receipts for all payments are returned to the Committee, and kept in possession of the branch; he shall not on any account pay, lend, or appropriate any of the funds to any member, cause, or purpose whatever, beyond the rules, resolutions, or Minutes of the Council; he shall attend all meetings, answer all questions relative to money matters, if such questions be asked at the Committee or branch meetings, and by members. And he shall forward to the General Treasurer for the time being of the Association all moneys received by him on behalf of the Association within 72 hours." I believe it was proved here or admitted that what in fact happened with regard to the moneys collected at a branch was that such moneys as were required for the purpose of the branch were kept by the branch, and the residue was forwarded to the Association. Of course an account had to be rendered for it. I think 37 is a rule to which I should call attention.

Lord DAVEY. It says that the Secretaries of every branch shall be elected or re-elected every six months. I presume that means by the branch.

Mr DANCKWERTS. Yes, that is so. You are referring to Rule 32, my Lord.

Lord DAVEY. Yes, Rule 32. The President, they say, shall be elected or re-elected by a majority of the Branch, and I suppose the meaning must be the same in Rule 32.

Mr DANCKWERTS. I think so. These Friendly Societies and Trade Union rules, as you know, are not always framed with that degree of clearness and lucidity which is desirable.

Lord DAVEY. They have not a monopoly in that respect.

Mr DANCKWERTS. No, but I have always found peculiar difficulty with Friendly Societies and Trade Unions. "All local branches shall be conducted by a Committee of not less than five or more than nine financial members, President, Secretary and Treasurer included, whose duty shall be to attend all meetings whether regular or special, and shall at all times transact the business of the Branch as directed by the rules and minutes of the General Council" Now surely Mr Bankes fell into a great fallacy over that What are they to do? They are to conduct the business of the branch that is all, not the business of the Union, but the business of the branch as directed by the rules and minutes of the General Council

Lord DAVEY What rule is that?

Mr DANCKWERTS Rule 37, and I submit that the final words simply relate to the mode of conducting the business

Lord DAVEY That means by the rules and resolutions of the General Council

Mr DANCKWERTS Governing the transaction of business.

Lord DAVEY "As directed by the rules and minutes of the General Council" It only applies to minutes

Mr DANCKWERTS To minutes—that is all, my Lord Then there is the re-election of the Local Committee I submit that the Local Committee are elected for the purpose of the branch and for nothing else Rule 40 prescribes the business 'The Committee of Local Branches shall meet once in every fortnight (unless warned by the Secretary after consultation with the President that there is no business to transact), to investigate all grievances and complaints of members, and deal with them as per rule" "Rule" there, I think, means the rule of the Association So far as the rules give them any power, there it is "They shall attend to all moneys being received and paid in accordance with these rules and minutes of Council and Executive Committee they must know the amount of income and expenditure at all committee meetings, and shall lay all transactions and business of the branch and the Association before the general meeting of the branch, which shall be held once in every fortnight, or oftener if required Rule 41 In the event of any alteration at any of the collieries in the mode or working that tends in any way to take away the interest or the members, the branch (through the committee) shall at once investigate the matter, and shall lay all facts before the Council of Executive Committee or General Secretary immediately"

Lord DAVEY That must be wrong It ought to be "of the members," clearly.

Mr DANCKWERTS I am told it is "or" in the original I think it refers to attempts made to lead members to leave the Union and things of that sort

Lord DAVEY It is a very curious expression "That tends in any way to take away the interest of the members"

Mr DANCKWERTS There is an "of" obviously left out there, anyhow

Lord DAVEY I do not understand it with regard to the members

Mr DANCKWERTS Probably it is a misprint altogether, but it might mean that attempts might be made to get them to leave the Union

The LORD CHANCELLOR We have had a note that a correction has been made The "of" is to be "or" and the "or" is to be "of"

Lord JAMES of HEREFORD It is transposed

Mr DANCKWERTS May I hand an official copy of the rules to your Lordship? What appears to be the case is this Do you see "of" in the ante-penultimate line there? It may be that the "of" and the "or" have been transposed

The LORD CHANCELLOR Yes. We need not spend time on it It has been corrected before, and it is as I said

Mr DANCKWERTS It is not alone in this that it has been done

The LORD CHANCELLOR No

Mr DANCKWERTS "In all cases of emergency arising at any of the branches where prompt action is required, such branch shall forthwith lay all information before the General Secretary, who shall report the same to the Council or Executive Committee as early as possible" That shows that beyond being collectors of information in order to lay it before the proper authorities, the branches have no power whatever of this sort to commit the Association to any illegal acts, or anything of that kind

I do not think the next is material Rule 46 shows what matters can be paid for by the branch out of the funds of the Association You will see that it says "shall be paid out of the funds of the Association and shall be the property of the Association" That only refers to certain things Then there is the ballot box.

Then Rule 60, on page 110, my Lords, is this ' No branch shall be allowed to make use of the funds of this Association for processions, flags, banners, or any other personal or public use not specified in these rules, unless the same be submitted to the Council and approved by a majority" There is something on page 94, Rule 4, which I passed over by accident I was looking for it It is rather important "Each delegate appointed to attend Council meeting shall present to the President a credential from his branch, empowering him to act as their representative before being allowed to take part in the business of such Council meeting"

The LORD CHANCELLOR I had marked it already two or three days ago We have been through the whole of these Will you just give your criticism upon them? It is not necessary to go through them again

Mr DANCKWERTS If you look at Rules 64 and 65, what I submit upon those two rules is that the function of the Council is if certain things have been done to pay "If any branch member or members have grievances affecting their wages, mode, or manner of working, if the employers refuse to remedy those grievances, and after all proper and peaceful means have been tried, to effect a settlement by deputations from members, with the advice and assistance of Council, and such member or members be permitted to cease work by the sanction of the Association in accordance with the rule

Lord DAVEY What rule does that refer to?

Mr DANCKWERTS To be quite frank with your Lordship, it has puzzled me very considerably unless it means Rule 72

Lord DAVEY I have been looking carefully to see whether there is anything which enables or obliges

Mr DANCKWERTS The only thing that I can see that it refers to is Rule 72

Lord DAVEY Very well, we will come to that

Mr DANCKWERTS I think that is the only rule that I know of and can find that it refers to

Lord DAVEY I had not seen that

Mr. DANCKWERTS "Such members shall receive nine shillings per week and so forth ' You will see that it says "shall receive" There is no option there All that the spending authority has to do, I suppose, is to find out if those conditions have been complied with and if they have been complied with, there is an end of it "Any branch or portion of any branch which may be locked out, or otherwise thrown out of employment, in consequence of any action that may legally have been taken by the Association to keep up the price or remedy any grievances either at that or any other colliery connected with the Association, the members of such branch shall be supported after the same rate as the members on strike, until such time as they can get work, or the Association decide otherwise." There again, once the fact occurs, there is a title to the pay. Then the same is the case under 66. If certain things are done they shall be supported from the funds of the Association. Again, it does not rest with the Council there to say what those things shall be, and whether those things shall exist, or come into existence rather. "If any member or members should be discharged from their employment in consequence of adhering to the rules of the Association, or for holding any office, or sitting in Committee, or attending on deputations to employers (if properly appointed), or collecting contributions, or in any other legal way advocating the claims and furthering the objects of the Association, without interfering with the employers, or the liberty of their fellow workmen, such member or members shall immediately communicate (through the Branch Secretary) the particulars of the case to the General Secretary, who shall promptly investigate the matter, with a view of restoring such member or members back to their work, but if found impossible to do so, they shall be supported from the funds of the Association. But no member or members will be supported as victims who may have been discharged from their employment for neglecting their work, swearing or using abusive language to the owners, managers or other officers, violating the special and general rules stealing or hiding their fellow workmen's tools, and no victim will be accepted whose case has not been made known to the District Secretary within seven days from the time he loses his work. Any member or members who may have been acknowledged by the Association as victims, in accordance with the foregoing rules shall receive," and so on. Then 69. "no branch member or members who may be on strike, locked out, or victimised, shall be entitled to the support of the Association until such branch member or members have been out of work six clear days, after which they shall be paid according to rule for every working day they remain unable to find employment, or, in case of strikes, are unemployed by the sanction of the Council." The way in which that has been interpreted in this Union is, that they wait until six days have passed, and then they pay them for the six days as well as for the future. 71. "That courts of conciliation and arbitration be acknowledged by this Association, and recommended in the settlement of all disputes where they can be adopted with justice to all parties concerned." Rule 72 is the only place where a strike with the sanction of the Association can be got, and there it is rather a misnomer, because it is not the Association that sanctions the cessation of work really. "No branch or portion of a branch shall be allowed to strike or leave off work with a view of causing the works to stand, unless sanctioned by two-thirds of the members composing the branch, when such strike shall be determined by registered ballot, such vote to be obtained by the branch officials calling a special meeting of said branch for that purpose, and each member shall have delivered to him," and so forth

The LORD CHANCELLOR Upon this, which is a very crucial part of the case, as to where the power resides of initiating or protracting strikes, I have been thinking about it, and I want you to help me The power of initiating strikes appears to be in the branch

Mr DANCKWERTS Yes Rule 72 is the only one, as far as I know, where a strike with the sanction of the Association can be found

The LORD CHANCELLOR By a sufficient vote

Mr DANCKWERTS You are not referring to lock-outs, my Lord?

The LORD CHANCELLOR No, I am talking of strikes

Mr DANCKWERTS Of strikes only, not lock-outs?

The LORD CHANCELLOR The power of initiating strikes is with the branch

Mr DANCKWERTS Yes, my Lord

The LORD CHANCELLOR You think that is so?

Mr DANCKWERTS Yes, I think that is so

The LORD CHANCELLOR Then it seems that the adoption or prolongation of it by Rule 12 depends upon a registered vote of the whole Association

Mr DANCKWERTS Yes

The LORD CHANCELLOR Then the payment of the money follows, and is payable by the Council Look at Rules 64 and 65

Mr DANCKWERTS Rule 65 relates to lock-outs and things of that sort, and does not relate to strikes

The LORD CHANCELLOR You say that it does not, but I do not assent to that, as at present advised

Mr DANCKWERTS Rule 65 says, "which may be locked out, or otherwise thrown out of employment"

The LORD CHANCELLOR "In consequence of any action that may legally have been taken by the Association to keep up the price"

Mr. DANCKWERTS It does not relate to strikes

The LORD CHANCELLOR I see what you mean

Mr DANCKWERTS I think it means that there may be a lock-out which is not due to the Association

The LORD CHANCELLOR I understand

Mr DANCKWERTS In that case it does not come within the rule

The LORD CHANCELLOR Rule 64 provides that they shall receive the money practically as long as they are out with the sanction of the Association, that is to say, until the Council otherwise determine Now, if your view is right, as I understand it, the Council have nothing but ministerial functions in connection with the strike The initiation is with the branch, the sanction is by the vote of the whole Association, and the ministerial duty of paying, according to that, rests with the branch Is that your view?

Mr DANCKWERTS Yes, except that the Council, I think, would have to ascertain whether the facts existed

The LORD CHANCELLOR Yes

Mr DANCKWERTS You asked me about it before, my Lord, and I think I answered it in the same way

Lord MACNAGHTEN Rule 12 is only put in operation when there is a number of branches, numbering one-fourth of the Council, demanding such a vote What do you say to that?

Mr DANCKWERTS That strengthens my view, my Lord

Lord MACNAGHTEN What is the meaning of it That is what I want to know

Mr DANCKWERTS I think it has to be demanded through the delegates.

Lord MACNACHTEN Supposing there is no demand, what happens?

Mr DANCKWERTS In that case, nothing

Lord MACNAGHTEN Does the strike fall to the ground?

Mr DANCKWERTS No, it will go on

The LORD CHANCELLOR It would not be a strike supported by the sanction of the Association, and therefore would not get strike pay Is not that the machinery?

Lord MACNAGHTEN It looks like it

The LORD CHANCELLOR First you have to get the majority With regard to what Lord Macnaghten pointed out you have to get a number of branches amounting to one-fourth

Lord MACNAGHTEN It rather looks as if what has been put to you was the position If the other branches refuse to allow their money to be applied to the purposes of supporting a strike, if there is no such demand made, then can a strike go on?

Mr. DANCKWERTS I think so, my Lord

Lord MACNAGHTEN Can the Association pay strike pay?

Mr DANCKWERTS I think not, unless you can find the sanction of the Association somewhere else

Lord MACNAGHTEN I only wanted to know your view

Mr DANCKWERTS I said that it had puzzled me considerably Rule 64 is a very difficult one, but it works out somewhat in that way, and it would seem to circumscribe strikes and the power of striking enormously

The LORD CHANCELLOR They seem in this case to have treated it as being a lock-out, and to have purported to act under Rule 65, which is a lock-out rule Then they are to continue paying until the Association decides otherwise That seems to be the real position

Mr DANCKWERTS That is how we tried to put it under Rule 65

Lord JAMES of HEREFORD That there was a lock-out?

Mr DANCKWERTS Lord James will remember, perhaps, because he was one of the noble Lords who decided the Howden case, that we had a great discussion about what "thrown out of employment" meant

Lord JAMES of HEREFORD. I do not recollect

Mr DANCKWERTS Your Lordship particularly discussed that question with me, and that is why I have a recollection of it

Lord JAMES of HEREFORD I recollect discussing many questions with you, but I do not recollect that one

Mr DANCKWERTS I was more impressed by it

The LORD CHANCELLOR That seems to be the end of the relevant rules

Mr DANCKWERTS I do not think there are any more relevant rules, my Lords

Now, I think, with all submission, I have made my point good with which I started, namely, that the Association itself cannot sanction strikes except in the particular manner indicated by Rule 12 The Council has no power over the matter, and therefore cannot bind the Association, and, further, I submit that the local branches are perfectly at liberty to do anything by common consent, which does not contravene these rules, and I presume if men struck contrary to the rules the penalty would be that they stood no chance whatever of getting strike pay but I do not see anything in these rules which prevents the members of the Committee, like members of the Committee of any other assembly of workmen, doing what they think fit The penalty is that they do not do it on behalf of the Union, and cannot do it on behalf of the Union, and the officials of the Union cannot sanction it or adopt it From beginning to end that is the view which was taken in the Court of Appeal, certainly by Lord Justice Cozens-Hardy and Lord Justice Mathew, and I think also by the Master of the Rolls with regard to the first part of the case, although I think he lost sight of it in regard to the second part of the case.

Now I would like to draw attention, with your Lordships' permission, to the case of Poulton and the London and South Western Railway, which is reported in Law Reports, 2 Queen's Bench, at page 534.

Lord DAVEY For what proposition ?

Mr DANCKWERTS For this proposition—that where the alleged principal is himself incapable of doing the act, no servant of his can do it on his behalf, nor can he ratify it In that case a stationmaster had demanded payment for the fare of a horse which the Plaintiff had in his custody, and there was no payment, and he detained the Plaintiff in custody, and it was sought to make the Railway Company liable for the illegal act of the stationmaster What the Court held was that the Company, having no power to do anything of the sort, could not be made responsible for the act of the stationmaster   The point is put very shortly by Lord Blackburn, my Lords, who gives a long Judgment   I refer your Lordships to page 539   "Then comes the question we have to determine can there be said to be any evidence from which it may be inferred that the Railway Company authorised the stationmaster to do an act which it appears, on every view of the facts, he would be utterly unauthorised to do?   We think not, we do not think it is within the scope of his authority in what he was authorised to do, so to bind the Company   It was an act out of the scope of his authority, and for which the Company would be no more responsible than if he had committed an assault, or done any other act which the Company never authorised him to do"   On the succeeding page, at the end, in his Judgment, he says this   "In the present case an act was done by the stationmaster completely out of the scope of his authority, which there can be no possible ground for supposing the railway company authorised him to do, and a thing which could never be right on the part of the company to do   Having no power themselves, they cannot give the stationmaster any power to do the act   Therefore the wrongful imprisonment is an act for which the Plaintiff, if he has a remedy at all, has it against the stationmaster personally, but not against the Railway Company"   Mr Justice Mellor says   "I am entirely of the same opinion   I think the distinction is clear   it limits the scope of authority, to be implied from the fact of being the stationmaster, to such acts as the Company could do themselves, and I cannot think it ever can be implied that the company authorized the stationmaster to do that which they have no authority to do themselves, and that seems to me to be the boundary line   It was well put by the Counsel for the Plaintiff, and no doubt there is a difficulty at first in seeing where the distinction begins and where it ends, but I cannot help thinking it is analagous to an action against magistrates   If the stationmaster had made a mistake in committing an act which he was authorized to do, I think in that case the Company would be liable, because it would be supposed to be done by their authority   Where the stationmaster acts in a manner in which the Company themselves would not be authorised to act, and under a mistake or misapprehension of what the law is, then I think the rule is very different, and I think that is the distinction on which the whole matter turns"   Then Mr Justice Shee said   "As pointed out by my learned brothers, an authority cannot be implied to have been given to a servant to do an act, which, if his master were on the spot, the master would not be justified in doing, or the assumption of a particular state of facts'

Lord JAMES of HEREFORD   It says "Authority to be implied"

Mr DANCKWERTS   Yes, from his position of stationmaster   You see if it had been within the scope of the man's authority it would have been otherwise   "It is clear from the construction of

S 103 of 8 Victoria, chapter 20 (1) that the Company had no power to arrest this passenger because he had not paid the price for the carriage of his horses" There is a case of Charlebois, a Canadian case, to which I will refer your Lordships Of course the Ashbury Railway v Riche is itself an authority for this proposition There Lord Cairns said that was *ultra vires* the Company is simply void That case was cited by my learned friend, Mr Bankes This case is the Great North West Central Railway Company v Charlebois, 99 Appeal Cases, page 114, in the Privy Council It is a very strong case, and I ask your Lordship's permission just to read the first part of the headnote "Where by contract *ex facie* legal and regular, the Appellant Company purported to incur liability to the Respondent for railway construction in an amount which was in reality calculated to cover the amount of bonus and of price of issued shares payable by agreement between the Respondent and all the Shareholders of the Company irrespective of either actual or estimated cost of construction Held that the contract was *ultra vires* of the Company Held, further, that a consent Judgment obtained on the contract declaring the Respondent's lien on the Company's railway and other property, the question of *ultra vires* not having been raised either in the pleadings or on the facts stated, was of no greater validity than the contract" Judgment there was that of Lord Hobhouse, Lord Macnaghten, Lord Morris, Sir Richard Couch, and Sir Henry de Villiers It is a very long Judgment, but I think the pith of it is given in the head-note

My Lords, there was the case of the Hornsey District Council and Islington There the Court of Appeal laid down the same proposition It is reported in 1900, 1 Chancery, at page 695 I am sorry that I have not the book here, but Lord Lindley there delivered the Judgment of the Court He quotes several cases where he says that no amount of ratification of an act which is itself *ultra vires* can possibly bind the Company Now here you will remember that Mr Justice Farwell in the Taff Vale case himself reserved the question of *ultra vires*, and simply decided the other point You will remember that the whole of his Judgment was that it was neither a partnership nor a Corporation, but he said that it was analagous to a Corporation Therefore I submit the analogy by which the question of *ultra vires* is to be tried here is the analogy of a Corporation It is something which Mr Justice Farwell says has no existence according to the ordinary common law It is some monstrosity created by statute, a particular kind of entity, and he solves the questions by analogy to a Corporation I submit, therefore, the question of *ultra vires* and the consequences of *ultra vires* are equally to be determined by the analogy to a Corporation, and that these cases of Hornsey Urban District Council, of Charlebois, and of The Ashbury Railway Company v Riche all apply

My Lords, the case which I had in my mind is Saint Mary, Islington v Hornsey Urban District Council, 1900, 1 Chancery, at page 695 The question there was whether or not the Islington

Vestry were estopped from permitting certain acts to be done which, if they had done them directly, would have been *ultra vires* Lord Lindley says this "If this were an information by the Attorney-General instead of an action by the Islington Vestry, the Defendants would, in our opinion, have no defence whatever to the claim for an Injunction Considering who the Plaintiffs are, we cannot think that they are estopped at law or in equity from obtaining the relief they seek In Fairtitle v Gilbert, some turnpike trustees who had power to mortgage their tolls, but not toll-houses, mortgaged both by deed They were, nevertheless, held entitled to recover the toll-houses from their mortgagees, and the doctrine of estoppel was held inapplicable to the case on the ground that the Plaintiffs were a public body with limited powers conferred by statute, and could not exceed those powers Many other decisions to the same effect are to be found in the books, the most recent being the Great North-West Central Railway Company v Charlebois in the Privy Council, where a public Company, which had entered into an agreement beyond its powers and had consented to a judgment against it in an action brought on that agreement, was nevertheless entitled to impeach both the agreement and the Judgment, and both were set aside For similar reasons the Plaintiff cannot, in our opinion, be treated as precluded from obtaining relief on the ground of laches and acquiescence" Now this doctrine of your being bound by the acts of your servant done without your command in the course of his duty is very analogous to estoppel

The LORD CHANCELLOR But it is very clear surely with regard to contracts that you cannot ratify a contract made *ultra vires* of the Company We are dealing here with an alleged tort It seems to me that those cases do not apply

Mr DANCKWERTS But I submit that the principle is the same In the Ashbury case the question was one of a tort having been done The principle is the same, I submit Poulton's case is a question of tort Your Lordships will remember that He falsely imprisoned a man there I submit that the doctrine is exactly the same A body of a limited capacity such as this is, with limited powers, and given by the law a sort of——

The LORD CHANCELLOR What I meant was that if you quote authorities of that kind it would be better to quote them with regard to tort because the questions with regard to that really involves wholly different considerations

Mr DANCKWERTS I am obliged to your Lordship I submit that the principal is very analogous, because in both cases it is because you cannot do the Act yourself

My Lord, there was a question raised at the trial with regard to the question of bag dirt The argument that was made there was

this They said that bag dirt was a mere pretext for a strike, and
that the whole object of the strike was, if I may use the expression,
to kick against Lord James' award, and further that the other
question which arose on 17th July about the Home Secretary's rule
was also a mere pretext I do not know that it is so very material,
but I submit that the whole thing having been dragged in for the
purpose of showing *mala fides* on the part of the parties, and as I
understand for that purpose alone the only way of meeting that is
by showing that this bag dirt question was a *bona fide* question It
had been in dispute ever since the year 1894 and it had gone through
various phases As I understand it the price lists prescribed certain
prices for getting coal and prescribed another price for doing a thing
which included dropping bag dirt The original view of the colliers
was that they were entitled to get both sums That dispute lasted
for some years, until, I think, in 1897 there was a County Court
action in which it was decided, against the colliers, that they were
not entitled to both. Then came the question of what was the real
meaning of this price list and where had the bag dirt been taken
into account The Colliery Company alleged that the halfpenny in
the 1s 4½d represented the dropping of bag dirt There was an
arbitration, or conciliation meeting about that, the result of which
was that Mr Chambers's view was held to be right, namely, that
the halfpenny was originally included for dropping bag dirt Then
came another action in the County Court The real grievance of
the miners was that the circumstances had completely changed, so
much so that the getting of bag dirt imposed upon them far greater
labour than had been contemplated when the price list was originally
fixed The County Court Judge in delivering his Judgment, as I
shall show your Lordships, made a long statement to the effect that
in his opinion the men had a genuine grievance and that the time
had come to revise the price list That was in February of the year
1902, I think Accordingly, some months in the year 1902 were
spent in trying to persuade Mr Chambers to agree to a new price
list Various proceedings were taken to that end to which I shall
have to call your Lordships' attention, I am afraid The final result
was that Mr Chambers would not budge He said he had had
actions, and he had had an arbitration as to the existing price list,
and he was satisfied with that and he declined to do anything He
admitted that himself in cross-examination by my learned friend,
Mr Rufus Isaacs I shall show that Then came the question with
regard to the 28th June, the pay day There was a considerable
reduction from the pay of a certain number of men at the Cadeby
Pit, I think, with the result that the men were exasperated and took
things into their own hands and nobody was more surprised, I think,
than the Association I contend that it was a genuine grievance as
I shall show your Lordships, and not a mere pretext With regard
to the other point the Home Secretary's rule, the position of things
as to that as far as concerns the great majority of the men certainly
was this the Home Secretary's rule was promulgated about six
months before these events, somewhere in the early part of the year

or the summer of 1901 My learned friend says that it was the summer The men found that the strict enforcement of the Home Secretary's rule was exceedingly oppressive to them and prevented them from earning as much as they would have earned if it had not been so strictly enforced That was the position

The LORD CHANCELLOR You mean the timbering rule

Mr DANCKWERTS Yes, the timbering rule There is no doubt whatever that representations were made to Mr Chambers from time to time There was a great deputation to him in March, 1902, about these timbering rules The fact was he could not be moved The idea of the men was to get rid of the rule because they rightly or wrongly believed it to be *ultra vires* The mischief was that when they were asked to sign on on the 17th July, 1902, the thing which they were asked to sign contained a reference to the contract book which was delivered to them which incorporated this rule of the Home Secretary The view which they took, whether it is right or wrong, I do not think is very material, but they genuinely took it, was this They said, " If we sign on and agree to a book as governing the contract which contains this, it then no longer remains a matter of the rule of the Home Secretary, but it becomes a matter between us and the Colliery Company " and hence the objection to signing on under a contract which they thought incorporated this rule As my learned friend reminds me it never was brought to the notice of the men individually except in the sense that it was posted up somewhere about the mine When Mr Chambers was notified that this was the real objection to signing on on the 17th July, he had that notice put up which has already been commented upon and which certainly was bald and was not calculated to persuade the men that their point of view was wrong That was the whole point about not signing on then Undoubtedly they should have signed on on the 17th July, and having signed on they could subsequently have given their notices for fourteen days I take it that a man has a perfect legal right, and I so submit, to enter into a contract under which he is entitled to give fourteen days' notice, and to give the notice at once It is simply entering into a contract for fourteen days The other party has a right to refuse to enter into that contract too, that is perfectly true, but I submit that there is no wrong, and to characterise it as a sham is to use language which is not fit to describe what was done on this occasion If the men had signed on, and had then given their notices, and the object was to negotiate in the interval with Mr Chambers, no doubt it would have resulted in further proceedings possibly, but it would have been legalised, and there would have been no excess at all

Now with regard to the question of bag dirt, I would like to refer your Lordships to page 776 first, but I hope I shall be permitted to read to your Lordships the evidence of Mr Chambers in cross-examination It is a little bit long The reason why I ask that permission is that in that cross-examination the whole case of bag dirt and of the Home Secretary's rule is expounded, and the facts are brought out Mr Wadsworth is asked at Question 2201 on page 776 "You have been acquainted with the circumstances relating to the bag dirt question in these two collieries, almost from the beginning, I think?—Well, I have known about them for a considerable number of years—nine years, I should think, something like that Q Did you first of all attend the meeting—I will not go further back than that, but do you remember in 1895 the agitation started at Cadeby after the opening of the Cadeby Colliery?—I do" You will remember, my Lords, that the price list had shortly before that been brought into force by the adoption of the Denaby list in Cadeby "They raised the question there, although I think the question was not so serious at the Cadeby Colliery as it was at the Denaby."—No, I do not think it was Mr Justice Lawrance Was it in 1895?—Mr S T Evans In 1895, my Lord Mr Justice Lawrance I thought Cadeby Colliery was opened after that?—Mr Eldon Bankes Yes it was opened in 1896 Mr Rufus Isaacs I think 1896 at any rate It is confirmed by a minute" Then there is a discussion There is a reference on page 778 to the correspondence of March 23rd, 1895 "Mr Chambers also wants the men to get down and shift the bag dirt in their tonnage rate This the men object to do, and rightly so, inasmuch as it states very clearly on the price list what the men have to do for the 1s 4½d per ton"

Lord JAMES of HEREFORD You will pardon me, but I have never been able to understand how the question of bag dirt bears on the question here

Mr DANCKWERTS In this way, my Lords, that I am dealing with it to meet a point made against us

The LORD CHANCELLOR No Mr Bankes opened it in this way He said "The Plaintiffs have always said that it is not material to consider whether these were or were not real grievances well founded, but inasmuch as the other side maintain this I do" Now you say that you maintain it because he does

Mr DANCKWERTS My learned friend, Mr Bankes, is utterly mistaken there

The LORD CHANCELLOR I do not say that he is not, but I point out to you that both of you seem to agree that it has no relevancy except that the other side rely on it Do you think that it has?

Mr DANCKWERTS In answer to that, may I be quite candid with your Lordships about it

The LORD CHANCELLOR Yes Tell us exactly what you think

Lord JAMES of HEREFORD You will make an effort

Mr DANCKWERTS Yes I will unbosom myself about it, if I may The position with regard to it is this the father of this point is my learned friend, Mr Lush Mr Lush has, in both the actions, made a great point of it, and in each case has said "Why, your bad faith throughout the transaction is shown by your making the bag dirt question a pretext The real truth is that you want to get rid of Lord James's ten per cent award That is his point, my Lords, and whenever he has addressed a Court or a Jury he has rubbed that in, if I may be allowed to use the expression

The LORD CHANCELLOR If you or anyone thinks that it is material, by all means deal with it Whether or not it was a thing put forward in good faith may be material, but with regard to the actual merits, whether $\frac{1}{2}d$ is right or whether anything else is right I cannot understand the materiality That is how it strikes me

Mr DANCKWERTS As to that I agree, and we have never said that, on the contrary The way in which we put it, as your Lordships will see, when we cross-examined Mr Chambers (my learned friend, Mr Rufus Isaacs, cross-examined him) was this and always this "You accused us of bad faith in the opening speech of Mr Lush Very well What we have to show is that the bag dirt question was not a mere pretext"——

Lord ROBERTSON My impression, and I attended very closely to Mr Bankes' argument, was that he did advance the point that you are going to combat, although not with very great salience

The LORD CHANCELLOR Then we had better go into it

Mr WADDY If I may, without impropriety, my Lords, intervene here, may I tell your Lordships the reason why it was introduced into our case It was met by us in the course of the case because it was pleaded in the defence and particulars given in the defence as one of the grievances from which the men were suffering, grievances which led them to take the step which they did on the 29th June That is the way in which it came to be introduced

Mr DANCKWERTS It was also used in another way

The LORD CHANCELLOR I daresay it was

Mr DANCKWERTS May I state this? It was said that this was an important test whether the strike was spontaneous on the part of the men or procured on the part of the Association

The LORD CHANCELLOR You need not labour it You will proceed with your argument

Mr DANCKWERTS If your Lordship pleases I think I rather apologetically referred to it at the beginning I do not know that I care much about it, but may I tell your Lordship our point of view with regard to it?

The LORD CHANCELLOR Yes

Mr DANCKWERTS Our point of view is that it does not matter a bit whether the men were right, or whether Mr Chambers was right All that is material is that there was a substantial dispute on both sides

Lord JAMES of HEREFORD I do not see any evidence that the men were acting in order to get rid of the 10 per cent Award This was no doubt a very strong point

Lord DAVEY It seems that they were very much irritated and angered on account of the reduction made in their wages on account of the bag dirt, which seemed to be a large amount, no doubt by reason of arrears of previous weeks The largeness of the amount apparently had had an effect upon them and they thought, rightly or wrongly, that Mr Chambers had no right to make those deductions

Mr DANCKWERTS That is it I may say at once that I could satisfy your Lordships, I think

Lord DAVEY Probably they were wrong in what they thought

Mr DANCKWERTS I think I can satisfy your Lordships at once that under the Coal Mines Regulation Act, the deduction is legal That of course is not material

The LORD CHANCELLOR We have not to determine that

Mr DANCKWERTS No, you have not, my Lord

The LORD CHANCELLOR I am sorry I interrupted you

Mr DANCKWERTS I am exceedingly obliged to your Lordship

The LORD CHANCELLOR Kindly proceed with your argument

Mr DANCKWERTS Yes, my Lord I was telling your Lordships how the case was put My learned friend Mr Rufus

Isaacs said "It is not material at all to show on which side the merits of the disputes lie I am entitled to satisfy the Jury that there was a substantial *bona fide* dispute' The deductions had been as much as forty pounds sometimes

Now, I was reading the letter on page 778 of March 23rd, 1895 It is a letter from Mr Hall "Mr Chambers also wants the men to get down and shift the bag dirt in their tonnage rate This the men object to do, and rightly so, inasmuch as it states very clearly on the price list what the men have to do for the 1s 4½d per ton, and in another item on the price list, which refers to cutting tops and dropping bag dirt, 11d a yard is to be paid Mr Chambers says it is in their contract, and we say it is not, and I trust the district will insist on the work being paid for' That is as far back as 1895, from Mr Hall, Then "It goes through 1896, but in September of 1897, I think, you attended a meeting from the Denaby and Cadeby men, when the bag dirt question was introduced amongst other grievances? —Yes, assuming those dates are correct I cannot very well remember the dates My memory is very bad Q Before that deputation, do you remember yourself giving attention to the question of the thickness and hardness of the bag dirt with Mr Murray, who was sent down to examine and to make sections on behalf of the men of the Association?—I did not attend with Mr Murray Q. You attended a meeting, I think, with him afterwards?—Yes, afterwards Q Mr Murray had been sent down on behalf of the men to investigate the matter," and so on And then on page 779, about the letter A, there is this letter "Dear Sir,—As ordered, I have been down the Denaby Main Pit, and taken sections of the bag dirt, which had to be cut down in all the gates but one, and was very hard Then he gives eight sections, showing that it varied in places from 1ft 5½ins to 2ft 1in in thickness (To the Witness) That came to your knowledge before you attended the deputation in September, 1897?—Yes (Mr Justice Lawrance) On an average about 1ft 10ins (Mr S T Evans) About 1ft 10ins (Mr Justice Lawrance) That is near enough" There is a lot more there, but as I have to read it in Mr Chambers' evidence, I do not want to read it here.

Then there is the evidence of Mr Parrott at page 847, Question 2821 "Now have you from time to time been concerned with deputations to the Denaby and Cadeby mines?—Yes Q And have you been aware of this agitation with reference to the bag dirt?—Yes Q I need not go again through the details connected with it You know that the men's contention was that it was getting harder and more difficult to get?—Yes Q And you knew, did you, that up to June of 1902, no agreement had been arrived at between the masters and the men upon it?—Yes Q With regard also to the timbering question" Then comes the question as to the meeting of the 30th June Then Mr Hall, on page 882, question 3071 "In that price list" (that is the Denaby price list)—"I am going to take this very shortly—there was an item of coal getting, wooding, packing and top-cutting, large coal, 1s 4½d '—There is Q Then there is another one 'Cutting tops in gates (including dropping bag dirt) per yard, 11d '—Yes Q Now, rightly or wrongly, was it your view that the 1s 4½d did not include that for which the 11d was to be paid?—Yes Q The 11d you understood was to do the bag dirt in gates?—Yes, and cutting the tops, Q As far back as the year 1895 was that question a matter of discussion between you and Mr Chambers?—It was "

Lord JAMES of HEREFORD Were there one or two suits about this in the County Court

Mr DANCKWERTS Two, one in 1897, and one in 1902 With regard to the 1902 suit, the County Court Judge's observations, which have come before your Lordship, were very strong in favour of the men, and so much did Mr Chambers believe that the bag dirt was the real cause of what happened on the 29th June, that he took the trouble to write a letter to the learned County Court Judge, explaining to him that he had been all round, and saying that the men were relying on his Judgment to support them in their contention, that there ought to be a new price list, and so on There was an offer

Lord JAMES of HEREFORD There was an offer to do the work and make a certain deduction for it

Mr DANCKWERTS A halfpenny

Lord ROBERTSON As I understand it, the argument which was advanced to us by the Appellants on this, it was this they quite admit that there was this bag dirt question, and also that the question was what you now say it was, but they say that it affected a comparatively small number of the men, and it had not such a hold on the mass of the miners that they would ever have struck as a body with regard to that It is suggested that other pressure and other motives operated upon them than the bag dirt, and that, that although an existing grievance, was not an operative grievance to the extent of bringing about a strike——

Mr. DANCKWERTS I understand that, my Lord They did try when they found they could not go to the full extent to make some point like that, but there is no doubt whatever that it was an operative grievance The only other point which they made in order to show that Lord James's Award had something to do with the strike was this There were other collieries in which there were boys I forget what the number of the other collieries was In due time the boys reached a point when their wages should have been slightly increased under the provisions of the contract, and the effect of Lord James' Award was to neutralise that increase in the boys' wages. What the boys in the other collieries thereupon did was that they struck because of not getting the increase which they had expected. They struck with the result that those collieries were thrown idle because the men could not get on without the boys. The boys were essential to enable the men to get on with their work. My learned friends said "because that happened in other collieries therefore we were entitled to say that in this colliery it was a mere pretext." I do not quite follow the argument myself, but that is what they said.

Lord JAMES of HEREFORD. What had the men to gain by putting forward the bag dirt point as the cause of the strike compared with that with regard to the deduction?

Mr DANCKWERTS. I think it was a good deal more than 10 per cent.

Lord JAMES of HEREFORD. With reference to the statement that you have made as to the strike in other collieries, why should the men of this colliery have put forward the bag dirt point if it was not their real case. Why not state boldly, "We have come out because of the deduction?"

Mr DANCKWERTS. I do not know. There is not any reason at all that we know of or can find for what my learned friends say. The difficulty is that in these cases the whole thing rests upon innuendo rather than evidence upon which you can put your finger, and the only way of meeting that kind of allegation is by telling you the whole story.

Lord JAMES of HEREFORD. If an innuendo is made, there must be some ground for it before it becomes worthy of argument.

Mr DANCKWERTS. There is really none. I believe the sole bit of possible suggestion or foundation for an innuendo is that one of the speakers at one of the meetings mentioned 10 per cent.

Lord JAMES of HEREFORD. Yes, he did.

The LORD CHANCELLOR. I am unable myself to see how it would advantage you to show it was not bag dirt. What does it signify whether it was bag dirt or anything else, provided it was in good faith? Even then, if it was in good faith, it would not help you very much, because it was undoubtedly illegal.

Mr DANCKWERTS. It was undoubtedly illegal. Everybody admits that.

The LORD CHANCELLOR. I do not say these things are not worthy of consideration especially from the point of view put by

Lord Robertson just now as suggestive of some influence behind to get the men to act in this way. I understand that, but to discuss this whether it is right or wrong seems to me to be remote.

Mr DANCKWERTS. I do not know of any way of meeting it except by putting the whole facts before you which slay it.

Lord JAMES of HEREFORD. Suppose you meet it as the Lord Chancellor has suggested to you by saying it is not of the slightest consequence which way it is taken.

Mr DANCKWERTS. If that is so, if that is your view, that is sufficient for me.

Lord JAMES of HEREFORD. Why not meet it in that way?

Mr DANCKWERTS. I cannot myself see any evidence of procurement of any sort or kind whatever. Perhaps you would allow me to consider seeing the stage at which we have arrived, whether I cannot shorten it.

(Adjourned to to-morrow at half-past 10.)

FOURTH DAY.

Friday, 16th March, 1906.

Mr DANCKWERTS My Lord, with reference to what happened yesterday at the adjournment, my friend Mr Isaacs can be here to-day, and as it is no use both Counsel dealing with the facts, it has been arranged that Mr Isaacs will deal with the facts before you I just want to cite one or two authorities, my Lord The authorities which I am about to cite are bearing upon this proposition with regard to ratification in cases of torts My Lord, in the case of Wilson v Tumman—that is in 6 Manning and Granger, page 236—the headnote is this "Where A does an act as agent for B, without any communication with C, C cannot, by afterwards adopting that act, make A his agent and thereby incur any liability or take any benefit under the Act of A "

Now, my Lord, that was a case where a sheriff had committed a tort in the course of making a levy under a writ of *fi fa* (I think it was), and Chief Justice Tindal, in delivering the opinion of the Court, lays down the principle in this way He says "The question, therefore, is a dry question of law whether the subsequent ratification by this Defendant of a taking under such circumstances is the same, in its consequences, as a precedent command of the Defendant And we think, under the authorities, and upon the reason of the thing itself, that it is not That an act done for another, by a person, not assuming to act for himself, but for such other person, though without any precedent authority whatever, becomes the act of the principal, if subsequently ratified by him, is the known and well-established rule of law In that case the principal is bound by the act, whether it be for his detriment or his advantage, and whether it be founded on a tort or a contract, to the same extent as by, and with all the consequences which follow from the same act done by his previous authority "

My Lord, that passage was cited by Lord Macnaghten in his Judgment in Durant v Keighley with approval, my Lord, that same case was approved in Woollen v Wright, 1 Hurlstone and Coltman, 555 Woollen v Wright was a case where 'an execution creditor does not, by becoming a party to an interpleader issue, ratify or adopt the act of the Sheriff so as to render himself liable in trespass for the seizure of the goods which are the subject of the interpleader issue " And, my Lord, the ground upon which it was put by Mr Justice Wightman, who delivered the Judgment of the Court, was based on the rule laid down in Wilson v Tumman

o

Lord JAMES of HEREFORD   That is Exchequer Chamber is it not?

Mr DANCKWERTS   This is Exchequer Chamber, my Lord   The Court were (rather a strong Court it was) Justices Wightman, Williams, Crompton, Wills, Byles and Blackburn   and it was the unanimous opinion of the Court that he delivered

My Lord, the next case in which a similar question was discussed is Ancona v Marks, 7 Hurlstone and Norman, 686   That was a case where an action had been commenced in the name of a person without his authority, and it was held that he might subsequently ratify that and it would then become his action   The same principle was put by all the Judges on the same ground   It was again based on Wilson v Tumman, and the Judges laid down the rule in substantially the same terms   I will not trouble your Lordship by reading it

My Lord, then there is a case in Godbolt, page 109, but your Lordship will find it mentioned in a note to Wilson v Tumman, at page 238   There are several cases quoted there   It is quoted there, my Lord, but it is in Godbolt   I think I have got another place where it is also quoted more fully   It is in the 4th Edition of Story on Agency at the bottom of page 305 in a note   This point arose as long ago as in the Year Book, 7 Henry IV, page 35   "There a party justified as bailiff taking a heriot for service due to the lord," &c (reading down to) "the subsequent ratification by the lord made him bailiff at the time"

Now, my Lord, as I have it now before me in the same book— Story on Agency, 4th edition, section 242—I will read it   My Lord, what I wish to say about this is that when Durant and Keighley was before the House here we verified it (Lord Davey will remember it), and this particular section is Mr Justice Story's own writing, and this is it   "But whatever may be the force of this distinction," &c (reading down to) 'an original authority"

Lord DAVEY   What was the case in which that passage occurred?

Mr DANCKWERTS   In Durant v Keighley, my Lord— Keighley, Maxted and Co, my Lord   My Lord, what I read from Godbolt is from Chief Justice Anderson, and you will find it on page 243 of Wilson v Tumman   I will read it, my Lord "If one have cause to distrain my goods, and a stranger of his own wrong, without any warrant or authority given him by the other, takes my goods not as bailiff or servant to the other, and I bring an action of trespass against him, can he excuse himself by saying that he did it as his bailiff or servant?   Can he also father his misdemeanour upon another?   He cannot, for once he was a trespasser, and his intent was manifest " Then Chief Justice Tindal goes on to say that he must act in the name of a principal

My Lord, in the Phosphate of Lime Company *v* Green, Law Reports 7, Common Pleas, pages 56 and 57, Mr Justice Wills discusses the proposition He says (that is the late Mr Justice Wills) "It remains to consider whether or not the Defendants have established the second branch of the alternative, viz that the Company did ratify and adopt the act of the directors Now, the law with respect to ratification is clear, and applies equally to cases of contract and of tort The principle by which a person on whose behalf an act is done without his authority may ratify and adopt it is as old as any proposition known to the law But it is subject to one condition In order to make it binding it must be either with full knowledge of the character of the act to be adopted, or with intention to adopt it at all events and under whatever circumstances."

My Lord, in Buron *v* Denman (2 Exchequer——

Lord DAVEY That is the case you have cited already, is it not?

Mr DANCKWERTS Yes, my Lord, but I had not it with me yesterday Page 167 is the beginning It was a trial at Bar before Barons Parke, Alderson, Rolfe, and Platt, and on page 188 Baron Parke, who charged the Jury on behalf of the Court in Banc, says this "Therefore, the justification of the Defendant depends upon the subsequent ratification of his acts A well known maxim of the law between private individuals is ' *Omnis ratihabitio retrotrahitur et mandato aequiparatur* ' If, for instance a bailiff distrains goods, he may justify the act either by a previous or subsequent authority from the landlord : for, if an act be done by a person *as agent*, it is in general immaterial whether the authority be given prior or subsequent to the act. If the bailiff so authorised be a trespasser, the person whose goods are seized has his remedy against the principal Therefore, generally speaking, between subject and subject, a subsequent ratification of an act done *as agent* is equal to a prior authority That, however, is *not* universally true In the case of a tenant from year to year who has, by law, a right to half year's notice to quit, if such notice be given by an agent without the authority of the landlord, the tenant is not bound by it Such being the law between private individuals, the question is, whether the act of the Sovereign, ratifying the act of one of his officers, can be distinguished On that subject I have conferred with my learned brethren, and they are decidedly of opinion that the ratification of the Crown, communicated as it has been in the present case is equivalent to a prior command I do not say that I dissent, but I express my concurrence in their opinion with some doubt, because, on reflection, there appears to me a considerable distinction between the present case and the ordinary case of ratification by subsequent authority between private individuals If an individual ratifies an act to be done on his behalf the nature of the act remains unchanged , it is still a mere trespass, and the party injured has his option to sue either , if the Crown ratifies an act the character of the act becomes altered, for the ratification does not give the party injured the double option of bringing his action against the agent who committed the trespass or the principal who ratified it, but a remedy against the Crown only (such as it is), and actually exempts from all liability the person who commits the trespass "

My Lord, in Phillips v Eyre (Law Reports 6, Queen's Bench, page 1), a passage appears at page 23   It is also in the Exchequer Chamber   The Court there consisted of Chief Baron Kelly, Barons Martin, Channell, Pigott, and Cleasby, and Justices Wills and Brett, and the Judgment was delivered by Justice Wills   At page 23 he says   " But to affirm that it is naturally or necessarily unjust to take away a vested right of action by act subsequent is inconsistent both with the common law of England and the constant practice of legislation   If (for instance, from the common law) a mere stranger, acting without authority at the time, takes upon him to do an act of trespass in the name and for the benefit of an absent person, such professed agent becomes liable for his unauthorised act, and a right of action is acquired by the person against whom the wrong was committed , and yet the general rule of the common law, borrowed from the civil law, is that the person in whose name the act was done may, if he thinks fit, afterwards ratify and adopt it " In every case, therefore, it must be done in the name or on behalf of (expressed in some way by words or by conduct, it is immaterial which) the absent person

My Lord, I think I have read nearly all the cases now   There is another one, Freeman v Marshall, 13 Queen's Bench, 789, which I have not here, but there on that page the learned Judge who delivered the opinion of the Court (I think it was) said that an act could only be ratified in such cases after full knowledge, or by a person who says I do not care what the act was, I am going to ratify it, which he says is equivalent to knowledge

Then, my Lord, there is one further case, Firth v Staines, 1897, 2 Queen's Bench, page 75, which is somewhat germane here from another point of view   (It was the Rural District Council of Staines, I think—no, it was a private individual) The question in particular there was whether an act of a committee of the Rural District Council committed without any prior delegation to them of authority, but subsequently adopted and affirmed by the Council was a binding act, and they held it was, and the late Mr Justice Wright says this " I think the case must be decided upon the ordinary principles of the doctrine of ratification To constitute a valid ratification three conditions must be satisfied first the agent whose act is sought to be ratified must have purported to act for the principal , secondly, at the time the act was done the agent must have had a competent principal, and, thirdly, at the time of the ratification the principal must be legally capable of doing the act himself" My Lord, that lays down in addition to Poulton the doctrine, namely, that where an act is done for somebody who cannot himself do it—being an infant, for example, or being a Corporation with limited powers, or a quasi Corporation with limited powers In that case it cannot be ratified, because the principal could not originally do the same act himself Then there is a case in America—in the Court of Missouri I think it is It is Rowland r The City of Gallatin—12, American Reports, at page 399 The head-note is this "The Street Commissioner of the city, under direction of the Mayor, took earth from the Plaintiffs' premises and used it in the construction of a street There was no authority in the charter or elsewhere to warrant such a proceeding *Held* that the city was not liable for the trespass," because they could not ratify it, I think, and because they could not do the act themselves

My Lord, I have now cited two English cases—Poulton and Firth r Staines—that the principal must be a person competent to do the act done by the agent before he can ratify it My Lord, there is a considerable paucity of authority on that question, but I think the explanation is that which is given by Lord Macnaghten in Durant r Keighley Maxted At page 245 Lord Macnaghten says this "And when your Lordships are told that there is no actual decision, nor even any carefully considered expression of opinion in favour of the view which the Master of the Rolls took to be settled law, I cannot help recalling the observation of a great Judge 'The clearer a thing is,' said Lord Justice James, 'the more difficult it is to find any express authority or any dictum exactly to the point'"

Lord DAVEY Where is Durant reported?

Mr DANCKWERTS 1901 Appeal Cases, pages 240 My Lord, in the Court below in Keighley Maxted (which you will find in 1900, 1 Queen's Bench) your Lordship will find a complete collection—a very careful collection of the authorities by the late Lord Justice Smith, and he says it is not based in particular upon its being a contract or its being a tort or anything of that sort but the way it is always put is An act done may be ratified by a principal if it purports to be done for him or in his name

Now, my Lord, I submit that there is really no distinction in regard to these matters between tort and contract and the reason why the cases mostly deal with the case of contract is, I submit that the question has never been really seriously doubted in connection with tort, and in the case of contracts they have always tried to make out somehow or other that there has been something done which takes it out of the rule rendering acts *ultra vires* invalid

My Lord, there is a case which my learned friend Mr Bankes cited yesterday, and that is Giblan r The National Amalgamated

Labourers' Union of Great Britain, which is reported in 1903, 2 King's Bench, page 600 That case is really an authority in the Respondents' favour when you come to look at it In that case the Union were sought to be made liable for an act which is undoubtedly within their power to commit, and which had been done by one of their officers and had afterwards been ratified and adopted formally by resolution of the Union

Mr S T EVANS Done by the chief officers ?

Mr DANCKWERTS It was done by the chief officers of the Union in that case

Lord DAVEY Has that been reported ? Mr Bankes quoted it from the *Times* I think

Mr DANCKWERTS No, my Lord, that is another case you are thinking of That is Wayhill and something This is in 1903, 2 King's Bench The passage which conclusively shows that I am right is at page 617 in Lord Justice Vaughan Williams' Judgment "There remains the question of the liability of the Union and Toomey I think they are both liable The Union, Williams and Toomey were all parties to acts constituting an actionable wrong—namely, interference with Giblan in the exercise of his undoubted common law right to dispose of his labour according to his will It is said that the rules did not authorise the acts of Williams and Toomey, but, be that how it may, the acts were not *ultra vires* of the Union, but only of its officers, and the Union in General Meeting undoubtedly adopted the acts of Williams and Toomey and took the benefit of them ' Therefore that so far from being a case tending in any way against the Respondents shows that the reasons are exactly what we contend for, namely, that it must be *intra vires* in order to be chargeable against the Union

My Lord, the other case that I promised to give your Lordship the reference to is the Royal British Bank *v* Turquand, an Exchequer Chamber decision which is in 6 Ellis and Blackburn, page 327, and at page 332 Chief Justice Jervis in delivering the opinion of the Court (which was formed of Chief Baron Pollock, Barons Alderson, Cresswell, and Justices Crowder and Bramwell) said this "We may now take for granted that the dealings with these Companies are not like dealings with other partnerships, and that the parties dealing with them are bound to read the statute and the deed of settlement " And, my Lord, similar propositions were laid down in the following cases Balfour *v* Ernest, 5 Common Bench (New Series) 624, *Re* the Athenæum Life Company, by Vice-Chancellor Wood, 4 Kay and Johnson, at page 559, and Ernest *v* Nichols, 6 House of Lords Cases, by Lord Wensleydale My Lord, I submit, therefore, that in dealing with these Unions people have always to remember what are then powers at the time by their statutory rules which anybody can get for a shilling

Mr RUFUS ISAACS If your Lordship pleases My Lords, I propose to deal with the facts of the case, and what took place at the trial before making any observations to your Lordships upon the law, or quoting any cases, in fact I may say after the decisions that have been referred to, the observations that I shall have to make upon the law may be very short, as I only propose to deal with the principles which I contend are really laid down by the authorities which have been referred to, and I shall not trouble your Lordships with further reference, to the authorities, but, my Lord, it is of great importance that one should understand what took place at the trial, how this case was tried, and indeed what was left to the Jury and what was the direction to the Jury, upon which the Jury did arrive at the conclusions of fact upon which my learned friend's argument is based My contention is that there was no evidence to support any of these findings of the Jury—that so far as they can be used against the Defendant Association for which I am appearing—there was no evidence, and then further I desire to call your Lordship's attention to this that I do not think has yet been brought before you, that should it turn out that your Lordships should think that there was some evidence (as the Master of the Rolls thought) upon one part of the case, as he in his dissenting Judgment explains—then I have to consider the summing-up, because my submission is that in that case this verdict and Judgment could not stand, and that though your Lordships came to the conclusion that I was not entitled to Judgment for the Association—that there must be a new trial because the verdict and Judgment given as they were could not be allowed to stand—and it is that that makes it essential, and also some criticisms which I have to direct to the Master of the Rolls' dissenting Judgment—that makes it necessary that I should go, I will not say at length, because I do not think it really becomes of importance to do that, but at some detail into what I consider the vital parts of the case The rest of it, I think, I shall be able to deal with very shortly, indeed, but in the Master of the Rolls' Judgment, which has already been read to your Lordships, it is very significant that he there comes to a conclusion which I submit from any point of view cannot be supported The Jury having been asked to find one conspiracy, that is a conspiracy dating as from the 29th June 1902, that is conspiring to injure and molest the Plaintiffs in their business, and in that way to entitle the Plaintiffs to recover damages for all the injury or damage which has been sustained by the Plaintiffs, that is Question No 9, which I shall have to refer to in more detail directly, and that is far the most important question of all these findings, it is far the most important question, much more far-reaching than any of these questions on the subject of damages, because if that finding were to stand, which is based upon the decision of your Lordships' House in Quinn v Leathem, if that finding stands it has the effect of making the Association responsible for all the loss occasioned to the Colliery Company by reason of the strike and of the continuation of the strike, and it is upon that, that in the main, the Plaintiff's case must rest for his claim for the £150,000 damages which he has launched against the Defendant My Lords, that finding has not been affirmed by any of the Judgments of the Court of Appeal In the Court of Appeal I respectfully contended that the Court of Appeal could not set aside the verdict of the Jury on one conspiracy, and substitute for it a finding on another conspiracy which had not been before the Jury If I may make my meaning clear, my submission was that supposing the Court of Appeal came to the conclusion that we were right in the view that we were presenting to them,— that is, that the Association had had no part in what has been described, and what your Lordships will understand when I refer to it, as the first period,— that is from what took place, including the 29th June, 1902, up to the 15th July, 1902—that period depending upon the view which your Lordships may take of the agency—that is as to whether the branch officials were the agents under the rules, it not being contended that there was any express authority—and then also upon the ratification point which is found in the Plaintiffs' favour in Question 5, those are questions which relate entirely—or, at least, I may be wrong in saying that—which may be sustained in relation to the first period, and in respect of which it cannot be contended that the Association itself (I mean upon the view of the Court of Appeal) was taking part The Association only interfere at a subsequent stage, but the Court of Appeal came to this conclusion two of the learned Lord Justices, as your Lordships know, found that there was no evidence to support the finding, but the Master of the Rolls said that although he agreed with our contention that there was no evidence to support the finding of the Union having taken part—being responsible for anything that took place up to the second period (that is the period from the 15th July onwards) yet that from that date he did find for reasons which he gave that they had interfered or intermeddled with the strike in some way which made them liable for all the subsequent events, and upon that he finds a conspiracy—because that is what the Master of the Rolls does find—that they were acting in concert, he says, from that date Now if that is true it cannot make them responsible—nor does the Master of the Rolls in his Judgment take the view that the Association were responsible for acts which preceded these acts of the Union from the 17th July onwards, but he then proceeds to say that as there was an acting in concert by them from that date he thinks there was an actionable conspiracy upon which the Plaintiffs would be entitled to damages

Lord JAMES of HEREFORD Is not that merely a convertible term with respect to the question that you put of the date? The Master of the Roll says No evidence for the Jury of procuring, but evidence of maintaining

Mr RUFUS ISAACS Yes, my Lord, I think it is, so long as it is borne in mind that maintaining can only refer in that connection to the second period

Lord JAMES of HEREFORD I put it as a convertible date, it represents rather what is meant by the alleged action of the Defendant.

Mr RUFUS ISAACS Yes, my Lord, I am quite prepared to accept that, as I say, always provided that the same thing is meant, and I think it is What the Master of the Rolls means by his Judgment is, that you having as from the 17th July on paid strike pay That is really the main thing——

Lord JAMES of HEREFORD Yes

Mr RUFUS ISAACS And there being, as he thought (I shall have to deal with it), some evidence of intimidation and molestation for which in some way he thinks the Union may be made responsible— those three constitute unlawful acts, and being unlawful acts for which you are responsible, and having been in concert with yourself and damage having resulted you have an actionable conspiracy

Lord JAMES of HEREFORD For maintaining.

Mr RUFUS ISAACS Yes Well, an actionable conspiracy to injure and molest the Plaintiffs in their business The maintaining and the intimidation and the molestation are the acts by which the conspiracy is proved

Lord JAMES of HEREFORD Exactly

Mr RUFUS ISAACS That is the view, but I shall have to call attention more definitely to what the Master of the Rolls says with regard to it I only wanted to indicate how the case will stand so that your Lordship might, if I might say so, follow with regard to what I intend to say later on on some of the passages in the evidence to which I must call attention The substance of this point that I am now making being that the Master of the Rolls by his Judgment has substituted a finding of another conspiracy which I maintain was not really before the Jury at all There may be some controversy with regard to it, and I shall have to call attention to what took place, but that is the way that the case stands My Lord, of course that arises only if we fail to establish to your Lordship's satisfaction that the Judgment of the majority of the Court of Appeal was right, that is that there was no evidence to support the finding, and it is to that part that I propose to direct in the main the observations which I have to make

May I point out further in regard to the way the case was tried what happened in the Court below, because that again is rather important to follow in order to appreciate some of the observations which were made in the Court of Appeal, and indeed some of the arguments which have been addressed to your Lordship's House on this hearing I certainly do not intend to weary (because I am quite sure that it must weary) your Lordships by going in detail through all this evidence about the bag dirt, I am only going to refer to it for the purpose of showing what happened I can summarise the position which I have taken from the first moment with relation to the bag dirt by saying this—that I am not seeking a finding that our view with reference to the bag dirt was right All I am saying is that there was a grievance which the men honestly thought a legitimate grievance, and that is the height to which I have ever sought to take the findings, or to ask for any finding with reference to the bag dirt That again, in the view which I put forward to the Court below in the Court of First Instance and in the Court of Appeal, was quite irrelevant The view as to the bag dirt and why the men struck is, I say with the greatest respect, a matter which is outside the consideration of Courts altogether So long as the men struck, they were perfectly entitled to strike, although it may be that in law they took a wrong view of their position, but in dealing with the case before a Jury—as your Lordships will appreciate—I could not leave the case with that statement, because the case had been opened against us dealing with this 10 per cent point and that the basis of this statement was that the 10 per cent reduction was the real ground of the strike

Mr ELDON BANKES It was used as an argument

Mr S T EVANS It is the whole of the summing up

Mr RUFUS ISAACS My learned friend says it was used as an argument I do not really mind much whether it is used as an argument or whether it is a statement All I can say is, if it is an argument it was not based upon the evidence, and there it is one that ought not to have been adduced, but now what my learned friend is——

Mr ELDON BANKES I do not mean that I used it as an argument, but that the men used it as an argument

Mr RUFUS ISAACS If the men used it as an argument, what is the materiality or bearing of that unless it was intended to be used in some way against the Association for the purposes of this case ? I am quite sure my learned friend would not have put before the Jury all the arguments the men used when there is a question of whether they are to go out on strike or not, but this is far more important than perhaps your Lordships might think for the moment, having regard to my learned friend's interruption (of which I am not in the slightest degree complaining) because the learned Judge thought that this was such an important point, being lured to that view by my learned friend in the Court below—he was so impressed with this view—which I had sought as strenuously as I was able to remove from his consideration so that he might direct the Jury that the view which we were putting forward was right—that is, that whether it was the 10 per cent grievance, or whether it was the bag dirt grievance the Jury had nothing to do with the merits of the strike, but although we laboured hard for this purpose, my learned friends triumphed in this, that they succeeded in getting the learned Judge to take the view that it was really the most important point in the case, and when I call your Lordships' attention to his summing-up, you will see that what he says is this Really a very important question is, was this bag dirt question a legitimate grievance, or was it a mere pretext, as has been put forward by the Plaintiffs? That is the question you have to answer yourselves The learned Judge's view is that that was the basis upon which the Jury had to form an opinion as to the whole of the rest of the case, if they once came to the conclusion that this bag dirt grievance was not a *bona fide* grievance but had been used by the men or by the Association in some way for the purpose of manufacturing some colourable pretext, and, my Lord, be it observed that not only does the learned Judge take that view but, I think, I am right in the observation that the Master of the Rolls uses the same language in his Judgment, he talks of it being a colourable grievance

Lord JAMES of HEREFORD Where, I think, the ratification may be of some importance (I took rather a different view yesterday) is in this way If the 10 per cent reduction was the real cause of the strike that would be a general cause

Mr RUFUS ISAACS Yes

Lord JAMES of HEREFORD A cause which would give the Barnsley people more interest in it than if the bag dirt was the real cause, which would be a local grievance

Mr RUFUS ISAACS Yes, my Lord, and if my friends are right in saying that the 10 per cent was the cause, it makes my case far stronger really than if it was the bag dirt, because if they are right in saying that the 10 per cent was the real grievance then the branch certainly could have had no right to have struck without the Council—without the Association coming to the conclusion that they should Then you would get into operation Rule 12 and the other rules under which there would be a strike for the general benefit of the Yorkshire miners, and I quite appreciate that would be if that was the fact——

Lord JAMES of HEREFORD If you get a strike for the general benefit what is the deduction from that? what is the effect of it in law?

Mr RUFUS ISAACS Then the branch had no right to have struck at all

Lord JAMES of HEREFORD No, it is colourable

Mr RUFUS ISAACS This one branch out of 150 branches could have had no right to strike, that is to say, the men there could not have been authorised by the Council—by the Association—to strike, and more particularly to strike to redress a grievance under the pretext of something else

Lord JAMES of HEREFORD It might have been so in fact, and it might have been maintained in fact, though it would not have been proper under the rules

Mr RUFUS ISAACS Of course, I suppose one might conceive—dealing with what I think is in your Lordship's mind—this, that the various branches might have been told to manufacture some grievance—to put it forward as a pretext for the purpose of a strike because it might be thought that it was not desirable to strike against a decision which had just been given I can understand that

Lord JAMES of HEREFORD Can you tell me, Did the 22 or 23 other branches that struck strike in the name of the 10 per cent or not?

Mr RUFUS ISAACS Oh, no, nothing whatever to do with it That is what we relied strongly upon Nobody did

Lord JAMES of HEREFORD Did they not give other causes—the other branches?

Mr RUFUS ISAACS Yes, my Lord, every one of them That had nothing whatever to do with it, and indeed in one sense they were not strikes at all We had to go into it because so much was made of it They were not strikes at all In the case of the other collieries—the branches—what happened was this—that there was some difficulty with the boys—nothing to do with the colliers The boys would not work, the consequence was that the colliers could not work, and the Association would not pay and did not pay strike pay My friend says—and I rather think that he is right in making this one correction—I will call attention to the evidence of it directly—I think I am putting it rather too high when I say they did not pay any strike pay, I think in some instances they did, but whatever the value of that may be it had nothing whatever to do with it None of the strikes were strikes in respect of the 10 per cent reduction or against the 10 per cent reduction, and if it became a question of fact of importance in this case whether or not the strike was against the 10 per cent and that the bag dirt was merely a pretext—then, my Lord, surely upon a point of that kind it was of the utmost importance that there should be a definite finding. You must have a finding of the Jury before that can be inferred. My Lord, may I say I do not think that that was the case, with respect, but that was put forward by the Plaintiffs, and I say *that* for this reason—that they never asked for a finding on it, and after carefully formulating their questions, this which if they were right was the most important question, never was put at all—obviously the question which was at the threshold of the case and which the Jury would have to decide upon

Lord JAMES of HEREFORD: Will you tell me, Did your opponents put it as high as that the Barnsley Central knew of the false pretence—knew that this bag dirt was only put forward formally as a pretext?

Mr RUFUS ISAACS: I think the way it was used against me—and the only justification there could have been for introducing the 10 per cent at all—the only justification apart from pure prejudice—no doubt prejudice which would operate very strongly upon the minds of a special jury, but the only legitimate ground upon which it could be put, and on which I think it was put, and the reason why my learned friends introduced it—though they may have been tempted to magnify it a little owing to the presence of the Jury, but the reason of it was this. They said, we can show that in truth it was the Association that was behind it, because if it was the 10 per cent grievance then the Association was interested in it; if it was the bag dirt grievance then the Association was not interested in it, it was a mere question as affecting the local branch. If that is not the way in which it is put then there could have been no justification at all for introducing it. That is the only defence I have heard put forward.

Lord JAMES of HEREFORD: I will tell you why I asked you whether the Association knew of it, it was for this reason. Mr Pickard was, apparently, the moving spirit at Barnsley.

Mr RUFUS ISAACS: Yes.

Lord JAMES of HEREFORD: Mr Pickard being a member of the Conciliation Board he represented the workmen, and I think it is a very hard thing against him (he is dead) to say that he was not perfectly loyal to the decision of the Board. If it is true, as was put forward, he must have been plotting against the decision.

Mr RUFUS ISAACS: It was called attention to when this case was before the Court below—the Court of Appeal—and it was admitted that there was no reflection of any sort or kind, or imputation upon Mr Pickard—it was expressly said and I am quite sure it could not be made and would not be made. It was really perhaps too tempting a morsel for my learned friends to leave when they had to get findings of fact from the Jury because I do not know that it would be easy to find in a case of this kind anything which would be more tempting to inflame the Jury's mind against the Association than to say Here they go to a Conciliation Board composed of employers and men and presided over by your Lordship, and then when they have got a decision which they do not like they immediately set to work to get rid of it Although we were contending that it was not really material, we could not allow that statement to be made, because, as set out, it would have had such a very serious effect upon the minds of the Jury

The LORD CHANCELLOR Was that case put?

Mr RUFUS ISAACS Oh yes Oh, most certainly, my Lord, and I have complained of it on every opportunity I have had, I have said in the words I have just used to your Lordship that nothing could be more inflammatory to the Jury than that, and that has always brought from my learned friends an explanation of why they used it, because I contended—certainly in the Court of Appeal (and as I think I was right in contending) that it had been introduced as prejudice which affected the case very much My learned friends said—and, of course, I accept their statement at once—that they did not introduce it for prejudice, that they introduced it because they thought they were legitimately entitled to introduce it, and that it had some bearing upon the case, because it enabled them to say—or gave them some ground upon which they could ask the Jury to find—that what had happened when the men were induced to break their contracts was the work of the Association That is how it was used

Lord JAMES of HEREFORD Because the Association was interested in one view and not the other

Mr ELDON BANKES I am loth to interrupt, but, my Lord, this question has been under discussion between my learned friend and myself as to the purpose for which the reference to this 10 per cent was made, and in the Court of Appeal I read from the Shorthand Note my opening to the Jury about it

Mr S T EVANS Not Mr Lush in reply

Mr RUFUS ISAACS You did not read Mr Lush's reply I absolve my learned friend almost entirely He introduced it in the first instance with a very slight reference I think my learned friend used it with the greatest discretion —I am bound to say that although I quite agree and do not for a moment suggest that my learned friend Mr Lush in replying did not think he was perfectly justified in using it and pushing it to the extreme,—I can only say it was used in the strongest possible way against us, and in the way which would most prejudice the Jury's mind,—and not only the

July's mind, but it prejudiced the Judge's mind, because the learned Judge was so captivated by what had been said by my friend Mr Lush in reply, that he seemed to take it that the important question (as I was saying just now) was whether or not this was a pretext My Lord, he says it at page 962

Mr ELDON BANKES Your Lordship will understand that the matter was in conflict between us, and my learned friend will refer to it

The LORD CHANCELLOR I quite understand, but you will have an opportunity, Mr Bankes

Mr RUFUS ISAACS Later on I am going to read the summing up,—I shall leave to, but I only just want to make this point that I am referring to at page 962—E to F—this is what the learned Judge said—I am reading from D "Now that being so, then we come to the disputes which arose Taking it broadly, the first question that arises is—I am not putting this as a question for you, but a question which you will have to settle in your own minds" (therefore that is the basis), "though it is not one of the questions I am going to leave to you, but one of the questions upon which greater time has been probably spent than upon any other —was the bag dirt question the real reason of the strike which took place upon the 29th of June, as said by the Defendants, or was it, as alleged by the Plaintiffs, a mere pretext for the strike which took place upon that occasion?"

Now, my Lord, certainly nothing could have been more complete than the triumph of my learned friends for the Plaintiffs in taking the Judge along the road which they themselves had wished to travel, and had to travel, but, of course, the question is whether that was right

Lord JAMES of HEREFORD Has your junior got a short summary of how Mr Lush on the part of the Plaintiff put the materiality of this question?

Mr RUFUS ISAACS My Lord, we have got the reports of all the speeches, and your Lordships shall have a short summary of it, and my learned friends, if they have not it, shall have a copy

Mr ELDON BANKES We have the Shorthand Note

Mr RUFUS ISAACS Very well, you can refer to it Of course, as my learned friend, Mr Bankes, rightly says, this is brought up at every hearing on further consideration, and there has been a hearing in the Court of Appeal, and on every hearing there has been some discussion with reference to this—I always maintaining the view—accepting explicitly, of course, what is said by my learned friend with regard to it, but still maintaining that the effect of this was prejudice, and that it had no real materiality or bearing upon the case

Now, my Lord, in the Court of Appeal I contended for this view and submitted to the Court of Appeal that it was wholly irrelevant to this case to consider whether it was the one cause or the other that had brought about the strike   I said there is evidence, and I am prepared to go into it, but I contended in the Court below that it had nothing to do with it and I contend that now, and the Court of Appeal really stopped me upon that point and agreed at that time that that was the view that they held, that it could have no bearing upon the case because upon either of the grounds clearly the men would have been entitled to strike, although, no doubt one can quite understand that it would be in a sense a wrong thing, although it would not have been legally wrong—it would have been a wrong thing to have had a strike against this decision after they had joined in getting it   The evidence, my Lord, upon it is really rather curious because so far as I have been able to follow what my learned friends have proved and have said upon this matter, their evidence consists upon this point of three references in speeches—out of a great number—to the 10 per cent, accompanied in each case by a much longer reference to the bag dirt grievance which was the immediate necessity   That is the evidence in the case, and it was upon that slender material that the whole edifice was built and that we have the learned Judge stating what he did state at page 962   There is not a tittle of evidence upon this point except those speeches which have been referred to, and which my learned friend called your Lordships' attention to yesterday or the day before   My Lord, they were the speeches which were made on the first occasion   May I just call attention to how the matter stands—and now I am going to put facts which are not in dispute up to this point—facts I mean upon which there can be no controversy, because every single fact which I am going to refer to now is contained in documents   I will give the references, if I may, to them without going through them, but I am going to summarise the position as it was in relation to this bag dirt   That this grievance had existed for a number of years is made plain from what my learned friend stated in opening the case to your Lordship, and from every witness whom he called I cannot do better than say this - that Mr Chambers admitted that it had been a legitimate grievance—that is, legitimate in the sense that the men believed it to be a grievance—of course, not that they were well founded, but that the men had believed it to be a grievance for a number of years   There had been two County Court actions, one, I think, in 1897, the other in 1901, in which the points had been tested, and in both of which the men had failed, there had been numberless deputations, there had been numberless letters upon the point, and there had been references to the Joint Committee to deal with this matter, and it culminated in the year 1902, when, after the trial at the County Court at Doncaster, when the learned Judge made some observations with the intention of bringing about a settlement of this long existing dispute between the parties, whereupon the men asked that they should have an interview with Mr Chambers, and they did have it. They had interviews in February of 1902 and in March of 1902, and were stimulated by what the learned Judge had said to get what they called a revision of the price list, the revision of the price list being to the effect of altering this cutting in "tops" from the 1s 4½d., so that they might be paid more where the bag dirt was extra thick and hard.

Now, my Lord, in that position of affairs we get to June of 1902, the grievance constantly being agitated, and your Lordships will remember there was early in 1902 a ballot taken upon this very point, and the requisite majority—the requisite number—did not vote in favour of it. There was a good deal of diversion of opinion at that moment. Then, later on at the week ending the 28th June, 1902—which was a Saturday—came the climax, and as one can understand—because the men were touched in what was a very vital point—a number of the men (16 of the men) who were working had £8 15s deducted from their wages. £8 15s was deducted from their wages by Mr Chambers because he contended that he had had this work done and was therefore entitled to deduct it from the pay which the men would be entitled to. In other words he said I have done part of the work that you ought to have done. I am not for a moment attempting to ask your Lordships to say which was right in the dispute, but that led to a feeling of great aggravation on the part of the men—those men whose wages, as they thought, had been unlawfully stopped—wrongfully stopped—by Mr Chambers, and they were quite powerless in the matter—must be powerless in the matter—unless they got the colliers in the other collieries to join them in what would be the only effective protest against this reduction of wages, and for that purpose the meeting is called on the 29th June.

Mr S T EVANS. The next morning.

Mr ELDON BANKES. There were many more than 16—a great many more.

Mr RUFUS ISAACS. I want to avoid controversy if I can with regard to it. My learned friend says it is a great many more—that it affected more than 16. It really does not matter for the purpose of the point I am putting. It would not matter to us if it was 160. My learned friends have said at one time 25, and there is some doubt as to how many men were affected, but it really does not matter at all for the purpose of the point I am putting. I suppose to whatever amount the wages are stopped it has to be made up—and was made up by the other men, and they were affected by it, the amount is immaterial that would come out of each man's pocket, but the consequence of this was that there was this meeting

P

called for the 29th June (that was the next day, the Sunday) of 1902
And my Lord at that meeting the speeches are made which are
relied upon as containing the only evidence against my clients of
having attempted to bring about the strike against this 10 per cent
reduction, and at that meeting on the 29th June—I am just going
to state the salient facts with regard to it, because it is very important
in relation to an argument which I am going to address to you upon
the first and third questions which were submitted to the Jury—
that is the procuring point, because what happened was this The
bellman is sent round to call a meeting, he calls a meeting which
takes place at the Croft, the evidence is (of Mr Chambers and
everybody in the case) that the meeting was called in respect to this
bag dirt grievance There is no doubt about that That was the
point that necessitated the calling of the meeting, and indeed as my
learned friends say in one part of their case, although it cuts against
them on another—that is why they got so few to attend the meeting,
because your Lordship will remember it was stated by my learned
friend, and I take the figures from him as far as they are material—
they are sufficiently accurately stated—there was between 4,000 and
5,000 men employed at these collieries

Lord JAMES of HEREFORD When you say between 4,000
and 5,000 men, do you mean "men" or "hands," including boys and
everybody ? It is not very material

Mr. RUFUS ISAACS I rather meant "hands," my Lord I
did not mean to draw a distinction Out of those 4,000 or 5,000
employed, 2,000 only were members of the Union On the question
of the procuring, my submission is that this becomes of some
importance The meeting is called for the 29th June, and at that
meeting 200 to 300 men and boys attend, and it is from that meeting
and what takes place at that meeting that the case is launched—
which is the point from which my friends must start and upon
which they must rely for the whole case that the branch delegates,
Nolan and Humphries, and, under Question 3, some members of
the Committee, and Mr Croft the President—that those branch
officials procured the men to break their contracts

Now I am going to say something in a moment, when I come
to that part of the case about the procuring of 4,000 or 5,000 hands
to break their contracts The only evidence of it which was before
the Court, and which is before your Lordships, are the statements
which are alleged to have been made—are proved to have been
made—at this meeting called on the 29th June, at which 200 to 300
were present—men and boys, and from that the extraordinary jump
is made—as I respectfully submit—the extraordinary jump which
everybody seems to have made with my learned friends, that
because it is proved that there is a meeting at which 200 to 300
men and boys were addressed by the branch officials and assuming
(as I do against myself for the moment) that those 200 to 300

were induced to break their contracts with the Company, that therefore you are to assume without anything further that 4,000 to 5,000 did the same. I submit it is an extraordinary fallacy. It does not even stop there, because what happened with relation to this matter was this. The men were addressed by these officials, and the men passed a resolution—when I say "the men" I mean those present—they passed a resolution, and I suppose it can hardly be doubted that that resolution must have a good deal of effect upon some of the men. No doubt a good many of the men again may have had other causes operating upon their minds, but the only way in which it can be suggested that what the branch officials had said had procured the men to break their contracts is by saying that having procured the men to pass a resolution, and that resolution (I suppose it would be said) affecting the minds of other men, that therefore you are entitled to make a jump and say that the statements which had been made by the branch officials — which never were communicated to the other men—had operated upon the other men's minds, so as to induce them to break their contracts. My submission is that that is a complete fallacy, and that there is not a tittle of evidence to support that excepting what took place at this particular meeting.

Now, my Lord, on the 29th June, page 388—I am referring now to what my learned friend Mr Bankes read as evidence upon which he bases his case of the 10 per cent, and he addressed an argument to your Lordships upon it—if I quite follow he must have found some ground for putting forward that view, and he called attention to this speech for the express purpose of pointing out to your Lordships that what was operating on the minds of the men—what was bound to operate on the minds of the men—was the 10 per cent.

Now, my Lord, Mr Fred Croft, who was the President of one of these two branches, deals with this matter at page 388, and he makes some observations at "D" to "E" about the 10 per cent. Perhaps I may remind your Lordships that the decision had been given, I think, at the end of June, and it would be operative as from the 12th July, that is to say, it would come into operation one week after what was called the first "making-up day," which would be the 12th July, 1902.

Lord JAMES of HEREFORD. I think, Croft, before you come to "D" and "E," goes into the other cause of the strike—that is the bag dirt cause.

Mr RUFUS ISAACS. I am much obliged to your Lordship. I had lost the reference to it for the moment. "B" to "C" is "as to whether anything should be done with regard to the 'bag dirt' question." Then he goes on. "When it came to nearly £10 on a Saturday being stopped from their fellow working men" (the exact amount was £8 15s.) "it was time something was to be done, when

18s went out of a man's wage it was hard lines. It was hard lines when a penny was deducted, but when it came to £3 12s being stopped from four men it was a bit thick" (the four men worked in one stall or gang, as, I suppose, it would be called, and they were paid in that way—£3 12s came from one settlement). "It was for them to say what they were going to do. 'If any speaker treads on your toes this morning don't cry out, but bear it.' The district was prepared at the previous meeting in September. He had told them then as a gentleman had said, they had winter before them and he said if they had, they had summer still. It was beautiful weather and they could stand it. They stood it in '93" (Then he goes on) 'for about 10 weeks without anything and the feeling had been throughout the Federation that they would suffer again before they would suffer a 10 per cent reduction." All I can say is that this gentleman appears to have felt that it was rather a hardship upon them—he does not seem to have been particularly pleased that their wages were to be reduced under the decision, the 10 per cent, and he travels—as people have done who make speeches in other places—from the point which is immediately under discussion to another grievance which is not relevant to the matter which is then before the meeting, the discussion of this 10 per cent.

Lord JAMES of HEREFORD. Croft was the President of Denaby only, I think.

Mr RUFUS ISAACS. Yes, Croft was the President of Denaby only, the Denaby branch, and all these men—I rather think this has been stated, your Lordship will forgive me if I am repeating it—all these Committee-men and branch delegates were working people in the collieries, which forms another rather important matter, having regard to some observations I want to make later. "The wage question was a one-sided affair. When Judge Ellison was then Arbitrator he had given another 10 per cent advance," and so forth. Now I do not need to read all that takes place upon that. The next one, I think, is Mr Harry Humphries, who is a Cadeby official. That is at page 389. He said "So far as the 'bag dirt' question was concerned, it had always been contended that they had nothing to do with it."

Lord JAMES of HEREFORD. I am sorry to interrupt you, but if you look at 389 it is "If they would support them, they would support the men in getting a fair wage on Saturday." Is that "bag dirt," or is that 10 per cent?

Mr RUFUS ISAACS. I think that is "bag dirt." Your Lordship will see what he says in the next passage. "It was time that the 'bag dirt' question was settled."

Lord JAMES of HEREFORD. Yes.

Mr RUFUS ISAACS "There was not another colliery where they got coal so cheap as they did at Denaby Main" Then he goes on

Lord JAMES of HEREFORD I beg your pardon You have got on to Humphries now

Mr RUFUS ISAACS Yes, my Lord I am about to refer to Humphries Then Humphries begins "So far as the 'bag dirt' question was concerned, it had always been contended that they had nothing to do with it save in the getting of it down or in the removing of it as it was not on the price list, according to the contract under which they worked The bag dirt some years ago was not so thick then, as it was now, neither was it so hard to get down He remembered the time when they were only too glad for the bag dirt to stop up, so that they could get the coal from under it They had had to set props under it to hold it up, and when they took the props away the stuff fell It was the same now as then in some districts" (that is the district which led to the difficulty) "the 'bag dirt' had stiffened and took four times the amount of labour to get it down as it used to do Formerly it was so handy to get in for the 'packs' and came down so easy that they never took the question into consideration" Then he goes on—I do not want to read right through it, but he goes on for a considerable time dealing with the whole of this matter I think, my Lord, that this gentleman, Mr Humphries, only deals with this matter, he does not say a word about the 10 per cent It is rather important, he is a delegate for Cadeby, and he is at this meeting making a speech at which it is said the 10 per cent was the important matter which was discussed He makes a speech of some length, but he never says a word about the 10 per cent All his observations are directed to the bag dirt

My Lord, I do not think I need read anything more of what he says except at letter "C" After dealing with the facts about 18 or 19 being stopped from the men he says "It was time that the men should not have this to contend with, and if it was then cause they should want the men to fight the cause for them They were met there to ask the men" (now this is what he says the meeting has been called for) "who were not affected to help these men The reason was because of a principle, and he thought every Union man, when one man had a grievance, should make every man's grievance his own There were two large districts, and where there were a lot of men to deal with, there was a lot of trouble to get all the men in one mind" Then he argues to try and get all the men to make common cause with those who had the money stopped from their pay, but not a word, as I say, about the 10 per cent

Then Nolan, who is the other delegate, and was a Defendant who put in no defence—Nolan was the Denaby delegate—he deals with it, and your Lordship will remember these are the men—Humphries and Nolan are the two men who are said to have induced,—or rather the word "procured" is the word used in this case—"procured" the men to break their contracts, and the important thing is that Humphries never says a word about the 10 per cent and only deals with the bag dirt, and Nolan also deals entirely with the bag dirt question, so that the men who procured the breach—both of them—only deal with the bag dirt and never say a word about the 10 per cent. They are both men who would be affected in conjunction with the other men working at the collieries by the stopping of pay for bag dirt, they themselves being workers.

Now, I am not going to read Nolan's speech, my Lord, it deals entirely with bag dirt, and deals with it at some length. It states the facts which have been stated to your Lordships several times, and I do not want to go through it again. If your Lordships would look at page 392, at "C," he winds up by saying what I submit is of great importance as explaining the view that the men took of the case. "Since the Judge had made his decision" (that is the decision of the Doncaster County Court in February, 1901), "they had collected £30 to put the men right who were suffering from the deductions." I can hardly want better evidence than that that the men thought that there was a legitimate grievance that they collected among themselves £30 for the men.

Then a resolution is passed. Now, my Lord, may I just pause there? May I point out that the resolution is an important matter, because it is only from that resolution and what happened after the resolution that my learned friends are able to base the argument that there was a procurement by the branch delegates of the breach of the contract? Now, all the speeches that have been made there are those three, one of them only contained a reference at the end of the speech (which begins by dealing with the bag dirt question for which the meeting was called) to the 10 per cent. The other two, and the two which are said to have "procured," never mention the 10 per cent from beginning to end. That is how the matter stands in evidence.

Lord ATKINSON. There is the evidence of Hurst immediately after.

Mr. RUFUS ISAACS. I am much obliged to your Lordship. I just stopped at that moment because I was calling attention to the resolution which was then passed. There is the resolution, and the resolution only deals again with the bag dirt, so that the extraordinary part of it is that it is said against these men that they have got some deep Machiavellian scheme in their heads, which I should have thought was far beyond the reach of a collier, that they had some idea in their heads of putting forward "bag dirt," but in reality wanting to get rid of the 10 per cent, so that all the resolutions they pass are totally ineffective, and, if my learned friends are right, are really fraudulent, in the sense that they are bogus resolutions, passed entirely with the object of throwing dust in the eyes of somebody—I do not quite know who   Then comes the resolution about the bag dirt   After the resolution is passed, Hirst, who was a Cadeby official, says "The question had been labouring in his own mind and he thought it had been explained very well   There was an understanding that they ought to have a few words with reference to the wages question"   Now it shows that that is something which was outside the matter of discussion , there ought to be a few words said about the wages question. " With regard to the 10 per cent reduction when they were about to enter on it he would refer to it in a few remarks "   Then he goes on   " Some few weeks ago they had held a Joint General Meeting of the Denaby and Cadeby Main workmen including surface men   The question before them was with reference to the recommendation from their officials connected with the Association to accept the 10 per cent   His opinion was, at that time, that they should not hear of the reduction   In Northumberland and Durham their wages had gone down very seriously   The wages had gone down 33⅓ per cent ," and then he goes on to explain—I do not want to read it all , he is dealing with this question of the reduction which had been made, but it is after the resolution is passed, and it is only because the men are there and it is another matter which was affecting the men's minds, and he says he thought some few words ought to be said with reference to the wages question   Now, my Lord, I think that really that is all that there is of evidence of the 10 per cent My learned friend says I have omitted the most significant passage I thought I had referred to it, that is on page 389   I thought I called attention to everything that there was there   I do not want to be taken back to it   I think your Lordships are well aware——

Lord JAMES of HEREFORD   What is it ?

Mr RUFUS ISAACS   What my friend is very anxious that I should read is the words " When Lord James gave in his decision against them they ought to say we will not stand it "   That is what Croft said   This is what has been read, and as to which I have said already that Croft had dealt with the bag dirt question, and then had passed on to the 10 per cent

Now, my Lord, so that there may be no misunderstanding about this matter what I submit concludes this against my learned friend— at least in your Lordships' House—are the questions that they framed so carefully to put to the Jury   There are four speeches made—one is Croft's—dealing with the 10 per cent , the others are Nolan and Humphries and Hirst—made after the resolution   Now, who are the persons they so induced ?   My Lord, at 1009 they put their questions, and they never suggested for a moment that Croft had induced the men to break the contract, nor did they suggest that Hirst had induced the men to break the contract   Their case is this   Did the Defendants Nolan and Humphries procure the men to break their contracts of employment by going out on strike?

That is the matter to which they direct attention. That is in the forefront of their case. It is quite true to say this, that they subsequently put another question which would include Croft.

Lord DAVEY: It is Harry Humphries.

Mr RUFUS ISAACS: Yes, my Lord.

Lord JAMES of HEREFORD: One has a nickname.

Mr RUFUS ISAACS: It is the same one, and it is the Cadeby official.

Lord DAVEY: Yes.

Mr RUFUS ISAACS: As I was saying (I do not want to mislead in reference to it), it is quite true that subsequently they put another question, which would and does include the Committee, and would include Croft, because they put Question 3. I will show directly what that was. The point I am making about that is that this first question is the question upon which they base their case. Their case was: The branch delegates have induced the men to break their contract, and then they say: Not only the branch delegates but the Committeemen interfered and intermeddled with the strike, and therefore the branch Committeemen also took some part in this procuring; and it is upon that that they base the view that the Association is responsible for these acts.

My Lord, I will just read the two or three passages my learned friend is kind enough to give me the references to, of what my learned friend Mr Lush, said. I will give the references so that my friend may follow. At page 629 he says, first of all, this: "If this was, as I am going to demonstrate to you it was a Union strike, that is to say a strike for which the Trade Union were responsible, I succeed here if I show that the object of it was in itself an improper object—an unlawful object. If, for example, I show, as I shall, that the object of it was because of this 10 per cent. reduction to bring the employers to their knees and raise prices, if the object was to molest the employers, to injure the employers, then, the object of the combination being unlawful, the Union are liable in damages." Well, I must not pause to criticise my friend's language to the Jury, but there your Lordship sees the extraordinary confusion of terms that are used; but the whole point of what he is saying is that he is going to show that the object was because of the "10 per cent. reduction to bring the employers to their knees." This was a point he argued strenuously that therefore it was an unlawful object for which they had struck, and therefore an unlawful strike. The point which my learned friend, Mr Lush, argued strenuously for was that if the men struck for an object of that kind it was unlawful, and that the protection of the Trades Unions Acts given to combinations of men in furtherance of their disputes did not avail them, because he said, all that that means is that it must be for a lawful purpose My Lord, I think what he meant was this—it eluded me at various stages, but I think that what my friend meant, and was eventually putting, was this—that if they had got a decision against them which they did not like and they struck against that decision, then it was an unlawful thing to do, because, having got that decision, they were bound to act on the decision that they were bound to conform to it, and that combining for the purpose of getting rid of a decision which had just been given—refusing to abide by the decision—would be an unlawful purpose, and, therefore, would be a conspiracy

Then, my Lord, my friend says further (page 634) "I think I can best assist you by taking the various issues one by one, pointing out to you what are the considerations on the one side and on the other, and then dealing with each of them, endeavouring to help you by focussing the evidence as far as I can, and showing you what the true conclusion to arrive at in respect to those different issues is The first one in point of date, and the first one in point of importance is this We say that this strike on June 29th, when the men broke their contracts and came out, was not the spontaneous and voluntary act of the men at all We say that it was a strike which was procured and induced by the officers of the Union acting on the Denaby and Cadeby branches and we say that it is a subterfuge for them to pretend that it was the voluntary act of the men, because we say it was the officials who got them out, and not the men who wanted to come out They say, on the other hand, that is not true They say the men came out voluntarily, because they wanted to come out, and they say the reason for their doing it was their discontent about the bag dirt"

Mr WADDY Do you mind reading on from the next line?

Mr RUFUS ISAACS By all means "Now, gentlemen, I will tell you at this point the importance of this 10 per cent question under the Award of Lord James of Hereford, and I beg you to bear this in mind, that in itself it is a matter of no importance By that I mean this That it matters nothing what it was that induced the officials to call them out Whether they were actuated by one motive or another is immaterial, and even if we were wrong in asking you to believe that the 10 per cent was the cause, it would not affect our right to succeed if you still thought it was the officials who called the men out" That is to say my friend says it is of no importance to my case, because although I may fail in proving to you that the 10 per cent was the real cause, it does not affect my case—it does not hurt me, because you still may come to the conclusion that it was the officials who called the men out "But it has this most important bearing upon the question which you have got to determine The whole defence of the Union to this action is that the men came out because of the bag dirt dispute, and if I satisfy you that this is a mere pretext, that what induced the officials to do what they did was this grievance of having their wages reduced by 10 per cent, it has this important bearing on the case that it will convince you this thing they rely upon was, as I say it was, a subterfuge, because if Lord James of Hereford's Award was the real cause it shows that the defence they put forward was a sham defence, and it gets rid of the only answer that they make to this first contention of ours, namely, that it was the officials who got the men out. Therefore it is idle to pretend", he is dealing now with points I had been making to the Jury, and he says "Therefore it is idle to pretend that this question of the 10 per cent is only imported to prejudice your minds. It is one of the strongest arguments on which I am going to rely in asking you to come to the conclusion that we are right in saying that this was the officials' strike, and not a strike of the men at all." Then it goes on. Then my friend, at page, 637 says———

Lord JAMES of HEREFORD. Before you pass on, will you tell me this. What happens before the speech is made? In the first place, the speech is made, as I understand, at the meeting by Cadeby and Denaby men—the branch, and not by men from the general Association.

Mr RUFUS ISAACS. Yes.

Lord JAMES of HEREFORD. Had any single official spoken before the resolution?

Mr RUFUS ISAACS. No, it it is not suggested.

Lord JAMES of HEREFORD. Any central official?

Mr RUFUS ISAACS. No, it is not suggested. All the evidence that there is about the resolution indicates that. There may be one more speech, it may be two at most, but the important point as to what took place before the 29th is contained in those passages I have given to your Lordship. There is no other evidence.

Lord JAMES of HEREFORD. Croft and Humphries.

Mr RUFUS ISAACS. Yes, and Nolan.

Lord JAMES of HEREFORD. And Nolan.

Mr RUFUS ISAACS. All the other evidence is on the "bag dirt" question. This is the only evidence as to the 10 per cent, and that consists in the references made, as I submit, by Fred Croft, because Hirst is in favour of and determined to do it.

Lord JAMES of HEREFORD   Hirst is in favour

Mr ELDON BANKES   At page 637 again my friend comes back to this question; there have been pages in between on this question which I have not read—pages of it

Lord MACNAGHTEN   What was your last reference?

Mr RUFUS ISAACS   Page 637 of the book of the speeches It is not in the book before your Lordship, it is page 637 in *this* book   "First was the bag dirt really at the bottom of this dispute? Secondly, did the bag dirt people take part in the strike at all? and Thirdly, was it thicker or harder so as to give them a more moral claim to more payment?"   Then my friend says, later on, this "Now, gentlemen, let me show you beyond doubt that the real grievance was one that they did not dare to put forward"   That had reference to pretending that it was something else   Then it goes on again—pages more—and at page 640 it goes on again What I read just now was at page 637   Then I come to page 640, but I will not read that because it is only repetition, and at page 675—having gone on for some 40 pages now—my friend is coming to the conclusion and he says "Gentlemen the cause of this strike, now that these men are not obliged to work upon the men, as they were originally, is no longer this suggested complaint about the bag dirt   It is the price list—the getting of bigger wages   It is getting more than they had got before   That really caused these people to call upon the men to persist in the strike, and I will challenge my learned friends to find after this period was entered upon, and the intimidation was well in play, any reference to the pretended cause that had brought them out   Gentlemen, the price list is the explanation   What has become of friend bag dirt—the friend that they had used on June 29th, and forgotten when the strike was settled? Poor bag dirt!   He was brought in, like people often are, and used for a purpose, and flung aside, and I say I think the least they can do for him is to put up some slab to his memory at Denaby, because when once they have made him serve their purpose they fling him away, because I say the men know that it is wages and wages alone which keeps them out   Now, Gentlemen, about the ejectment notices, it really seems to me absurd, and I will not discuss that The men stopped in their houses   Of course, I do not say that I have proved that the officials have induced the men not to go out, but it is all part of the same thing, and by inducing the men to stop out on strike and not to work it obviously follows that the Denaby Company were losing the benefit of these houses and losing the rent which the people there ought to have paid and were obliged to pay   Now, Gentlemen, of course, there is this aspect of the case with regard to the 10 per cent, and I do say this, that if in fact the 10 per cent was the cause of the strike, they were through the Union in that respect procuring the men to break their contract, because I suppose it is always implied as a term of every arbitration that the parties to it will abide by the Award If in fact they were inducing the men to come out in order not to abide by the Award, they were inducing the men to break their contracts, and they would be liable on that ground even if there were no other grounds upon which we say they are liable" I am much obliged to my learned friend for the references That proves what I had stated from recollection as to what had taken place at the trial, and what my learned friend was putting forward as the unlawful ground upon that bearing was the decision—the Award I called it, it is not properly an Award, but it is a decision—and a decision to which the men have conformed without question, but there it was used, and as your Lordship sees, used again and again and again, and with the effect that I have already indicated to your Lordships, and it is not to be wondered at, if I may so, with the greatest respect to the learned Judge, that the Jury were carried away by these observations against the Defendants, when my learned friend had the effect upon the learned Judge that he desired to have upon the Jury, and when I come to read the summing-up your Lordship will see that the learned Judge's Judgment is coloured throughout by this, which had very strongly impressed his mind The view that he took was that they had put forward, or at least that there was good ground for saying it, and that it was an important matter in the strike and an important matter in the consideration of this case, to find out whether it was a mere pretext or subterfuge, as my friend said

Lord JAMES of HEREFORD What do you say is the effect of this? Is this tribunal to come to the conclusion that Mr Lush did by his eloquence lead the Judge astray, and that the Jury were led not to take a due sense of the importance of this question? What effect has that upon the finding of the Jury?

Mr RUFUS ISAACS If I am right, my Lord, it would cause them to be set aside

Lord JAMES of HEREFORD A new trial?

Mr RUFUS ISAACS Yes, they fail on the first point

Lord JAMES of HEREFORD You cannot go further?

Mr RUFUS ISAACS No, not on this point Of course, I do go further, but it would not entitle me to do more than that

Lord DAVEY You may explain how they came to give this finding and this verdict

Mr RUFUS ISAACS It is for that purpose that I am referring to them now As I was saying, one has to bear in mind in view of these findings what had happened at the trial so as understand really how it was that the Jury came to the conclusion which they did arrive at

Lord JAMES of HEREFORD   We shall have to determine whether there was or was not evidence to go to the Jury

Mr RUFUS ISAACS   Certainly, and if I fail to convince your Lordships that there was no evidence to support the finding—suppose I fail in that, and, therefore, that I should not be entitled to Judgment—then your Lordships would have to say whether the summing-up was satisfactory or whether there was not misdirection, as I contend there was—in which case I should be entitled to a new trial

Lord JAMES of HEREFORD   You use Mr Lush's argument in support of that argument

Mr RUFUS ISAACS   Yes   Then I say that what my learned friend said had that effect

Now, my Lord, so far I really think that I have said all that I want to say for the time being about this 10 per cent point which has to my mind (I say it with the very greatest deference) occupied infinitely more time in every court which has had to do with this matter than it merited , but the difficulty has always been that one has had to face that, and as my learned friend Mr Bankes said, when he was opening this case, he rather put that forward in support of the bag dirt question   I say   That is perfectly true, and it was very ingenious, but your point was the introduction of something which was wholly irrelevant , but your Lordship sees the only reason why we introduced the bag dirt question was to counteract the effect of their having introduced something prejudicial to us which we were contending was immaterial   That is the only reason why we did it at a very early stage of the case, I think my learned friend Mr Danckwerts quoted it, but certainly I said it was quite immaterial to me what the merits of dispute in the bag dirt question were once it was admitted that it was a *bona fide* dispute, and the reason why I had to go into it was to counteract the effect of my learned friend's observations upon the 10 per cent , and, as I say, every time I have had an opportunity to speak upon it I have always maintained to Judge, to Jury, to the Court of Appeal, that the merits of the strike have no relevance to the matter under discussion   My submission is that all that a court of law will look to is whether an unlawful act has been committed and that it is of no value to say to a court of law (even supposing my friend could establish that it was a right thing in one point of view on which nothing could be said) that having got a decision which they did not like they engineered a strike against it   The way in which it was used is shown by the last passage which I quoted from my learned friend's observations It has taken a long time to get to that, but eventually he does say that the way in which he uses it is for the purpose of showing that it was a strike engineered by the Association and for an unlawful object. Those are the words he used. And, of course, I make this last comment upon this part of the case, from which I propose to pass now, that it is a very remarkable thing that my learned friends having devoted so much time—and they having devoted so much time—to this question when they came to frame the questions of fact (the questions of fact upon which it was necessary to have a finding), and when, presumably, they were away from the tribunal and were discussing as lawyers the questions which would have to be put to the Jury, it never occurred to them that this question of subterfuge or pretext was of any relevancy at all, and it never was a question for the Jury at all

Lord JAMES of HEREFORD. The learned Judge takes that point himself, he says. I am not going to ask you that question

Mr RUFUS ISAACS. Yes. The learned Judge if I may say so of him, found the questions handed up to him by my learned friend, and took those questions as they were handed up. He certainly gave me the opportunity of suggesting any other questions, but I took the view, as I submit now, that as I contended there was no evidence to go to the Jury I should take no part in framing questions that I said ought not to be presented to the Jury, and thereupon after giving me that opportunity, he took the questions—carefully framed by my friend—and put them *en bloc* as my learned friend had framed them. He did not put any questions of his own. He adopted my friend's argument upon the point, and that really I think lies at the root of the whole thing, and it is for that reason that I attach so much importance to it, because my respectful submission to your Lordships is that every one of these findings of fact is coloured by the view that the learned Judge has put to them with the assistance of my learned friends. At the passage I read just now he said. That is what you have got to find first

Now, my Lord, that is the position on the 29th June, and I call attention to this, that at that meeting this small number of men had attended, and that so far the Association had had nothing to do with it, and it is not pretended that the Association had had anything whatever to do with it, it is not pretended, I say, except in so far as this 10 per cent point may affect the consideration of this question I confess that I do not understand even now—I know that I am open to the reproach of my learned friends, who have made it before upon this—it may be my fault, but I confess I do not understand now how the 10 per cent question can affect the consideration of the first question as to the inducement to break the contract, it can have no bearing upon it, because my learned friend Mr Bankes admitted in your Lordships' House in opening the case that he did not suggest that there was anything in the nature of authority to the branch officials from the Association to procure the breach of contract, except in so far as you may get it—and as he contends he is entitled to get it—from the rules. That is entirely a question of construction upon the fact in answer, I think, to my Lord Chancellor, who said—what he was bound to say upon the case as it stands—that there was no evidence of it and he could not see that the Association had taken any part at all, so that that part of the case (the first part of the case and the most important part) depends entirely (absolutely, my submission is) upon the construction of the rules and that there is nothing else which is relevant to the consideration of this issue

Lord JAMES of HEREFORD: Would it suit your proposition to call that a "procuring"?

Mr RUFUS ISAACS: Yes, my Lord, if under the rules the branch officials were the agents of the Association, and (I must add what my learned friend omitted in his proposition with reference to this) "for that purpose." Then if they were the agents of the Association for that purpose that is a procuring of the breach of contract—in other words for the procuring of a strike—and if that was done on behalf of the Association, as my learned friend contends, then he has gone a long way in establishing his case, and he has established a very important element in his case. I shall have something to say with regard to that later, but that is the first question of fact, and with reference to that question of fact I want respectfully to take these two points. The first of them is—and this, I say, applies to the first four questions which are asked, because for this purpose I am going to draw no distinction (it is only to avoid repetition) between branch delegates and branch committee men—the first two relate to branch delegates only, the second two—that is, the third and fourth questions—relate to the committeemen, and on those four questions my submission is that there is no evidence to support the finding of the Jury upon those questions of fact—no evidence. I say there is no evidence to support the finding, and then I say, as a matter of law—assuming that, in fact, these persons did do what is alleged and what the Jury have found, then there is no evidence upon which the Association can be held liable.

The LORD CHANCELLOR: Are you not dealing with the Questions 2, 3, 4 and 5?

Mr RUFUS ISAACS: I intended to deal with 5, it is really covered, and I am going to say that 5 is covered by four.

The LORD CHANCELLOR: I only want to know what you mean.

Mr RUFUS ISAACS: I think some other observations would have to be made with reference to 5 which would not apply to 1 and

4 Questions 1 to 5 are questions which deal with the first period, the procuring period, only, and I have divided them so as to keep Question 5, which is the ratification point, separate, because some observations I am going to make upon that would not apply to these other four questions, although they apply to what I am going to say on those four questions equally to the fifth question

Now, my Lord, I want to say why I submit no evidence of the facts found as apart from the responsibility of the Association What is it that is asked there? The carefully framed questions, purposely framed with the object of hitting (if I may use the expression) the Association—it is of no value to them to get a verdict against Nolan and Humphries, who indeed have not put in a defence—what they want is to get a finding of fact upon which they can say the Association are liable Now it would not do for them to get a finding that the 200 to 300 persons or some of them who were present at the Croft on the 29th June were induced to break their contracts That would not suit my friends My submission is that that is the utmost extent to which they can go upon this evidence They could only say at the highest that all the 200 to 300 who were present at that meeting were induced to break their contracts by the statement of the officials But that is not the question they put, and it is not the question they meant to put for the reasons I have just given It would not help them at all What they want to get is, that the 4,000, to 5,000 persons of whom my learned friend Mr Bankes stated to your Lordship in opening, all except an insignificant number did not go to work on the 29th June or on the 30th June—he wants a finding that all those persons broke their contracts, and that is why the question is put in this way "Did the Defendants Nolan and Humphries or either of and which of them unlawfully and maliciously procure the men to break their contracts of employment by going out on strike on June 29th without giving notice" Now what he means by that—and what the whole case is launched to mean is all the men who did not go to work on June 29th, all the 4,000 to 5,000, less some 40 I think it was said, who did continue to work for some little time If I may, I will just illustrate why it is that it is necessary for them to get that finding This is a claim in which they seek to recover from the Defendants £150,000 damages for loss occasioned to them as from the 29th June Now, of course, if they only get a finding that 200 to 300 men and boys, or some of them, did not go to work on the 29th or 30th June because of the statements of Nolan and Humphries the damages are infinitesimal as compared with the amount which has been claimed That would not suit them at all

Lord JAMES of HEREFORD What did cause the men not to go into work?

Mr RUFUS ISAACS I have no doubt the bag dirt question.

Lord JAMES of HEREFORD   It was brought in some way to their knowledge

Mr RUFUS ISAACS   I have no doubt there would be a resolution passed

Lord JAMES of HEREFORD   But they called a public meeting, the bellman went round

Mr RUFUS ISAACS   Yes, I stated it just now   I said they most probably dealt with the thing from the general point of view   What happened was this   They knew of the bag dirt grievance, it became bruited about in the neighbourhood, because in this place they are all colliers—people engaged in the collieries

The LORD CHANCELLOR   Suppose it to be the case that the speeches procured the resolution and the resolution procured the breach of contract, do you say that that is not sufficient causation?

Mr RUFUS ISAACS   Yes, my Lord, I do   That is the point I was making   I say, supposing you take it at the highest against me, that the speeches brought about the resolution and that the resolution brought about the men not going to work, I submit that that would not be sufficient

Lord JAMES of HEREFORD   I should like you to expand that

Lord MACNAGHTEN   I did not catch what you said last

Mr RUFUS ISAACS   I said that that would not be sufficient to make the Association responsible for the refusal of the men to go to work who had not been present at the meeting

Lord JAMES of HEREFORD   The Association is one thing   What the Lord Chancellor asked you was the cause of the strike

The LORD CHANCELLOR   Let me put it in order that you may see it clearly   I am asking you the question whether the Association is responsible for the speeches   If you please, let us assume that the Association is responsible

Mr RUFUS ISAACS   Yes, my Lord

The LORD CHANCELLOR   Then you would say that the speeches caused the resolution, we will suppose

Mr. RUFUS ISAACS   Yes

The LORD CHANCELLOR   And the resolution caused the absence of the whole 4,000 or 5,000 men from their work   Could you say that the speeches were not substantially in that case the cause of the absence of the men from the work ?

Mr RUFUS ISAACS   My Lord, I should submit, yes

Lord JAMES of HEREFORD   You mean you should submit not

Mr RUFUS ISAACS   I mean I should submit what my Lord said, not submit that it would be the cause

The LORD CHANCELLOR   That is your contention   Now we can get on

Mr RUFUS ISAACS   That is the point   That is what I meant to have answered   I passed then imperceptibly into the Association in answering my Lord's question   I did not mean to Really I think I might put it in this way   Did what Nolan and Humphries said cause the men who were not present and did not hear it to refuse to go to work on the Monday ?   That is the question That is the real question put in another way   So far as I know I submit that no case has ever gone so far as that, because here what we are dealing with is procurement   Now, I understand "procurement" to be operation on the mind with effect   It really is persuading with effect   If you procure a breach of contract, it means that you persuade a man not only to come to the conclusion that he shall break his contract, but you persuade him to do it and he does it   You must have the two things   You must have persuading him and you must have the result   That is the procuring of the breach of contract   Then here, in order to reach the men's minds, the statements which are relied upon as having been made at the meeting and contained in these speeches which are before your Lordships, are statements made by Nolan and Humphries to those who were present, and it is those statements that persuaded the men (I am assuming against myself for the moment) and boys who are there present to pass the resolution which they did pass , but there is an end of it when we have arrived at that, at any rate, they are not statements which have caused the men who have not heard them

Lord JAMES of HEREFORD   Is not that very limited ? If a man makes a statement in a community, it is not only the people in the room who are affected by it, it overflows amongst the community, you cannot limit it to those who were present when the statement was made

Mr RUFUS ISAACS   My Lord, I suppose that must depend Of course, if you could show that the statement is repeated, no doubt that may be effective

Lord JAMES of HEREFORD The bellman goes round and says "Come to the meeting, and there they listen to the speeches," then the men go home—they are workmen living near each other—they are men who go down the pit together, surely you cannot limit it to the persons present?

Mr RUFUS ISAACS In one sense I do not care very much about this for the purpose of the Appeal I am now arguing, because I do not think it becomes of great importance, having regard to other points, but I do desire, so far as I can, to guard myself from making any admission that that would be the result, because the effect of it is really very far reaching If your Lordships were to say that in consequence of a statement made by a delegate to 200 men—if after that it turns out that a number of men do not go to work, that therefore you are entitled, as a matter of law and evidence, to say that that is evidence that these men do not go back to their work because of a statement made by a delegate to somebody else, I do submit that that is travelling rather further than hitherto we have been able to travel under the rules of evidence

Lord ATKINSON Mr Isaacs, I should like to draw your attention to the last two lines of that resolution "having tried to come to some amicable understanding and failed, the only thing that is left for us to do is to stop the wheels at both collieries"?

Mr RUFUS ISAACS Yes

Lord ATKINSON How could the men addressed stop the wheels of both collieries, except by enlisting other workers in the movement?

Mr RUFUS ISAACS My Lord, I think this is what must happen—that these men would persuade other men, and did no doubt persuade other men

Lord ATKINSON Then is not express authority given by the resolution to the men then and there present to start upon that propaganda?

Mr RUFUS ISAACS The difficulty is that what one has to arrive at is the cause of action here being the inducement It is not the breach of contract That is the importance of it The cause of action is the procurement of breach of contract, and what you have to arrive at is What is it that did procure it? Take, for example, the repetition of a slander, it is an analogous case Suppose a slander uttered and repeated? That is not sufficient

Lord JAMES of HEREFORD Take your case——

Mr RUFUS ISAACS Vickers and Wilcox is an authority in my favour on that point

Lord JAMES of HEREFORD Take the case of slander A man in a public room where there are a hundred people present slanders another, then he says Special damage, I have lost all my trade throughout the district, could you give damages in respect of the loss of trade as regards anybody except the hundred people who heard it ?

Mr RUFUS ISAACS No

Lord JAMES of HEREFORD Why not ? You must take the nature of ordinary things

Mr RUFUS ISAACS Surely Vickers v Wilcox is the authority for that particular proposition My Lord, I have not it here May I call attention to it another time, I will if I may

Lord JAMES of HEREFORD Can you give evidence of general loss of business ?

Mr RUFUS ISAACS Yes

Lord JAMES of HEREFORD That includes the neighbourhood ?

Mr RUFUS ISAACS Evidence when given of general loss is really because it is said that it is the result of the statement made— of the statement published

Lord JAMES of HEREFORD Would the one hundred people agree to that ?

The LORD CHANCELLOR It seems to me you are going rather far when you say you cannot consider the resolution as operative beyond those who heard it

Mr RUFUS ISAACS My Lord, I do not think I am saying that with respect—at least I have not made myself clear I do not mean to say that the resolution may not have done it

Lord DAVEY It is said that the men were called out on the 10 per cent question, there is nothing in the resolution about the 10 per cent

Mr RUFUS ISAACS Not a word

Lord ROBERTSON Are not you rather mixing up two separate propositions ? I quite understand your view on the question between the 10 per cent and the other thing, but is not the gravamen against you of what you are now discussing not any specific statements of reasons given for striking, but the fact that these officials of the

Defendants told them to strike? Now that does not require any analysis of motives or arguments

Mr RUFUS ISAACS My Lord, I have no doubt if your Lordship thinks that I am confusing the two I must be, I did not mean to I was rather passing from the 10 per cent

Lord ROBERTSON I do not ascribe "confusion" to you at all

Mr RUFUS ISAACS What I meant was I had passed from the 10 per cent and was dealing with the first and third questions The only reason that I am concerned in arguing this is that I want to guard myself (perhaps I may be travelling outside the necessities of the particular case) against its being thought that by merely giving evidence of a statement of certain men—as in this case of a resolution arrived at by these men—that that is evidence that a number of men who were not present and did not hear the statement—who could not have heard all the statements and to whom it was not proved that they were repeated—have been induced to break their contracts by the mere statement that it has induced men who were present to break theirs, or rather to pass the resolution With great respect it seems to me a very considerable jump to say (when you analyse it, it is put in this way) that because Nolan makes a statement to one man the effect of which is to cause that man to make up his mind to break his contract, and then this man goes and repeats to other men what Nolan has said to him I submit would not be evidence that Nolan had procured other men to break their contracts That is the point I am upon

Lord JAMES of HEREFORD May not the Jury infer that Nolan wished the one man to repeat to the other?

Mr RUFUS ISAACS And even if they did repeat, would it be sufficient, with respect?

Lord JAMES of HEREFORD He would be sent forth then as a repeater of the words

Mr RUFUS ISAACS We still get two questions It is one thing to wish—there are very few statements that one wishes to be repeated that are repeated as one would wish them to be repeated Suppose the statement made by Nolan was transmitted by one of the persons present at the meeting with some elaboration and exaggeration, the question is as to whether that would operate I do not want to take up time in discussing this further, because I have said all I want to say, and I say again with deference, my only object in saying it is not so much for the purposes of this case because I have the other argument, but because I do desire to guard against any admission that this could be evidence of inducement to those who were not present and did not hear the statement

The LORD CHANCELLOR I do not ask you about that any more You have been kind enough to answer it Upon this resolution and these speeches, I may have overlooked something, but did the resolution or did the speeches ask the men to strike so as to break their contracts?

Mr RUFUS ISAACS Oh, no, it did not What it asked them to do was to "stop the wheels" We have got to that point

The LORD CHANCELLOR Then the question is whether "stopping the wheels" would import stopping them at once, without notice?

Mr RUFUS ISAACS Yes

Lord JAMES of HEREFORD Then Mr Isaacs, I think, you must reduce it to that—that they did stop them

Mr RUFUS ISAACS Yes, I think so—they did, and I think I am right in saying it was the intention that they should

The LORD CHANCELLOR That they should stop them at once

Mr RUFUS ISAACS Yes, from what happened I think it must have been so No doubt the men, having come to the conclusion at this meeting—whatever the operating clause in their minds was—to strike, the effect of it was that they did not present themselves for work on the night shift on the Sunday as the result of this, and I think one must take it that they understood it to mean that they were to strike at once

The LORD CHANCELLOR Yes

Mr RUFUS ISAACS And indeed it is because of that very fact that they did strike in breach of the contract that the Association refused from the very first to countenance it until they had put themselves right If they had struck—if they had given their notices and then refused to go to work, the Association would have been in a different position, because then under the rules if the Association had come to the conclusion that every peaceful means had been adopted—that everything had been done that could be done to arrive at an amicable understanding and had failed, and the men set up a breach of contract, then the Association would have been entitled to grant them strike pay

The LORD CHANCELLOR Yes, I understand

Mr RUFUS ISAACS That being so, here the difficulty that arises in the Association, and which curiously enough is proved and relied upon by my learned friends for one part of their case, is, I submit, the conclusive answer to the point which they make upon Question 5 and ratification, a conclusive answer in fact, because as your Lordship may know from the evidence—and I shall have to call attention to it, and will call attention to it in a moment—as to what took place after the 29th June, immediately the Association knows of it the Association says This is wrong, you are out in breach of contract, you have to give 14 days' notice and you have not done it, you have come out in breach of the rules, you have no right to do this, go back, put yourselves right at once I submit that was very proper advice from every point of view, and one does not quite understand how it can be said to be ratification of an inducement to break the contract That is what takes place, and that attitude is continued right up to the end of the first period— the procurement period That is, the Association is taking that point of view from first to last The Association never swerves from that point of view, and indeed it is part of my friends own case, but whether it is so or not does not matter, because it all depends upon the documents The case, as proved beyond all question, is that the Association was informed, and that the Association gave them the notice, and then, before I call attention—as I am going to do—to a few of the documents, it certainly will not be necessary to trouble your Lordship to go through any number of them, because I am going to submit that the thing is so plain upon the documents that it admits of no doubt, and therefore I need not multiply the evidence of it, but the history of what took place, quite shortly put, and as found by your Lordships in Howden's case—in which these facts were under review and discussion—what was found there was this, and what was proved and what I take to be new ground which is beyond all debate—it is the differences between the same parties, because although in name Howden was the Plaintiff it is not disputed, and could not be disputed after the statements which my learned friend frankly and rightly made when Howden's case was being fought, that it was really the employers' action, they had to have Howden as Plaintiff in order to bring it, and a good deal of argument took place upon it in this House as to whether under the circumstances Howden could obtain the injunction; it was held that he could notwithstanding those facts, but it was the employers who had "bought"—I do not mean it in any offensive sense in the way of bribery or anything of that kind—I will not say that, but who had paid him a sufficient amount per week to induce him to refrain from doing the work of a collier to live in London the life of a gentleman for some time, while they had got their proceeding on its way to your Lordships' House, or to lend his name as he was lending his name—to bring this action to stop the paying of the strike pay Now the importance of Howden's case, I submit, is difficult to exaggerate, because Howden's case decided this, that when the men had refused to go back to work (which was the breach of contract complained of, because under their contract they were bound to give 14 days' notice and did not) they committed a breach and the employers were entitled to rescind the contract and did rescind the contract, and the last point is, as I submit, of very great importance. That was the argument upon which much turned in Howden's case, because in that case I put forward the argument, or rather the Counsel for the Association—it is immaterial—put forward the argument that the contract never was broken—that there was merely a suspension, by consent of the parties, of the contract, but that it had always remained the same contract—that it never had been broken—and, therefore, there being no breach, the Association were entitled to pay the strike pay (which they did) under the rules—the point in Howden depending upon whether or not the men had struck, whether, in fact, there had been a breach of contract. If the men had struck in breach of contract, then under the construction of the rules which your Lordships took the Association was not justified in granting the strike pay. It was an essential condition that there should have been no breach of contract. In order to meet that the Association argued: We are entitled to grant strike pay because there has been no breach. It was said then: How can you say that when the men were out from the 29th June and never re-presented themselves till the 17th July? and then the Association answered that, and this was the point which it was essential for them to maintain in order to justify their view— the view they were putting forward to your Lordships—that there was no breach of contract. They said that between the 29th June and the 17th July there were negotiations proceeding for an amicable understanding, and at the end, in a telegram which I shall read in a moment, Mr Pickard said to Mr Chambers: Will you let the men resume work? And Mr Chambers said: The men may resume work at any moment. The men then, by orders of Mr Pickard, who had said to them: You must go back and get back to work, re-presented themselves, or presented themselves, for work on the 17th July, and in doing so gave their notices. The difficulty that arose was that they were asked to "sign on again"—as the expression is. The men said they would not sign on again. The manager, Mr Chambers, said: You shall not be allowed to come back to work unless you do sign on, and apparently the difficulty between signing on and not signing on was not worth, as it turned out, much discussion, if any. The result of it unfortunately was that between these two views there was no *media via*, and the conclusion was that the men refused to sign on, the manager refused to let them go back to work. Then the men from that time were out of work for a very considerable time, and what was said by the Association was: When the men presented themselves for work, as they did on the 17th July, they were resuming work under the contract the purpose of which had been suspended by mutual consent and were not really presenting themselves to enter into a new contract, and indeed to some extent that seems to have been one of the reasons which operated upon the minds of those who refused, or were advised to refuse, to sign the new contract Now that has passed beyond all discussion now

Lord JAMES of HEREFORD Can you tell me why in this case, as in many others I have known Why did the men insist on stopping the wheels at once and break their contracts, instead of giving notice and putting themselves in a legal position?

Mr RUFUS ISAACS My Lord, I should think the answer to that is—Temper I know of no other I am afraid that is what happens When men's money is stopped, their angry passions rise, and the consequence of it is that they were annoyed about what had happened and they did stop, but certainly there was no necessity to stop, and that is what Mr Pickard and the Council were saying to them That is the very view they were taking

Lord JAMES of HEREFORD Not only in this case have I known it, but in many others, they will break their contract

Mr RUFUS ISAACS They do—a lot I am afraid the answer must be in most cases something like the answer I have given, although I may have put it somewhat crudely, but I think that is really what happened in this case and indeed I think your Lordship will find it in other cases, it is the case that the rules of the Trades Unions are framed for the very purpose of meeting this The object of the Trades Union rules is usually to prevent the men going out in a temper—hastily—on strike The rules are framed—certainly these rules in this case are, and in many other cases with the express object of preventing that and for a very good reason—without the necessity of putting it upon high moral grounds—it is sufficient to say that it is very much to their material interest, because otherwise what would happen would be that when men had grievances at branches they would be striking, and the result would be a serious matter for the Union if the branches every time there was a grievance struck They have a right to do it and do do it But then comes the important matter If they strike in breach or in any unlawful way then the Association cannot help them, and that operates, I think one may say, as a very salutary check

Lord JAMES of HEREFORD The men know that When they strike they know they will not get strike pay

Mr RUFUS ISAACS I am afraid, my Lord, when men do that they forget the rules and they forget that when they strike under these circumstances it is not possible for the Association to give them the strike pay That is what happens This case is one of various cases which illustrate that the Union really operates to prevent the men from breaking their contracts and to make them do what is lawful—to make them follow what is the lawful course—the right to give their notices, and when they have given their notices, to refuse to work any further

Now, my Lord, the 29th of June is the date with which I have dealt, and now I want to call attention to this. That immediately a telegram was sent, which I think your Lordship will find at page 334. I do not know whether your Lordship might find it convenient in referring to these documents to refer to the case presented by the Respondent—we are only dealing with documents in this—and that will be at page 21, paragraph 46. I refer to that because it sets out the material documents, and it gives the reference to the appendix, and as it means going backwards and forwards for the speeches and minutes and letters, I think perhaps your Lordship might find it the more convenient course in dealing with the arguments to take that Paragraph 46 is this——

Lord JAMES of HEREFORD. Did any communication take place before that? Was nothing done, on the resolution being passed, by the central body?

Mr RUFUS ISAACS. No your Lordship will see they did not know of it. They knew nothing about it. I am now giving you the reference to that telegram. D to E, page 21, there there is a telegram from the Denaby men and a telegram from Conisbro, which is Cadeby to Pickard. "Pickard, Miners' Office, Barnsley"—Pickard being the General Secretary, Smith and Hirst being the secretaries respectively of the branches—"Denaby Pit playing over stoppages. Bag dirt question"

Now, my Lord, may I just make this observation, with apologies for repeating anything with reference to bag dirt, I will not make it again, but here you have got the first statement made by the men—or the secretaries of the branches—to the central Association

Lord JAMES of HEREFORD. Are you quite right? Look at paragraph 42. The telegram did not come about till the 30th

Mr RUFUS ISAACS. That is what I am referring to, my Lord

Lord JAMES of HEREFORD. That is the 30th June

Mr RUFUS ISAACS. That is the one I am referring to

Lord JAMES of HEREFORD. I thought you said the 30th July

Mr RUFUS ISAACS. No

Lord JAMES of HEREFORD There is no question about it—this is the 30th June

Mr RUFUS ISAACS I thought your Lordship meant before the strike

Lord JAMES of HEREFORD No, you referred me to paragraph 46

Mr RUFUS ISAACS The strike is mentioned, the moment the strike takes place there is a communication on the 30th June, and I am going to call attention to what took place I was saying in passing—and I do respectfully submit—that they are absolutely destructive allegations that are made by the Plaintiffs, they completely destroy the case they make about the pretext, or subterfuge, if you like The notices given by the Secretaries of the branches to their central Association are on page 21, both of which say that it is the bag dirt question on which they are "playing" and, my Lord, all these things were before the learned Judge Of course, these telegrams are not for publication It is obvious that they are sent to Mr Pickard, the General Secretary, for his information and nothing else It is the first intimation of a strike—the first thing they know about it—"Denaby Pit playing over stoppages Bag dirt question" Now, these were laid before a meeting of the Executive Committee, and this resolution was passed 'That Mr Cowey" (Mr Cowey was the President then of the Association) "be instructed to wire them" (the secretaries of the Denaby and Cadeby Main branches) "stating that in the opinion of this Executive they ought to have a meeting and agree to resume work at once as they are out contrary to the rules and regulations of this Association,' and he immediately complied with the instruction, he did send the telegram The telegram is at page 334, and it was in these words— it is at "F" on page 334—the telegram He telegraphs him the whole of the resolution "That Mr Cowey be instructed to wire the secretaries of Denaby and Cadeby Main Collieries stating that in the opinion of this Executive they ought to have a meeting and agree to resume work at once as they are out contrary to the rules and resolutions of this Association" That is sent, of course, to both Smith and Hirst, who were the secretaries of Cadeby At the same time, on the same day, a letter is sent to Chambers (this is also on page 334) from the secretary of the Denaby Main "If convenient a joint deputation will wait upon you on Tuesday, at 4 p m , to try and arrive at some amicable arrangement re the stoppages that have taken place at Denaby Colliery" Now, that is what they did at once This is on Monday morning, June 30th There is no doubt that came to nothing

Lord MACNAGHTEN He was away

Mr RUFUS ISAACS He was away at that time, and he could not see them Then, my Lord, I think the next thing that happens is that he came back on the 2nd July, and he then wrote a letter, which is at page 335, to the Judge of the County Court, who had made observations which it was said had led to the strike Now, I am not proposing to read the letter It is there before your Lordships The effect of it is this—it is rather a protest by him against the learned Judge having made statements which, according to Mr Chambers, had led to difficulties with his men The only reason that I am referring to it is because it follows in the order of date, and it shows what Mr Chambers' view was as to the reason of the strike having taken place That is the only importance which I am attaching to it It is all the bag dirt question I will keep the matter in chronological order if I may On the 5th July, 1902, Mr Chambers wrote a letter to the *Sheffield Independent* (it is at page 338) for the purpose of stating what his view was as to the dispute "I have seen so many contradictory statements made with reference to this strike that I think it is incumbent upon me to place those facts which are not in dispute before the public, and before the men, for I believe that numbers of the latter are entirely in the dark as to the truth of the matter I avoid technical details " Then, my Lord, he says "In some parts of our pits the strata known by the name of ' bag dirt' comes in between the upper portion of the seam of coal called the 'day bed,' and that portion of the seam immediately below it technically known as the 'bags' There is no dispute as to the fact that where this substance exists it must at some time or other be got down, and when got down is used by the men for building the pack walls which support the roof and roads " Well, my Lord, I do not think that I am doing any injustice to my friends or myself if I do not read the whole of the letter unless my friends require it, because my view with reference to it is —the point of my reading is— that it shows very definitely and clearly Mr Chambers's view, and the whole question there is that he is pointing out that it is the bag dirt, and he gives the various events that have happened in relation to bag dirt so as to justify the position he has taken up That is Mr Chambers He admitted to me—and had to admit—under cross-examination that this was right—that when he wrote this letter he believed it, he was telling them that this was the view he had taken of this question from beginning to end The only thing said was (in re-examination I think it was) that from something he heard afterwards he thought it was the 10 per cent, and that is as far as we got in the evidence

Now, my Lord, I do not think it is necessary for me to go more into detail with regard to that The matter is made so plain by that letter and, as I respectfully submit, has already been made plain by the documents to which I have called attention, that I will not do more than refer to them My Lord, my main reason for referring to them—and, indeed, my excuse for referring to them after the observations that I have made upon this part of the case, is because

I know that my learned friend is going to follow me—Mr Lush—and I am not to reply to him, and as this has always been a pet point of his, he will no doubt deal with it, as the burden of it rests upon him. I only want to give the reference to the documents that are material without elaborating them at all.

That takes us up to the 7th July. Now, on the 7th July, 1902 (that is the minute), Hall and Annables attended a joint meeting of the Denaby and Cadeby men, and that was in consequence of a resolution which had been passed on the 18th June to explain why they had signed a document on the 9th February, 1901. It is not necessary to go into detail with reference to that, but that meant that on the 18th June, 1902, there had been a resolution passed that Hall and Annables should be called upon to explain the document of the 9th February, 1901. That was a document under which the men contended that Hall and Annables had given away their case—the bag dirt case—as to the halfpenny. That is why they came. I refer to that simply with the object of calling your Lordships' attention to what happened when they attended. It is on page 393. These were speeches which my learned friend had relied upon. That is why I am drawing attention to them.

The LORD CHANCELLOR. We have had the speeches, of course.

Mr RUFUS ISAACS. If your Lordship pleases. It is for that reason I am referring to this.

The LORD CHANCELLOR. You wish to make a criticism upon them.

Mr RUFUS ISAACS. Yes. It begins by saying they had behaved very properly. I think upon the evidence so far—perhaps I ought to have mentioned that in passing, as I rather wanted to deal with the matter in its chronological order—there is evidence of one assault, that is an assault on Bury, which I think I am right in saying took place on the 2nd July. That is an isolated assault. According to his view, the evidence has been read to your Lordship—I am not going through it again, but a general observation I am going to make upon the whole of that evidence—I will refer to it later—but upon the evidence, as it stands, his statement was, with reference to it, that it began with an old woman pushing him down— "shoving him down" was the expression.

The LORD CHANCELLOR. Quite an indefensible thing.

Mr RUFUS ISAACS. Quite, and I am not seeking to justify it for a moment. I am only recalling it so that your Lordship may recollect the particular man's evidence—that is all. That is all I am saying about it, and neither in that respect nor in any other assault that took place, am I suggesting for one moment that there is anything to be said in defence of it Those were acts which I call attention to for the moment as being indefensible acts—as having taken place on the 2nd July, and there is no evidence of any kind (that is the point here) that my Association either knew or took part in it, or that the Committee took part in it That is the observation I wanted to make upon that.

Now that brings us to the 7th July First of all Fred Hall is called upon to make a speech My Lord, I am not going to refer again to these speeches—and Croft dealt with the same question—this bag dirt, and I will not say anything more about it It is all "bag dirt" All Croft's speech I think I am right in saying is "bag dirt"—certainly it is all "bag dirt" or a great part of it, "324" shows it very plainly, and here we have got to the point as to who is keeping the men out We know now who has brought them out Now this is what is keeping them out on strike—why it is the men are not going back to work, and there you have Croft's statement as to the reasons of it Then Mr Fred Hall had to make a statement, and no doubt he was not in a very enviable position because he was there to explain what has already been indicated to your Lordships, and he had to meet a rather hostile demonstration as the men were angry with him and with Annables for what they thought had been a sacrifice of their interests, but the whole of his speech relates to "bag dirt" and nothing else It is long, but that summarises it I think accurately It is all a justification of the position which he had taken with regard to the bag dirt, and that was the reason, as I have already said, why he went down He went down in pursuance of that resolution of the 18th June, 1902, under which he had been called up That is the resolution on page 226 "That Messrs Annables and Hall attend a meeting of the men and explain to them the agreement with regard to the $\frac{3}{4}$d per ton' Then Mr Annables tried to explain, and he was met apparently with a very hostile demonstration, there were interruptions, and the result of it was that he was prevented from proceeding in consequence of the uproar That is at the end of the speech—"F" to "G" Now again that is all "bag dirt" and nothing else but "bag dirt"

Now, my Lord, that takes me from the 7th July to the 11th July, at paragraph 49, in which an application was made by the branch secretaries for strike pay

Now, my Lord, those are two letters in which Smith and Hurst state their view to Mr Pickard, and what they say is (I will read one of them, they are not in exactly identical terms, but the substance is the same) "You will have heard that the pit has been stopped owing to the excessive tyranny that has been imposed upon the men and also through the stoppages that have been made off the men's wages for the so-called bag dirt It was unanimously agreed at a meeting of 3,000 men and boys to put the pit down" (Well, that does not seem to be the case—it was 200 to 300, but this mentioned

that a large number had come out, therefore entitled to strike pay.)
"This was done. At General Joint Meetings which have been held
this proposition has been unanimously confirmed with the addition
that we have a revised price list, something that will be definite, not
(as Mr Chambers calls the present one) a myth to work on as we
are at present. I am instructed to ask you to put before the Council
our case with a view to obtain strike pay for the men and boys
affected. I wish to bring to your notice and before Council that
Mr Chambers repudiates the revised price list signed by you in 1890
and falls back upon Mr Chappell's agreement that was made in
1885, a thing which we cannot entertain." Both of those are
"bag dirt," Chappell's and the other. I cannot help making this
observation with reference to this. Is it not somewhat startling that
it should be said that either one of those letters is a pretext—a
subterfuge—that they are varied; that is what is suggested now,
and the one from Hirst is "I am instructed by a Joint meeting of
Denaby and Cadeby Main workmen to write asking you to bring this
letter before the Council Meeting on Monday, July 14th. Our men
along with Denaby men set the pits down on Monday, June 30th,
without giving any notice, through the action of the Colliery
Company by deducting £8 15s 6d from the men's wages in one
particular district in the Denaby Main pit which amounted in some
cases to 17s 6d per man for (as the management alleges) refusing
to do work that the price list tells them to do. But we say that it
is not in the contract. We have tried all that lays in our power to
get the grievance remedied but have failed, Mr Chambers saying
that if it was only 2½d we wanted he would not give it us to settle
the case, so our branches think that the time has come when some
stand should be taken to get a revised price list, a list that the men
can understand, and seeing that we are now out in the field it ought
to be thoroughly gone into before we commence again, and we are
now making application for strike pay. Hoping that the Council
will grant us pay, and oblige." "P.S.—Anything further you may
want our delegates will be able to explain." That letter shows very
plainly that there you have got the report of what had happened
from Hirst to the General Secretary, a report which is made by them
to their own officials stating what the view is—of which so far they
had only the knowledge that has been referred to in these documents.

Now, that led to a meeting of the Association being called, and
the meeting of the Association was called for the 14th July, 1902.
This was a meeting which came in the ordinary course—this meeting
of the 14th July was an Association meeting. What I mean by that
is that it was not called specially, but it was a meeting in the ordinary
course. I make that observation because apparently some argument
was addressed to your Lordship upon the fact (my learned friend,
Mr Bankes, addressed it) that the Association had not called a
meeting. The Association did not require to call a meeting, because
on the 11th July the Association gets an application for strike pay.
The Association had done all it could up to this moment, the

moment it gets the news it has given notice to the men to go back to work   That is the first thing that is done   It has sent Hall and Annables down in order that they may explain the position to calm the men down   That has all along, as your Lordship will see, been the object of Mr Pickard, who was the General Secretary, to calm the men so that they might arrive at some understanding with regard to it   That is on the 7th July   Then on the 11th July, when they got the application stating the facts from the two secretaries of the branches, then came the meeting of the Council on the 14th July, 1902, and then they passed the resolution   The resolution is set out in paragraph 50, and is also at page 228   Paragraph 50 states it accurately   "That Messrs Wadsworth and Walsh accompany Messrs Nolan and Humphries to a meeting to be held to-morrow morning at 11 o'clock and tell the men they must resume work and then take a ballot of Denaby and Cadeby Main Colliery the first day they work as to whether or not they will give in their notices to terminate their contract of service to get their grievances settled, also that Mr Pickard be instructed to wire Mr Chambers asking him to meet a deputation along with Messrs Wadsworth and Walsh to-morrow afternoon to try and arrange for the men to resume work"   Now, my Lord, that is an important resolution   That is the first resolution which my learned friends can point out in which anything is done by officials of the Association, properly so called (I mean to distinguish them from the branch officials) in which the officials are going to take any part (whatever the effect may be) at all in the strike   The part that they are to take is, not to carry the strike on, but the resolution is that they shall go and persuade the men to go back   That is the whole point   The whole point of the resolution is to get the men to resume work, and they said—and, I submit, rightly said— Wadsworth and Walsh said this   If you have a grievance, your proper course is to give notice   If you have a grievance and you, at the branch, desire to strike, we, the Association have no power to prevent your striking   Neither have they   There is nothing in the rules which would take away the independence of the men at the branches   The men had a perfect right, if they choose, to "play," as they call it, or to "stop the wheels" and not to work—a perfect right to do it—but that has nothing to do with the Association   Then when the Association are called upon to pay the strike pay they say   This is not right , you must go back and you must put right what you have put wrong   when you go back to your work you must resume your work and then take a ballot, that is to say, ascertain then by means of the ballot whether you are to give your notices, in which case you will be in the right so far as the law is concerned   If you have given your notices to terminate the contract then you may strike as much as you like   It is another question whether you would get strike pay , that depends upon whether you have exhausted the means of arriving at an amicable understanding in the opinion of the Association, but at least you will be within the law , you will not be trespassing against the law if you give your 14 days' notice and so commit a breach of contract, and that is the way you ought to terminate your contract of service, but, of course, what the Association officials had in mind, not only in this, but in all the resolutions, as I think your Lordship will see certainly here, is the same thing from beginning to end; Get the men to go back to work, then, if they give 14 days' notice, they will have time to think about it, and during that 14 days we may be able to arrive at a satisfactory settlement; we may be able to prevent this dreadful waste of money by arriving at some sort of arrangement. Chambers took the view that he would not have anything to do with the men until they had resumed work, and Pickard says: You ought to go back to work, and then take another ballot. He is not even satisfied with the resolutions that the men have passed. He says: You must go back—not only get back into your work, but take a ballot as to whether you are to terminate your contract so as to get the benefit of the rules which are framed, again with the avowed purpose as is shown when one reads them, of avoiding anything like hurried and hasty action by the men, involving the Association if they had to grant strike pay in enormous expense, which comes out of the pockets of the other 149 branches, in order to assist the one branch. That is why it is that it is so very essential that there should be this great control—that these great safeguards should be introduced for the purpose of preventing hasty strikes by the men and these hasty conflicts with their employers.

(Adjourned for a short time.)

Mr. RUFUS ISAACS: My Lord, I had just called attention to the resolution of the 14th July, and the result of that was that a telegram was sent by Mr. Pickard to Mr. Chambers, which is at page 344, but set out at paragraph 51 of our case, page 22. "In accordance with these instructions Defendant Pickard wired to Mr. Chambers, 'I am desired by our Council Meeting to ask you to meet a deputation of your men along with Messrs. Wadsworth and Walsh to-morrow afternoon to try and arrange for the men to resume work.'" Mr. Chambers replied to that: "No need to wait for meeting; the pits are open when the men wish to resume work." Then Messrs. Wadsworth and Walsh upon that proceeded to Conisbro' to instruct the men to resume their work, and Wadsworth wired to Pickard and got the telegram (I do not think it is necessary to trouble your Lordships with that) repeated from Mr. Pickard which Mr. Chambers had sent to Pickard. Thereupon Wadsworth, who had succeeded in the view that he was desired to advocate by the Council that the men should resume work, sent a telegram: "Men agree to resume work" (page 344) "and terminate notices." It is set out in paragraph 52. That means that the men agreed to go back to work, and to terminate the contract by giving notices, in other words, that they would resume work, and when they had resumed work they would give a fortnight's notice, which would

R

enable them then to leave the employment of the Company without committing an unlawful act

The LORD CHANCELLOR   I think that is common ground, rather, is it not?

Mr RUFUS ISAACS Yes, my Lord, I think so

The LORD CHANCELLOR , It was not opened in a different sense, I think

Mr RUFUS ISAACS , If your Lordship pleases   But a good deal turns—or rather a good deal was made—I do not propose to spend much time over it—of the point that it was said that the return to work, or the offer to return to work, was a sham offer, and again that it was a colourable offer   Now, in one sense, that is true , I mean in one sense I do not dispute it, giving it the sense, and the only sense, I think which the events meant—that is, that the men meant to go back to work, and did mean when they had got back to work apparently to give notices   What they meant was to go back to perform their contract, and to terminate the contract then in a lawful manner by giving the notice, and not only by giving the notice, but serving under the notice , and, of course, that was, as I submit, perfectly proper, and it does not in the slightest degree detract from the effect of what took place—the men offering to resume work and to terminate by a notice, and to say that it was a sham is really, I think, rather playing with words , I do not know that it conveys a true impression of what had happened   It was a sham if you mean by that that the men did not intend to resume employment and continue the employment indefinitely, no doubt they did not   What the men did do was to put themselves right , that is what they intended to do—by giving the notices so as to put themselves right, in order that they might comply with the advice that had been given

Now, your Lordships notice at page 229, B to C, on the 15th July, 1902, there is a minute of the Cadeby branch at which Walsh and Wadsworth, who were officials of the Association, attended, and the result of it is that Walsh and Wadsworth get their way, the resolution is passed "(1) That we take a ballot to decide whether our men are in favour of returning to work with a view to giving 14 days' notice   (2) That the ballot be taken at once   (3) That the whole of the Committee assist with the ballot boxes and giving ballot papers out"   There is the same thing in the Denaby book, there are similar minutes in the Denaby book, and it simply means that the same thing was carried out

Now, my Lord, we come to what I call the second period   At this point we have got to the end of the first period   As my learned friend, Mr Bankes, opened it he drew the same distinction I draw between these two periods, and I pause for a minute there to see what the position of the Association is up to this. I am dealing with facts only. The only observations that I have to address myself to of my learned friend upon the facts in this part of the case are with reference to Question 5, because it is in Question 5 that they have the finding that there was a ratification. I understand—and I think it has been so agreed by my learned friend—that that ratification is intended to mean that there was a ratification before the second period. If it does not mean that, I do not quite follow what the importance of the question is, because the facts are then ascertained by Question 6. It has been acquired, and I think it is intended to cover this ground—the first five questions, as I think my learned friend Mr Banks admitted to your Lordships, deal with the first period. Now we have got to see what ratification there is and whether there is any evidence in what I have read so far of any ratification of the acts of Nolan and Humphries to procure the men to break their contracts. I think, my Lord, I have given your Lordships all the evidence there is on the point. I have given you all the evidence up to the 16th July, which is the beginning of the second period. I am dealing with the question of verification, of course, by the Association of the acts; if any of the acts of Nolan and Humphries make the Association liable, you do not want ratification. I am only seeing whether there are any further acts upon which they can rely so as to support the finding under Question 5.

Now, my Lord, my submission is upon Question 5 that the facts not only are no evidence of ratification, but prove the direct opposite. The facts proved by my learned friends refute absolutely the contention they are now putting forward. One may summarise the whole of the period from the 30th of June, when the Association first had notice of what had happened, to the end of the first period—that is, up to the 15th July—by this observation, that all the efforts of the Association were directed, not to procuring breaches of contract, but to curing breaches of contract, if they could cure them. That is the whole of the position. I trust I am not dealing with this matter with undue confidence when I say that I do submit that upon the evidence which I have referred to, which is all the evidence upon this point, I do not require to spend another moment upon that part of the case, as regards ratification. I have dealt in that with the acts of the Association.

Now my learned friends cannot point to any act which would amount to ratification; they cannot point to any act done by the Association which adopted or ratified the procuring of the breach of contract by Nolan and Humphries. But my learned friend's argument, if I have correctly apprehended it, was directed to this although there was some difficulty in dealing with this point he still maintains that the question was right, and that the answer was supported by evidence; but the evidence upon which he sought to justify the answer in argument to your Lordships was that the Council had the opportunity (of course I am only professing to state what I understand was the effect of his argument) but that the Council had by not interfering, as he used the expression, ratified, or as it was sometimes said adopted, the acts of the delegates and officials

Now, my Lords, I wish to say in answer to that, first, that it is not supported by the evidence, but that the contrary is proved by the evidence. That is the first point. And, further, that even though my friends were able to establish that there had been in fact a ratification, by which I mean a standing by or interfering or so intermeddling as to enable them to say that that is evidence that they adopted the act as their own, then I say they fail in law upon this point—that in law there could be no ratification, because this act which it is said they ratified was an act which the Association could not ratify, it was *ultra vires* the Association as well as *ultra vires* the Council of the Association

Now my learned friend Mr Danckwerts has addressed an argument upon the law on this point which makes it unnecessary for me to quote the authorities of your Lordships, but which enables me to say this, that the authorities referred to support the proposition that a Corporation taking the Trades Union at its highest as a Corporation, cannot ratify an act which it had not the power to commit. It cannot ratify an act which it never had the power to authorise, and the various authorities referred to support that view, Wilson v Tumman is certainly an authority upon the point—the case in 6 Manning and Granger that is—and the observations which were made particularly I think by Lord Macnaghten in dealing with Keighley Maxted and Company v Durant, and Mr Justice Wright in the very careful and considered Judgment in Firth and Staines, the case in 1897 in 2 Chancery, makes plain that you cannot ratify that which there was no power to authorise

The LORD CHANCELLOR Upon that, if you are to pass from that, do you say that supposing the Council of the Association had met and passed a resolution in terms ratifying the act of leaving the pit without giving notice, in law they could not be held responsible?

Mr RUFUS ISAACS: Yes, my Lord, I do

The LORD CHANCELLOR: That is your proposition?

Mr RUFUS ISAACS Yes, that is the proposition in law, of course, as your Lordships know I only say it to show that the persons injured are not without a remedy. The individuals of course are liable, but not the Association, I mean the persons who come to the conclusion would be liable. I do not suggest that it is a very valuable remedy in some cases, of course it may not be——

The LORD CHANCELLOR Of course, after all that does not affect the point of law

Mr RUFUS ISAACS No

The LORD CHANCELLOR What I mean is this there is a distinction between an act which is *ultra vires* because the subject matter is not within the competency of the Council

Mr RUFUS ISAACS Yes

The LORD CHANCELLOR That is not at all the same thing as saying that if the subject matter is within their competency the act illegal in excess of their rights is *ultra vires* It does not follow

Mr RUFUS ISAACS My Lord, I appreciate what your Lordship is putting, and if I may I will deal with that when I have finished with the evidence I quite follow that that is a part of the proposition which has to be dealt with

The LORD CHANCELLOR So long as you are conscious of it

Mr RUFUS ISAACS If your Lordship pleases My Lord, that is so far, but the answer I make and the answer which I submit disposes of this part of the case altogether, and makes it unnecessary to deal with the question of law, is that that the facts do not support but, on the contrary, are against the views which my learned friends put forward, and I cannot help making this further observation Questions 2 and 4 are questions directed to "purporting," that is, with regard to Nolan and Humphries and the Committeemen the Jury were asked whether they purported to act as agents of the Association There has been a good deal of discussion as to what was really the meaning of purporting in that connection, and the Jury found it unhesitatingly and apparently without any difficulty, and I am bound to say this, without any assistance from the Court as to what the meaning of purporting was, or what the reason was for introducing——

Lord DAVEY There is no finding of that kind in the questions is there?

Mr RUFUS ISAACS Yes, my Lord, Questions 2 and 4, page 1010 There is a good deal of confusion as to the reason why it was introduced At one time it was put in order to bring the case within Limpus v the General Omnibus Company and that class of case, but I should have thought that the question of purporting was not so material for that purpose, it became material on the question of ratification, but not on the question which would really be involved

in the question which my Lord Chancellor put to me just now
Supposing that the subject matter was covered and that the act
which was done to carry out something which the Association had the
power to do, was done in a wrongful manner, that would be Limpus
i The General Omnibus Company and that class of case which I
am going to deal with, but you do not require "purporting" for that
"Purporting" as I understood the question which was here put was
for the purpose of leading up to 5, which was the ratification, so as to
come within Keighley Maxted v Durant

The LORD CHANCELLOR That is another matter which no
doubt you will deal with, but people may purport to act as agents,
and do often so do, and rightly so, but it does not follow there is no
finding I can see at present that they did in fact act as agents

Mr RUFUS ISAACS I was going to call attention to that,
they were never asked to find that they did in fact act as agents,
and I am going to comment upon the fact

Lord DAVEY What were they supposed to have done to
purport to have acted as agents?

Lord JAMES of HEREFORD Those speeches

Mr RUFUS ISAACS I think what was meant by it was the
fact that they were officials, and that they made the speeches at the
meetings

Lord DAVEY That they were officials of the branches, and
made speeches at the meetings?

Mr RUFUS ISAACS Yes, and I am going to say, and I do
say while I am upon it now with reference to that, of course, these
men were in a dual position since it is true they were branch
delegates, but their position as branch delegates did not make them
persons who were not interested themselves personally in the matter
of the bag dirt, or in the matter that was being discussed as a
grievance because they were fellow workers with the other men at
the colliery

Lord ROBERTSON Mr Bankes's point is that the agency is
proved by the rules

The LORD CHANCELLOR That is so, Mr Bankes said the
agency was proved by the rules of course, that is another matter
altogether

Mr RUFUS ISAACS That would not require ratification?

The LORD CHANCELLOR If so it might not require to be left to the Jury at all, it might be a conclusion of law?

Mr RUFUS ISAACS Certainly, as to whether in fact they were.

Lord DAVEY I understood Mr Bankes's argument to be, that by the rules they were appointed agents, but that is, that they were agents in fact

Mr RUFUS ISAACS Yes

Lord DAVEY Then you will have to enquire whether they were agents for the purpose for which they are supposed to have acted

Mr RUFUS ISAACS Quite

Lord DAVEY This is not that they were agents in fact, but that they were in persuading the men or inducing the men to break their contracts purporting to act on behalf of the Association

Mr RUFUS ISAACS Yes, "purporting to act for the Association and for its benefit" is the question in each case This is the learned Judge's only direction upon this—and again I am referring to it now, for the purpose of showing how the Jury arrived at this conclusion it is at page 992 "If you say 'Yes' to this" (that is the first question) "if you say that they did' (that is that they did procure the breach of contract) 'then 'Were Nolan and Humphries or either and which of them in so doing purporting to act as agents of the Association and for its benefit?' Now if a person who is acting as an agent for another does an unlawful act in the course of his employment and for the benefit of his employer, the employer is responsible—you see what I mean—if a man does an act purporting to do it for his employer and for the benefit of his employer, it is not necessary to prove direct authority from the employer—you see what I mean—it is necessary that he should be acting for the employer, and that it should be for the benefit of the employer For instance, you might have a servant who was doing something for you, you order him to go and do a particular thing, he goes and does it in some unlawful way, which you would not have allowed him to do if you had known Still he does it, he does something for your benefit, and you would be responsible " (That is Barwick v The Joint Stock Bank and that kind of case) 'That affects that particular part of the question with regard to agency 'Were Nolan and Humphries, or either, and which of them in so doing purporting to act as agents of the Association and for its benefit?' —which means this Were they acting for the interests of the Association, acting on behalf of the Association, and for its interests in doing these acts' That is assuming you answer the first question in the affirmative' That is the only direction that there is upon this matter, and when I come to deal with the summing up I shall with the greatest respect to the learned Judge say, that that displays a confusion of mind with regard to the real point of the matter, and that the Jury really were never properly directed upon this question at all

Lord JAMES of HEREFORD Purporting to act as regards the general liability seems to me very unimportant if a person purports to act as an agent unless it is done with the knowledge of the principal but here in this case as to ratification if you confine the question of purporting to ratification it may become important

Mr RUFUS ISAACS Yes, and it is only on that point that I think it is of any importance, it is only on that point and with reference to the matter which was so much discussed in Keighley Maxted & Durant as to whether it was necessary for the person to have purported to be acting as agent in order to enable the ratification in law to be made

Lord JAMES of HEREFORD If you confine it to that it becomes very important

Mr RUFUS ISAACS Yes, and I think that is the whole importance of it It does not seem to me—of course I am speaking with deference to your Lordships—that it is necessary to have purporting if you authorise a man to do an act and he does that act, it is one of the class of acts which you put him there to do, and he does that act, but in doing it commits a wrong whilst acting for his master if he does that, then he is liable and you have covered all the ground as to purporting to act by the proposition which I have put

Lord ROBERTSON Mr Isaacs, I am rather afraid after my last experience to say anything, but it occurs to me that it has this separate importance, apart from the question of ratification a man may be an agent and yet he may have another quality beside that of agency, to wit that of a workman, and he might be acting, not *qua* agent but *qua* workman Now, this is important, on the question of liability, apart from ratification altogether, because the Jury by affirming the purporting affirm that he acted in the quality of agent, and not merely that he represented himself to be an agent I allow that the word "purporting" has evidently been chosen, and Mr Bankes said so frankly, in reference to the ratification, but it has that double importance I suggest that——

Mr RUFUS ISAACS My Lord, I quite appreciate what your Lordship says and, of course, it might, I do not think that I should be justified in dissenting from what your Lordship is putting upon that - that it may be that the Jury thought that in what they did, not only were they workers, but they were purporting to act as the agents of the Association, or rather as the agents of the branch, which is a more neutral term

Lord JAMES of HEREFORD That makes all the difference when you come to ratification, the agency of the branch is a very different thing from the agency that is required for the ratification of the Association

Mr RUFUS ISAACS Yes, my Lord As far as I am able to follow, the Jury, in dealing with the question which was then put to them, had, I think, probably in their minds, or may have had, what Lord Robertson put to me just now—I do not know The only direction upon the point is the direction I have read, and what exactly they meant to find it is somewhat difficult to say but supposing that I take that as a finding, that they purported to act as agents of the branch, I submit, my Lord, that that could not cover on the evidence that they were purporting to act as agents of the Association , because all that we have on it—and assuming that the Jury ever were considering this—the only evidence we have of it is the evidence which I have read as to what they were doing, and in that they are only purporting to act as the branch delegates, and in consequence of their position as branch officials, but of course it leaves open the question as to whether they were, by being the branch officials, the agents of the Association Although I quite appreciate that it might be put in the way Lord Robertson put it to me just now, that is not the way in which it was put to the Jury, and if it was, as I have pointed out, the result of it would be that I should submit that there was no evidence to support it

Upon this question of ratification, therefore, your Lordships see that the question which is asked is whether the Association " by its Executive Council or by its officials " (I do not quite know what is meant by "officials" there, it cannot mean branch officials because it would not be necessary to have ratification if the acts of the branch officials were sufficient, and it must mean, therefore, the Executive Council or the officials of the Association, apart from the branch officials) " did ratify the acts of Nolan and Humphries, or of the members of the Committees, in so procuring the men to break their contracts " That being confined to the first period I do submit to your Lordships upon the evidence which I have read, and which is beyond all controversy, because really there is no controversy upon the facts here, except in so far as inferences of fact may have to be drawn, here are the facts as stated in the documents and I say that those facts negative the finding of the Jury which is contained in Answer 5 to Question 5

Now, my Lord, Questions 2 and 4, before I pass from that part of the case, deal not only with the purporting to act as agents of the Association, but also with the words " for its benefit, that is to say those words were introduced and that certainly would involve the consideration of the question as to whether what the branch delegates were doing was intended by them to be in the interests of the Association, whether what they were doing was intended to be for the benefit of their principal, which was the Association. My Lord, I submit the answer to that is that so far from its being in any way for the benefit or in the interests of the Association, in a sense it is contrary to the interests of the Association. it is in the interests of the men themselves, it is in the interest of those who are employed, but it is not in the interests of the Association. I submit to your Lordships that there is no statement by them which would show that what they were doing was for the benefit of the Association. What they wanted to do was to do something which was for the benefit of the men who were working at the Cadeby and Denaby pits and in particular to get the grievance redressed relating to the bag dirt. If they could once get the men to combine for the purpose of redressing those grievances, then the result would be that they had all that they wanted, but, in what they were doing so far from its being for the benefit or in the interests of the Association, they did not consult them or profess to consult them, and I submit, on the evidence which is before your Lordships, they did not profess to have acted for them. They profess to have acted for themselves, that is for the two particular branches, and in the interests of those who are employed in those branches. My submission is that really this part of the case must stand or fall—Questions 1 to 5 stand or fall really—upon the Rules, and if the Rules do not give a mandate to the officials, if the Rules do not make the branch officials the agents of the Association, then all the facts that have been proved fail to establish that there was any agency or any ratification.

Now, my Lords, that exhausts what I have got to say on the facts with reference to the first period, and the second period I can deal with, I think, very much more shortly. The question there is in reference to the three points which are mentioned in Question 6, whether there is any evidence (I submit there is none) to support the finding of the Jury against the Association, and that really involves also Questions 6 and 7. Question 6 is "Did the Defendant Association by its officials or by the members of the Committees of Denaby and Cadeby Branches maintain or assist in maintaining the strike by unlawful means, that is to say"—and these are the unlawful means "(A) By molesting or intimidating men who were working for the Plaintiffs with a view of inducing them to cease from so working?—Yes. (B) By inducing or attempting to induce men who were willing to enter into contracts of service with the Plaintiffs or to work for them to refrain from so doing?—Yes. (C) By the grant of strike pay against the rules of the Association?—Yes." Now, I take that to involve three different points. Upon the first, molestation and intimidation, there the question involved would be whether the Association can be made responsible for any of the proved acts of molestation or intimidation. That is a question of fact, because, of course, if the answer is against me on the first point in the case that the branch officials were the agents of the

Association, then all these questions, I think, would become unnecessary. If there is evidence that the branch officials did the acts complained of, or can be made responsible for them, and if under the rules they were agents of the Association, then these questions, I say, are quite unnecessary and irrelevant.

Now, the second question really (B) of Question 6 is putting something which I submit is not *in eodem negotis*. Your Lordship will observe that what is intended to be put in Question 6 is: Did they maintain the strike by unlawful means? (A), (B), and (C) are the instances of unlawful means. (A), I agree, if proved and proved against the Association, would show unlawful acts. (B), my submission is, does not, as stated, involve an unlawful act, and (C), I submit, also does not involve an unlawful act in the sense of a tort; it does not involve that a tort was committed. Of course, those elements are necessary in order to find the answer to the question that the strike had been maintained by unlawful means. A great deal can be said, and no doubt will be said, upon the point of granting the strike pay against the rules of the Association which is a matter which I shall deal with particularly in reference to your Lordships' decision in Howden's case, but as regards the other two, I want to make this observation as to (A) that there is no evidence, as far as I know, not a tittle of evidence, of the Defendant Association having taken part in any way in the molestation or intimidation.

Again, if I have correctly followed what my learned friend Mr Bankes put with regard to this, he does not suggest that there is any evidence of their having taken part or being present when the acts were committed, but what is relied upon are the speeches, and it is said that the speeches were an incitement to the molestation or intimation that took place. Now, my Lord, again I submit that the answer to that is that the evidence proves the contrary. The molestation and intimidation that took place in the main was from the 13th to 18th August of 1902, there was a period at that time when there was a considerable amount of disturbance. It lasted for a short time, feeling seems to have run high and during that period several persons were assaulted, and there was what may be properly called—rightly called—unlawful acts, such as molestation and intimidation. But my submission with regard to those is that the Association was not responsible for those acts of molestation and intimidation, and that not only is it not suggested that the Association authorised them, but they did not incite any one to commit the acts of molestation or intimidation; not a word can be shown to establish it. The evidence set up in support of it was like a passage in Parrott's speech, which was made on November 24th, 1902, in which Parrott made use of the word 'devilish' in connection with the evictions which had been taking place, but that is at a late period and as is pointed out by Lord Justice Cozens-Hardy in his Judgment, even although you attach meaning to the word which he decline to attach to it, no harm resulted from it, nothing happened, and the mere fact of the use of the expression, even assuming that it was an expression which ought not to have been used, resulted in no injury No act was proved to have been committed in consequence of what he had said, and therefore that in itself amounts to nothing

Upon this part of the case my learned friend is quite entitled to say that no evidence was called to rebut the evidence which he put before the Court for the simple reason that as far as the view we took with regard to it went first of all we did not dispute the facts as proved, and the case which we put forward was that unless it was brought home to the Association that did not make the Association responsible Now that was dealt with—or perhaps I ought first to deal with (B) before I make an observation which will cover both of those It was said further that what the Association did was to induce, or attempt to induce, men who were ready to go to work not to go to work

Now, my Lord, I do submit that that is not in itself a wrongful act If unaccompanied by a wrongful act such as molestation or intimidation or some other form of tort, it has been laid down, and I submit laid down by your Lordships' House, that it is not an actionable wrong to induce, or attempt to induce, a man not to enter into a contract of service That was really the point which I think was discussed at great length in Allen v Flood, and, of course, in the Mogul case, but I prefer to refer to Allen v Flood because it was rather a development of what had been laid down in the Mogul case Your Lordships may remember the short history with reference to that, because having regard to the fact that it has been decided, I do not propose to spend time over the point, but what had happened was that in Temperton v Russell this point had been raised for the first time, and it was there said that it was a very small jump from inducing a man not to enter into a contract of service to inducing a man to break a contract, and that the one thing went to very much the same as the other in so far as it should make a cause of action It was said that it was a cause of action to induce a man to break a contract, and equally that it was a cause of action to induce a man not to enter into a contract, that view was put forward, but that view was disposed of really by Allen v Flood, because in that case the whole case turned upon that, and in order even to make an argument with regard to it, in order that it should be put forward as a legal proposition, that statement of fact had to be supplemented by this, that it was a malicious inducement, that it was a malicious act done with the object of injuring, and that it resulted in damage My Lords, the result was this, that, as laid down in that case in 1890 Appeal Cases page 1, it was made perfectly plain that that is not an actionable wrong when you are dealing with a Trade Union If it is not an actionable wrong—an unlawful act as it is called in paragraph 6—to induce, or to attempt to induce, men not to enter into contracts of service, then it follows logically, and, I submit, must follow inevitably, that every strike is unlawful, because the continuance of any strike does depend to some extent upon one man or upon some of the men inducing other men not to enter into contracts of service, not to work for certain people—for their employers My submission is that (B) is not actionable, it is not an unlawful act, and it assists not at all in the discussion of this subject, but really only rather confuses it

I will call attention later on, if I may, to the Summing-up (C) Involves another point, (C) involves the consideration of what I respectfully submit is the only substantial point upon this part of the case, because I agree that from the 24th July, 1902, the Association paid strike pay to the members of the Association I agree that in Howden's case it was held that the Association could not pay this strike pay, that is to say, it was *ultra vires* of the Association to pay the strike pay in view of what had happened, and an Injunction was granted to restrain them, and, of course, from that moment they did not pay any strike pay The action was not started in Howden's case until the end of 1902 the strike pay had been continued from the 17th July till somewhere about the end of 1902, and it came to trial early in 1903, the only relevance of which is to enable me to make this observation, that the officials of this Association legitimately believed that they had a perfect right under the circumstances that had happened to grant the strike pay It has been pointed out by my learned friend, Mr Danckwerts, I think, that they had some ground for that view—some ground for holding that they had the right to do it, inasmuch as Lord Justice Stirling thought they were justified I can give higher authority than that, because in your Lordships' House both Lord Davey and Lord James dissented from the view of the majority in Howden's case, and thought that it was not *ultra vires*

Lord DAVEY No, I think the point we dissented on was whether an action could be maintained

Mr RUFUS ISAACS I beg pardon, your Lordships dissented on the point whether an action could be maintained directly enforcing

Lord DAVEY Yes

Mr RUFUS ISAACS The effect of which might be said to be the same, but I will not labour it because I have got the view which Lord Justice Stirling put forward in the Court of Appeal as to what he thought was the meaning of the rule, and all that was held—the effect of what was held—in Howden's case, as I submit, was that under those rules there was a breach of contract because they were paying away strike pay under circumstances which did not justify the paying of it under the rules, in other words, what it meant was, "Before you, the Association, can pay the strike pay you must show that you come within the rules" Then came the argument as to whether or not we were within the rules, and your Lordships' House held that we were not, but Lord Macnaghton stated the view very much as I have stated it, with reference to the contract being an agreement between the parties, and I submit that really was the whole foundation of the case. The question, and the whole question in that case was whether under a particular subsection of the Trade Union Act of 1871, under Section 4, it could be said that this action which was brought was brought for the purpose of directly enforcing the agreement. The argument on the part of the Trade Union Association was that it was directly enforcing the agreement, and that therefore the action was not maintainable, and it was held that although it was enforcing the agreement it was not directly enforcing the agreement, that you must give effect to every word in the statute, and therefore that "directly" meant something different from merely saying "enforcing the agreement." The consequence was that it was held that under this agreement we had not the power to grant the strike pay.

I refer to that for this reason. That establishes, I think, under the Judgment of your Lordships' House that to pay this strike pay was a breach of agreement between the members of the Association and the Association, but, I submit, nothing more. It really does not do, and never was intended to do, anything more. It was in that sense, no doubt, a breach of contract to do it and in that sense being a breach of contract, it was contrary to law and therefore in that sense an unlawful act, but, my Lords, I submit it was never intended to say that that was a tortious act and the Judgments show that it was dealt with by your Lordships as really something which was a breach of the agreement and therefore the agreement had to be enforced and could be directly enforced.

I think use has been made—a good deal of use was made in the Court below—both before the learned Judge and before the Court of Appeal—of the word illegal which was used by Lord Macnaghten in the form of Order which Lord Macnaghten said should be the form in which the Order should go and that is at pages 266 and 267 of Howden's case which has already been referred to. What my Lord said there was that the resolution purporting to authorise such payment was *ultra vires* and illegal and I submit that all that my Lord meant (and Lord Macnaghten's Judgment is very plain on the point except it says it all turns on the agreement) was that it was a breach of contract between the parties. What I have to say with reference to that is that that would give a cause of action, assuming that the Trade Union Acts did not prevent it.

Lord DAVEY. It was more than that, it was *ultra vires*, that is to say, the act of the Treasurer or Trustees in paying the money was not an act which bound the members of the Association.

Mr RUFUS ISAACS. Yes, it was not an act which bound them because they had no power, but I was directing——

Lord DAVEY It was a misapplication of their money

Mr RUFUS ISAACS Yes, whatever the precise Judgment was, as between the member of the Association and the Association, all that your Lordships meant to do, as I submit, was to say with reference to this that this was a breach of the agreement because it did not come within the rules, and if that is what it meant, then it cannot give a cause of action to a person who is not a party to the agreement If I might put it in this way, supposing the money had been paid in pursuance of the rules, of course it is quite plain, then, no cause of action would be given, assuming that all that is done and all that is relied upon in maintaining the strike is the payment of the money Suppose that had taken place, that would give no cause of action, it could not be contended that it would What is said is, " Yes, you did pay the money, and it turns out as between you and your members you had no right to pay the money, therefore, because as between you and your members it was a breach of the agreement, we have got a cause of action, although we should have had no cause of action if it was in pursuance of the agreement between you and your members " That rests apparently upon this view that if what has been done by the payment of the strike——

Lord DAVEY If it was not the act of the Association you might say

Mr RUFUS ISAACS Yes I am much obliged to your Lordship, and I mean to deal with that point as to its not being the act of the Association, because it is *ultra vires*, and that therefore no action can be maintained against the Association for it, but just for the moment I was dealing with this unlawful act which is what is alleged against me in paragraph 6, and I do submit that it is not the law that the mere fact that there is a breach of contract between two persons will convert that as regards a third person, which would otherwise be a lawful act, into an unlawful act The question is Is it an unlawful act *qua* the third person, not as between the two parties?

My Lord, might I give an illustration Supposing a man entrusted with £5 to pay something on behalf of his principal, and instead of using the money as he ought to do as between him and his principal he were to pay that money to the Association, that, of course, is a breach of contract—a wrong as between the principal and the agent, but that would not make the payment of the £5 a payment maintaining the strike by unlawful means It would not convert the lawful act by a person paying——

Lord JAMES of HEREFORD Could you not carry your example further, and say that instead of paying it to the Association, he subscribed to support the strike direct, placing the £5 into the hands of the men.

Mr RUFUS ISAACS   Yes, supposing he subscribes the £5

Lord JAMES of HEREFORD   There have been subscriptions to strikes, when the case of the men has been thought to be meritorious, the public have subscribed

Mr RUFUS ISAACS   Yes, supposing he subscribes money that does not belong to himself, if my learned friends are right in the view they are putting forward, the fact that he has done that converts the operation from a lawful act into maintaining the strike by unlawful means, and I submit that is really a confusion, with great deference of the notion that the unlawful means must be in this case unlawful as between the person affected and the person doing the act   It must mean in an action as between the Plaintiff in the action and the Defendant in the action, and it cannot mean that the unlawful means are not as between the Plaintiff and the Defendant, but that the Defendant is responsible to the Plaintiff because the Defendant has committed some breach of agreement with a third person who has nothing whatever to do with the case My Lord, my submission is that that is really a confusion of ideas

Now, my Lord, what is said against me in the whole of this paragraph 6, which is really the important one because the other questions follow upon this to some extent (and I have very little to deal with upon those) is that this molestation and intimidation complained of were the acts of the Association   I do not want to go through the evidence to which attention has been called by my learned friend and I do not want to go through it for this reason (I hope it will not be thought that I am in any way avoiding what may be said against me with reference to it) that my submission is that there is not one of the acts complained of which can be brought home, to use the compendious expression, to the Association   There is not one of the acts which are relied upon as the molestation and intimidation which do constitute intimidation, which is an act in which the Association by its officials as distinguished from the branch officials had any part   All that can be said against me in this connection is, as I have indicated, the speeches, and as I rather gather the argument is put forward against me that by the fact that the Association (and I attribute very great importance to this part of the case) was granting strike pay to the members they were maintaining the strike and that they became responsible for all the unlawful acts which were committed   That, I submit, is the startling proposition which is involved in this case   I am dealing with it now apart from the later question which arises as to conspiracy, but what is said?   "Because from the 24th July you paid strike pay as from the 17th July, 1902, you were maintaining the strike, first of all by the unlawful means" (which I have just discussed) "that is by payment of money, which you ought not to have paid, but apart from that you were maintaining a strike, during which in the course of about nine months some acts of molestation and intimidation occurred, and in consequence of your having done that if you interfere with a strike" (this is the kind of proposition which was put forward) "or intermeddle with the strike in which there are some acts of molestation and intimidation, however isolated, if those acts happen you become responsible not for the consequence of those acts of molestation and intimidation, but you become responsible for the strike as from the date when you intermeddled or interfered" The chain of reasoning by which they arrive at that is, I presume, this if you interfere to maintain a strike that is perfectly lawful and you may go on maintaining the strike indefinitely as long as you do not commit an unlawful act, but the moment unlawful acts are committed, then you are maintaining a strike, which is an unlawful strike, because it is a strike carried on in which some unlawful means are used, and, therefore (and this is again, as I submit, the extraordinary conclusion that is arrived at), you not only become responsible for those particular acts, but for all the acts which succeed those acts, and, more important still, for all the acts that precede those acts

Now, I do submit that those are startling propositions of law, and that those are the propositions which my learned friends have to support in order to give even (A) of Question 6 Assuming I am right in saying that (B) is of no use to them and that (C) is of no use to them *per se*, they are thrown back then to the molestation and intimidation, and besides the point I have already indicated of no evidence against the Association they are seeking to point by that, not that I am liable for the damages (if your Lordship looks at the question in 6) of molesting or intimidating the men, but I am liable for maintaining or assisting in maintaining the strike by unlawful means—a very very material difference, because if the Association is liable for maintaining or assisting in maintaining the strike by unlawful means then no doubt the damages will be very very great, but if all that can be shown against them is that there have been those acts of molestation and intimidation, and assuming that they could be made responsible for those acts, the damages are comparatively trifling

Lord JAMES of HEREFORD What you are saying may have a very wide application Of course, if you recollect, a short time ago there was, whether rightly or wrongly, sympathy shown with a strike in a Welsh colliery in the North of Wales, and the public did subscribe, and individuals subscribed, to assist those strikers to maintain the strike I suppose no one would say there was any error or any liability because they sent in their subscriptions to maintain those strikers

Mr RUFUS ISAACS No, I think my learned friend had to admit that would not give a cause of action

ㄅ

Lord JAMES of HEREFORD   Then it would come to your point that the strikers, one or more at different times, did show acts of violence

Mr RUFUS ISAACS   Yes

Lord JAMES of HEREFORD   Does each and every subscriber become liable ?

Mr RUFUS ISAACS   That is the point that I crave in aid

Lord JAMES of HEREFORD   If liable for something, what does he become liable for ?

Mr RUFUS ISAACS   It does not convert the strike, as is sometimes said, into an unlawful strike   What it does do is this, and this is the only legitimate use, I submit, that can be made of it—if it can be shown that there was a combination to do these unlawful acts, then you get an actionable conspiracy, and there you have got, I agree, an actionable wrong, assuming you have damage with it, you have all the elements of a civil wrong, and that would give a cause of action, but that is a totally different thing, that involves the finding of a conspiracy

Lord JAMES of HEREFORD   Would it be enough in the instance I have put if, before the parties sent in their subscriptions, they became aware that there were systematic acts of molestation going on ?

Mr RUFUS ISAACS   I submit it would not affect the case at all   My submission is that unless you go further and say that in what they were doing they were combining so as get a conspiracy——

Lord JAMES of HEREFORD   Who were combining ?

Mr RUFUS ISAACS   That the persons who sent the money were combining with those conducting the strike to commit unlawful acts, or, in other words, conspiring

Lord JAMES of HEREFORD   Would not the sending in of the money, with the knowledge that the unlawful acts were going on, and a reasonable deduction that they would be continued, be evidence of conspiracy

Mr RUFUS ISAACS   It might be some evidence, although I should say if the only evidence was the evidence your Lordship puts to me, I should have submitted it was not evidence of conspiracy at all

The LORD CHANCELLOR It would be evidence of a conspiracy to do the unlawful acts, not evidence of a conspiracy to maintain the strike

Mr RUFUS ISAACS That is all, my Lord

Lord JAMES of HEREFORD Excuse me, Mr Isaacs if the strike was being maintained by the unlawful acts, that is by preventing men going into the works, that would be a combination of the two, would it not, both a conspiracy to carry on the acts and to maintain the strike?

Mr RUFUS ISAACS If the evidence shows (if I may put an instance) that the men are actually molesting and intimidating in the course of a strike, and a person goes up to those men, and seeing what they are doing, committing unlawful acts, gives them money, I think it might be said that is evidence against him of inducing them to commit the acts It might be said that is some evidence, and it might be said that is some evidence, perhaps, of conspiracy

Lord JAMES of HEREFORD To maintain that strike, because that is the Lord Chancellor's point is it not evidence of both—to carry on the acts and to maintain the strike, or is it only evidence of one of them?

Mr RUFUS ISAACS It can only be to maintain the strike at the particular moment

The LORD CHANCELLOR There are two things, the combination and the agreement To maintain a strike per se is not an unlawful thing The agreement to do anything or to contribute towards riot or assault and so on, is of course, actionable and in some cases indictable If you give money, if it is for a strike it is a lawful thing and you cannot have a conspiracy of that kind The only conspiracy of which it is evidence is the conspiracy to do an unlawful act and to encourage the doing of an unlawful act

Mr RUFUS ISAACS Unless, of course, you can supplement it by some other facts, that is all it can amount to, it is helping them to commit a particular act of molestation or intimidation, and in that sense for that time they might be said to be maintaining the strike, I suppose, to that extent It is only a question of words then, it is helping to maintain, but only for that moment

Lord JAMES of HEREFORD Then comes in the question of damage

Mr RUFUS ISAACS Yes, and of course the whole of this case and the whole importance of this case as regards the question of damages depends upon my learned friends being able to establish the view which they are putting forward that really the whole of this strike was maintained by the Association and that the Association is liable

The difficulty in this part of the case is really intensified when your Lordships come to deal with Question 8, because Question 8 asks whether the Defendants conspired to do any and which of the matters mentioned in Question 6. Those are the matters I have just been dealing with. I have passed over 7 because it adds nothing to it. It is rather difficult to understand what the answer to Question 7 means, one does not see how these persons can be made liable, or can have done the acts which are complained of as servants of the Association without doing them personally, because it is only by them doing them personally that it is sought to make the Association liable for the acts of those men. What the precise view with regard to it is, I take it, rather affects my learned friend, Mr Atherley Jones, who represents these gentlemen, more than it does me, but all I say with regard to it is that it seems to be a contradiction if you take the answer as given by the Jury, because the whole that was suggested was that these were the men through whom the Association had acted. They are the persons by whom the acts had been done and through whom the Association was responsible

Now, my Lord, Question 8 is the one I was dealing with, and that question involves a conspiracy to do the (A) (B) (C) of Question 6. This and the next question become important more especially by reason of the dissenting Judgment of the Master of the Rolls, and again, as your Lordship will see, by reason of the summing-up of the learned Judge. Now, after 6, I take it—I think it must be so—that Question 9, and the answer to Question 9, are the most far reaching of all the questions and answers in the case. If Question 9 is right, and the answer to it is right, then the damages would date from the inception of the strike to its conclusion. That is the big question undoubtedly upon which the case was to a great extent based. Now, Question 8 cannot be the same thing; it specifies the unlawful acts. Question 9 does not specify the unlawful acts, but adds the words " to molest and injure the Plaintiffs in the carrying on of their business." The point of that question is based on the decision of your Lordships in Quinn v. Leathem, to which I shall have to call attention, but, as I have said, these questions of conspiracy, more especially 9, are the most important of all the Questions in the case

Now, my Lord, 8 is a conspiracy to do the matters mentioned in Question 6—that is, there comes in again the same idea that I was just dealing with as to being an unlawful act. As your Lordships will see when the learned Judge deals with this he says that conspiracy is a combination to do—and he gives the three well-known variations of what a conspiracy is—" a lawful act by unlawful means," and so forth, and he explains that you must find in it some unlawful means, some unlawful acts committed, but if you find those then it is sufficient and you may find a conspiracy Now, supposing your Lordships came to the conclusion that (B) of 6, that is the inducing, or attempting to induce, men not to enter into contracts of service, could not make an actionable conspiracy, I mean that that could not be an unlawful act which would make a conspiracy, which would make a combination unlawful, I might eliminate that In order to make such an act unlawful you must either get some unlawful act in itself, or you must get such a finding as there is in Question 9, the intention to molest or injure If you get that I agree that that would make a cause of action if your evidence supports it If you could find that there was a combination with the intention to injure the Plaintiffs, to induce men not to enter into contracts of service, that would be undoubtedly (at least I say so with the greatest respect) within the principles laid down by your Lordships' House in Quinn v Leathem, because you have got to find by the intention to injure, which covers "molest," the elements of conspiracy, but if you have merely, as is said here, an inducing or attempting to induce men not to enter into contracts of service, that gives no cause of action Your Lordships will observe that I am drawing this distinction because in Question 8 you have not the element which is present in Question 9 Question 8 is framed without intention to injure or molest Question 9 is framed on Quinn v Leathem Question 8 is intended to group together the three acts referred to in Question 6 by including them in a combination and goes no further, it adds nothing more to it It says "Those are unlawful acts, and you conspired together to do those unlawful acts '

Now, I have said all that I propose to say upon (B) in respect of the conspiracy alleged in Question 8 (C) is again the old question of the grant of strike pay against the rules of the Association Now, that would not make a conspiracy an actionable combination without the intent to injure or molest, and I submit that is a very important element, because here I think it must be plain there was no intent to injure There was an intent in this case to protect the men, and that is the utmost that can be said I mean this strike was not engineered, and nobody has ever suggested that it was for the purpose of injuring or molesting, with the intention of injuring or molesting the Plaintiffs in their business

Lord JAMES of HEREFORD If the natural result is to injure the employers, is not that enough ?

Mr RUFUS ISAACS No, my Lord, with the greatest respect every strike—most strikes—will have the effect of injuring the employer's business, but that will not give a cause of action

Lord JAMES of HEREFORD Not if it is a lawful strike, I thought you were upon this strike as it occurred on the 30th June

Mr RUFUS ISAACS No, I am much obliged to your Lordship for making this observation because it reminds me that I have not made clear what I very much wanted to make clear, that is, the reason why I am drawing a distinction between the two periods It is really my fault for I ought to have made it plain because I do draw the very broad distinction that I have indicated before, but meant to refer to again at the end of the first period, that from the time that the men ceased to be in the employment of the Plaintiffs, the colliery proprietors, the Association were entitled to induce them not to enter into contracts of service, were entitled to advise them not to "sign on" as the expression is, and were entitled to do everything that they thought right, always assuming they acted within the law, for the purpose of inducing the men to continue on strike I submit that is inconvertible law

Lord JAMES of HEREFORD Not in an unlawful strike

Mr RUFUS ISAACS No, my Lord, I make this observation with this exception always assuming that there is no unlawful act Now may I say with reference to what your Lordship put to me that a strike does not continue to be (I am submitting this to you with the greatest respect) an unlawful strike because when the men cease work they break a contract You have not, by the men having ceased work under breach of contract, tainted the whole of strike however long it may continue The men have no right to break their contracts, but once there is a breach of contract which is accepted by the employer as a recission of the contract existing hitherto between him and the employed, once you have that, then my respectful submission is that these men are free men in the sense that they are not under contract, and they are entitled to go to work or not just as they please, and any one is entitled to advise them to go to work or not as he pleases That is a point which, I submit, has to be borne in mind in connection with this case as it is so important in relation to the second period, because when you get to the second period upon which I have been dealing with the facts, it is common ground now—it has been their contention all along, but it was not ours always, and we have been defeated upon it—since Howden's case that the contract was at an end when the men left and the employer accepted it

Now, if I may put that for the moment and follow it up closely, if the men leave on the 29th or 30th June we will assume (the exact date is not material really whether it is the 30th June or the 1st or 2nd July) that the employers elect to treat the contract as at an end, and that from that date I assist the men in maintaining the strike without using unlawful means, could it be said that I am maintaining an unlawful strike? The strike is no longer unlawful A strike is unlawful in the sense that it might be, and would be, said, that to combine to cease work in breach of your contract with a Company is to combine to do an act which is unlawful *qua* that Company, and, therefore, that being an unlawful act, you have a combination to do an unlawful act, and therefore an actionable conspiracy I quite appreciate that that might be said.

Lord JAMES of HEREFORD To carry out your argument I think you must define—I have always thought it would be necessary—what a strike is.

Mr RUFUS ISAACS I was just thinking so, my Lord.

Lord JAMES of HEREFORD Really as it stands on your proposition having left the employment, and that leaving having been accepted by the employer, this strike means merely a determination to stop work and not return to their employment.

Mr RUFUS ISAACS Is not that all it does mean? I suppose the origin of the word probably must be from the fact that the men strike work when they refuse to work any longer.

Lord JAMES of HEREFORD You procure that to be done. You have put in the proposition that the employer has accepted the non-attendance of the servant.

Mr RUFUS ISAACS I put in that proposition because your Lordships have held it.

Lord JAMES of HEREFORD That being so your first ground is that what has been done is to persuade persons not to return to their employment, which they might or might not do.

Mr RUFUS ISAACS My submission is that so long as they only use lawful means to persuade them not to return to work, they are perfectly entitled to do it.

Lord JAMES of HEREFORD "Maintaining the strike" are scarcely the proper words when the employment is accepted to be at an end.

Mr RUFUS ISAACS No doubt what happens is, if there is a breach of contract, as happened in this case, that the man would become liable to the employer, notwithstanding that he has rescinded the contract, with an action of damages for a breach of contract, and he did in this case. Damages were recovered against several hundred men, I do not know exactly the number, and it is not very material, but actions were started against several hundreds of men in the Police Court under the Employers and Workmen's Act which gives the right to bring the action for damages there. At the moment the rescission of the contract had taken place and from that moment the men are free. The breach of contract does not run with the men, if I may say so, it is not like a covenant running with the men, and the moment you have got the men freed by the recission of the contract they would be free to go and offer themselves to some other employer, and the moment they are free to offer themselves to some other employer everyone is free to induce them not to go to a particular employer, even although it be the employer from whose service the man has improperly severed himself

Lord JAMES of HEREFORD I should like to get this point clear, assuming there was no provocative act of the masters and that, as they state, these men simply did not go back to work on the 30th, when would they be free from their obligation—after two or three shifts?

Mr RUFUS ISAACS That is rather a difficulty and it is a point that was a good deal discussed in Howden's case, because it might be said and was said, that as the men were under offer of 14 days' notice the contract must continue for that 14 days if the masters had not elected to treat it as rescinded before, but on the facts of this particular case it was held that Mr Chambers had elected, and for the purposes of the point we are now discussing it matters not whether it is the 30th June or whether the 13th or the 14th July, because equally it would not come within the beginning of the second period

Lord JAMES of HEREFORD Apart from Mr Chambers's election, was it contended on the other side that at the end of the second shift the men would have to "sign on" again?

Mr RUFUS ISAACS Not after the second shift, my Lord, I think what is said is that they would have to "sign on" after two or three days unless they were absent through illness

Lord JAMES of HEREFORD That would be well within the 14 days

Mr RUFUS ISAACS Yes, my Lord No one has contended, and it could not be contended, from any point of view, even if there was no rescission, that the contract lasted more than the 14 days, and as I said in this case we are beyond all that now because it has been so decided

Lord JAMES of HEREFORD You got to the 17th July

Mr RUFUS ISAACS Yes In fact, as the Court of Appeal held in Howden's case "It is argued that the proper inference is that that was not a termination of the employment" Those are the facts I have represented to your Lordship "I should say it was impossible to come to any other conclusion on the facts than that it was" And then there was what happened in fact, and your Lordships held exactly the same upon the point, and there was an end of it So that for the purposes of this period what I submit as the result of the evidence is, that the acts relied upon as to conspiracy to induce, or attempting to induce give no cause of action because of the absence of the intention to injure and in the same way the grant of strike pay against the rules gives no cause of action even although done in concert, because there is no intention to injure

Lord JAMES of HEREFORD If it comes to damage how will you manage as regards 8 and 9, because everything will depend upon when these acts were done? If they were done on the 30th June or 2nd March, the measure of the damages would be very different

Mr RUFUS ISAACS I am going to say something in reference to that when I come to deal with Question 9 The question is so framed, and intentionally so framed as to cover everything, and to entitle them to recover damages as from the inception of the strike That is why I say 9 is the most serious question, and 9 if it stands is certainly capable of that view and it was so put The case as put against us was, that we were liable, as your Lordships will see when we come to the summing-up, if the Jury thought that there had been this combination for everything that had happened from the inception of the strike That would be under 9, but I was just really dealing with 8, and that leaves me with the only other question with which I have got to deal on 8, and that is (A) I do not want to repeat what I have said about (A), because I think really I might summarise the observations with reference to 8 by saying that as you have not the intent to injure or molest found in 8, it carries you really no further than 6 That is the point

Now, my Lord, I come to the important Question 9, and that becomes so very important for the reason that the Master of the Rolls has differed from the view taken by the learned Judge and the Jury in so far that he agrees in the conclusion as to liability from the 29th June and he thinks that the Association were not liable The Court of Appeal were unanimous upon this, that the rules do not impose any liability and do not make the delegates or officials of the branches agents and that there was nothing to make the Association responsible for anything that had happened during the first period and that the conspiracy as dating from that first period was not sustainable That is the conclusion he came to, and my submission is that when he has come to that conclusion he must go further, because that was the conspiracy which was put against us upon which the Jury were asked to find, and if he finds that there was no evidence to support that, he is bound to enter judgment in my favour, and, I submit, is not entitled to find another conspiracy which has never been submitted to the Jury

Then, my Lords, supposing that there is evidence, when is the conspiracy to date from if it is not from the 29th June? Upon the questions as found it is very difficult to say, and in fact, I submit, it is impossible to say. Perhaps it would only be right with reference to this criticism I am directing to the Master of the Rolls' Judgment, to which I shall have to refer to say this, that presumably the Master of the Rolls was not very precise about it and did not indicate very clearly his views upon the matter because the rest of the Court were differing from him, and his Judgment would be ineffective except as his reasons for differing. That is probably the explanation of it, but it does not get away from this, that the conclusion to which the learned Master of the Rolls does come involves us in the difficulty of ascertaining when the conspiracy arose for which the Association is to be held liable.

Lord JAMES of HEREFORD: Why do you say the Master of the Rolls' conspiracy does not come within Question 9?

Mr RUFUS ISAACS: Because I say it is not a question which was put to the Jury.

Lord JAMES of HEREFORD: I am looking to the terms of Question 9.

Mr 'RUFUS ISAACS: I think in terms, as there is no date given, if you found your conspiracy on the 17th July you might find it under Question 9—in terms I agree, but what I mean is after all the conspiracy is a concerted action—something which is supposed to have taken place from the 29th June, and that is the case which is presented against me, and that is the case which is put to the Jury, and that is the case upon which the learned Judge sums up, has there been concerted action with the intention to injure as from the 29th June? That is the case, and the Master of the Rolls says, "No, I do not think there has, but I think there is some evidence upon which the Jury might have found that there was' (that is the effect of his Judgment) "as from the 17th July, and therefore I shall find that there is a conspiracy as from the 17th July." If you once eliminate from the consideration all the antecedent facts I do submit that it would have had a most material bearing on the finding of a Jury. The Court cannot say that the Jury were bound to find that there was a conspiracy, and that is what the effect of the Master of the Rolls' Judgment is. "You have found conspiracy (A), which is wrong, but I think there is evidence upon which you might have found conspiracy (B) which has not been submitted to you, but as I think you might have found that, and that is a different conspiracy from conspiracy (A), therefore I find the Jury would have been entitled to find conspiracy (B), and I treat it as if they had so found it.'

Lord JAMES of HEREFORD: Why is not conspiracy (B) included in conspiracy (A)?

Mr RUFUS ISAACS Because they are two different conspiracies, for this reason, the one is a combination to procure the breaches of contract, an element of the utmost importance—you have that element in it which is absent from the subsequent events

Lord JAMES of HEREFORD But if conspiracy (A) was procured and then went on and was maintained, would not the Master of the Rolls be right then?

Mr RUFUS ISAACS I should submit not I am looking at the substance of what was put to the Jury, and the question was put to them as to whether there was a combination to procure and maintain I submit it really could not be the same conspiracy because if it is the same conspiracy, I think, if I may with respect say so, it might be between the same people, but it might not It certainly is not the same conspiracy, because the one conspiracy is to procure a breach of contract as from the 29th June, which involves, undoubtedly, committing what your Lordships have already held to be a wrongful act—an actionable combination, and the other is to do something quite apart from that, to do the acts which start as from the 17th July

Lord JAMES of HEREFORD No, they commence on the 30th June and then continued That is maintained

Mr RUFUS ISAACS Yes, no doubt if you find that there was a conspiracy from the 30th June, that will cover the 17th July

Lord JAMES of HEREFORD Assuming that you are right in saying that there was no evidence of the 30th June conspiracy, and that you get evidence not of the procuring, but of the maintaining, would not the Master of the Rolls' Judgment then come in and say "It has been found by virtue of the finding that the 17th July does come in"?

Mr RUFUS ISAACS He could come in on the other question as to maintaining—yes, but it would not entitle him to transform this finding of conspiracy into a finding that there was a conspiracy on the 17th July, or frame a conspiracy out of the acts on which reliance is placed as from the 17th July.

Lord JAMES of HEREFORD That might depend on the way the case was presented in substance, but as that Question 9 is framed I should have thought that it could have contained both periods

Mr RUFUS ISAACS I agree that if you once come to the conclusion that the conspiracy dated from the 30th June, Question 9 would cover all the subsequent acts, undoubtedly, it would cover the maintaining, it would cover the acts referred to in 6, and it is for that reason I say that it is the largest question involved in this action, it would cover everything, and, of course, if the Jury thought we had conspired to induce breaches of contract they would have found all the rest *Non constat*, that if they thought we had not conspired to induce breaches of contract they would have found we had conspired to molest and injure by paying strike pay to men who were out without any means of subsistence

(Adjourned to Monday next)

FIFTH DAY.

Monday, March 19th, 1906.

———

Mr RUFUS ISAACS May it please your Lordships When your Lordships adjourned we were just dealing with the period which began on the 16th and 17th July, what is called the second period Just before I get to that may I point out that now upon the first period the whole question as now standing upon the evidence is first as to the rules, that is whether the rules made the branch officials or the Committeemen the agents of the Association for the purpose of inducing the men to break contracts, and the other question of fact, as I know it is merely the question of fact as to ratification, upon which I have made my submission, and I say the evidence tends all the other way

And now, my Lord, may I say with reference to the third question involved in the five questions dealing with the first period— and by that I mean the questions contained in Questions 2 and 4 to the July—that is as to "purporting," the questions involved being whether Nolan and Humphries or the Committeemen purported to act for the Association, and for the benefit of the Association I have looked at that rather carefully since the matter was before your Lordships on Friday, and what I submit is the true view with regard to that is this There is a confusion in putting that question as to "purporting" and "for the benefit" in the one question, I mean by that that unless "purporting" means with the intention of acting for the Association, then it has really no place in that question, and I think if it does mean with the intention of acting for the Association, which is what I submit it is intended to mean, then it really carries one no further than the last words, that is "for the benefit of" Whichever way you may put that question it resolves itself into this Was the act done being done by the person for the benefit of the principal? That is what it is intended to cover, and in that no doubt you must have, I think, three things, you must have first of all that it was in fact done for the employer, then that it purported to be done for the employer, and, thirdly, that it was for the benefit of the employer—in the interests of the employer

Now, my Lords, I think I am justified in that view by certainly what took place in the Court of Appeal, because there was some discussion with reference to this question—a discussion between my learned friends and myself and eventually with the Court—and the result of it seems, I submit, to establish what I have just put because otherwise it would mean this The purporting, which is the first limb of those two questions, Questions 2 and 4, are both of

them questions which really relate to ratification If they are
intended to relate to ratification, then properly they must be asked
independently of the question as to whether they were for the
benefit of the employer I mean "for the benefit of the employer,"
has no relation, I submit, to ratification That is a question quite
apart That question becomes of importance having regard to the
principle laid down in Barwick *v* The English Joint Stock Bank
and that class of case, but that is entirely independent of
ratification That question always depends upon this—an act
done which is one of a class of acts which the servant is put
there to do, and if done by him for his employer—purporting
to act for his employer—that is, whilst appearing to be acting
for his employer—the question comes whether in fact what he
was doing was done in the interests of his employer or was
done in his own interest It is in that relation that the question
becomes of importance and only in that relation, but it pre-supposes
the authority to do the class of acts There is no necessity for
ratification then and ratification does not assist it in the slightest
degree if a man is employed, if I may take as an instance a case
which your Lordships had to deal with in which this question was
discussed, certainly at, I am afraid, considerable length, namely the
case of Whitechurch, Limited, *v* Cavanagh, in which the point arose
whether the Secretary of a Limited Liability Company who had
certified transfers fraudulently for his own benefit and not for the
benefit of his employers—notwithstanding that it was one of a class
of acts which he was employed to perform, which he was put there
by the Company to perform, the Company could be made responsible
for those acts That was discussed undoubtedly at very considerable
length, and it was eventually decided by your Lordships, that if, in
fact, he was not acting for his employer, but for himself, if he was
committing a fraud to benefit himself, the employer was not liable,
notwithstanding he was put there to do the particular class of acts
My Lord, the reference to that is Whitechurch, Limited, *v* Cavanagh,
1902, Appeal Cases, page 117, and it is following that case that the
Court of Appeal have held in Ruben and another *v* Great Fingall
Consolidated and Others, a case quoted by my learned friend, Mr
Bankes, in opening this Appeal to your Lordships upon this branch
of the case—it is upon Whitechurch *v* Cavanagh, and the view
taken there, that Ruben *v* The Great Fingall Company has been
decided, and that is a case which is only, I think, some four or five
out of the list of Appeals for hearing before your Lordships at the
present moment, it is on Appeal here So really Ruben *v* Fingall
has no value because it only professes to follow Whitechurch *v*
Cavanagh, and is dealt with upon the principle of Whitechurch *v*
Cavanagh My Lord, there is a great number of those cases, and
the Charnwood Forest Case is another one in 18 Queen's Bench
Division, which has been referred to as a similar class of case
There the whole question was the secretary of a Company who was
the proper person to answer questions which were put by a shareholder, answered some questions falsely—made false representations

with regard to them—upon which there was a loss incurred by the shareholder who acted on the faith of the answers to the questions which were given, and the question there arose as to whether upon that false statement and fraudulent statement made by the secretary the company could be held responsible and it was said no, because the secretary in doing this was acting for his own benefit and not for the benefit of the Company.

The LORD CHANCELLOR: Have you the reference to the Charnwood Forest case?

Mr RUFUS ISAACS: 18 Queen's Bench Division.

The LORD CHANCELLOR: That will do.

Mr RUFUS ISAACS: I think your Lordships have already got the reference, my friend, Mr Bankes, gave it in opening, but it is in 18 Queen's Bench Division, page 714 the name of the case is The British Mutual Banking Company v Charnwood Forest Railway Company. Upon that class of case it is of importance always to know whether the act done was done for the benefit of the employer or whether it was done for the benefit of the servant. There is another, as I submit, rather difficult question what has not yet had to be dealt with upon that aspect, and that is: Supposing it is both for the benefit of the employer and for the benefit of the servant, what is the position in law? That, I submit, is the kind of case that may very easily happen, and upon one assumption of facts in this case—assuming the facts found against me—which would arise for consideration, because I put it in this way: Nolan and Humphries in this case in inducing the men to break their contracts were as much interested as the rest of the men who came out, they were employed at work at the collieries, and they were making common grievance with the rest of the men who were employed there, just the same as the several thousand men came out because a few were affected, by this bag dirt question, so Nolan and Humphries were in the same position, and my submission is that they were really, in fact, acting there entirely for themselves, and not for the Association at all. But if I am wrong in that, and if it is said "Well, there is evidence that they were acting for the branch"—using a more neutral expression for the moment, then they were acting for the branch, but they were also acting for themselves. They were acting for both. The question which is involved in that and the two questions that are put are, as I submit, two totally different questions, if you give them their true meaning, and then, when you come to the question of purporting, what I think my learned friends say now with reference to it is that what they meant by purporting, what they intended to cover, was purporting which was necessary for ratification. If that is the case one can only say this, and I make this observation so as not to repeat it when your Lordships come to deal with the Summing-up, that there is not one single word in the learned Judge's Summing-up which deals with this question, or which explains what would be necessary, or upon what basis the Jury are to decide this question of purporting, it is a matter upon which we commented in the Court of Appeal, and in which the Court of Appeal all agreed with the view we were putting, that there was no such direction of the learned Judge, and, so far as I can follow, the learned Judge does not seem to have understood the question as meaning anything else but what the second branch of the question meant—that is, whether these men in doing what they did do (Nolan and Humphries or the Committeemen) were acting in the interests of their employer

On this branch of the case, of course, the rules are of the utmost importance Strictly I ought to deal with the rules, and follow out the line I laid down for myself I ought to deal with the rules in this first part of the period, but, if your Lordships would allow me, I would prefer to finish the facts, which I can do very shortly, upon the second part, and then come back to some observations I want to make upon the rules; they have been read, and I am not going to refer in detail to them; but, as a good deal of what I have to say on the rules is mixed up with the authorities, with your Lordships' permission, I will come back to it and finish the facts first

Now, my Lords, I am coming to the second period, as I have always ventured to put it There are two separate periods, and in considering this case it is always necessary to bear in mind that there are the two separate periods My learned friends objected to my attempting to distinguish between the two periods in the Court below and before the learned Judge, but I am glad to find, at any rate for convenience, my friend Mr Bankes adopts it for the purpose of the argument which is now being addressed to your Lordships' House At this date (the date with which I was dealing, that is the 15th of July) I had got as far as that, I had called attention to this, that on the 14th of July there had been a telegram by Mr Pickard to Mr Chambers asking that there should be a meeting with Wadsworth and Walsh on the next day, the 15th, and the documents referring to this—certainly all that are material I think—are set out at page 22 paragraph 51 of the Respondents' case—it quotes them He sent the telegram which is there set out, and Mr Chambers replied, "No need to wait for meeting, the pits are open when the men wish to resume work" That was in answer to the telegram which had been sent by Mr Pickard saying "I am desired by our Council Meeting to ask you to meet a deputation of your men along with Messrs Wadsworth and Walsh to-morrow afternoon to try and arrange for the men to resume work" No doubt a great deal of discussion has taken place as to what was meant by resuming work, the one side contending that it meant simply going back to work under the old contract, and the employers contending that it meant going back to work under a new contract, but really there is no importance in that now after what your Lordships have held in Howden's case Then, in consequence of that, Messrs Wadsworth and Walsh went the next day as arranged, on the 15th, to Conisbro', where the meeting took place, and Mr Pickard telegraphed to them the answer that he had had from Mr Chambers which I have already read Then came the speeches on that date, the 15th July, of Wadsworth and Walsh, with reference to which so much comment has been made I want just to call attention to what they said, because these speeches are relied upon I think rather strongly against the Respondents, because it is said, as I follow the argument At this date, on the 15th July, whatever may have been the position before, Wadsworth and Walsh were sent by the Council Now that is perfectly true, that appears from the resolution of the 14th July which I have already referred to, they were sent, but they were sent for this purpose—and I place strong reliance upon this, they were sent as the resolution states in terms in paragraph 50 of the Respondent's case, to tell the men to resume work and then take a ballot of the Denaby and Cadeby as to whether or not they would give in their notices Wadsworth and Walsh were sent down not to incite the men to continue out of employment In one sense it had already passed outside, as I submit the proper meaning of the word "strike" was no longer applicable, because the men, as we now know, within a few days of the 29th June were no longer in the employment of the Colliery, so, although I might use the word "strike," if they only interfered at that moment, and assuming they had not interfered before, they were interfering at a time when the men were not committing a breach of contract They were not inciting the men to break a contract, they were simply then interfering with men who were not in the employment of the Plaintiff Company That was the view which was taken by Mr Chambers himself Wadsworth and Walsh then go, and the burden of what they say—I am not going to refer in detail to the speeches, because your Lordships' attention has been called to them, and I am afraid it would take an interminable time if I had to read the speeches again—but the effect of what they say is that they are trying to induce the men to go back to work, because they point out that so long as the men are out in breach of contract the Association will not and cannot recognise them Now, a very great attack has been made upon the Association about this matter, upon Wadsworth and Walsh, and upon the Council

Lord JAMES of HEREFORD Is it quite right to say that the men are out in breach of contract ? Is it not right to say they went out breaking their contracts, but when their time expired they are not still out under breach of contract ?

Mr RUFUS ISAACS I am much obliged, my Lord, they are not, what your Lordship says is what I meant, only one unfortunately falls rather into the colloquialisms that are used in connection with this matter, or were used during the hearing, the men struck in breach of contract and when the few days had elapsed and the

T

masters had determined that the contracts were at an end, then so
far as the men were concerned from that day they were no longer
breaking a contract, but they were doing what they were entitled
to do—they were not resuming employment and not tendering
themselves for fresh employment

Lord JAMES of HEREFORD Of course, the colloquial term
"out on strike" is recognised and we know what it means legally
and technically, the men were not returning back to make a second
or fresh contract

Mr RUFUS ISAACS That was it, my Lord, they would not
return Of course, by this time they were already being sued for
breach, but that is, perhaps, immaterial When Wadsworth and
Walsh therefore go on the 15th July it is under the circumstances I
have described, and perhaps your Lordships may think that I am
laying under stress upon this part of the case as drawing a distinction
between the period before the masters had elected to treat the
contract as at an end, and the subsequent period, but according to
the view which I am putting to your Lordships, it is of the utmost
importance, and it is really the key of the whole case It once the
case is understood from that point of view, I will not say that it
disposes of it because there are other questions no doubt to be dealt
with, but it disposes of the main difficulty, and it disposes of the point
which is made against the Respondents that they are responsible for
the strike *ab initio* if that view is right Now, in order to meet
this and to make their case of conspiracy against the Defendant
Association effective as from the 29th of June, what my learned
friends did was again to crave in aid, and very effectively, the words
"pretext, subterfuge and sham," which were used in connection
with the reason for the men breaking their contracts on the 29th
June—or rather for their being induced to do it, because what was
said and what was contended at considerable length—and I have the
address of my learned friend before me which I have read, upon this
matter, and to which I can give references if it is challenged, but it
cannot be challenged in view of its having been put forward, and I
have no doubt my learned friend will remember its being put forward
by him both in Howden's case and in this case to the Jury—what he
contended was that this offer to return to work on the 17th July was
a mere sham, a pretext, a subterfuge, a mere blind, and he said that
putting themselves back to cure the breach of contract was a position
which the men never could get into, and the Association never
intended they should occupy, that the Association apparently knew
that the men would not be accepted by the employers as their
workmen, and that all this was a mere device

Now, I am afraid that there is a good deal of playing with words
in this question, because I say perfectly frankly that by that is
meant that the Association intended that the men should go back to
work to get into the employment, into the service again of the

Plaintiff Company, and that when they were once there, as Mr Wadsworth says, everything would be done to effect a settlement of the dispute, but that the men had the right and could if they chose exercise their right by giving notices after they had once resumed the service. So that if during that fourteen days that they would have to serve for the notice the employer and employed did not come to terms, then if the men came out at the end of 15 days, which is what is put forward by Mr Wadsworth, the result would be that the men would not have ceased work in breach of contract. Then if that had happened, the result would have been that the Association if it thought fit, and if it thought every reasonable means had been taken to conciliate and had failed, then they would grant the strike pay. But what is said against us, and what was used with the Jury, as all these suggestions were, I am afraid, with deadly effect, was that really this was all nonsense, it was part of a device which was being resorted to with the knowledge that the men would never be allowed to get back to work, and simply in order that the Association might have a colourable pretext for saying it would grant strike pay.

Now, my Lords, I do submit that again upon this question, looking at the evidence—and I am going to call attention to the documents that passed at this time—it is really impossible to contend that this was anything else but a *bona fide* attempt on the part of the Association to do what it thought it could do, that is cure a defect by getting the men back again to work, and then if no settlement was arrived at, putting the men in the position of coming out of the employment lawfully instead of unlawfully.

Lord DAVEY What the resolution of the Council advised was that they should return to work and then take a ballot whether they would hand in Notices or not.

Mr RUFUS ISAACS Yes, that would be the right course under the rules and that is what they did do.

Lord DAVEY They did not advise that they should go in merely for the purpose of serving notices, but that they should go in and take a ballot as to their future action which would be determined by the result of that ballot.

Mr RUFUS ISAACS That is so. What Mr Wadsworth said very definitely and plainly when he was cross-examined upon this point was that what he had to do, the desire they had and what they wanted to do, was to persuade the men to go back to work, the words they used were "humble yourselves", one of them said "humble yourselves", another one said "you must eat humble pie," and so forth, "you must go back, you are wrong," and that is what they were sent down to do, and as Mr Wadsworth explained the whole point of it being once they were there never mind what the result of the ballot was, if the men resolved by the ballot that they would terminate by notice, it still gave you 14 days during which there could be deputations, and as your Lordships see, the main difficulty in seeing Mr Chambers was that Mr Chambers would not meet a deputation, because he said he would not meet a deputation of men who were out on strike without a notice. Therefore Mr Wadsworth thought "if we can only get the men back we shall be able to have a deputation, and there ought to be no difficulty in settling this matter with Mr Chambers"

The result of the meeting was that Mr Wadsworth and Mr Walsh persuaded the men to return, and a telegram was sent to the Association "Men agree to resume work and terminate notices"

Lord JAMES of HEREFORD. What is the date of that?

Mr RUFUS ISAACS. On the 15th July, page 23, paragraph 52, B to C, one of the passages from Mr Wadsworth, whether the men liked it or not, that was the view he was putting forward to them

The LORD CHANCELLOR. Page?

Mr RUFUS ISAACS. It is really page 106 at D "He trusted that every man at that particular meeting, and those away from it, would try, and especially at that particular time, to keep a cool head. They had got to a crisis, and it was now felt absolutely necessary that they should discuss without any opposition or feeling, but to come to the best decision in the interests of the whole of the men, women and children. They all knew that they had had this particular dispute about 'bag dirt,' and other disputes on hand for a considerable time. He had been down at Denaby on one or two deputations, but he had never been able to get Mr Chambers to do what, in his opinion, he ought to have done as a colliery manager over an important firm like the Denaby and Cadeby Collieries." Then he says at the bottom of the page at G "They were outside the law, and there was not the slightest doubt but what Mr Chambers was trying all that he possibly could to play that card to the uttermost" Then B to C is the passage I particularly wanted "Whether they liked it or not they would have to swallow the pill. They would have to put themselves within the rules of the Association. If they took the advice which had been given to them by Mr Walsh, and which they had come down from the Council to advise them, they would then put themselves in a legal position and would be able all the better to deal with Mr Chambers and his firm than what they were at the present time" And then at page 408, from A to B "They had to recommend to them what was not a very nice thing, but when a man took a position he ought to be in a position to assist his Union and carry out the rules of his Union. In the meantime they should ballot the whole of the men whether they are disposed to give in a 14 days' notice to terminate then contracts They would then be within the rules of the law and their Association" Then the resolution was passed, at G "That this meeting of the Denaby and Cadeby workmen agree to resume work at the earliest convenience, and that the men be balloted as to whether they are prepared to serve 14 days' notice to terminate their contract of service"

Now, up to that, my Lord, I submit that what is being done by Wadsworth and Walsh is all perfectly proper, that it cannot be suggested that they were doing anything unlawful in that for one moment on that 15th July, and if the Association had done nothing wrong up to then, it certainly did nothing wrong by what it did on the 15th July in saying what I admit in the fullest and frankest way may be said with reference to this "That if you go in and give your notices and then are not able to get your grievances settled and have to strike, then the Association would be in a position to give you strike pay, but not as it is at present" That was the argument, a very powerful argument, that was used by Wadsworth and Walsh to get the men to go back, and they succeeded, they got the men then to make up their minds that they would go back

Lord JAMES of HEREFORD Here you do get some action, do you not, inducing a strike which I would call the second strike, that is "Go back so that you will be enabled to strike legally"

Mr RUFUS ISAACS If it becomes necessary

Lord JAMES of HEREFORD 'So that you may be able" (is my term) "to strike if you think right so as to bring you under our rules to obtain strike pay"

Mr RUFUS ISAACS That is so

Lord JAMES of HEREFORD Therefore there is a leading up to the strike in the second instance, I do not say for a moment that it is illegal

Mr RUFUS ISAACS Oh yes, there is

Lord JAMES of HEREFORD It is advice given that they may go in in order that they may strike if they think right

Mr RUFUS ISAACS Yes, they may strike if they think right, but if they strike, if they think right under those circumstances, after having taken their ballot and given their notices, then the Association would be in the position to do what it could not do at present—that is, consider the granting of strike pay That is what I think it fairly means, and I submit that is the fair inference to be drawn from these facts, and certainly not that it was, as is suggested, a subterfuge or pretext

Lord JAMES of HEREFORD I think your opponents admit that there is no cause of action arising upon counselling a strike unless unlawful means are employed

Mr RUFUS ISAACS Yes, they must admit that, and your Lordships see how they have always met that by saying that this strike—this is again a matter one has to bear in mind, as it colours the whole of the case—was an unlawful strike from the beginning, and they say that for two reasons Unlawful, first, because breaches of contract were committed, and they say, further, that being unlawful from the start it remained unlawful to the end That is one way in which it is put Another way in which it was put was this, to show that it was an unlawful strike " Because you, the Association, really have not put forward the right view to the men, but you have induced them to come out really on the ' bag dirt ' grievance, whereas, what you really intended was to get this 10 per cent reduction altered—a revision of the price list—so far as the 10 per cent was concerned, the strike was unlawful, and continued unlawful right up to the end '

Lord JAMES of HEREFORD They must say that they are advising them to go in so as to give them notices, in order to get the 10 per cent reduction

Mr RUFUS ISAACS They must say that to carry out what they put forward throughout the case Of course, I dealt with that on the last occasion, and I do not want to go back to the facts upon them

Lord JAMES of HEREFORD Supposing they had wished to obtain the 10 per cent reduction, how does the unlawful character come in in taking that course even ? It may be an untrue statement they made, but where is the unlawfulness ?

Mr RUFUS ISAACS It is only unlawful in that way, my Lord, it is said it was not *bona fide*, that was the kind of argument that was used to the Jury,—that it was not *bona fide*, but was, as your Lordships may remember, I read out from my learned friend's address several passages —" a mere blind," as the learned Judge says in his Summing-up, a subterfuge, a pretext, and so on, and was in that way made to appear to the Jury as if from the first this strike was unlawful, because it was carried out by the officials, whoever they were, as a subterfuge I confess, as I have said in the Court of Appeal and elsewhere with reference to this, I have never been able to appreciate how striking to alter the 10 per cent reduction would have made the strike unlawful, but that was the kind of view that was put forward I have got some passages——

Lord DAVEY It was suggested—I seem to remember having seen it somewhere—that that would have been an unlawful strike because it was a breach of contract—that the men had contracted to observe the terms of, I will not call it the award, but the decision of the Chairman of the Conciliation Board, and, therefore, to strike against it and refuse to perform it was a breach of contract I think that is the way it was put

Mr RUFUS ISAACS I read a passage from my learned friend Mr Lush's speech on a recent occasion with reference to it in which it was put in that way, because at first it was put as an award, and it was pointed out that it was not strictly an award, and they said " Well it was a decision and equally they were not entitled to strike against that" in fact that was the burden of the whole of the argument on this part of the discussion of the question It had no importance except for that reason It was said " You have agreed to abide by the decision, you have got the decision of Lord James, and having got the decision you then want to get rid of the decision because it is not in your favour " That was the engine which was so powerfully wielded against the Defendants with the Jury

The LORD CHANCELLOR Can you refer me to the evidence showing what the terms were under which the parties entered into the so-called arbitration ?

Mr RUFUS ISAACS I am afraid I cannot, my Lord, because they were never proved, all that was done with reference to it, and it was common ground between us, was that there had been a decision of Lord James of Hereford on June 14th, which would come into effect on the first pay day after the first making-up day, which would have made it July 12th

Lord JAMES of HEREFORD If I may answer the Lord Chancellor, I suppose they were not proved, but I do not think you will find anything more than can be found in the rules establishing the Conciliation Board

Mr RUFUS ISAACS I do not think it was contended that it was anything more than that, my Lord, certainly nothing more was proved than that that was the common ground between us

The LORD CHANCELLOR Thank you

Mr RUFUS ISAACS And this was only another way in which my learned friend created throughout the hearing of this case an atmosphere of unlawfulness surrounding everything that the Defendants were doing, of course, it made it very difficult for the Defendants to deal with it before the Jury It was that reason that made it so essential to the Defendants to deal at some length with the " bag dirt " question, in order that the Jury might be satisfied that whatever had been done with reference to the strike was at least with the *bona-fide* desire to redress a grievance which was a legitimate grievance

Lord DAVEY I think that all that could be made out of this was that to take it one stage further they would have to give notice that they ceased to abide by the decision of the Conciliation Board I think in the case of another Conciliation Board, in an important district with which I am acquainted, that is the position In fact, in Durham, they did give notice once, and there was no Conciliation Board for a whole year, because they did not like the decision which the Umpire had given

Mr RUFUS ISAACS Of course that would not have affected, and could not have affected the position with which we had to deal as between the employers and ourselves

If I may just proceed to show what happened now, on the 16th July was the date when the men presented themselves for work again that is at paragraphs 53 and 54 When the men presented themselves there arose this difficulty about signing the contract There again, unfortunately, there is a great deal of evidence and a good deal of conflict, but my submission is that that is really immaterial Whether the men were right or whether they were wrong in refusing to sign, or whether Mr Chambers was right or wrong in asking them to sign, is wholly immaterial for the purposes of this case, it does not affect it, because by that time the men were perfectly justified—whatever motive was prompting them, whatever reason they had—in saying to the employer "We will not sign the new contract" It may have been the most ridiculous thing of them to do, it may have been the most arbitrary act to have done, but they were entitled to do it

Lord JAMES of HEREFORD Yes, but they would not go back into the employ

Mr RUFUS ISAACS No

Lord JAMES of HEREFORD They chose to keep out of the employ then

Mr RUFUS ISAACS Certainly

Lord JAMES of HEREFORD By that refusal

Mr RUFUS ISAACS Yet, they did not go back to the employ, but the point that really arose upon that was this Unfortunately there were differences of opinion, because it was thought that the men in signing the new contract, that is to say signing again in the contract book, would be signing something under which they had not been contractually bound before and there is no doubt that is so The importance of it I must say I think is slight when one considers it, but the fact is right What had happened was this As your Lordship may know, with reference to these matters, there is a book kept in which the men sign, there is a heading to the book, and at the time the men sign there are certain statutes that have to be shown to them, and certain bye-laws, and they have to sign incorporating all those in the contracts which they make The heading of that is at page 196, so far as it is of any importance, No 45 is the document from B to D This is the heading "We, the undersigned, having each received a copy of the Abstract of the Mines Regulation Acts, 50 and 51 Vic Cap 58, 57 and 58 Vic Cap 52, 59, and and 60 Vic Cap 43, General and Special Rules, Regulations and Bye-laws now established and in force at the Denaby Main Colliery, belonging to the Denaby and Cadeby Main Collieries, Limited, Denaby Main, near Rotherham, hereby undertake to obey, fulfil and agree to them, and the owners of the said Colliery hereby undertake to fulfil and perform the same on their part" Well, now, it is not really to be wondered at that some difficulty arose when the men went back, not knowing at that time that they would have to sign again when they were asked to sign on in these books which were given, and of which we had copies before the Court which were certainly very voluminous, and would require a good deal of study even by those who have spent their lives in the study of Statutes and Bye-laws, that some question did arise with reference to them and some suspicion, I do not say that the suspicion as it turns out from the facts was well founded, but the suspicion did arise in the men's minds that they were being asked to sign something new, and there is no doubt that they were to this extent In August of 1901 there had been some special rules promulgated by the Home Secretary under the Act of Parliament, and a question had been raised certainly as to whether the Home Secretary had the power to make those special rules under the Act and, so far as the men were concerned, that they thought they had grievances with regard to these matters is shown by deputations which waited upon Mr Chambers with reference to these very timbering notices In February and March, 1902, there were deputations which waited upon Mr Chambers, which he admits in cross-examination, and which appear upon the documents which I have already quoted relating to the bag dirt At least one strike occurred at another colliery objecting to these timbering notices, the point being so far as it is material—I do not think it is necessary to trouble your Lordships with any detail with regard to this—that in these rules it was only necessary to bring the timber up to a certain distance, I think 30 yards, from where the men were working, and questions arose as to whether that was sufficiently near

Now, it turned out that in fact according to the evidence which was given there had been a notice given by Mr Chambers with reference to this matter of the timbering, and which he contended brought the men under a contract to perform what was stipulated for in the special rules promulgated by the Home Secretary both contractually and under the Statute, or rather under the rules made by the Home Secretary. The point that was raised here was that it was said "Well, there is a question about this matter." The men were raising undoubtedly in the Association, I will not say throughout but in certain parts of the Association, and notably in the Denaby and Cadeby, questions about these timbering rules, and it was thought by the officials that if the men signed new contracts they would be contracting to abide by the rules which the Association were contending were *ultra vires* of the Home Secretary's powers to make. And there is no doubt now from the evidence given—that to any man who presented himself for work on the 16th July, 1902, and was asked to sign again and who had been in the employ of the Company before August, 1901, that is before the promulgation of the Home Secretary's Rules, when he did sign a new contract in July, 1902, if he did sign it, he would have been making himself liable—he would have been agreeing by that contract to abide by those Rules and would have been giving them therefore the force of an agreement between the parties which would have prevented him ever complaining that those Rules were *ultra vires*.

That was one of the questions, I do not know that it was all, but it was one of the questions that undoubtedly arose. Again I say with respect it was of no real importance in the matter except to get rid of this atmosphere of suspicion which is thrown around all the acts of the Defendant Association and of the men at this time. That very likely they were unduly sensitive about this is quite possible, that they would have been giving up nothing in substance is also quite possible, but it was the view that was taken, and equally Mr. Chambers who thought that there was some substance in these matters—I do not say in this particular form of complaints, but who desired that the men should sign on again, insisted upon it, he was just as insistent of his rights as the men were insistent of theirs, and I do submit with respect that it does not serve any very useful purpose really to discuss in this very unfortunate controversy that arose at that time which caused the continuation of this strike for so long or to decide who was right or who was wrong in the view that was taken by the two. But that was the unfortunate position that was adopted, and on this 16th July there is a letter which is written by Smith, the secretary of one of the branches, to Pickard, telling him what had happened, I refer to that because it is much better than going back to the evidence, because it gives a contemporaneous record of what did take place. It is at page 23 of the Respondents' case. He says I have to inform you that when our men present themselves asking for their lamps to be got ready for Thursday morning they are told they cannot start work until they have signed a Contract Book with a heading on it which we have not heard of before. According to the information received they will not be allowed to resume work for the purpose of serving their notices. Shall we be in order in refusing to sign a fresh contract? The result of the ballot is '—then he gives the result of the ballot Now, unfortunately, what the men did do, having passed the resolution to which attention has been called on the 15th of July that they should resume work and then take the ballot, when they found apparently that they were not allowed to resume work without signing the contract, they took a ballot, and the effect of the ballot was that there was an overwhelming majority as stated here for giving the notices

Lord JAMES of HEREFORD What value would the notice be under these conditions if they did not sign on the new contract?

Mr RUFUS ISAACS The notice was of no value whatever

Lord JAMES of HEREFORD A notice of nothing

Mr RUFUS ISAACS Notice of nothing The men were taking the view then that they were not bound to sign on, and if they were right, if the contract was still in existence, then they would have to give the notice in order to put an end to it If the contract was not in existence then, of course, unless they entered into the new contractual relationship it was utterly useless to give the notices Then, at page 24, the letter continues "We are intending serving the notices out on each shift, and have urged the men and boys to present themselves for work on their respective shifts, and if their lamps are refused to return home after giving in their notices" Then on the next day, Thursday, Mr Pickard wired to Mr Chambers asking him to meet a deputation Mr Chambers replied on the same day "Discussion impossible with men on strike without notice" Mr Pickard answered that telegram "I have no advice to give to the men, but I hold you to your telegrams as follows 'No need to wait for meeting, the pits are open when the men wish to resume work'" (that is quoting from the telegram of Mr Chambers, which is at the top of page 23), "and if you do not carry it out so far as I know" (this is Mr Pickard's own view) "you place yourself in an awkward position" Then Mr Chambers answered that "I adhere to my telegram Pits are open, and all men who have applied and signed on have been employed Every effort will be made to prepare the stalls for turning" (That is for getting to work) Then, on the same day, July 17th, in paragraph 56, Mr Pickard sends to Smith the telegrams that had been sent to him from Mr Chambers and adds these words—and I submit these words are of importance as showing that he legitimately intended that the men should go back to work—"Present yourselves for work at every shift Consulting solicitors Either send or bring first thing in the morning the two copies of rules" Those are, of course, the rules which were referred to as included in the contract heading which I called attention to just now

Then, on the 18th July, Mr Pickard writes to Mr Chambers " Why should men sign on again? is not the contract they previously signed still existing?"—and Mr Chambers replied, " Regular custom at these collieries when men have left to sign again before restarting " Then Mr Pickard responds by this telegram " The men have not left your employ, and therefore why should they sign on again?" Now I stop at that moment, because that brings us to the point of the refusal by Mr Chambers to let the men work without signing on, and the view taken by Mr Pickard, that the men were not bound to sign on, but that simply going back to work was all that was required of them, and all that Mr Chambers had the right to demand in view of his previous telegram

Then, on the 18th July, the men having presented themselves for work, wrote to Mr Pickard applying for strike pay My Lord, I am sorry, but that reference is one which is of no importance in this case, it applies to a matter which is outside, and your Lordship might please not take that date of the 18th, it comes a little while after On the 21st July Mr Pickard wrote a letter to Mr Smith stating what had happened, and that, my Lord, is on page 25 of our case and at page 347 of the Appendix He says this " We cannot recommend you to sign on again, but earnestly recommend you to continue presenting yourselves for work I am also of opinion that whilst you are not entitled to pay, and which the Council considers also at the same time, I think from the time you presented yourselves for work, and they refuse to allow you to do so, according to Mr Chambers' first telegram, from that date you will come within our rule However, under the circumstances, you as secretary must present a requisition to come within rule from the date you offered to resume work and were refused " I must refer to the page in the Appendix, as there is just a sentence there which is not quoted in the case It is at the bottom of page 347 " We are also of opinion that your contract is not broken, and if Mr Chambers persists in refusing to allow you to re-start without signing on, he comes under the same law he brought you under, namely, he summoned you for leaving work without notice, and we shall be able to sue him for wages for the whole of the time he refuses to allow you to resume work " That seems to be the view he was taking of the law then

Lord JAMES of HEREFORD How is that? " We are also of opinion that your contract is not broken " Was he right, according to you?

Mr RUFUS ISAACS No, my Lord, he was wrong What he meant was the old story that the contract was only suspended, and that Mr Chambers said they could resume work, that they could go on with the contract, the operation of which had been suspended during the time the men were out

Lord DAVEY That they were ready and willing to perform their contract

Mr RUFUS ISAACS That was their view, and that is what he is referring to when he says the contract was not broken

Lord DAVEY He regarded it as a continuous contract which they had broken for a week or a fortnight, but were willing to go on with

Mr RUFUS ISAACS Yes That same sort of thing sometimes happens when a collier does not present himself for work for two or three days, when he returns he does present himself for work and is allowed to take his turn at the shift, and to do his work, his contract really has been broken by his absenting himself for the two or three days, but notwithstanding no notice is taken of that except that he is not paid He goes on and resumes his contract without signing on again Mr Pickard's view was that what had happened here was the same thing, and that the men ought to be allowed to go back without signing a fresh contract

Lord JAMES of HEREFORD For the purpose of this case it is admitted, I think, that after two or three days' absence from work, the practice was for the men to sign on

Mr RUFUS ISAACS Yes—well, it varies from two or three days to a week

Lord JAMES of HEREFORD A period that had expired in this case

Mr RUFUS ISAACS Certainly

The LORD CHANCELLOR Mr Isaacs, we have in fact had our attention drawn to all these telegrams, if you wish to read them again I do not want to stop you, but would it not be better if you were to summarise any differences of opinion

Mr RUFUS ISAACS Yes, my Lord, I was only anxious to get as far as this with the telegrams, and I will not go further, but to these I attributed a considerable amount of importance, because what I wanted to point out was probably a matter to which your Lordship's attention had not been directed hitherto, that is that in this letter of July 21st what Mr Pickard is writing is " We earnestly recommend you to continue presenting yourselves for work ", so that the view he was taking was that " notwithstanding the fact that the Company refused to allow the men to work without signing on again you must go on presenting yourselves for work, you must not be satisfied with that, but I earnestly recommend you to go on presenting yourselves for work at every shift " The men continued to do that throughout the period. After some days no doubt the numbers got fewer, because it became a matter of form, but they did persist for some time, and Mr Pickard is always persisting in saying to them " You must not stop, you must go on presenting yourselves for work." I rely upon that for the purpose of showing this, that Mr Pickard did really mean that the men should present themselves and should resume their employment, and then of course should at the end of the 14 days, after they had given notice, determine whether or not they would leave the work again.

Your Lordships have had the various documents which followed upon this referred to, and I think one may say the substance of it was that the men after presenting themselves for a considerable number of shifts did not return, and they continued out of employment, and I think from the 24th July the Council thought that the men were entitled to be paid the strike pay, and from that time they paid it as dating from the 17th.

I think, my Lord, there is some importance to be attached to the rules——

Lord JAMES of HEREFORD. Did the pay start from the 24th, or did it not run back to before the 24th? The order was made on the 24th, but when did it commence to run from?

Mr RUFUS ISAACS. It was made on the 24th to commence from the 17th. The view taken by the Association, rightly or wrongly, was that from the time the men presented themselves to work and the employers refused they came within the rules. Now, may I call attention to these rules, because I think the matter is a little difficult to follow, and I want to say a word in reference to it by just calling attention to the particular rule under which it was thought the men came. That your Lordship will find, if I may just keep to the case where it is set out, on page 10 of the Respondents' case, all the material rules are set out there. It is Rule 65, and what the Association did was to pay what is called strike pay, which again is not the right term, because what they really meant and thought they were doing was paying lock-out pay. It is always called lock-out pay in the books. It has been called strike pay during the course of this case, and the name does not matter, but the view taken by the Association was that the employers, having refused to let the men work the employers were locking the men out, and it was upon this that so much discussion took place in Howden's case. Rule 65 is "Any branch, or portion of any branch, which may be locked out, or otherwise thrown out of employment, in consequence of any action that may legally have been taken by the Association to keep up the price or remedy any grievances either at that or any other colliery connected with the Association, the members of such branch shall be supported after the same rate as the members on strike, until such time as they can get work, or the Association decides otherwise."

Now, of course, if Mr Pickard's view was right that the contract was still subsisting, and the employers had refused to let the men return to work then Rule 65 undoubtedly would have applied, but it did not apply because he was wrong in that view. Well then, my Lord, if he was wrong in that view the payment of strike pay was justified, or rather ought to be justified under another rule, which was Rule 64, which was the strike pay, and when we were beaten from the ground of lock-out what was said was "If that is the view the Court takes of what had happened we can justify it under Rule 64." Then a great question turned on the word "cease." I will read the rule "If any branch member or members have grievances affecting their wages, mode or manner of working or the hours of labour, if the employers refuse to remedy those grievances and after all proper and peaceful means have been tried to effect a settlement by deputations from members, with the advice and assistance of Council and such member or members be permitted to cease work" (that is what the point turns on) 'by the sanction of the Association in accordance with the rules such members shall receive 9s per week for all full members, 4s 6d per week for all half members and 1s per head per week for all children under 13 years of age, until such time as they can resume work." What was said was "Very well, if the masters are right and we are wrong in the view we take the members have been permitted to cease work by the sanction of the Association from the 17th July" That was the view put forward It was said "No, they have not, because they had ceased work from the 29th June" and, therefore, and this, my Lord, I again respectfully submit is conclusive against my learned friend by your Lordships decision in Howden's case, upon the first period They said, "No, the ceasing of the work is not by the sanction of the Association of the 17th July, but the work ceased on the 29th June without the sanction of the Association, and therefore you cannot pay strike pay", and so your Lordships held The same rules were quoted, the same facts were given in evidence, and the same arguments were used, and as I submit really the arguments used there and your Lordships' decision are conclusive against my learned friend upon this point If I may make this observation upon it now that I am dealing with this rule and have called attention to what the decision was in Howden's case, if it is right now to say that under these very rules which were under discussion, under your Lordships' consideration, in Howden's case the Branch officials were the servants of the Association, and it being admitted I assume that the Branch officials had induced the men to come out, if the act of the Branch officials was the act of the Association under the rules, as is now contended, why then the men do cease work with the sanction of the Association, and the decision ought to have been in the Association's favour and not in Howden's favour

Lord JAMES of HEREFORD That would have been a ceasing of work unlawfully if on the 29th June.

Mr RUFUS ISAACS Yes, but it would have been ceasing with the sanction of the Association

Lord JAMES of HEREFORD I quite agree, and it must be taken that the Branch were the servants and that they sanctioned the unlawful act

Mr RUFUS ISAACS I think if the men had ceased to work with the sanction of the Association notwithstanding that they were committing a breach of contract they could come within Rule 64

Lord JAMES of HEREFORD Yes, but are the Association coming forward here now and saying they did sanction a breach?

Mr RUFUS ISAACS No, not at all, my Lord, but on the contrary what we are saying is that we did not, what I am saying is that if the Appellants' argument is right now then the decision in Howden's case must have been wrong, which they cannot say

Lord JAMES of HEREFORD What do you say the decision in Howden's case was bearing on this point?

Mr RUFUS ISAACS The decision in Howden's case was that the men had not ceased work with the sanction of the Association on the 29th June, that is the decision, and the point I am making, and I respectfully submit that it is clear, is that if the Branch officials were the servants of the Association under the rules, as is now suggested, under the same rules as were being discussed in Howden's case, then the men had ceased work with the sanction of the Association, because the basis of the argument in Howden's case was this—this was the decision upon which the whole point turned The Branch officials caused the men, as then said, to cease work and the Association was no party to that, therefore it cannot be said that the men ceased work with the sanction of the Association, and therefore you cannot bring yourselves within Rule 64   Then the argument against it which was put forward was The men on the 17th July having presented themselves for work they had ceased work as from that date with the sanction of the Association , and your Lordships held that would not do, that that could not be said and that in fact they had ceased work on the 29th June, and had not ceased work with the sanction of the Association What your Lordships are asked to say now is that they had ceased work on the 29th June with the sanction of the Association.

The LORD CHANCELLOR Will you give the reference to Howden's case

Mr RUFUS ISAACS Yes, my Lord, I am going to quote it—it is reported in the House of Lords in 1905 Appeal Cases, page 256, but the facts there are not really dealt with—the facts are dealt

with in 1903, 1 King's Bench, page 308   The reason why the facts
are not dealt with was because your Lordships did not call upon the
Respondent Howden to deal with the facts, having heard them
argued   They were dealt with, of course, in the Court of Appeal,
and in the Court of Appeal they are set out at great length and
discussed at great length   My learned friend, Mr Lush, in arguing
the case for Howden at page 321 of that case says " With regard
to the construction of Rule 64, that rule only authorises the granting
of strike pay where the men have been permitted to cease work by
the sanction of the Association   Here, admittedly, the men ceased
work without that sanction "   Now that is the position upon which
the whole case proceeded

Lord JAMES of HEREFORD   Just read those words again—
" Here admittedly "

Mr RUFUS ISAACS   " Here admittedly the men cease work
without that sanction "   That is what he said in that case, and
what was held in that case was that when the men ceased work on
the 29th June they were ceasing work without the sanction of the
Association   What they are contending in this case is that when
the men ceased work on the 29th June they ceased work with the
sanction of the Association, because they are saying that the
Association procured the men to break the contract   They are
putting forward, as I say, contrary propositions   The Judgment
proceeds upon that ground   Had it been otherwise, had it been the
fact that under the rules the branch officials were the servants of
the Association, inasmuch as in that case, in Howden's case, it was
not in controversy for the purposes of that case, that the branch
officials had induced the men to cease work on the 29th June, the
consequence must have been that if the branch officials were the
agents of the Association it was the Association that was ceasing to
work with the sanction of the Association, and an Injunction never
could have been granted

In the case which came before your Lordships' House this is
what they say with reference to that in their reasons (their case on the
facts which were admitted was not in dispute at the trial)   " The
men ceased work without the sanction of the Association within the
meaning of Rule 64, and had ceased to be in the employment of the
employers at the time they pretended to offer themselves for work
on July 17th "

The LORD CHANCELLOR   Page, please

Mr RUFUS ISAACS   It is the 7th Reason—on page 30 of
the Respondents' case in the Yorkshire Miners' Association v
Howden

All these rules which we are now discussing are the very rules which are discussed and dealt with in the Court of Appeal Judgment, and which formed the subject of so much discussion in this House, and it is in connection with that very Rule 64 that the element of doubt arose as to the construction of the rule, because, as my learned friend Mr Danckwerts pointed out when he was addressing your Lordships in this Appeal, Lord Justice Stirling gravely doubted whether we were not right in our contention as to ceasing, but he would not differ from Lord Justice Vaughan-Williams, and Lord Justice Mathew took the same view, that is, these two Lord Justices took one view, and Lord Justice Stirling was very doubtful as to whether our contention was not right, and whether it might not be said that we had come within one or other of these two rules 64 or 65 I do not think that it is much use reading the Judgment upon this point It appears very plainly from Lord Justice Stirling's Judgment upon this that he had the doubt which I have just referred to Lord Justice Stirling's Judgment is at page 340

I pass from what was said there, but I do venture to submit that it cannot be that the employers, the Colliery Company, are right in both contentions, one or other must be wrong The view which has been held already by your Lordships in Howden's case is, I submit, quite conclusive against the Appellants on the part of the case which relates to the first period I do not say that it is conclusive as regards the second part

The LORD CHANCELLOR On that I should like to ask you a question for information I do not see that in the House of Lords the decision turned at all upon the word "cease" It may be that there was a good reason

Mr RUFUS ISAACS May I point out why, my Lord? Because your Lordship's House took the view, a strong view, that we were wrong as to the point turning on the question as to whether or not the contract was broken on the 17th July We were contending, and contended here, as we had contended below, that the contract was not at an end, but your Lordships thought that the contract was at an end on the telegrams and statements of facts which were made, and did not call on my learned friends to argue that, all that they had to argue was the question of law under the Trade Union Act

The LORD CHANCELLOR Thank you

Mr RUFUS ISAACS Page 259, at the beginning of the argument, states that the Respondent was requested to argue only the question whether the action could be maintained under Section 4 of the Trade Union Act, and that is why it does not supply the necessary information upon the other point

Lord DAVEY It was not very much argued, all their Lordships took a strong view

Mr RUFUS ISAACS Certainly

Lord DAVEY The late Lord Chancellor was very emphatic

Mr RUFUS ISAACS Yes, very emphatic that we could not come within either of these two rules for the reasons given in the Court of Appeal, and as we could not come within 64 (the only argument on 64 was the one I am just putting forward), and we could not get within the lock-out or thrown out of employment, we could not come within any rule, and therefore we were driven to the point of law that this was an action for the purpose of directly enforcing an agreement That was the matter which was discussed at some length

It I pass now from the period of the payment of strike pay I think I can pass to the 13th to the 18th of August From the 13th to the 18th of August it is said, and it is proved, there was some intimidation and some molestation in the shape of assault The 13th to the 18th of August appears to have been a period when feeling seems to have run somewhat high in this part of the world, and where there were 4,000 or 5,000 people grouped together at the colliery, and undoubtedly there were unlawful acts committed—acts for which I have not a word to say in defence, but those are acts for which it cannot be said that the Defendant Association was responsible, unless we get back to the old point of the branch officials' acts binding the Defendant Association All I want to say with reference to this—I am not going to refer in detail to the evidence—I have been through it again—is that I submit, and my learned friends agree (my learned friend Mr Bankes certainly did so in this statement of the case to your Lordships on this point) that so far as the members of the Council of the Association were concerned there is no evidence that they took any part or were present in any way What is said against them, and the way in which the case is made against them, is this it is said, "you were granting strike pay and therefore you are responsible" and it is said also, "you made statements subsequently which would have the effect of inciting the men to acts of this character" Now I want to make this observation with reference to it, that these acts of violence between the 13th and the 18th August are, except for this isolated one on the 2nd July which I have already dealt with, Berry's case, really the only acts of violence which were committed during the course of this strike I rely upon that, not for the purpose of excusing the acts, but for the purpose of saying this, that it is quite plain that this was not one of those cases in which you can say that the granting of pay or the granting of money to a man must necessarily involve your giving him money to enable him to commit acts of violence or other unlawful acts That is the reason for which I refer to the few acts that were committed, and the short space of time during which they lasted. Upon the evidence of the Appellants in this case, in this district where there were these 4,000 or 5,000 excited persons grouped together in a place which existed only upon the work which was done in the collieries, they were able to maintain peace throughout the time except for this isolated period from the 13th to the 18th August, with the assistance of seven policemen—in one instance it was five, and at another seven—seven is the highest, and I take that against myself—and I do submit that when you have that state of facts proved it would be idle to say that any one who was giving money must have been conspiring with the persons to whom he gave the money to commit the acts of violence, because that is what my learned friends have to say.

Lord JAMES of HEREFORD. They were branch officials, were they not, and it is brought home to them?

Mr RUFUS ISAACS. It is brought home to them that they were present and did nothing. That would involve the old question of agency. All that is brought home to them, may I observe, is that one or other of the branch officials is seen in the crowd when the assault is committed. That is what is proved against them.

Lord DAVEY. They were not acting as committeemen though.

Mr RUFUS ISAACS. No, but I wanted particularly to call attention to that—it is never suggested that they were actually doing the thing, nor is there any evidence that they were themselves instigating the assault, and again in this connection not even in the branch books is there any payment to any man for picketting or any of these acts, the kind of entry which one usually finds in these matters as to the payment for picketting and so forth is absent, the accounts are complete and there was no such payment made. I do submit that it might just as well be said that because a director of a company is present when something takes place the company is responsible because the director does not state that he, as a director, disapproves of what is being done at the time. What is contended in this case is that because a branch official was present when an assault was committed, although not taking any part in it, therefore the Association is to be responsible.

Now, my Lords, at page 477 a speech was made on this very 13th August, 1902, at the Station Hotel, Croft. The Chairman of this meeting was Phil Humphries, and one has to bear in mind that that is not the Humphries who is a Defendant, the branch official, this is Phil Humphries, and Mr Croft makes a speech. "The Chairman's opening remarks were brief. He said the time had come when they ought to throw away the password 'Be calm,' and get another. It was 'Be calm,' in 1885, and they lost." See what

Mr Croft says in answer to that "Mr Croft took a different view" (He was the President) "He said in regard to 1885, what he witnessed and experienced taught him that the moment they began rioting, their case was over, and they were beaten As he said at the last meeting, the quieter they were the more uneasy someone else was That was what those they were opposed to were waiting for The moment they began to kick up a disturbance, the sympathy of the public and of their own Association would be gone, and they did not want that He would not like to see any man in that audience have to go to Wakefield for six months" (that is where the prison was) "He urged upon them not to interfere with any man when they left the meeting All they could do was to stand in the road and watch those who were coming from the collieries pass by, but they need not say a word to them He had every confidence that they would not lose the fight, but if they lost he would say 'God help every man at Denaby and Cadeby Main' There were a hundred summonses for Saturday, but he urged them to never mind summonses They need not meet trouble, but take it as it came "

The LORD CHANCELLOR Mr Isaacs, I want to say a thing which is on my mind as to this if they all went and watched those coming from the colliery passing by, supposing there were hundreds of them lining the road, would you say that was a proper act

Mr RUFUS ISAACS My Lord, it depends, of course, if they simply stood there seeing the men without there being any reasonable apprehension of violence on the part of those who were coming from work, I submit that would be a proper act If they were simply watching, I submit that could not make it a wrongful act, but if what is meant, and what might be meant, was watching for the purpose of intimidating, either threatening to commit violence or causing apprehension of violence, of course that would be a totally different thing, and I do not contend that would be a rightful act I think the very question your Lordship has put to me has been discussed in a recent case in the Court of Appeal, and I think I am right in saying that that is the distinction that would be drawn

Now, that is what took place on that date, and, my Lord, from the 18th of August, the period at which the disturbances ceased, until the 29th October no question arises of any wrongful act There was nothing complained of either in the Court below or in my learned friend's opening, but in the meanwhile there had been attempts made by the Respondents to get a settlement of this dispute In paragraph 61, at page 25 of our case, the documents are referred to which show this I think I might summarise those, and they are only of importance as showing that during this time the Respondents were doing all they could to bring this matter to a satisfactory settlement Paragraph 61, at the bottom of page 25, shows what had happened "The Council suggested new price lists, which were submitted from the Denaby and Cadeby men, and it was resolved 'that Mr Cowey be instructed to write to Mr Chambers asking him to meet a deputation in order to discuss the suggested price list, and, if possible, settle grievances amicably' Accordingly Defendant Cowey wrote on the 11th September, 1902, to Mr Chambers, to which Mr Chambers replied on the 15th September, 1902, as follows 'In reply I have always been willing to meet deputations with or without a Union official with a view of arranging amicable settlements of disputes At the moment, however, there is no dispute between the Denaby and Cadeby Main Collieries, Limited, and their men The miners lately in the employ of the Company left their work without giving notice, and are therefore not now in the Company's service If they are re-engaged the question of any matters with which they are dissatisfied can be dealt with in the usual manner' To this Defendant Cowey replied on the 17th September, 1902 'I am rather disappointed with your reply I thought that perhaps we might have met and come to an understanding It appears this is not to be until the men resign I have sent your communication on to our men at Denaby and Cadeby for their consideration'" Then the men replied this was sent on to the men, and Smith replied that he was instructed by a joint General Meeting that the men were determined to fight the dispute to a successful issue The documents are at pages 357 and 358, but I will not trouble your Lordship with a reference to those Then at the end of October there was another meeting at which again attempts of a similar character were made with the result that the letter was written which appears at paragraph 64 Paragraph 63 states the steps that were taken again to secure settlement, again there was a request to meet a deputation, and paragraph 64 sets out the letter from Mr Chambers in which he says "In reply to your request that I should meet a deputation of our late workmen I am unable to comprehend that any good result would be attained by it I have previously endeavoured to make perfectly clear it is quite impossible for the Company to give any advance on the standard rate of wages, or to interfere with the price lists which have existed for many years and on which the men entered the Company's employment, and the Company desire there should be no misapprehension on this point If the men are disposed to resume work they are at liberty to do so If afterwards any matters arise which cause dissatisfaction I will try to remove them Failing that the men can appeal to the Joint Committee appointed by the South Yorkshire Coal Owners' Association and the Yorkshire Miners' Association for the purpose of settling disputes" Well that was very idle, because as we know from Mr Chambers' admission made in cross-examination the Coal Owners' Association was supporting the Plaintiffs and was bearing a share of the damage which was done to the Plaintiffs' collieries, they had some arrangement as between them, and, of course, if the Coal Owners' Association was supporting the Company, it was idle for the men to apply to the Coal Owners' Association

Lord MACNAGHTEN There is no suggestion of applying to the Coal Owners' Association is there? It is only the Joint Committee

Mr RUFUS ISAACS Yes, the Joint Committee of the two, but the difficulty would arise

Lord MACNAGHTEN That may be

Mr RUFUS ISAACS That is all I meant, that is the only relevance of it All I meant was that it was not very much good, if you have a number of men on each side, and they are each committed to a view at this time, and determined not to allow any settlement to be made, it was not much good applying to them That is all, of course, that had been done—and that appears from documents which were read before—at an earlier stage, there had been an application made to the Joint Committee What had happened so far as it was material was that an application had been made in June 1902, and Mr Chambers had said, "Oh, no, I cannot have that reopened, it is not a matter that ought now to go before the Joint Committee"

That having taken place, I think the next thing that is said against my clients is on the 24th November, 1902 That is Mr Parrott's speech, in which your Lordship will remember there was the word "devilish" used What happened there again as appears from paragraph 68, was that steps were taken, but they were of no avail, and there the same view was taken which is repeated again and again almost every month "That if Mr Chambers will not agree to meet a deputation we stand firm to the resolution of June 29th, 1902," and to that view the men adhered Then the 24th November was the date at which the question was raised about the evictions

Lord JAMES of HEREFORD Where does the "devilish" speech occur, Mr Isaacs

Mr RUFUS ISAACS I am just going to give your Lordship the reference, it is at page 434 that Mr Parrott is present and makes a speech on this date What he says is, just at B, page 436 "To turn people out of their houses and let them remain empty was a most devilish thing in his opinion" Where it begins leading up to that passage is at F of 435 "They were giving them notice to quit the Company's houses They knew that winterly weather had already set in, and they would have very severe weather to contend with between now and spring" and so forth What he is referring to is the notice of eviction which were given Now that really was the strongest thing that there was in language used against the Association Of course, Mr Parrott himself was a member of the Council and as to what he said with regard to it he was cross-examined, he stated in reference to it that he was dealing with this question of the eviction of the men No doubt feeling was running high at the time and he used that expression in relation to the evictions which have nothing whatever to do with this case There is no finding and although there are certain allegations about it in the Statement of Claim, no claim for damage was made, it is not one of the unlawful acts complained of here I mean and it is not said that the men did not go out when they were evicted or that the men were induced to remain in after they had received notice We have nothing of that kind to deal with, and as Lord Justice Cozens-Hardy says "If he did say it nothing happened as the result of it" That is the evidence—nothing did happen

Lord DAVEY Of course although he is an individual member of the Council, one is in a little difficulty in seeing how that binds the Association The members of the Association which is a widespread organisation, have the right to say "We have established a Council by which we are bound," but he was only an individual member of the Council

Lord JAMES of HEREFORD He went down by virtue of his office

Lord DAVEY Was he sent there?

Mr RUFUS ISAACS I think so, there was a resolution which I will read to your Lordships It is at page 238, apparently that seems to have been a resolution of the Executive Committee, not of the Council There was to be a meeting held on Monday the 24th, they had notice of it, and he attends and makes this speech Now, may I make this observation with reference to what Mr Parrott said, not only did no injury or damage result from it, no illegal act was done in consequence, but I submit that it is extravagant to say that because he makes that statement on the 24th November, 1902, therefore his Association is to be liable for acts committed as far back as 29th June, 1902, or as the 17th July 1902 That is what is said, it is said that this is evidence, that he said something which was wrong, which was inflammatory, is evidence from which the Jury are asked to find that this strike was the result of a conspiracy to injure or molest the employers, or was the result of a conspiracy to do unlawful acts My Lord, I do submit that that is very extravagant, and that that is the utmost that can be said with regard to it At the most, what can be said about this matter is that a strong word, inflammatory language, is used Granted that it ought not to have been used, granted that it would be better to use more moderate language under these circumstances, what is the effect of it? No damage is sought for that particular act, no damage is sought for anything which resulted from that speech, nor is it said that that speech is one of the unlawful acts That was not molestation or intimidation, nor did any molestation or intimidation follow it, but as I understand the argument, and this was the use that was made of it, and it is the use always made of these instances in these cases, what is said is "If you prove something which is wrong, however late it may be in the stage of the strike, the Jury may infer from that that all the preceding unlawful acts have been done in pursuance of a preconceited arrangement and you should therefore find a conspiracy"

Now, my Lord, that is the way in which the conspiracy is sought to be established. I do submit with great deference, that really it is extravagant to maintain any such proposition as that I could understand its being said that, assuming you can make the Association liable at all, if an official has said something on behalf of the Association which is wrong, the Association might be made liable for that particular wrong I could understand that, but I do submit that it cannot date back and prove that because he has lost his temper or his calmness on a particular date and uses inflammatory language in November, therefore without any other evidence the Association of which he is the official must have been conspiring ever since 29th June or the 17th July with the men to do these particular acts

I think, my Lord, that brings me really to the end of the evidence, so far as it is material upon this point I have not gone through the subsequent dates because the subsequent dates show only what took place with reference to the Injunction, and throw no light on the matter which we are now discussing

Perhaps I ought just to call attention to some passages in Mr Wadsworth's evidence, I will not read more than Mr Wadsworth, because I think from reading one one may get a view of the attitude of the others, but this is the evidence of the Defendants which I think has not yet been read to your Lordships, I think you have only had some of the evidence which was selected by the Appellants All the Defendants who were in the land of the living were called, that is the Defendants who were represented, and stated what had taken place Wadsworth's evidence begins at page 776, I can pass over a great deal of it, and I only want to trouble your Lordships with reading material passages At the time of being examined he was the President of the Yorkshire Miners' Association, he had been elected that year, but he had been Vice-President for about 15 years in succession The Association covers the whole of the Yorkshire coalfield and there are altogether about 150 branches Then he is asked the total membership and he says "About 63,000, roughly speaking Q You have been acquainted with the circumstances relating to the bag dirt questions in these two collieries, almost from the beginning, I think?—Well, I have known about them for a considerable number of years—nine years I should think, something like that" Then he is asked about the bag dirt and as that part has been read I do not want to go through it again May I in passing over it call attention to a discussion which takes place between my learned friend and myself as to the materiality of this evidence as contained in the shorthand note, which helps one to understand how the point was material. At page 783 questions were being asked about the bag dirt, and this is just after Question 2232 "(Mr Eldon Bankes) I desire as far as possible to keep this within limits. I opened my case that the merits of the dispute were not material. My learned friend has also opened his case by saying that the merits of the dispute are not material. The fact of the existence of the dispute I understand my friend to say is material, and of course I understand that. (Mr Rufus Isaacs) I am glad to hear from my friend at any rate something that seems to me very near a recognition of the point I argued yesterday and the day before, that all this was really immaterial" (I had been arguing that at considerable length, and with such strenuousness as I could command) 'I have been saying so all along, but my learned friend introduces rather curiously this in opening his case. Your Lordship may recollect he suggests that there was no *bona fide* intention to strike on the bag dirt question, which he treats as a small matter, and one which would not have led to a strike. (Mr Justice Lawrance) I am not excluding it. (Mr Rufus Isaacs) I only wanted to clear the ground. I agree it makes a good deal to go into which I have always contended is immaterial. Then my learned friend says in opening. I do not touch this bag dirt question, except I admit there was something with reference to it, and then passes from it, but he then goes on and continues the suggestion. Really what you were trying to do was to get back the 10 per cent. Therefore it is most material to my case so long as he persists in that suggestion, which I submit is not material to his case or mine, that I should go on and show there was a real dispute. (Mr Eldon Bankes) I do not intend to go into it. (Mr Rufus Isaacs) Very well. (Mr Eldon Bankes) I desire to be consistent. I said it did not seem to me to be material, and I say still it does not seem to me to be material, and I understand my learned friend to agree with me, but he will go into it. I am not going to follow him or else we shall be here for months. (Mr Rufus Isaacs) If you withdraw the suggestion that has been made as to the 10 per cent being the real thing—— (Mr Eldon Bankes) Certainly not. (Mr Rufus Isaacs) And as to its being a sham dispute, of course I am ready to withdraw the question as to the bag dirt. As long as you say, it is a sham strike and a sham dispute I must go on" That is how the matter stood, and that really is how the matter stood throughout the trial. If your Lordship sees what is happening there, how could we for the Defendants avoid going into this question and be content with the statement that there was something with reference to it when they were saying all along that we were putting this as a pretext and a subterfuge.

Lord JAMES of HEREFORD. Would you give me the date of the decision of the Conciliation Board?

Mr RUFUS ISAACS. Your Lordship means your Lordship's

decision—14th June, 1902 It is at page 190 if your Lordship
wants it

Now I am going on to page 785, and the only point I am going
to call attention to there is that from Question 2238 and onwards it
is evidence as to the timbering rules, the documents are referred to
which relate to it, and that goes on for some few questions, but I do
not propose to trouble your Lordships with reading these

Now, at page 787 we get to the material date of the 28th June,
Question 2252 "I have put before you quite shortly some of the
proceedings with reference to this bag dirt question and other
grievances Were they grievances which were seriously entertained
by the men at the colliery?—They were very seriously entertained by
the men Q We now know—you did not at the time—that on the
28th June there were deductions in four stalls amounting to £8 15s
altogether in respect of this bag dirt work?—Yes Q And we know
that the result of that was that the men came out on strike?—They
said they came out on strike——" Mr Bankes objects Question
2255 "You were not aware, at all at this time of the deductions on
the 28th June, at the time they were deducted you were not aware
of the deductions?—Certainly not, I was not there" (your Lordship
sees later what really had happened was that Mr Wadsworth and a
number of others were at this time away at Southport where there
was a federation meeting in connection with some other matters and
they did not get back until the 5th July) "Q You knew nothing
about the strike of the men until it had actually taken place?—We
got to know through the letters from the secretaries, &c Q On the
29th June, there was a meeting of your Council, but I think you were
not present?—That is the executive Q At the Executive Council
meeting?—That is the Executive Committee on the 29th June, not
the Council" "Q You were not present at this meeting yourself?—
No Q But the result of the meeting we know by the minute'
That we have had, that was the minute that the men were to resume
work at once That was the view "That was confirmed at a
Council meeting on July 14th?—That is right Q I think at
the meeting of July 14th you yourself were present?—Yes (Mr
Justice Lawrance) At Denaby? (Mr S T Evans) At Barnsley'
Then at Question 2264 the resolution is referred to under which
Messrs Wadsworth and Walsh were to go to the meeting
which we have been discussing, and to which I have been
referring this morning Then at Question 2266 "Q That is
on the 14th July, and the men had been out on strike we know
since the 29th June?—Yes Q Is there any truth at all in
the suggestion that you in any way encouraged or took part in
the strike, or did anything in connection with the strike until
after this meeting of the 14th July to commence with?—Not in the
slightest We did everything we possibly could to avoid it
In fact, I had been myself for two or three years trying to prevent

these collieries being set down" ("set down" means having a strike) "Q You and your colleagues had done all you could to prevent any strike taking place at the colliery for two or three years?—Certainly, either legally or otherwise We did not want a strike Q Is there any pretence at all for saying that you encouraged the strike in order to protest against the Award of Lord James?—There is not the slightest truth in it Nobody knows better than Mr Chambers and the Coalowners' Association there is not the slightest truth in the statement Q You know a great deal of what took place afterwards, we know Did you during the strike at all, or at any time, until after the hearing of the Howden action, hear any suggestion made by Mr Chambers or anybody that the strike was due to the 10 per cent reduction by Lord James' Award?—Never They knew perfectly well that it was not Q Your Association, as you said, covers a very large field Lord James' Award, as I understand it, which was made on the 14th June, applied to the whole of that coalfield?—It applies to the whole of the Midlands, Yorkshire, Derbyshire, Nottinghamshire, Stafford-shire—— Q The whole of your coalfield and other coalfields as well?—All of the Midland coalfields, all except Durham and Northumberland Q Now, with reference to your own Association, did you do anything at all to encourage the men to quarrel with Lord James' Award then or at any other time?—Not at all We told the men to accept Lord James' Award In fact, they are bound to accept it They have never objected They never made a single objection "

Now, my Lords, except for what may be gathered from the speeches which have been read by Mr Bankes, this evidence is uncontradicted except so far as they may be entitled to say that there was some evidence in the speeches of an objection to the 10 per cent Question 2276, "They never objected?—Not at all Not any colliery" (That disposes of the point my learned friends have been making), "And if they had they would not have been paid" (That is strike pay) "Q You as an Association, represent-ing the men, had taken part for some time in this Conciliation Board, with Lord James of Hereford, the independent Chairman, and you have observed always his Award, whether in your favour or against you?—Certainly Q Now, putting it shortly, were about 58,000 or 59,000 persons, who were members of your Association, affected by Lord James' Award, in addition to those at these collieries?—Yes, the whole of the members were affected Q You attended this meeting on the 14th July, and the resolution was passed that you and Mr Walsh should go down to a meeting to be held at Denaby?—Yes" Question 2283 "Did you have any idea in your mind at all, or did you have any instructions from your Council when you went down otherwise than to do your best to get the men to resume work?—Certainly not We went purposely to try to get the men to resume work" Then at Question 2285 "Did you advise the men that they had struck illegally?—Yes"

(This is the 15th July meeting) " Q And did you do your best to influence the men (we have your speech, I will not read it again), to resume their work, and then in the ordinary way to take a ballot to see whether or not it was the desire of the necessary majority to put an end to their employment by giving the proper notice?—Yes (Mr Eldon Bankes) I assume you are not suggesting any other than what is in the speech which we have seen (Mr S T Evans) No (Mr Eldon Bankes) I do not want to object (Mr S T Evans) Except generally his conduct down there Is there any truth at all in the suggestion that your advice to the men was a sham and a pretence?—There is no truth at all I went down there with the determination to try to get these men back to work on any conditions really, because, as I have already told you, I had been trying, along with my colleagues, for two or three years to keep the pits at work These men had been agitating nearly at every Council meeting I have had to fight the two delegates from these two particular firms to prevent them coming on strike even legally We did everything we possibly could, and Mr Walsh and myself talked the matter over when we were going down I asked Mr Walsh to support me, and we agreed to do all we possibly could to get these men back to work, because I was of this opinion, that if we could only get the men to resume work under any conditions we should be able in the meantime to get the disputes settled either with Mr Chambers or with the joint committee at Sheffield, because it was such a frivolous thing, in a sense, for the whole of these men to be on strike that we thought it would be a disaster " Question 2291 " We know that the ballot was taken by means of papers?— Certainly Q Is that quite ordinary?—Yes "

Now, may I make an observation with regard to the ballot to get rid of that once for all My learned friend Mr Bankes made a great point, or a point, at any rate, and argued at some length that this was an unlawful act, that all this must be looked upon as an unlawful strike or as an unlawful combination, because the ballot had not been taken in the manner prescribed by the rules Now, may I say with reference to that, that that is not one of the acts complained of, or as to which a question is asked, it is not one of the unlawful acts There was some discussion between us during the trial——

Lord DAVEY What Mr Bankes said rather was that the ballot was not a real secret ballot, that the ballot papers were filled up at the table which the men passed, and anybody could see how they were filled up

Mr RUFUS ISAACS Yes

Lord DAVEY That was his observation

Mr RUFUS ISAACS And, my Lord, he founded the observation upon it—I was not present, but I have read the note, and that is what makes me say it—that that was one of the ways in which this strike was being unlawfully or illegally conducted

Lord DAVEY   Engineered

Mr RUFUS ISAACS Yes, it was one of the ways, and again may I with great respect point out that that was another of the kind of suggestions that were made throughout the case, an atmosphere again being created, it was said, " Look at this ballot ' Why instead of the ballot should men have to sign ' papers '   Why was that done ?"   And it is said that it was an illegitimate pressure which was being brought to bear upon the men, and because of that it was said in the same way that this was an unlawful act, that is to say that the strike became unlawful or the Association became responsible for unlawfully conducting the strike   That was really ruled out in this way by the learned Judge because there was a discussion about it, and as to whether it was covered by the proceedings of which very voluminous particulars have been given, but so far as that was concerned no question was asked about it, and I therefore pass from it with that observation   I mean no question was asked of the Jury, and that is why I make the observation   When my learned friends, after we had been at the trial a good many days, framed their questions, they did not rely upon this ballot as an unlawful act

The LORD CHANCELLOR They would not put to the Jury a thing which was a matter of evidence merely

Mr RUFUS ISAACS If it is an unlawful act, with great respect, my Lord, I submit in this case you would, if you are relying upon it as an unlawful act as they did in this case

Lord JAMES of HEREFORD   It was not the unlawful act which caused the injury

Mr RUFUS ISAACS No   All I meant by it was that of course they have to say in these cases what are the unlawful acts which they say were committed which rendered this an unlawful combination   The answer to that was " Intimidation or molestation," " Inducing the men not to enter into contracts," and " paying strike money ", all those three things were the things of which they had given us particulars and which we tried and upon which questions were put to the Jury   All I meant, and all I intended to say about the ballot matter, was to get rid of it, because it has been introduced on every occasion I am afraid, and I have always had to get rid of it, and I want to get rid of it now by this statement, that no question was ever framed upon it and it is not relied upon as an unlawful act   At most it might create an atmosphere.

Lord DAVEY You who have got the Shorthand Notes of course know that the impression on my mind—and I endeavoured to listen as attentively as I could to Mr Bankes' speech—is that what he said was that it was not a real ballot or a secret ballot

Mr RUFUS ISAACS, What is the object of that statement, my Lord? What is the meaning of that statement unless it is intended to suggest that it was not properly carried out, and therefore was an unlawful act in some way, otherwise I do not suppose my learned friend could introduce it here, whatever may have happened below for the purpose of mere prejudice but apart from that what is the value of it unless it is relied upon as an unlawful act?

Lord DAVEY I think Mr Bankes used it to show that the large majority in favour of continuing the strike or giving notices was obtained by pressure of the local Union officials

Mr RUFUS ISAACS Unless, of course, it is said that there is something wrong in what they were doing——

Lord DAVEY I do not think anybody was called to say that he put his cross in favour of giving the notice from fear of the local officers

Mr RUFUS ISAACS No, there was no evidence as regards the ballot, there was some evidence with regard to the notices that some of them were written out in the presence of one of the Committee-men—that is the most —but not as to the ballot, and I do submit I may get rid of the ballot point and not encumber this already somewhat complicated case by discussions with regard to that, particularly when I have got this piece of evidence about it, that it was quite the ordinary way to do They did not at the Association, like clubs and some other institutions, always follow out very carefully what their own rules were as to the form of taking the ballot, and that is all it amounts to I do not intend to say another word about the ballot

At page 792 attention is called to the 17th July incident, and at the top of page 793 I think I might read the minutes "That the financial members"——

Lord DAVEY 24th July, is it not?

The LORD CHANCELLOR That we have had had repeatedly

Mr RUFUS ISAACS It is only in order to found a question it is only the resolution of the 24th July which is called attention to

Lord DAVEY I suppose "financial members," an expression I see very frequently, means subscribing members

Mr RUFUS ISAACS Yes it does, members who have duly paid their subscriptions, if they are in arrears for a certain time they are not financial members, and that is explained at Question 2296 Question 2301, " You decided you could not give them any strike pay or any help, but you recommended that the branch should do what they could voluntarily to help the men in reference to the time when they were out illegally when you could not help them at all?—That is right " (that means that the men who were working at a particular branch could have a voluntary levy, as appears from the speech which has already been read, in order to help the men who had suffered) " Q At that meeting of the 24th July, when you were in the chair, was any letter from Mr Smith containing a reference to breaking away, read at all before the resolution to give the strike pay?—No " I do not think there is any importance in that Then on page 795, at Question 2310 " At the time that you voted in favour of that resolution to give strike pay, did you honestly believe that the men under your rules, in accordance with the rules, were entitled to strike pay, from you?—After the 16th Q Yes, at the time you passed this resolution?—After Mr Chambers refused the men, yes certainly Q You thought so?—Yes, or else they would not have had it Q Did you honestly believe that up to the time of the decision in the case of Howden against your Society?—I did " Then Question 2321 " Did you in fact believe the strike was a legal one after the men had been refused work when they went back to work?—After Mr Chambers refused to take them on? Yes?—We believed then it was a legal strike '

Now, my Lord, I do not think it is necessary to read more of the evidence, that is the evidence of Mr Wadsworth, and the evidence of the others is to the same effect There was a good deal of cross-examination of Mr Hall, in particular upon a point which really is so immaterial to the matter we are discussing, that I cannot take up time reading it, but I can give the references to it It is the point, again, as to the 10 per cent, and it is laboured at length, the names of the collieries are given at which there had been strikes, and throughout that part of the case it is suggested that the strikes which had been taking place at other collieries at the same time, were really due to the men's objection to the 10 per cent Even if that had taken place, it is difficult to see how it could bear upon this

In Hall's evidence he stated that there were about 300 collieries included in the Yorkshire Miners' Federation In point of fact it was elicited that at this time, or about this time, there were about 18 or 20 collieries either on strike or not at work The suggestion was that the 18 or 20 were on strike as part of some preconcerted arrangement as against the 10 per cent and the cross-examination took place about that With regard to the explanation of it by Mr Hall, the only possible colour that there was for the suggestion, and what seems to have been the foundation of the suggestion was

this, that when Lord James's Award came into force, which would
be at the date I have just stated at the beginning, that is about 12th
July, the lads who were under contract to get an advance of some
penny-halfpenny in their wages in consequence of the Award or
decision of Lord James having taken place, and the reduction having
taken place, were told by the masters that they would not give this
six months' advance which had been agreed with the lads At these
collieries the lads objected, they would not work, and in consequence
of the lads not working the men were not able to work, and that is
all that happened with regard to it It proceeds over a number of
pages, and if your Lordship will look at page 894 it begins, and one
gets a very good idea——

Lord JAMES of HEREFORD Where does Mr Hall speak
about the boys?

Mr RUFUS ISAACS I am just coming to it, it gives really
a very good idea of what one had to meet in reference to this At
page 893, it begins Question 3205 "Did you have a very busy time
in July with strikes at your collieries?—We had Q From what I
think you told us you must have been kept briskly busy?—Very
busy Q On strike questions in July?—Yes Q There was an
epidemic among the various associated pits in your Union?—There
was, there seemed to be (Mr Justice Lawrance) Amongst the
boys?—Amongst the boys (Mr Justice Lawrance) It all broke out
in the boys?" and my learned friend says "They got it first, and
then the men followed suit?—No Q I am going to ask you about
that Were the men locked out because the boys struck?—They
were Q Can you suggest any common cause for this striking in
these various collieries, anything that affected them all?—With
the boys, do you mean? Q Never mind the boys I will not limit
myself for the moment Can you suggest any common cause for the
discontent at the various collieries in July, 1902?—The discontent
was only amongst the boys save and except at the Denaby and Cadeby
Collieries Q At about how many collieries altogether in your
Federation were there strikes in July, 1902—30?—Well, no, not so
far as Yorkshire was concerned"

The LORD CHANCELLOR Is that statement qualified
afterwards? It seems that he practically agrees with that question
I am referring to the answer to 3212 Is it qualified afterwards?

Mr RUFUS ISAACS No, my Lord, it is not The particulars
are given The only modification, I think, is that at the top of page
897 he gives a reference to the strike about the timbering rules
Now they had asked for a list, and we gave them a list of every
colliery in which there had been a strike, and what had happened in
reference to it My learned friend has the list here, and he is going
through it He said, "All I want to know is, was there a strike?"
Then, my Lord, at the top of page 897, to conclude this matter, I

V

will read only for the purpose of showing that at one of these collieries the strike was about the timber, which shows that they had what they thought was a grievance about these timbering rules, Question 3265 'There was a strike at several of the collieries with regard to the new timbering rules Q With regard to the timbering rules?—Yes ' Now on page 899 he is asked to go on and state what the explanation is of these strikes Question 3288 "There is an arrangement in existence throughout the whole of Yorkshire whereby the boys' wages shall be a certain wage when they first commence to work in the pit, and an advance of $1\frac{1}{2}$d per day every six months, and it so happened that a very large number of the advances became due the very week that Lord James's Award took effect (Mr Justice Lawrance) That was in the beginning of July?—Yes, my Lord Their wages should have been advanced as and from the last day of June, so that the wages were entitled to be advanced by $1\frac{1}{2}$d per day at the least the same week as Lord James's Award took effect The reduction was taken from the lads' wages, but the $1\frac{1}{2}$d 's were not put on Consequently the lads said 'We are not going to work until we get our $1\frac{1}{2}$d per day advance' (Mr Montague Lush) Is that the explanation?--That is the explanation." It has really nothing else to do with Lord James's Award

Mr MONTAGUE LUSH Will you read the next one?

Mr RUFUS ISAACS Yes Then my learned friend says, "May I ask was it a mere coincidence, according to you, that that grievance was prominent, and led to a strike at the same time that Lord James of Hereford's Award came into operation?—No It has occurred more than once or twice or thrice at many collieries in the County of Yorkshire, that when the owners have not put on the $1\frac{1}{2}$d a day when it became due, the boys have set the pits down for one or two days in succession, until the matter has been rectified That has occurred over and over again, so that there is no coincidence about it "

Lord JAMES of HEREFORD What about the boys at Denaby? Was there a question there with the boys about the advance?

Mr RUFUS ISAACS The $1\frac{1}{2}$d point did not affect the boys at Denaby, it did not arise, because I suppose that was not the period when their six months advance began It was only at these other collieries that the point arose, because Mr Hall's explanation is that the time happened to coincide with the taking effect of your Lordship's Award, and that is the sole ground for the suggestion which is made

(Adjourned for a short time)

Mr RUFUS ISAACS My Lords, may I make one further observation, and the last, upon the evidence? I am not going to refer to the detail of it because the material upon which it is founded has already been called to your Lordships' attention. It is said that the Association paid for the bellman and for the notices determining the contract. The answer to that is that that is not accurate; what happened was that the branch, as it was bound to do, paid for this bellman and for the notices being printed and simply paid for them in the ordinary way, and that so far as the Association is concerned they had nothing to do with the payment except in so far as you may deduce from that that the act of the branch officials was the act of the Association, which is the old question. So that it really carries us no further. May I say, in case of any difficulty, that some confusion was caused in the Courts below owing to this, in those accounts to which reference has been made—that the word "organising" occurs, and that there are charges for organising. In some cases "organising" has been used to mean something else. It has been said that it means picketing and things of that description. There is no foundation for that, my Lords, in this case. It means the work done for the purpose of and in connection with the organisation of the branch, and the word "organising" occurs every week long before the strike arises. I just mention it to clear away the confusion. My learned friend, Mr Bankes, did not make a point of it, but the Court of Appeal were in doubt in reading through the accounts as to what was meant by the word, and we had to clear it away. That disposes of what I have to say upon the evidence.

Now may I call your Lordships' attention to the Summing-up. I purposely have not read Mr Chambers cross-examination, but it confirms the view which we are putting forward. He admits the legitimacy of the grievances which we are making, that is to say that they were thought by the men to be legitimate grievances, and he admits in substance the case that we are putting. Therefore I do not think it would serve a useful purpose to go through the cross-examination in detail which necessarily was rather lengthy as it was by that means that the Defendants developed their case.

Lord JAMES of HEREFORD Were not the rules (I am not speaking of 74 and 75) generally used against you as showing the authority, the agency, of the branch against the central body?

Mr RUFUS ISAACS In this case, yes, but in the last case the contrary, my Lord.

Lord JAMES of HEREFORD In this case I mean.

Mr RUFUS ISAACS Yes, in this case it is said that the rules show authority.

Lord JAMES of HEREFORD Have you more to say on that?

Mr RUFUS ISAACS Yes I am going to call your Lordships' attention to that, and I would rather do it after I have referred to the Summing-up when I am dealing with the Judgments I want to avoid reading what was necessarily a somewhat lengthy Summing-up, and which naturally travels over ground which we have traversed before your Lordships in argument, or some part of it I will call your attention to some of the salient passages—to what are really the passages of the law The reference to the facts is not very material perhaps The Summing-up begins at page 957, and after dealing with the rules as the learned Judge did, he proceeds at page 962, to formulate a question for the Jury, which is a question that I have already read once and which I do not mean to repeat, but I will call your attention to it It is E to F at page 962 I have already addressed an argument to your Lordships on that, showing that according to the learned Judge it is the basis of the whole case At page 966 D to E the learned Judge says "Now the question is—not the question to be decided in this case, but the question upon the point we are on now—was the real cause of the strike this bag dirt question, which had already been three times settled and decided against the men Now it is said (and this is what you have to consider, and consider very carefully) by the Plaintiffs—it is a matter entirely for you—that this was not the real state of things at all" It is really very difficult to understand that, my Lords The learned Judge says "It is not a question to be decided in this case, but it is the question upon the point we are on now, and you have to consider it very carefully and really must make up your minds upon it It is said that there had been an Award made by Lord James in another procedure" Those are the references to the facts in reference to it, my Lord I pass over those because they add nothing to what you already know upon the point The whole of page 967 deals with the 10 per cent award It is following out the question which I have already indicated At page 973, B to C, at the beginning of the paragraph "Now was this a *bona fide* strike by the men or was it a strike suggested by their delegates and ratified and adopted by the Miners' Association?" I am not quite sure that I understand what that means I am trying to avoid reading the learned Judge s statements of the facts and am only going to passages where he formulates questions I confess that it is rather difficult to understand what the learned Judge meant by that Did he mean, did the miners want to strike? Does he mean that, or was it that the delegates suggested it to them and it was ratified and adopted by the Miners' Association? That I think must be what the learned Judge has in his mind In other words, presumably he would say, "Was this idea put into their heads by the branch delegates and then ratified and adopted by the Association, or was it an idea that came to the men in consequence of grievances which they thought they had?" Your Lordships are in possession of the evidence upon this point, and here again I desire to avoid repetition of it

Now, at page 978, C to E, the learned Judge gets to conspiracy. This is very important, I respectfully submit, for the purpose of finding out what was in the Jury's mind and what it was they meant to find when they answered the questions. "Now what is said by the Plaintiffs, whether they are right or not, is this. That you not only conspired together, but if you did not conspire the persons acting as your agents, Humphries and Nolan acting as your agents, acting with the knowledge of the officials of the Society, induced the men to break their contract upon the 29th June. What they say is that the bag dirt question was a mere pretext, that that was not the real question; that the real object was to get a revision of the price list which they did not like, because of the reduction of 10 per cent. by Lord James. And in support of that they adduced evidence from two or three witnesses who were called by the Defendants, that there were no less than 30 or 40 or 50 collieries that had all struck about the same time" (That is inaccurate, it is 18)—"In the beginning of June, and they had all struck in consequence of Lord James's Award in this sense, that that affected the boys—you remember the lads—and that in all these cases the lads were affected or said to be affected in their rise of 1½d. a day, I think it was, at the end of six months.' Then the learned Judge goes on with that. Then B and C at page 979. "We have trouble enough with this Denaby Main Colliery, and you need not trouble about other collieries; but, at all events, all these things did take place at that particular time, and that is relied upon by the Plaintiffs as showing that this was not a *bona fide* strike about the bag dirt." That is the important point that the learned Judge is making throughout the case.

I think I can pass over a good many pages now until I get to page 990. Now, so far the greater part of the learned Judge's summing up, except for these references to the bag dirt and pretext point, consists of the speeches which were made which have been referred to my learned friend in opening the case. The learned Judge after referring to Parrott's speech of the 24th November, the "devilish" speech, says at A to B. "Gentlemen, those are all the speeches I think I need bring under your notice. You remember the other speeches. As to the question of the injuries done to the men, I do not propose to go over them. You remember them. I have forgotten their names. It does not matter what their names were. You remember men who are said to be injured. That there was molestation and that there was injury done there can be no doubt. These persons had to come from their work through a great crowd reaching through the whole of the streets and had to be escorted by police and so forth, and three or four of the men were injured and intimidated and molested, if you believe them. It is a question entirely for you whether you believe them, whether they were or not." We never contested the facts with regard to that, my Lords. "The other question is, of course, whether that molestation had anything to do with the people against whom this action is brought. Now, that is all I am going to say about the facts. I do not think there are any other facts I need mention to you which I have in my mind at present." Now, I come to what the the learned Judge says as to the law. "Now, let me say a word to you with reference to the law on this subject. 'Any person who has intentionally, that is to say, knowing what he is doing, interferes with the legal right of another, such as procuring a breach of contract, commits an actionable wrong unless there is sufficient justification for the injury done.' I have given you that in the very words of one of the learned Judges in one of the recent cases, in order that there may be no doubt about it. Any person who intentionally interferes—it is not necessary that he should maliciously interfere or that he should have a design to do an injury to the other person if the effect is to injure him—you see what I mean—unless he has got a sufficient excuse for doing it. The answer made here is that they were acting in the interests of the men, and that would be an excuse. The answer on the other side is. You were acting in your own interests, because you were afraid your men would break away, and because you were afraid you would lose them. Then, with regard to such an interference as that, 'it is necessary,' to use the words of the same learned Judge, 'to have in your mind the nature of the contract broken.—that you have got, that you have heard of often enough—'the position of the parties to the contract, the grounds of the breach, the means employed to procure the breach, the relations of the person who procures the breach to the person who breaks the contract, and the object of procuring the breach'—That almost hits every point that has been taken in this case. That is why it was so necessary that the door should be open wide enough for any evidence that could be forthcoming either on the one side or the other. Now, with regard to the conspiracy acts, you can take it conspiracy has been defined by the Court to mean the doing of an illegal act by legal means, or a legal act by illegal means, or an illegal act by illegal means, that is to say, that there must be illegality on one side or the other, and in order to make a conspiracy actionable damage must result. That is the only difference between a civil and a criminal proceeding for conspiracy. Of course, a criminal proceeding is out of the question, from what I have read to you from the Statute. That was taken away so far as this is concerned. Therefore, in civil actions for conspiracy, it is neccessarily actionable only if damage results. The damage which is said to have resulted here, if these people did conspire, is the loss which the Plaintiffs have suffered by being prevented from carrying on their business." My Lords, it is observable that throughout, as you see, that is always the conspiracy, and always the damage which is made the subject of discussion, it is the total of the loss which they have suffered. "Now let me put to you these questions. I will give you these questions so that you may take them with you, but I will say one word or two as we go along on the questions you have to answer, 'Did the Defendants Nolan and Humphries,' those are the two delegates, you remember, of the branch——'or either of them unlawfully or maliciously procure the men to break the contract of their employment by going out on strike on June the 29th without giving notice?" He reads the questions. Then copies of the questions were handed to the Jury. This is the learned Judge's direction as to this. The second question is " 'Were Nolan and Humphries or either and which of them'——it is only them—— 'in so doing purporting to act as the agents of the Association and for its benefit'" These are the questions upon which I have made some criticism. "Now, if a person who is acting as an agent for another does an unlawful act in the course of his employment and for the benefit of his employer"—I should have thought, my Lords, that there was something more necessary than that. That a man purports to act as agent and that it is for the benefit of his principal is not sufficient to make the principal liable. He must be, in fact, acting for him and he must have his authority to do the act. "For instance, you might have a servant who was doing something for you, you order him to go and do a particular thing; he goes and does it in some unlawful way which you would not have allowed him to do if you had known. Still he does it, he does something for your benefit and you would be responsible. That affects that particular part of the question with regard to agency." That bears out the view that I was putting in argument, that really the learned Judge understood this question to be within Barwick and the Joint Stock Bank, and Limpus and the London General Omnibus Company. Purporting in reference to ratification apparently is something which has not occurred to him at all. "That affects that particular part of the question with regard to agency. 'Were Nolan and Humphries or either, and which of them in so doing purporting to act as agents of the Association and for its benefit?'—which means this." (This makes clear, I think, what he thought) "Were they acting for the interests of the Association, acting on behalf of the Association and for its interests in doing these acts?—that is, assuming you answer the first question in the affirmative. Of course if you do not the second question falls to the ground. Then the third question is 'Did the members of the Committees of the Denaby and Cadeby branches or any of them unlawfully and maliciously procure the men to break their contracts of employment by going out on strike on June 29th without giving notice?' It is the members of the Committees of the Denaby Main and Cadeby branches. Then, if you answer this in the affirmative, 'Were the members of the Committees in so doing purporting to act as the agents of the Association and for its benefit?'" You will observe, my Lords, that there is not any direction of any kind or description as to purporting. Whatever it is, it is all to be found in this passage I have read at page 992. There is no other assistance to the Jury than what I have just read. "Then the fifth question is 'Did the Defendant Association by its Executive Council or by its officials ratify the acts of Nolan and Humphries or of the members of the Committees in so procuring the men to break their contracts?' That is to say, if they did not know the contracts, and if they had nothing to do with the breaking of the contracts themselves, when they found they were broken, did they adopt then act That is what ratification means Did they adopt their act themselves and treat it as if it were the act of the Association?" That is all the direction there is on ratification "Then the sixth is 'Did the Defendant Association by its officials or by the members of the Committees of the Denaby and Cadeby branches maintain or assist in maintaining the strike by unlawful means?' That is to say Did the Defendant Association by its officials or by the members of the Committees maintain the strike 'by molesting or intimidating men who were working for the Plaintiffs with a view of inducing them to cease from so working or by inducing or attempting to induce men who were willing to enter into contracts of service with the Plaintiffs and to work for them to refrain from so doing, or by the grant of strike pay against the rules of the Association?' That strike pay was against the rules of the Association has already been found ' Then there is the seventh question as to the Defendants Wadsworth, Parrott and Frith Now, there I finish, if I may, the Summing-up, because I want to say something about those questions

Then at the bottom of page 993 comes the conspiracy Did the Defendants or any and which of them conspire with each other or with workmen in the employ of the Plaintiff to do any and which of the matters mentioned in Question 6 May I call your Lordships' attention respectfully to the distinction between Question 8 and Question 9? Question 8 is founded upon workmen in the employ, Question 9 is founded upon workmen formerly in the employ As I understand it, Question 8 is directed entirely to the 29th June, because that is "Workmen in the employ" Question 9 is different That is the conspiracy count, as you can see Page 994 "And lastly did they all agree to combine for the purpose, that is to say, it depends upon whether you take the view which was put to you that the whole thing was a blind only"—(That is one of the words adopted by my learned friend Mr Lush)—"and that the intention was to call these men out and that the effect of what the Association did was to call them out on the 29th" Now, my Lords, if they conspired to do that, then the question is put "Did the Defendants or any and which of them unlawfully and maliciously conspire together and with workmen formerly in the employ of the Plaintiffs to molest and injure the Plaintiffs in the carrying on of their business, and were the Plaintiffs so molested and injured" I submit that that last passage I have read of the learned Judge's Summing-up, as he understood the contention put forward by my learned friends, and as he put it to the Jury, warrants the observation that I made in opening the case to your Lordships, that what was being dealt with was a conspiracy as from the 29th June That is exactly what the learned Judge says there And not only that, was it a conspiracy? He seems to think that an important thing in determining the conspiracy was that the whole thing was a blind only, in other words, that they had struck ostensibly on a bag dirt grievance, but really to get rid of the 10 per cent reduction, and

that is what he means by those references at page 994   If you take
the view which was put to you—that is what my learned friends
have been strenuously arguing for—that the whole thing was a blind
only and that the intention was to call these men out (that is the
27th June) and that the effect of what the Association did was to
call them out on the 29th June—if they conspired to do that, then
he seems to take the view that it must follow that they conspired to
molest and injure the Plaintiffs in the carrying on of their business
Then the learned Judge makes some observations at the end, which
I do not complain of in one way, but they were rather prejudicial to
to the Association when it was before the Jury, because they suggest
really that it was the Association's fault that there had not been a
settlement of the matter, whereas one cannot help thinking it is
not very easy to determine whose actual fault it is and it does not
really assist in the determination of this case   That my Lords, is
the Summing-up

Now, my Lords, on the law with reference to the Summing-up,
I say, with the greatest deference to the learned Judge who summed
up the case, that there is no assistance of any kind or description
given to the Jury, and that such assistance as the learned Judge
does give is, with deference to him, wrong in law   So far with
regard to what I have have read to your Lordships and the direction
as to Questions 2 and 4 that were submitted to the Jury   The
questions entirely presuppose the agency, on which he gives no
direction, they presuppose the agency and presuppose that in fact
the acts were done as agents, upon which there is no finding   This
assumes that fact and then simply asks the question whether it was
done in the interests of the Association and on behalf of the Association,
which is really begging the whole question   That is as to Questions
2 and 4   As to ratification, which is really somewhat a difficult
question to deal with in law, all that the learned Judge has attempted
to do with the Jury is to change the word ratify to the word adopt
That is the solitary direction, if direction one can call it, that there
is   Of course, I quite readily concede, for what it may be worth,
that whatever question had been put to the Jury they would have
found against the'Association   Whatever the questions were that
were put, they would have simply answered them in favour of the
Plaintiffs   But to say that they understood or that it was brought
home to their minds what was meant by this ratification or what
they had to be satisfied about if they could find it is, I submit,
clearly wrong, having regard to what the learned Judge says

Then I come to what is said about Question 6, and here I want
to make an observation founded upon my learned friend, Mr Bankes
argument before your Lordships   Question 6 is founded upon
"maintaining or assisting in maintaining a strike by unlawful
means" It is really remarkable, I say, with the very greatest deference,
that there is not the slightest assistance to the Jury as to what
is the meaning of "maintaining" a strike or "assisting in

maintaining" a strike   There is not a direction, as I submit, we ought to have had, from the learned Judge, to point out to the Jury that as from a certain date the contract was at an end and determined, and that from that date totally different considerations applied   The Jury had to bear that in mind and deal with it in that way   The most that can be said about that is that I contended it so far as I was able before the Jury, and my learned friends contended that you must treat the whole thing as one period, and refused to accept this division of periods, and the learned Judge does the same thing   The learned Judge deals with it as if the whole thing was one period dating from the 29th June   That you have to consider   What is contended and what the Jury are invited to find is, that the Association were responsible for everything that happened from the start   It is not unfair to say that there was not the faintest discrimination in the way this was left to the Jury in regard to the periods or the acts of the Association   There was not the faintest attempt at it   It was left to the Jury, who answered every question, as you see when they are read, without any attempt to deal even with the matters which are put to them in those questions   Now, on Question 6, there is a rather important factor   A good deal had been made in the course of the case of the fact that my clients, it was said, had induced or attempted to induce men not to enter into fresh contracts   I argued on a recent occasion (on Friday last) that that was not a cause of action and that that was not an unlawful act   I find that my learned friend, Mr Bankes, now admits that that is so, and we therefore must strike out, as I respectfully submit, on my learned friend's own showing, B from Question 6   It is not supportable, according to my learned friend's own argument

Lord JAMES of HEREFORD   What is the page where the questions are?

Mr RUFUS ISAACS   1009, my Lord, and the question that I am reading is on page 1010

Lord JAMES of HEREFORD   You say that B must be struck out from Question 6

Mr RUFUS ISAACS   Yes   Six is the important question, as you will see, with regard to the unlawful means used to maintain the strike   B is "by inducing or attempting to induce men who were willing to enter into contracts of service or to work for them to refrain from so doing"   Now that has been admitted in your Lordships' House—but, as far as I know, not before—to be something which cannot be supported   May I, so as to put this beyond all question, read to your Lordships what my learned friend, Mr Bankes, said in opening this appeal in your Lordships' House on this point at page 134, where he is dealing with the question of assisting or maintaining the strike by unlawful means?   It is on the third day

First of all, he deals with the granting of strike pay, and he agrees that there are serious questions of law to deal with as to that. Then he says "The third alleged unlawful means" (the other being the intimidation) "the inducing or attempting to induce men who were willing to enter into contracts we do not rely on and never have relied on." That is rather extraordinary in view of the question put to the Jury "Did the Defendant Association, by its officials or by the members of the Committees of Denaby and Cadeby branches, maintain or assist in maintaining the strike by unlawful means, that is to say (C) By the grant of strike pay against the rules of the Association." That justifies me, plainly, in the observation which I make, that we must strike out (B) so far as Questions 6 and 7 are concerned. It gets rid of one point that I was arguing on the last occasion. You will remember that I quoted Allen v Flood as the authority for the proposition. Now, it is a little difficult to understand how my learned friend says that it never has been relied upon. It formed a great subject of discussion in the Court below and in the Court of First Instance most distinctly, because it was one of my learned friend's points about the sham, the pretext, and the subterfuge.

Lord JAMES of HEREFORD. It is on the Note here that at the request of the learned Judge, Mr Bankes handed up these questions to his Lordship to read to the Jury so that this question came from the Plaintiffs' Counsel

Mr RUFUS ISAACS. Certainly, my Lord. These are questions framed by my learned friends, Mr Lush and Mr Bankes. They put this question, and it was a substantive complaint of an unlawful act. The first that I heard of its being given up was what Mr Bankes said in opening the case to your Lordships last week. That gets rid of one point which has been the subject of so much discussion, and which I respectfully submit seriously prejudiced my clients in the Court below. The learned Judge did not take the view that this was not actionable. Following the view that was put forward by my learned friends, led as he was by them, if I may respectfully say so, he thought that it was actionable, and the passages which I have read show that he thought so. My learned friend's argument and my learned friend's speech to the Jury all show that they were relying upon this. It is upon this part of the case that the observations with regard to sham, and so forth, are used in order to show that the attempting to induce them not to enter into a contract, that is not to go back and sign on again, was a mere blind, as the expression was, and a mere sham. It is in that respect that we are dealing with this question. Once I have got rid of that I have only two classes of unlawful acts to deal with in the case. The one is the molestation and intimidation, as to which I have said all I intend to say. I have dealt with the facts, I agree very generally, because from my point of view the facts as proved do not touch the Defendant Association. As regards the molestation and intimidation, there is nothing that assists further I suppose it must depend upon the view as to whether or not we are responsible for the branch officials—whether the branch officials can make the branch, and from the Association, responsible for those acts by being present when some of them have taken place, and whether my learned friends are able to establish that these acts were in any way incited or induced by any act of the Council of the Association I have said what I desire to say in reference to that, and my submission is that there is not really one tittle of evidence upon this point, and that nothing that has been brought before your Lordships justifies the view that we were maintaining the strike by those unlawful means of molesting or intimidating the men So far from that, the passages which I have read show that the desire was to keep the men calm One cannot wonder that under such circumstances, however wrong it is and however indefensible it is, now and again some one man or some two or three men may lose control of themselves and commit some act of violence Of course nobody disputes but what they are punishable for that, and that any person who has induced it may be made liable for it, but to say that because of those particular acts having happened on the days I have mentioned, isolated as they were in this case, therefore you are able to say that this strike was maintained by unlawful means is, I submit, a very great stretch, and what the meaning of maintaining a strike is must be a very important element in this case There is all the difference in the world between maintaining a strike, that is to say, inducing the men to come out in breach of contract, and helping them when they are once out and when the contract is at an end either to put themselves right or helping them to means of subsistence during the time that they are out of work Totally different considerations apply I respectfully call your Lordships' attention to this—that there is not a word from the learned Judge which would draw any distinction which would in the slightest degree help the Jury to discriminate or to indicate to them that they could look at the case in any other light than as dating everything to the 29th June No doubt that is what the Jury were thinking of

Now with regard to the granting of strike pay against the rules of the Association, upon that there was a good deal said, and a great deal made as to what was meant by Lord Macnaghten's view in saying that it was illegal—by the addition of the word "illegal" at the end of the Injunction which was granted in Howden's case

Lord MACNAGHTEN You speak of an addition at the end of the Injunction The position was that the Injunction had been granted in the Court below as a general Injunction to restrain them from doing anything contrary to the terms of the rules

Mr RUFUS ISAACS Yes

Lord MACNAGHTEN There was no particular alteration in that, except that it was confined to what they had actually done, and what was called in question in the suit

Mr RUFUS ISAACS I think that your Lordship added the word "illegal"

Lord MACNAGHTEN That was part of the ordinary form

Mr RUFUS ISAACS That is all that was intended

Lord MACNAGHTEN That is part of the ordinary form of Injunction

Mr RUFUS ISAACS I think what your Lordship intended was, and what you said was, that you objected to the form in which it was granted, and you put it in the right form

Lord MACNAGHTEN Yes The form in which it had originally stood pointed to nothing

Mr RUFUS ISAACS Yes, that is so That was all that your Lordship intended Now, great use has been made of it It has been pressed against us really very severely Considerable use was made of it by my learned friends What is said and said again and again? I am afraid your Lordships have not what I am going to read now, but it is from what took place in the Court of Appeal when my learned friend, Mr Lush, was arguing He objects to its being dealt with as I have been dealing with it in the Court of Appeal and in the Court of First Instance in two periods He says "Our case all along was"—and this is what I am going to endeavour to show your Lordships there was not only evidence, but conclusive evidence of—"our case is that there were no two such periods; there was no curing of the wrong; there was no intention to cure the wrong, the Union, under very great pressure which was being put upon them, which was indicated by the fact that something like 20 other collieries were out on strike at the same time for this cause, not the bag dirt, but the question of wages owing to the reduction of 10 per cent, our case was that the Union, under this tremendous pressure, unfortunately allowed themselves to be swept along with the tide that was setting in, and gave instructions, as I am going to show your Lordships in a moment, to the men not to go back to work" (that is dealing with the 17th July) "at all on July 17th—to pretend to go back, and not to go back That is my case" Then that is continued, but I do not want to keep reading passages My learned friend impresses that upon the Court

Lord JAMES of HEREFORD A good many of these men from the central body were called, I suppose Was any question, in fact, of conduct put to any of them to show that they were pretending to do a thing which they did not mean to do ?

Mr RUFUS ISAACS I submit not, my Lord

Lord JAMES of HEREFORD I have looked and I cannot find it

Mr RUFUS ISAACS No, and indeed so far as Mr Pickard was concerned it was admitted all along that no such suggestion could be made against him if it was intended to be suggested seriously that all these transactions were a fraud, because that is what the suggestion amounts to—that they were shams and subterfuges, and that documents were brought into existence for the purpose of concealing the true facts Then I submit that definite questions ought to have been put with regard to that

Lord JAMES of HEREFORD There is one other point I do not quite see at present how, if the hidden intention was to get rid of the 10 per cent reduction, that question is affected in the slightest degree by putting forward the strike as in respect of the bag dirt

Mr RUFUS ISAACS It did not touch it It did not assist them in the slightest degree The suggestion which my learned friends made with reference to it was—I do not say that anybody actually said it, but the idea evolved from somebody who was not called with regard to why we must put forward the bag dirt was, that the 10 per cent question was something which we could not put as the ostensible reason because it would alienate the sympathy of the public That was the view—that the public would think that it was very wrong, as they no doubt would have thought, that the men should immediately strike against an award made by the Conciliation Board, and therefore that would alienate all sympathy

Lord JAMES of HEREFORD That is not quite an answer to the question Was it their case that the real motive of the strike was in some way to get rid of the 10 per cent reduction ?

Mr RUFUS ISAACS Yes

Lord JAMES of HEREFORD How do they in any way assist in getting rid of the 10 per cent reduction by putting forward the bag dirt point ?

Mr RUFUS ISAACS They did not assist it, and they never could.

Lord JAMES of HEREFORD We may have an explanation of it, but at present I do not quite see how they did.

Mr RUFUS ISAACS The Master of the Rolls says "What is the precise point that you are making—that this strike never got rid of its initial illegal character?" and my learned friend says "Yes" That is the point made against us from beginning to end of the case, my Lords I rest upon it because with submission it seems to me that that is so important on the question of conspiracy as a question for your Lordships' consideration My learned friend's case from beginning to end is that there has been a breach of contract, and nothing can cure the wrong—that nothing else that happens can ever make it anything else but an illegal strike, that you cannot alter it He says that anything that happens afterwards, whatever you may do afterwards cannot be justified on the ground that you are interfering in a strike which is lawful, because the strike is from its initial character and continues for evermore an unlawful strike That is the argument and that is what my learned friend put definitely My learned friend says 'I want to show and will show when I go through the documents, that the Unionists were parties to a mere device "

The LORD CHANCELLOR We have heard that argument also here, therefore we are familiar with what you are reading

Mr RUFUS ISAACS If your Lordship pleases

Lord DAVEY And, no doubt, we shall hear it again

Mr RUFUS ISAACS Yes, my Lord What I wanted to find in the book and what I referred to it for, unfortunately I have not been able to find

The LORD CHANCELLOR The passage that you were referring to was with regard to the alleged use made of the fact that the word "illegal" had been inserted

Mr RUFUS ISAACS, That is the passage that I wanted, but I cannot find it

The LORD CHANCELLOR You can supply it afterwards

Mr RUFUS ISAACS Now, my Lords, I have shown sufficiently the character of the case that we had to meet May I go to the Master of the Rolls' Judgment for a moment, and then I have a very few observations to make upon the rules and other questions, and I shall have concluded The Master of the Rolls' Judgment proceeds, in so far as it is against us, as I submit, upon a complete error with regard to the facts You will, of course, have observed that upon the first period point, up to ratification, the Master of the Rolls is in entire agreement with the other two Lords Justices, and is in our favour Then when he comes to deal with the conspiracy it is there that he takes a view against us, and, as I think I can show he takes the view under a complete misapprehension

Lord DAVEY I thought that on the sixth question he was against you

Mr RUFUS ISAACS Yes, on the sixth question, which is the beginning of the second period and the conspiracy which is founded upon it The sixth question really covers the facts He seems to have been under the impression, as I will show you, that there was in that second period an inducement to break a contract, and, of course, if that was so, and you could bring that home, it is an unlawful act, for which, no doubt, the parties to it could be made responsible But there is not a word of the kind in the evidence there is not a suggestion of it in the evidence there is not a finding of the Jury upon it, and it never took place In order to make my meaning clear, would your Lordships refer to the bottom of page 1033, in the Master of the Rolls' Judgment, where he is dealing with what is, for the purpose of his Judgment, the vital point —"There are three distinct elements of illegality in the maintenance of this strike"—he formulates them and he formulates the one which my learned friend has given up in a form in which it would have been actionable if those had been the facts ' There are three distinct elements of illegality in the maintenance of this strike, two of them affecting the means actually used, the third affecting the immediate object aimed at They are (1) Aiding the strike by• misapplying to its maintenance funds which the law expressly forbade to be so applied, (2) Intimidation in different forms, (3) Inducing the men to break existing contracts " Where is that got from ?

Lord DAVEY He misunderstood B

Mr RUFUS ISAACS Yes, my Lord, he must have misunderstood B, and that has coloured his whole Judgment It is not simply in formulating it As you will see, he deals with it later He goes on to say at the end of (3) it is quite true "Inducing the men to break existing contracts, an illegal act in itself, and not mitigated by the fact that the means used to bring it about were themselves illegal I have dealt with the first and second heads I will add a few words as to the third Passing over the cases of those men who did not join the strikers in the first instance, but who were forced to come out afterwards, of whom there were several, but who may have come out before the date at which it may be inferred that the co-operation of the Association in the common movement began, I will confine myself to the case of those who had signed on after the meeting of July 15th, where the majority refused to do so There can be no doubt that these men were induced to break their contracts and come out at a time when there was evidence that the co-operation between the Association and the branches in a common purpose had begun How is it possible to say that the Association, who were finding funds for the carrying out of such a purpose, that is, of inducing or compelling those who had returned to their employment to break their contracts and come out, how is it possible to say that they are entitled to have Judgment entered for them?" That is a complete misapprehension, my Lords, there is not a word to support that

The LORD CHANCELLOR There is no finding of the Jury to that effect?

Mr RUFUS ISAACS No finding and no question put, and no such suggestion is put forward by my learned friends It is a misapprehension of the arguments My learned friend's view was including B, which is a very different thing, which is now given up, but this is a point with regard to which, as I say something or other, the learned Master of the Rolls has made a mistake upon a very material matter of that character He has said, ' When you have breaking of contracts, and when you have the Association inducing men to break contracts, how can you say that Judgment can be entered for them?" I agree that if you had that element, you could not say it By the decision of your Lordships' House in the Glamorgan case, if you have once the breaking of contracts it is an actionable wrong to induce a man to break a contract Now the learned Master of the Rolls says also on page 1027 between C and E "I am of opinion as to the issues raising the question of the responsibility of the Union for the maintenance as distinguished from the initiation of the strike, that there was evidence fit for the consideration of the Jury of concerted action between them and the officials of the branch to maintain the strike by illegal means It is not my province to decide anything more, unless it is made out that there was misdirection which may have affected the verdict Of this on this part of the case I can find no trace" There is no direction at all Then you will observe, my Lords, what the Master of the Rolls says—"evidence fit for the consideration of the Jury of concerted action between them and the officials of the branch to maintain the strike by illegal means" That begs the whole question, What is desired is to make the Association responsible apart from the rules If the rules make it responsible you do not want this question I submit that the learned Master of the Rolls is there dealing with a question which does not arise so far as the Association is concerned, by saying that there is evidence of concerted action between the officials of the branches to maintain the strike by illegal means "It is not my province to decide anything more, unless it is made out that there was misdirection which may have affected the verdict Of this on this part of the case I can find no trace On this second branch of the case it becomes necessary to examine the evidence in somewhat greater detail" Then the learned Master of the Rolls discusses the evidence, with which I will not trouble your Lordships Then he says on page 1029 after referring to the speeches at D (that is the speeches of the 15th July) "These

W

speeches coupled with the resolution, seem to me to furnish very cogent evidence—it is not necessary to say more—that matters had thus far developed that the Association now intended that the men should resume work, not with a view of ending the strike, but with a view of legalising their position so as to enable them to strike effectually with the resources of the Union behind them It will be seen from what follows that the position never was legalised, but that nevertheless the resources of the Union were thrown into the scale " You will observe that word at page 1029 "It will be seen from what follows that the position never was *legalised*" But you do not require the position to be legalised It was already legal If the contract was at an end, there was no legalising of the position necessary What the learned Master of the Rolls has in mind there is my learned friend's argument, that once a breach always a breach, continuing until the end of the strike, and that the breach ran, as I said, with the strike so long as the men did not go back to work

Lord JAMES of HEREFORD But did not Mr Pickard and the others think that to entitle them to give the men strike pay, the men ought to go back to work and then give notice?

Mr RUFUS ISAACS: Certainly

Lord JAMES of HEREFORD Does not this mean that to give pay without that would have been illegal?

Mr RUFUS ISAACS I think that what was meant by the view that my learned friend was putting was, that you could not legalise the strike, because you could never cure the wrong by which the strike had been started

Lord JAMES of HEREFORD But legalising the strike means, I think, that you could not legalise the payment of the funds of the Association for the strike

Mr RUFUS ISAACS Probably that is so, my Lord, but is it not, with respect, the same thing—because it is the same argument that the Master of the Rolls is dealing with He means by that, that as they never could legalise the position, that is to say, never could cure the original breach so long as the men being out of work continued, therefore they never could pay the strike pay, because he goes on to say "It will be seen from what follows that the position never was legalised, but that nevertheless the resources of the Union were thrown into the scale, and life blood supplied to the strike in the shape of strike pay furnished week by week from the funds of the Association "

Lord JAMES of HEREFORD It was contended that a proper legal ballot had never been taken, and, therefore, strike pay ought never to have been given

Mr RUFUS ISAACS I went a little further than that What was said was, in the words which I have just read, that this was an illegal strike because it was in breach, and you never could put it right

Lord JAMES of HEREFORD I only wanted to ascertain if we could see with what intention the words were used

Mr RUFUS ISAACS "I think there is cogent evidence that from and after the stage which I have now reached, the Association itself directly intervened in guiding the source of the strikers in such fashion as to give such a colourable semblance of legality to their proceedings as should make it possible for them, the Association, to assist the movement by the granting of strike pay" I do not think I need to read any more there That is pursued On page 1,030 the Master of the Rolls says something more at B to C "It had not occurred apparently to Mr Pickard or any one else up to that time that having been on strike for a fortnight they were, nevertheless, in a position to give valid notices without resuming work Mr Pickard was at once informed of what had happened Then followed a correspondence by letter and wire between him and the branches and the manager of the collieries, which is strongly relied upon by the Plaintiffs as evidence of malice That is to say, of persistence in an illegal course with full notice of facts which must have brought home to the minds of the Executive a sense of the illegality had they not allowed their judgment to be disturbed by their desire to attain the end in view, namely, to maintain the strike" I have said really enough upon that point "The position assumed originally, viz, that the men on strike were out of employment and must get back into it before they could legally give notice, was not at first abandoned when the new emergency of the men not having signed on arose, but objection was taken that a new condition was sought to be imposed When this suggestion was proved to be unfounded, Mr Pickard does not withdraw his direction given to the men on the 17th July, 1902 'Do not sign any new rule,' and, writing in the name of the Council on the 21st July, 1902, he says, 'We cannot recommend you to sign on again' Why should such advice be given, unless for some reason it was thought undesirable then that the men should be allowed to go back into employment at all?" That really, my Lords, misses the whole point of the contention If it was as Lord James was putting to me just now, that the Master of the Rolls meant that Mr Pickard thought that the men should be allowed to go back into employment in order that strike pay might be paid to them, how could this question on page 1030 be asked by the learned Master of the Rolls? "It was thought undesirable that the men should be allowed to go back into employment at all"

Lord JAMES of HEREFORD I do not think you have told us why the men were not allowed to sign on, unless it was because of the timbering question

Mr RUFUS ISAACS I did really tell your Lordships It was because they were making themselves contractual parties to the timbering

Lord JAMES of HEREFORD They could never dispute the *ultra vires* point

Mr RUFUS ISAACS They could never contest that point That is the ground There are suggestions of grounds but it is difficult to trace them One of the men said that he was told that they would be signing for twelve months and a great attack was made upon us with regard to that I daresay that he was told that, but, my Lords, mining centres are not the only places where that sort of thing takes place, and colliers are not the only people who misrepresent what has been told to them, exaggerating or misstating from their own points of view what has been imparted to them

Lord DAVEY They are not the only people subject to panics

Mr RUFUS ISAACS No, they are not, and certainly nobody said that this statement had come from any one for whom the Association were responsible I do not know that there is anything else just here that I need read

The last point in the learned Master of the Rolls' Judgment to which I think I must call attention is at page 1032 I will read from C to D "Passing for a moment at this stage, it is quite clear that the course thus adopted by the Association was illegal It has been so held by the House of Lords As pointed out in Lord Macnaghten's speech, it was not merely *ultra vires*, but (if that makes any difference) positively prohibited "

Lord MACNAGHTEN That seems to be a complete misapprehension The position with regard to it is that originally it was not in the form of a Declaration, but if I recollect rightly it was in the form of an Injunction

Mr RUFUS ISAACS Yes, my Lord

Lord MACNAGHTEN The Injunction was in a very peculiar form—to restrain them, not from doing anything in particular, but from acting contrary to the Rules of the Association without saying what they were to do or what they were not to do Then the House put it in the ordinary form of a Declaration I have sent for Seton on Decrees, and it is in the ordinary form It is in the only form given —" Declaring that the said agreement was and the resolutions for carrying the same into effect were *ultra vires* and illegal " That is page 720 They seem to have built upon that ordinary form of declaration an extraordinary argument.

Mr RUFUS ISAACS Yes, my Lord, they have built an extraordinary argument upon that—that because your Lordship said that therefore it could not be said that the granting of strike pay was an act which we could in way justify It was said with regard to this by the Plaintiffs "The mere fact that you had done it and that it was illegal, as Lord Macnaghten said, makes it actionable, because it is a wrongful act" That is the argument "It is an unlawful act which you have done, and it is a conspiracy, because we have shown that you have done a lawful act by unlawful means" (I have now, my Lords, the passages from the argument which took place in the Court below, which I wanted to find out but could not) You will see what sinister use was made against us in the Court of Appeal of what, if I may say so with respect, was a very innocent observation

Lord MACNAGHTEN It was not an observation at all It was merely making it take the ordinary form of a declaration That was all

Mr RUFUS ISAACS Very well, my Lord I will say the insertion of a word, if your Lordship pleases

The LORD CHANCELLOR Lord Macnaghten has shown me the form of declaration It is a declaration that an intended agreement for transfer and so forth is *ultra vires* It relates to a contractual transaction

Lord MACNAGHTEN *Ultra vires* and illegal

The LORD CHANCELLOR Yes, *ultra vires* and illegal It is with regard to a contractual transaction

Mr RUFUS ISAACS We contended, my Lords, in the Court below, with regard to the drawing up of the form of declaration, that Lord Macnaghten only meant it to be a correction of a vague and indefinite form of injunction

Lord MACNAGHTEN The insertion of a declaration for an unmeaning injunction

Mr RUFUS ISAACS Yes We contended that your Lordship never meant it to be anything more than that I have the passages now from what my learned friend said in the Court of Appeal in dealing with this On page 345 he says "I was only going to say that in the arguments in the House of Lords in Howden's case, which I have here, there was a considerable part of the argument devoted to this very contention, namely, that not only was the payment of this money *ultra vires*, having regard to the construction of the rules, but it was unlawful, because the money was paid to maintain a strike which we contend was unlawful, because it procured breaches of contracts, and had molestation as one of its methods "

Lord DAVEY   Unlawful because of the application of it

Mr RUFUS ISAACS   Yes   Your Lordships never dealt for a moment with this part of it   All that you did was to say that it was unlawful because it was contrary to the rules

Lord DAVEY   Now they are saying that it was an illegal act because it was originally unlawful, and they say that it was unlawful because it was applied to a purpose which was unlawful

Mr RUFUS ISAACS   Lord Justice Mathew says   " I think you may be content with saying it was *ultra vires* without getting the exact meaning of his Lordship when he used the phrase ' illegal ' "   Then Mr Lush says   " I will tell your Lordships frankly our view was, when this declaration was added, that it was really a confirmation of my contention in the House of Lords that in point of fact the payment was not only *ultra vires* but unlawful, because made to maintain an unlawful strike "   Nothing could be plainer or clearer than that, my Lords

The LORD CHANCELLOR   That was in the Court of Appeal, who dealt with the legal point of view purely, but was any argument of that kind used before the Jury ?

Mr RUFUS ISAACS   Most certainly it was, my Lord   It was used as an argument, but not Lord Macnaghten's alteration, that was not before the Jury

Lord MACNAGHTEN   I wish that you would not call it my alteration

Mr RUFUS ISAACS   I beg your Lordship's pardon

Lord MACNAGHTEN   It was merely the substitution of a declaration in place of an unmeaning injunction, as I have said I took the form from Seton

Mr RUFUS ISAACS   It was always referred to as what your Lordship said

The LORD CHANCELLOR   If it was used before the Court of Appeal, although it was erroneous, it would not do much harm Was it used before the Jury ?

Mr RUFUS ISAACS   The argument was used before the Jury ?

Lord DAVEY Was the trial before the hearing in this House, or after?

Mr RUFUS ISAACS It was before the hearing in this House, and therefore we had not the alteration of the word "illegal," but the argument was used That is what I am saying That was the argument, but they could not say that they were supported The argument was used that it was an unlawful strike, and that the money was paid for the purposes of an unlawful strike, but they could not use the substitution that was made in your Lordships' House because that had not yet been made

That is all that I desire to say upon the Master of the Rolls' Judgment May I point out the result of it, my Lords? Founded as it is on a definite misconception of the acts which were charged, it goes on to find a conspiracy which has never been put to the Jury I am justified in that observation by what I have read to your Lordships from the learned Judge's summing-up, in which he makes it quite plain that the question is as from the 29th June If you look at Questions 8 and 9, which are the two conspiracy questions which are put they make it plain to manifestation, because there you have the distinction drawn between men in the employ and men formerly in the employ, in the two questions, so that Question 8 would be directed to the workmen in the employ and Question 9 to the larger question

Now, my Lords, I want to say something about these questions from another aspect It is a very noteworthy feature of this case that the Jury have never attempted to answer the questions as they are put— I mean by that, that they have simply answered these questions, "Yes," without giving the only answer which I submit would make them intelligible For example, take question 8 "Did the Defendants, or any and which of them conspire with each other or with workmen in the employ of the Plaintiffs to do any and which of the matters mentioned in Question 6?" The only answer made to that is "Yes, they did" I do not know whether it means that they conspired with each other, or that they conspired with workmen in the employ of the Plaintiffs, or which of the matters it is said they did under Question 6, of which, as I say we know now one of them has had to disappear

The LORD CHANCELLOR Mr Bankes told us that it was understood between you at the trial to be a comprehensive answer in the affirmative in regard to all the alternatives put That is what he said

Mr RUFUS ISAACS I cannot assent to that at all Certainly what we understood the Jury meant and what they found was——

The LORD CHANCELLOR Did you say that you gave no assent?

Mr RUFUS ISAACS No assent of any kind or description On the contrary I submitted that there was no question to be put and no evidence to support the findings, and that the learned Judge was still bound to enter Judgment for me We assented to nothing What I have been calling your Lordship's attention to runs right through these questions May I now call your attention to perhaps what is the most important question in one sense although not the most far reaching, and that is Question 6? "Did the Defendant Association by its officials or by the members of its Committees of Denaby and Cadeby branches maintain or assist in maintaining" That is the whole point in the case

Lord DAVEY Did they answer "Yes," to that?

Mr RUFUS ISAACS Yes, they simply answered that question in that way

Lord DAVEY It would make a great difference to your argument whether the first alternative or the second alternative was adopted

Mr RUFUS ISAACS Certainly, my Lord, it would make all the difference, but they answered A, B, and C, by "Yes"

'Lord DAVEY It would be the argument over again that the branch officials are your agents

Mr RUFUS ISAACS Yes, that would be going back to the argument on the first point I am reminded on looking at these questions that Question 7 would almost seem to negative the view that it was the Defendant Association by its officials that had been doing it Will your Lordships look at page 1,010 You get the question put as to the specific persons Did they "maintain or assist in maintaining the strike by unlawful means," that is to say, by any and which of the above means The answer is "Not personally but as servants of the Association" The only way in which I can make sense of it is to say that what they meant was that the Association was liable because the branch officials had done it, and they thought therefore that the Association was liable, and that as these gentlemen had been taking part for the Association, therefore they were liable as the servants of the Association Apparently the Jury believed the evidence which was given by the Defendants themselves, and they took the view that they had not taken part in anything unlawful personally

Lord ATKINSON That becomes very important now owing to the omission of B

Mr RUFUS ISAACS Yes, I am much obliged to your Lordships.

LORD ATKINSON It is "Any or which of them" There may be a reference to B

Mr RUFUS ISAACS Yes Now that B has gone, it becomes of great importance, and I am very much obliged to your Lordship for calling my attention to that The same thing applies to 8— "Any and which of the matters mentioned in Question 6" As to the facts of B there was no real dispute, the only question was whether it did give a cause of action or not

Now, my Lords, the last criticism that I desire to direct to these questions is with regard to Question 9 at 1011 One cannot overrate the importance of that question As it stands it makes my clients liable for about £150,000 damages as the case is now presented My learned friend's case upon that is that the Defendant Association (it does not state it in terms here, but it is meant to include them) have conspired to molest and injure the Plaintiffs in the carrying on of their business Of course, that introduces Quinn v Leathem and that kind of case I submit there is not the faintest vestige of evidence to support in this case a finding that there was an intention to molest and injure the Plaintiffs in the carrying on of their business, unless, of course, you mean by that unlawful acts A and C in 6 If you mean that the conspiracy was to do the unlawful acts A and C of Question 6, then you do not require the finding of the intention to injure and molest I do not know whether I make myself clear to your Lordships If you have the doing of an unlawful act, if it is an unlawful act done by one, or if you have a combination of several to do it, it is equally actionable, but supposing that it is not actionable if done by one, then it does not become actionable if done by two, unless you get the intention to injure or molest That is the distinction Therefore, if your conspiracy is founded upon those unlawful acts A and C, as I say, the conspiracy, paragraph 9, is not wanted at all The reason why I am seeking to draw the distinction is because, apart from those questions, apart from the unlawful acts A and C of Question 6, the only unlawful act that is alleged to make this an actionable conspiracy, making my clients liable for this amount, is an intention to injure the employers, and I submit that there is not a tittle of evidence to support that An intention to injure means having some spite against the employers, some ill will, such as is found in Quinn v Leathem and in that class of case So that paragraph 9 is an entirely new and most far-reaching conspiracy which is found in the case of a trade dispute in which really no one can suggest that these Defendants were acting otherwise than in what they conceived to be the true interests of the men The Association is found guilty of a conspiracy to injure and to molest All I can say is, if that is right, if the finding could stand, then with great respect there is no strike that can ever take place in which you would not have the same finding I mean, if you look at that question apart from unlawful acts, apart from any combination to do any act which is unlawful in itself, then as I say every strike must be a conspiracy in civil law, because every strike to the extent of this strike may be said in one sense to be done to injure the Plaintiffs In one sense it is true, inasmuch as there is a dispute between them, and what they want to do is to guard themselves and maintain their own position To that extent, and to that extent only, it may be said But that there is any evidence to support such a finding as would be necessary under Quinn *v* Leathem I deny There is not, I submit, a word May I make this further observation, my Lords, that in dealing with a case of this kind, of this far-reaching importance, there is not a word of direction, as far as I am able to find, upon this point, except the direction which I read to your Lordships, which is merely with regard to whether the Jury believed that this had taken place on the 29th May I read the direction? It is only four lines, at page 994 This will be the last I shall say upon it "Did they all agree to combine for the purpose, that is to say, it depends whether you take the view which was put to you that the whole thing was a blind only, and that the intention was to call these men out, and that the effect of what the Association did was to call them out on the 29th If they conspired to do that, then"—then he reads the questions That is what has happened with regard to it, and my submission is that the learned Lords Justices Mathew and Cozens-Hardy, were right in the view that they took of this, and that indeed not only could the verdict and Judgment not be supported, but that there was no evidence upon which the Defendant Association could be made responsible, and therefore Judgment was entered for them

Now may I say just a word or two about the rules? I have already referred to Rule 64 and Rule 65 Those deal with the payment of either lock-out pay or strike pay, and prescribe the only events upon which it can be granted I am not going to refer to these rules in detail, my Lord, having regard to the fact that your attention has been already called to them My submission is that the whole scheme of the rules is that the branch is quite independent as to a strike It may strike or not, as it pleases There is no control of any kind or description by the Council of the Association over the branch or over the branch officials The men meet and the men determine whether they will strike or whether they will not They have a perfectly free right to do it or not as they please, and it is no business of the Association It is no business of the other branches It does not concern them in the slightest degree Whether the men at one particular colliery choose to work or not is not the business of the other 149 branches or of the Council Where it does become of importance, and the only importance to the Association, to the other 149 branches, is with regard to whether the strike pay is to be granted by the Council of the Association to the branch which is on strike It is only in that connection that it ever becomes necessary for the Association to look at the matter at all or to consider it I do not dispute, and it would be idle to dispute before your Lordships, that the granting of strike pay may be, and, no doubt, is a very useful adjunct to whatever weapons they may have or whatever forces they may have at their command at a branch in a strike, but that is prescribed by very strict rules, and rules which I submit are framed obviously in the interest of peace, one cannot read them without seeing that, and in the interest of conciliation, the interest of the Association always being to avoid a strike and not to have a strike

Lord ATKINSON What force do you give to the words in the 72nd Rule, "No branch or portion of a branch shall be allowed to strike, or "——

Mr RUFUS ISAACS· What that means is, that it regulates the branch It is as between the members of the branch These rules regulate what is going to happen at the branch What it says is that no branch or portion of a branch shall be allowed to strike unless two-thirds of the members composing it shall agree, when such strike shall be determined by registered ballot

Lord ATKINSON. If it is independent and acts for itself, what is the meaning of the word "allowed"?

Lord DAVEY Who is to prevent them?

Mr RUFUS ISAACS I think it means as between themselves as members of the branch

The LORD CHANCELLOR Do these rules regulate the internal arrangements of the various branches as well as the relation of the branches to the Association?

Mr RUFUS ISAACS Certainly they do, my Lord There are a number of rules showing that—quite a number The point of it is this Suppose for example—to take again the bag dirt question, and use that as an illustration—the men are affected to the extent of 40, and suppose that those 40 men wish to come out on strike, they are not allowed to do that unless two-thirds of the members of the branch agree

Lord DAVEY How can they be prevented?

Mr RUFUS ISAACS You cannot really prevent them

Lord DAVEY. It is a counsel of perfection

Mr RUFUS ISAACS It means that as between themselves they are not to do it What your Lordship says would describe it It is to prevent what actually happened here The meaning is that as between themselves they should not be allowed to strike without taking a poll.

Lord DAVEY It may mean that the Council of the Association will not sanction the strike so as to enable them to get strike pay?

Mr RUFUS ISAACS It may mean that, my Lord

Lord DAVEY I have been looking at the rules a good deal with regard to that point of view I think that "adoption" means nothing more than that It is all with regard to strike pay The only function which the Association has with regard to a strike, as far as I can see, is to pay strike pay

Mr RUFUS ISAACS Nothing else?

Lord DAVEY When you speak of "sanction," it means nothing more than that they think fit to allow strike pay

Mr RUFUS ISAACS At a certain point they say, "We have exhausted all means of conciliation" What happened in this case——

Lord DAVEY I cannot see that any consequences follow from what is called "adoption" The word is only used in one rule and that in an indirect manner When they "sanction," it refers, I think, to what I have said

Lord ATKINSON In Rules 60 and 61 the same word is used in reference to the jurisdiction which the Association have over the branch

Mr RUFUS ISAACS "No branch shall be allowed to make use of the funds of this Association"

Lord ATKINSON And again in Rule 61?

Mr RUFUS ISAACS That prohibits the branch from using the funds

Lord ATKINSON That provides for the control of the Association over the action of the branches

Mr RUFUS ISAACS Does it, my Lord?

Lord MACNAGHTEN The Association has some authority over the branches, because apparently it can suspend a branch I do not know what that means quite

Lord DAVEY A branch may be suspended

Lord MACNAGHTEN It can suspend a branch if it acts in defiance of its orders

Mr RUFUS ISAACS I suppose the effect would be to suspend it from some benefits to which it might be entitled, but Rule 60 seems to be dealing with the funds

Lord DAVEY Yes

Mr RUFUS ISAACS The object is to restrain them from making use of the funds for these purposes unless the Council has approved In the same way Rule 6 uses the word " allowed "

The LORD CHANCELLOR Look at Rule 80 "That no unfinancial member of any branch shall be allowed to vote or speak upon any subject being discussed at the meeting" That is for internal management

Mr RUFUS ISAACS I had in mind Rule 6, which says, " No branch shall be allowed to send more than one delegate to the Council meetings, and each recognised branch having 50 members or under have one vote " Then it " shall be allowed one extra vote for every other clear 50 members or fractional part of 50 members," and so forth

Lord JAMES of HEREFORD In Rule 37 you find " shall at all times transact the business of the branch as directed by the rules and minutes of the General Council " We had a discussion on the word " Minutes "

Mr RUFUS ISAACS That occurs in various rules It occurs in Rule 40, and I think you will find it throughout the rules It means this You have certain rules and certain resolutions which have been passed, and you must transact the business according to the manner prescribed by the rules and minutes

Lord JAMES of HEREFORD I suppose that the Council from time to time can alter the rules and say that the branches shall do so and so?

Mr RUFUS ISAACS No, I do not think it can alter the rules, my Lord. It can only be done by the members

Lord JAMES of HEREFORD The central body as distinguished from the branch body, at any rate

Mr. RUFUS ISAACS I do not think the central body could alter the rules Under the Act it must be done by the members There is no doubt that that is so

Lord JAMES of HEREFORD By the members generally, not by the branch members?

Mr RUFUS ISAACS It could not be done by the branch, and it could not be done by the Council It would have to be done by the members

Lord JAMES of HEREFORD Very likely

Mr RUFUS ISAACS Rule 2 says so, and it is also dealt with by the Statute Rule 12 has been referred to That is the only way it can be suggested that there is any control of any kind over a strike, and that is not a control by the Association either An argument has taken place with regard to that What it really means is that when there is a discussion about a strike, taking the whole of the Association, when a number of branches numbering one-fourth of Council demand a vote as to the adoption or prolongation of the strike, it shall be taken in a certain way To put an illustration, if I may, my Lords, it is very much the same as if a certain number of shareholders demand a general meeting to be called You must call it in a certain way That is what that is intended to deal with, and I submit only that

Lord DAVEY Do you think that "adoption" means making a local strike a general strike of the Association?

Mr RUFUS ISAACS No, I do not think it does

Lord DAVEY I may have overlooked some passage, but this is the only place in which I have found the word used

Mr RUFUS ISAACS I think that what it has in mind is Rule 64, which is the important rule

Lord DAVEY Sanctioning the strike for the purpose of giving strike pay

Mr RUFUS ISAACS That is what it has in mind, my Lord It has to be sanctioned in accordance with the rules, and if you have to have a vote taken under Rule 12, you would have to have it taken in pursuance of 12, in order to come within Rule 64

Lord DAVEY That is only when one-fourth of the branches demand it

Mr RUFUS ISAACS Yes, my Lord

Lord DAVEY If one-fourth of the branches say " We will not go on paying strike pay,' then they must proceed under this rule.

Mr RUFUS ISAACS Only in that case It does not apply to the strike of a branch, it only applies when there is strike pay granted or when it is to be granted Then they say "We object, and we will have a vote of the whole Association as to whether all the branches are willing or not that the strike pay should be paid" It might be said, "It is really too trumpery a matter and we will not pay strike pay"

Lord DAVEY It gives a kind of appeal from the acts of the Council

Mr RUFUS ISAACS What is intended, I submit, is that you should have a vote of the delegates upon this question to decide it

Now, my Lords, I have not called attention to the authorities further than what I indicated on Friday My learned friend, Mr Danckwerts, has referred to them with regard to ratification, the point upon which there is no doubt most difficulty in argument Upon that point your Lordships have the arguments on the question of law which we have put before you and which my learned friends have put Apart from that, I submit that it does not arise in this case You cannot have ratification proved by facts such as they are in this case, every one of which is against ratification, and not in favour of it

The only other observation on the law is in reference to the question of *ultra vires* There are one or two cases which follow the case which was referred to of Poulton v The London and South Western Railway Company, in which it has been held that if there is no authority to do an act, then the Association or the Company cannot be made responsible I respectfully ask your Lordships, does not all this question come to this, that you cannot make a Corporation or Association responsible for an act the doing of which it never had the power to authorise? You cannot do that If it was once *ultra vires* the Association, as we contend it is in this case and as in that case you have found, when once you have that, then there cannot be authority to do an act which you have held could not be done by the Association It never had the power

The LORD CHANCELLOR You, Mr Atherley Jones, appear for the other Defendants We have heard an argument on the merits of the case Your case, I understand, will be strictly directed to differentiating between the personal case and the case of the other Defendants

Mr ATHERLEY JONES Yes, my Lord, it will be strictly

confined to that, and my argument will necessarily occupy a comparatively short time

Lord JAMES of HEREFORD It is to be hoped so

Mr ATHERLEY JONES Do your Lordships wish me to commence now ?

The LORD CHANCELLOR No, it is not worth while You will not cover ground which has been already covered, and very fully covered ?

Mr ATHERLEY JONES No, my Lords

————

(Adjourned to to-morrow)

SIXTH DAY.

Tuesday, 20th March, 1906.

Mr ATHERLEY JONES I appear before your Lordships in this Appeal with my learned friends Mr S T Evans and Mr Compston on behalf of the Union officials

My Lord, I am only concerned unfortunately at this stage through the death of Mr Pickard and Mr Frith and Mr Cowey for three Defendants—for Mr Parrott who unfortunately has died since the Judgment in the Court of First Instance, and Mr Hall and Mr Wadsworth, my Lord, as I indicated last night, my observations need only be very brief because so far as the general issues in this case are concerned they have been traversed at very great length by my learned friends Mr Isaacs and Mr Danckwerts, and indeed some part of that case which was peculiar to my clients in a sense has unavoidably been dealt with by my learned friend

Lord JAMES of HEREFORD Would you kindly give the names of the Defendants affirmatively for whom you appear?

Mr ATHERLEY JONES The names of the Defendants originally——

Lord JAMES of HEREFORD Never mind originally, but now

Mr ATHERLEY JONES Mr Wadsworth, who is now the President of the Association and was the vice-president at the time this action commenced ; Mr Hall, the treasurer of the Association, and Mr Parrott, who died after the Judgment in the Court of First Instance I am corrected , it is not material, but it was after the Judgment in the Court of Appeal that Mr Parrott died

My Lord, as I understand, the allegations against the Defendants whom I represent are summed up in this—that they by unlawful means assisted in maintaining the strike , in other words, that they were participators in the intimidation and molestation which marked certain stages of this trade dispute, and therefore I shall confine myself to an examination of what was done by these gentlemen whom I represent during the course of this dispute My Lord, I wish to make this observation, that the sole evidence against these Defendants is confined to one or two letters and telegrams which have already been before your Lordships, I think all, or at any rate, all with the exception of one, to which I shall draw your Lordships'

X

attention later, to the speeches which were made on three several occasions, and to the oral evidence which they gave at the trial There is no oral evidence presented by the Plaintiffs against any one of these gentlemen, and there was no charge, other than the general charge to which I have referred—I mean there was no specific act alleged against them, except a suggestion by inference made, I think, by my learned friend, Mr Lush, to be drawn from the speeches which were made by persons who were present at the meeting of the 15th July when Mr Wadsworth spoke, and the speech of Mr. Parrott, which he made at a later date

My Lord, it is also to be noted, I think, that these Union officials, all of them, had no voting power at the Council, or what might be called the Parliament of the Association They had, with the exception of Mr Wadsworth, who was not, curiously enough, an official of the Union, the vice-president being a sort of honorary office not recognised by the rules, they all had a vote at the Executive Council or Executive Committee. But the functions of the Executive Committee did not extend to any control over strikes, lock-outs, or trade disputes, nor to the dealing with money beyond the amount of £5

I will not trouble your Lordships to read to you the rules which deal with the officials Perhaps, however, I might mention the rules which, so far as I understand, are alone material They are Rules 4, 22 28, and 29 those are the only rules which are important, and the substance of what I have just said is set forth in those rules

I will deal in the first place with the case against Mr Hall so far as the evidence relates to his actions Your Lordships will remember that in February, 1901, Mr Hall, with Mr Annables, made what is described as an Award in respect to the bag dirt, and which Award was the subject of resentment on the part of the men That Award, my Lords, was made in February, 1901 Now, your Lordships remember after the strike had taken place Mr Hall went down for the specific purpose of giving some explanation to the men as to the circumstances under which that Award was made, and, my Lord, the speech of Mr Hall—again I refer to it in the briefest possible way—is set out on page 395 of the Appendix I hope your Lordships, if I may respectfully say so, will check me if I am dilating on any matters as to which dilation is unnecessary

The LORD CHANCELLOR You are just referring to them, that is quite enough to bring our memory to them, we know them all

Mr ATHERLEY JONES Thank you, my Lord The speech which is set out on page 395 deals with nothing but the bag dirt question—does not trench upon the strike—offers no advice whether of a questionable or unquestionable character—is received on the whole—although Mr Hall is an experienced and popular official of the Association - with resentment, and results after a few words have been spoken by Mr Annables, his colleague, in their both having to quit--or, I will not say, having to quit, but both quitting—the meeting amid general disapproval, and, as my learned friend, Mr Evans justly reminds me, before the other speeches, which may or may not be open to question, were made I also ought to observe that no comment has been made by either of my learned friends—either in their addresses to the Jury or in their arguments to the Court of Appeal—as to anything in Mr Hall's speeches which pointed to conduct on his part for which he might be made amenable

My Lord, the evidence of Mr Hall is contained at page 880 of the Appendix and there again I wish to avoid reading to your Lordship any portion of that examination and cross-examination unless your Lordships think I should be guilty of any negligence in not doing so but I wish to point out to your Lordships that Mr Hall, being challenged as to the strike and his conduct in reference to the strike declares, and gives the reasons for his declaration, that he was most anxious to bring the strike to an immediate termination, and that that was the attitude of his colleagues My Lord, I do not think I can usefully occupy your Lordship's time by reading passages from that evidence, I think it is enough for me to say that the cross-examination is wholly ineffective in drawing from Mr Hall anything in the nature of an admission that he was either privy to the strike at its origin, or that he did anything to encourage the action of the men in its maintenance or in its completion As to its completion, he went down, of course, on the 7th July, and the notices, if there had been notices, would not have terminated until the 14th or 15th July

Lord JAMES of HEREFORD What was relied upon as evidence of Hall's participation by Mr Lush or Mr Bankes in reply?

Mr ATHERLEY JONES I am bound to say I have been very carefully through the speeches of my learned friends, and the arguments of my learned friends, and I am unable—I speak subject to correction by my learned friend here—to discover anything in the speeches which points in the smallest degree to Mr Hall having done anything which fell within the allegations contained in the Statement of Claim I shall draw your Lordship's attention, if you will allow me, a little later to the Summing-up so far as it deals, if it can be said to deal with either of these gentlemen, and I think I may make bold to make the same observation in relation to the Summing-up as I do in regard to the conduct of the case as regards Mr Hall on the part of my learned friends

I draw your Lordship's attention now to the case as against Mr Wadsworth, and Mr Wadsworth your Lordship will remember by a decision of the Council of the Association which was made on the 14th July, was directed to go down on the following day, which

was the 15th July, to the scene of this dispute, and give advice to
the men for the purpose of bringing that strike to an end, and
I think there was also—I speak now subject to correction—a direction
that he should see Mr Chambers with a view of bringing the strike
to an end

My Lord, his speech at that meeting is set out at page 406
The speech is so short that I hope your Lordship will allow me,
unless your Lordship have it fully in mind at the present moment—
to read it through, because I am going to suggest to your Lordship
that if one were hypothetically to suggest a speech which ought to
have been made in the interests of concord, no more apt speech
could have been made than the speech which I am going to read to
your Lordships now   He says he was sorry——

Lord JAMES of HEREFORD   This is Wadsworth?

Mr ATHERLEY JONES   Yes

Lord JAMES of HEREFORD   Have you left Hall altogether?

Mr ATHERLEY JONES   Yes, my Lord   I said except the
Summing-up, which I would deal with both together, I have left
Mr Hall   I have exhausted Hall

Lord JAMES of HEREFORD   He was called as a witness

Mr ATHERLEY JONES   Yes

Lord JAMES of HEREFORD   You say nothing occurred in
the evidence

Mr ATHERLEY JONES   Nothing occurred in the evidence
my Lord   My Lord, I have exhausted everything, in answer to
your Lordship's question, against Hall   Of course, be it understood
that Mr Hall paid the strike pay   Of course, he merely paid that
strike pay as an instrument of the Association, having no power of
directing whether the strike pay should be paid or objecting to the
strike pay being paid, and perhaps in answer to your Lordship's
question I ought to say this, that my learned friend in cross-
examination challenged Mr Hall as to whether Mr Hall when he
went down to give that strike pay did not see exhibitions of violence
or molestation   There was no evidence adduced that Mr Hall was
ever present when there was violence or molestation, whatever
inference in law might be drawn therefrom

Lord JAMES of HEREFORD   Just assume hypothetically
that the strike pay on the part of the Association constitutes a cause
of action—assume that purely hypothetically—are you quite content

to leave it that the person who carries out himself that illegal act of paying the strike pay is exempted from the consequences ?

Mr ATHERLEY JONES I do not quite follow

Lord JAMES of HEREFORD You have just put it to us that all that Hall did he did as an officer of the Association

Mr ATHERLEY JONES Yes

Lord JAMES of HEREFORD And that, therefore, he was personally not liable

Mr ATHERLEY JONES Yes

Lord JAMES of HEREFORD Therefore I ask you to assume hypothetically that the act of the Association in paying the strike pay would constitute a cause of action—are you willing to leave it as it stands that the officer of the Association who carries out individually that illegal act is exempt from all legal consequences ?

Mr ATHERLEY JONES I do not know that I could, supposing it was an illegal act of the Association to pay strike pay, I do not know, but I think that might depend upon the knowledge of the official as to whether it was a tortious act or not

Lord JAMES of HEREFORD Of course, you must fall back upon the argument of your colleagues that that was not an illegal act

Mr ATHERLEY JONES Yes, my Lord Of course, I am very anxious not to trench—and I am sure your Lordship would not wish me to do so—upon the province of my learned friend Of course he has taken upon himself the burden of the contention that the payment of strike pay was not an illegal act—I mean, illegal otherwise than as between the members of the Association

Lord JAMES of HEREFORD You ought to make your position clear

Mr ATHERLEY JONES Mr Hall was a mere instrument for the purpose of conveying—physically conveying the money to the men

Now I was telling your Lordship my learned friend put to him whether he did not see acts of molestation Now it appears that the strike pay was paid at a place somewhat remote from the colliery, and therefore it was not necessary for Mr Hall to go to the scene where there might, or might not be disturbance, and he emphatically stated that his sole knowledge of disturbances was confined to reading some references thereto in the daily papers, and that he did not see on the occasions when he went down there any act of violence or molestation Therefore it is not necessary for me under these circumstances I apprehend to take upon myself the burden of asking how far a person in Mr Hall's position might see acts of molestation

The LORD CHANCELLOR I do not think it would be open to anything against Hall personally in the least

Mr ATHERLEY JONES No

Lord ROBERTSON I thought you were dealing with Wadsworth ?

The LORD CHANCELLOR I think you have put the position of Hall plainly, indeed I do not think there was anything specially urged against Hall as apart from the others

Mr ATHERLEY JONES No

The LORD CHANCELLOR And you have told us the material points at any rate

Mr ATHERLEY JONES Yes In answer to Lord James, my Lord, I just stated so far what was done by Mr Hall

Lord JAMES of HEREFORD I only wanted you to state your proposition as regards Hall clearly—not to go into detail about it for a moment

Mr ATHERLEY JONES My proposition with respect to Hall is this, that there is absolutely no evidence whatever against him upon any of the issues which are raised in this case—that so far as Hall is concerned his functions were confined, so far as his active functions were concerned, his active functions were confined to going and explaining the bag dirt question and the cause of the Award, and as an instrument of the Association, the mere physical act of the payment to the men of the strike pay which the Council of the Association directed to be paid There is no evidence whatever that he took any personal part, and I have a word to say in respect of the finding of the Jury—no evidence whatever in relation to the strike other than in respect of those matters which I have just mentioned

My Lord, I was turning to the case with regard to Wadsworth

The LORD CHANCELLOR We have had this speech of Wadsworth, Mr Jones, we really have had it read over, I think, twice.

Mr ATHERLEY JONES   Then, my Lord, I will not read it
I had the idea of reading it, because I was suggesting, my Lord, that
no speech could have been more moderate in tone, or more reasonable,
or more proper, than the speech which Mr Wadsworth made

Then Mr Wadsworth is, of course, examined, and the examination is at page 776, and there again, although I have marked passages
which might be proper to draw your Lordship's attention to, yet I
think probably it will be sufficient for me to draw your Lordship's
attention to the evidence, and to ask your Lordships, if you kindly
will to take it from me that there is no admission whatever by Mr
Wadsworth of any impropriety of conduct, or anything which would
render him amenable in this action

I am very anxious, however, because he was very much
challenged in cross-examination—in a very effective cross-examination,
so far as it covered every possible point—which was made by my
learned friend, Mr Bankes, I think, of Mr Wadsworth, in order to
try and establish that he, being present at meetings where speeches
of a more or less inflammatory character were made, in a sort of
sense made himself an accessory to anything which was wrong in
the advice tendered in these speeches or in the opinions expressed
in these speeches   I think, my Lord, I will draw your Lordships'
attention to this—I do not think it is immaterial   Mr Wadsworth
pointed out in the course of his cross-examination that there were
some things in those speeches to which he could not extend his
concurrence, but he pointed out what I cannot help thinking, with
great respect, will impress your Lordships—that, although it is
perfectly true that some things were said by, I think, Mr Nolan or
Mr Walsh, which might be impolitic, he said, " We came down there
with an express purpose to get these men back to work, and in
dealing with a body of men—men of strong passions, and men who,
of course, were not highly educated men—it is necessary to humour
them", and, he said, no doubt, Mr Walsh in his speech was anxious,
and they had so decided when they went down to this colliery, to
get the men back to work, and they hoped and believed that if they
got them back to work they would be able to settle this controversy
with Mr Chambers   " Therefore," he said, " I took no exception,
and I take no exception now "   I am giving you the substance of
what he said--"to any too strong language which was used by Mr
Walsh or by anybody else, because I believe that if he had spoken to
the men in a different tone or in a different manner, if he had done
nothing but reprimand them he would have produced the very
opposite results to those which he aimed at "   My Lord, I cannot
help respectfully suggesting to your Lordships that that is an element
in considering these speeches which is well worthy of your
consideration

Now the next speech which I shall refer your Lordship to is the
speech which was made by Mr Parrott, and which has given rise to
some animadversion on the part of my learned friends in reference

to a particular phrase which was used about turning these people out of their houses (the speech is at page 434), and that something would be a devilish thing to do—to turn people out. Now, of course, I remember my learned friend Mr Rufus Isaacs pointed out to your Lordships that even if the construction which was sought to be put upon that language by my learned friends were the correct construction, at any rate after that date no damage had resulted therefrom, that is to say, after the date when that speech was delivered, which was on the 24th November, no violence is recorded nor alleged. My Lords, I make bold to ask your Lordships to regard that language as perfectly innocuous. What is the language? Of course at that time, quite within their right, the Colliery Company had given notice of their intention to evict the people from their houses, at any rate I think the notice was this—that it was to evict all those people who would not agree to come back to work, and it was perfectly legitimate pressure very likely for the colliery officials to exercise. Now what Mr Parrott said was this. "To turn them out of their houses"——

Lord JAMES of HEREFORD. What is the reference to that?

Mr ATHERLEY JONES. I beg your Lordship's pardon, page 436, A to B. To turn them out of their houses if he required them would be a different thing, but then it would be nothing like what was expected in a Christian age, but to turn people out of their houses and let them remain empty was a most devilish thing in his opinion. The Coal Owners' Association were supporting their owners in that stoppage.

Now, of course, your Lordships are far more competent than myself to form an accurate estimate of what the value and proper proportions of that language may be, but I respectfully suggest to your Lordships this. That it was not an unnatural thing and not an unreasonable thing to suggest with regard to turning these men, women and children out of their houses, because, of course, the obvious result of being turned out of their houses would be that they would probably camp out, as, in fact, happened on adjoining land, although it might be an unwise expression to use, I am not going to enter into any casuistical argument with regard to that, but at the same time, I suggest to your Lordship that to put the interpretation that that was the means of inciting, and was intended as the means of inciting the men to further acts of violence or to the prolongation of this unfortunate trade dispute, whatever legal effect that might have is, to my mind, an unreasonable and false interpretation.

The LORD CHANCELLOR. May I ask, as regards Parrott, has the action abated against him since his death?

Mr ATHERLEY JONES. Yes, my Lord.

The LORD CHANCELLOR Have any other persons been substituted ?

Mr ATHERLEY JONES No, I think not

Mr MONTAGUE LUSH Yes   May I say with regard to Parrott, we ask no relief against the executors either for damages or costs ?

The LORD CHANCELLOR If so, we surely need not pursue the case against them

Mr ATHERLEY JONES Of course there is the Judgment

The LORD CHANCELLOR In his favour   What I mean is that no practical consequences can ensue

Mr MONTAGUE LUSH I can explain this, if your Lordships would let me, because there has been an arrangement   My learned friends do not appear for Parrott, I think   Mr Parrott died, and his executors were added, and as the Order of the Court of Appeal stands we have to pay the costs of Parrott   All we ask is, if we should succeed, not to get any damages or costs against the executors, but to be relieved from paying costs

The LORD CHANCELLOR Does Mr Atherley Jones appear for Parrott or his executors ?

Mr ATHERLEY JONES Yes

Lord JAMES of HEREFORD He made a claim for costs against Mr Lush's clients   What does Mr Jones say about that ?

The LORD CHANCELLOR That is enough Mr Jones   I am sorry I interrupted   Pray proceed

Lord DAVEY The question of costs of these personal Respondents must depend on the general decision

Mr MONTAGUE LUSH Yes

The LORD CHANCELLOR If there is no practical use in it, of course you must remember we have already considered it very fully for five days

Mr ATHERLEY JONES I hope it is not altogether worthless that I should have referred to this, because undoubtedly one would not wish a stigma to rest upon a man who was a Defendant in this action and against whom Judgment has been recorded   I could deal

more with the action and attitude of Mr Parrott, but there is no
necessity to do so after what has fallen from your Lordship

That exhausts the whole of the evidence against these
Defendants whom I represent, I only ask your Lordship's attention
to the Summing-up of the learned Judge   Now, my Lord, the only
references—I speak subject to the correction of my learned friend—
in reference to these gentlemen are at page 978, where the learned
Judge says "Now what is said by the Plaintiffs, whether they are
right or not, is this   That you not only conspired together, but if
you did not conspire, the persons acting as your agents, Humphries
and Nolan, acting as your agents, acting with the knowledge of the
officials of the Society, induced the men to break their contract
upon the 29th June" I suggest to your Lordships, in view of the
answers which were given to the questions that direction to the
Jury, or that allegation of fact to the Jury, would entitle these
gentlemen to a new trial, because as a matter of fact there was
absolutely no evidence that any one of these gentlemen on whose
behalf I appear had any knowledge of the strike until after the event
Therefore there is no foundation for the statement that they induced
the men to break their contract upon the 29th June

That is one reference and the next reference, my Lord, is where
he refers at page 983, at the top of the page, to Mr Hall's address to
the men on the 7th July with reference to the bag dirt question
The learned Judge did not say and, indeed, could not give any
suggestion to the Jury that anything that was said by Hall at that
meeting had anything to do with the proper issues in this case, but
he confines himself, my Lord, to reading to the Jury a portion of the
speech which dealt with the bag dirt controversy   I will not trouble
your Lordships with reading it, but I refer your Lordships to page
983 and some portion of the following page   That exhausts Hall
either expressly or collectively in connection with the other officials,
that exhausts all the references made to Hall either individually or
collectively

Now, my Lord, he then refers on page 984 to Annables   that is
at F G   He says "So much in respect of that meeting" (that is
the Hall meeting) "I do not think there are any other meetings
which I need call attention to excepting the one that Mr Wadsworth
was present at, which is important   I do not know—it is a question of
morals altogether, it is a question I have often had to debate myself
not of low but of political morality—how far a man sitting in a
chair and occupying the position of chairman should bear without
contradiction the man on the right hand or his left saying that which he
knows is not quite true, and taking no steps whatever to let the
people know which way the truth is   It is a question   Now let us
see what takes place when Mr Wadsworth goes down   I think
you know what Mr Wadsworth went down for, and Walsh   He
went down to get the men to come back to ballot and to send in their
notices   That was the object of his visit   However, he came on

July 15th, with Walsh, whom Mr Bankes called the orator Mr Wadsworth was the president, I think, of the Association" (He was then vice-president, my Lord) "The Chairman of the meeting was Mr Croft I need not read what Mr Croft said"

Then, my Lord, the learned Judge reads Mr Walsh's speech, or a portion of Mr Walsh's speech, and he does not refer to what Mr Wadsworth said beyond a single passage on 986 D to E—or rather C it begins at, nearly at D He said "Then Mr Wadsworth says 'He was sorry that they were not on a better mission He was sorry that the men at those two large and important collieries and in that great industrial centre were not that morning within the rules and regulations of their own society and outside altogether the clutches of the law' That is Mr Wadsworth view of the matter"

Lord JAMES of HEREFORD Give me again, Mr Jones the date when Mr Wadsworth made that speech, you have given it to us once

Mr ATHERLEY JONES It was on the 15th July, he went there in accordance——

Lord JAMES of HEREFORD With the resolution of the 14th?

Mr ATHERLEY JONES Yes 'That is Mr Wadsworth's view of the matter Then 'For the time being the manager had the advantage They were outside the law, and there was not the slightest doubt but what Mr Chambers was trying all that he possibly could do to play that card to the utmost It was not always a matter of getting everything at the time being, but it was a question of whether it was right, just and equitable, whether it would succeed in the future If Mr Chambers had met them and put aside the supposed document'—supposed document—'which Chappell signed'

"Now Mr Chappell has come down and sworn to it, and here is the President of the Miners' Federation comes and addresses the men who are affected by it and calls it a supposed document, meaning to throw some doubt upon it The man himself who signed it had been there and sworn that he signed it, and said he signed it, and that it had the marks and all upon it 'If Mr Chambers had met them and put aside the supposed document which Chappell signed which he ought to have done and dealt with the price list in a proper and fair manner they would have met him in a fair, honest and amicable spirit Instead Mr Chambers had pushed everything to the gate'" That is all My Lord, those comprise the whole of the references made by the learned Judge to these Defendants on whose behalf I appear There is no discrimination on the part of the learned Judge between the acts of these gentlemen, one as between the other or as between them and the Council And now if I might suggest to your Lordships this—drawing my remarks to a conclusion now—that the finding of the Jury on Question 7, if I remember right is a finding that I am not prepared to assent to—is a finding directed against these chief officials because the word "officials" has been used throughout this case in the loosest possible sense, it has been used as applying to the local officials and it is used——

The LORD CHANCELLOR Does not the answer to that question mean that they were not necessarily, as apart from the Association, responsible at all, but as being servants of the Association

Mr ATHERLEY JONES If that means anything it means that they were a sort of principals of the Association who were bound by the acts of the Association as their agents, which, of course, is a proposition absolutely untenable I rather suggest to your Lordships that what might have been, and what probably would have been, on the minds of the Jury was this "We find nothing wrong in these men, but still they were members of the Association, and therefore we will include them in our finding against the Association"

' My Lord, apart from trespassing on the ground which has been so well covered by my learned friend, I do not know that I can usefully add anything I should like to say, my Lord, with regard to the allegation that they maintained the strike, that my learned friend did deal with that point Of course it very materially affects my clients, and therefore, perhaps, it will not be impertinent if I say this with regard to it that I resent the use of the word "strike" in any legal sense in which it has been indiscriminately used in relation to this case I understand that the proper view with regard to the whole of this matter is whether there was breach of contract or not, and I venture to urge upon your Lordships this— that so soon as the contract was rescinded, whether it was rescinded before the 14th July, as in fact it was, by the action of the managers— immediately after the rescission of that contract there was no strike

Lord JAMES of HEREFORD What was the action of the managers that caused the rescission?

Mr ATHERLEY JONES The action of the manager was saying that he would not take back the workmen—in the first place he said, "I will not meet the workmen as they are no longer in our employ" and in the second place he said that they must enter into fresh contracts

Lord JAMES of HEREFORD But was there not a previous rescission by the absence of the workmen from the works?

Mr ATHERLEY JONES The absence of the workmen from the works was a breach of contract on the 29th June It need not have been treated by the employer as a determination of the contract

Lord JAMES of HEREFORD No, but you must take the evidence that the practice was that if they were away more than three or four days they had always to sign on again

Mr ATHERLEY JONES They could have signed on again no doubt

Lord JAMES of HEREFORD And they had always so done, that was the practice

Mr ATHERLEY JONES Some few of them signed——

Lord JAMES of HEREFORD No, no, but that was the general practice in the colliery—that if the men were away more than a certain number of days the first contract came to an end and they had to sign on again

Mr ATHERLEY JONES Yes, that is so—they had to enter into fresh contracts of service

Lord JAMES of HEREFORD Yes Does not that constitute rescission?

Mr ATHERLEY JONES Yes, that in itself would constitute rescission obviously I think probably there was evidence of rescission before that date, but it is quite enough for my purpose to accept that as the rescission

What I venture respectfully—although I hope your Lordships will check me if I am intruding in referring to it—to press upon your Lordships is this—that talking about maintaining a strike has no meaning in law—that although in popular language you might say there was a strike at a colliery or at works, while a number of men are living contiguous to the premises, and are not in course of employment at these works, yet these men were no more strikers after the rescission of the contract than any people who were living 100 miles away from the place, and that therefore when you come to test whether there was maintenance or whether there were illegal acts or whether there was advice not to enter into contracts, or whatever it might be, you have got to deal with it from this standpoint—that there was no responsibility upon the part of any of these workmen to the owners of the Denaby and Cadeby mines after the date of the rescission of the contract, and therefore I respectfully——

Lord JAMES of HEREFORD I suppose your point is that what these Defendents did at most was, they committed acts which encouraged the workmen not to return to the employment

Mr ATHERLEY JONES If they did

Lord JAMES of HEREFORD At the most I say

Mr ATHERLEY JONES Yes, the most that could be said

Lord JAMES of HEREFORD They encouraged the workmen and assisted them not to return to the employment

Mr ATHERLEY JONES Yes, my Lord, and I say that since the case of Allen *v* Flood was decided, you may advise people not to enter into employment or advise people by lawful notice to determine employment unless there is an antecedent conspiracy to do injury, which was Quinn *v* Leathem If there is an antecedent conspiracy you may do the most lawful acts, but if it is in furtherance of that conspiracy, that would render you amenable Unless there is an antecedent conspiracy to injure and to do harm to the employers or to the owners of these works, the mere advice to men not to enter into contracts, whether it be by payment of pay to persons on the employ who were lawfully entitled to it, or not lawfully entitled to it, is immaterial, is an act which the law does not recognise as a tort

That, I think, is all I need trouble your Lordships with

Mr S T EVANS My Lords, the case has been so fully put before your Lordships that it would be unpardonable for me to take up any time in argument I did, as your Lordship will see at page 1005, submit to the learned Judge at the trial that there was not even a finding of the Jury which justified Judgment against us We still take that position, there is no finding of the Jury and no evidence at all against us

Mr MONTAGUE LUSH If your Lordships please My Lords, I desire to compress what I have to say in reply into the smallest possible space that I can, but after the powerful and forcible arguments that my learned friends have addressed to your Lordships, necessarily ranging over a good many points, I hope your Lordships will be indulgent to me if I seem to take a little time in dealing with them

My Lords, the first point I wish to deal with is one which I am sure must have impressed your Lordships when my learned friend Mr Rufus Isaacs put it, and that was that in the Howden case we contended, and got the benefit of the contention, that the branch officials when they called the men out on the 29th June, were acting without the sanction of the Association, and it is said, *prima facie* with great force, that that is inconsistent with the contention that we are raising now. My Lords I think a few minutes attention to the rules will show your Lordships that that is not inconsistent I fully admit I said that, and I should submit it again, that on the 29th they were acting without the sanction of the Association, but the answer to it is to be found really in an examination of three rules. I hope your Lordship will not be wearied by my referring to them again as they are very important.

The LORD CHANCELLOR Not the least, Mr Lush

Mr MONTAGUE LUSH At page 113 we find Rule 72 This is the rule which deals with the power of the branch officials to initiate or conduct a strike, and your Lordships will observe that it has no reference to obtaining strike pay—it has nothing to do with the pay, it is merely what I may call the strike rule. "No branch or portion of a branch shall be allowed to strike," and so on, "unless sanctioned by two-thirds of the members composing the branch, when such strike shall be determined by registered ballot" Now, that is independent of getting the sanction of the Association; there is nothing in that about getting the sanction of anybody except the sanction of the members of the branch, and, therefore, when you are only considering—and, I submit, that is all we have got to consider here—as to whether the branch officials were the agents or officers of the Union to initiate the strike and conduct it, one must bear in mind that they had to get nobody's sanction but that of two-thirds of the members. When you come to what follows, namely, to getting the strike pay which they might or might not get, one turns back to Rule 64, which relates only to strike pay This Rule 64 is not a rule which regulates or defines the authority to call the men out. Now, this does require the sanction of the Association "If any branch, member, or members have grievances affecting their wages, mode or manner of working, or the hours of labour, if the employers refuse to remedy those grievances, and after all proper and peaceful means have been tried to effect a settlement by deputations from members, with the advice and assistance of Council"—now we come to the other clause, which is important as to strike pay—"and such member or members be permitted to cease work by the sanction of the Association in accordance with the rules, such member shall receive" so much

Now, the strike may be conducted by the officers of the Union under their authority under Rule 72, it may not follow that the men may get pay. To entitle them to pay they must show that they have obtained the sanction of the Association, and I think it is conceded—I gather it was in Howden's case—that that sanction may be given afterwards. The whole contest in Howden's case was as to whether the Association did afterwards really give their sanction to what the branch officials had done, but whether it was to be obtained before or afterwards does not affect my point, and in saying, as I did say in Howden's case, "You have not got the sanction of the Association," I was only dealing with their right to get the strike pay, obviously, and I say that is perfectly consistent with my contention that this strike was initiated by agents of the Association so as to bind them, although it was initiated without their sanction, because, as I submit, their sanction was not required for the initiation of a strike   My contention was and is, even in this case, that when you consider whether the payment of strike pay was lawful you then for the first time introduce the element of obtaining the sanction of the Association   I entirely repel the charge of inconsistency   It is not inconsistent, it is my contention here   I say when you come to deal with the question of whether strike pay was lawful you must see whether they obtain the sanction, it does not touch my argument as to whether the officers of the Union were or were not the agents to call the men out

Now, the last rule which throws light upon it is Rule 12, at page 96, and I think these three rules show how very carefully the framework of these rules has been applied with a view to regulating the power to call the men out and the power to get strike pay   Now, Rule 12 gives the power to the whole of the branches, if they are not content with the attitude that the Association may have adopted in sanctioning a strike for the purposes of strike pay—this Rule 12 gives power not to the branch officials, but to every single member of the Trade Union to call a meeting and outvote their own delegates, because Rule 12 says that "A registered vote shall be taken throughout the entire Association whenever any number of branches numbering one-fourth of the Council demand such vote on the following questions, viz   "The adoption or prolongation of a strike," and so on   So that if the branch officials had initiated a strike, and if the Association, which consists of the Council attended by the delegates, have sanctioned it, this Rule 12 gives power to the men to meet together and by their vote overrule what the Council have done, and therefore I ask your Lordships to bear in mind——

Lord DAVEY   It must be one-fourth of the branches represented on the Council

Mr MONTAGUE LUSH   Yes, only, my Lord, the point of Rule 12——

Lord DAVEY   They would need a ballot, because naturally the expense of strike pay falls on the whole Association

Mr MONTAGUE LUSH   Yes

Lord DAVEY   It is a kind of appeal?

Mr MONTAGUE LUSH   Yes, it is a kind of appeal in which the men may really reverse the decision of their delegates

Lord DAVEY   A referendum ?

Mr MONTAGUE LUSH   Yes, it is a power given, and therefore it is very carefully drawn ; the branch officials may create a strike ; the Association may support them——

Lord DAVEY   May sanction it ?

Mr MONTAGUE LUSH   May sanction it for the purpose of strike pay only

Lord ROBERTSON   I should like very much to hear your proposition on this completed, Mr Lush

Mr MONTAGUE LUSH   Yes   I will begin and put it again, if I may   The branch officials without getting the sanction of the Council at all, may under Rule 72, initiate a strike ; they may bring the men out   They may not get strike pay, that is another matter Under Rule 64, the Association may sanction what they have done, the effect of which would be to give strike pay   It will not touch the validity or invalidity of their calling the men out at all, it merely affects the payment of money   Thirdly, the men may, after that has been sanctioned, reverse the ruling or the decision of the Council and decide against the prolongation or the adoption of the strike— the effect of which will be to neutralise, from the time they so vote, the sanction of the Association, and make strike pay no longer payable   I submit that is the code under these three rules

Now, my Lords, I will turn to deal with a wider question than that   I wanted to deal with that because it looked very much at first as if I had been inconsistent, but I ask your Lordships to say that I have not been   Now my submission is that first of all I quite agree with my learned friend, Mr Atherley Jones—I was going to say the same thing myself—that in dealing with legal liabilities the less one falls into conventional or colloquial language about a strike and maintaining a strike the better, and I am going to avoid it as far as I can because it is apt to mislead   One asks the question, " What is a legal strike and what is an illegal strike ?"—and I will use language which will avoid that altogether in order to assist your Lordships if I can to see whether we are right or wrong in saying the Union are responsible for what was done

Now, my Lord, I want most strongly to say this—that my submission is that it is impossible to understand the history of this Denaby strike or to legally arrive at a proper conclusion as to who is responsible for it unless one takes care to see whether my learned friend's contention is right, which amounts really to saying that the

y

only element of illegality in what was done on June 29th was the procuring of breaches of contracts I submit that is a misapprehension That it was an element of illegality of course we not only agree but we allege, it is one of what we say are the unlawful methods that were adopted If I can show that the procuring of the men to come out was in itself unlawful in its object, then I not only have the unlawfulness of the method of procuring the breach of contract but I add to it the unlawfulness of the object, and I think I can show your Lordships that that is the position of things when this calling out took place

My Lords, Lord James of Hereford did ask my learned friend, Mr Rufus Isaacs, " Why is it that sometimes you find these things commence by procuring a breach of contract ? Why do not the men give them notices ?" Mr Rufus Isaacs replied, " Temper " Well now I venture respectfully to disagree It is that, but it is something more The difficulty to branch officials, or whoever the people may be, to bear in mind is that as long as the men are at work talking to each other and earning their wages, if they are going to initiate one of these trade movements by serving notices, the men will not be willing to do it, or at all events many of them will not, and, if I may use a metaphor taken from quite a different sort of subject matter, you have got to get up sufficient head of steam or sufficient head of water, to rush down your obstacles, and my submission is that it is closely analogous to what took place here when the men were asked to resume their work, because I say that the branch officials who wanted the strike recognised that if the men were at work talking to one another and earning their money it would be very difficult to get them to strike The reason why this procuring of breaches of contract was resorted to was, as I submit it usually is when a strike is the result of what the leaders do, that you must get the men out in a moment and use angry language and get up their tempers In that sense when Mr Rufus Isaacs says " temper " I agree, but it is the temper of the men you want to get at

Lord JAMES of HEREFORD Is not that shown by the ballot ? They would have to ballot first would they not ?

Mr MONTAGUE LUSH That is shown by the ballot and that is the importance of it When I come to deal with what took place with the ballot here ——

Lord JAMES of HEREFORD If the men by ballot struck, would not that give them the headway to go on with ?

Mr MONTAGUE LUSH Not quite, because they have to go back to work out their notice—you have to get the men to work properly so as to have a ballot Here the appeal is made to the men on the Sunday night to get them to commit themselves on the spot to come out, use angry language, and then you will get a sort of what I call coercion, or whatever the language is, which will enable the leaders to carry their will. That is what I submit is the reason why the strikes in these cases are initiated by getting the contracts broken instead of giving notice. I only suggest it to your Lordships—I submit it is the true answer really to the question why the men resorted to that which they knew from their speeches would expose them to liability. I submit that the only reason was they wanted to get as I say a sufficient head of force to overcome the obstacles which the men who wanted to work would oppose.

Now let me ask your Lordships to follow me while I just refer to the language which was used not only on the 29th June, but throughout the whole period down to December, just shortly before the strike pay was stopped, when Howden's action was commenced. May I say in passing that we do not contend as a cause of action that the Union paid strike pay to the men who were not at work. If the men had gone to their homes—if they had gone to Lancashire we will say it does not hurt my clients that the Association should pay them £1,000 a week at all. The point we make with regard to the payment is only one of the instances of unlawful methods, but the point we make with regard to it is not that they were paying their money to support and maintain the men, but that they were paying their money as one of the methods they used to support the men in doing what the men resolved to do under the guidance of the officials of the Union of June 29th, and what they reiterated every time resolutions were passed—at least, that is not literally true, I do not want to overstate it, but it was almost every time, and if your Lordships will turn to page 392 and read again what, I am afraid, has often been read already, this is the point I am going to make, the resolution that the men came to on the Sunday night was, not that they would not go on working—certainly not that they would not go on working until the bag dirt grievance was remedied but that they would stop the wheels at both collieries. There was evidence given about stopping the wheels, and one of the witnesses explained it as stopping the pulleys which work the wheels.

Lord JAMES of HEREFORD. That does mean stopping the work.

Mr MONTAGUE LUSH. Yes. Now the resolution they came to on June 29th—and I am going to show how they reiterated this every time they discussed the matter—was that they would not let anybody work, they would stop the wheels in the sense that they would prevent people working, and, therefore, if that is true (and I think I can show it is) why we complain of the payment of strike pay, among other things is that the men were not merely being kept from starving when they were not at work, but the men were being assisted in preventing the Colliery Company getting their mines worked at all by anybody.

Lord DAVEY The only way of stopping the wheels was by not going to work

Mr MONTAGUE LUSH Yes, and by preventing others That is an element of illegality

Lord DAVEY I mean, there was no intention physically to interfere with or injure the plant of the Colliery

Mr MONTAGUE LUSH I did not mean that, I meant stopping the wheels in the sense of preventing anybody going down the mines

Lord DAVEY In the sense of not going to work themselves and persuading others not to go to work

Mr MONTAGUE LUSH The question of whether that is "persuasion"—— ——

Lord DAVEY I did not use the word in any technical sense—inducing, if you like—not going to work themselves, and inducing others not to go

' Mr MONTAGUE LUSH If I might use the word "procure," I should prefer it '

Lord DAVEY I do not care what the phrase is, it does not make any difference in substance

Mr MONTAGUE LUSH My point is that the resolution was to stop the wheels in this sense—that they would prevent the Colliery Company from working

Lord JAMES of HEREFORD As I understand, by the one overt act only—not going to work themselves

Mr MONTAGUE LUSH More than that, I submit

Lord JAMES of HEREFORD What else?

Mr MONTAGUE LUSH By the coercion and intimidation of others

Lord JAMES of HEREFORD That was not in the works, I was applying it more to within the works, you refer to molestation

Mr. MONTAGUE LUSH Yes

Lord JAMES of HEREFORD That is not what was in my mind, as far as the works were concerned, nothing was done except not going to work

Mr MONTAGUE LUSH Quite If your Lordships would turn to page 227, you will see on the next day, June 30th, the Cadeby and the Denaby Branches both met and confirmed the resolution of the previous day—that is, to stop the wheels Turning over the page, on the next day, July 2nd, again they confirmed the previous resolution to let the pits lie idle On page 394, on July 7th, five days later, in Croft's speech—which my learned friend, Mr Rufus Isaacs, said yesterday was only counselling the men only to do what was lawful and to avoid violence—he and Nolan had told the manager time after time that unless the grievances were remedied the wheels would stand, and the reply was, "Let them stand" Then lower down, at E, he said, "They would have strike pay, no one could stop them Grass would grow over the top of the wheels before they would work if they got strike pay"

On July 17th, at page 230, there is a joint meeting, and the fifth clause of it is, "That we still adhere to the old resolution of June 29th" That is to say, at a time when they were pretending—as I shall show they were merely pretending—to resume work—they were adhering to the resolution that the wheels should be stopped until their grievances were remedied And at page 410 your Lordships will find a speech on the same day in which Croft said at the top of the page, that "If they did not get their grievances remedied they would stop out at Denaby" Then there is the language which has been referred to before and which I need not repeat On July 23rd, page 231, the day before they got the strike pay, they passed a resolution (Clause 2), "That we still adhere to the resolution of June 29th" Turning over the page, on the next day, July 30th, we find this "That we stand until we get a fresh price list" I will show your lordships in a moment what that referred to on the evidence And at the bottom of the same page at a meeting on August 7th (Clause 3), they resolve "That we still adhere to the resolution of June 29th, 1902, until we get a new price list On August 13th, at page 233, the next page, at letter C "That we stand firm to the old resolution of June 29th, 1902, till all our grievances are remedied Over the page, on August 21st (Clause 6) "That we adhere to the resolution of June 29th, 1902' Then on September 3rd, on the next page (Clause 4) "That we adhere to the resolution of June 29th, 1902, and stand firm until our grievances are remedied" On September 17th, at the bottom of the same page "That we adhere to the resolution of June 29th' Now turning for a moment again to the speeches, at page 414, on the 17th September, the same date as letter B Hirst says "He hoped every man would still be as loyal as on the 30th June, when he assisted in passing the resolution to stop the wheels On page 458, which I think is the last I need trouble your Lordships with, we come to the date in December when Nolan talked about "The blazes out of the top of the shaft before any men should go to work"

Now, my Lords, of course I may say in passing it is obviously material to know what the grievances were which the men said they would have remedied before they would allow the wheels to go round, the evidence, your Lordships will probably remember, with regard to it   On page 513, at the bottom of the page, Chambers said what this new price-list was, it was not bag dirt, and had nothing to do with bag dirt, because the Cadeby Main, which was the larger of the two, had no bag dirt, and it did not affect the Cadeby Main   As to the new price-list, this is the uncontradicted evidence at Question 174   "I want to know generally," said Mr Bankes, "with regard to that price-list, how did it compare as a whole with the price-list in existence at the time of the strike ?—There was a very considerable advance in the standard rates they were asking for   Q An advance all round ?—Not on all items, but the general effect of it was to advance the rate of wages that they had been having about 28 per cent —at least that   Q At least 28 per cent over and above the standard rate ?—Yes "

Lord DAVEY   Surely the price list was in direct connection with the bag dirt question ?   The objection they made to the price list-- that is, the standard of wages—was that they said it was ambiguous, there was a decision against them too, but they said it was an ambiguous decision, and the men put one interpretation upon it and Mr Chambers put another, and they thought Mr Chambers' interpretation of the price list was unfair

Mr MONTAGUE LUSH   That is only about bag dirt

Lord DAVEY   Certainly

Mr MONTAGUE LUSH   This new price list they formulated and said they meant to have was not only about bag dirt   With great respect, that is an inaccuracy my learned friend has fallen into

Lord DAVEY   That is my impression, and I think you will find it rather difficult to remove it   I will not say that, but that is my impression although you may remove it

Mr MONTAGUE LUSH   That is my learned friend's impression   Take Cadeby, it had no bag dirt, and no change about bag dirt in the price list would affect the larger proportion of the men   As to the point about alteration of the price list—and the price list is exhibited in the Appendix—it touched bag dirt, of course, but it touched everything else, and I think the evidence is " none at Cadeby "

Lord DAVEY   On the question of the rise and fall, Mr Chambers says an alteration in the price list retaining the present rate of 50 per cent above standard would mean so much more above standard   That is what I understood

Mr MONTAGUE LUSH But the point that I want to make good is that the new price list they wanted not only dealt with bag dirt but other things, so that the result would have been to give an increase of 28 per cent   The price list is set out in the Appendix, at page 129, and your Lordships will find it there

Lord DAVEY Is this the one they wished for or the old one?

Mr MONTAGUE LUSH This is the old one of the 18th June, 1890   I think your Lordships will find the new one at page 354

Lord DAVEY They have had two decisions against them on the old one

Mr MONTAGUE LUSH Yes   My learned friend, Mr Danckwerts, may be right, if he says so   I will not tender my view to the contrary, but I certainly thought if there was any in Cadeby it was very small, and that the whole thing affected only about 50 or 60 men

Lord JAMES of HEREFORD Were Denaby and Cadeby federated? Were not they in the Federation?

Mr MONTAGUE LUSH Yes, both

Lord JAMES of HEREFORD Could they move for any general rate of wages without the sanction of the Federation?

Mr MONTAGUE LUSH No, I think not

Lord JAMES of HEREFORD I do not quite understand what they are doing now, unless it is for the bag dirt or some special thing they are referring to at that particular colliery

Mr MONTAGUE LUSH The point is this—I am coming to deal with it, but still I will answer it at once   The point we made was—and that is why I am going to show whether the bag dirt or the 10 per cent was material—that there was ample evidence to the Jury, which is all very conclusive that the boys' wages in the 20 collieries that were out on strike at the same time were admittedly affected by your Lordships' decision or Award

Lord JAMES of HEREFORD Indirectly?

Mr MONTAGUE LUSH I forget if directly or indirectly, and therefore our case was that the new price list which these leaders wanted was not confined to what Mr Wadsworth, I think, or one of the witnesses for the defence said was frivolous it was not confined to this paltry question of bag dirt which affected so few

It was the desire they had to raise wages all round the Federation, and, therefore, I think I can show your Lordships really when I come to deal with it that that is correct. Therefore this new price list which the men insisted on getting before they would allow the resolution to be altered about stopping the wheels was not at all confined to the bag dirt. It was an organised intention, if they could, to get an increase of wages which would wipe out the 10 per cent and give them something beyond.

Mr Chambers's evidence, inasmuch as there is no contradiction of it—because my learned friends had an opportunity of calling evidence about it—is at page 513, Question 175. It is quite clear I submit. "An advance all round?" Mr Bankes puts, and his answer is, "Not on all items, but the general effect of it was to advance the rates of wages that they had been having about 28 per cent—at least that." Now, it is impossible to say after that, as I submit, considering that that is the only evidence on the point, that the men decided to stop the wheels until the bag dirt question was remedied. It was an organised movement, and the leaders of the branches, acting as we submit within their authority (that is another question, but they had in fact got the men out on the 29th June, and committed two illegalities in doing so) got the men out by getting them to break their contracts, and they got them out as the first step in a movement which on every important occasion reiterated the old resolution which would not have been necessary if they did not mean to keep that constantly before the minds of the men "We adhere to the old resolution of the 29th, which is that we will stop the wheels"—and they explain that in their speeches to mean "until our grievances are remedied"—"an intolerable tyranny," one of them said which means— "until we get a regular advance of wages all round." I submit that when one remembers the strikes that were going on elsewhere it is manifest—at all events there was evidence for the Jury that that was what they meant.

Lord DAVEY You said it was illegal on two grounds

Mr MONTAGUE LUSH The first is breaking their contracts

Lord DAVEY, What is the second?

Mr MONTAGUE LUSH Secondly it was illegal because they meant that they would prevent the Colliery Company carrying on its work at the colliery. Therefore, I submit that it was for the Jury to say whether the stopping of the wheels did not mean that When your Lordships remember that these men stopped on in the houses which were wanted to enable other men to work the mines— they would not go out—they stopped in the houses from June 29th right away until we got eviction orders against them about Christmas time—the object of that was not, I submit, that they wanted to save rent, but it was a step taken with a view to the common end they had—to stop the wheels and prevent the Colliery Company getting their coal We submit that is all a question for the Jury—that is all, of course, your Lordships have got, as I submit, to deal with If that is right the Court of Appeal have held—and I submit that it is perfectly good law—it is not very long ago—is Lyons v Wilkins, 1896, 1 Chancery, page 811, that that is in itself (the desire to prevent business being done) actionable

The LORD CHANCELLOR If you put it so broadly as that it means that every strike is actionable

Mr MONTAGUE LUSH A strike may not be actionable if all the men do is that they resolve that they will not any longer work

The LORD CHANCELLOR Perhaps you had better tell us the language of it

Mr MONTAGUE LUSH It is Lord Lindley's language Mr Justice North held that, and the Court of Appeal affirmed, and Lord Lindley, in a passage at page 882, says this, after saying what the difficulty is in strikes—that they may be legal or illegal "Now Parliament has not yet conferred upon Trade Unions the power to coerce people, and to prevent them from working for whomsoever they like upon any terms that they like, and yet in the absence of such a power it is obvious that a strike may not be effective, and may not answer its purpose Some strikes are perfectly effective by virtue of the mere strike, and other strikes are not effective unless the next step can be taken, and unless other people can be prevented from taking the place of the strikers That is the pinch of the case in trade disputes, and until Parliament confers on Trade Unions the power of saying to other people, 'You shall not work for those who are desirous of employing you upon such terms as you and they may mutually agree upon,' Trade Unions exceed their power when they try to compel people not to work except on the terms fixed by the Unions " I need hardly say that up to the present moment no such power as that exists By the law of this country no one has ever, and no set of people have ever had that right or their power If Parliament chooses to confer it on Trade Unions it will do so as and when it thinks proper and subject to such limitations as it thinks proper, but it is idle to pretend not to see that this struggle exists Trade Unions have now been recognised up to a certain point as organs for good They are the only means by which workmen can protect themselves from tyranny on the part of those who employ them, but the moment that Trade Unions become tyrants in their turn, they are engines for evil they have no right to prevent any man from working upon such terms as he chooses " Then Lord Justice Kay and Lord Justice A L Smith concur

Lord JAMES of HEREFORD What was the nature of the interference with the work there?

Mr MONTAGUE LUSH In Lyons v Wilkins it was picketing

Lord JAMES of HEREFORD The question was whether, as the picketing was carried out, it was legal or not?

Mr MONTAGUE LUSH Yes, and it was said there, "You are using an unlawful method of affecting your purpose," and the test was, the Court of Appeal held, that as the picketing was done there it was done with the view of preventing other people from working

The LORD CHANCELLOR By coercion?

Mr MONTAGUE LUSH Yes, in substance by coercion, and the Court of Appeal said, "When once you find that step proved, you have a cause of action" If you prevent other people from working by coercion——

Lord JAMES of HEREFORD That is by molestation?

Mr MONTAGUE LUSH Yes My reason for quoting it is to show that it is a mistake, as I submit here, to deal with this as if the only illegality we complained of on the 29th June was breaking contracts, because our case is—and I must go through my case before I confirm my reasons for saying it is right—that there was evidence for the Jury here that from the moment this strike was initiated, and right through down to the very end of it, the real object was not only a combination not to work, but a combination to prevent other people from working, and a combination to prevent the Colliery Company from getting work done in their mines

The LORD CHANCELLOR To prevent other people by molestation?

Mr MONTAGUE LUSH To prevent by molestation other people from working

The LORD CHANCELLOR I understand you

Mr MONTAGUE LUSH Now, my Lords, I will give your Lordships just one instance here on the evidence At page 659 (I am not going through the evidence, but I am just going to take passages as illustrative of what I say), Question 1044, one of the men—Chapman—was giving evidence, and when he goes up to the so-called resuming of work he is asked "Was anything said about signing on"? He had said the committee were standing there and were shouting at the people that were going by "Here, come here and fetch this paper—sign this notice paper" Then Question 1044 "Was anything said about signing on?—'You must not sign on' We were told not to sign anything Q Were you willing to sign on?—Yes Q. Did you sign on?—No Q Why not?—I was afraid of signing on" That is only an illustration, there is other evidence like it, but it is anticipating the date Of course this is later, but I submit this is an instance of how they were carrying out the purpose they formed on the 29th June—that they would prevent as far as they could until their grievances were settled——

The LORD CHANCELLOR Do you mean by molestation?

Mr MONTAGUE LUSH Yes, by threats

The LORD CHANCELLOR Let us distinguish If you persuade persons legitimately and peacefully, I imagine there is no objection to it

Mr MONTAGUE LUSH I agree

The LORD CHANCELLOR If you do anything in the nature of molestation or of threat, of course, that is unlawful

Mr MONTAGUE LUSH Yes, I quite accept that.

The LORD CHANCELLOR You mean that all through?

Mr MONTAGUE LUSH Yes

The LORD CHANCELLOR Then I will not ask any further question

Mr MONTAGUE LUSH If I may, in passing, refer to the language used in the speeches, at which Mr Wadsworth was present, when that word "rats" was used—that there were many rats present and they would come out of their holes—it sounds innocent, possibly, afterwards, but it must have been intended to frighten those who wanted to work to call them by that name I think Lyons v Wilkins was a case where there was a publishing of a black list by the men, which was treated as in itself an element of coercion If you do that which is intended to terrorise men into doing what you want them to do, it is all for the Jury, although I would ask your Lordships to say that we proved it I was giving these two questions, which are enough to justify, as I submit, my contention that it is not right to confine the illegality to the first movement, which is the breaking of contracts, but one must bear in mind that there was evidence here of an intention from the first—perpetually reiterated—to stop the wheels

Lord JAMES of HEREFORD It is very important I think you will only repeat yourself in your answer, but by stopping the wheels you mean preventing the work in the factory being carried on by any one?

Mr MONTAGUE LUSH By any one.

Lord JAMES of HEREFORD You have established that point

Mr MONTAGUE LUSH Yes—if I may put it again, because it is very important, of course, to prevent the Colliery Company from carrying on its business by making it impossible for the Colliery Company to get men to go down

Lord JAMES of HEREFORD Making it impossible to go down—is that in consequence of a portion of the works not working or in consequence of the molestation?

Mr MONTAGUE LUSH In consequence of the molestation and the combination of the men

Lord JAMES of HEREFORD The combination of the men effective in what degree—in doing what?

Mr MONTAGUE LUSH In preventing by threats, or intimidation or molestation

Lord JAMES of HEREFORD It comes round to molestation?

Mr MONTAGUE LUSH Yes, it comes round to that, if I may include in that calling men "rats" or "blacklegs", as long as I understand your Lordship to understand me to include that in "molestation"

Lord JAMES of HEREFORD. Yes, I do

Mr MONTAGUE LUSH The molestation of language

Now, my Lords, I come to what is really the important and vital question here Who is responsible for the illegalities which we submit were perpetrated? That is the real question, because Nolan and Humphries, of course, have Judgment against them The real question here, and that is what makes this case, of course, of first importance, is, Who is responsible? Are we right in saying that there was evidence that the Association were responsible? That is the real vital question Or are my learned friends right in saying that the only people responsible were the people who actually are proved—like Croft and Humphries for instance—to have intimated or been present when intimidation went on—or Nolan and Humphries who were present when the men were called out on the the 29th? That is the real contest between us Who is responsible for what was done?

My contention is that if the Association by its officers called the men out on the 29th and induced them to pass that resolution, I submit there is an end of the case—that the Association are responsible for all that followed because they acting through their officers did it

Lord JAMES of HEREFORD This would be what I think Mr Rufus Isaacs called the first period

Mr MONTAGUE LUSH Yes

Lord JAMES of HEREFORD And the Court of Appeal were against you on all

Mr MONTAGUE LUSH Yes, quite true Then of course they are equally responsible if they by their officers authorise unlawful things to be done as soon as they interfered I am afraid I have not put that very well

Lord JAMES of HEREFORD As you say they interfered from the first

Mr MONTAGUE LUSH Yes I was putting the second on the hypothesis that I am wrong in the first, I say if I am right in my first statement there is an end of the case, and I am right all the way through Now I ask your Lordships to wipe out that No 2, and let me put it again This is No 2 I must assume, I may be wrong, in saying their officers did it on the 29th, but on the assumption that I am wrong, then the Association would be liable if it ratified what these people did on the 29th That would cover the whole period, of course

Then there is the third alternative, which is the one the Master of the Rolls adopted—that if I am wrong in both these propositions— that is to say, if the officers were not their agents on the 29th, and if they did not ratify, then they would be responsible for a part of the period if they by their agents supported the men in carrying on this unlawful combination, either unlawful in object or unlawful in methods

Now comes the importance of appreciating where we differ— where our roads part—because my learned friend's case is, with regard to it, that you must divide this period into two They say that all that happened up to the—I forget the exact date, but the 15th July is roughly right—they say that all that happened up to that date happened through the acts of persons who were not agents of the Association at all, and they say that they could not in law, and did not, in fact, ratify Now they come to what is extremely important They say all that the Association did was exactly the opposite to what the Appellants say, they say the Association, so far from assisting in doing what was wrong, cured what was wrong—cured the wrong, the breach of contract that had been perpetrated, by persuading the men to go back to their work That is their case—that they put the wrong right—that they persuaded the men to go back to work, and that all they did afterwards was to advise them not to make fresh contracts That is the importance That is why I am going to ask your Lordships to let me a little closely analyse the evidence with regard to it They admit with regard to the payment of strike pay that the payment of it was wrong, because your Lordships have already decided that, but they say that was only a wrong as between the Association and its members, and that it was not an unlawful act I say it is one of the unlawful acts we rely upon I do not put in the foreground, but it is one As I submit, my Lord, it is not fair to take it only as a wrong between the Association and its members I say it was a wrong because it was a violation of the statutory rules which they were bound to follow But I do not want to put too much stress upon it Our case is strong enough, I submit, without it My learned friend, Mr Rufus Isaacs, read naturally enough the first part of my argument in the Court below Of course, if one reads a few lines apart from its context, it would look as if I put my whole case upon it in the Court of Appeal It is far from that, we do, and have always, relied on the wrongful payment of strike pay as one of the unlawful methods employed, but if we were wrong about that, it does not very seriously hurt my case

Those are the two views, and I want to ask your Lordships now to follow me as I endeavour to deal with them In order to deal with them I must defend myself for the third or fourth time— I forget which—against my learned friend's perpetually reiterated statement that we have introduced this 10 per cent to prejudice— he does not say intentionally, of course—I am sure he would not— but with the result of prejudicing the Jury, because he says it is irrelevant As I tell your Lordships, I have dealt with it three times before, and if your Lordships order a new trial I may have to deal with it again, but I submit it is an utterly erroneous conception I believe my learned friends—one of them—said I even opened this case to the Jury violently on the 10 per cent, but, inasmuch as I did not open it all, and Mr Bankes did, I do not think I need deal with that As a matter of fact, my Lord, there is one aspect to this case which makes it almost impossible even to suggest that this was not relevant Mr Rufus Isaacs read a bit of my speech, may I read a bit of his? Mr Rufus Isaacs made use of the contention against us that it was Mr Chambers's obstinacy in not meeting the men about the bag dirt after the 29th June that made the masters really responsible for this strike. This is what he said "One really would have thought that there was room, in what was to the employer a trumpery matter such as this, for making some trifling allowance, when the bag dirt was of this very hard, rocky character that we have heard it was, and which led to this discussion. But Mr Chambers would not have it. He would not have deputations about it, he took the stand of saying 'No, there is an end of the matter, I stand by my contract, I stand by my bond, you get nothing more'" A little later he said "The men apparently who were firmly determined and had made up their minds that there was no chance of getting their grievances settled, because they could not get Mr Chambers to do anything, took the view that their grievances would not be settled, and they said 'Very well, we will go back to work, but we shall have to give in our notices'" Now, if Counsel for the Defendants are asserting that it is the obstinacy of the employers in not meeting the bag dirt difficulty, and suggesting that if they had this strike would never have occurred to this length, if I am not at liberty in answer to that to say, "But that was not your reason, Mr Chambers said he knew the bag dirt was an excuse," surely it is legitimate for me in answer to that to retort and say, "You must be sure first that the bag dirt was your grievance, because you are asserting against the employers that they were so obstinate, and we say it was not your grievance at all, and everybody knew it"

Lord Justice Mathew has been strongly affected by that contention of my learned friend, because the part of his Judgment at page 1040 is only founded upon this assertion, that the bag dirt was all that was the trouble, and if we had only met them the strike would have ended. At the top of page 1040 Lord Justice Mathew says "The Council could exercise no control over the men, who were as obstinate as their employers" Now, the evidence is all one way. Mr Chambers tells us that he knew this to be an excuse, and knew it from the moment he heard of this strike. At page 605 he says so—Questions 576 and 577. So far from blaming the masters for not meeting the men, Mr Chambers took this view I said to him "Now, you were asked as to whether you believed, when you had the telegram announcing the strike, that the bag dirt was really the cause of it?—I did not believe it. I knew it was not. Q. What did you believe to be the cause?—What I said at the time I said, 'Here is that 10 per cent, that is the result of it'"

Lord DAVEY How is this evidence—that Mr Chambers thought?

Mr MONTAGUE LUSH I think I was re-examining him on his cross-examination. If your Lordships will look back to the cross-examination, you will see how it was introduced at page 569 Mr. Rufus Isaacs was cross-examining him at pages 569 and 570

Lord DAVEY   He may have thought that the agents were at the bottom of it

Mr MONTAGUE LUSH   But if you cross-examine a witness with a view to getting the Jury to think that it was his obstinacy in not meeting the men that caused the trouble

Lord DAVEY   His belief may prove that he was not obstinate

Mr MONTAGUE LUSH   That is the only reason

Lord DAVEY   But it does not prove the fact

Mr MONTAGUE LUSH   Not the least, absolutely not, I do not for a moment suggest it   At the moment I am showing that the charge of obstinacy against the masters which was not introduced by us was not well founded   I quite agree it does not touch the truth, at all events, I say, if it stood there alone, it is rather difficult to see that I can be blamed for repelling the statement

Lord DAVEY   I thought you referred to it as showing that the real cause of the strike was the 10 per cent?

' Mr MONTAGUE LUSH   No, I did not mean that for a moment   The reason why it was relevant was this   our case was that the branch officials got the men to come out and pass that resolution—that they procured the men of both branches to come out and stop the wheels until their grievances were remedied—it is necessarily very material to know what are the grievances, what is the thing they are to see put right before they will let the mine work   It is apparent that you must see what the grievance is   They were asserting that it was bag dirt, our case was that that was not the thing   "You never said you would go back to work, and you never meant you would go back to work when the bag dirt grievance was settled   What you were asserting and intending was to organise a strike at these branches just as had been going on at about twenty others, and to make the pits be idle until your whole wages were increased "   That was our case, and it is strong evidence that the men were not coming out voluntarily because they were affected by bag dirt, if we are right in saying there was something behind which was urging their leaders to get them out, not because of the bag dirt question at all, their leaders were getting the men out because they were discontented with the alteration in the wages   It shows why it was that the leaders chose the bag dirt, and I think I can make it, at least I will endeavour to make it, clear   The 64th Rule which I have read this morning made it a condition that before they got strike pay they should be able to show the Association that all possible means of remedying their grievances or to effect a settlement, as it is called, had been tried   If the employers refused to remedy the grievances, and if all proper means had been tried they could get strike pay if they could get the sanction, but they knew they had to say that of course. Now the bag dirt was a grievance they had been trying by peaceable means to settle, there had been deputations previously, and if your Lordships look at the resolutions at page 392, your Lordships will appreciate that the leaders of the branch were well aware of the importance in order to get strike pay, that they should choose something as to which they had endeavoured to remedy their grievance, and they put it themselves in their resolution at page 392 " That this meeting is of the opinion that the time has now arrived when some steps should be taken with reference to the reduction of men's wages for 'bag dirt,' and fines for different things at Denaby and Cadeby Collieries, and that having tried to come to some amicable understanding and failed, the only thing that is left for us to do is to stop the wheels ' So that they are putting into the resolution the statement that they had complied with that part of the rule which is one step towards strike pay. Having done that and passed the resolution, Mr Harry Hirst uses a most strange expression on this same page 392 " There was an understanding," he said to the men after the resolution had been passed, " that they ought to have a few words with reference to the wages question "—and then, having got the resolution put on bag dirt, he discussed the 10 per cent reduction. I submit that certainly there is strong evidence there that they got the men out on the bag dirt question, in order to make it possible to get strike pay by complying with that condition, but having done it they began to discuss with the men this 10 per cent difficulty

Lord JAMES of HEREFORD. Mr Lush, is it part of your case that the central body, the Barnsley people were a party to this, what we will call, substituted case

Mr MONTAGUE LUSH. No, my Lord, my case is that they were a party—the Master of the Rolls put it in much better language than I can—to cleverly getting an apparent healing of the wrong doing by getting the men back to work and then turning them into locked-out men

Lord JAMES of HEREFORD. That is not my point, were they party to putting forward ostensibly the bag dirt grievance, but intending to ask for the 10 per cent ?

Mr MONTAGUE LUSH. No, I do not think the Barnsley people knew at the time this took place what was going on, they could not

Lord JAMES of HEREFORD. Were the Barnsley people always kept in the dark ?

Mr. MONTAGUE LUSH. Of that I am not sure, there are reasons for answering it both ways. I do not want to make it part of my case, because I think it is left in obscurity

Lord JAMES of HEREFORD I will tell you why I ask you about it, both in relation to the central body and in relation to the branch body, inasmuch as Denaby and Cadeby were federated, they never could get any alteration of the 10 per cent reduction without the whole Federation coming in

Mr MONTAGUE LUSH No, but they could get the price list altered without disturbing the Award?

Lord JAMES of HEREFORD You must alter your form of argument, because you have been taking it as the 10 per cent argument

Mr MONTAGUE LUSH It may be my infirmity in answering, I rather avoid the 10 per cent, and what I meant was, that the real motive of the branch officials in getting the men out was to raise the wages I will not use the 10 per cent now

Lord JAMES of HEREFORD You must give us something definite, because they must ask for a definite end, and, mind you, you could not alter the 60 or 50 per cent, or whatever it was, except by a general alteration

Mr MONTAGUE LUSH Quite, but you could get the same result by altering the price list in other things, that is the point Might I just complete the answer,—that if you are discontented with the reduction of your wages by 10 per cent you will get that and something more if you can alter the price list on things which have not been the subject of the Award Every colliery has different price lists

Lord DAVEY Surely this new price list was not formulated or published or, that I can find, spoken of until September?

Mr MONTAGUE LUSH It was certainly spoken of, but that it was not formulated is I think very likely I want to make it quite clear what I mean, and I am not to go a bit further than I meant to go, what I say is that the materiality of the bag dirt being the real cause is this whether you say that the branch officials procured the men to come out, and resolved to stop the wheels until higher wages were got all round, or only until the bag dirt question was settled Our case is the former and it is very material to see that there were strikes at 22 collieries at this time when this reduction of wages was just coming into operation, and you find they were all affected by it because the boys were affected by it at the other 20 collieries There is a general spirit of striking and you find the leaders at these two branches saying "We will stop the wheels until our grievances are removed," which is not of course until the new price list be obtained, and you will find in September a new price list being published which is to give them the 10 per cent and something more

Your Lordship will remember the speech—I am not sure if it is Hirst—at page 392 When the resolution on the 29th June was passed, you find a reference by the speaker Nolan to the other strikes, which seems to me unintelligible unless they have some organised movement of this kind At letter B "They had men as good at Denaby and Cadeby as well as they had at South Kirkby, Hemsworth, or anything else" Now if your Lordships turn to Hall's cross-examination you will see those are places where these other strikes have just broken out At page 896, running through the places South Kirkby at letter B is one of them I do not know where Hemsworth is There is no evidence at all, and I am dealing with this evidence South Kirkby is one of the places where these strikes have broken out, and when the witness Hall was asked at page 898, Question 3284, the learned Judge puts the question "The Jury want to know" (because the Jury appreciated the point) "upon that Were the boy's wages dealt with by Lord James's Award," and the answer is, "They were, my Lord Q They had been reduced by his award?—They were reduced by his award" Of course, Mr Hall said that was not the point in dispute, but that was the question between us, and that is why I asked if it was a mere coincidence in the passages Mr Rufus Isaacs read

Lord JAMES of HEREFORD Is not the evidence that there was no absolute affirmative reduction by that vote, but that it was in consequence of the reduction of 10 per cent they did not get the rise of 1½d ?

Mr MONTAGUE LUSH Yes, quite true

Lord JAMES of HEREFORD. That is the only effect of it ?

Mr MONTAGUE LUSH Yes, but that is enough for my purpose, it was for the Jury who had the whole of these facts in mind, and I wanted this question answered, whether it was a mere coincidence, as the witness put it, that these strikes were breaking out all over the Federation at the time that your Lordships' decision was just operating The boys did not get a rise, and Mr Hall said that they were on six months' notice, but I pointed out that cannot have been the reason, because then six months' notice would expire at different times, the different boys were engaged on different notices

The LORD CHANCELLOR My impression is that if you develop your argument we will see it, I think there is probably a point where we will see it when your argument is developed Please develop it

Mr MONTAGUE LUSH At present I want to point out again why Nolan should have told the bag dirt strikers, if that was the real cause, that they had as good men as they had at South

Kirkby, when the men knew that the South Kirkby people were out on strike for wages and nothing more, and I submit that is at least evidence for the Jury—I do not want to put it higher than that—upon which the Jury could have come to this conclusion "You are putting the bag dirt forward in order to get strike pay, nothing more, you are choosing a grievance about which you have had, we agree, attempts to settle, and if you are to get the sanction of the Association for strike pay you must satisfy them that you have endeavoured to settle the grievance" Now, here is one ready to hand—bag dirt Now it is most important surely for me in supporting my case that this was a calling out of the men by the procurement of the branch officials with the intention that they would stop the wheels in the sense that they would prevent work until they could get the employers forced to raise wages It is most important for me, surely, to show that the way they set about it was by putting forward a shown pretext and getting the men to listen to an inflammatory speech and break their contracts, because they knew that if they had let the men consider this and ballot for it when they were at work, putting the bag dirt before them, which they were bound to do if they wanted strike pay, in 1901 the ballot had been against a strike and it would be again That is the force, as I submit, of our contention

Now, my Lords, that being so, I come now to deal with what is the evidence of procuring My submission is—I do not know if it is seriously contested—that the evidence that the branch officials, whatever the consequence may be in law, procured the men to come out, is overwhelming If your Lordships look at page 409, you will see in the presence of Wadsworth, who was sent down from the Union, and in the presence of Walsh, who was sent down from the Union, a statement was made and never contradicted, so that the Union knew it Harry Hirst said in their presence "They had brought the men out to prove to the district that they had grievances, and that they intended if they could get strike pay to get those grievances remedied before they took the men back to work" That is not the language which you would use if this was a voluntary strike by the men coming out because of bag dirt, it is a statement in the presence of gentlemen sent down specially by the Association that the branch officials had brought the men out and it was the branch officials who were to take the men back, and it is stated in the presence of these two representatives of the Barnsley Council that they would not take them back until they had got these grievances remedied That must, as I submit, have opened the eyes of Mr Wadsworth and Mr Walsh it must have led them to ask the question "What are the grievances which you are to get remedied before you are to take the men back?" I think I am right in saying that they had gone down from Barnsley accompanied by Nolan and Humphries, they had gone down in company of the men who had brought the men out on the 29th June, and they must have talked about it The Jury must have been entitled, as I submit, to say what I have done about this and therefore, I submit we have got here on July 15th notice, knowledge, that there was some movement on foot in connection with which the delegates had brought the men out, not that they had wanted to come and that they would not take them back until they got their grievances remedied, and, of course, they must have known, at least the Jury might well infer that they knew, that these same people, Nolan, had been telling the men on the 29th, "We have got as good men as there are at South Kirkby." So that at least these two gentlemen had the opportunity of knowing that this was an organised movement which was not going to end with bag dirt at all and was not going to end until wages were increased

If your Lordships again look at page 414 at letter B you find in September an appeal to the men's loyalty "He hoped every man would still be as loyal as on the 30th June, when he assisted in passing the resolution to stop the wheels" And again on page 442, at letter C, when Mr Walsh again says, "It was their duty now to stand by the strike Committee" (Walsh sent down again from Barnsley) "The Committee were men highly respected at head quarters, and it was the least they could do to support them"

Lord JAMES of HEREFORD Were the Strike Committee certain named persons of the branch?

Mr MONTAGUE LUSH They were the branch committee I think my Lord, we have their names in evidence Now, your Lordships have to add to that these two facts that the ballot was worked by the Committee in the sense your Lordships have heard, how they sat at a table and gave the papers out and so on, and the serving of the notices by the men when they went through the mere colourable device of pretending to go back to work without meaning to work The notices were served by the Committee On page 642 the witness Soar is asked at letter D "The men were going up to the table, were they?" (that is the working men) —"Yes Q And getting the notices?—Yes Q And then coming on?—Yes Q Did you see any of the Committeemen as you went up to work that morning?—Yes, I did Q Where did you see them?—I saw them running about amongst the men" Then he is asked if there had been anything said by the Committeemen, but that is not pursued I think, and at page 763 your Lordships will find Scott giving evidence about this, "I want to ask you about the 17th July—the day when the men signed the notices Were you going to the pit on that day, —Yes Q On your way to the pit did you see any of the Committeemen?—Yes Q Who were they?—Smith, James Birch and a man named Stokes Q Where were they when you saw them?—On a little plot of land that lies off the highway, just by Mr Soar's house Q Had they got a table?—They had a table there, and Smith and these men were round it, and they called me and said 'Scott come here, we we want you to sign one of these notices to go and give your notice, us will get our Union pay if we sign these notices' I said

'What are you giving notice for, you are not employed here, you have left their employ' Q What did you say when he said he wanted you to give notice?—I said how can you give notice when you are not employed there I said, 'You must work there before you can give notice,' and they made an answer to me as the reason they were not going to sign on was that the Company had brought a new rule out, which was to the effect that any one signing on signed on for 12 months" (of course, nobody suggested that this was true, they were telling the men this, but nobody suggested that they were doing other than misleading the men for the purpose of preventing them going back to work, there was no 12 months at all) "I asked them if they had seen that rule, and they said 'Yes,' I said 'Well, I cannot believe you I shall go and see for myself, and shall believe myself It is ridiculous if I have got to sign on for 12 months I can understand giving 14 days' notice, but as far as regards signing for 12 months, I cannot agree with it' Q What happened then?— I left them and proceeded through the crossing, and I met a man called Nolan Q Is that a Committeeman?—Yes He asked me if I had got my notice I said, 'No, I do not need one' He said, 'You b ——— y old cripple, you want to take a notice,' and I said, 'I shan't take one' I said, 'I do not see what there is to give notice for I have not got anything to include your grievances at all, as far as it concerns me, they have been all right to me, and I am going to see what is the difference between signing on now and signing on before,' He told me I should have to sign on for 12 months," and so on I only quote that as one instance There is one more I can give your Lordships about it at page 709, where Gill says he is "a dataller,' a man employed not to get coal, but to look after the roads

The LORD CHANCELLOR Both those passages have already been read

Mr MONTAGUE LUSH Then I will not trouble to read them again except to refer your Lordship to the fact that Nolan again tells this man when he is coming out that they had had the meeting that morning and settled to stop the wheels

I need not read your Lordships more, but may I without reading it call your Lordships' attention to page 42 of the Appellants' case, because we have there collected at some trouble and given pages, if they would be any assistance to your Lordships, of the references to all the cases in which the branch officials of both branches were present when anything was done about the men's giving notice or intimidation being exercised, and so on From page 42 to page 47 of the Appellants' case your Lordships will find the evidence that there is with the pages against it showing, and I think I may say it is correct, all the instances in which the officials of the branch took part in these various matters

So far I submit we have given evidence which entitled the Jury to find, and I submit they could not do other than find, that the branch officials, whatever it is worth, procured the men to pass these resolutions about stopping the wheels Now comes the first important question If that is true were they the officers and agents of the Union to do it? Or again, to put it more accurately, was there evidence on which the Jury could find that they were? Were they the officers and agents of the Union to do it? As I said before, If I prove that, I submit we prove all we have got to prove

Now, I would remind your Lordships—Mr Bankes put it very clearly—how the matter stands with regard to this The Act of Parliament requires in the schedule a registered Trade Union to provide for the appointment of officers of the Union, and your Lordships find here that the constitution of this Union is a mere assemblage of branches and nothing more There is no central controlling body at all, as I submit It is not as if there was a central board of directors, and that the branch officials were mere managers or employees—that is not the constitution, in this Union there was no centre and it is mere branches, it is governed in that way Taking the officers appointed under the rules here, the treasurer or the secretary of the Union is no more of an officer of the Union than the secretary of the branch, they merely perform different functions They are all the officers of the Union, which the Act of Parliament requires them to fill in

My Lord, my submission is—it is for your Lordships of course to deal with this—that this is the real important point of law perhaps in the case, the first important point of law, that the agents, or rather the officials of the branch are the Union for the purpose of performing those duties which are by the rules delegated to the officials of the branch There is nobody else Now, Rule 72 is the rule which shows how a strike shall be initiated and conducted This is one of the Union rules, it is not a rule of the branch but a rule of the whole Association, and Rule 72, which I have read a few minutes ago provides for the branch officials being the only persons, the directors, not the servants, who can under the rules initiate a strike or call the men out If it is to be done at all nobody else can do it, and the central body have nothing to do with it The function of the Central Advisory Board, which consists of the delegates who alone can vote with the assistance and advice of a few other paid officials, begins when the question of strike pay is considered, not before, and they have nothing on earth, I submit, to do with the strike If the men were out on strike, and they did not want strike pay the Council would never be consulted, and therefore in calling the men out, in inducing them to break their contracts, and in getting them to pass that resolution, my humble submission to your Lordships is that it was the Union doing it through their officers

Some criticism, I think, has been passed, or some suggestion has been made (I would rather put it in this way) that there was no finding of the Jury that in doing that the branch officials were acting as agents of the Union But, my Lords, I submit that that follows without saving if I am right in the first positon If the Directors of a Company, or any other head of the Company, not a servant, if the head of the concern does an act, the only ground upon which you can name assistants is to know whether these men were doing it merely as item units, as workmen, or the antithesis, whether they were doing it as the branch officials That is the only possible antithesis, of course, I quite agree that some of these men who are both workmen and officials might be doing something in their capacity as workmen to earn wages, and so on, but when once you have got that antithesis answered there is nothing else left My learned friends are always treating the branch officials as if they were in the position of the paid employees at directors' meetings, but that is not their capacity, they are not servants but principals If one is to compare principal and agent or master or servant it is the paid officials, if anybody, who only advise, and who are subordinate to them, but I say they are subordinate to nobody, and that these general branch officials when they act are the Union acting No question can be asked as to whether they are acting within the scope of their authority, because they are not servants, they are heads Then secondly, I submit that, although I quite agree, and I think Mr Bankes has already stated it, that that question—I forget which it was, but I think it is No 5, in which we suggested that the Jury should be asked whether in doing what they did they purported to act——

Lord DAVEY Two and four

Mr MONTAGUE LUSH I beg your Lordship's pardon I quite agree, as Mr Bankes said, because of course we considered these questions before they were formulated, that what we had in mind was with a view to our being wrong upon the point we are now taking and having to fall back upon ratification Then it covers this ground as well, I think Lord Robertson pointed out that it covers the ground as well, because if one wants to know whether these people were acting in their capacity of officers of the Union, it is obvious that if the Jury found they were purporting to do it they did do it If you only want to find out in what capacity they intended to act, the answer to 2 and 4 cover it, but my submission is that we did not need it if once we realised that they were principals and not servants

That being so I would ask your Lordships to bear in mind what was decided by the Court of Appeal in what has been called Giblan's Case—Giblan v The National Amalgamated Labourers' Union reported in 1903, 2 King's Bench 600 That very point was decided by the Court of Appeal, and I submit that your Lordships are, in effect, being asked to say it is wrong Lord Justice Vaughan Williams there at page 617 [said 'There can be no doubt but that the Plaintiff Giblan was prevented from getting or retaining work, by reason of the facts which I have narrated, at various works where members of the Union were employed, but not elsewhere On this two questions seem to arise First, can the action of those who brought about this result be justified " (I need not trouble about that) "There remains the question of the liability of the Union and Toomey I think they are both liable The Union, Williams and Toomey were all parties to acts constituting an actionable wrong—namely, interference with Giblan in the exercise of his undoubted common law right to dispose of his labour according to his will It is said that the rules did not authorise the acts of Williams and Toomey, but, be that how it may, the acts were not *ultra vires* of the Union but only of its officers, and the Union in general meeting undoubtedly adopted the acts of Williams and Toomed and took the benefit of them

I submit that I do not know that it has been contended here that in bringing the men out on the 29th the branch officials were acting *ultra vires* of the Union, they could not be May I point out how inconsistent such a contention as my learned friend's argument about the strike pay is They say with regard to the illegality of the strike pay that these rules are nothing but contracts, and if you are paying money wrongly you are only breaking contracts and nothing more If that is true of that it is *a fortiori* true of the Strike Rule 72, because if it is not more than a breach of contract paying the strike money, how much more true is it to say that they were only as officers doing what under their contractual obligations towards the members they ought not to have done in calling the men out in the way they did In any case, my Lords, inasmuch as they are the Union who have delegated to them by the rules the responsibility of initiating a strike and deciding under what circumstances to initiate it, it is, as I submit, clear, as Lord Justice Vaughan Williams in Giblan's case said "If they are doing that class of acts in a way which is contrary to their real duty, they may be acting *ultra vires* themselves, but it does not show the Union were not competent to do it " And I submit, therefore, we have got now to this stage, that the initial act was the act of the officers of the Union acting within their powers under the rules, that they were certainly acting in the capacity of officers of the Union their references to strike pay for the men and so on demonstrate it, and thirdly they were agents acting in that capacity, and if they were not performing their duties under the rules until the strike was started, that is merely that they were committing a breach of duty, and an access of power, and it was not in the least true to say that what they did was beyond the powers or competency of the Union itself

The LORD CHANCELLOR Before you finish your argument, as we are now going to rise, will you just consider this one point which has troubled me According to your argument supposing that these branch officials procured this strike, and supposing the central officials knew nothing of it, deprecated it and did their best, as found by the Jury, to stop it and refused to pay any strike pay in support of it, your argument, I suppose, is that still they are liable for damages caused by the strike

Mr MONTAGUE LUSH I am much obliged to your Lordship

(Adjourned for a short time)

Mr MONTAGUE LUSH My learned friend, Mr Danckwerts, has asked me to call attention to something which he thinks would a little correct my statement about the price list I will just give your Lordships the reference to it, I do not propose to read it or argue it, and I think my learned friend will be content if I just give your Lordships the pages At page 314 there is the price list set out, which was introduced apparently in April, 1901 The page before, page 313, shows how it came about, and your Lordships will find, if I again may only refer to the page, that Mr Chambers is cross-examined about it, and gives explanations with regard to it, at page 545 and the following pages There are certain small details in which it differs from the September one, I do not do more than call your Londships' attention to it

Lord JAMES of HEREFORD What I did want to know is, is it a general price list, or a Denaby price list?

Mr MONTAGUE LUSH Denaby and Cadeby only I did endeavour to make the point this morning, my Lord, that the alteration of the price list would only affect the particular colliery, and that it would not mean an alteration all through

Now, if I may go back and just finish what I had to say about the question of agents *ad hoc*, I have submitted what I have to submit about it, but in the case of Nevill *v* the Fine Art Company, 1897, Appeal Cases, page 68, your Lordships will find, at page 76, the Lord Chancellor expressing his view as to what should be done if a question has not been left to the Jury which ought to have been left, to explain another that has been left It is said against me, or it has been suggested that we ought to have asked the Jury to find that these branch officials were acting within the scope of their power or authority My submission is that we were not obliged to do so for the reasons I have endeavoured to give, that they are not mere servants, but they are the officers If it be true it ought to have been left, my view is that what the Lord Chancellor says at page 76 of this case of Nevill would apply, "That would, but for what I am about to say, give the Appellant only a right to ask for a new trial, which, though he has not asked for it, it is no doubt within your Lordships competence to give him, but what puts him out of court in that respect is this, that where you are complaining of non-direction of the Judge, or that he did not leave a question to the Jury, if you had an opportunity of asking him to do it and you abstained from asking for it, no Court would ever have granted you a new trial, for the obvious reason that if you thought you had got enough you were not allowed to stand aside and let all the expense be incurred and a new trial ordered simply because of your own neglect " What I would submit here is that if it was necessary in fact to put a question which would tend to cut down the authority and showing they were not acting *ad hoc* as agents, my submission is that it was for those who would rely upon that and who had the opportunity because the learned Judge did consult them to ask that that question should be put

Now, if I might pass to the next point, assuming I am wrong in what I have said, namely, that the branch officials were officers, I submit at all events there was confirmation or ratification of what they did by the Association Your Lordships, the Lord Chancellor, asked just before the adjournment what should I say if a case like this occurred the branch officials initiate a strike, and the Central Council (I do not like to call them central, because I submit it is not accurate, but the Council) are all opposed to it, and they will not sanction strike pay but do their best to stop the strike while the branch officials persist in it I gather that is the question your Lordship put Well, my submission is that until the body can put in force Rule 12, and get a vote which will effectively put a stop to it, they are from the necessities of the case liable for the wrong doing of the branch officials It often happens, of course, that a person who has a co-ordinate jurisdiction with others, like an executor with his co-executors or a director with his co-directors, a managing director, say, may do a thing which may be utterly opposed to the wishes of the rest of the board or the wishes of the other executors, but until they can get it set right it is no answer to say if the whole body are sued, " we were opposed to it," and my submission here is that the key to this problem, the key to this position, lies in the fact that these various branch officials are officers of the Union

Now, I come to this question of ratification, and that embraces two questions—first, could they in law ratify, second, did they, in fact, assuming they could, do it? Now, with regard to the question, could they in law ratify, my submission is that by the case of Keighley Maxsted *v* Durant in your Lordships' House, although you have not, of course, expressly said they could, your Lordships have by implication said so Might I put two illustrations apart from authority? The law with regard to contracts is clear, of course, since your Lordships decided the Keighley Maxsted, that if a person means to be making a contract which another can ratify, he must say so either expressly or impliedly to the other contracting party, and the reason is this, that the contract consists of the consensus of two minds, and it is obvious that it is irrelevant to say what was in the mind of one if not communicated to the other Consensus being the foundation of the right to adopt, or ratify, rather, it stands to reason that that which you conceal in your own mind can be no evidence at all of the consensus of the two, and, therefore, your Lordships held in Keighley Maxsted that it had always been the law that if it is intended to contract on behalf of B without authority it is not enough to think it, he must convey the impression to the other, because it is contract, it is consensus   But if you take another case, take the case of the ratification of a tort, which has always been possible at law, let me put a case and show how it is impossible to do it, and how irrelevant it would be to do it   You do not want the consensus of the two minds to create a liability for a tort, it is your own wrong doing and not the mind of another that is concerned   Suppose A owns a private road and that the public think it is a public road, and somebody acting with that intention puts a barrier across it, and a friend of A, knowing that A is asserting it is a private road, thinking A may lose some benefit if it is not removed, removes it for A, tells him at once he has done it and has incurred expense, and A pays the expense and says to the person who put it up " I will take proceedings against you for putting it up ; I have had it removed," it is obvious upon facts like that that if the public assert a right to it he can assert a right to have an Injunction to stop its being done again, or if they issued a writ against him for removing their barrier, he has adopted that act, and it is impossible in law to say that, because the man who removed it did not say in the air—there was nobody to say it to—" I am doing this for A," he is not purporting to do it for A   He has got nobody to say it to, and there is no need to say it   He is not asking another to consent, which is the case of a contract   He is intending to do something for A's benefit ; he tells A at once that he has done it, and A recoups him his expenses and adopts what he has done   It has always been the law ; I submit that is a ratification

Take another case, the case of a distress for rent, which is a common case in which these questions have occurred   If somebody were to put in a distress for rent for the landlord, knowing that the landlord wishes it, although he has not authorised it, but he does it intending to do it as a distress for the landlord's rent, tells the landlord he has done it, and the landlord retains the proceeds, can it be said that he has not adopted it ?   In the case of Keighley Maxsted, I am sure Lord Robertson, and I think some of your Lordships in addition, expressly pointed out that what your Lordships were deciding did not touch the case of a tort   At page 260 of 1901 Appeal Cases, where Keighley Maxsted's case is reported, Lord Robertson says, " The other texts from the Digest cited by Collins, L J , relate to torts, and the juridical considerations which ought to determine liability or non-liability for a tort acceded to *ex post facto* by the person in whose interest it has been committed are not the same as apply to a man being introduced into a contract with a third party, although the word ratification in its Latin equivalents may with propriety be applied to describe his accession in the one case as in the other   But again I must add that I fail to find in any of those passages any discussion of the question now agitated, or anything implying that the person injured did not know that the wrong was done in the service of the person who ultimately ratifies." If the word "adoption" were used instead of "ratification" that apparent confusion between contracts and torts might, I submit, have been avoided.

Then, in Wilson v Tumman, the case which has been referred to by my learned friend Mr Danckwerts, in 6 Manning and Granger, page 236, the Lord Chief Justice at page 242, dealing with this question of the ratification of a tort, says this: "That an act done *for another* by a person, not assuming to act for himself, but for such other person, though without any precedent authority whatever, becomes the act of the principal if subsequently ratified by him, is the known and well established rule of law. In that case the principal is bound by the act, whether it be for his detriment or his advantage, and whether it be founded on a tort or a contract, to the same extent as by, and with all the consequences which follow from, the same act done by his *previous* authority. Such was the precise distinction taken in the year book 7 Henry IV, fo 35—that if the bailiff took the heriot, claiming property in it himself, the subsequent agreement of the lord would not amount to a ratification of his authority as bailiff at the time; but if he took it at the time as bailiff of the lord the subsequent ratification by the lord made him bailiff at the time." That refers to intention, and that being so my submission is that in law it could be done. The question is has it been done? Assuming again that the officers of the Union were not their agents when they called their men out, have the Association adopted what they did? Now my submission is that there was ample evidence on which the Jury could find that they did. It is enough, as I submit, for me to call attention as I have already done to the fact that they were even at the very first speech on June 29th referring to the fact they would get strike pay for the men, and referring to the fact that it would be a Federation job, as they did at page 389. "They would stop throughout the Federation, and they would do right if they never started until they got 60 per cent." And on the page before they said "It was beautiful weather and they could stand it. They had stood it" before, and so on. At page 410 the speaker Croft says "Mr Pickard had the opinion that it would have to be a Federation job again as it was in 1893. (A Voice 'That's what we want.') It would soon be all over then. If they did not get their grievances remedied they would stop out at Denaby."

On July 7th they had already said they would get strike pay, which means they were doing it in their character as officials. They could not get the strike pay unless they showed that the men had been called out under the rules, that is to say, that all possible means had been used, and so on; and at page 404 Mr Walsh uses language which I submit is only possible if in fact they considered they were ratifying what had been done. Mr Walsh had come down from Barnsley, and he said at page 404, F "Your grievances are burning grievances, and your management" (that means the branch officials) "have not been so discreet as the majority of managements are in Yorkshire" Then he refers to what should happen about their taking a ballot, and then he refers to there being rats in the branch

Then, my Lord, I submit that that payment of the strike pay, if one considers how it was paid, is evidence of ratification, because your Lordships will remember that at one of these earlier speeches the speakers had referred in Mr Wadsworth's presence to the difficulty that the Taff Vale decision had created, and they said 'You would have had your strike pay now if it was not for that" It is impossible to say they did not ratify if they were entitled in law to ratify

Now, my Lord, I am getting towards the end, and I now come to a very important chapter indeed in the history of this case, and I shall have to ask your Lordships to kindly let me a little analytically refer to documents and a little of the evidence, not very much The case for the Respondents, as I have said, is "The Association when they interfered, put the wrong right, they urged the men to go back to work and they never allowed strike pay to be given until they had gone back and the masters would not take them in" I am now going to show, as I submit I can, to your Lordships that those who were responsible at Barnsley at the time—Mr Pickard was very ill, and your Lordships remember he was too ill, as was said in a speech, to go down—but those who were in fact acting as the Advisory Board at Barnsley did in fact delegate to these branch officials if they were not the officers before, as I say they were, the carrying on of this strike and when it was found that strike pay was clamoured for and could not be got unless the sanction of the Association was given, the Association, as I shall endeavour to show, gave their sanction to that which was merely colourable, merely a sham They never got the wrong put right, they could not, they were swept along by the strong force that was being brought to bear and they lent themselves to what the Court of Appeal have already called a sham pretence of going back to work

My Lords, when Howden's case was before the Court of Appeal we were obliged to go into this same matter that I am going into now, and Lord Justice Mathew, who has taken a different view in this case, expressed himself in this language with regard to this pretended curing of the wrong It is 1903, 1 King's Bench, page 333, about two-thirds of the way down the page "But the resolution passed by the men and the correspondence clearly show that the men never meant to resume work as before the strike, but only intended to go back for the purpose of putting the strike which had already commenced in order under Rule 64 It would have been a sham return and a sham resumption of work The employers, knowing from the statement of the men themselves what their object was, positively declined to restore the old contract, the repudiation of which they had already accepted." I find that is Lord Justice Vaughan Williams, but at page 343 Lord Justice Mathew uses similar terms, at the bottom of the page "The proposal to resume employment was a sham under such circumstances, and the men never got back to their employment." Now, I want to ask your Lordships to follow and see how the Council under this pressure were obliged to act. At page 342 your Lordships will find the first reference to a communication to the Barnsley Council. It began with the application for strike pay—lock-out pay, rather—for three men. "These men are locked out from the pit," said Mr Smith, the Denaby official, and in the case of one letter of the 11th he says to Mr Pickard, "I am instructed to ask you to bring before Council meeting"——

Lord DAVEY. It was stated in the evidence that this letter did not come before the Council when they determined to send Mr Wadsworth.

Mr MONTAGUE LUSH. I had forgotten that, I was not here at the time, but there were two letters of that date. I think I am right in saying that there is no evidence at all that those two letters did not come before the Council. I think that must have been suggested under a misapprehension.

Mr DANCKWERTS. It is quite right, these letters did not come before the Council.

Mr MONTAGUE LUSH. Either of them? I think my learned friend is wrong. I do not think he is right about this.

Lord DAVEY. Do not let me interrupt you.

Mr MONTAGUE LUSH. I think Mr Danckwerts is referring to a different letter. The evidence, as I understand it, is that these letters did come before the Council. This letter I am referring to is "I am instructed to ask you to bring before Council Meeting the case of the Denaby Main Miners. You will have heard that the pit has been stopped owing to the excessive tyranny that has been imposed upon the men and also through the stoppages that have been made off the men's wages for the so-called bag dirt."

The LORD CHANCELLOR. These letters have been read twice?

Mr MONTAGUE LUSH. Yes, I will not read them again.

The LORD CHANCELLOR. I want to follow your point.

Mr MONTAGUE LUSH. I wanted to read that to show your Lordship that Barnsley is told that the bag dirt is not all they have struck for "excessive tyranny," and also during the speeches other subjects than bag dirt The second letter on page 343 is a little more important, and that has not been read I am told and I attach some importance to that

Lord DAVEY It has been read

Mr MONTAGUE LUSH Then, my Lord, the only passage I wish to remind your Lordships of is between D and E "We have tried all that lays in our power to get the grievance remedied" (that is a reference to the same thing again, and as I pointed out they knew they would have to give it) "but have failed, Mr Chambers saying that if it was only 2½d we wanted he would not give it to settle the case So our branches think that the time has come when some stand should be taken to get a revised price list, a list that the men can understand, and seeing that we are now out in the field it ought to be thoroughly gone into before we commence again, and we are now making application for strike pay," and then there is the statement that they hope the Council will grant the strike pay

Turning back now to page 228, you find the resolution of the 14th July, the language of which is important "That Messrs Wadsworth and Walsh accompany Messrs Nolan and Humphries to a meeting to be held to-morrow morning at 11 o'clock, and tell the men that they must resume work and then take a ballot" That is what Barnsley, in the presence of Mr Wadsworth requested "You must not let the men while they are on strike take a ballot, let them get back to work and then ballot" Now at the meeting itself on page 404 your Lordships will find how that advice was really thrown to the winds by Messrs Walsh and Wadsworth They had gone down with Nolan and Humphries, and the advice given by Walsh and Wadsworth, backed up as I say by references to "rats," people who were not going to vote for a continuation of the strike, was exactly the opposite of what had been recommended by the Council and at the bottom of page 404, at the last line Walsh says "What you try and do is to take a ballot of yourselves within the rules, give in your notices and come out" He does not say "go to work first," and Mr Wadsworth carries it a step further, because he at page 408 puts it point blank that they are to take a ballot before going back to work That is just the opposite of what he had come down to do They really wished to quiet the men He says at letter D "If they took their advice they would agree to return to work at as early a date as possible, and in the meantime they would take a ballot of the men Take a ballot to-day" It did not matter as trade unionists whether they balloted in work or out, but it made all the difference, as I endeavoured to point out this morning, when the Council see the necessity, if they wish to stop the strike, of getting the men back to work first and balloting afterwards, Messrs Wadsworth and Walsh, who had come with Nolan and Humphries, and clearly intended that the strike should go on, give the exactly opposite advice to the men "Go back to work at any early date, and in the meantime ballot take it to-day"

Now, my Lords, the ballot was taken, and I need not remind your Lordships of the importance of the difference of phraseology. The usual form of ballot, as it has been pointed out, was to take a ballot as to whether you would give the notice to terminate your contract of employment. I will just give your Lordship the page— 189 I think it is, and your Lordship will find there the usual form of ballot. The usual form of ballot is "Are you in favour of giving 14 days' notice to terminate your contract?" which implies the men are at work. The one given in this particular case is on page 195 "Are you in favour of giving 14 days' notice, until such time as your grievances are remedied?" The men could not terminate their contracts—they were not at work. That is the ballot paper that is given.

Now, turning back to the correspondence and seeing how it is worked out, at page 344, on the 15th July there were a few telegrams that passed, in which Mr Chambers was saying "The pits are open when the men wish to resume work", and Mr Wadsworth telegraphs. "Men agree to resume work and terminate notices"

Now, my Lord, why I said the meeting was in the morning is a little important, this telegram was sent after the meeting, and Mr Wadsworth has been present at the meeting, at which he has advised the men not to go back to work first and then ballot, but precisely the opposite. To ballot first, and he is sending this telegram "Men agree to resume work and terminate notices" That is on the 15th. Over the page, the next day, comes now for the first time an intimation that there is a difficulty said to have arisen about signing on. Mr Smith from Denaby writes to Mr Pickard saying that they had been told the men "cannot start work until they have signed a 'Contract Book' with a heading on it which we have not heard of before" Your Lordship has read it?

The LORD CHANCELLOR Yes, it has been several times read, I do not for a moment want to prevent your referring to it, but tell us the point on it?

Mr MONTAGUE LUSH The point is that the men are said to be asked to sign a contract book with a fresh heading on it, that is the point That is followed by the telegrams which your Lordships have already read, and which I do not want to read again Turning to page 230 on the same date, July 17th, when the men are presenting themselves at the lamp room, comes this resolution of the Cadeby Branch, which shows that Croft and Humphries are agitating for the continuation of the strike, it shows that they have seen Mr Pickard and have discussed with him about the employers refusing to let them resume work until they have signed a fresh contract. You will observe at the end of the resolution there is an adherence to the old resolution to stop the wheels.

On the same date, 17th July, page 409, Mr Croft makes a speech to the men saying that Mr Pickard "was heart and soul with them" (at letter D) "Mr Pickard said 'They had done perfectly right not to sign, and telling the men not to sign on under any circumstances, and to go every morning to the pit to every shift, and they would see what they could do'" That is the position on the 17th. Now, my Lords comes a very important little incident. On page 663 your Lordships will find that a man named Smeaton had been on the 16th to the lamp room. Question 1102 "What happened after you told them that?—I showed them these rules that I had" (these were new printed books of rules which now had printed among the ordinary print the Home Secretary's Order which had come into force in 1901 about having the timber within 30 yards) "One of them read them. Then I took them home after he had given me them back. Then in the night I was down again at the Ferry Booth and a party asked me 'Have you got these rules'"? Then after some discussion the learned Judge said "The short question would be where is the book now?—The last time I saw the book it was in Messrs Raley's office in Barnsley" (these were the Solicitors to the Association). So that your Lordships observe that Mr Pickard had seen it. On going back to page 346 Mr. Pickard writes or telegraphs to Smith on that same date that the rules were sent to the solicitor's office, at letter C "I adhere to my telegram" (he is quoting Mr Chambers now) "Present yourselves for work at every shift. Consulting Solicitors. Either send or bring first thing in the morning the two copies of rules, those you are working under and the new one you are expected to sign. Don't fail to go to work, and don't sign any new rules."

Now, my Lord, he consults the solicitor. Having got the rules sent up from the men, if there was any truth or substance in the suggestion that they had got a new heading on, Mr Pickard and the solicitors saw it for themselves. You see Mr Pickard absolutely throws away this suggestion about their being asked to sign a new contract with a new heading on. After he must have looked at the rules he telegraphs on Page 346 on the next morning, July 18th a totally different reason for advising the men not to sign. "Why should men sign on again? Is not the contract they previously signed still existing"? He has thrown over this point, because nobody can suggest there was any reality in this story about the heading.

The LORD CHANCELLOR: I do not see the throwing over in the least.

Mr MONTAGUE LUSH He does not mention it in the telegram, he takes a different point

Lord DAVEY What did they want to sign a new contract for?

Mr MONTAGUE LUSH The evidence is all one way about that

Lord DAVEY· And I say that is what Mr Pickard says

Mr MONTAGUE LUSH But he gives his reason

Lord DAVEY Yes.

Mr MONTAGUE LUSH His reason is this—not that you are altering the contract, but he says "The old contract is still existing"

Lord DAVEY It is still existing

Lord JAMES of HEREFORD That makes the new one immaterial

Lord DAVEY He evidently did not wish them to sign the new one.

Mr MONTAGUE LUSH But the point is he says it is not a new contract now

The LORD CHANCELLOR Mr Lush, because he says there is no occasion to sign any contract that is not abandoning the position that if they had signed it it would be signing a new contract, at least I respectfully suggest that

Mr MONTAGUE LUSH I am much obliged, but that is not the point

The LORD CHANCELLOR That is all I meant by the question

Mr MONTAGUE LUSH That is not the point I mean, the point I make is this, that there were two reasons given at different times for the men not signing I am going to show they were neither of them reasons which could have been thought to be sound The first one was "There is a new heading on the book now,' and that could not be thought to be sound because there was not, and the evidence is all one way about it—the timbering rules which are the new element of contract suggested were not new because the men had had their books with those gummed on them since the Home Office passed them in 1901, there was no new heading, but it was simply that these rules were printed in ordinary type instead of being gummed on The second reason was that the men had never ceased to be servants which is totally different

Lord JAMES of HEREFORD Will you show where their signatures have been attached to the first set of rules with these Home Office Regulations which are referred to?

Mr MONTAGUE LUSH We have got the book and your Lordship will see how they sign The contract book has got the heading on it In the book are actually bound the Acts of Parliament which were in force under the Mines Regulation Act, and the men signed The men go on working for a couple of years when a new rule comes into force, and unless you are to reprint the book and make everybody re-sign it, you have got to give them something which will show them the new rule, and yet not require the necessity of their signing the book again

Lord JAMES of HEREFORD That is the point, they do not sign that they will be subject to these conditions whether it is within or without the power of the Home Office to make them

Lord DAVEY They did not sign a book as I understand which contained either gummed on loose or otherwise this particular Order of the Secretary of State, but they did sign a book to abide by all the regulations made under the Mines Regulation Act?

Mr MONTAGUE LUSH · True

Lord DAVEY All this was one?

Mr MONTAGUE LUSH Yes, but this would equally show them whether they sign it or not The question is whether the Jury could upon this evidence come to the conclusion that this difficulty about signing the book with a new heading was a sham or not a sham The Court of Appeal have held that the whole thing was a sham in Howden's case, and your Lordships are now asked to say there was no evidence on which the Jury could find it, and I suppose no evidence on which the Court of Appeal in Howden's case could hold it

Lord DAVEY But they had not this evidence before them.

Mr. MONTAGUE LUSH. The evidence on this point was the same, my Lord, the witnesses were called and the same point was gone into in Howden's case precisely. Here is the book, and the point is this. Supposing these men were asked to re-sign the book, as the evidence shows they were bound to do, if they went back to work they could not help themselves as they could not be away for three days, my point is that inasmuch as Mr. Pickard after looking at the rules does not say to Mr. Chambers "Let them sign the book without this new timbering rule at all," but states his ground, and says "They have never left your employ,' that is, I submit, evidence that the Barnsley Association did not in earnest expect the men to go back. That is all. The answer is that it is the regular custom to sign again, that is what Mr. Chambers answers. If Mr. Pickard had meant "That is not the point, you are putting a new rule upon them," he would have said so, but his answer is not that, his answer on page 347 is "The men have not left your employment, and therefore why should they sign on again?" I submit there is evidence on which the Jury could find that that was not genuine, because men who have been out since the 29th June who have resolved to stop the wheels and who have reiterated that resolution, could not, as I submit, really seriously be said to be still in the employment of the Colliery Company.

That is the evidence with regard to it, and the answer is that the Jury were well warranted in inferring from that the fact, as they did infer, that this never was an intended sending back of the men to work at all, but that it was a desire to bring the men, if they could, within the privileges of strike pay without rendering themselves liable to the action which they said themselves would lie. My Lords, that is confirmed by two or three letters that passed at the end. On the same page 347 comes an important letter of the 21st July, after all this attempt to patch up the difficulty has been gone through. The letter has been read, but Mr. Pickard, as your Lordship sees, told Mr. Smith there, "We cannot recommend you to sign on again." His only reason, as shown in the telegram above, was that the men had never ceased to be in the employment of the Colliery Company, which I suppose was the men's view, but he says, "We cannot recommend you to sign on again," and then he speaks as he does in that letter. On the next day Smith replies in a very important letter, dated July 22nd "I am instructed to ask you if it would be possible to get a week's strike pay for our men. We have played six days on Wednesday, July 23rd, 1903, and seeing that our men have not had a pay day for one month, they are getting uneasy and will doubtless break away and sign the contract book." That shows the men were willing enough to sign.

Lord DAVEY. There is the letter which was not brought before the Council, it is shown at page 794.

Mr MONTAGUE LUSH   I was not aware, but I follow what your Lordship says   I am told by my learned friend Mr Waddy that Mr Isaacs accepted full responsibility for the letter   At page 868 there is a reference to it where Mr Isaacs says, "Whether it was produced or not, it was intended to be produced, and it no doubt, at any rate, was before Mr Pickard, and I take the responsibility of it for the Association"

Lord DAVEY   Who says so?

Mr MONTAGUE LUSH   This is Mr Rufus Isaacs conducting the Trade Union so that I am entitled to rely on the letter   I submit that letter is really conclusive of the case   I have pointed out how the Barnsley Councillors first of all saw the rules, secondly in their telegrams they adopt a new contention which I submit is bad on the face of it, and now I have got the fact that they are told the men were willing enough to sign the contract book and that they would break away if they did not get strike pay   Then on the next day, on the following page, Mr Hurst writes asking for strike pay   "When we presented ourselves to work the management refused to let us start until we signed the contract book again"   (There is no reference to any new rule there)   "So our men refused"

That being so, if your Lordships will now turn to page 231 you will find that a special meeting is summoned for the next day   Here are the Council being told the men will break away and that the men will sign on   I am told this is an ordinary meeting but at all events the next day the Council are in this position that they have been told the men will break away and sign on, and under the operation of that threat they pass the resolution for strike pay, and Mr Wadsworth asserts again, "Mr Chambers would not allow them to resume work unless they signed a new contract   That this Council meeting recommend every branch to do what they can in a voluntary manner to help the Denaby and Cadeby Main men during the time they were out illegally"   Now my submission is that it is only a question whether there was evidence for the Jury there, I submit there is abundant evidence for the Jury there, that looking through these matters and reading between the lines the Council never meant the men to go back   They were told they would and the Council did not wish it, and therefore the Council voted strike pay for them

Now at page 616 there is a reference to this in the evidence—I have referred to it before at the bottom of the page—that in order to get the men not to sign the officials who were now conducting it told them they would have to work for 12 months if they did   Is it not manifest that they did not want them to sign?   I submit it is almost impossible to draw any other conclusion, but that certainly there was evidence on which the Jury could proceed

Mr DANCKWERTS Unwittingly, no doubt, you said that Mr Isaacs had accepted the responsibility for that letter, but that is a letter of July 23rd

Mr MONTAGUE LUSH My Lord, my learned friend, Mr Danckwerts, calls my attention to the fact that at page 868, when Mr Rufus Isaacs accepted responsibility for a letter it was the letter of the 23rd July

Lord DAVEY It does not matter very much

Mr MONTAGUE LUSH It does not much matter, because if that is right there is no question they received the other one

The LORD CHANCELLOR Whether Counsel accept responsibility or not, if they did not receive the letter it did not affect the matter at the time, and I do not think it very much matters

Mr MONTAGUE LUSH Perhaps not

Lord DAVEY Mr Wadsworth says it was not before the Council when they passed the resolution to send him and Walsh

Mr MONTAGUE LUSH Of course, the whole matter was before the Jury and they would have to draw their inference Then there is that other passage on page 659, in which I have shown that the Committeemen were saying that the men must not sign on, not that the men did not want to sign because there was a new contract, but the Committeemen said "You must not sign on"

My Lord, at page 865, Question 2963, Mr Parrott said the letter was read "Had you seen the letter which had come from Mr Smith, of the Denaby Main, on the previous day?—It was read at the Council meeting Q That is important? (Mr Rufus Isaacs) Would you read the letter? (The Witness) When I say I think it was read at the Council meeting, I would not like to be positive (Mr Eldon Bankes) I will take your impression You told me positively just now it was, but I will accept your amended impression that you think it was?—Yes, but my mind is not very clear this morning I do not want to explain, but the death of Mr Pickard has affected me," and Mr Rufus Isaacs repeats what he said before, "I accepted the responsibility for it—and I do it again" That is how it stands

Mr DANCKWERTS That is the 23rd July, the date of the other letter is the 22nd July

Mr MONTAGUE LUSH I said the 23rd, Mr Danckwerts

Mr WADDY There is no letter from Mr Smith of the 23rd July

Mr DANCKWERTS The letter which was not read, according to Mr Wadsworth, was the letter of the 22nd July

Mr MONTAGUE LUSH There is no letter of July 23rd from Smith, and there is not one in existence, there never was one and there is not now I think it is clear there was evidence for the Jury to say that the letter was read

Lord DAVEY I am afraid I have raised this controversy, for which I am sorry

Mr MONTAGUE LUSH I am sorry, too, but I do not think there is any real doubt about it

As to the question which Mr Bankes raised as to whether if the branch officials were not agents, and assuming their conduct was not adopted, Mr Bankes pointed out that in any case as soon as the Association did interfere they did treat them and appoint them as the persons to conduct the strike That is supported by the passage on page 437, in which Mr Parrott, who was from Barnsley, and had come down to address the men, when Pope's circular had been before them, appealed to them to go back to work Mr Parrott's advice to the men is at letter C "They should always obey the advice of their officials, and never take it into their own heads that they knew how to settle disputes better themselves than those who had been in the work 20 or 30 years or more" That is a recognition of these branch officials as the official whom the men were to obey, and, at page 408, Mr Wadsworth says practically the same thing at letter B, talking of the continuation of the strike, "They would have officials the whole of their delegates and collieries in the county to help and assist them in fighting this battle"

Now the last point on the facts is about the intimidation and coercion I say with regard to that that it has been said that the assault on Berry was isolated, but the position was this, that the colliers had nearly all come out, and Berry was intimidated and prevented going on with his work These expressions in the speeches about "rats" having to come out of their holes were calculated to terrorise the men and the evidence about that is uncontradicted, because my learned friends did not call one of the branch officials Croft was not at the trial nor any of these men, and there was no evidence from anybody who knew anything about what was going on. At the trial we find that the Committeemen were present when the men wanted to sign on, and told them they should not do it, they were present when the men went to give them notices, and the notices were given to the men by the Committmen For example, the evidence of Legge and Gill, which I read this morning, is that they were prevented when they wanted to work from working Then there was a passage in a speech "God help the man who will sign" Your Lordships had from me a list of the different officials who are identified on the evidence as having been present when these various acts took place Your Lordship remembers what Mr Bankes said—I am not going over the ground again—how, whenever there was need for it, from August 13th to 19th, the assaults and intimidation began with lines of people down the road through which the workers had to pass, and how in November a fire broke out The same thing was repeated when Mr Parrott, coming down from Barnsley specially to address the men, used the expression about the "devilish" conduct in turning the men out of their houses

Therefore, my submission is that these acts of coercion or intimidation, or terrorising were to be seen from the commencement to the end, and they were one of the instruments by which the wheels were procured to be stopped, and inasmuch as the working of this struggle had been entrusted by the Barnsley Council to the agents on the spot, and Mr Hall admitted in cross-examination that he read in the papers about these attempts, although he did not see them, my submission is that it is impossible to say that this strike was not maintained in fact by means which would make it what is called an unlawful strike, or in other words, to put it into more correct legal phraseology, it is impossible to contend, as I submit, that the methods used in inducing persons not to contract were unlawful methods, and your Lordships will remember that side by side with the inducing persons not to work was the making it impossible which led to their breaking their contracts, and therefore, you have the additional element of lawlessness here, not only inducing men not to contract by unlawful means, but preventing those who had contracted to work from carrying out their contracts

The result was that the colliery was closed on the 19th August, and my submission is therefore that the whole conduct of the strike, and the whole mode by which it was made effective, was the use of means which would really render it impossible for the Colliery Company to get men to get the coal, and if that is true, I submit that this has become from first to last a carrying on of an object, and a combination—combined efforts for the carrying on of a scheme which had for its object the preventing of my clients from getting coal, and that the methods used for doing it were unlawful methods

Now, my Lords, I have travelled over, I hope, all the ground I think I have "I am not sure, but I have endeavoured to answer

your Lordship's question put to me, and therefore I will just say a
few words with regard to the criticisms which have been passed upon
the Judgements and upon the Summing-up, but just to summarise
my contentions, I say you must look at the object of its movement
It was not only to work, it was more—it was to stop the wheels
You must look at the methods employed to attain that object   It
was not merely not working they were the methods, the ordinary
instruments of coercion, or terrorising, or intimidation, or whatever
language one uses   Thirdly, one must look at the necessary result,
there was the injury to the Plaintiffs, the owners of the Colliery
You must look, fourthly, among the methods, at the payment of the
strike pay   There I say as I said before, we do not put that as an
unlawful act   I say it was an unlawful method for this reason, if
money had only been paid to men to support them, I should not have
been able to complain, and it would not have affected me, but if
money is paid to enable men to carry out this combined object—if
that money is paid in a manner contrary to the statutory rules, I submit that is one of the unlawful methods which would vitiate the
whole of this combination, and make it unlawful

If there is any part of these rules which may be likened to a
Memorandum of Association, I suppose it is the one which relates to
the objects of the Trade Union, because it is only by the objects in
the rules that you can tell often if a society is a friendly society or a
Trade Union, you look at its objects   The objects are the disposition
of the funds, and if there is one part of the rules which is funda-
mental, it is the disposition of the funds, and I submit therefore that
the payment of strike pay illegally is far more like an unconstitutional
act than anything else that has been done in the course of this case.

Now, my Lords, with regard to the questions—I do not propose
to trouble your Lordships with them, because I think, in effect, as I
have passed along I have endeavoured to refer to them   As to the
criticism that has been passed with regard to Number 6 (page 1014),
Question 6 looks, I agree, a little defective   I do not attach the least
importance to it and I ask your Lordships not to do it   I confess I cannot
recollect—although, Mr Bankes, and we all considered these questions
I cannot quite recall how it was that this letter was put in as apparently it is as an unlawful means, and I think the explanation is
this—that if you start with the assumption that the object of the
strike was to stop the wheels and prevent people working, then if you
are attempting to induce people not to contract with that object in
view, it would become an unlawful method   A combination of persons
to induce others not to contract can do it with impunity if they have
justification for doing it—That is Quinn v Leathem, and all these
cases   If they have not justification it is an unlawful method, and if
you start, as we submit you must start with the real resolution they
passed on the 29th June, and not merely the one of not working,
then the attempt to induce men not to contract would become un-

lawful, because it has got an unlawful object in view. That is how I submit one can justify that part of Question 6.

Then, my Lord, with regard to Question 9, that is the only other one I need trouble about. "Did the Defendants or any and which of them," when the Jury say "Yes." I think it is obvious that means all. When they say "Yes" to the first they do not go on to discriminate. The fact that they do not discriminate is, I think, shown by the fact that they have answered the question as a whole with the answer "Yes." It was easy for them, or for my learned friend, to say, "Well, but the Jury have not answered Question 9," but no difficulty was raised about that, it could have been cured if my learned friend had thought there was any faultiness in the answer, and I think it is manifest that the Jury meant to answer this question altogether. The reason why workmen formerly in the employ are put in is this: we wanted to cover by this ninth question the case of our failing to prove the agency in law or the ratification, which was what is called the first period, and if we failed to prove either of these things, then doubtless we wanted if we could to get a finding that after the man has ceased to be in the employ—that is to say, after the first period was over—when the strike had got into full swing, we wanted to get a finding if the Jury thought fit to give it that the Defendants did conspire at all events with workmen who had been in our employ to injure. The Jury found that they had, the Master of the Rolls has adopted that view, because the Master of the Rolls, Judgment is based entirely upon this second period as your Lordships recollect. The Master of the Rolls has held as we respectfully submit wrongly, that the officers of the Union are not agents at all. He has held you cannot in law ratify what they did, but he has held that with regard to this later period there was evidence that these unlawful methods were used with the cognisance of those who were really at that time undoubtedly directing the strike, with the full assent of the Barnsley Council, and I submit it is impossible to say on the evidence that there is no evidence upon which a Jury can so find.

Then, my Lord, with regard to Lord Justice Mathew's Judgment, which is the one I would rather respectfully turn to, because I submit that is founded on a misapprehension, he says at page 1036, letter C (he takes the view which I submit is right about the agency), and at B C he says: "The rules gave the Council no control whatever over the refusal of the workmen to continue in the service of the employers. They" (that is the Council) "had no power to prevent or to terminate a strike. In that respect, each branch was independent of the Council." Now, Lord Justice Mathew took that view, which is our submission—that the branch was independent for the purpose of the strike—and I submit you cannot look at the rules without seeing that is right. But when the learned Judge came on later to deal with the question of responsibility, on page 1037, Lord Justice

Mathew deals with the difficulty in this way at letter E "The men were told that they might go back if they signed fresh contracts"—which I understand to mean either new terms or merely a re-signing of old ones—"but no explanation satisfactory to them was given for this requirement" This is letter E My Lord, there is no evidence of that—no explanation was given to them The evidence is all one way, they were told they must not sign No men were called at the trial, there was no evidence given at the trial that anybody asked for an explanation and could not get one "Meanwhile it was not disputed that every exertion was being made on the part of the Council to induce the men and their employers to settle this dispute amicably"

Now, my Lord, our whole contention, so far from not disputing it, was that the Council only wanted the dispute settled in the sense that I have said the men were going to break away, the branch officials had all made up their minds to continue the strike, and I submit that is a misapprehension on the part of the learned Lord Justice Then over the page at 1038, "They were advised to take this course"—that is to tender their services I submit it is not a case of advice According to our case, they had no alternative It was not advice "Their demand, as between them and their fellow members of the Association, would seem not to be unreasonable, having regard to the advice which had been given" Then over the page the Lord Justice sums it up thus "In this state of things it was clear there was no ground for the allegation that the strike in question was referrable to Lord James's Award The men acted loyally by the decision of Lord James"

My Lord, it is not necessary to decide it, but my submission is that the Lord Justice could not, as I submit, correctly say that it was clear The evidence is, as I submit, the other way Then he speaks of the contemptuous treatment the men considered they had received from the Plaintiffs and their managers I submit that Judgment is founded on a misapprehension of the facts

I have concluded all, but dealing with the case of Wadsworth and Hall, and I will only occupy a few minutes, and then I have I think travelled over the whole ground Our case with regard to Mr Wadsworth, and our case with regard to Mr Hall lies, I agree, in a very narrow compass I quite accept the position that the Jury have found, whatever it means, that they did do what they did, not personally, but as servants I think they say

The LORD CHANCELLOR As agents

Mr MONTAGUE LUSH As servants of the Association Of course my submission is that that does not in the least protect them, if I succeed in showing that what was done was wrongfully done—that is to say, if there is a combination, and the Jury have found in the answer to 9 that they all, as I submit they have, joined in this movement, the fact that the Treasurer pays money in the course of his duty as a servant, if in fact it is a step in an unlawful combination, does not protect him any more than if the Trustees paid the money away, it would protect them if they were called to account for it It is not necessary to say "I committed a trespass, or whatever it was, because I was told to do it,' and, of course, the whole case really comes back to whether I am right in saying as against the Association and as against the individual Defendants there was a wrongful combination, a wrongful purpose The case against Wadsworth has this strength in it, that Wadsworth was present on the 15th July, and that in a sense he had got to choose between counselling peace or counselling continuation of the strike He was sent to get the men back to work, and he advised the men to do the opposite, as I have pointed out He says, "Do not go back to work until you have had your ballot"—in substance, he says, "Ballot at once and go back to work afterwards" He is taking the first step, as I submit, towards doing that which will encourage the men to go on with the strike He is departing from the resolution which had been passed the day before, which was just the opposite, and my submission is that it is impossible to say that the Jury were not warranted in saying that Mr Wadsworth was in fact a party to the carrying on of this combination, and that he not only did not use the means which he was told to use to get the men back, but counselled exactly the opposite

With regard to Mr Hall, the evidence against him, no doubt, is only that he paid away the funds of the Union contrary to the rules, and one must take it now, I suppose, that he knew it was contrary to the rules Your Lordships have held it, and the Court of Appeal have held it, and, in addition to that, he knew from the papers which he said he saw that unlawful methods of intimidation were being used, and my submission is that with regard to himself also there was evidence upon which the Jury could find as they did Your Lordships are only asked to say there was none, of course, you cannot be asked to say that on the evidence the verdict was wrong

We, of course, do not ask as against Mr Parrott's executors or any of the individual Defendants that these heavy damages should be paid in fact by them, or the costs, but we do assert a right as against them all, at least to pay them none We say they were properly joined as being parties to this movement, the leading members of this great Association, and we say they have rendered themselves liable by what they did to have an action brought against them, and if so, of course, there would be no possible ground for saying they ought to get relief.

Now, my Lords, I think I have travelled over the whole ground—I am afraid at some length—and I ask your Lordships to reserve the Judgment appealed against

The LORD CHANCELLOR We are much obliged for your argument Their Lordships will take time to consider their Judgment

———

ENOCH EDWARDS, President

THOS ASHTON, Secretary,

925, Ashton Old Road,

Manchester

In the House of Lords.

MONDAY, 14th MAY, 1906

LORDS PRESENT—
THE LORD CHANCELLOR
LORD MACNAGHTEN
LORD DAVEY
LORD JAMES OF HEREFORD
LORD ROBERTSON
LORD ATKINSON

BETWEEN

The Denaby and Cadeby Main Collieries Limited,
Appellants,

AND

The Yorkshire Miners' Association and Others,
Respondents

JUDGMENT.

The LORD CHANCELLOR My Lords, the litigation out of which this Appeal arises relates to a strike at the Denaby and Cadeby Collieries, which commenced on the 29th of June, 1902, and ended about the month of March, 1903 It will be convenient to summarise at the outset the main facts which led to this dispute

For some years before 1902 there had been a controversy between employers and workmen at these collieries in regard to the right of payment for removing what is called bag-dirt The controversy related to the price-list obtaining in these particular collieries, and not elsewhere, though the men had the sympathy of the Defendant Association and of their Secretary, the late Mr Pickard, who assisted them in negotiating for a settlement In fact, however, no satisfactory settlement was reached.

On the 14th of June, 1902, another dispute, not confined to these collieries, but applied to all the collieries in the Defendant Association, was for the time, ended by the casting vote of Lord James of Hereford, after a meeting of the Conciliation Board Lord James awarded, to use a phrase sufficiently accurate for the present purpose, a reduction in wages of 10 per cent It is said that the men at the two collieries were dissatisfied with this Award

In that condition of things, when some bitterness undoubtedly existed, on Saturday, 28th June, certain officials of the Denaby and Cadeby Branches of the Defendant Association summoned a meeting of the men in both collieries for the morning of Sunday, 29th of June Only 400 or fewer out of 5,000 attended the meeting It was addressed by officials of both branches, who advocated an immediate strike Unhappily the men followed this advice and passed a resolution to stop the wheels Pickets were placed, and on the night shift of that Sunday, 29th of June, all except four refused to work On Tuesday, the 2nd July, one of the four was assaulted in a cowardly fashion, and then the other three ceased working also Few, if any, of the others worked from the 29th of June until the end of the strike in the following March.

Inasmuch as the men were all working under contracts which could not be terminated except after 14 days' notice, it is manifest that the abrupt cessation of work on the 29th June involved a breach of contract and was unlawful

This was fully recognised by the Council of the Defendant Association, to which many of the strikers belonged I shall discuss later on the relations between the Denaby and Cadeby Branches of the Association, and the Association at large At present it is enough to say that the Council of the Association constituted its supreme governing body, and controlled its funds At this stage the Council refused to maintain the strike by giving strike pay Further, they sent representatives at once to the two collieries, who told the men they had acted illegally in breaking their contracts and must return to work, and that then they could take a ballot according to the rules of the Association to decide whether they should resume the strike after working out their 14 days of contract service The men consented, and, but for an accident, would have resumed work.

In August, 1901, the Home Secretary had issued some new regulations in regard to timbering, which, rightly or wrongly, were by some persons supposed to be *ultra vires* Those who had been employed in these two collieries, before August of 1901, had signed contracts which left them free to contest the legality of these regulations because the regulations were not embodied in their contracts, and therefore had no contractual force upon them, when on the 17th July, 1902, the workmen offered to resume in compliance with the advice of the Defendant Association, they were required to sign fresh contracts in accordance with the practice always observed in those collieries in regard to workmen who had been absent from their work These fresh contracts especially embodied the new regulations of the Home Secretary, and the men declined to sign them, a proceeding in which they were supported not only by the officials of their branches but also by the officials of the Defendant Association Accordingly the strike continued

After this incident the Council of the Association treated the case no longer as a case of strike, but of lock-out, and claimed that they were entitled, under the rules of the Association, to grant at these two collieries strike pay Strike pay was granted by the Defendant Association from the 24th of August (dating back to the 17th August, 1902) down to February, 1903, when one Howden, a member of the Association, obtained an injunction against the Association prohibiting any further grant of strike pay on the ground that the rules did not admit of this payment under the circumstances That view was upheld on an appeal to this House As soon as the injunction was granted the men in both collieries submitted , and the strike ended in March, 1903

After the strike ended the Denaby and Cadeby Main Collieries, Limited, brought this action Though there were many Defendants, the chief purpose was to fix the Defendant Association, who alone were in the position to pay damages, with a liability for the loss that had been incurred by the Plaintiffs For the present, therefore, I will deal with the case only so far as it relates to the Defendant Association

The Pleadings are of great length, and state the contentions in various forms, but after the evidence had been given, Counsel for the

Plaintiffs asked the learned Judge to leave nine questions to the Jury Counsel for the Defendants, claiming that there was no evidence to go to the Jury, refused either to suggest questions for themselves or to take responsibility for those suggested on behalf of the Plaintiffs The learned Judge accordingly left the Jury all the nine questions as they stood The Jury answered all of them in favour of the Plaintiffs, and they embody the ultimate form in which the case against the Defendant Association was shaped

Taken from this source, the first head of claim by the Plaintiffs may be stated as follows —The Defendants Nolan and Humphries unlawfully and maliciously procured the men to break their contracts of employment by going out on strike on 29th of June without giving notice In so doing Nolan and Humphries purported to act as agents of the Defendant Association and for its benefit The members of the Committee of Denaby and Cadeby Branches of the Defendant Association also unlawfully and maliciously procured the men to break their contracts of employment by going out on strike on 29th of June without giving notice They also, in so doing, purported to act as agents of the Association and for its benefit And the Defendant Association, by its Executive Council, or by its officials, ratified these acts of Nolan and Humphries or of the members of the Committees In short, the Plaintiffs say that the Defendant Association by its agents instigated the commencement of the strike and ratified the acts of its agents in procuring the breach of contract This head covers Questions 1 to 5 inclusive

Now it is quite clear that the Central Council did not know the strike had begun till Monday, 30th June When they learned of it they at once declared that it was illegal If we yielded to the suggestion that the strike of 29th June must, nevertheless, from its very suddenness, have been engineered by the Central Council behind the scenes we should be acting on pure imagination Nor can I see any evidence that the persons who procured the men to break their contract purported to act as agents of the Defendant Association, or that the latter at any time ratified that proceding All the proof is that the breach of contract was from beginning to end disapproved at headquarters.

Another view, however, was presented in regard to this first period. Mr Bankes contended that Nolan and Humphries, delegates of the two branches, and the committees of the two branches, had, as the Jury found, in fact, procured the strike on 29th June in breach of contract, and that the Defendant Association was, under its constitution and rules, liable as principals for this wrongful conduct of their agents, apart from any ratification. It is necessary to ascertain the relations of the Association with its branches and their respective officials in order to decide this point of agency.

In substance, the position is as follows:—The Defendant Association comprises about 150 branches, extending, we were told, over Yorkshire and the Midlands. The Denaby Branch and the Cadeby Branch consist of men working at each of these two adjoining collieries, both belonging to the same owners, and, I suppose, roughly speaking, that each branch of the Association consists of men working in the same colliery or under the same employers. Certainly in the present case it is so.

Every member of the Association contributes according to a fixed scale to its funds. These funds are collected by the branch, and, after defraying its local expenses, the balance is handed over to the Association to be applied in paying the general expenses, the benefits, such for example as funeral allowances, and also, in case of need, in maintaining a strike. There are branch officials elected by members of the branch, and central officials of the Association elected by the branches.

The supreme government of the Association is vested in the Council (Central Council, I will call it) which consists of officials, the President, two Secretaries, the Treasurer, and also of Delegates, one from each branch, each with a voting power, proportioned to the number of members in the branch. It is unnecessary to mention the Central Executive Committee, which only acts on emergencies in the interval between council meetings, and has no authority in regard to strikes.

Besides these central bodies, each branch has a committee of its own, consisting of persons elected by members of the branches. Careful provisions are to be found in the rules dealing with the rights and duties of the Association and the branches respectively in cases of strikes and lock-outs, and for a very obvious reason Strikes or lock-outs may be, and generally are, local in their character, and arise out of disputes relating to the local conditions of service If one branch were able without control to call out its members on strike in consequence of a local dispute, and to claim the financial support of the entire Association as a matter of right, then the caprice or folly or selfishness of a few men might dissipate the common funds of all Hence the necessity for strict rules

No branch is allowed to strike unless two-thirds of its members, voting by ballot, so determine, nor unless three-fourths of the members composing the branch record their votes And even if that majority is procured the members of the branch are entitled to strike pay only "if the employers refuse to remedy their grievances, and after all proper and peaceful means have been tried to effect a settlement by deputations from members with the advice and assistance of the Council, and such member or members be permitted to cease work by the sanction of the Association in accordance with the rules" Another rule authorises a registered vote to be taken throughout the entire Association whenever any number of branches numbering one-fourth of the Council demand such vote on (among other things) " the adoption or prolongation of a strike "

The net result of these provisions is that all strikes of a branch are prohibited unless the prescribed majority of branch members is obtained, that no strike pay is to be granted except the strike be sanctioned by the Council after peaceful efforts have been exhausted, but that a plebiscite of the entire Association may adopt a strike after it has commenced.

On the other hand, if any branch is locked out in consequence of any action lawfully taken by the Association to remedy grievances, the men are entitled to maintenance equal to strike pay

Can it be said in the face of these rules that the Association is liable in damages for the action of delegates, or of branch officials or committees in procuring a strike (whether accompanied or not by a breach of contract) without a ballot, without the sanction of the

Council, and without a registered vote of the entire Association ? In my opinion the Association is not so liable

The delegates are agents of the branches, to represent them in the Council When acting in the Council they are agents of the entire Association, to do the business of the Council They are not agents of the Association to represent it, or act for it in their localities, either as to strikes or other matters

Branch officials and committees are elected by members of the branch who are engaged in a common service under one particular employer If they quarrel with the employers about the conditions of their service, they have a right to strike The Association does not confer that right which is derived from the general law, but it restricts the right by rules requiring a prescribed majority as the indispensable preliminary I do not see how either the officials or committees thereby become agents of the Association to procure a strike even if it were lawful and regular, still less to procure it contrary to the rules and contrary to the law in breach of existing contracts

It is true that on certain conditions the Association is bound to furnish strike pay Will that circumstance create the agency for which Mr Bankes contends? I will suppose that the employers also are members of an Association of Coalowners, as we were told they are, and that the Coalowners' Association bind themselves to support each other with money in the event of any one member locking-out his workmen after certain conditions had been observed If such member locked out his men without giving the notice prescribed by contract, it would seem very strange to suppose the other members were liable to damages for an act over which they had no control and which was contrary to the conditions Yet the cases are precisely the same

In my opinion the first head of claim entirely fails

The second head of claim advanced by the Plaintiffs is to be found in Questions 6, 7, and 8, and relates, not to the initiation of the strike, but to its maintenance by the Defendant Association after it had been commenced

It amounts to this, that after the strike had commenced, the Defendant Association, by its officials or by the members of the committees of Denaby and Cadeby branches, assisted and maintained the strike by means of intimidation, in order to prevent the men who were still working from continuing to work, by inducing others not to enter Plaintiffs' service and by granting strike pay against rules of the Association It also charged, as appears by Question 8, against all Defendants, that they conspired with the other Defendants or with the Plaintiffs' workmen to do all these things This later point really adds nothing to the charge, and in no case could any judgment be entered in respect of the 8th Question, because the answer leaves it quite open which of the many Defendants were guilty, and of which, among the several accusations made against them, any of the Defendants were guilty

I find no evidence in support of any material part of this charge against the Defendant Association That also was the view of the Court of Appeal, though the Master of the Rolls dissented

As to the charge that the Central Council granted strike pay against the rules of the Association, that is certainly true, and the fact was finally established in Howden's case, decided by your Lordships in 1905 The Association was restrained at the instance of one of its members from applying its funds for strike pay upon the ground that such payment was not authorised by the rules I fail to see how the fact that the rules were contravened can confer upon the Plaintiffs any ground of action which otherwise they would not have possessed The wrong committed by the Central Council of the Association was against its own members in dissipating their funds, not against the employers, who had no interest in the funds Had the rules permitted it, the grant of strike pay would have given the Plaintiffs no cause of action It seems a novel argument that they should acquire a right of action from the fact that the money so paid was derived by breach of trust from the funds of the Association whom they sue It is an attempt by persons who are no parties to the trust to sue for breach of it those who are parties

The third and last Head of Claim was formulated in the 9th Question put to the Jury, which was as follows "Did the Defendants, or any and which of them, unlawfully and maliciously conspire together, and with workmen formerly in the employ of the Plaintiffs, so molest and injure the Plaintiffs, and were the Plaintiffs so molested and injured?" To this question the answer of the Jury was "Yes." There, again, no Judgment could be entered against any Defendant upon this answer, for this simple reason that the Jury have not informed us which of the Defendants took part in the conspiracy In the view, however, that I take, this circumstance will not affect the result The question itself relates entirely to an alleged conspiracy after the commencement of the strike to which workmen formerly in the employment of the Plaintiffs were parties

No unlawful methods were used by the Defendant Association or sanctioned by it And if we were to hold that those who maintained the strike by helping with money the men on strike and their families are liable in damages merely because it caused loss to the employers, we should in effect be saying that every strike is an actionable wrong

Accordingly, I am of opinion that no case has been established against the Defendant Association

In regard to the other Defendants, Nolan and Humphries suffered Judgment to go by default, and are not before your Lordships' House The remaining Defendants and the representatives those who are deceased have hardly been the subject of attack in this House, and no separate argument directed against one or more of them apart from the Defendant Association has been advanced It is sufficient to say that their case stands upon substantially the same footing as the Defendant Association, and that in regard to them also I think the Judgment of the Court of Appeal ought to stand

Lord MACNAGHTON My Lords I have had the advantage of reading in print the Judgment which has just been delivered, and I entirely agree with it I do not think I could usefully add anything to what the Lord Chancellor has said

Lord JAMES of HEREFORD My Lords The facts controlling the case have already been so fully stated to your Lordships that I shall not refer to them beyond the extent necessary for explaining the Judgment I have arrived at

The action was brought to recover damages from the Defendants, an Association registered under the Trades Union Act of 1871, and from certain individuals the Trustees and other officers of the said Union

Substantially, the cause of action (as alleged in the Pleadings) was that the several Defendants had wrongfully employed the funds of the Defendant Association in wrongfully and maliciously procuring and inducing workmen employed or formerly employed by the Plaintiffs to break the contracts with the Plaintiffs and not to enter into contracts with them, and unlawfully to remain in possession of the Plaintiffs' houses, and for wrongfully and maliciously aiding and carrying on by unlawful means a strike of the Plaintiffs' workmen A claim was also made to recover damages on account of a conspiracy to effect the same unlawful acts

The case as presented by Counsel at the Bar on behalf of the Plaintiffs sought to establish the liability of the Defendants on various grounds   It was argued —

(1) That the Defendant Association—central body—by themselves or their agents, molested the Plaintiffs in carrying on their business

(2) If this was not established, then in the alternative that Defendant Central Association ratified the acts of the branches of the Association

(3) That the Defendant Association, by themselves or their agents, supported and maintained the Plaintiffs' workmen in carrying out certain illegal acts

(4) That the individual Defendants were personally liable in respect of the above alleged causes of action

The solutions of the questions raised by these propositions depends upon the construction to be put upon the constitution of the Defendant Trades Union under its rules, and also upon the result of certain facts given in evidence   This Union is registered under the Acts of 1871 and 1876   Certain rules declare and provide the objects, government, and constitution of the Union when registered under the Act of 1871

The Union had at the time of the committal of the alleged cause of action upwards of 60,000 members   The central governing body had its headquarters at Barnsley, consisting of a Council and an Executive Council with certain paid officials   There were some 150 branches, of which those at Denaby and Cadeby were important and numerous in membership   The government and business of the Union and of its branches are controlled by a body of rules, of which the principal and most material may be summarised as follows —

(4) The supreme government of the Union is vested in a Council consisting of certain named officers

(5)—The Council to meet once in every six weeks

(28) and (29) create an Executive Committee of not less than 13 members, elected by branches of the Union   The duty of this Committee is to deal with all matters of emergency arising between the meetings of the Council, but the Committee has no power to decide upon questions relating to strikes or lock-outs

Rules 31 to 47 deal with the constitution and management of the branches   Rule 37 is as follows —All local branches shall be conducted by a Committee of not less than five or more than nine financial members, President, Secretary, and Treasurer included, whose duty shall be to attend all meetings, and shall at all times transact the business of the branch as directed by the Rules and Minutes of the General Council

By Rules, 38, 39, 40, and 41, the mode of electing the Branch Committees and the method of dealing with the business of the branches are dealt with   Rule 46 deals with the manner in which the financial business of the branches shall be carried on   Rule 64 provides for the strike pay to members permitted to cease work by the sanction of the Union in accordance with the rules, and by Rule 72 no branch is allowed to strike or leave off work with the view of causing the work to stand, unless sanctioned by two-thirds of the members composing the branch, when such strike shall be determined by registered ballot

The effect of these rules seems to be very concisely and correctly stated by Lord Justice Cozens-Hardy, and I adopt the following portion of his Judgment "Now, under these circumstances it is clear that it is competent to the Union to order and adopt a strike— such action would ordinarily be taken only when the interests of the members as a whole are considered to be affected But it is quite clear that it is contemplated that a branch as distinct from the Union may strike In that case great care is taken that the branch members shall have no claim for strike pay out of the Union funds unless certain forms are complied with, and the sanction of the Council obtained A local strike will naturally be engineered by the local branch officials, but, in my opinion, the branch officials are not agents of the Union with authority to bind the Union by their acts in a local strike Such agency must be founded on something outside the rules, and its existence must be proved by those who rely upon it " Accepting this view it becomes necessary to consider the facts proved outside the rules in order to determine whether the liability of the Defendants is established by such facts and occurrences apart from the effect of these rules

It seems, that in the spring of 1902, the local workmen in the Denaby and Cadeby collieries were in a state of discontent in consequence of the employers' attitude in relation to what was called the bag-dirt question On Sunday, June 29th, 1902, a meeting of the operatives at the two collieries was summoned and was attended by some 300 or 400 miners The following resolution was passed by them "That this meeting is of opinion that the time has now arrived when some steps should be taken in reference to the reduction of men's wages for bag dirt and fines for different things at Denaby and Cadeby Collieries, and that having tried to come to some amicable understanding and failed, the only thing that is for us to do is to stop the wheels at both collieries "

The grievance as stated in this resolution appears to have been of a local character, but it was urged in argument on behalf of the Plaintiffs that this resolution did not correctly set out the cause for the intended stoppage of the wheels, and that the real cause was the hostility entertained by the men throughout a large district towards the action of the Conciliation Board, which had lately, by the casting vote of the Chairman, directed a reduction of the workmen's wages by 10 per cent throughout the whole of the federated districts. But in my view this allegation was not supported by evidence. It is true that the decision to reduce the wages had lately been arrived at, and that in some twenty other collieries about this time strikes took place, but causes for these strikes were shown to exist, and to be unconnected with the decision of the Conciliation Board. It must, therefore, be taken that the resolution correctly stated the grievance complained of, and that grievance was of a local and not of a general character.

The resolution thus passed was promptly acted on. According to the evidence of the manager of the collieries the first shift after the meeting was at 10 o'clock the same night. But the men at the two collieries did not go to work, and having given no notices of discontinuance they broke their contracts, committing an unlawful act, and the strike commenced. So far the decision to commit the unlawful act of breaking the contracts made by the individual workmen was the act of the two branches and not of the central body. The latter, however, were promptly informed of the step that had been taken, and promptly dealt with. On the next day, June 30th, the executive committee met at Barnsley, Mr. Cowey, the president, presiding, and passed the following resolution. "That Mr. Cowey be instructed to wire the secretary of Denaby and Cadeby main branches, stating that in the opinion of this executive they ought to have a meeting and agree to resume work at once, as they are out contrary to the rules and regulations of the Association." This resolution was confirmed at the Council Meeting of July 14th, when it was arranged that certain members of the central body should proceed to the collieries and tell the men that they must resume work, and then take a ballot the first day they worked as to whether they would send in their notices to terminate their contract of service.

The representatives of the central body attended at the collieries in pursuance of the resolution, and in consequence of the advice given the workmen at the collieries resolved to resume work, but were met by a demand to sign a new contract of service. This contract contained a new term recognising the validity of some rules recently made by the Home Office, and thereupon the men refused to sign it. The employers declined to allow the men to return without a fresh contract, and so the collieries continued idle for many months

At this time, Mr Pickard, the President of the Association, and other members of the council, appear to have been advised that the men had not broken their contracts, and that, therefore, the masters by refusing to allow them to continue their work under the original contracts had locked them out Apparently this view, however incorrect, was acted on, and on July 24th a resolution was passed granting strike pay from the day when the men offered to resume work and were refused unless they signed a new contract

It should be noted that before any strike pay was voted the unlawfulness of the acts of the men had been clearly established They had absented themselves from their work for a fortnight, whilst it was proved that an absence of some two or three days was regarded as establishing a discontinuance of service "The strike" had thus commenced, but this word is of an artificial character, and does not represent any legal definition or description The legal effect of what had occurred was that the men had wrongfully left their employment without giving the necessary 14 days' notice, that therefore the contract between them and their employers was broken, and that the latter had the right to treat, and did treat, the different contracts of service as at an end They also required, as I have said, that if the men sought to return to their work they must do so under fresh contracts of service which, however, the men refused to recognise, and thus the non-employment and the idleness of the mine continued until January, 1903

Now in respect of the period from June 29th to July 15th the members of the Court of Appeal were unanimous in holding that no liability attached to the trade union central body, and in such view I concur I do so because I think that there is nothing to be found in the rules that makes the officers of the branches the agents of the central body, and also because I can find no evidence from which it can be shown that authority was given to the branches to act between those dates as such agents

But the determination of the case is not yet arrived at It was further contended on the part of the Plaintiffs, that the acts of the Defendant Union in granting strike pay, and some individual acts established liability on account of what was termed maintaining the strike existing at the Denaby and Cadeby Collieries Importance must be attached to this argument in consequence of the Judgment given by the learned Master of the Rolls upon the point thus raised In relation to it consideration should be given to the term 'maintaining the strike" If one assists in procuring the commission of an unlawful act, doubtless liability follows, and so if the Defendants had done anything by assistance or otherwise to induce the branch workmen to break their contracts, the Union would have been liable But no such inducing to break a contract was proved. When the assistance was given, that is, when strike pay was voted, the unlawful acts had been committed, all the contracts of employment were terminated, and employers and employed were in respect of contracts entirely unconnected So that the effect of the grant of strike pay was not to cause or induce the commission of an unlawful act, but to place the workmen in the position of being able to maintain themselves without entering into a new contract of labour with the Plaintiffs or with anyone else This is no more than the subscribing to a strike fund Within the last few years we have had instances of the public contributing largely towards the maintenance of men who had ceased to work, under conditions which constituted what is called a strike Were these subscribers liable to an action? It surely must be admitted that they were not—even if the workmen had broken their contracts

Some other grounds of liability were alleged, but may be briefly dealt with It was urged that the money of the Union was unlawfully expended when applied to the strike pay granted That may be so, as between the members of the Union and those who made the grant, so that an injunction could be obtained to restrain such payments But this faulty application does not confer any cause of action upon the Plaintiffs, who have no interest in the money misapplied If the subscribing to a so-called strike fund is legal, the source from which the money so subscribed is derived, however tainted, cannot create illegality

I concur also in the Judgments given in the Court of Appeal, that no acts of molestation were brought home to the Union, and also that there was no legal ratification of the acts of the branch officials by the central body

In relation to the liability of Parrott, Wadsworth and Hall, I think it follows that of the Union Those men were not guilty of independent tortious acts Nolan and Humphries did not appear, and must be held to be liable, but probably that liability is of no importance to the Plaintiffs

For these reasons I think that the Judgments of the majority of the Court of Appeal must be affirmed

Lord DAVEY My Lords, I have prepared a Judgment of my own in this case, but I find that the views which I have endeavoured to express concur so entirely with those which have been expressed in the Judgments of the Lord Chancellor and my noble and learned friend who has last addressed your Lordships that it is unnecessary for me to trouble your Lordships by reading mine I therefore content myself with expressing my entire concurrence with those views

Lord ROBERTSON My Lords, I agree that this Appeal should be dismissed, and I shall add a few words only on that part of the case on which the court of Appeal was not unanimous

From the first part of the case, however, I carry forward this, which is my ground of Judgment upon it, that the branch officials were not, as such, officers or agents of the Respondent Association, and this must be steadily kept in view on the question of maintenance, and, indeed, directly affects it We start then with this—that the Respondents were not responsible for the original breach of contract, or for those who caused it, and, in fact, although on a somewhat narrow ground, they disapproved of what was done on the 29th June

Now I do not profess to decide, and have no occasion to decide, more in favour of the Respondents than that on the specific questions to which the findings of the Jury on maintenance relate, the

Appellants have not established liability   Those findings are in answer to the sixth question, and are lettered A, B, and C, and I shall consider C first as it charges the only act which the Association is said to have done directly by itself, viz , the grant of strike pay   Now this grant was never made except to men whose contracts were at an end, and the payment was, therefore, not to induce men to break contracts, but to induce them not to enter into new contracts   So far there is no illegality   Nor do I see how the fact that the payment of this strike pay was held to be a violation of the internal constitution of the Association turns it into an invasion of any right of third parties like the Appellants

The answer to the charge lettered B (menacing or attempting to induce men who were willing to enter into contracts of service with the Appellants, or to work for them to refrain from so doing) is that it is not a legal wrong

The Question lettered A charges the Respondents with molesting or intimidating men who were working for the Appellants with a view of inducing them to cease from so working   The theory upon which this charge is made can only be that by giving financial support to the strike the Respondents made themselves liable for all that was done during the strike by the officers of the branches I am unable to adopt that view, and I do not find any other valid ground for attaching such liability

The 9th query raises substantially the same questions under the form of conspiracy, for the *media concludendi* are in substance the same

The answers to the 7th and 8th queries are hopelessly ineffective, for the reason given by my noble and learned friend, the Lord Chancellor

Lord ATKINSON   My Lords, I concur in the views that have been expressed by my noble and learned friends who have preceded me, and as both the law and the facts have been so fully dealt with by them, I do not think it necessary to go over again the ground which has been traversed   I may, however, say shortly that I beg to adopt, if I may, the Judgment delivered by Lord Justice Cozens-Hardy in the Court of Appeal   I concur in the conclusion at which that learned Judge arrived, and in the reasoning by which he arrived at it

Questions put—

That the Order appealed from be reversed

The Not-Contents have it

That the Order appealed from be affirmed and the Appeal dismissed with costs

The Contents have it

———

ENOCH EDWARDS, President

THOS ASHTON, Secretary,

925, Ashton Old Road,

Manchester

E~ 11/3C

C W·A·

CPSIA information can be obtained
at www.ICGtesting.com
Printed in the USA
LVHW021152260623
750796LV00005B/405